Mastering Public Speaking

SIXTH EDITION

George L. Grice
Radford University

John F. Skinner
San Antonio College

PEARSON

Boston   New York   San Francisco
Mexico City   Montreal   Toronto   London   Madrid   Munich   Paris
Hong Kong   Singapore   Tokyo   Cape Town   Sydney

Editor-in-Chief: Karon Bowers
Series Editor: Brian Wheel
Senior Developmental Editor: Carol Alper
Editorial Assistant: Jenny Lupica
Associate Editor: Deb Hanlon
Senior Editorial-Production Supervisor: Karen Mason
Marketing Manager: Suzan Czajkowski
Composition and Prepress Buyer: Linda Cox
Manufacturing Buyer: Megan Cochran
Cover Administrator: Linda Knowles
Cover Designer: Susan Paradise
Text Designer: Carol Somberg
Photo Researchers: Larissa Tierney and Naomi Rudov
Project Management/Composition: Omegatype Typography, Inc.

For related titles and support materials, visit our online catalog at www.ablongman.com.

Between the time website information is gathered and then published, it is not unusual for some sites to have closed. Also, the transcription of URLs can result in typographical errors. The publisher would appreciate notification where these errors occur so that they may be corrected in subsequent editions.

Library of Congress Cataloging-in-Publication Data

Grice, George L.
    Mastering public speaking / George L. Grice, John F. Skinner. — 6th ed.
       p. cm.
    Includes bibliographical references and index.
    ISBN 0-205-46735-0
     1. Public speaking.   I. Skinner, John F.   II. Title.

PN4129.15.G75 2007
808.5'1—dc22

                                       2005054981

Printed in the United States of America

10 9 8 7 6 5 4 3 2 1   RRD-OH   10 09 08 07 06

Credits appear on page 447, which constitutes an extension of the copyright page.

To Wrenn, Evelyn, Carol, and Leanne

To Suzanne, Drew, and Devin;
Beverley, G. W., Rick, Randy,
and the memory of my grandmother,
Gertrude Viola Wallace

and

To the memory of Robert C. Jeffrey,
our teacher and friend

Brief Contents

Contents

chapter *5*   **Analyzing Your Audience   85**

chapter *6*   **Selecting Your Speech Topic   109**

chapter *7*   **Researching Your Topic   129**

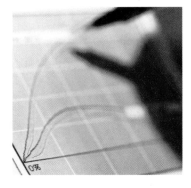

chapter *10* **Introducing and Concluding Your Speech   197**

chapter *11* **Outlining Your Speech   215**

chapter *12* **Wording Your Speech   233**

chapter *13* **Delivering Your Speech   255**

chapter *14* **Using Presentational Aids**   **275**

chapter *15* **Speaking to Inform**   **295**

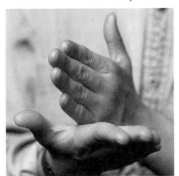

chapter *16* **The Strategy of Persuasion**   **317**

chapter *19* **Speaking in and as a Group**   389

Preface to the Student

The word began as the spoken word. Long before anyone devised a way to record messages in writing, people told one another stories and taught each other lessons. Societies flourished and fell, battles were waged and won—all on the basis of the spoken word. Ancient storytellers preserved their cultures' literature and history by translating them orally to eager audiences. Crowds might wander away from unprepared, unskilled speakers, but the most competent, skilled storytellers received widespread attention and praise.

After the development of script and print, people continued to associate marks on the page with the human voice. Even today, linked as we are by television, computer, and radio networks, a speaker standing at the front of a hushed room makes a special claim on our attention and our imagination. As you develop and deliver speeches in class—and in future years as you deliver reports, sell products, present and accept awards, or campaign for candidates—you continue an ancient oral tradition. This book is about the contract that always exists between a speaker and an audience, and about the choices you make in your roles as speaker and listener.

We developed this book with two principles in mind. First, public speaking, like ancient storytelling, requires a level of competence that develops from skills handed down from patient teacher to interested student. Yet this is more than a skills course. Although a working knowledge of skills is fundamental to your mastery of public speaking, the master speaker is principled as well as skilled. We want to instruct you in how to make wise choices as you select topics and then research, organize, practice, and deliver your speeches. Just as important, we want to spur you at each point in the speech-making process to think about why you make the choices you do.

Our second guiding principle has been most economically stated by British journalist and author Gilbert K. Chesterton: "There are no uninteresting subjects, there are only uninterested people." This book is for those who believe, as we do, that the lessons we have to teach one another can enrich the lives of every listener. The student of art history can learn from the business major, just as the business student learns from the art historian. This course will give you the chance to investigate subjects that appeal to you, but it demands far more than telling what you already know. We admire the advice of the author who said, "Teachers of creative writing have got it all wrong when they say, 'Write about what you know.' You should write about what you don't know about what you know."[1] We challenge you to keep that advice in mind as you research and develop speech topics creatively, and then to listen to one another's speeches expecting to learn.

Public speaking is an important part of communication, and communication is not only part of your education but also the way you gain and apply your learning. A liberating and lifelong education occurs only through communication, with ourselves and those around us. We wish each of you the kind of education Steve C. Beering, former president of Purdue University, described so eloquently:

> Education is dreaming, and thinking and asking questions. It is reading, writing, speaking, and listening. Education is exploring the unknown, discovering new ideas, communicating with the world about us. Education is finding yourself, recognizing human needs, and communicating that recognition to others. Education is learning to solve problems. It is acquiring useful knowledge and skills in order to improve the quality of life. Education is an understanding of the meaning of the past, and an inkling of the potential of the future. Education represents self-discipline, assumption of responsibility and the maintenance of flexibility, and most of all, an open mind. Education is unfinishable. It is an attitude and a way of life. It makes every day a new beginning.[2]

An Invitation

We are interested in your feedback about this edition of *Mastering Public Speaking*. Please contact us by email at the following addresses:

ggrice@radford.edu

jskinner@accd.edu

We look forward to hearing from you.

—George L. Grice and John F. Skinner

Preface to the Instructor

In 1993 we published the first edition of *Mastering Public Speaking* to show students both the hows and the whys of public speaking. Ours was the first major public speaking textbook to devote an entire chapter to speaker and listener ethics and another to managing speaker nervousness. We also introduced students to the "4 S's," a practical mnemonic device for organizing each major idea in a speech.

The text's instructional approach mirrored our view of the public speaking instructor as a "guide on the side" rather than a "sage on the stage." Our goal is to empower students with responsibility for their own learning by challenging them to make all the decisions required of public speakers. By incorporating into our text many credible examples, both actual and hypothetical, we hoped to inspire and encourage students to achieve the full potential of public speech.

To support our goals, we also wanted to help instructors shape the public speaking classroom into a community of caring, careful thinkers. We sought to improve the quality of feedback in the classroom by analyzing in our text the elements of sound critiques and providing a helpful model for discussing speeches.

Though we certainly live in a changed world in the early twenty-first century, in our view, little of consequence has changed in the discipline since that first edition. Although new media have altered our expectations of what a public speech can accomplish, and new research tools have sent us scrambling to ensure that we know as much about these emerging technologies as do most of our students, the fundamentals remain the same. Sensitive audience analysis, adequate research, clear organization, and forceful delivery remain the key ingredients for effective speeches. Therefore, our basic instructional approach in this text has also remained constant: We seek to engage students in the principles, practice, and ethics of public speaking—both as speakers and listeners.

Changes in the Sixth Edition

Although our basic approach remains the same, we have made changes and improvements to strengthen it. Instructors who have taught from previous editions suggested some of these changes. We made others to help students navigate through the technological advances that have broadened the menu of research and presentational aid options for public speakers.

Two new features reinforce the text's basic instructional emphases:

- Theory into Practice, a boxed feature that appears in every chapter, helps students understand and apply concepts and strategies of public communication to enhance their speaking competence.
- Try This boxes, also in each chapter, engage students in specific assignments that

Theory into Practice

TIPS

Gaining Perspective

In this chapter we present eleven strategies (listed on page 44) for building your speaking confidence. You incorporate these suggestions as you prepare and deliver your speeches. However, what should you do *after* your speech? You've heard the expression, "Experience is the best teacher." Well, there's some truth in that folk wisdom; you can use your public speaking experiences to build your confidence.

After each speech, assess your performance by asking and answering important questions. Your instructor will give you feedback for some of these questions; oth-

munication convey as you delivered your speech? What feedback did you receive from your classmates and instructor following the speech?

Remember, don't be too critical as you evaluate your performance. You will do some things well, and this should build your confidence. Other aspects of your speech you can improve, and you should work on these.

Suppose, for example, that you do encounter a serious problem: You lose your place, your mind goes blank, and so you bury your head in your notes and race to the end

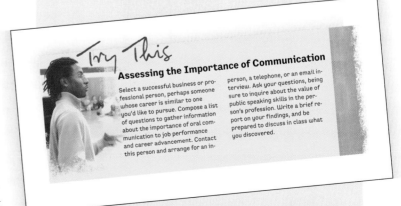

Try This

Assessing the Importance of Communication

Select a successful business or professional person, perhaps someone whose career is similar to one you'd like to pursue. Compose a list of questions to gather information about the importance of oral communication to job performance and career advancement. Contact this person and arrange for an in-person, a telephone, or an email interview. Ask your questions, being sure to inquire about the value of public speaking skills in the person's profession. Write a brief report on your findings, and be prepared to discuss in class what you discovered.

will prepare them for speeches they give in and outside of class. Students may self-select these activities, or they may be assigned by their instructors.

In addition to these new features, we've given a new title to an old resource. Exploring Online is so named because it captures the creativity and commitment necessary to master public speaking. These sidebar features, which were updated and checked for accuracy at the time of this writing, appear several times in each chapter, directing students to a wealth of Internet information that we consider especially interesting or useful.

Several of the student speeches included in the text are available online in video format on the accompanying MySpeechLab website.

Throughout this edition we've replaced and updated many student and professional examples, using actual classroom and contest speakers for most of these. In addition, we have incorporated changes specific to chapter content. The most significant changes are as follows:

- Chapter 1, "An Introduction to Public Speaking," more clearly illustrates how students use critical thinking skills as they research, construct, and deliver their speeches.
- Chapter 4, "Responding to Speeches," extends what is already the most thorough discussion of critiquing speeches in any textbook. The chapter now includes a student critique of a classroom speech; the transcript of that speech is included in the Appendix. We have annotated the critique to illustrate how the student used the critiquing guidelines discussed in the chapter.

- Chapter 5, "Analyzing Your Audience," more clearly focuses the discussion of using an audience questionnaire in the Theory into Practice feature.
- Chapter 7, "Researching Your Topic," now recognizes that most students research primarily online. We have added new information on searching the deep web while continuing to emphasize the quality of library subscription databases and academic and subject-specific search engines.
- Chapter 8, "Supporting Your Speech," expands its already strong emphasis on how to cite sources, especially from the Internet, with additional examples of poor versus good oral footnotes.
- Chapter 9, "Organizing the Body of Your Speech," provides expanded coverage of applying the "4 S's" strategy of developing key ideas. This chapter includes a new annotated example of a "4 S's" module, as well as an extended example discussed throughout the explanation of the "4 S's."
- Chapter 11, "Outlining Your Speech," features a new extended example of the stages of outlining undertaken by one person developing a speech.

- Chapter 12, "Wording Your Speech," elevates the importance of using inclusive language and using oral style.
- Chapter 14, "Using Presentational Aids," includes several new examples of visual aids, and provides clearer instruction for designing transparencies and slides.
- Chapter 16, "The Strategy of Persuasion," and Chapter 17, "The Structure of Persuasion," enhance already extensive coverage of persuasion theory and application. Chapter 17 includes a new student speech, annotated to illustrate the steps of Monroe's motivated sequence.
- This edition includes three new student speeches, complementing eight speeches retained from the previous edition.

Special Features

There are many special features that are an integral part of the learning materials in this book. We've included these to help students understand and learn pubic speaking concepts. In addition to the new Theory into Practice and Try This boxes, we have retained the following popular instructional features:

- **Key Points** boxes appear throughout the book to reinforce instruction and aid student review. They summarize important material and offer helpful guidelines throughout the public speaking process.

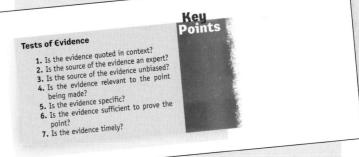

Key Points

Tests of Evidence

1. Is the evidence quoted in context?
2. Is the source of the evidence an expert?
3. Is the source of the evidence unbiased?
4. Is the evidence relevant to the point being made?
5. Is the evidence specific?
6. Is the evidence sufficient to prove the point?
7. Is the evidence timely?

- **Ethical Decisions** boxes deepen students' understanding of the difficult choices speakers and listeners can face. These boxes present mini cases and ask students to choose between controversial courses of action. Thought-provoking questions follow each scenario, providing springboards for engaging classroom debates.

Ethical Decisions

The Privacy of Public Information

Jeanine was researching a speech on the problem of child sexual abuse. While she was searching the Internet, she discovered a series of forums devoted to this topic, including a newsgroup, a listserv, and a live chat group. She found thought-provoking and useful discussions in the newsgroup and listserv, but the chat discussions were the most intimate and revealing. There, sexual abuse survivors described their memories of actual incidents and talked about how the trauma affected their adult lives.

Jeanine took notes on some of the most remarkable stories and decided to recount one in her speech to add drama. Is this a legitimate way for Jeanine to use her research? Should stories told on the Internet be considered public property, available for anyone to write or speak about? Should Jeanine try to find out whether the speaker would feel comfortable about having the story repeated in a speech? Should she try to verify that the story is true?

- **Speaking with Confidence** boxes feature the voices of real students from public speaking classes throughout the country explaining how this text helped them build their confidence in public speaking.

Speaking with Confidence

Though informative speaking sounds like a simple concept, it is more complicated than it may first appear. It is all too easy to fall into the trap of biased speaking. I selected the hotly debated topic of standardized testing for my informative speech. I then began my research. Throughout the process I would write down notes, only to realize that the information could be interpreted as leaning toward one side of the debate. In order to remain objective, I made an outline to plot the main points that needed to be discussed. I carefully chose ideas that were purely informative, such as "What exactly is standardized test-

ing?" and "When did standardized testing become widely used?" As I constructed my speech, I made sure to use reliable, objective websites that were not gung-ho for either side of the debate. Also, if I had a piece of information that had the slightest inclination of bias, I took it out and saved it for my persuasive speech. Researching an informative speech proved to be more challenging than I anticipated, because it's human nature to be biased in any hotly debated issue. But all this work kept me focused. When I delivered my speech, I felt confident that it was strictly informative.

—**Patty Pak,** *Virginia Tech University*

Sustainable Giving[18]

James Chang, Cypress College

1 Beatrice Biira, a nine-year-old girl in Uganda, lives in abject poverty. Living in a shanty home where the rain seeps through the roof every night, neither she nor any of her siblings has ever stepped foot in a school. Her story, sadly, is not unique. The World Bank in 2001 concluded that nearly three billion people live on less than two dollars a day. We hear this and we want to help, so we write checks to groups who claim that they will make a difference by donating food, clothing, and other short-term essentials, and we feel like we have helped make a difference in Beatrice's life, and, indeed, we probably have.

2 But what happens after the food runs out? Despite our best intentions, by donating to charities that offer short-term aid, we inadvertently perpetuate the cycle of poverty. Thus, I am advocating today that potential donors to charities should give to organizations that provide solutions that are sustainable in nature and that, furthermore, we change our very conception of the role of charities in fighting poverty. First, we will evaluate the problems caused by traditional conceptions of charitable giving, and then we will take a look at two examples of the solution—sustainable charity program. Finally, we will see how we can personally take steps to implement these solutions.

3 The American Association of Fundraising Counsel reports that Americans gave $212 billion to charity in 2001, and while that money was certainly donated with good intentions, much of it went to short-term causes that don't solve for poverty in the big picture. Certainly, charities that fight poverty see those horrors on a daily basis. The UN Food and

Attention
In his introduction (paragraphs 1 and 2), James focuses his audience's *attention* on the pervasive problem of poverty. He appeals to his listeners' self-interest (values) by suggesting that they are, unintentionally, part of the problem.

Need
James discusses the problems of traditional charitable giving in paragraphs 3 and 4. He es-

■ **Sample speeches** appear in selected chapters and in the Appendix as models for students to learn from or critique.

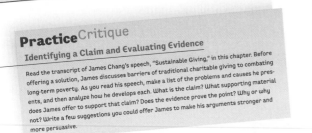

Practice Critique

Identifying a Claim and Evaluating Evidence

Read the transcript of James Chang's speech, "Sustainable Giving," in this chapter. Before offering a solution, James discusses barriers of traditional charitable giving to combating long-term poverty. As you read his speech, make a list of the problems and causes he presents, and then analyze how he develops each. What is the claim? What supporting material does James offer to support that claim? Does the evidence prove the point? Why or why not? Write a few suggestions you could offer James to make his arguments stronger and more persuasive.

■ **Practice Critique** activities at the ends of chapters give students an opportunity to learn how to provide helpful and thoughtful evaluations of others' speeches. These activities correlate with student speeches that appear in the Appendix.

Instructor Supplements

For this edition, we have enlisted the help of a number of talented colleagues in revising existing supplements and developing new ones. The following resources are available to help instructors plan and teach the public speaking course.

Print Resources

■ NEW! *Mastering Public Speaking Instructor's Classroom Kit,* **Volumes I and II:** Our unparalleled classroom kit includes every instructional aid a public speaking professor needs to manage the classroom. We have made our resources even easier to use by placing all of our print supplements in two convenient volumes, and electronic copies of all of our resources on two CD-ROMs found within the print volumes. Organized by chapter, each volume contains an Instructor's Manual, Test Bank, Grade Aid study guide, and slides from the *Mastering Public Speaking* PowerPoint presentation. Electronic versions of the Instructor's Manual, Test Bank, Grade Aid, PowerPoint, images from the text, and video clips—all searchable by key terms—are made easily accessible to instructors on the accompanying classroom kit CD-ROMs. The Instructor's Manual and Test Bank were prepared by a team of three professionals: Trudy Hanson and Jason Teven, West Texas A&M University (instructor's materials), and Ryan Loyd, West Texas A&M University (test questions). The Instructor's Manual provides suggestions for constructing the course syllabus, assignments, and sample exercises and activities; critiquing strategies; techniques for conducting in-class reviews; detailed chapter outlines; and a teaching tool section that gives strategies, ideas, and examples of how to integrate the Companion Website Plus into your course. The Test Bank includes more than 1,500 test questions, including multiple choice, true/false, short answer, and in-depth essay formats.

- *A Guide for New Public Speaking Teachers: Building toward Success,* **Third Edition,** by Calvin L. Troup, Duquesne University, is designed to help new teachers teach the introductory public speaking course effectively by covering such topics as preparing for the term, planning and structuring the course, evaluating speeches, using the textbook, and integrating technology into the classroom. The third edition includes a brief guide on teaching ESL, as well as teaching suggestions and student activities designed to accompany the Allyn & Bacon Classic and Contemporary Speeches DVD.
- *ESL Guide to Public Speaking,* by Debra Gonsher Vinik, Bronx Community College of the City University of New York, provides strategies and resources for instructors teaching in bilingual or multilingual classrooms. It also includes suggestions for further reading and a listing of related websites.
- *Great Ideas for Teaching Speech (GIFTS),* **Third Edition,** by Raymond Zeuschner, California Polytechnic State University, provides descriptions of and guidelines for assignments successfully used by experienced public speaking instructors in their classrooms.

Electronic Resources

- NEW! *Mastering Public Speaking Classroom Kit CD-ROM:* This exciting new supplement for instructors will bring together electronic copies of the Instructor's Manual, the Test Bank, the PowerPoint presentation, images from the text, and video clips for easy instructor access. This CD-ROM is organized by chapter and is searchable by key terms.
- *Computerized Test Bank:* The printed Test Bank is also available through Allyn & Bacon's computerized testing system, TestGen EQ. This fully networkable test-generating software is available on a multiplatform CD-ROM for Windows and Macintosh. The user-friendly interface allows you to view, edit, and add questions; transfer questions to tests; and print tests in a variety of fonts. Search and sort features allow you to locate questions quickly and to arrange them in whatever order you prefer. Free on request to adopters. Also available electronically through the Allyn & Bacon/Longman Instructor's Resource Center.
- *PowerPoint for Mastering Public Speaking,* **Sixth Edition,** prepared by Ilene Benz, Monroe Community College, is a text-specific package that consists of a collection of lecture outlines and graphic images keyed to every chapter of the text. These are available electronically through the Allyn & Bacon/Longman Instructor's Resource Center.
- *MySpeechLab* is a state-of-the-art, interactive and instructive online solution for introductory speech and communication courses. Designed to be used as a supplement to a traditional lecture course, or to completely administer an online course, MySpeechLab combines multimedia, video, activities, speech preparation tools, research support, tests, and quizzes to make teaching and learning fun! Video footage of several of the student speakers included in the text is included in MySpeechLab. Contact your Allyn & Bacon sales representative for additional details and ordering information.
- *VideoWorkshop for Public Speaking,* **Version 2.0,** prepared by Tasha Van Horn, Citrus College, and Marilyn Reineck, Concordia University, is a way to bring video into your course for maximized learning in public speaking. This total teaching and learning system includes quality video footage on an easy-to-use CD-ROM, plus a Student Learning Guide and an Instructor's Teaching Guide—both with textbook-specific correlation grids. The result? A program that brings textbook concepts to life with ease and that helps your students understand, analyze, and apply the objectives of the course. VideoWorkshop is available for several course areas and can be ordered only

when value-packaged with participating Allyn & Bacon textbooks. Visit www.ablongman.com/videoworkshop for more details.

- *Allyn & Bacon Classic and Contemporary Speeches DVD* presents a collection of more than 120 minutes of video footage in an easy-to-use DVD format. Each speech is accompanied by a biographical and historical summary that helps students to understand the context and motivation behind each speech. Contact your Allyn & Bacon sales representative for additional details and ordering information.

- *Mastering Public Speaking Video: A Student Speech with Critiques,* prepared by Julie Benson-Rosston, Red Rocks Community College, provides a model for students and instructors to learn to provide effective speech critiques. Included are critiquing guidelines, an informative student speech, an interactive session offering student and instructor feedback on the speech, and an improved student speech. Contact your local Allyn & Bacon sales representative for ordering information. Some restrictions apply.

- The *Allyn & Bacon Student Speeches Video Library* includes three two-hour American Forensic Association videos of award-winning student speeches, and three videos with a range of student speeches delivered in the classroom. Contact your local Allyn & Bacon sales representative for ordering information. Some restrictions apply.

- The *Allyn & Bacon Communication Video Library* contains a collection of communication videos produced by Film for the Humanities and Sciences. Contact your local Allyn & Bacon sales representative for ordering information. Some restrictions apply.

- The *Allyn & Bacon Public Speaking Video* includes excerpts of classic and contemporary speeches as well as student speeches to illustrate the public speaking process. One speech is delivered two times by the same person under different circumstances to illustrate the difference between effective and ineffective delivery based on appearance and nonverbal and verbal styles. Contact your local Allyn & Bacon sales representative for ordering information. Some restrictions apply.

- The *Allyn & Bacon Student Speeches Video III* includes student speeches covering a variety of topics that illustrate informative, persuasive, after-dinner, and eulogy topics. Contact your Allyn & Bacon sales representative for ordering information. Some restrictions apply.

- The *Allyn & Bacon Public Speaking Key Topics Video Library:* Adopters of Allyn & Bacon communication texts may receive one video from this series. Video topics include Critiquing Student Speeches, Addressing Your Audience, and Speaker Apprehension. Contact your local Allyn & Bacon sales representative for ordering information. Some restrictions apply.

- The *Allyn & Bacon Digital Media Archive for Communication,* Version 3.0, CD-ROM contains electronic images of charts, graphs, maps, tables, and figures, along with media elements such as video, audio clips, and related web links. These media assets are fully customizable to use with our preformatted PowerPoint outlines or to import into your own lectures (Windows and Mac). Contact your Allyn & Bacon sales representative for additional details and ordering information.

- The *Allyn & Bacon Public Speaking Transparency Package,* Version II, contains 100 public speaking transparencies created with images and text from our current public speaking texts. The transparency package is useful for providing visual support for classroom lectures and discussion on a full range of course topics. Contact your Allyn & Bacon sales representative for ordering information.

- *CourseCompass for Public Speaking,* powered by Blackboard and hosted nationally, is the most flexible online course management system on the market today. By using this powerful suite of online tools in conjunction with Allyn & Bacon's preloaded textbook and testing content, you can create an online presence for your course in under 30 minutes. The public speaking course features preloaded content such as quiz questions; video clips; instructor's manuals; PowerPoint presentations; still images; course preparation; instruction materials; VideoWorkshop for Public Speaking, Version 2.0; websites; and more! This course provides an abundance of resources to help you effectively teach and manage your class in the CourseCompass environment. Go to www.coursecompass.com for more information.

- *CourseCompass for Public Speaking, Professional Development Edition,* is a collection of helpful instructional materials that feature public speaking teaching strategies, resources, and video examples that you can access on the Internet using CourseCompass, our dynamic, interactive teaching and learning environment. For course coordinators working with adjuncts and/or teaching assistants, our *CourseCompass for Public Speaking, Professional Development Edition,* helps you provide training materials to your instructors— whether they're on campus or not. You can access our preloaded instructional materials, add your own materials, and make the resulting combination available to the other instructors for their own instructional development and for the continued benefit of their students. Go to www.coursecompass.com for more information.
- The *Allyn & Bacon PowerPoint Presentation Package for Public Speaking,* available electronically, includes 125 slides that provide visual and instructional support for the classroom including material on communication theory, visual aids, and tips for organizing and outlining speeches. A brief user's guide accompanies this package.

Student Supplements

The following resources are available to help students learn and study the material for the public speaking course.

Print Resources

- The *Study Guide,* prepared by James Benjamin, University of Toledo, contains a set of comprehensive review questions for each chapter in *Mastering Public Speaking,* as well as a set of PowerPoint lecture outlines so students can take notes as they follow along with each chapter's lecture.
- *Research Navigator Guide for Speech Communication,* prepared by Terrence Doyle, Northern Virginia Community College, is designed to teach students how to conduct high-quality online research and to document it properly. Pearson's new *Research Navigator* is the easiest way for students to start re-searching their speeches. Complete with extensive help on the research process and exclusive databases of credible and reliable source material, including EBSCO's ContentSelect Academic Journal Database and the *New York Times* Search by Subject Archive, *Research Navigator* helps students quickly and efficiently make the most of their research time. The guide is available on the web at www.researchnavigator.com or value packed with any of Allyn & Bacon's public speaking texts.
- *Speech Preparation Workbook,* prepared by Jennifer Dreyer and Gregory H. Patton, San Diego State University, takes students through the various stages of speech creation—from audience analysis to writing the speech—and provides supplementary assignments and tear-out forms. Contact your Allyn & Bacon sales representative for ordering information. Some restrictions apply.
- *Preparing Visual Aids for Presentations,* **Fourth Edition,** prepared by Dan Cavanaugh, is a 32-page visual booklet that provides a host of ideas for using

today's multimedia tools to improve presentations, including suggestions for planning a presentation, guidelines for designing visual aids and storyboarding, and a PowerPoint presentation walk-through. Contact your Allyn & Bacon sales representative for ordering information. Some restrictions apply.

- *Public Speaking in the Multicultural Environment,* **Second Edition,** prepared by Devorah A. Lieberman, Portland State University, helps students learn to analyze cultural diversity within their audiences and adapt their presentations accordingly. Contact your Allyn & Bacon sales representative for ordering information. Some restrictions apply.
- *Outlining Workbook,* prepared by Reeze L. Hanson and Sharon Condon, Haskell Indian Nations University, includes activities, exercises, and answers to help students develop and master the critical skill of outlining. Contact your Allyn & Bacon sales representative for ordering information. Some restrictions apply.

Electronic Resources

- *Mastering Public Speaking CD-ROM,* prepared by Edward Lee Lamoureux, Bradley University, is a fully interactive CD-ROM that allows students to critique speeches; plan, outline, and write their own speech; and view professional speeches. Students can watch speeches while writing their critiques, save their critiques to share with classmates or submit as assignments, and practice their speech-writing skills while they watch professionals in action. This CD-ROM brings to life the concepts and best practices detailed in the text.
- The *Companion Website Plus with Online Practice Tests,* accessed at www.ablongman.com/grice6e, prepared by Kane Madison Click, University of Nebraska–Lincoln, provides a wealth of activities to help students practice their critiquing techniques by linking to archived speeches on the Internet, and to help students learn to identify effective evidence and support for their speeches by critically evaluating scholarly websites. Web links include sites with speeches in text, audio, and video formats. The site also contains online learning objectives, flashcards, and a fully expanded set of practice tests for each chapter.
- *VideoWorkshop for Public Speaking,* **Version 2.0,** prepared by Tasha Van Horn, Citrus College, and Marilyn Reineck, Concordia University, includes quality video footage on an easy-to-use CD-ROM plus a Student Learning Guide with textbook-specific correlation grids. The result? A program that brings textbook concepts to life with ease and that helps students understand, analyze, and apply the objectives of the course. VideoWorkshop is available for introduction to communication, interpersonal communication, and public speaking courses. Visit www.ablongman.com/videoworkshop for more details.
- *Allyn & Bacon Classic and Contemporary Speeches DVD* presents a collection of more than 120 minutes of video footage in an easy-to-use DVD format. Each speech is accompanied by a biographical and historical summary that helps students to understand the context and motivation behind each speech.
- The *Allyn & Bacon Public Speaking Website,* **Second Edition,** prepared by Nan Peck, Northern Virginia Community College, can be accessed at www.ablongman.com/pubspeak. This website contains modules built with enrichment materials, web links, and interactive activities designed to enhance students' understanding of key concepts. The website helps students build, organize, and research speeches while learning about the process of public speaking.
- *Interactive Speechwriter Software,* **Version 1.1,** prepared by Martin R. Cox, is an interactive software package for student purchase that provides supplemental material, writing templates (for the informative, persuasive, and motivated sequence speeches, as well as for outlines), sample student speeches (text only), and more! This program enhances students' understanding of key

concepts discussed in the text and is available for Windows and Mac. Contact your Allyn & Bacon sales representative for ordering information. Some restrictions apply.

■ ***Speech Writer's Workshop CD-ROM,* Version 2.0,** is interactive software that will assist students with speech preparation and will enable them to write better speeches. The software includes four separate features: (1) a speech handbook with tips for researching and preparing speeches plus information about grammar, usage, and syntax; (2) a speech workshop that guides students through the speech-writing process and includes a series of questions at each stage; (3) a topics dictionary containing hundreds of speech ideas, all divided into subcategories to help students with outlining and organization; and (4) a citation database that formats bibliographic entries in MLA and APA styles. Contact your Allyn & Bacon representative for ordering information. Some restrictions apply.

■ **Public Speaking Tutor Center,** www.aw.com/tutorcenter (access code required): The Tutor Center provides students with free, one-on-one interactive tutoring from qualified public speaking instructors on all material in the text. The Tutor Center offers students help with understanding major communication principles as well as methods for study. In addition, students have the option of submitting self-taped speeches for review and critique by Tutor Center instructors to help prepare for and improve their speech assignments. Tutoring assistance is offered by phone, fax, Internet, and email during Tutor Center hours. For more details and ordering information, contact your Allyn & Bacon sales representative.

Acknowledgments

We are, first and foremost, grateful to the many university, college, and community college educators whose enthusiasm contributed to the success of previous editions of this textbook. This edition of *Mastering Public Speaking* is the product of more than just two authors. Although we have tried to speak with one voice for the sake of our readers, the truth is that many voices resonate throughout this text: the voices of our teachers, our colleagues, our editors, and our students. What we know, what we value, and what we write is shaped in part by their influence and insights. Wherever possible we have tried to acknowledge their contributions. For all their influence on this manuscript, we are thankful.

Our collaboration began at the urging of a former student, Pam Lancaster, when she was a publisher's representative at Prentice Hall. We are grateful to Prentice Hall and Allyn & Bacon for allowing us to make previous editions of *Mastering Public Speaking* the book we wanted it to be. We are especially indebted to Steve Dalphin, Virginia Feury-Gagnon, Paul Smith, Carla Daves, Helane Manditch-Prottas, Marlene Ellin, and Karon Bowers for their faith in the project, their patience, and their suggestions.

We thank the entire editorial and production staffs at Allyn & Bacon for their contributions to this sixth edition. We have benefited from the unflagging encouragement and accommodation of Brian Wheel. We are especially grateful to Carol Alper for her guidance and suggestions and for carefully supervising the editing process for the past three editions of this book. Her professionalism and patience provided us the time to explore and evaluate new ideas, while keeping the project on schedule. These colleagues in cyberspace were always just an email away from providing us their input and support. Carol and Brian, thanks for helping to make writing fun.

We would like to acknowledge the individuals at Allyn & Bacon who contributed to the production of the sixth edition of *Mastering Public Speaking*. Karen Mason guided the process very capably. Heather Hawkins completed many tasks along the way with efficiency and enthusiasm. Larissa Tierney and Naomi Rudov artfully chose the photographs that adorn the pages. Thanks to Robert Tonner for securing necessary permissions. We are also grateful to Shannon Foreman and the team at Omegatype Typography, who masterfully guided our manuscript into page proofs. Thanks for keeping all the plates spinning.

Many students, authors, and publishers graciously allowed us to quote material in this book. Especially helpful were the comments from students and their instructors. Five advanced public speaking students—Stuart Howlett, Erin King, Danny McLean, Amanda Radley, and Caitlyn Rancourt—provided input to make this book more reader friendly. Our graduate teaching assistants—Johnny R. Doane, Melissa Janoske, Callie S. Robertson, Hannah L. Shinault, Melissa Short, and Emilie L. Tydings—tested our ideas in their classrooms and coordinated feedback from students. A number of students responded to our call for feedback about classroom experiences or topics in *Mastering Public Speaking* that increased their confidence. We thank them all, particularly the students selected for the Speaking with Confidence features in this edition. We are grateful to Heather Toro Derrick, Dante Morelli, Paula Schlegel, Suzanne Skinner, and Emily Wilkinson Stallings for introducing us to several of these students.

John Deosdade joins colleague Stephen Dingman of the San Antonio College Learning Resource Center on the list of reference librarians whose expertise has strengthened our research chapter. Thanks for your close reading and expert suggestions that helped us monitor changes in research sources and technology. We thank James McCroskey for permission to reprint his "Personal Report of Public Speaking Anxiety" featured in Chapter 3.

We have benefited immensely from the encouragement and advice of our fellow faculty members at Radford University and San Antonio College, particularly Gwen Brown, Barbara Strain, Suzanne Skinner, David Mrizek, Jolinda Ramsey, and Melody Hull. Leonard Ziegler, Debra Coates, Lora Gordon, and Gary O. Smith, many thanks for your help with photographs. Chris Skinner, thanks for your help in transferring a number of videos to DVD.

In addition, *Mastering Public Speaking* has been shaped and refined by the close readings and thoughtful suggestions of a number of reviewers. We would like to thank the following reviewers for their comments on this edition:

Hope E. Bennin, Big Sandy Community and Technical College

Kathy Lee Berggren, Cornell University

David L. Bodary, Sinclair Community College

Kane M. Click, University of Nebraska–Lincoln

Ellen Karsh, Florida International University

Marianne L. Palmisano, Glendale Community College

C. Thomas Preston, Jr., University of Missouri–St. Louis

Kirk Puckett, Alamance Community College

We would also like to acknowledge reviewers of previous editions:

Linda Anthon, Valencia Community College

Barbara L. Baker, Central Missouri State University

Elizabeth Bell, University of South Florida

Jim Benjamin, University of Toledo

Tim Borchers, Moorhead State University

Sue E. Brilhart, Southwest Missouri State University

Carl R. Burgchardt, Colorado State University

Sharon Cline, University of North Dakota

Dolly Conner, Louisburg College

Pamela Cooper, Northwestern University

Michael Cronin, Professor Emeritus, Radford University

Thomas E. Diamond, Montana State University

Terrence Doyle, Northern Virginia Community College

John Fritch, Southwest Missouri State University

Robert W. Glenn, University of Tennessee

Trudy L. Hanson, West Texas A&M University

Dayle C. Hardy-Short, Northern Arizona University

Deborah Hatton, Sam Houston State University

Kimberly Batty Herbert, Clovis Community College

Leslie A. Klipper, Miramar College

Mary Kaye Krum, formerly of Florence-Darlington Technical College

Bruce Loebs, Idaho State University

Sean McDevitt, Lakeland College

Patricia Palm McGillen, Mankato State University

David B. McLennan, Peace College

Eileen Oswald, Valencia Community College

Rosemarie Rossetti, Ohio State University

Jim Roux, Horry-Georgetown Technical College

Edward H. Sewell, Virginia Tech University

Frances Swinny, Professor Emerita, Trinity University

Cory Tomasson, Illinois Valley Community College

Beth M. Waggenspack, Virginia Tech University

Doris Werkman, Portland State University

Dianna R. Wynn, Midland College

We enlisted the help of several talented individuals to prepare the supplemental materials for *Mastering Public Speaking*. We would like especially to thank Trudy Hanson, Jason Tevon, and Ryan Loyd at West Texas A&M University for preparing the Instructor's Manual and Test Bank; James Benjamin of University of Toledo for preparing the printed study guide; Kane Madison Click of the University of Nebraska–Lincoln for his work on the Companion Website; Julie Benson-Rosston of Red Rocks Community College for her work on the *Mastering Public Speaking* Video: A Student Speech with Critiques; Ilene Benz of Monroe Community College for her work on the PowerPoint package; and Edward Lee Lamoureux of Bradley University for designing the interactive *Mastering Public Speaking* CD-ROM.

Finally, we are indebted to all our public speaking students, who have crafted their messages, walked to the front of their classrooms, and informed, persuaded, entertained, and challenged us. Without their ideas and experiences, writing and revising this book would have been impossible, just as without tomorrow's students it would be unnecessary.

An Invitation

We are interested in hearing your feedback about the sixth edition of *Mastering Public Speaking*. Please contact us by email at the following addresses:

ggrice@radford.edu

jskinner@accd.edu

We look forward to hearing from you.

—*George L. Grice and John F. Skinner*

An Introduction to Public Speaking

chapter

1

All the great speakers were bad speakers at first. —RALPH WALDO EMERSON

Why Study Public Speaking?

By anyone's standards, Deep Springs College is an unusual two-year school. A self-sustaining cattle ranch and alfalfa farm in a remote, far eastern California valley, its entire student body is a couple of dozen young men; its faculty, half a dozen residents. The nearest town of significant size is an hour's drive away. The average combined SAT score for applicants is high.[1] After two, sometimes three, years at Deep Springs, students transfer to the "safety net" schools that accepted them fresh out of high school: Harvard, Cornell, Berkeley, Swarthmore, Princeton, or MIT, for example. Students, who attend free of tuition in return for 20 hours a week of labor, govern the school, evaluate the progress of their peers, and select each year's professors and incoming students.[2]

L. L. Nunn, industrialist and founder of Deep Springs, wanted to prepare young people of exceptional aptitude for lives of public service. He knew that would require them to be articulate. For that reason, the only two required courses are English composition and public speaking. Deep Springs president Jack Newell notes that "Monday evenings have become major events in the community as faculty, staff, and their families gather to hear students speak on topics ranging from international affairs to institutional concerns. Always lively, these sessions provide a natural setting for the exchange of ideas and the unification of the community."[3]

Public speaking required each semester? That, you may think, is the most unusual fact of all. Yet the people of Deep Springs—past and present—seem keenly aware of how important public speaking can be, both in the college classroom and beyond.

Today, beyond the relative security of the college or university classroom, thousands of speakers will stand in front of American audiences and deliver speeches. And during those same 24 hours, people will make millions of business presentations. These speakers will express and elaborate their ideas, champion their causes, and promote their products or services. Those who are successful will make sales, enlist support, and educate and entertain their listeners. Many will also enhance their reputations as effective speakers. To achieve these goals, each will be using the skills, principles, and arts that are the subject of this textbook.

Consider, too, that somewhere on a college campus right now is the student who will one day deliver an inaugural address after being sworn in as president; the student who will appear on national television to accept the Heisman Trophy, a Tony Award for Best Performance—Leading Actress in a Play, or the Academy Award for Best Director; and the student who will present breakthrough medical research findings to a national conference of doctors and medical technicians, or whose words will usher passage of important legislation.

You may be taking this course as an elective because you want to improve your public speaking skills in the relative security of a classroom. Chances are, however, that, like the students at Deep Springs, you are in this class because it is a requirement for graduation. If that's the case, you may rightfully be asking, "Why should I take a course in public speaking?" The answer, suggested in the preceding real-life examples, is that studying and practicing public speaking benefits you personally, professionally, and publicly.

Personal Benefits

This course can benefit you personally in three ways. First, mastering public speaking can help you acquire skills important to your success in college. According to a Carnegie Foundation report,

> To succeed in college, undergraduates should be able to write and speak with clarity, and to read and listen with comprehension. Language and thought are inextricably connected, and as undergraduates develop their linguistic skills, they hone the quality of their thinking and become intellectually and socially empowered.[4]

Look at some of the chapter titles in this textbook. They include words such as *analyzing, researching, organizing, wording,* and *delivering.* These are skills you will use in constructing and delivering your speeches. They are also *transferable* skills; they can help you throughout your academic studies, as well as in your chosen career.

Second, public speaking can help you become more knowledgeable. According to one study, we remember:

10 percent of what we read,

20 percent of what we hear,

30 percent of what we see, and

70 percent of what we speak.[5]

Consider for a moment two different ways of studying lecture notes for an exam. One method is to read and reread your notes silently. An alternative is to stand in your room, put your lecture notes on your dresser, and deliver the lecture out loud, pretending you are the instructor explaining the material to the class. Which method do you think promotes better understanding and retention of the course material? You will not be surprised to learn that it's the second, more active method.

Speaking is an active process. You discover ideas, shape them into a message, and deliver that message using your voice and body. The act of speaking is a crucial test of your thinking skills. As author E. M. Forster observed, "How do I know what I think until I've seen what I've said?" In this course, you will learn a lot about the topics on which you choose to speak. By learning how to construct an effective speech, you will also become a better listener to others' speeches, oral reports, and lectures, and this will further increase your learning.

A third personal benefit of this course is that it can help build your confidence. We devote Chapter 3 to discussing the most common fear of adult Americans: the fear of speaking to a group of people. In this course, you will learn how to turn this apprehension into confidence. You will do so by reading this textbook, by listening to your instructor, and, most important, by doing. The confidence and poise you gain as you begin to master public speaking will help you when you give that oral report on "Gender Roles in the Plays of Shakespeare" in your British literature class or when you address your school board urging them to retain the district's music education program. As the Emerson quotation at the beginning of this chapter suggests, great speaking requires practice, but your efforts will bring you these three personal rewards.

Professional Benefits

Studying communication, and specifically public speaking, is also important to you professionally. Numerous studies document a strong relationship between communication competence and career success. Effective speaking skills enhance your chances of first securing employment and then advancing in your career. In a 1999 report, the National Association of Colleges and Employers listed characteristics employers consider most important when hiring an employee. At the top of the list was communication skills.[6]

In another study three speech and business professors surveyed 1,000 randomly selected human resource managers to determine the "factors most important in helping graduating college students obtain employment." Oral communication skills ranked first, with written communication second and listening third.[7] The researchers concluded:

> From the results of this and the previous study, it appears that the skills most valued in the contemporary job-entry market are communication skills. The skills of listening, oral communication (both interpersonal and public), written communication, and the trait of enthusiasm are indicated to be the most important. Again, it would appear to follow that university officials wishing to be of the greatest help to their graduates in finding employment would make sure that basic competencies in oral and written communication are developed. Courses in listening, interpersonal, and public communication would form the basis of meeting the oral communication competencies.[8]

This course will instruct you in two of those vital skills: public speaking and listening.

Once you are hired, your speaking skills continue to work for you, becoming your ticket to career success and advancement. A survey of 500 executives found that speaking skills "rated second only to job knowledge as important factors in a businessperson's success." That same study also showed that effective communication helped improve company productivity and understanding among employees.[9]

Although you are likely to spend only a small portion of your communication at work giving presentations and speeches, your ability to stand in front of a group of people and present your ideas is important to your career success. One survey of 66 companies found that 76 percent of executives gave oral reports.[10] Another survey found that, while on-the-job public speaking accounted for only 6 percent of managers' and technical professionals' time, it nevertheless ranked as more important to job perform-

Try This

Assessing the Importance of Communication

Select a successful business or professional person, perhaps someone whose career is similar to one you'd like to pursue. Compose a list of questions to gather information about the importance of oral communication to job performance and career advancement. Contact this person and arrange for an in-

person, a telephone, or an email interview. Ask your questions, being sure to inquire about the value of public speaking skills in the person's profession. Write a brief report on your findings, and be prepared to discuss in class what you discovered.

ance than did time spent reading mail and other documents, dictating letters and writing reports, and talking on the phone.[11] Oral communication and public speaking clearly play a critical role in your professional life.

Public Benefits

Finally, public speaking can help you play your role as a member of society. Public speaking is an important part of creating and sustaining a society of informed, active citizens. A democratic society is shaped, in part, by the public eloquence of its leaders:

> *Speech is civilization itself. The word, even the most contradictory word, preserves contact—it is silence which isolates.*
> —THOMAS MANN

A mayor who reveals hidden strengths by mourning the dead and comforting the living

A noted talk show host who encourages parents "to jumpstart a child's imagination" through the power of reading

Two former presidents who tap a nation's generosity to aid tsunami victims in southern Asia

But a democratic society is also shaped by the quiet eloquence of everyday citizens:

The police officer who informs residents of a crime-plagued area how to set up a neighborhood watch program

The social worker who addresses the city council and secures funding for a safe house for abused and runaway children

The student who consoles grieving students and faculty at an assembly remembering classmates fatally shot at their school

In each of these instances, the speaker used the power of the spoken word to address a need and solicit an appropriate audience response.

While we recognize effective speaking when we meet the person who always says "just the right thing" or who says things in funny and colorful ways, few of us have been trained to speak well. To appreciate the power of communication, you must understand just what it is. That requires a look at some definitions of communication and at some of its essential components.

Definitions of Communication

The word *communicate* comes from the Latin verb *communicare,* meaning "to make common to many, share, impart, divide."[12] This concept of sharing is important in understanding communication and is implicit in our definition of the term. Simply stated, when you communicate, you share, or make common, your knowledge and ideas with someone else.

You can understand communication best when you view it as both a *process* and a *product.* Some scholars believe that communication is basically a process. For example, Thomas Scheidel provides a process perspective when he defines communication as "the transmission and reception of symbolic cues."[13] Other scholars see communication as an outcome or a product and define it simply as shared meaning. We believe both of these perspectives are valid. **Communication,** then, *is the sharing of meaning by sending and receiving symbolic cues.*

> **communication:** the process of sharing meaning by sending and receiving symbolic cues.

FIGURE 1.1
The Triangle
of Meaning

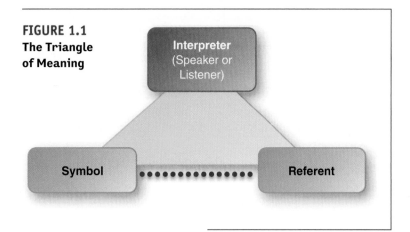

You can understand how meaning is shared by studying Figure 1.1, Charles Ogden and I. A. Richards's triangle of meaning.[14] This figure illustrates the three elements necessary when someone communicates; those elements are interpreter, symbol, and referent. The word interpreter refers to both the sender and the receiver of a message. The **interpreter** is simply the person who is communicating, with words or other symbols.

The second element of this model, the **symbol,** is anything to which people attach or assign a meaning. Symbols can be pictures, drawings, or objects. Even colors can function as symbols: Political pundits reduce us to living in red states or blue states. The police officer's uniform and squad car are symbols of the authority of the police. The most familiar symbols, however, are words in a particular language. Many words refer to particular objects, places, and people: *chair; Long Beach, California;* and *Eudora Welty,* for example. Some words refer to concepts, such as *freedom of expression, existentialism,* and *fair play.*

The third and final element of the triangle of meaning is the **referent,** the object or idea for which the symbol stands. Both the sender and the receiver of a message have a referent for the symbols used. This referent depends on each individual's knowledge and experience. People cannot exchange referents in the way they can exchange objects. For example, someone can hand you a paper clip, and that paper clip is the same in your hand as it is in your friend's. Your friends, however, cannot transfer their ideas or information to you. All they can do is to code their ideas into symbols and hope that, as you decode them, the ideas you receive will be similar to the ones they intended. In short, as senders we select a symbol based on our referent. That symbol, in turn, triggers the receiver's referent.

Countless jokes and situation comedy plots revolve around interpreters who attach different referents to the same symbol. The *New Yorker* cartoon on page 7 illustrates one such outcome. Yet the consequences can also be serious and divisive. Consider the experience of Muslim-American Zayed M. Yasin, the Harvard student whose graduation speech emerged from a competitive process as one of the three choices of the selection committee in the spring of 2002. The furor began when the campus newspaper, the *Harvard Crimson,* published the titles of the three student commencement speeches. Yasin's speech, to be delivered less than nine months after September 11, 2001, was titled "Of Faith and Citizenship: My American Jihad." His aim, he said, was to rescue the word *jihad* from extremists who had co-opted it to justify terrorism. He defined the term as a spiritual quest, "the determination to do right and justice even against your personal interests."[15] Among the definitions of the Arabic word are "striving," "effort," and "struggle," but many of those who protested the selection of Yasin's speech equated the term *jihad* with a "holy war." After the protests began on his campus, Yasin met with members of the selection committee, retitled his speech "Of Faith and Citizenship" for the printed program, and delivered the text of the speech without changing a word.[16]

As this example demonstrates, communication is clearest only when the interpreters involved attach similar referents to the message being communicated. You can, no doubt, think of experiences you have had when people misinterpreted what you said because they attached different referents to your words. The most important thing to remember about the triangle of meaning and the process of communication is this: *Words and other symbols have no inherent meaning. People have meaning; words do not.* The word takes on the meaning that each interpreter attaches to it.

interpreter: any person using symbols to send or receive messages.

symbol: anything to which people attach meaning.

referent: the object or idea each interpreter attaches to a symbol.

Public meetings provide citizens with a forum for public debate, an essential ingredient for a democratic society.

What does the triangle of meaning have to do with public speaking? As you will discover throughout this book, this model applies to public speaking just as it does to all other forms of communication. If speakers and listeners always used specific symbols, interpreted them objectively, and attached similar referents to them, we would

experience few if any communication problems arising from the content of the message. As a result, your work in a public speaking class could be limited to improving your organization and polishing your style of delivery. Yet many of our communication problems can be traced directly to difficulties in the relationships between interpreters, the symbols they use, and the referents behind those symbols.

As a public speaker, you must try to ensure that the message your audience hears matches as closely as possible the message you intended. You do that by paying particular attention to your content, organization, and delivery, major subjects of this book. To understand the complexity of public speaking, you need to realize how it relates to other levels of communication.

Levels of Communication

Communication can occur on five different levels:

1. intrapersonal
2. interpersonal
3. group
4. public
5. mass communication

Each level is distinguished by the number of people involved, the formality of the situation, and the opportunities for feedback. One level, public communication, is the subject of this book and the focus of the course you are now taking. Yet public speaking incorporates elements of the other four levels of communication, and a brief look at each will help you better understand public speaking.

Intrapersonal Communication

Simply stated, **intrapersonal communication** is communication with yourself. The prefix *intra-* means "within." Intrapersonal communication serves many functions, and we all practice it every waking moment. If you woke up late this morning, for example, and panicked because you overslept for a class, you were communicating intrapersonally. If in the middle of a public speech you tell yourself, "This is really going well," or "I can't believe I just said that," you are also communicating intrapersonally.

As these examples demonstrate, much intrapersonal communication is geared toward a specific, conscious purpose: evaluating how we are doing in a particular situation, solving a problem, relieving stress, or planning for the near or distant future. Though we all have probably uttered something aloud to ourselves at times of stress, joy, puzzlement, or discouragement, intrapersonal communication is typically silent. We sit quietly as we reflect on a speaker explaining the difference between ambient and progressive jazz. We are attentive as we hear another speaker explain the preparations for a first sky dive. Both as public speakers and as audience members for others' speeches, we communicate intrapersonally a great deal. Key features of intrapersonal communication to keep in mind are that it is a continuous process of self-feedback and that it involves only one person.

Interpersonal Communication

As soon as our communication involves ourselves and one other person, it moves to a second level. **Interpersonal communication** occurs between people, usually two of

INTRAPERSONAL COMMUNICATION
www.cdm.uwaterloo.ca
The communication that is central to your career success begins with effective intrapersonal communication. If you're uncertain about your ultimate career, the University of Waterloo's *Career Development eManual* will help you assess your strengths and interests, research various occupations, decide on career objectives, make employment contacts, measure your success at work, and reevaluate your goals in later life.

intrapersonal communication: cognition or thought; communicating with oneself.

interpersonal communication: communication between individuals in pairs; also called dyadic communication.

them. Interpersonal communication is sometimes called dyadic communication; *dyad* is Latin for "pair." Face-to-face conversations between friends, colleagues, or acquaintances are a common form of interpersonal communication. Yet even strangers communicate interpersonally: A police officer questioning a witness to a crime and a new student talking to a teacher are both communicating interpersonally. Even keyboard to keyboard communication—two friends instant messaging, for example—is interpersonal.

Whenever two communicators are face to face or speaking over the telephone, the opportunity for verbal interaction always exists. If someone had secretly tape-recorded your last conversation with your best friend and typed a transcript of it for you to read, you would probably be surprised by the number of incomplete sentences each of you spoke. Ideas that do not appear to make much sense in writing were likely quite clear in conversation. Your best friend, someone who is really on your wavelength, often knows how you are going to finish a sentence and either finishes it for you or nods agreement and switches to another idea.

In some interpersonal situations, of course, the verbal interaction is less frequent and more self-conscious. We do not interrupt the interviewer sizing us up for a job or the police officer who has just pulled us over for a traffic violation as easily as we do a close friend. Yet the opportunity for verbal interaction exists in even those relatively stressful situations and is always a characteristic of spoken interpersonal communication.

Group Communication

As we add to the number of people involved, the next level is group communication. Although we discuss group interaction more thoroughly in Chapter 19, we will present some important points about it here. **Group communication** generally takes place with three or more people interacting and influencing each other to pursue a common goal. Although researchers place varying limits on the size of a group, everyone recognizes that a sense of cohesion or group identity is essential to any definition of this level of communication.

Seven students who get together and spend half the night reviewing material and quizzing one another for an upcoming exam are obviously engaged in group communication. When you present your speeches in class, you will not be engaged in group communication. However, if your presentation on a particularly interesting topic generates questions and discussion, your public speaking class might qualify as an example of group communication.

The important thing to remember about group communication is that the people involved must have a sense of group identity. A group of 14 people, for example, is not just seven dyads or pairs of people. They must believe and accept that they belong together for some reason, whether they face a common problem, share similar interests, or simply work in the same division of a company.

Group communication may be informal, with all group members free to discuss issues as they wish, or formal, operating under the rules of parliamentary procedure. As long as members are relatively free to contribute to the discussion, what occurs is clearly group communication. However, once someone stands up and begins to present a report or make a speech, the communication shifts to the fourth level, public communication.

Public Communication

Public communication, the subject of this course, occurs when one person speaks face to face with an audience. That audience may be as small as your public speaking class or as large as the masses of people who fill stadiums and other public areas to hear certain speakers. As the size of the audience grows, the flow of communication becomes increasingly one directional, from speaker to audience. When the audience is large, individual members have less opportunity for verbal interaction with the speaker.

group communication: three or more people interacting and influencing one another to pursue a common goal.

public communication: one person communicating face to face with an audience.

Former Presidents Bill Clinton and George H. W. Bush used their visibility and voices to enlist support for tsunami victims in South Asia and East Africa. The following year they once again mobilized public support for Hurricane Katrina relief in the United States.

For example, your public speaking class is probably small enough that you feel free to have your instructor answer any questions you have during class. In a lecture class of several hundred students, however, you might feel more pressure to keep silent, even if you had a legitimate question. If you were part of an audience of several thousand people, not only would you feel pressure to keep quiet during a speech, but even if you did voice a question the speaker probably could not hear it.

The key characteristics of public communication, therefore, are a more one-directional flow of information and a more formal feeling than the other types of communication we have discussed so far. Whether the audience is a class of 20 or an assembly of 20,000, public communication always involves one person communicating to an audience that is physically present.

Mass Communication

But what happens if we sit in front of our television sets or computer monitors and see video clips from that small class or large public assembly? In such a situation we have entered the fifth and final level of communication, **mass communication.** Once the audience becomes so large that it cannot be gathered in one place, some type of print or electronic medium—newspaper, magazine, radio, television, or computer, among others—must be placed between speaker or writer and the intended audience. The physical isolation of speaker and audience severely limits the possibilities for spontaneous interaction between them. In fact, an important characteristic of mass communication is that audience feedback is *always* delayed. If a print or electronic article inspires or angers you enough that you write a letter to the editor or post a response, you will be slowed as you compose your message and mail or email it. You have the opportunity to send feedback, but it is delayed.

A second characteristic of mass communication is that the method of message transmission can become very important. Advertising agencies, political consultants, and the people who use them know very well that the *way* a message is sent can be as impor-

mass communication: one person or group communicating to a large audience through some print or electronic medium.

tant as the *content* of that message, something public speakers should also remember. Advertisements for products, services, and political candidates reach different sizes and types of audiences via radio, television, billboards, magazines, newspapers, or Internet websites. We devote a portion of Chapter 18 to the special challenges of speaking before a video camera, because future technology will surely expand the importance of mass media in getting messages across to the public.

You will master public speaking skills more quickly and easily if you remain aware of the connections between public communication and the four other levels of communication. In this class, you may use interpersonal and group communication to determine your speech topics and how you approach them. You may interview an expert on a topic you are considering for a speech. Through informal conversations with your classmates, you will form a clearer picture of your audience by discovering their interests, attitudes, and values. You may offer others feedback on their speeches and receive their comments regarding your speech. If you have the opportunity to videotape one or more of your speeches, you will gain experience with one of the important electronic media of mass communication, even if your speech is not broadcast publicly. Certainly, you will consult print and electronic media resources as you research your speech. And all the time you are delivering your public speeches, you will be giving yourself intrapersonal feedback about the job you are doing and the positive responses we hope you are receiving.

Elements of Communication

Now that you understand the different levels of communication, let's look at the elements of communication to see how they apply, specifically, to the complex activity of public speaking. Remember, the better you understand how communication works in general, the better you will be able to make it work for you in specific speaking situations. Just as important, knowing these elements will let us see where some common communication problems arise.

Today, the most widely accepted model of communication has seven components, as illustrated in Figure 1.2, the communication elements model. Although we can identify the individual elements of the communication process, we cannot assess them in isolation. Contemporary scholars emphasize the transactional, interactive nature of communication. Each element simultaneously influences, and is influenced by, the others.

Speaker

Though other animals certainly communicate, human communication starts with a person, the **speaker**. We could also call this person who initiates communication the sender, the source, or the encoder. **Encoding** is the process of putting ideas into symbols, and we encode so much and so well that we are aware of the process only when we find ourselves "at a loss for words" while either speaking or writing.

Message

Inextricably linked to the speaker is the **message**, the ideas actually communicated. Speech communication scholar Karlyn Kohrs Campbell captures the connection between messages and people when she writes:

> Ideas do not walk by themselves; they must be carried—expressed and voiced—by someone. As a result, we do not encounter ideas neutrally, objectively, or apart from a context; we meet them as someone's ideas.[17]

speaker: the sender, encoder, or source of the message.

encoding: the process of selecting symbols to carry a message.

message: ideas communicated verbally and nonverbally.

FIGURE 1.2
The Communication Elements Model

A speaker encodes a message, sending it through a channel to a listener, who decodes it. The listener provides feedback, sending it through a channel to a speaker. This interaction takes place in an environment with varying levels of internal and external noise.

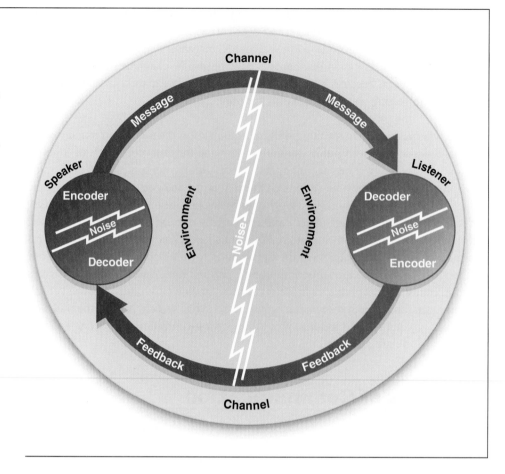

Exploring *Online*

COMPARING COMMUNICATION MODELS

http://web.sfc.keio.ac.jp/~masanao/Mosaic_data/com_model.html

Visit this site, maintained by Keio University in Japan, to view and compare a variety of communication models. The site includes linear, interactional, and transactional models. For explanations of each model, you will need to consult the sources cited.

The ideas of the message originate with the speaker, who determines the form that the message will initially take. However, that message is further shaped by others who may participate in the communication process.

Listener

Unless the communication is intrapersonal, the message is sent to a **listener**—the decoder, or receiver. This person shapes the message by **decoding** it, that is, attaching meanings to the words, gestures, and voice inflections received. Is each listener's decoded message identical to the one the speaker originally encoded? Remember our earlier discussion of the triangle of meaning; communication involves more than a single message. The truth is that there are as many messages as there are communicators involved. As long as these messages are similar, communication is usually effective.

Nor does the message stop as it is received. Instead, it is transformed—added to or diminished—as it is joined by other messages that originate with each listener. It is a mistake to assume that a person in the communication process is either a sender or a receiver of messages. The truth is that we perform both roles simultaneously.

Feedback

The interactions between listeners and senders provide a fourth element in our model of communication. **Feedback** includes all messages, verbal and nonverbal, sent by listeners to speakers. If you tell a joke, your listeners will tell you through laughter and visual feedback whether they understood the joke and how they evaluated it. If you are

listener: the receiver or decoder of the message.

decoding: the process of attaching meanings to symbols received.

feedback: verbal and nonverbal responses between communicators about the clarity or acceptability of messages.

paying attention, you will know who liked it, who didn't, who hasn't understood it, and who was offended by it. "If you are paying attention" is the particularly important phrase, for, in order to be effective, feedback must be received and interpreted correctly.

Because public speaking is an audience-centered activity, you as a speaker must be sensitive to feedback from your audience. Some feedback is deliberate and conscious; some is unintentional and unconscious. But your audience will always provide you with feedback of some kind. If you are paying attention to it, you will know when they appreciate your humor, understand the point you are making, disagree with the position you advocate, or are momentarily confused by something you have said.

Channel

The fifth element of our model is the **channel** or medium—the way the message is sent. Each speaker sending a message and each listener providing feedback uses a channel. In public speaking, the medium is vibrations in the air between speaker and listener, set in motion by the speaker's voice. Vocal elements such as rate, volume, voice quality, and changes in pitch level also carry part of the message. Visual elements, another channel for the message, include eye contact, facial expression, gestures, movement, and even the use of presentational aids. As a public speaker, you must learn to use and control all these channels.

Environment

The sixth element of the model of communication is the **environment.** Two factors shape an environment: (1) the occasion during which the communication occurs and (2) the physical setting where the communication occurs. The occasion refers to the reasons why people have assembled. Circumstances may be serious or festive, planned or spontaneous. Occasions for communication may be as relaxed and informal as a party with friends, as rule-bound as a college debate, or as formal and traditional as a commencement address at a graduation ceremony.

The physical setting for your classroom speeches is probably apparent to you. You know the size of the room and the number of people in the audience. You know whether the seating arrangement is fixed or changeable. You know whether the room has a lectern or Internet access. You know, or may soon discover, potential problems with the setting: The table at the front of the room is wobbly, the air seems stuffy about halfway through each class meeting, one of the fluorescent lights flickers. Each of these distracting elements is a form of noise, a final element for which any accurate model of communication must account.

Noise

Noise is anything that distracts from effective communication, and some form of noise is always present. Three forms of noise exist, distinguished by their sources. First, much noise is **physical**; that is, it occurs in the physical communication environment: the sounds of traffic, the loud whoosh of an air conditioner or a heater, the voices of people talking and laughing as they pass by a classroom. Some physical noise may not involve a sound at all, however. If your classroom is so cold that you shiver or so hot that you fan yourself, then its temperature is a form of noise. If the lighting in the room is poor, then that form of noise will certainly affect the communication occurring there. If your classroom is near a construction site and the smell of creosote disgusts you, then that odor is a form of noise. Anything in the immediate environment that interferes with communication is physical noise.

A second type of noise is **physiological**: A bad cold that affects your hearing and speech, a headache, and an empty, growling stomach are examples. Each of these

channel: the way a message is sent.

environment: the physical setting and the occasion for communication.

noise: anything that distracts from effective communication.

physical noise: distractions originating in the communication environment.

physiological noise: distractions originating in the bodies of communicators.

Effective public speakers adapt their speaking styles to the physical settings and the occasions for their speeches.

bodily conditions can shift your focus from communicating with others to thinking about how uncomfortable you feel, a form of intrapersonal communication.

A third and final type of noise is **psychological.** This type of noise refers to mental rather than bodily distractions. Anxiety, worry, daydreaming, and even joy over some recent event can distract you from the message at hand. Each of these forms of noise—physical, physiological, and psychological—can occur independently or in combination and, as we have said, some form of noise is always present. As a speaker, you must try to minimize the effects of noise in public communication: by varying your rate, volume, and pitch, for example, or through lively physical delivery that combats noise and rivets the audience's attention to your message.

As you can see, public speaking, like every other level of communication, is more complicated than just saying the right words. Rather than being a linear process—with one speaker sending one message to one or more listeners—communication is dynamic and transactional. Speaker, message, listener, feedback, channel, environment, and noise all interact to influence each other. Unlike that paper clip—the same in every hand that holds it—the message that emerges in communication will never be identical to what any one speaker intended.

Part of mastering public speaking begins with basic skills: organizing a presentation with an identifiable introduction, body, and conclusion; providing previews, summaries, and transitions; deciding whether the oral message needs the support of visual aids; and using appropriate grammar, pronunciation, and articulation.[18] To design, develop, and deliver a speech that is appropriate to you, your audience, and the communication context requires some higher-order thinking, however. Public speaking involves choices, and to choose appropriately you must sharpen your thinking skills.

The Public Speaker as Critical Thinker

We began this chapter by discussing benefits you gain from studying and practicing public speaking. One of those benefits is that public speaking not only uses but also *develops* your critical thinking ability. **Critical thinking** is "reasonable reflective thinking that is focused on deciding what to believe or do."[19] Is it important? If you are perfectly satisfied with your daily routine, with dealing with others in relative isolation, and with accepting the obvious without question, then critical thinking may seem unimportant to you. If, however, you have ever questioned obvious answers you were offered, viewed yourself as part of a larger group, looked for patterns you thought no one else had noticed, or followed a hunch to solve a problem in your own way, you have already begun to cultivate your critical thinking ability.[20] You probably also recognize its importance to your personal and professional life.

psychological noise: distractions originating in the thoughts of communicators.

critical thinking: the logical, reflective examination of information and ideas to determine what to believe or do.

In a world overloaded with information, both a business and a personal advantage will go to those individuals who can sort the wheat from the chaff, the important from the trivial. . . . Quality of life is directly tied to our ability to think clearly amid the noise of modern life, to sift through all that competes for our attention until we find what we value, what will make our lives worth living.[21]

Drawing from the works of Stuart Rankin and Carolyn Hughes, Robert Marzano and his colleagues have identified eight categories of critical thinking skills. As a public speaker you will exercise all of these as you develop and deliver your speech.

This skill . . .	enables you to . . .
Focusing	Define problems, set goals, and select pieces of information
Information gathering	Formulate questions and collect data
Remembering	Store information in long-term memory and retrieve it
Organizing	Arrange information so that it can be understood and presented more effectively
Analyzing	Clarify existing information by examining parts and relationships
Generating	Use prior knowledge to infer and elaborate new information and ideas
Integrating	Combine, summarize, and restructure information
Evaluating	Establish criteria and assess the quality of ideas[22]

In order to exercise and develop these critical thinking skills, you must care enough to do so. Educator Barbara Thayer-Bacon explains why caring is so important:

Caring is a necessary characteristic of critical thinkers for ideas and arguments do not have a life of their own; they are generated by people and critical thinking is an activity performed by people. *What* a knower brings to the knowing and *how* a knower relates to the knowing is as important as the knowing itself.[23]

Caring helps us both as speakers and as listeners. Caring means "being receptive to what another has to say and open to hearing the other's voice more completely and fairly" than we otherwise might.[24] The fact that you are reading this sentence—so close to the end of the chapter—is evidence that you care to expose yourself to all of our message, that you care about being able to answer any exam question about this chapter, or both. The critical thinker is, then, a person who cares enough to be reasonable and to think clearly. These abilities can help overcome prejudices and foster a community of caring, careful thinkers in your classroom. We can't imagine a better climate in which to exercise your critical thinking as you study the remainder of this textbook and put its principles into action.

Summary

Public speaking offers personal, professional, and public benefits for the individual. On a personal level, public speaking teaches you skills you can use in other courses of study. It is also an active form of learning and can increase your retention of information. Finally, gaining public speaking skills and experience will build your confidence and self-esteem. On a professional level, public speaking is an important form of communication, and excellent communication skills increase your chances of getting the job you want and advancing in it. On a public level, public speaking binds people into groups and propels social movements and social change.

Theory into Practice

Tips

Thinking about Speaking

Effective public speakers care about their topics and their audiences. As they research, construct, and deliver their speeches, they use the critical thinking skills discussed in this chapter. Consider how one student employed each of these skills in developing her speech.

■ Generating

Wanda's first assignment in her public speaking class was to prepare and deliver a speech about someone she admired. She immediately began generating a list of names: her mother, who held down two jobs to help raise five children; a high school teacher who inspired Wanda to go to college; Coretta Scott King, First Lady of the Civil Rights Movement; and Thurgood Marshall, the first African American to serve on the U.S. Supreme Court.

■ Focusing

Wanda recalled how Marshall's commitment to justice for all was one of the reasons she decided to become a prelaw major. So she decided to focus her speech on Marshall.

■ Information gathering/Remembering

She devised a research plan and began to gather her supporting materials. Remembering the moving tributes following Marshall's death, Wanda located some of these articles and also found several books about him.

■ Analyzing/Focusing

She analyzed her audience, the occasion, and the information she had collected and began to focus her speech further. Wanda decided that a biography of Marshall's life was far too encompassing for a three- to five-minute speech. She also chose not to discuss his more controversial decisions on abortion and capital punishment.

■ Organizing/Focusing/Integrating

Wanda organized her key ideas and integrated her supporting materials around two central images: closed doors and open doors. First, she would describe some of the doors closed to African Americans during much of Marshall's life: equal education, housing, public transportation, and voting. She would recount that Marshall, the great-grandson of a slave, was denied admission to the University of Maryland Law School.

Second, she would tell how Marshall fought to open these doors by expanding access to housing, public transportation, and voting. And she would, of course, note that it was Marshall who successfully argued the case of *Brown v. Board of Education of Topeka* (1954), which declared racial segregation in public schools unconstitutional. She would conclude her story by observing that it was Marshall who litigated the admission of the first African American to graduate from the University of Maryland Law School.

■ Evaluating

Wanda evaluated each of these examples as she prepared her speech to ensure that her ideas were well supported.

■ Remembering

As she constructed her speaking notes, Wanda used only a brief outline to help her remember her ideas.

■ Evaluating

After delivering her speech, she evaluated her speaking strengths and weaknesses to help her improve her next speech.

■ Caring

Caring about how she could inform and inspire her classmates, Wanda approached her topic critically and creatively. She developed an interesting, accurate speech and delivered it well.

We may view *communication* as either a process or a product, but the most accurate definition of the term probably includes both perspectives. Effective communication is the sharing of meaning by sending and receiving symbolic cues.

Public communication, the focus of this textbook, is one of five levels of communication. *Intrapersonal communication* refers to the communication we do with ourselves individually. *Interpersonal communication* is that carried out between pairs of people. *Group communication* involves three or more people communicating for some purpose and with a clear sense that they belong together. *Public communication* occurs when one person speaks face to face with an audience, either large or small. *Mass communication* involves one person communicating to a large audience through some print or electronic medium. These five levels of communication are differentiated by the numbers of people involved, the direction of communication flow, and the opportunities for audience feedback.

At whatever level it occurs, communication involves seven key components. The *speaker* or sender is the person originating and encoding the *message,* or the ideas communicated. The *listener* is the person receiving and decoding the message. *Feedback* refers to all verbal and nonverbal responses between the people communicating. The *channel* or medium of communication is the way the various messages are sent. Public speaking involves verbal, vocal, and visual channels. The *environment* includes the speaking occasion and the setting where communication occurs. Finally, *noise* is the name given to anything that interferes with communication. Noise can be physical (environmental), physiological (bodily), or psychological (mental).

The process of developing and delivering a public speech requires you to sharpen and use eight categories of critical thinking skills. You use *focusing* skills as you select your speech topic and narrow it to key points. You use *information gathering* skills as you conduct research, identify your key ideas, and decide how you will support them. You use *remembering* skills as you tap personal knowledge and experience relevant to your topic and as you practice speaking only from key words and phrases. You use *organizing* skills as you outline your key ideas and develop your speech introduction, body, and conclusion in a logical way.

Throughout the speech-making process, you use *analyzing* skills as you study your audience, your research, your main points, your supporting materials, and the ideas or arguments you develop. As you brainstorm for topic ideas, draw conclusions from your evidence, and predict the effect of what you propose, you are using *generating* skills. You use *integrating* skills as you arrange your supporting material to reinforce your specific purpose and as you summarize your main points for your listeners. Finally, you use *evaluating* skills as you assess the validity of what you say and your effectiveness in saying it. Caring enough to think clearly, to be reasonable, and to remain open to other people's ideas is the quality that activates all these critical thinking skills. A community of caring and careful listeners is the ideal environment for improving public speaking.

Exercises

1. If your class includes international students, ask them to describe the roles speaking plays in their native cultures. Are students encouraged to speak in class? Or are such behaviors discouraged? Are speaking skills considered more important for one gender than for the other? What differences do international students notice in the speaking skills of U.S. students compared with those of their own nationalities?

2. Jot down a few of your most embarrassing experiences. Review your list, noting incidents that resulted from a breakdown in communication because you did not share similar referents with someone else. Can you think of other examples of miscommunication based on individuals' having different referents for the same message?

3. List examples of words that trigger referents that are different because of the users' ages, genders, religious experiences, educational backgrounds, political affiliations, economic status, and so forth. Discuss how a speaker could enhance shared meaning in each of these examples.

4. Using the communication elements model (Figure 1.2) as a guide, analyze a lecture given by an instructor in one of your classes. Focus specifically on the listeners and feedback. Was the instructor attentive to the verbal and nonverbal behaviors of the students? If your answer is no, what could the instructor have done to make the communication event more of a two-way experience? If your answer is yes, give examples to illustrate the instructor's attentiveness to student feedback.

5. Find an article in a magazine or journal discussing speech communication in business and professional environments. Write a one-page summary and attach it to a copy or print of the article.

6. Analyze the physical noise present in your classroom. As a listener, how does this affect your reception of your instructor's message? As a speaker, how might you minimize the effect of this noise? If you were redesigning the classroom, what changes would you make to minimize this type of noise?

*T*he Ethics
of Public Speaking

chapter

Knowledge is not a loose-leaf notebook of facts. Above all, it is a responsibility for the integrity of what we are, primarily of what we are as ethical creatures. —JACOB BRONOWSKI

Commercial cartographers once produced maps containing small errors, such as nonexistent streets or bodies of water with funny, fictitious names. Known as "copyright traps," these errors were used to establish ownership and to serve as grounds for legal action against anyone copying the maps without permission.[1]

Today, digital cartographers, photographers, musicians, artists, and software creators are likely to place electronic watermarks or fingerprints in their original works using the techniques of steganography.[2] With perfect copies so easily produced and shared, claiming and proving creation and ownership become more important. The ID tag hidden in an MP3 file and the electronic watermark on a DVD have the same purpose: to protect the value of the original works and the reputations of their creators.

Unlike yesterday's mapmakers or today's electronic wizards, as a classroom public speaker you create a product that leaves no permanent record, except possibly in the memories of some of your listeners. Nevertheless, the speeches you deliver will have a unique value, reflecting your originality, exercising your critical thinking, and building your credibility.

In Chapter 1 we observed that ideas cannot be separated from the people who voice them. Everything you do or say affects the credibility your audience assigns you; that credibility in turn affects the believability of your ideas. Of course, as important as the perceived credibility you have with various audiences is your personal integrity. One of your goals as a speaker, in this class and beyond, should be to make choices that develop and maintain that integrity.

Effective, ethical public speakers understand and respect their audiences. They demonstrate this respect by honoring an unwritten contract with their listeners. Terms of this contract require that audience members listen expecting to learn, that they listen without prejudging you or your ideas, and that, ultimately, they evaluate your message and provide you feedback. As a speaker, you assume responsibility for being well prepared, communicating ideas clearly in order to benefit the audience, and remaining open to feedback that will improve your speaking. In this chapter we focus on these mutual responsibilities as we examine ethical speaking, ethical listening, and the issue of plagiarism.

Definition of Ethics

It is virtually impossible to read a newspaper or listen to a newscast today without encountering the topic of ethics. We hear of politicians selling out to special-interest groups, stockbrokers engaged in insider trading, accountants "cooking the books" of corporations they advise, contractors taking shortcuts in construction projects, and college professors falsifying résumés. We read stories of people who agonized over the decision to allow, and in some cases even to help, a terminally ill loved one to die. We watch news clips of rallies and demonstrations by constituents accusing their elected officials of abusing the public trust. Society is so concerned with unethical behavior that many professions even include the term *ethics* as a component: medical ethics, business ethics, bioethics, journalistic ethics, environmental ethics, and so forth.

When we talk about **ethics,** we are referring to the standards we use to determine right from wrong, or good from bad, in thought and behavior. Television's fictional Frasier Crane once offered a surprisingly serious and useful definition: "Ethics is what you do when no one is looking."[3] Our sense of ethics guides the choices we make in all aspects of our professional and private lives. You should not be surprised that your academic studies include a discussion of ethics. You are, after all, educating yourself to function in a world where you will make ethical decisions daily. In Chapter 1, we established the importance of speech communication in our lives. We will now examine why it is important for you to ensure that you communicate ethically.

Principles of Ethics

In discussing communication ethics, Donald Smith notes that communication is an ethically neutral instrument: "[S]peaking skill per se is neither good nor bad. The skill can be used by good persons or bad persons. It can be put to the service of good purposes [or] bad purposes. . . ."[4] In this course you will learn fundamental communication skills that will empower you as both a speaker and a listener. How you exercise these skills will involve ethical choices and responsibilities.

Two principles frame our discussion of ethics. First, *all parties in the communication process have ethical responsibilities.* Assume, for example, that college administrators had denied one of your instructors a requested leave of absence. Assume as well that this

© 1992 by P. S. Mueller. Reprinted by permission.

ethics: standards used to discriminate between right and wrong, good and bad, in thought and action.

instructor, without revealing his or her true motives, used class time to provoke and anger you about inadequate parking or poor food quality in the student center at your school, then led you across campus to take the school president hostage, barricade yourselves in the administration building, and tear up the place.

Anyone who knew the facts of this case would agree that the instructor acted unethically; it is wrong to manipulate people by keeping your true motives hidden from them. Yet students who let themselves be exploited by participating in such a violent and destructive episode would also share ethical responsibility for what happened. College students, no matter what their age, know that their actions have consequences. As this outlandish example demonstrates, all parties involved in communication share ethical obligations.

In spite of this, public speaking textbooks often discuss ethics only from a speaker's perspective, presenting ethical standards as a list of dos and don'ts for the sender of the message. Certainly, a speaker has ethical responsibilities, but a speaker-centered approach to ethics is incomplete. Communication, as we suggest throughout this textbook, is an activity shared by both the speaker and listener. As such, both parties have ethical responsibilities. For that reason, we will discuss the ethics of speaking and listening.

Second, *ethical speakers and listeners possess attitudes and standards that pervade their character and guide their actions before, during, and after their speaking and listening.* In other words, ethical speakers and listeners do more than just abstain from unethical behaviors. Ethics is as much a frame of mind as it is a pattern of behavior. Ethics is not something you apply to one speech; it is a working philosophy you apply to your daily life and bring to all speaking situations. Consider the actions of the speaker in the following incident that one of us witnessed in a classroom.

> Lisa presented a persuasive speech on the need for recycling paper, plastic, and aluminum products. To illustrate the many types of recyclables and how overpackaged many grocery products are, she used as an effective visual aid a paper grocery bag filled with empty cans, paper products, and a variety of plastic bottles and containers. After listening to her well-researched, well-delivered speech, with its impassioned final appeal for us to help save the planet by recycling, the class watched in amazement as she put the empty containers back in the bag, walked to the corner of the room, and dropped the bag in the trash can! After a few seconds, someone finally asked the question that had to be asked: "You mean you're not going to take those home to recycle them?" "Nah," said Lisa. "I'm tired of lugging them around. I've done my job."

Try This

Developing a Code of Ethics

Ethical behavior is something we should demand in national, state, and local political campaigns. We should also expect it of candidates and the electorate in campus politics. Investigate to see if your college or student government association has a code of ethics. Using that information and the ethical guidelines discussed in this chapter, develop a code of ethics that you think should govern speech in student government campaigns on your campus. Also, suggest specific guidelines for the voters, the receivers of these messages.

You may or may not believe that people have an ethical responsibility to recycle. But regardless of your views on that issue, you likely question the ethics of someone who insists, in effect, "Do as I say, not as I do." Lisa's actions made the entire class question the sincerity with which she spoke. Ethical standards cannot be turned on and off at an individual's convenience.

Ethical Speaking

Maintaining strong ethical attitudes and standards requires sound decision making at every step in the speech-making process. In this section we present six guidelines to help you with these decisions.

Speak Up about Topics You Consider Important

First, ethical public speakers make careful decisions about whether or not to speak. In many public discussions outside the classroom, silence is often an option, and if the issue is trivial, it is sometimes the best option. There are times, though, when people have an ethical obligation to convey information or when they feel strongly about an issue or an injustice. *Ethical communicators speak up about topics they consider important.* Our nation's history has been shaped by the voices of Thomas Jefferson, Frederick Douglass, Susan B. Anthony, Martin Luther King, Jr., Cesar Chavez, and other advocates. You may never have the sweeping historical impact of those famous speakers, but you do have an opportunity to better the communities of which you are a part. This class provides you with an opportunity to share information your classmates can use to help them get more from their college experience or function better in their careers and personal lives. You also have a chance to educate others about problems you feel need to be confronted. This class provides you with the training ground to hone your skills as speaker and listener. Use these skills as you move from involvement in class and campus issues to improvement of your community.

> *"A speech is a solemn responsibility. The man who makes a bad thirty-minute speech to 200 people wastes only a half hour of his own time. But he wastes 100 hours of the audience's time—more than four days—which should be a hanging offense."*
>
> —JENKIN LLOYD JONES

Choose Topics That Promote Positive Ethical Values

Second, *ethical speakers choose topics that promote positive ethical values.* Selecting a topic is one of the first ethical choices you will make as a speaker. Unless you are assigned a topic, you can choose from a wide range of subjects. In a real sense, you give your topic credibility simply by selecting it. As an ethical speaker, your choice should reflect what you think is important for your audience.

In the course we teach, many student speeches have expanded our knowledge or moved us to act on significant issues. But consider this list of informative speech topics:

How to get a fake I.D.

How to "walk" (avoid paying) a restaurant check

How to get a faculty parking permit

How to get out of a speeding ticket

Former U.S. President Jimmy Carter was awarded the Nobel Peace Prize for his efforts to promote the ethical values of freedom, social justice, and global peace.

We have heard speeches on each of these topics. Even though they were informative rather than persuasive speeches, each of these how-to topics implies that its action is acceptable. We do not know why students chose these topics, but we suggest that all of those speakers disregarded their listeners, failed to consider the values they were promoting, and presented unethical speeches.

Speak to Benefit Your Listeners

Third, *ethical public speakers communicate in order to benefit their listeners.* Speakers and listeners participate in a transactional relationship; both should benefit from their participation. As the Jones quotation on page 23 suggests, listeners give speakers their time; speakers should provide information that is interesting or useful in return.

Informative speakers have an obvious obligation to benefit their audiences. As in the following example, however, students sometimes lose sight of that duty.

> Assigned to give an informative speech demonstrating a process or procedure, plant lover Evelyn decided to show how to plant a seed in a pot. Her instructor, who had asked students to write down their topic choices, was privately worried that this subject was something everyone already knew. Evelyn was, after all, speaking to college students who presumably could read the planting instructions on the back of a seed packet. The instructor did not want to discourage Evelyn but wanted the class to benefit from her speech.
>
> Without saying, "You cannot speak on this topic," the instructor shared her concerns with Evelyn. She found out that Evelyn had several other plant-related topics in mind. Evelyn agreed that a more unusual topic would be more interesting to the class and more challenging for her to deliver. On the day she was assigned to speak, Evelyn presented an interesting speech demonstrating how to propagate tropical plants by "air layering" them. Evelyn got a chance to demonstrate her green thumb, and her classmates learned something most had never heard of before.

Evelyn finally paid attention to her audience and rejected the simple, familiar topic that would probably not have taught her listeners anything.

You may often speak for personal benefit, and this is not necessarily unethical. You may, for instance, urge a group to support your candidacy or to buy your product. There is nothing wrong with pursuing such personal goals, but ethical speakers do not try to fulfill personal needs at the expense of their listeners. As one popular book on business ethics states, "There is no right way to do a wrong thing."[5] Speakers whose object is to persuade should do so openly and with the goal of benefiting both the audience and themselves. To do otherwise is manipulative. Allan Cohen and David Bradford define manipulation as "actions to achieve influence that would be rendered less effective if the target knew your actual intentions."[6] A public speaker may try to inform, convince, persuade, direct, or even anger an audience. Ethical speakers, however, do not deceive their listeners. They are up-front about their intentions, and those intentions include benefiting the audience.

Use Truthful Supporting Material and Valid Reasoning

Fourth, *ethical speakers use truthful supporting materials and valid reasoning.* Listeners have a right to know not only the speaker's ideas, but also the material supporting those claims. Ethical speakers are well informed and should thus test the truthfulness and validity of their ideas. They should not knowingly use false information or faulty reasoning. Yet we sometimes witness students presenting incomplete or out-of-date material, as in this example:

> Janet presented an informative speech on the detection and treatment of breast cancer. Her discussion of the disease's detection seemed thorough, but when she got to her second point, she said that the only treatments were radical mastectomy, partial mastectomy, radiation therapy, and chemotherapy. She failed to mention lumpectomy, a popular surgical measure often combined with radiation or chemotherapy. Her bibliography revealed that her research stopped with sources published in the early 1980s, explaining the gap in her speech content.

Janet did not necessarily act unethically; she was simply uninformed and ended up being embarrassed. But what if Janet had known of the lumpectomy procedure and had just not wanted to do further research to find out about it? Then we would question her ethics.

In this case, certain listeners did not notice the factual errors and the lapses in content while others did. Not getting caught in a factual or logical error does not free the speaker of ethical responsibility to present complete, factual information. If you speak on a current topic, you need to use the most recent information you can find and to try to be as well informed as possible.

Consider the Consequences of Your Words and Actions

Fifth, *ethical speakers concern themselves with the consequences of their speaking.* Mary Cunningham observed, "Words are sacred things. They are also like hand grenades: Handled casually, they tend to go off."[7] Ethical speakers have a respect for the power of language and the process of communication.

It is difficult to track, let alone to predict, the impact of any one message. Statements you make are interpreted by your immediate audience and may be communicated by those listeners to others. Individuals may form opinions and behave differently because of what you say or fail to say. Incorrect information and misinterpretations may have unintended, and potentially harmful, consequences. If you provide an audience with inaccurate information, you may contaminate the quality of their subsequent decisions. If you persuade someone to act in a particular way, you are, in part, responsible for the impact of the person's new action.

Strive to Improve Your Public Speaking

Finally, *ethical speakers strive to improve their public speaking.* Speakers who use the guidelines we have presented accept their obligation to communicate responsibly in the communities of which they are a part. Their ideas have value, are logically supported, and do not deceive their listeners. We would argue, however, that this is not enough.

Ethical speakers are concerned not only with *what* they speak but also with *how* they speak. As a result, they work actively to become more effective communicators. This course provides you with an opportunity to begin mastering public speaking. You will learn how to select, support, evaluate, organize, and deliver your ideas. Your professional and public life beyond the classroom will extend your opportunities to speak publicly. Speakers have "the opportunity to learn to speak well, and to be eloquent [advocates of] truth and justice." If they fail to develop these abilities, they have not fulfilled their "ethical obligation in a free society."[8]

Key Points — Responsibilities of an Ethical Speaker

1. Speak up about topics you consider important.
2. Choose topics that promote positive ethical values.
3. Speak to benefit your listeners.
4. Use truthful supporting material and valid reasoning.
5. Consider the consequences of your words and actions.
6. Strive to improve your public speaking.

Ethical Listening

The guidelines for ethical speaking we've just discussed probably make perfect sense to you. If some seem intimidating, if you feel that the future of free expression in a democratic society rests squarely on your shoulders, remember that no individual bears such a responsibility alone. Members of your audience also have obligations as ethical listeners, and you share these same four ethical responsibilities as you listen to the speeches of others.

> "A mind that is stretched to a new idea never returns to its original dimension."
>
> —OLIVER WENDELL HOLMES

Seek Exposure to Well-Informed Speakers

The ethics of listening involves four basic principles. First, *ethical listeners seek out speakers who expand their knowledge, increase their understanding, introduce them to new ideas, and challenge their beliefs.* These listeners reject the philosophy, "My mind's made up, so don't confuse me with the facts." A controversial speaker visiting your campus can expand your knowledge or intensify your feelings about a subject, whether you agree or disagree with the speaker's viewpoint. Even in situations in which students are a captive audience for other students' speeches, such as this class, ethical listening should be the standard.

Avoid Prejudging Speakers or Their Ideas

Second, *ethical listeners listen openly without prejudging speakers or their ideas.* This may be difficult. Listening without bias may require that we temporarily suspend impressions we have formed from the other person's past actions. But the rewards of doing so can be great, as in this example.

ETHICAL DECISION MAKING
www.scu.edu/ethics
Ethical speakers and listeners should consider the values that shape their decision making. The Markkula Center for Applied Ethics at Santa Clara University is devoted to the study of ethics. Access articles, case studies, and other resources relating to business, global, government, and technology ethics.

> Linda's first speech in class completely confused her classmates. She seemed nervous and unsure of herself and what she was going to say, and the point of her speech really eluded everyone. Class discussion after the speech focused primarily on Linda's delivery, and some of the distracting mannerisms she exhibited and needed to control. When she went to the front of the room to begin her next speech weeks later, no one was really expecting to be impressed. But they were.
>
> Linda's second speech dealt with the problem of homelessness. Her opening sentence told the class that three years before she had been living on the street for a time. She had their attention from that point on. In addition to citing recent newspaper and magazine articles, Linda had conducted a great deal of original research. She had interviewed the directors of local shelters and a number of the homeless people who took refuge there, and she quoted these individuals. Her speech was well organized and well delivered. It was both educational and inspiring.
>
> When discussing the speech later, classmates kept referring to her first speech and noting the remarkable improvements Linda had made. One person was blunt, but apparently summed up the feelings of a number of listeners that day: "Linda, I wasn't expecting much from you because your first speech was so unclear to me, but today you had a topic that you obviously care about, and you made us understand and care about it, too. I can't get over the difference between those two speeches!"

When listening to your classmates, you should assume that you may learn something important from each speaker and therefore listen intently. Information and ideas are best shared in such an atmosphere of mutual respect.

Evaluate the Speaker's Logic and Credibility

Listening eagerly and openly does not imply a permanent suspension of evaluation, however. A third standard is that *ethical listeners evaluate the messages presented to them.* A listener who accepts a premise without evaluating its foundation is like someone who buys a used car without looking under the hood. The warning "let the buyer beware" is good advice not only for consumers of products but also for consumers of messages.

As a listener, you should critically evaluate the ideas of a speaker. Is each idea logically constructed? Is each supported with evidence that is relevant, sufficient, and authoritative? In Chapters 8 and 17, you will learn specific strategies to help you answer these questions as you evaluate a speaker's evidence and logic.

Beware of the Consequences of Not Listening Carefully

Fourth, *ethical listeners concern themselves with the consequences of their listening.* As the following example illustrates, listeners who assimilate only part of a public speaker's message because they fail to listen actively are responsible for the distorted message that results.

> Eduardo, a staff writer for *The Clarion,* the campus newspaper, mentioned in a speech that the online version of the paper was sponsoring a contest for best research

Ethical listening involves thinking critically about a speaker's message. How often do you make a conscious effort to evaluate the meaning and logic behind the messages you hear and read each day?

suggestions. The student emailing the HTML page with the most useful research links, as judged by the publication staff, would win first prize: a new BlackBerry. Ted listened to his classmate Eduardo, but the only words that stood out were the name of the paper and the prize. At the next class meeting, Ted told Eduardo, "I called the paper yesterday asking how to get my free BlackBerry and they told me I had to develop a web page and enter some kind of contest." Eduardo replied, "I told you about that contest in my speech. Weren't you listening?"

Ted may have been embarrassed, but he didn't suffer greatly as a result of not listening to Eduardo. In other cases, however, the consequences of not listening are more serious. When you fail to listen to someone's directions and are late for an interview, you miss an employment opportunity. In both of these examples, the listener, not the speaker, bears responsibility for the breakdown in communication.

At other times, listener and speaker may share responsibility for unethical behavior. For example, audience members who become victims of scams because they did not listen critically share with the speaker responsibility for their behavior. Voters who tolerate exaggerated, vague, and inconsistent campaign statements from those who ask to represent them similarly become part of the problem and not the solution.

Most of us begin learning ethical principles as children: "It's wrong to lie." "It's wrong to deceive others." "It's wrong to blame others for what we say and do." In the past, views of communication ethics implied a dotted line across the front of a classroom, with ethics being solely the speaker's responsibility. In contrast, we view ethics as a shared re-

Exploring *Online*

CHECKING FAIRNESS IN NEWS REPORTING

www.fair.org/whats-fair.html

Interested in journalistic ethics? Visit this website maintained by Fairness and Accuracy in Reporting (FAIR) for critiques of the stories you may be getting in mainstream media. A media watch group, FAIR works aggressively to highlight bias and censorship in establishment media and to advocate greater diversity in the press.

Key Points

Responsibilities of an Ethical Listener

1. Seek exposure to well-informed speakers.
2. Avoid prejudging speakers or their ideas.
3. Evaluate the logic and credibility of the speaker's ideas.
4. Beware of the consequences of not listening carefully.

sponsibility of the speaker and each listener. An absence of ethical motives among speakers and listeners devalues the currency of communication. Two aspects of ethics, however, do begin as the speaker's responsibility: understanding fair use guidelines and avoiding plagiarism. These two topics deserve special attention.

Fair Use Guidelines

If the person behind the counter in a copy shop has ever made you feel like a criminal for asking to have a magazine or journal article copied—never mind a few pages or photographs from a book—you have experienced one of the quirks of copyright law. The copy shop operates to make a profit; you probably don't have any commercial use of the material in mind. "[A] nonprofit educational institution may copy an entire article from a journal for students in a class as a fair use; but a commercial copy shop would need permission for the same copying."[9] As a result, the person behind the print shop counter may direct you to a self-service copy machine, where you assume full responsibility for respecting copyright law. That law places restrictions on uses of copyrighted materials, but also grants you important rights to specific uses of them. Section 107 of the Copyright Law of the United States, commonly called the **fair use provision,** says that the fair use of a copyrighted work—"including such use by reproduction in copies or phonorecords or by any other means . . . , for purposes such as criticism, comment, news reporting, teaching (including multiple copies for classroom use), scholarship, or research—is not an infringement of copyright."[10]

The law also specifies four factors to consider in determining whether your specific use of copyrighted material is fair. The law is ambiguous and can vary depending on the specific nature of the work you wish to use. We are not lawyers and cannot offer assurances that will apply to every case. However, attorney Georgia Harper, copyright expert and manager of the intellectual property section of the General Counsel's office for The University of Texas system, has translated these four factors into rules of thumb that "describe a 'safe harbor' within the bounds of fair use."[11] If you are planning to use any copyrighted material in a speech, ask the following four questions:

- *What is the character of the use I plan?* If your intended use is personal, educational, or nonprofit, chances are it is fair use. Use of copyrighted material for purposes of criticism, commentary, or even parody also weighs in favor of fair use.

- *What is the nature of the work I plan to use?* Use of a published work that merely reports facts weighs in favor of fair use. You need to seek permission, however, if you are planning to use an unpublished, creative work, such as a story or poem.

- *How much of the work do I plan to use?* Noncommercial use of a small portion of a copyrighted work—or even more than a small portion—likely qualifies as fair use. Commercial uses that exceed strict length limits, however, require permissions.

- *If the use I plan were widespread, what effect would it have on the market value of the original?* This question can become particularly important if you use copyrighted material in a presentation that is preserved electronically or transmitted by electronic means for distance learning.[12]

fair use provision: section of U.S. copyright law allowing limited noncommercial use of copyrighted materials for teaching, criticism, scholarship, research, or commentary.

Using these guidelines can help ensure that your use of copyrighted material in a speech is fair. Note, though, that the fair use provision does *not* give you the right to use another's work without crediting that person. Unattributed use—even fair use—of someone else's work leaves you open to charges of plagiarism, an issue that seems to grow more important in these days of cut-and-paste Internet research.

Plagiarism

> *"You must renounce imagination forever if you hope to succeed in plagiarism. Forgery is intention, not invention."*
>
> —HORACE WALPOLE

> *"Your manuscript is both good and original; but the part that is good is not original, and the part that is original is not good."*
>
> —SAMUEL JOHNSON

The word *plagiarize* comes from a Latin word meaning "to kidnap," so in a sense a plagiarist is a kidnapper of the ideas and words of another. A modern definition of **plagiarism** is "literary—or artistic or musical—theft. It is the false assumption of authorship: the wrongful act of taking the product of another person's mind, and presenting it as one's own."[13]

When you write a paper and submit it to a teacher, you are in effect publishing that work. If, in that paper, you copy something from another source and pass it off as your own work, you are plagiarizing. This act is such a serious offense that in most colleges and universities it is grounds for failing the course or even for dismissal from the school. Yet recent history has shown us numerous examples of politicians, educators, historians, and other public figures caught plagiarizing materials, either consciously or unconsciously. An offense serious enough to derail a candidate's campaign for office, to force the resignation of a corporate officer, or to end a student's academic career certainly deserves the attention of students in a public speaking class.

Just as you publish the paper that you write and submit to your teacher, when you deliver a speech in this class or on any other occasion, you are also "publishing" your material. Even without putting your words in print or placing a copyright notice on them, you hold the copyright on your ideas expressed in your own words. The current copyright law is interpreted to say, "Even if a speech has merely been delivered orally and not [formally] published, it is subject to copyright protection and may not be used without written permission."[14]

Plagiarism of well-known speeches or speakers is both unethical and foolish. Repeating a joke a friend tells you is one thing; memorizing and reciting a comedy routine by Caroline Rhea, Chris Rock, or Robin Williams is quite another. Repeating distinctive, well-known material as though it were your own may be the most foolish type of plagiarism. No less serious, however, is plagiarizing from obscure sources. If you deliver a speech someone else has researched, organized, and worded, you are presenting another's work as your own. You are plagiarizing.

Plagiarism applies to more than simply the copying of another's words, however. You may also plagiarize another's ideas and organization of material. For example, if you presented a speech organized around the five stages of dying (denial, anger, bargaining, depression, and acceptance) and did not give credit to Elisabeth Kübler-Ross, you would be guilty of plagiarism. On the other hand, if your speech analyzed the political, economic, and social implications of a pending piece of legislation, you would prob-

plagiarism: the unattributed use of another's ideas, words, or pattern of organization.

ably not be guilty of plagiarism. Kübler-Ross developed, explained, and published her framework or model in her book *On Death and Dying*, whereas the second example relies on a commonly accepted pattern of analyzing public policy initiatives. As you can see, the line between legitimate appropriation of material and plagiarism is sometimes unclear. As a speaker, you must always be on guard to credit the source of your ideas and their structure.

Plagiarism can be intentional or unintentional. **Intentional plagiarism** occurs when speakers or writers knowingly present another person's words, ideas, or organization as their own. **Unintentional plagiarism** is "the careless paraphrasing and citing of source material such that improper or misleading credit is given."[15] Intentional plagiarism is considered the more serious offense. Widespread use of the Internet for research may be blurring the distinction between deliberate and accidental plagiarism, however. Web pages are ephemeral; page content and design can change from one day to the next. That quality, together with the ease of browsing numerous sites in a short time, lets readers pick up phrases, ideas, or even organizational patterns almost unconsciously. If a researcher has not printed, bookmarked, or jotted down the URLs for key sites, retracing steps and finding those sites again may be difficult. Unintentional plagiarism may be committed due to ignorance or sloppy research methods, but the effect is still the same: One person is taking credit for the work of another.

Unintentional plagiarism sometimes occurs because of a common misconception that by simply changing a few words of another's writing you have paraphrased the statement and need not cite it. Michael O'Neill refers to this "hybrid of half textual source, half original writing" as a "paraplage."[16] Note the differences and similarities in the original and adapted passages of the following statement.

Exploring *Online*

COPYRIGHT VIOLATIONS
www.benedict.com
The Copyright Website contains some interesting recent examples of alleged copyright violations in the visual, audio, and digital arts. Enter the site at this address, and then click on the tabs to see and hear these examples, read about the allegations, and discover how they were resolved.

intentional plagiarism: the deliberate, unattributed use of another's ideas, words, or pattern of organization.

unintentional plagiarism: the careless or unconscious, unattributed use of another's ideas, words, or pattern of organization.

Statement by Carolyn Kleiner Butler

Black-only baseball squads had existed since before the Civil War, but there was no organized competition until former pitcher Rube Foster helped form the Negro National League in 1920, which was relaunched in 1933 and joined by the Negro American League in 1937. Clubs such as the Birmingham Black Barons, Indianapolis Clowns and New York Cubans often held games at off times in Major League stadiums or barnstormed across the country to challenge community teams. By the mid-1940s, black baseball was pulling in more than $2 million a year.

Then, on April 15, 1947, former UCLA track and football star Jackie Robinson, who had played one season with the Negro American League's Kansas City Monarchs, suited up for the Brooklyn Dodgers, integrating Major League Baseball. Others followed, and over the next 12 seasons African-Americans—including Robinson, Roy Campanella, Willie Mays and Hank Aaron—won nine Rookie of the Year and nine Most Valuable Player awards.[17]

Speaker's Paraplage of Carolyn Kleiner Butler

African American baseball teams are older than most of us imagine. And African Americans made a strong impression quickly once baseball was integrated. Though there were black-only baseball squads even before the Civil War, they hadn't competed in an organized way until the formation of the Negro National League in 1920. By 1937 the Negro American League was also operating. Some of the earliest clubs were the Birmingham Black Barons and the New York Cubans. Even though they played for big crowds only when major league stadiums weren't being used, by the mid-1940s, black baseball was bringing in more than $2 million a year.

Then in 1947, just ten years after the launch of the Negro American League, Jackie Robinson joined the Brooklyn Dodgers, integrating major league baseball. Others quickly followed, and over the next twelve seasons African Americans with names as familiar as Willie Mays and Hank Aaron would win nine Rookie of the Year and nine MVP awards.

Speaker's Appropriate Citation of Carolyn Kleiner Butler

African American baseball teams are older than most of us imagine. And African Americans made a strong impression quickly once baseball was integrated. Carolyn Kleiner Butler, a contributing editor for *U.S. News & World Report* and a frequent contributor to *Smithsonian Magazine,* notes that though there were black-only baseball squads even before the Civil War, they hadn't competed in an organized way until the formation of the Negro National League in 1920. In her article in the April 2005 issue of *Smithsonian Magazine,* Butler notes that by 1937 the Negro American League was also operating. Some of the earliest clubs were the Birmingham Black Barons and the New York Cubans. Even though they played for big crowds only when major league stadiums weren't being used, by the mid-1940s, black baseball was bringing in more than $2 million a year, according to Butler.

Then just ten years after the launch of the Negro American League, in 1947, Jackie Robinson joined the Brooklyn Dodgers, integrating major league baseball. Others quickly followed, and Butler points out that over the next twelve seasons African Americans with names as familiar as Willie Mays and Hank Aaron would win nine Rookie of the Year and nine MVP awards.

Notice that the appropriate citation above not only tells the listener something about Butler's credentials, but also explains exactly where her words appeared. With that information, any listener wanting to read the entire article could find it quickly.

To avoid plagiarizing, let the following five simple rules guide you.

1. *Take clear and consistent notes while researching.* As you review your notes, you should be able to discern which words, ideas, examples, and organizational structures belong to which authors.

2. *Record complete source citations.* Each sheet of notes, each photocopied article, and each printed page of a document you have accessed should indicate its source or sources.

3. *Clearly indicate in your speech any words, ideas, examples, or organizational structures that are not your own.* If you cite a source early in your speech and then use another idea from that author later, you must again give that author credit. You do not need to repeat the complete citation, however. Use an abbreviated citation, such as "according to Butler" in our earlier example, if you have provided the full citation earlier in your speech.

4. *Use your own words, language style, and thought structure when paraphrasing.* Remember that both content and structure distinguish another person's statements. When paraphrasing what another person has written or said, you should use not just your own words, but also your own language style and thought structure. Otherwise you are "paraplaging."

5. *When in doubt, cite the source.* If you are unsure whether you really need to acknowledge a source, it's always wise to err on the side of caution.

We have discussed some reasons *not* to hide the true authorship of words and ideas. There are also at least two reasons why speakers *should* mention their sources. The first reason may seem self-serving, but it is nevertheless true that speakers who cite their sources increase their credibility or believability with the audience. When you quote from a book, an article, or an interview and name the author or speaker of those words, you show the audience that you have researched the topic and that you know what you are talking about. Second, and far more important, acknowledging your sources is the right thing to do. It is honest. Good ideas and memorably worded thoughts are rare enough that the original writer or speaker deserves credit.

Guidelines to Avoid Plagiarism

1. Take clear and consistent notes while researching.
2. Record complete source citations for notes or photocopied pages.
3. Indicate any quoted material as you deliver the speech.
4. Use your own words, style, and structure when paraphrasing.
5. Cite the source when in doubt.

Theory into Practice
TIPS

Effective and Ethical Paraphrasing

The Purdue University Online Writing Lab (OWL) offers several suggestions to help writers quote, summarize, and paraphrase materials for their papers. Their "6 Steps to Effective Paraphrasing" are also excellent suggestions for speakers.

1. Reread the original passage until you understand it fully.
2. Set the original aside; write your paraphrase on a notecard or on paper or type it into a computer file.
3. Below your paraphrase write a few words to remind you later how you might use this material in your speech. Near your paraphrase write a key word or phrase in all capital letters to indicate its subject.
4. Check your version against the original to make sure that your paraphrase accurately expresses all the essential information in a new form.
5. Use quotations marks to identify any unique terms or phrases you have borrowed exactly from the source.
6. Record the source on your notecard so that you can credit it easily if you decide to incorporate the material in your speech.[18]

Visit http://owl.english.purdue.edu/handouts/print/research/r_paraphr.html for examples of plagiarized statements and legitimate paraphrases. You can also engage in an online exercise and paraphrase several passages and then compare them to samples provided by OWL.

Summary

Ethics and plagiarism are topics of concern to students and teachers of public speaking. *Ethics* refers to fundamental questions of right and wrong in thought and behavior. We offer some positive observations on ethics from the viewpoints of both speaker and listener. Ethics is not a standard for acceptable practice that we turn on before speaking and off after the speech is over; it is a value system pervading our lives. We believe that everyone involved in public communication should be guided by the following ethical considerations.

First, ethical speakers choose to speak about topics and issues they consider important. They make the decision to speak out, even when remaining silent might be easier. Second, ethical speakers choose topics that promote positive ethical values. Third, ethical speakers speak to benefit their listeners, not merely to fulfill their personal needs. Fourth, ethical speakers present audiences with ideas backed by logical reasoning and authentic, up-to-date supporting materials. Fifth, ethical speakers care about the consequences their words and actions may have for their listeners. Finally, ethical speakers seek to improve their public speaking.

Listening should be guided by four ethical principles. First, ethical listeners welcome challenges to their beliefs, just as they embrace learning. Second, ethical listening means listening openly, without prejudging the speaker's ideas. Third, ethical listeners evaluate the speaker's ideas before acting on them. Finally, ethical listeners care about and accept responsibility for the consequences of their listening.

Speakers planning to use copyrighted materials in their speeches need to be aware of the *fair use* provisions of copyright law. The four factors to consider in determining whether a particular use is fair are (1) the purpose of your use, (2) the nature of the work you want to use, (3) the quantity of the entire work that you want to use, and (4) the effect that widespread use such as you intend would have on the market value of the work. Both speakers and listeners also need to be aware of the issue of *plagiarism,* the unattributed use of another's ideas, words, or organization. Plagiarism may be either *intentional* or *unintentional.* To avoid plagiarizing sources, speakers should (1) establish a clear and consistent method of notetaking; (2) record a complete source citation on each page of notes or each photocopied article; (3) clearly indicate in the speech any words, ideas, or organizational techniques not their own; (4) use their own words, language style, and thought structures when paraphrasing; and (5) when in doubt, acknowledge the source. Careful source citation not only increases a speaker's credibility with the audience, but is also ethically right.

Exercises

1. Select two individuals prominent on the international, national, state, or local scene whom you consider ethical speakers. What characteristics do they possess that make them ethical? Select two people you consider unethical. What ethical standards do you think they abuse?

2. Consider the following scenario. State representative Joan Richards is running for a seat in the state senate. She worked hard as a legislator and was voted the best representative by the Better Government League (BGL). The BGL voted her opponent, incumbent Mike Letner, one of the ten worst senators in the state. Many political analysts think Richards would be the superior senator. Letner has taken a "no new taxes" pledge and has challenged Richards to do the same. Richards personally thinks taxes may have to be raised in order to keep the state solvent. Nevertheless, she knows that unless she promises to oppose any new taxes, she will lose the election. What should Richards do?

3. Answer each of the following questions and be prepared to defend your position
   a. Should a speech instructor have the right to censor topics students select for their speeches?
   b. Should students have the right to use profanity and obscenity in their speeches in this class?
   c. Should the Ku Klux Klan be allowed to hold a rally on your campus?
   d. Should public prayers be a part of opening ceremonies at athletic contests at publicly supported schools?
   e. Should lawyers defend clients they know are guilty?

4. Find an article on any subject written by an expert. Summarize the article in one or two paragraphs. Use appropriate source citation, paraphrasing, and quotations to avoid plagiarism.

5. In researching your speech on discrimination against women in the workplace, you discover two polls reaching conflicting conclusions. One shows that experts generally agree with your position; the other shows that they disagree. Is it ethical to present your listeners only the poll that supports your position, or should you acknowledge the other? On what basis should you make this decision?

Speaking Confidently

chapter

3

According to most studies, people's number one fear is public speaking. Number two is death. Death is number two. Does that seem right? This means to the average person, if you have to go to a funeral, you're better off in the casket than doing the eulogy. —JERRY SEINFELD[1]

Recognize That Speaker Nervousness Is Normal

Seinfeld may be playing a bit fast and loose with his facts and his logic, but the point of his humor is sound. **Communication apprehension,** the perceived "fear or anxiety associated with either real or anticipated communication with another person or persons," is widespread.[2] One form of communication apprehension, public speaking anxiety, affects even people with a great deal of public speaking experience.

Garrison Keillor, author and host of National Public Radio's *A Prairie Home Companion,* reflected on his teenage years in terms that may seem familiar:

> I had an awful rough time in high school. I was such a shy person. I was so terrified of everything, so afraid of being embarrassed in front of other people, afraid to speak up in class, afraid that I might have the wrong answer to a question that everybody else had the right answer to. . . . I was able to get up in speech class only because I could take off my glasses, and when I did I could no longer see faces. It was just a kind of an Impressionist tapestry.[3]

It is worth noting that, aside from his potential radio audience, Keillor was sharing these thoughts with hundreds of people from the stage of the 996-seat Fitzgerald Theater in St. Paul, Minnesota. Keillor has obviously managed his fear of speaking in public.

As you can see, if you are nervous about public speaking and experience what we sometimes call "platform panic," you are in good company. In fact, the first edition of *The Book of Lists* reported a survey that asked 3,000 Americans, "What are you the most afraid of?" "Speaking before a group" came in first, ahead of heights, insects, financial problems, deep water, sickness, and, yes, even death.[4] Psychiatrists John Greist, James Jefferson, and Isaac Marks contend that public speaking anxiety is "probably the most common social phobia."[5] Today, when so many people are apprehensive about even striking up a conversation with a stranger, is it any wonder that the fear of public speaking is so widespread?

Our experience and research confirm the prevalence of this common fear among college students. When asked to list their communication weaknesses, a clear majority of our students rank speaking before a group of people as their primary fear. James McCroskey has studied the anxieties of public speaking extensively. McCroskey's

communication apprehension: perceived fear or anxiety associated with real or anticipated communication with another person or persons.[2]

Personal Report of Public Speaking Anxiety (Figure 3.1) assesses the fear college students have about giving public speeches. His data, collected from several thousand students, confirm that public speaking generates greater apprehension than other forms of communication and that this fear spans several levels:

high anxiety	40%
moderately high anxiety	30%
moderate anxiety	20%
moderately low anxiety	5%
low anxiety	5%

Note that nearly three-fourths of college students fall into the moderately high to high anxiety range! This means that even the person who always has the quick response, who can make others in the class laugh, and who always looks together may be just as worried as you are right now about getting up in front of this class to give a speech. McCroskey and coauthor Virginia Richmond conclude: "What this suggests, then, is that it is 'normal' to experience a fairly high degree of anxiety about public speaking. Most people do. If you are highly anxious about public speaking, then you are 'normal.' "[6]

What is this platform panic and how does it affect us? Chemically and physiologically, we all experience stage fright in the same way. Adrenaline is suddenly pumped into the bloodstream. Respiration increases dramatically. So do heart rate and "galvanic skin response"—the amount of perspiration on the surface of the skin. All these things occur so that oxygen-rich blood can be quickly channeled to the large muscle groups. You may have heard stories of a 135-pound person who lifts the front of a car to help rescue someone pinned under it. Such incidents happen because the body is suddenly mobilized to do what must be done.

Yet the body can be similarly mobilized in stressful situations that are not life threatening. Musicians waiting for the start of the opening selection, athletes for the game to begin, actors for the curtain to go up, and speakers for their call to the lectern often feel their bodies marshalling all their resources either to perform to capacity or to get away from the threatening situation. This phenomenon is called, appropriately, the "fight-or-flight" syndrome.

Although our bodies' chemical and physiological responses to stress are identical, the outward signs of this anxiety vary from person to person. As the time approaches for your first speech in this class, you may experience any of several symptoms to varying degrees. Our students tell us that their symptoms include blushing or redness, accelerated heart rate, perspiring, dry mouth, shaking, churning stomach, increased rate of speech, forgetfulness and broken speech, and nervous mannerisms such as playing with jewelry, tapping fingers, and clutching the lectern. Realize that these symptoms are typical, not atypical, of a public speaker. If you experience any of them, you have plenty of company.

Control Speaker Nervousness

Before discussing what your goal should be regarding speaker nervousness, it is important to note what it should not be. Do *not* make your goal to eliminate nervousness. Such a goal is counterproductive for at least two reasons. First, as we have noted, nervousness is natural. Attempting to eliminate it is therefore unrealistic. Most experienced, successful public speakers still get nervous before they speak. In addition, focusing on

FIGURE 3.1
Personal Report of Public Speaking Anxiety (PRPSA)

Directions: This instrument is composed of thirty-four statements concerning feelings about communicating with other people. Indicate the degree to which the statements apply to you by marking whether you (1) strongly agree, (2) agree, (3) are undecided, (4) disagree, or (5) strongly disagree with each statement. Work quickly; record your first impression.

_____ 1. While preparing for giving a speech, I feel tense and nervous.

_____ 2. I feel tense when I see the words "speech" and "public speech" on a course outline when studying.

_____ 3. My thoughts become confused and jumbled when I am giving a speech.

_____ 4. Right after giving a speech I feel that I have had a pleasant experience.

_____ 5. I get anxious when I think about a speech coming up.

_____ 6. I have no fear of giving a speech.

_____ 7. Although I am nervous just before starting a speech, I soon settle down after starting and feel calm and comfortable.

_____ 8. I look forward to giving a speech.

_____ 9. When the instructor announces a speaking assignment in class, I can feel myself getting tense.

_____ 10. My hands tremble when I am giving a speech.

_____ 11. I feel relaxed while giving a speech.

_____ 12. I enjoy preparing for a speech.

_____ 13. I am in constant fear of forgetting what I prepared to say.

_____ 14. I get anxious if someone asks me something about my topic that I do not know.

_____ 15. I face the prospect of giving a speech with confidence.

_____ 16. I feel that I am in complete possession of myself while giving a speech.

_____ 17. My mind is clear when giving a speech.

_____ 18. I do not dread giving a speech.

_____ 19. I perspire just before starting a speech.

_____ 20. My heart beats very fast just as I start a speech.

_____ 21. I experience considerable anxiety while sitting in the room just before my speech starts.

_____ 22. Certain parts of my body feel very tense and rigid while giving a speech.

_____ 23. Realizing that only a little time remains in a speech makes me very tense and anxious.

_____ 24. While giving a speech, I know I can control my feelings of tension and stress.

_____ 25. I breathe faster just before starting a speech.

_____ 26. I feel comfortable and relaxed in the hour or so just before giving a speech.

eliminating nervousness is probably undesirable. In fact, the more you concentrate on your nervousness, the more nervous you may become.

A second reason why you should not try to eliminate nervousness is that some nervousness can actually benefit a speaker. Nervousness is energy, and it shows that you care about performing well. Use that nervous energy to enliven your delivery and to give your ideas impact. Instead of nervously tapping your fingers on the lectern, for

_____ **27.** I do poorer on speeches because I am anxious.

_____ **28.** I feel anxious when the teacher announces the date of a speaking assignment.

_____ **29.** When I make a mistake while giving a speech, I find it hard to concentrate on the parts that follow.

_____ **30.** During an important speech I experience a feeling of helplessness building up inside me.

_____ **31.** I have trouble falling asleep the night before a speech.

_____ **32.** My heart beats very fast while I present a speech.

_____ **33.** I feel anxious while waiting to give my speech.

_____ **34.** While giving a speech, I get so nervous I forget facts I really know.

Scoring: To determine your score on the PRPSA, complete the following steps:

Step 1: Add the scores for items 1, 2, 3, 5, 9, 10, 13, 14, 19, 20, 21, 22, 23, 25, 27, 28, 29, 30, 31, 32, 33, and 34.

Step 2: Add the scores for items 4, 6, 7, 8, 11, 12, 15, 16, 17, 18, 24, and 26.

Step 3: Complete the following formula:
PRPSA = 132 – Total from Step 1 + Total from Step 2.

Your score should range between 34 and 170. If your score is below 34 or above 170, you have made a mistake in computing the score.

Interpreting the Personal Report of Public Speaking Anxiety

For people with scores between 34 and 84 on the PRPSA, very few public speaking situations would produce anxiety.

Scores between 85 and 92 indicate a moderately low level of anxiety about public speaking. While some public speaking situations would be likely to arouse anxiety in people with such scores, most situations would not be anxiety arousing.

Scores between 93 and 110 indicate moderate anxiety in most public speaking situations, but the level of anxiety is not likely to be so severe that the individual won't be able to cope with it and eventually become a successful speaker.

Scores that range between 111 and 119 suggest a moderately high level of anxiety about public speaking. People with such scores will tend to avoid public speaking because it usually arouses a fairly high level of anxiety. While some public speaking situations may not cause too much of a problem, most will be problematic.

Scores between 120 and 170 indicate a very high level of anxiety about public speaking. People with scores in this range have very high anxiety in most, if not all, public speaking situations and are likely to go to considerable lengths to avoid them. It is unlikely that they can become successful public speakers unless they overcome or significantly reduce their anxiety.

From *Communication: Apprehension, Avoidance, and Effectiveness* 5th ed. by Virginia P. Richmond and James C. McCroskey. Copyright © 1998 by Allyn & Bacon. Reprinted by permission.

example, you can gesture. Rather than shifting your body weight from foot to foot, incorporate motivated movement into your speech.

Your goal, then, is not to eliminate nervousness but to control and channel it. The coping strategies we suggest in the next section and in Chapter 13 will enable you to control the symptoms of nervousness and to channel that energy into dynamic, effective vocal and physical delivery.

Nervous energy is a sign that you care about your speech performance. Try to channel that energy into gestures and body movements that will enhance your message.

Learn How to Build Speaker Confidence

We began this chapter by observing that public speaker nervousness is normal. We now suggest that it may actually be beneficial. James Belasco, professor and consultant to major corporations, describes how he uses nervousness as a transforming agent:

> Fear is a wonderful stimulant. It quickens the mind, sharpens the senses, heightens performance. I've learned to focus the stimulant on doing better, rather than worrying about doing worse. When fear runs through my system, I ask myself, "What can I do to remove the potential cause of failure?" "What can I do to ensure success?" I've evolved rituals to answer these questions constructively.[7]

The rituals Belasco then describes do not involve touching a lucky charm or intoning any magic phrase. Instead they are quite practical and make a lot of sense: Get up early, practice saying the first part of each main point in the speech while in the shower, get to the speech setting early and get the feel of the place.[8] Whether or not you develop your own "readiness rituals," the eleven suggestions on page 44 offer a systematic way of becoming a more confident communicator. If you consider each suggestion seriously, you will control your nervousness and channel it into a dynamic and effective speaking style.

Know How You React to Stress

Remember that nervousness affects different people in different ways. Perhaps you feel that your hands or knees shake uncontrollably as you speak in public. The people sitting next to you may not experience those symptoms of nervousness, but may have difficulty breathing comfortably and feel that their voices are shaky or quivery. Whatever your individual responses to stress, don't wait until you are delivering a public speech to discover them.

Knowing your reactions to stressful situations helps you in two ways. First, this knowledge lets you predict and cope with these physical conditions. Your dry mouth or sweaty palms will not surprise you. Second, because you are anticipating these physical conditions, you will be better able to mask them from the audience. How do you do this? Try these techniques.

Exploring *Online*

RELAXATION TECHNIQUES
http://ourworld.compuserve.com/homepages/har/les1.htm
Visit this site to study Bernd Harmsen's step-by-step directions for "Progressive Muscle Relaxation," a technique invented by Edmund Jacobson. The site also links to directions for a shortened version of the exercises.

If you know that your hands shake when you are nervous, don't hold a sheet of paper during the speech; the shaking paper will only amplify the movement of your hands and will telegraph this sign of nervousness to your audience. If your voice is likely to be thin and quivery as you begin speaking, take several deep, slow breaths before you begin to speak. If you get tense before speaking, try some muscle relaxation techniques: Tense your hands, arms, and shoulders, and then slowly relax them. If you get flustered before speaking, make sure you arrive on time or even a little early—never late. If looking at an audience intimidates you, talk to audience members before class, and when you speak, look for friendly faces in the audience.

Know Your Strengths and Weaknesses

Surgeons spend many hours learning how to use the equipment they need to perform operations. Each surgeon knows just what each instrument is capable of doing and strives to use it effectively. As a public speaker, your instruments are your voice, body, mind, and personality. You will use all these instruments together to create and communicate messages.

To know yourself, you must honestly assess both your strengths and your weaknesses. Use your strengths to communicate your message with force and impact. If you are a lively and enthusiastic person, channel that energy to reinforce your speech physically and enliven your listeners. If you have a talent for creating memorable phrases, allow that creativity to help your listeners attend to and remember your

> *The best speakers know enough to be scared. Stage fright is the sweat of perfection. The only difference between the pros and the novices is that the pros have trained the butterflies to fly in formation.*
>
> —EDWARD R. MURROW

EthicalDecisions

Being Yourself

Sondra is preparing a speech on defensive driving. A drama major, she is comfortable playing all sorts of characters on stage, but the thought of standing in front of an audience and delivering a speech terrifies her. She has visions of herself clutching the lectern, staring blankly at her notes, and mumbling inaudibly. "I'll feel so exposed—I don't think I can get through it just being my ordinary self," Sondra confides to her friends. She asks their help in brainstorming ways to steel herself before she comes to class on speech day.

"I bet a couple of glasses of wine would relax you," suggests her friend Amy.

"Amphetamines would perk you up; you'd zip right through your speech before you even had time to get scared," offers Edward.

"Maybe you could borrow some blood pressure medicine. My dad says it makes him feel less nervous," adds Michal.

"Or you could dress like a car crash dummy and deliver your speech in character," jokes her boyfriend, Steve.

What do you think of these suggestions? In Chapter 2 we noted that ethical speakers enter into and honor an unwritten contract with their listeners. How should the terms of that contract guide Sondra as she wrestles with how to control her nervousness? Could she follow any of her friends' advice and still "be herself" as she speaks? What advice would you offer if you were her friend?

ideas. Just as you can tap your strengths in these ways, you can minimize or avoid your weaknesses if you know them. If you are not effective in delivering humor, you probably should not begin your speech with a joke. To do so would risk failure at this critical point in the speech, and that would make you even more nervous.

The more you understand your strengths and weaknesses, the better you will be able to craft your speech to your abilities. The more confident you are that you can accomplish what you set out to do, the less nervous you will be. One note of caution, however: Don't be too critical of yourself and construct a "safe" speech because you have exaggerated your weaknesses. Instead, expand your abilities by incorporating new strategies into your speech making. Only through thoughtful, measured risk taking will you develop as a public speaker.

Know Speech Principles

If you are confident that you have constructed an effective speech, you will be more confident as you step to the lectern. This textbook and your instructor will assist you in learning speech principles. What are the five functions of an effective speech introduction? How should you construct the body of your speech, and how should you develop each key idea? What strategies help you conclude your speech? How can you use your voice and body to communicate your ideas dynamically? What strategies help you word ideas correctly, clearly, and vividly? We address all these questions, and many others, in this book. As you begin to answer these questions and apply what you learn, you will feel more confident about the content, organization, and delivery of your ideas.

Know That It Always Looks Worse from the Inside

Keep in mind the adage that it always looks worse from the inside. Because you feel nervous, you focus on your anxiety, exaggerate it, and become more nervous. Remember, though, your audience cannot see your internal state! Many times our students have lamented their nervousness after concluding a speech, only to learn that classmates

Speaking with *Confidence*

To get up and give a speech in front of class is really hard for me. One thing I learned that helped me is that even speakers who seem to have it all together are nervous inside just like I am. During the semester I tried to learn more about my classmates. I'd sit and talk to them before class, learn who they really are

through their speeches, listen to their oral critiques, and walk out with them after class. Knowing what my classmates looked for in a good speech helped me to prepare for my own speeches. Knowing that they also were nervous when they spoke made me more relaxed and boosted my confidence.

—Bo'don Wilson, *West Texas A&M University*

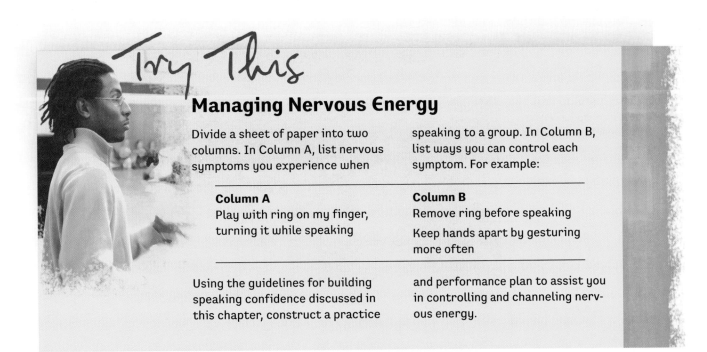

Try This

Managing Nervous Energy

Divide a sheet of paper into two columns. In Column A, list nervous symptoms you experience when

speaking to a group. In Column B, list ways you can control each symptom. For example:

Column A	Column B
Play with ring on my finger, turning it while speaking	Remove ring before speaking
	Keep hands apart by gesturing more often

Using the guidelines for building speaking confidence discussed in this chapter, construct a practice

and performance plan to assist you in controlling and channeling nervous energy.

---

envied them for being so calm and free from stage fright. The authors of a study of 95 speakers found that "untrained audiences are not very good at detecting the self-perceived anxiety of beginning speakers."[9] Even if you feel extremely nervous, then, your audience probably does not realize it. Knowing this should make you more secure and lessen your nervousness.

One of our students, Susan, wrote the following in her self-evaluation of her first graded classroom speech: "Too fast, too rushed. I forgot half of it. Yuck! Yuck! Yuck!" Yet here are a few of the comments her classmates wrote:

> "Wow! You seemed really relaxed! Your speech was organized, informative, and interesting."

> "Definitely the best speech given so far."

> "She seemed to know what she was talking about."

Susan obviously experienced her speech in a radically different way than her classmates and instructor did. Asked about her listeners' written comments, Susan responded, "Wow! What you said is definitely true. It does look worse from the inside."

If Susan had not received feedback from her audience, she would probably have retained her high level of fear of public speaking, perhaps even avoiding future opportunities to share her ideas with others. By offering honest evaluation, her classmates let her see her speech from "the other side," lessened some of her anxieties, and motivated her to continue to improve her public speaking skills.

Know Your Speech

Knowing your strengths and weaknesses, speech principles, and your audience gains you little, however, if you do not know your speech. This textbook will acquaint you with strategies to help you remember the ideas and supporting material of your speech. If you don't know what you want to say, you won't say it. If you think you will forget, you probably will. The more confident you are about your message, the less nervous you will be.

You certainly do not need to memorize the entire speech. Yet, if you are well prepared, you should have memorized the outline of major points for your speech and the

If you choose a subject you love, whether it be a favorite hobby, job, class, or poet, you will become deeply involved in developing your speech. This involvement, in turn, may reduce your inhibitions about speaking in public.

order in which you want to present them. If you forget your notes, or drop them on the way to the lectern and cannot get them back into proper order, you should still be able to deliver the speech. (Take a minute to number your notecards, of course, and you have one less worry.)

Believe in Your Topic

If you are giving an informative speech, you must believe that what you say will benefit your listeners—that hearing your speech will improve them in some way. If you are giving a persuasive speech, be committed to the belief you attempt to instill or the action you attempt to initiate in your audience. Convincing your audience that they should listen to your speech is easier if you believe that the topic is important. The more you believe in your topic, the more earnestly you will want to inform or convince your listeners. In short, if you doubt the importance of the topic, you will feel and seem tentative.

View Speech Making Positively

Poet Howard Nemerov has said about perception, "What we know is never the object, but only our knowledge."[10] In other words, we do not experience the world directly, but only through the various labels we have attached to things and experiences. More and more we are discovering and investigating the mind's ability to affect behavior. Doctors have learned, for example, that patients' attitudes about their illnesses significantly affect their speeds of recuperation or their chances for recovery.

One method for reducing communication anxiety is called **cognitive restructuring**. This approach recognizes that nervousness is, in part, caused by illogical beliefs. If speakers can restructure their thinking and focus on positive rather than negative self-statements, they reduce their anxiety. Cognitive restructuring involves two steps. First, you identify your negative self-statements ("Everyone will laugh at me when I give my speech"). Second, you replace the negative thoughts with positive ones ("My classmates understand what it's like to be nervous and will support my speaking efforts").

Exploring *Online*

COGNITIVE THERAPY
http://front.csulb.edu/tstevens/Cognitive%20
Therapy.htm
Dr. Tom Stevens of California State University, Long Beach, presents seven steps to cognitive restructuring, as well as an overview of other therapies.

cognitive restructuring: a strategy for reducing communication anxiety by replacing negative thoughts and statements with positive ones.

If you view public speaking as a tedious chore, your audience will sense it from your vocal and physical delivery and perhaps even from your choice of speech topic. On the other hand, if you look on public speaking as an opportunity, your positive attitude will help you control your nervousness. The following examples illustrate how you can replace negative thoughts with positive ones.

Replace the negative thought . . .	with a positive thought.
"My audience will probably be bored with my speech."	"I found the topic of how music affects our moods interesting, and my audience will, too."
"When I get up to speak, my mind will probably go blank and I'll have nothing to say."	"I've rehearsed my speech and I have a good set of speaking notes. If I momentarily forget a point, I'll just look at my note-cards and then continue."

Thinking positively can help turn anxiety into anticipation. Genuine enthusiasm about the chance to speak in public will guide your choice of topic and will reveal itself to the audience through your lively delivery. Seek out opportunities to test and develop your communication skills. Volunteer for oral reports in classes, speak out at organizational meetings, offer to introduce a guest speaker at your club's banquet. This positive attitude, coupled with practice and experience, will help make you less apprehensive and more confident.

Visualize Success

In football games, place kickers attempt field goals and extra points after touchdowns. Before taking the field, they stand on the sidelines, usually in deep concentration and away from the other players. They visualize the football being snapped and placed. They imagine themselves approaching the ball and kicking it. As they watch the football go through the goalposts, the referee lifts his arms to signal a field goal, and the crowd cheers. Through this ritual, place kickers focus on their task, visualizing how they can accomplish it.

Like athletes, public speakers can also use **visualization** to reduce their nervousness and improve their performance. A study of 430 college speech students revealed lowered speech anxiety among those who visualized themselves delivering an effective presentation.[11] Rodney describes how he used positive visualization to help build his confidence:

> The week before I gave my speech, I would find quiet spots where I could relax. I would close my eyes and visualize myself giving an effective presentation. I saw myself arriving at my classroom on the day I was to speak. Calmly, I would walk to my seat. I'd sit down, check my speaking notes to see that they were in order, and collect my thoughts. When Dr. Conner called my name, I got up from my seat and walked confidently to the front of the room. I put my notes on the lectern, looked at my classmates, and smiled. I paused, took a breath, and then began. I visualized myself being relaxed and delivering my speech as I had planned, with clarity and poise. I felt good talking about a topic that was so important to me. I visualized my classmates smiling at my humor and nodding in agreement as I explained my ideas. I concluded with a dramatic story that really drove home my point. I paused, then walked to my seat. My classmates applauded, and one of them even whispered to me, "Great speech, Rod!"

Project Confidence

Daryl Bem's theory of self-perception states that if you perceive yourself acting a particular way, you will assume that you feel that way.[12] Thus, if you want to feel

visualization: a strategy for reducing communication anxiety by picturing yourself delivering a successful speech.

confident, act confident. Begin by identifying characteristics of speakers who seem confident to you; then incorporate those behaviors into your own speaking. For example, instead of walking tentatively to the lectern, approach it confidently. Instead of avoiding eye contact with your listeners, look directly at them. Instead of leaning on the lectern or shifting your weight from foot to foot, stand erect and still. Instead of tapping your fingers on the lectern or jingling the change in your pocket, use your hands to gesture emphatically. Displaying confident behaviors such as these will not only make you *appear* more confident, it will also help you *feel* more confident.

Test Your Message

Confident speakers must believe that their speech content will interest listeners or satisfy an audience need. If your listeners are bored with your topic, you will sense it, and that will make you more nervous. If the audience is interested in the content of your speech, they will be attentive.

As a speaker, you can test your message by practicing your speech in front of friends. Can they restate your main points after listening to you? Do they find your supporting material believable? Does your delivery detract from or reinforce your message? Answers to these questions will guide your subsequent practice sessions. The more confident you are that your message will achieve the desired effect on your audience, the less nervous you will be.

Practice Your Delivery

The previous coping strategies have implied the importance of practice. Practicing your speech is so important, however, that it deserves a separate category. Jack Valenti, former presidential speechwriter, correctly observes, "The most effective antidote to stage fright and other calamities of speech making is total, slavish, monkish preparation."[13]

Your approach to your practice sessions will vary, depending on how your presentation develops. Sometimes you may practice specific sections of your speech that give you difficulty. But you should also practice your speech several times from start to finish without stopping. Too often when students mess up in practice, they stop and begin again. This is not a luxury you have when you address an audience, so as you practice, practice recovering from mistakes. Knowing that you can make it through your speech despite blunders in practice should make you more confident.

REDUCING ANXIETY
www.all-biz.com/articles/anxiety.htm
This article, "Overcoming Speaking Anxiety in Meetings and Presentations" by Lenny Laskowski, a Connecticut speech consultant, lists and briefly discusses ten steps for reducing speech anxiety.

You should also occasionally practice your speech in an environment laden with distractions. Students who practice only in the silence of an empty classroom may not be prepared for distractions that arise when they actually deliver their speeches—for example, a student coming into the classroom during the speech, a lawn mower passing by the window, or two students talking in the back of the room. These distractions, especially those stemming from rudeness, should not occur; in reality, though, they sometimes do. Practicing with the television on in the background or in your room with noise in the hallway forces you to concentrate on what you are saying and not on what you are hearing. You develop poise as a speaker only through practice.

The eleven coping strategies we've discussed will help you channel your nervous energy into dynamic, confident delivery. After your speech, reflect on the experience and gauge your success using the suggestions in this chapter's Theory into Practice feature. You can also read in the "Speaking with Confidence" boxes throughout this book

Theory into Practice

Gaining Perspective

In this chapter we present eleven strategies (listed on page 44) for building your speaking confidence. You incorporate these suggestions as you prepare and deliver your speeches. However, what should you do *after* your speech? You've heard the expression, "Experience is the best teacher." Well, there's some truth in that folk wisdom; you can use your public speaking experiences to build your confidence.

After each speech, assess your performance by asking and answering important questions. Your instructor will give you feedback for some of these questions; others you will need to answer for yourself, because you alone know the true answers.

- How did you react when you walked to the front of the room, turned, and looked at the audience looking at you?
- Did you remember what you planned to say?
- Did you have trouble finding your place in your notes?
- What techniques did you try in your speech that worked? What didn't work?
- Did you get less or more nervous as the speech progressed?
- How did your audience respond to your speech? What did their nonverbal com-

munication convey as you delivered your speech? What feedback did you receive from your classmates and instructor following the speech?

Remember, don't be too critical as you evaluate your performance. You will do some things well, and this should build your confidence. Other aspects of your speech you can improve, and you should work on these.

Suppose, for example, that you do encounter a serious problem: You lose your place, your mind goes blank, and so you bury your head in your notes and race to the end of your speech. Rather than trying to forget this, use it as a learning experience. Ask yourself *why* you forgot: Did you try to memorize your speech instead of speaking from a set of notes? Were your notes disorganized, or did they contain too little or too much information? Did you focus too much on your instructor and not enough on the entire audience?

Once you face a problem and determine its cause, you will be better able to plan so that it does not occur again. You don't *discover* confidence; you *build* confidence. Each public speech provides an opportunity to improve and enhance your confidence for your next speech.

how other public speaking students developed their self-assurance using some of these principles. For now, however, you can begin training those butterflies to fly in formation as you prepare your first speech in this class.

Prepare Your First Speech

This class will undoubtedly require you to give your first speech before you have read much of this textbook. What is absolutely necessary to know, then, in order to be able to deliver that first speech successfully? Preparing your first speech will be easier if you keep in mind two principles of public speaking. First, the more effectively that you prepare, the better the speech you will deliver and the more confident you will feel. Only then can you recognize what you already do competently and begin to identify skills you want to improve. In addition, your confidence will grow with each speaking experience throughout this course and later in your life.

Preparing thoroughly, practicing often, and wanting to communicate with your audience are keys to any successful speech.

The second principle is that every public speech is a blend of *content, organization,* and *delivery.* Each of these aspects affects the others. For example, choosing a topic you already know well or have researched thoroughly should easily translate into animated, confident delivery. Elements of speech delivery such as pause and movement can emphasize your speech's organization. Moreover, as you will soon learn, we believe that any speech on any topic should be well organized. The more you know about the principles of speech content, organization, and delivery, then, the better your first speech will be. The following seven guidelines will help you toward that goal.

Key Points

The Speech-Making Process

1. Understand the assignment.
2. Develop your speech content.
3. Organize your speech.
4. Word your speech.
5. Practice your speech.
6. Deliver your speech.
7. Evaluate your speech.

Understand the Assignment

For your first speech assignment, your instructor may prescribe a specific purpose or leave that choice to you. Often your first speech assignment is to introduce yourself or a classmate, and so is informative rather than persuasive. The speech may be graded or ungraded. Whether your instructor is trying an innovative assignment or using one that has been tested and proven, he or she is your first and final authority for the specific details of the assignment.

A primary, vital requirement for preparing any speech is to know exactly what you are to do. The following questions can help you identify your goals for the speech.

- What am I supposed to do in this speech: inform, persuade, or entertain?
- What are my minimum and maximum time limits for the speech?
- Are there special requirements for the delivery of the speech? If so, what are they?

Develop Your Speech Content

As you select a speech topic, you need to decide the number of main ideas you will cover. To determine what those ideas will be, think about what you would want to hear if you were in the audience. If your instructor assigns you a topic, the specific things you say and the order in which you say them will be uniquely your own. If you are asked to choose your topic, you have even greater creative latitude, of course. In either of these cases, you need to keep your audience in mind. The topic you select or the way you approach an assigned topic should be guided by what you think your listeners will find most interesting or useful.

If your assignment is to introduce yourself, begin by jotting down as many aspects of your life as you can. Audit your history, assess your current circumstances, and project your future goals. Among others, topics that apply to your life and the lives of all your listeners include:

accomplishments	people who have been significant influences
career plans	unusual life events
educational backgrounds	personal values
skills or aptitudes	prized possessions
hobbies	pet peeves
special interests	aspirations

In addition, you may have a particularly interesting work history or may have traveled to unusual places. You could decide to limit your speech to one of the preceding areas or to combine several that you think your listeners will find most interesting.

If the ideas you disclose are truly unusual, your speech will be memorable. But don't be intimidated or worried if your experiences seem fairly tame and ordinary. Some of your listeners will be relieved to find that they have backgrounds similar to yours. Whether ordinary or extraordinary, your background and your classmates' will provide the basis for conversation before class, for classroom discussion, and for audience analysis as you prepare for future speeches.

If your first speech is not one introducing yourself to the class, you may be allowed to choose a topic. If so, brainstorm for topics that are of interest to you and those that you think would benefit or be of interest to your audience. Your speaking occasion, the time of year that you speak, and upcoming or recent holidays can also suggest topic ideas. In addition, consider subjects that you discover as you conduct research. Don't settle for the first topic that comes to mind, however. If you generate a number of possible topics and spend some time reflecting on them, the subject you finally choose will probably be more satisfying for you and more interesting to your listeners. To make sure that you have a clear grasp of your speech topic, answer questions such as these:

■ What is my speech topic and why have I chosen it?
■ Who are the people in my audience?
■ What do I want my listeners to know or remember when I'm finished speaking?

The best way to answer that last question is to ask, "What aspects of my topic interest me and are likely to interest my audience?" Select only a few points to discuss. A time limit of two to four minutes, for example, may seem endless to you right now. It's not; it goes by very quickly. As you develop your speech content, check to be sure that everything you say is relevant to your purpose and to those few main points you want your listeners to remember. Limiting your number of main ideas should give you enough time to develop them with adequate supporting materials—definitions, stories, statistics, comparisons, and contrasts—that are interesting and relevant to your listeners. Once you have done this preliminary work, you are ready to assess your speech content by asking questions such as the following:

■ Have I selected a few key points that I can develop in the time allowed?
■ Is everything that I say relevant to my topic?
■ Do I use a variety of specific supporting materials, such as examples and stories, to develop my key points?

- Will my supporting materials be clear and interesting to my classroom audience?
- Do I acknowledge sources for anything I quote or paraphrase from other speakers or writers?

Once you begin to generate the main ideas of your topic and then to limit yourself to the ones you think the audience will find most interesting, you have begun to organize your content.

Organize Your Speech

Organizing a speech is similar to writing an essay. Every essay must have an introductory paragraph, a body, and a concluding paragraph. A speech has the same three divisions: an introduction, a body, and a conclusion. To determine whether your ideas are clearly organized and easy to follow, you must consider the organization of each of these three parts of your speech.

Organize Your Speech Introduction.   Though usually brief, your speech introduction serves five vital functions. First, it focuses the audience's attention on your message. You want to command the audience's attention with your first words. How can you do this? Question your audience, amuse them, arouse their curiosity about your subject, or stimulate their imaginations.

Second, your introduction should clarify your topic or your purpose in speaking. If your listeners are confused about your exact topic, you limit their ability to listen actively. To minimize any chances of this, state your purpose clearly in a well-worded sentence.

A third function of your introduction is to establish the significance of your topic, explain your interest in it, or reveal any special qualifications you have for speaking on your topic. Fourth, your introduction should help establish your credibility as a speaker on that topic. Your words, voice, and body should instill confidence in your listeners that you have prepared thoroughly. Finally, your introduction should highlight or preview the aspects of your subject that you will discuss in the body. Well-planned and well-delivered opening remarks will make the audience want to listen and will prepare them for what comes next. To check the integrity of your speech introduction, answer the following questions:

What are the parts of my introduction?

What is my attention-getter?

What is my statement of purpose?

What rationale do I provide for speaking about this topic?

How do I establish my credibility to speak on this topic?

What are the points I will cover in my speech?

Organize the Body of Your Speech.   The body of your speech is its longest, most substantial section. Though it follows your introduction, you should prepare the body of your speech first. Here you introduce your key ideas and support or explain each of them. You should develop only a few main ideas, probably only two or three in a first speech. Why? You can more easily develop a few ideas within your time limit. Your audience will also more easily grasp and remember a few well-developed ideas. Restricting your main points to a few is particularly important in a first speech, because it may be the shortest presentation you make during the semester or quarter.

Your organizational goal in the body of your speech should be to structure your main points so clearly that they are not just distinct but unmistakable to your listeners. To help you do so, we recommend a four-step sequence—the "4 S's"—for organizing each of your main ideas. First, *signpost* each main idea. Typical signposts are numbers ("first" or "one") and words such as *initially* or *finally.* Second, *state* the idea clearly. Third, the step that will take you the most time, *support,* or explain, the idea. Finally, *summarize* the idea before moving to your next one. These four steps will help you highlight and develop each of your main ideas in a logical, orderly way. The following questions and outline form should help you determine whether the body of your speech is well organized:

Do I have the body of my speech organized clearly?

    I. What is my first main idea?
      A. What will I say about it?
      B. How will I summarize it?

    II. What is my second main idea?
      A. What will I say about it?
      B. How will I summarize it?

    III. What is my third main idea?
      A. What will I say about it?
      B. How will I summarize it? and so forth.

Organize Your Speech Conclusion. Your speech conclusion is a brief final step with three main functions. The first function, the summary, is a final review of the main points you have covered. Summarizing may be as simple as listing the key ideas you discussed in the body of the speech. You should not introduce and develop any new ideas in the conclusion. When you summarize, you bring your speech to a logical close.

The second function of a conclusion is to activate an audience response by letting your listeners know whether you want them to accept, use, believe, or act on the content of your speech. Whether your speech is informative or persuasive, you want the audience to have been involved with your information and ideas. This is your last opportunity to highlight what you want your listeners to take away from your speech.

Finally, your conclusion should provide your speech with a strong sense of closure. To do this, end on a positive, forceful note. You can use many of the same techniques here that you used to get the audience's attention at the very beginning of the speech: Question the audience, amuse them, stimulate their imaginations, and so forth. Your final remarks should be carefully thought out and extremely well worded. Ask and answer these questions to test your speech conclusion:

What are the parts of my conclusion?

What is my summary statement?

What am I asking my audience to remember or do?

What is my closing statement?

If you answer each of the questions we've posed so far, you should have an interesting, well-developed speech that is easy to follow. Both your content and your organization are in good shape.

Up to this point, you have spent most of your time thinking about the speech and jotting down ideas. Now you have to word those ideas and practice getting them across to your audience through your vocal and physical delivery.

Word Your Speech

Unless your instructor requests that you do so, avoid writing out your first speech word for word. Even though having the text of your speech in front of you may make you

feel more secure, our experience has been that students who deliver speeches from manuscripts early in the semester or quarter often suffer two consequences. One is that what they say tends to sound like writing rather than speech. In Chapter 12 we'll examine some of the important differences between oral and written styles.

A second problem you may encounter if you deliver your speech from manuscript is a lack of eye contact. Effective speakers make eye contact with their listeners. If you are reading, you can't do this. Therefore, if you have a choice, speak from just a few notes, rather than from a prepared manuscript.

The language of your speech should be correct, clear, and vivid. To illustrate this, assume that you have been assigned a practice speech of self-introduction early in the course. Assume, too, that you have decided to make your travels one of your main points. "I've traveled quite a bit" is a vague, general statement. Without supporting materials, the statement is also superficial. But suppose you said, instead:

> I've traveled quite a bit. I had lived in five states before I was in middle school, for example. When I was seven, my father worked in the booming oil business, and my family even got a chance to live in South America for more than a year. My brother and I went to an American school in the tiny village of Anaco, Venezuela; we were students 99 and 100 in a school that taught grades one through eight. Instruction in Spanish started in the first grade, and by the time we returned to the States, I was bilingual. I have vivid memories of picking mangoes and papayas off the trees, swimming outdoors on Christmas day, and having my youngest brother born in Venezuela.

The second statement is a great deal clearer and more vivid than the first. It begins with the general comment, but then amplifies it with a more detailed story. The language is personal, conversational, and crisp. The following questions should help you test the language of your own speech:

- Does my speech sound conversational?
- Is the language of my speech correct?
- Will the language of my speech be clear to my listeners?
- Will the language of my speech be vivid for my listeners?

Practice Your Speech

Mental rehearsal is no substitute for oral and physical practice. Merely thinking about what you plan to say will never adequately ready you to deliver a prepared speech in class. As we said toward the beginning of this chapter, speech making is an active process. You gain a heightened knowledge of what you plan to say, as well as increased confidence in your abilities, just by practicing your speech out loud. Before you can do that, however, you must create the notes you will use to practice and deliver the speech.

Prepare Your Notes.   Make certain that your speaking notes are in the form of key words or phrases, rather than complete sentences. Remember, you want your listeners to remember your main *ideas,* not necessarily your exact wording. Your goal in preparing your notes should be the same: You should need only a word or phrase to remind you of the order of your ideas. As you elaborate those points, your specific wording can change slightly each time you practice your speech. Make sure that your notes are easy to read. If your speaking notes are on notecards, be certain to number the cards and have them in the correct order before each practice session.

Practice Productively.   Most of your practice will probably be done in seclusion. Practice any way that will help you, being sure to stand as you rehearse. Visualize your audience, and gesture to them as you hope to when giving the speech. You may even want to record and listen to your speech on audiotape or videotape, if you have access to that equipment. Give yourself the opportunity to stop for intensive practice of rough spots in your speech. Just make sure that you also practice the speech from beginning to end without stopping.

As valuable as solitary practice is, you should also try your speech out on at least a few listeners, if at all possible. Enlist roommates and friends to listen to your speech and help you time it. The presence of listeners should make it easier to practice the way that you approach your speaking position before you speak and the way you will leave it after finishing. Your rehearsal audience can tell you if there are parts of your speech that are so complex that they are hard to grasp. They may also be able to suggest clearer, more colorful, or more powerful ways of wording certain statements you make. A practice audience can point out strengths of your delivery, as well as help you eliminate distractions that draw their attention away from your message. Most importantly, serious practice in front of others should focus your attention on the important interaction involved in delivering a speech to an audience. The following questions make up a checklist for your speech practice:

- Have I practiced my speech as I intend to deliver it in class?
- Have I made my speaking notes concise and easy to use and read?
- Have I recorded my speech and made changes after listening to or viewing it?
- How many times have others listened to my speech, and what suggestions have they offered for improving it?
- Have I timed my speech? Is the average time within my overall time limit?
- What adjustments can I make in my speech if it is too long or too short?

Deliver Your Speech

Your speech delivery is made up of your language, your voice, and your body. Speaking in public should feel natural to you and seem natural to your audience. You want to be conversational and to talk with your listeners, not at them. Use a presentational style with which you are comfortable, but which also meets the requirements of your audience, your topic, and your speaking occasion.

Effective vocal delivery is energetic, easily heard, and understandable. Your voice should also show that you are thinking about what you are saying as you deliver your speech. With practice, your voice can communicate humor, seriousness, sarcasm, anger, and a range of other possible emotions behind your words. Check your vocal delivery by answering the following questions:

- Do I change the pitch of my voice enough to create a lively vocal delivery?
- Do I speak with enough volume to be heard easily?
- Do I vary my rate of speaking to match my audience's comprehension of what I am saying?

The message your listeners see should match the one they hear. Effective physical delivery is direct and immediate; effective speakers demonstrate their involvement in their topics and in their speaking situations by interacting with their audiences. You must make eye contact with listeners in all parts of your audience. Your facial expression should signal that you are thinking moment to moment about what you are saying. Physical delivery is not limited to your face, however. Gestures with your arms and hands and selective movement from place to place can emphasize what you say and mark important transitions in your speech.

If you are concentrating on your message and your audience's nonverbal feedback, your physical delivery will likely seem most natural. To gauge your directness, immediacy, and involvement, answer the following questions about your physical delivery:

- Are my clothing and other elements of my appearance appropriate to my topic, my audience, and the speaking occasion?
- Do I look at members of my audience most of the time I am speaking? Do I look at listeners in all parts of the room?
- Do my gestures add emphasis to appropriate parts of the speech? Do my gestures look and feel natural and spontaneous?
- Do my facial expressions show that I am thinking about what I am saying, rather than about how I look or sound?
- If I include place-to-place movement, does it serve a purpose?

Your goal should be delivery that looks and sounds effortless. Yet, ironically, that will require significant practice and attention to the vocal and physical elements of your delivery.

Evaluate Your Speech

Don't forget your speech as soon as you deliver your final words and return to your seat. While the experience is fresh in your memory, evaluate what you said, your organization, and how you delivered your speech. What sorts of feedback did you get from your listeners? In short, how did you respond to the challenge of preparing and delivering a speech? To evaluate the kind of speaker you are now and the kind of speaker you can become, answer the following questions:

- What did I do well?
- What areas can I target for improvement in this class?
- What specific efforts do I need to make in order to improve my next speech?

No matter what your level of public speaking experience, you will benefit from recognizing two concerns that you probably share with everyone in class. First, most of your classmates are probably as apprehensive as you are about the first speech. Almost everyone worries about questions such as, "Will I be able to get through my speech? Will I remember what I wanted to say? Will I be able to make my listeners understand what I want to say? Will I sound OK and look as though I know what I'm doing?" Your nervousness is natural, typical, and healthy. In fact, your nervousness is a good sign that you have reasonably high expectations of yourself and that you care about doing well.

Second, you should know that public speaking is a teachable skill, much like math, reading, and writing. So, yes, you can *learn* to speak well. We share responsibility for part of that learning with your instructor. You are also responsible for much of your learning through your own effort and initiative. If you skipped the student preface to this book, we urge you to take the few minutes necessary to turn back and read it. Written primarily for you, not just for your instructor, the preface condenses our philosophy about this course and about education in general.

We began this chapter by focusing on speaker nervousness because we know that it is a real worry for most people. We have suggested some techniques to help manage and channel your platform panic into a lively, enthusiastic speech. We have also sketched in broad strokes the process of developing and delivering an effective speech. If you stop to think about public speaking for a moment, though, you will realize that the worst thing that could happen to you is that you might embarrass yourself. Stop and ask yourself, "Have I ever embarrassed myself before?" Unless you never leave your house, the answer to that question will be yes. You may have even embarrassed yourself so badly that you thought, "I'll never be able to face them again" or "I'll never live this down." But you do. The sun rises the next day. None of us is perfect, and it is unreasonable to expect perfection of ourselves or the people around us. So the best advice of all may be, "Keep public speaking in perspective." Your audience is made up of colleagues. They are pulling for you. Use this friendly atmosphere as a training ground to become a more effective speaker.

Summary

The topic of this chapter is the widespread and normal phenomenon of speaker nervousness or stage fright. Caused by the body's preparation to perform to capacity, stage fright is a condition the speaker should try not to eliminate but rather to control. We offer eleven suggestions for controlling nervousness: (1) Know how you react to stress. (2) Know your strengths and weaknesses. (3) Know basic speech principles. (4) Know that it always looks worse from the inside. (5) Without memorizing your speech, know what you plan to say in it. (6) Believe in your topic. (7) Have a positive attitude about speech making. (8) Visualize yourself speaking successfully. (9) Project confidence. (10) Test your message prior to delivering it in class. (11) Practice as much as possible in a variety of situations.

You can also lessen your nervousness about your first speech by preparing thoroughly. To do so, you must understand the speaking assignment, develop adequate content of a narrow topic, organize the various sections of the speech, word your ideas effectively, practice productively, deliver the speech, and evaluate your performance. Preparing your first speech will also be easier if you realize that your nervousness is normal and that you can learn to be an effective speaker. Only by reflecting on your performance and on criticisms given by others can you develop as a speaker and deliver your next speech with less anxiety.

Exercises

1. Complete McCroskey's Personal Report of Public Speaking Anxiety (Figure 3.1), and determine your score. Into which group does your score place you, and how do you compare with other college students whose survey results we discussed early in this chapter? Which coping strategies discussed in this chapter seem most promising in building your confidence?

2. Interview someone who occasionally gives public speeches, asking how he or she handles speaker nervousness. Based on your interview, compile a list of suggestions for controlling nervousness. How does that list compare with the one in this chapter?

3. After you have presented your first speech in this class, answer the following questions.
   a. What were three strengths of my speech?
   b. What are two areas I should target for improvement?
   c. What are some specific strategies I can use to improve each targeted area?

Responding to Speeches

chapter

Listening is a magnetic and strange thing, a creative force. The friends who listen to us are the ones we move forward toward, and we want to sit in their radius. When we are listened to, it creates us, makes us unfold and expand.

—KARL A. MENNINGER, *LOVE AGAINST HATE*[1]

Effective public communication occurs in the charged space between a speaker and an audience, with each party leaning slightly toward the other. Within that space, for the duration of a speech, the contract binding public speakers and their audiences is in effect. We discussed that contract in Chapter 2. We maintained that, as members of a community of learners in the classroom, each speaker and each listener bear ethical responsibilities. Among the commitments of the ethical speaker are being well prepared, communicating information and ideas clearly in order to benefit the audience, and remaining open to feedback and criticism that will improve future speeches. Among the responsibilities of ethical listeners are listening openly, listening critically, and providing feedback to assist the speaker's thinking on the topic and to help him or her improve as a public speaker. If the mutual respect implicit in this speaker–listener contract exists, as we believe it should, then listening is the paper on which participants write their contract, and criticism is their ink.

In this chapter we focus on the related topics of listening and speech criticism. As we look at the process, problems, and potential of listening, we will provide you with the tools you need to improve your listening skills. We'll then discuss the nature of criticism, offer guidelines for making helpful comments, and suggest some ways that you can maximize the benefits of the speech critiques you receive from others.

Exploring *Online*

LISTENING
www.listen.org
Visit the website of the International Listening Association to find a host of excellent quotations about listening, as well as links to resources on the topic of listening.

The Importance of Listening

You probably remember playing the game of "telephone" when you were a child. Someone whispered a phrase or sentence to another person, who whispered it to the next one, and so on. The last person to receive the message then said it aloud. Usually, the final message bore little resemblance to what the first person whispered, and the group laughed at the outcome.

Unfortunately, examples of poor listening exist in areas of life where the results are often far from humorous. In fact, researchers estimate that U.S. businesses lose billions of dollars each year simply because of ineffective listening.

Of course, ineffective listening is not confined to commercial settings. You can probably think of several examples of problems, or at least embarrassing situations, caused by your own ineffective listening. You asked a question the teacher had just answered. You didn't realize that a complete sentence outline of your informative speech on the causes and cures of snoring was due a week before you were scheduled to speak. You arrived at a party dressed in jeans, a T-shirt, and Doc Martens only to find everyone else dressed formally.

Each day, you send and receive both oral and written messages. Of the four roles you perform—speaker, listener, writer, and reader—you spend more time listening than doing any of the other actions. College students, for example, spend approximately 53 percent of their communication time listening.[2] You listen to your parents, teachers, and friends; to television, radio, and movies; and to many other sounds around you. Yet, despite listening's monopoly on your time, you probably know less about this activity than about other forms of communication. While you have taken several courses teaching you to read and write, you have probably never taken a course in listening. In short, you have received the least training in what you do the most!

It will probably not surprise you, then, to learn that most of us are inefficient listeners. In fact, immediately after listening to your classmates' speeches, chances are high that you will remember, at most, only 50 percent of what you heard, and two days later only 25 percent. This doesn't surprise listening expert Robert Montgomery, who summarizes the sad plight of listening:

> Listening is the most neglected and the least understood of the communication arts. It has become the weakest link in today's communications system. Poor listening is a result of bad habits that develop because we haven't been trained to listen.

But there is good news, as Montgomery adds: "Fortunately, it is a skill that can be learned."[3]

Listening versus Hearing

Does the following situation sound familiar? You are watching *The Daily Show with Jon Stewart,* listening to a CD, or doing economics homework when one of your parents walks by and tells you to put out the trash. Fifteen minutes later, that person walks back to find you still preoccupied with television, music, or homework, and the trash still in the kitchen. Your parent asks, "Didn't you hear me?" Well, of course you did. You *heard* the direction to put out the trash just as you heard Stewart joking with Samantha Bee, Stevie Ray Vaughn playing a riff, the dog barking at a passing car, and the air conditioner clicking on in the hall. You heard all of these things, but you might not have been *listening* to any of them.

What is the difference between **listening** and **hearing?** The two activities differ in at least four important ways.

Listening Is Intermittent

Listening is not a continuous activity, but occurs only from time to time when we choose to focus and respond to stimuli around us. Hearing, on the other hand, is a continuous function for a person having normal hearing ability.

Listening Is a Learned Skill

Listening must be taught and learned. Unless you were born with a hearing loss, however, hearing is a natural capacity for which you need no training. We hear sounds

listening: the intermittent, learned, and active process of giving attention to aural stimuli.

hearing: the continuous, natural, and passive process of receiving aural stimuli.

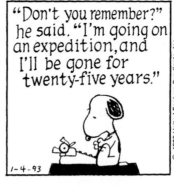

PEANUTS: © United Features Syndicate, Inc. Reprinted by permission.

before we are born; fetuses grow accustomed to certain voices, noises, and music. For this reason, pediatricians advise new parents not to tiptoe or whisper around the infant they have just brought home from the hospital. The child is already used to a lot of noise and must grow accustomed to the rest of it. Throughout our lives, we hear sounds even as we sleep.

Listening Is Active

Hearing means simply receiving an aural stimulus. The act of hearing is passive; it requires no work. Listening, in contrast, is active. It requires you to concentrate, interpret, and respond—in short, to be involved. You can hear the sound of a fire engine as you sit at your desk working on your psychology paper. You listen to the sound of the fire engine if you concentrate on its sound, identify it as a fire engine rather than an ambulance, wonder if it is coming in your direction, and then turn back to your work as you hear the sound fade away.

Listening Implies Using the Message Received

Audiences assemble for many reasons. We choose to listen to gain new information; to learn new uses for existing information; to discover arguments for beliefs or actions; to laugh and be entertained; to celebrate a person, place, object, or idea; and to be inspired. There are literally thousands of topics you could listen to: for example, regulating the Internet, the history of blue jeans, crimes of ethnic intimidation, preparing lemon-grass chicken, digital photography, and the life of Arthur Ashe. Some of these topics might induce you to listen carefully. Others might not interest you, so you choose not to listen. The perceived usefulness of the topic helps determine how actively you will listen to a speaker. Listening implies a choice; you must choose to participate in the process of listening.

The Process of Listening

In Chapter 1, we introduced the listener as one component of communication. Indeed, the listener is vital to successful communication; without at least one listener, communication cannot occur beyond the intrapersonal level. Remember that any time two people communicate, two messages are involved: the one that the sender intends and the one that the listener actually receives. As we discussed in Chapter 1, these messages will never be identical because people operate from different frames of reference and

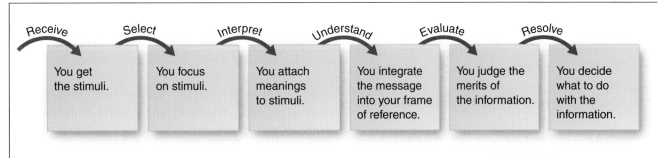

Receive	Select	Interpret	Understand	Evaluate	Resolve
You get the stimuli.	You focus on stimuli.	You attach meanings to stimuli.	You integrate the message into your frame of reference.	You judge the merits of the information.	You decide what to do with the information.

FIGURE 4.1
The Process of Listening

with different perceptions. As you examine the six steps in the process of listening shown in Figure 4.1, you will better understand this concept.

Receive

The first step in listening is to *receive* sounds. In face-to-face communication, we receive sound waves set in motion through the air by the speaker; on the telephone, those same sound waves are transmitted electronically. In both cases, the first step in listening to the speaker is receiving the sounds, the auditory stimuli. In other words, hearing is the first step in effective listening.

Some people, such as those with a hearing loss, unintentionally filter or leave out part of the stimulus. Whenever we filter, parts of the messages available to us will be lost.

Select

Individuals *select* different stimuli from those competing for their attention, a phenomenon sometimes called selective perception. When the police gather reports from various witnesses to a traffic accident, they often find conflicting information. Each bystander's report will be shaped by where the person was standing or sitting, what the person was focusing on at the moment of impact, how the person was feeling, and a host of other factors. Each witness has a selective perception of the event.

Exploring *Online*

TESTS OF LISTENING HABITS
www.highgain.com/SELF/index.php
www.isdesignet.com/Magazine/Apr'96/Commentary.html
To test your listening habits, visit either of these sites. At the first you can take a 28-item survey that rates your listening on the dimensions of attention, empathy, respect, response, memory, and open-mindedness. The second site contains a 25-item questionnaire with directions for self-scoring developed by Richard Ensman, Jr., a Rochester, New York, communication consultant.

Speaking with *Confidence*

Peer critics are so valuable when it comes to public speaking. Receiving constructive feedback and encouragement from my classmates increased my confidence. When ten audience members told me that I did a good job on some aspect of my presentation, I began to feel more comfortable getting up in front of people. My classmates were also helpful when they gently pinpointed areas I could work on for improvement.

I took their suggestions to heart more so than if my instructor was the only one critiquing me. Constructive comments from both my peers and my instructor helped me focus on what I needed to do in my next speech. Knowing that I was doing some things well and that I had the opportunity to improve other areas made me more confident and relaxed about giving a speech.

—**Julie Ruth,** *Radford University*

In public speaking situations, the audience reacts in a similar way. One person in the audience may focus primarily on what speakers are saying, another on their tones of voice or their gestures, still another on what they are wearing or even on the distracting hum of the heating system. If you are intrigued by the speaker's accent, you have selected to focus on that element of speech delivery, and you will probably hear a slightly different speech than the person sitting next to you. You may even be distracted by internal noise, such as worrying about an upcoming chemistry exam or trying to resolve a conflict with your roommate. As William James said more than 100 years ago, our view of the world is truly shaped by what we decide to heed.

Interpret

Not only do individuals choose differently among stimuli competing for their attention, they also *interpret* those stimuli differently. Interpreting is the process of decoding the message. When you interpret, you attach meanings to the cluster of verbal and nonverbal symbols the speaker provides—words, tone of voice, and facial expression, for example. At this stage, the listener is paying careful attention to those verbal and nonverbal symbols and their meanings. When a speaker introduced her speech on euthanasia, one listener heard "youth in Asia." Only after correcting this misinterpretation was the listener prepared to understand the speaker's message. As we noted in our discussion of the triangle of meaning in Chapter 1, the speaker's knowledge and experience must be similar to the listener's if communication is to be clear and effective.

Understand

Once you have decoded, or attached meanings to, a speaker's symbols, you begin fitting the message into your framework of existing knowledge and beliefs. To *understand* a speaker, you must consider both a message's content and its context. Is the speaker attempting to inform or persuade you? Is the speaker serious or joking? In short, what is the speaker trying to do?

It is easier to judge the context of communication when you listen to friends rather than to strangers. When you communicate with your friends, you can tell whether they are joking, upset, or teasing by their facial expressions or tones of voice, but you cannot always tell with strangers. You know your friends well and are more familiar with their cues. As you learn more about speakers, then, you enable yourself to understand their messages more accurately.

Evaluate

Before acting on the message you have decoded and understood, you *evaluate* it. Evaluating is the process of judging both the reliability of the speaker and the quality and consistency of the speaker's information. If the speaker is someone you know, you reflect on the history of that person's interactions with you. Has the person ever tried to deceive you? Or does the speaker have a track record of honest, open communication with you? If the speaker is a stranger, you often gauge the person's credibility based on the nonverbal cues of communication. Is the speaker making eye contact with you?

If you were unable to sense when your friends were serious or joking, you'd have a hard time interpreting and understanding what they told you.

Does he or she speak fluently, without unnecessary pauses or filler words? Do the speaker's gestures and other body language seem relaxed and spontaneous? In short, does the person seem well prepared, confident, and sincere? If your answer to any of these questions is no, you may wonder whether the speaker has ulterior motives for speaking to you. As you evaluate the speaker's message, you decide whether you believe the data presented and whether you agree or disagree with the position the speaker advocates.

Resolve

The final step in listening, resolving, involves deciding what to do with the information we have received. As listeners, we can *resolve* to accept the information, reject it, take action on it, decide to investigate it further, or just try to remember the information so that we can resolve it later.

Obviously, we do not consciously go through and dwell on each of these six steps each time we listen to someone. As the significance of the message increases for us, however, we become more involved in the process of listening—a point each speaker should remember.

Obstacles to Effective Listening

Speakers and audience members should recognize some of the reasons why effective listening is so difficult. Learning to listen better is easier if you know what you're up against. For this reason, you need to identify the major obstacles to effective listening. We list and discuss five barriers to listening in this section.

Physical Distractions

Have you ever told someone that he or she was being so loud that you couldn't hear yourself think? If so, you were commenting on one obstacle to effective listening: physical distraction. **Physical distractions** are interferences coming to you through any of your senses, and they may take many forms: glare from a sunny window, chill from an

physical distractions: listening disturbances that originate in the physical environment and are perceived by the listener's senses.

air conditioner vent, or the smell of formaldehyde in your anatomy and physiology lab. Like a diner whose enjoyment of a meal is spoiled by cigar smoke, you may have trouble focusing on the message of a speech on toxic waste if you concentrate on the speaker's outlandish clothing, on a PE class playing a vigorous game of touch football outside, or on the overpowering smell of aftershave on the person near you.

Physiological Distractions

Physiological distractions have to do with the body. Any illness or unusual physiological condition is a potential distraction to effective listening. A bout of flu, a painful earache, or fatigue after a sleepless night all place obvious and familiar limitations on our willingness and ability to listen.

Exploring *Online*

ACTIVE LISTENING
http://home.earthlink.net/~hopefull/active.htm
http://home.earthlink.net/~hopefull/active1.htm
Visit the first of these pages to review 12 blocks to effective listening and to read a suggestion for breaking that pattern. The second site briefly discusses three activities necessary to active listening: paraphrasing, questioning for clarification, and offering feedback.

Psychological Distractions

Your attitudes also affect your listening behavior. **Psychological distractions,** such as a negative attitude toward the speaker, the topic, or your reason for attending a speech, can all affect how you listen. If you are antagonistic toward the speaker or the point of view the speaker is advocating, you may resist or mentally debate the statements you hear. If you are coerced to be in the audience, you may also be more critical and less open-minded about what is being said. In short, if you are concentrating on thoughts unrelated to what the speaker is saying, you will receive less of the intended message.

Factual Distractions

College students, who should be among the most adept listeners in our society, find that they are often hampered by **factual distractions**, listening disturbances caused by the flood of facts presented to them in lectures. You may be tempted to treat each fact as a potential test question. But this way of listening can pose problems for you. For example, have you ever taken copious notes in your world civilization class only to find when you reread them that, although you have lots of facts, you missed the key ideas? Students and other victims of factual distractions sometimes listen for details, but miss the general point that the speaker is making.

Semantic Distractions

physiological distractions: listening disturbances that originate in a listener's illness, fatigue, or unusual bodily stress.

psychological distractions: listening disturbances that originate in the listener's attitudes, preoccupations, or worries.

factual distractions: listening disturbances caused by attempts to recall minute details of what is being communicated.

semantic distractions: listening disturbances caused by confusion over the meanings of words.

Semantic distractions are those caused by confusion over the meanings of words. Listeners may be confused by a word they have never before seen or heard, one they have seen in print but have never heard spoken, or a word the speaker is mispronouncing. If a student gave a speech about her native country, Eritrea, without showing that word on a visual aid, most listeners would probably begin wondering, "How do I spell that?" "Have I ever seen that word on a map before?" "Is this a new name for an established country?" "Is the speaker pronouncing correctly a word I've always heard mispronounced?" These thoughts divert you from the serious business of listening to a speech filled with new and interesting information. In Chapter 12, we will discuss some ways speakers can minimize misunderstandings about the meanings of words.

Promoting Better Listening

Once you understand the obstacles to effective listening, you can develop a plan of action to improve your listening behavior and that of your audience. A major theme of this book, as you no doubt are now aware, is that each party in the communication process has a responsibility to promote effective communication. Promoting better listening should be a goal of both the sender and the receiver of the message. How can you encourage better listening?

As a speaker, you can use many of the suggestions in the following chapters to help your audience hear and retain your message. You enhance the audience's retention, for example, when you select your ideas carefully, organize your ideas clearly, support your ideas convincingly, word your ideas vividly, and deliver your ideas forcefully.

As a listener, you must also work hard to understand and remember the speaker's message. So far in this chapter we have examined the process of listening and have discussed the obstacles to effective listening. The following nine suggestions will help you become a more effective listener. As you master these suggestions, you will find yourself understanding and remembering more of what you hear.

Guidelines to Promote Better Listening

1. Desire to listen.
2. Focus on the message.
3. Listen for main ideas.
4. Understand the speaker's point of view.
5. Reinforce the message.
6. Provide feedback.
7. Listen with the body.
8. Withhold judgment.
9. Listen critically.

Desire to Listen

Your attitude will determine, in part, your listening effectiveness. Some topics will interest you; others, no doubt, will not. Good listeners, however, begin with the assumption that each speech can potentially benefit them. You may not find a speech on how financial institutions determine a person's credit rating of great interest right now. Nevertheless, the first time you apply for a loan you may be happy that you paid attention and prepared for your visit to the bank.

Some speeches you hear in this class will be excellently prepared and delivered; others will not. Again, good listeners can learn something from any speech, even if it is poorly prepared and awkwardly delivered. For example, you can determine what the speaker could have done to improve the poorly developed speech. This experience enables you to apply speech principles you have learned and to improve your own speaking.

In your class you may also have the opportunity to offer helpful suggestions to your colleagues who present speeches. You will want to listen carefully so that you can help them improve. If you have a genuine desire to listen to a speaker, you will understand and remember more.

Speakers can promote better listening by demonstrating early in their speeches how the information will benefit their listeners. Let your audience know quickly just why it is in their interest to listen carefully to your speech. We believe this step is so important that we discuss it in Chapter 10 as one of the five functions of an effective speech introduction.

Focus on the Message

Your first responsibility as a listener is to listen attentively to the speaker's message. Yet a speaker's message competes with other, often quite powerful, stimuli for your attention. Often speakers themselves create distractions. They may play with change or keys in their pockets, dress inappropriately, sway nervously from side to side, use offensive language, or say "um" throughout their speeches. These quirks can be very distracting. We have had students, for example, who actually counted the number of "ums" in a speech. After a classmate's speech, they would write in their critiques, "You said 'um' 31 times in your speech." While this may have provided the speaker with some valuable feedback, we suspect these listeners learned little else from the speaker's message. You may not be able to ignore distractions completely as you listen, but you can try to minimize them.

Effective speakers can help listeners focus on the message by eliminating distracting mannerisms and by incorporating nonverbal behaviors that reinforce rather than contradict their ideas. For example, appropriate gestures can make a speech easier to remember by describing objects, providing directions, and illustrating dimensions.

Listen for Main Ideas

You are familiar with the cliché that sometimes you can't see the forest for the trees; well, that saying applies to listening. A person who listens for facts often misses the main point of the message. While it is important to attend to the supporting material of a speech, you should be able to relate it to the major point being developed. As in the simple game of tic tac toe, in which the evolving strategy is most important, "Listening for just the facts is like paying attention to only one O or one X without seeing the relationship or pattern that is emerging. You'll get beaten every time."[5]

When listening to a speech, pay close attention to the speaker's organization. The structure of a speech provides a framework for both speaker and listeners to organize the supporting points and materials of the speech. Speakers who clearly enumerate their key ideas and repeat them at several points in their speeches give their audience a better opportunity to be attentive listeners than do disorganized speakers. We discuss organizational techniques in Chapters 9 and 10.

Understand the Speaker's Point of View

As we discussed in Chapter 1, each of us has different referents for the words we hear or speak because we have different life experiences. These life experiences affect how we view our world.

Speaking in favor of agricultural programs that would preserve the family farm, our student Cathy tried to involve her audience in her speech by tapping their memories. She asked her classmates to think of the houses they grew up in and the memories created there.

> Think of Thanksgiving and family gatherings. Think of slumber parties and birthday celebrations. Of how you changed your room as you moved from child to teenager to young adult. Think of your feelings as you left home to come to college, and of your feelings when you return to those comfortable confines.

After the speech several students said they were moved by Cathy's eloquence and passion. She had tapped memories important to them. Others in the audience, however, said they were unable to relate to the topic in the way Cathy intended. Several had grown up in more than one house. Some were in military families and had moved often. Still others said they had lived in rented townhomes or apartments. And a few commented that their childhood memories were not fond ones. Both speakers and listeners need to remember that different experiences shape and limit our understanding of another's message.

An activist as well as a celebrity, Bette Midler spearheads drives to clean up and reclaim parks in New York City neighborhoods. Here she speaks to the media at the groundbreaking for a new community garden in East Harlem.

When speakers and listeners come from different cultures, the chances for misunderstanding increase. Differences in language, education, and customs challenge listeners to work especially hard at understanding the speaker's message and intent. These differences are often evident in today's multicultural classroom. Some foreign students, for example, come from educational environments that are more structured and formal than the typical American college classroom. They may interpret a speaker's casual dress and use of humor as an indication that the speaker is not serious about the speech. On the other hand, some American students may perceive the more formal presentations of some of their foreign counterparts as stiff and indicating a lack of interest in the topic. Understanding each other's frame of reference minimizes this distortion.

Speakers should do two things to clarify their points of view in speeches. First, explain early in the speech if you have some particular reason for selecting your topic or some special qualifications to speak on the subject. If you choose to speak on radio formats because you work at your campus radio station or because you are a media studies major, tell the audience a little about your background. Second, try to relate your subject to your listeners' frames of reference. Your use of technical jargon or complex explanations may limit their ability to listen effectively. Use examples and language your audience will understand.

Reinforce the Message

Most Americans speak at rates between 125 and 190 words per minute.[6] If you communicate simple ideas at a rate between 120 and 140 words per minute, your listeners may think you ill, reluctant, or uncertain.[7] Why? As listeners, we can process 400 to 500 words per minute. This means that, depending on the situation, we may be able to listen at a rate four times faster than a particular person speaks! As a result, we can get bored and move our attention back and forth between what the speaker is saying and some extraneous message, perhaps a personal problem that concerns us. Sometimes, the unrelated thought

> " . . . [L]istening requires something more than remaining mute while looking attentive—namely, it requires the ability to attend imaginatively to another's language. Actually, in listening we speak the other's words."
>
> —LESLIE H. FARBER

takes over and psychological noise, which we discussed earlier, drowns out the speaker's message. To be a better listener, you must make better use of this extra time.

You can fill some of this time and better focus on the message by mentally repeating, paraphrasing, and summarizing what the speaker is saying. You use *repetition* when you state exactly what the speaker has said. Consider, for example, a speaker who argues that a tuition increase is necessary to preserve educational excellence at your college or university. The first reason she offers is this: "A tuition increase will enable us to expand our library." If, after the speaker makes this claim, you mentally repeat her argument, you are using repetition to help you remember the speaker's message.

Using *paraphrase* is a second way of helping yourself remember the message. By putting the speaker's ideas into your own words, you become actively involved in message transmission. Suppose the same speaker offers this statement to justify one benefit of a tuition increase:

> A tuition increase would generate funds that could be used to enhance our library facilities and resources. In the chancellor's budget proposal, one-third of the tuition increase would go directly to the library. The chancellor estimates that this would enable us to increase our database subscriptions and audiovisual resources by 10 percent. Also, projected construction would create at least 12 new study rooms.

Obviously, it would be difficult to restate the speaker's explanation word for word. Yet you could paraphrase and summarize her message this way:

> A tuition hike would increase our library holdings by 10 percent and expand the number of study rooms by 12.

You use *summary* when you condense what a speaker says. The above paraphrase includes summary as it leaves out some of the specific information the speaker presented. As a speaker concludes his or her message, you should recollect the key points of the speech. Your summary might be, for example, "A tuition increase will help us expand the library, increase the number of faculty, and renovate some of the older dormitories." By getting you actively involved in the communication process, repetition, paraphrase, and summary increase your chances of understanding and remembering the message.

Provide Feedback

A listener can enhance the communication process by providing feedback to the speaker. Although there is greater opportunity for *verbal* feedback in interpersonal and group environments, it is nevertheless also possible in public speaking contexts. The effective speaker will especially read the *nonverbal* cues of the audience to assist in the presentation of the speech. If you understand and accept the point of the speaker and nod in agreement, the speaker can move to the next idea. If you appear perplexed, that signal should prompt the speaker to explain the idea more fully before moving to the next point.

Listen with the Body

We listen with more than our ears. In a sense, we listen with our entire bodies. If, as your instructor lectures, you lean back, stretch your legs, cross your arms, and glance at a fellow classmate, you detract from your listening effectiveness. Part of listening is simply being physically ready to listen.

You can ready yourself for listening if you sit erect, lean slightly forward, and place both feet flat on the floor. As you listen, look at the speaker. As important as the message you hear is the message you see. Remember, you want to detect any nonverbal messages that intensify or contradict the speaker's verbal message.

Withhold Judgment

You have probably listened to some political debates and heard discussions of them afterward. You and a friend may even have discussed the pros and cons of each candidate and differed over who won. What was important and memorable to you may have been quite different from what your friend found impressive. You may even have wondered if you had been watching the same debate.

In a sense, you and your friend did watch two different debates. Two people with contrasting perspectives receive two different messages while watching one communication event. You filtered what you heard through your set of beliefs and values. You began judging the candidates and the debate before it ever took place. This is quite common. Many of us have a problem withholding judgment. We hear something and immediately label it as right or wrong, good or bad. The problem is that once we do that we cease to listen objectively to the rest of the message.

It is difficult for you to withhold judgment, of course, when you listen to a speech advocating a position you strongly oppose. The following list includes topics student speakers sometimes discuss: legalization of drugs, capital punishment, abortion, flag burning, euthanasia, gun control, and embryonic stem cell research. We suspect you have some fairly strong opinions on most of these issues. You may even find it difficult to listen to a speech opposing your view without silently debating the speaker. Yet, as you mentally challenge these arguments, you miss much of what the speaker is saying. If you can suspend evaluation until after speakers have presented and supported their arguments, you will be a better listener.

Listen Critically

Even though listeners should understand a speaker's point of view and withhold judgment, they should nevertheless test the merits of what they hear. If you accept ideas and information without questioning them, you are in part responsible for the consequences. If the speaker advocating a tuition increase quotes from the chancellor's budget proposal before it has even been submitted, you have every right to be skeptical. "Will the final budget actually earmark one-third of the tuition increase for library use? Will the board of regents accept the chancellor's proposal? Or is this all speculation?" Decisions based on incorrect or incomplete data are seldom prudent and sometimes disastrous.

Critical listeners examine what they hear by asking several questions: Is the speech factually correct? Are sources clearly identified, and are they unbiased and credible? Does the speaker draw logical conclusions from the data presented? Has the speaker overlooked or omitted important information? Speakers help listeners answer those questions by presenting credible information, identifying their sources, and using valid reasoning.

John Marshall, Chief Justice of the United States from 1801 to 1835, once stated, "To listen well is as powerful a means of communication and influence as to talk well." If you use these nine suggestions, you will become a better listener.

Critiquing Speeches

Almost as important as the speeches you deliver in your public speaking course are the kinds of comments you can offer about the speeches others give. This textbook and your instructor will show you how to prepare and deliver an effective speech. You should

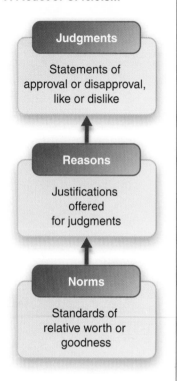

FIGURE 4.2
A Model of Criticism

Judgments

Statements of approval or disapproval, like or dislike

Reasons

Justifications offered for judgments

Norms

Standards of relative worth or goodness

use this knowledge as you comment on the speeches you hear others deliver. Appropriate feedback is crucial to your development as a public speaker. What you learn from your instructor and classmates about distractions caused by language, voice, or body will help you polish your speaking skills. You, in turn, want to be an incisive and sensitive critic when you write or speak about others' speeches.

For the purposes of this section, we define **criticism** as information (feedback) given to others in a way that enables them to use it for self-improvement.[8] Whether written or spoken, criticism, then, includes both positive comments that reinforce what a speaker did well and negative comments that point to potential improvements. If you say, "Your speech was well within the time limit at seven minutes and twelve seconds," you function as a speech critic as you spotlight a positive aspect of the speech. If you write or say, "I liked your speech a lot," you are also providing speech criticism. Notice, however, that while this last comment would no doubt make most speakers happy, it doesn't really teach them anything. In fact, finding out how long they spoke is probably more instructive for speakers than hearing simply, "I liked it." There is nothing wrong with saying to your classmates, "I enjoyed your speech," or "I didn't care for this speech as much as your last one." Just don't stop there. Explain why.

All criticism contains three parts: *judgments, reasons,* and *norms.*[9] Figure 4.2 illustrates the relationships between these parts. The most familiar and superficial level of critical comments consists of **judgments.** We make them frequently about many different subjects: "I loved the movie *Ed Wood,*" "Dr. Venkat is an excellent teacher," or "I always enjoy your speeches."

Underlying those judgments, whether we voice them or not, are **reasons** of some sort: "*Ed Wood* introduced me to this bizarre film director and Johnny Depp gave a memorable performance," "Dr. Venkat is an excellent teacher because her lectures make a course I dreaded lively and interesting," or "I always enjoy your speeches because you choose such unusual topics." Statements such as these specify reasons for the critics' judgments.

The statements in the preceding paragraph are instructive and useful because they help others infer your **norms,** the values you believe make something "good" or "effective" or "desirable." Such statements tell us that the individual critics value thought-provoking messages in movies, liveliness in class lectures, and unusual topics in public speeches. We may, of course, argue with the critics about whether these norms are actually valid. That is healthy and productive. The lesson for us as speech critics is to provide reasons for our judgments; only by doing so do we tell the speaker the basis of our reactions.

Here are some examples of helpful comments made by students about their classmates' speeches:

> Karen, your concern for children certainly shows in this speech on rating day care centers. Your personal examples really helped make the speech interesting.

> John, your speech on how to improve study habits was the best I heard. It was appropriate and beneficial to everyone in the class. Your language was simple and coherent. You explained just what we needed to know in the time you had.

> Lettie, one problem I saw was your use of visual aids. Once you have finished with the visual aid, you should put it away rather than leave it where the audience can see it. That way, the audience will focus their attention on you rather than on the object.

One value of receiving well-written or thoughtful oral comments such as these from classmates about your speeches is that repetition of a criticism will reinforce it. If your instructor or an individual classmate tells you that you need to speak louder, you may dismiss the advice as one person's opinion. If twelve people in the class write or say that they had trouble hearing you, however, the criticism gains impact, and you are likely to give it more attention.

criticism: feedback offered for the purpose of improving a speaker's speech.

judgments: a critic's opinions about the relative merits of a speech; the most common and superficial level of speech criticism.

reasons: statements that justify a critic's judgments.

norms: the values a critic believes necessary to make any speech good, effective, or desirable.

A second value of receiving criticism from many people, especially people from various cultures, is that different people value different aspects of a speech. Some may put a premium on delivery, others on speech content, and still others on organization. Individual classmates may notice different aspects of your speech simply because of where they sit in the classroom. With such a variety of perspectives and values, it would be a shame if all their criticism were reduced to "Good job!" or "I liked it." To provide the best criticism you can, just remember to specify the reasons for your judgments; ask yourself why a speech has the effect it does on you, and then try to communicate those reasons to the speaker.

We should also make a final note about the spirit in which you give speech criticism in this class. Your instructor may invite you to make oral or written comments about the speeches you hear others give. If your comments are written, they may be signed or unsigned. But whether your comments are written or oral and whether your written critiques identify you or retain your anonymity, you should never make criticisms that are designed to belittle or hurt the speaker. Target the speech, not the speaker. Focus on specific behaviors, rather than the person exhibiting those behaviors. You will probably never hear a speech so fine that the speaker could not make some improvement; and you will never hear a speech so inept or ill-prepared that it does not have some redeeming value. *Listen evaluatively* and then *respond empathetically,* putting yourself in the speaker's place, and you should make truly helpful comments about your classmates' speeches.

To help you become a better critic for your classmates, we offer ten suggestions you can use as you evaluate their speeches. One of our students, Susan, delivered an informative speech on three major tenets of the Amish faith. The text of that speech is included in Chapter 15. We asked other students to critique Susan's speech, and we have used their comments to illustrate our suggestions.

Guidelines for Critiquing Speeches

Key Points

1. Begin with a positive statement.
2. Target a few key areas for improvement.
3. Organize your comments.
4. Be specific.
5. Be honest but tactful.
6. Personalize your comments.
7. Reinforce the positive.
8. Problem-solve the negative.
9. Provide the speaker with a plan of action.
10. End with a positive statement.

Begin with a Positive Statement

Do you remember being told, "If you can't say something nice, don't say anything at all"? Well, that's good advice to follow when you critique your classmates' speeches. Public speaking is a personal experience. You stand in front of an audience expressing *your* thoughts in *your* words with *your* voice and *your* body. When you affirm the positive, you establish a healthy climate for constructive criticism. Demonstrate to speakers that what they said or how they said it was worthy. Fortunately, you can always find something helpful to say if you think about it. Be positive—and be sincere!

Two of our students began their critiques of Susan's speech with the opening statements below.

> I found your speech on the Amish to be very interesting; their beliefs are fascinating. They seem very simple but very committed to their group—what a unique way of living.

> I have lived near the Amish in Pennsylvania. Your speech explained the reasons for their behavior. You clearly explained why they do what they do.

Offering constructive feedback helps both the speaker and critic focus on ways to become more effective communicators.

Notice that while both critics compliment the speaker the second critic also demonstrates her involvement in the topic.

Target a Few Key Areas for Improvement

Sometimes students (and instructors!) think that the more mistakes they can point out to a speaker, the more helpful their critiques will be. However, seldom is this true. Imagine how you would react if your instructor told you, "There are seventeen areas you need to work on for your next speech." You'd probably feel overwhelmed: *How can I possibly do all that in time for my next speech? Which of the seventeen suggestions should I focus on first?* Susan's critics focused on the most important strengths and weaknesses of her speech. In so doing, they provided her with manageable goals for her next speech. After accomplishing them, she could begin to improve other aspects of future speeches.

Organize Your Comments

A critique, just like a speech, is easier to follow if it is well organized. You can select from several options to frame your comments, and you should select the one that is most appropriate to you, the speaker, and the speech.

For example, you can organize your comments topically into the categories of speech *content, organization,* and *delivery.* A second option is chronological; you can discuss the speech's *introduction, body,* and *conclusion.* A third option is to divide your comments into speaking *strengths* and *weaknesses* (remember, give positive comments first). You could even combine these options. You could discuss the speaker's introduction, body, and conclusion and within each of these categories discuss first the strengths and second the weaknesses.

Be Specific

Suppose, instead of this list of ten suggestions for offering criticism, we simply said, "When you critique your classmates' speeches, be as helpful as possible so that they can improve their speaking." Although that is good advice, it's not very helpful, is it? By being more specific and detailing ten guidelines, we hope to provide you a handle on how you can improve your critiquing skills. Similarly, you will help your classmates if you provide them with specific suggestions for improvement.

For speakers to become more proficient, they need to know *what* to improve and *how* to improve. One of our students told Susan: "I liked the way you presented the speech as a whole." That statement provides a nice pat on the back, but it doesn't give Susan much direction. The qualifying phrase "as a whole" seems to suggest that the listener noticed small problems that were minimized by the generally positive effect of Susan's speech. What were those problems, though, and what could Susan have done to minimize them? Remember, provide reasons for your judgments. In the two statements below, the listeners' comments are specific.

> I was really impressed with the fact that you did not use your notecards while you delivered the introduction or the conclusion. That suggests that you were confident and well prepared.

> Susan, you used good transitional phrases or words to move from subtopic to subtopic within each main point. An example of this was when you said, "Not only do the Amish have simple ways of dressing, but they also provide very simple toys for their children."

Be Honest but Tactful

Providing suggestions for improvement tests your interpersonal skills. At times you may be reluctant to offer criticism because you think it may offend the speaker. If you are not honest, however, the speaker may not know that the topic was dull, the content superficial, and the delivery uninspiring. Still, you must respect your classmates' feelings. The statement "Your speech was dull, superficial, and uninspiring" may be honest, but it is hardly tactful. It may provoke resistance to your suggestions or damage the speaker's self-esteem.

One of our students thought Susan's speech content and organization were excellent, but that her delivery was mechanical and lifeless. The student could have said, "Your delivery lacked excitement." Instead, she wrote: "The only problem I saw with your speech was a lack of enthusiasm. Maybe the speech was too rehearsed. It just sounded kind of like a newscast. I think it needed some humor to break the monotony of your voice."

> "Do not remove a fly from your friend's forehead with a hatchet."
>
> —CHINESE PROVERB

Personalize Your Comments

The more interest and involvement your critique conveys, the more likely the speaker is to believe in and act on your advice. You can personalize your comments in three ways. First, use the speaker's name occasionally, as in "Susan, your hand gestures would be more effective if you used them less. I found myself being distracted by them."

A second way of reducing a speaker's defensiveness and establishing speaker–critic rapport is by using "I-statements" in place of "you-statements." Tell how the speech affected you. Instead of saying, "Your organization was weak," say, "I had trouble following your key ideas," and then give some examples of places where you got lost. The following is an example of what one of our students could have said and what she actually did say in her critique of Susan's speech:

> *She could have said:* "You lost my attention during the first part of your speech because you spoke so fast that I couldn't keep up with you."

Instead, she said: "I had difficulty following your words at first because your rate seemed fast to me. After you settled down into the speech, though, I could listen with more attention."

A third way of personalizing your comments is by stating how you have benefited from hearing the speech. The following statement from a student critique let Susan know that her speech was interesting and helpful.

I found myself interested and saying, "Hmm," all through your speech. It especially caught my attention when you showed the toys, the quilt, and the artwork. And putting the visual aids down after explaining them helped in keeping me interested in the next area.

Reinforce the Positive

Sometimes we want so much to help someone improve that we focus on what the speaker did wrong and forget to mention what the speaker did well. As you enumerate how speakers can improve, don't forget the things they did well and should continue doing. One student was impressed with Susan's language and vocal delivery. She made the following comment:

Susan, your delivery was excellent. You used your voice to emotionally color your message. I really felt as if I was living in the pictures that your descriptions created.

Problem-Solve the Negative

If you are serious about wanting to improve your speaking, you will want to know the weaknesses of your speech. Only then can you improve. As a critic, you have a responsibility to help your classmates become better speakers. Don't be afraid to let them know what went wrong with a speech.

As a rule, though, you should not criticize behaviors that the speaker cannot correct. On the day she spoke, Susan was suffering an allergic reaction to molds and pollen in the air. As a result of antihistamines she was taking, her throat was dry. Even if this

EthicalDecisions
Right of Refusal

As she listened to Jeff's speech on the importance of rap music, Crystal found some of the lyrics he recited to be obscene and sexist. As she continued listening, she thought to herself, "These lyrics are offensive. I refuse to listen to them at home, so why should I be forced to listen to them now?" So, Crystal stood up and walked out of the classroom during Jeff's speech.

Was it appropriate for Crystal to leave the classroom? Should audience members in your class have the freedom to listen or not to listen to certain speeches? Are there some topics for which walking out is an acceptable form of feedback to the speaker? If so, what are some of these topics? What should guide a listener's decision to take such action?

had detracted significantly from her message, it would have been inappropriate for a student to comment, "I had trouble listening to what you said because your mouth seemed dry. Avoid that in your next speech." Such a request may well be beyond the speaker's control. On the other hand, it would be useful to suggest that Susan take a drink of water immediately before speaking, and several of our students did offer that advice.

You will help speakers improve their speaking if you follow two steps in your criticism. First, point out a specific problem and, second, suggest ways to correct it. Remember the title of this section is not "List the Negatives" but "Problem-Solve the Negative." You want to propose ways to overcome problems.

One student was impressed with Susan's visual aids, but offered her the following advice about one of them:

> You said that the Amish don't like to have their pictures taken, and yet you used a picture of an Amish man as a visual aid. Next time, if you'd explain how or where you got the picture, it wouldn't leave picky people like me wondering during the rest of your speech how you got that picture.

Provide the Speaker with a Plan of Action

When you give your comments, include a plan of action for the speaker. What should the speaker concentrate on when presenting the next speech? One student focused Susan's attention on her next speaking experience by suggesting the following action plan:

> Susan, your overall speech and style of presentation were very good. However, I detected two minor things that could be improved. First, except when you were moving toward or away from a visual aid, you remained in one place. I believe that taking a few steps when you begin a subtopic would emphasize your transitions and enhance your message. Second, take more time to demonstrate and talk about the boy's toy that you showed us. You said, "It has marbles and fun moving parts," but I didn't really get a chance to see how it operates. Your organization, your vocal emphasis and inflection, your eye contact, and your knowledge of the topic were all terrific. You're an effective speaker, and if you use these suggestions for your next speech, you will be even more effective.

End with a Positive Statement

Conclude your critique on a positive note. Speakers should be reminded that both you and they benefited from this experience. One of the highest compliments you can give a speaker is that you learned something from the speech. Two of our students concluded their critiques of Susan's speech as follows:

> Great job, Susan! You were very specific and enthusiastic about your subject, and your visual aids reinforced what was already thorough.

> Susan, you did an outstanding job. Your speech was well organized and very informative. You showed some signs of nervousness, but more practice will alleviate most of them. Whenever and wherever you will be speaking next, I'd like to be there.

To see how one student applied these ten guidelines, read Donika Patel's critique of classmate Melissa Janoske's speech. Melissa's speech is in the Appendix.

Theory into Practice

Critiquing a Classmate

Melissa Janoske delivered her informative speech, *Renaissance Fairs: The New Vaudeville* (see pages 409–410), in her public speaking class. We asked Donika Patel, a classmate of Melissa's, to write a critique of the speech. As you read Donika's critique, notice how she used the guidelines discussed in this chapter. Though most of the feedback you offer speakers may be less formal, more brief, or perhaps given orally rather than in writing, you should still use many of these critiquing strategies as you help others build their speaking competence and confidence.

Critique

1. Donika begins her critique by complimenting Melissa, establishing a supportive listener–speaker relationship.

2. She organizes her comments chronologically.

3. Donika offers specific examples to show how the speech engaged her.

4. Notice how she reinforces what Melissa did well.

Melissa,

I'm always impressed with your choice of topics. They're both interesting and informative. You definitely understand that public speaking is an audience-centered activity, and you actively involved all of us with the Renaissance culture throughout the introduction, body, and conclusion of your speech.

Introduction of Speech

Your introduction fulfilled the guidelines that we've studied in class. You captured my attention from the start with vivid narration. You painted a picture of a Renaissance scene and took us on a walk through the village. The use of the word *you,* combined with effective eye contact and movement, helped me imagine that I was actually in the sword fight. For example, you described how I won the fight with my sword, pinning my opponent to the ground.

After getting my attention, you introduced the topic of your speech, established the importance of people's interest in re-creating medieval England, and then previewed the key ideas you would discuss in the body of the speech. When you finished your introduction, I was ready to learn how I could participate in a Renaissance fair.

Body of Speech

The body of your speech was very well organized and easy to understand. Organizing your speech chronologically was appropriate, because it told us step by step how we could get involved in a Renaissance fair. You used the 4 S's to present your three key ideas. You signposted and stated your key ideas, using action verbs to tell us each step of the process. Melissa, I was impressed with your transitions and how they incorporated the theme of Renaissance culture. I really liked the image of "a potion from the apothecary" as you moved from your first to your second key idea.

Not only was your speech well organized, it was also well supported. You supported your ideas with examples, statistics, and testimony. When quoting experts, you told us who they were, and you gave us the URLs of a couple of interesting websites. Though you had good information,

I would like to have heard more. I was curious which university represents our kingdom in Virginia. I would also have enjoyed more descriptions of activities that women, as well as men, can participate in at Renaissance fairs. Maybe some pictures showing women and men in traditional costumes would make your speech content more vivid.

Melissa, in the introduction you had really enthusiastic vocal delivery and you used great hand gestures to describe the fight scene. You delivered that part of the speech without relying on your notes. I'd like to see that same delivery in the body of your speech. I noticed that you often glanced down at your notes, which sometimes disrupted the flow of the speech. Perhaps you had too many words on your notecards. Limiting your notecards to key ideas and supporting material, such as references, direct quotes, and statistics, might improve your eye contact. You also spoke a little quickly as you presented your key ideas. Try to include more and longer pauses to give the audience more time to understand each key point. Overall, I thought you had good poise and facial expressions that complemented what you were saying throughout your speech.

Conclusion of Speech

Your summary clearly reviewed the key points you discussed in the body of your speech. Remember that an important element of a conclusion is to activate audience response. What can we do next to get involved in Renaissance culture? Maybe you could give us the dates and locations of some upcoming fairs in our area, for example. I liked the way you used Mike the Truck Driver to connect your conclusion back to your introduction.

Melissa, for your next speech, I suggest adding some more content in the body, working on the conclusion to activate audience response, and practicing your delivery a little more to help slow your pace and to improve your eye contact. With greater attention to these areas, your future speeches will be even better!

As always, your topic was interesting, your speech was well organized, and your delivery was enthusiastic. Melissa, I learned a lot and look forward to hearing your next speech. Good job!

Donika K. Patel
Radford University

5. Even when Donika discusses areas for improvement, she does so tactfully and offers some specific suggestions.

6. Again, Donika helps Melissa problem-solve ways to relate to her listeners.

7. Throughout her critique, Donika targets a few key areas for improvement. Here, she offers a plan of action for Melissa's next speech.

8. Donika concludes her critique with a positive statement.

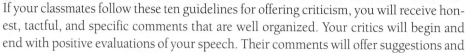

Acting on Criticism

If your classmates follow these ten guidelines for offering criticism, you will receive honest, tactful, and specific comments that are well organized. Your critics will begin and end with positive evaluations of your speech. Their comments will offer suggestions and plans of action for solving problems in your speech. Listening to or reading such critiques of your speeches will be helpful and reassuring. Your listeners' critiques will never be identical, however. Remember, listening is a complex activity, and each member of your audience may have heard a slightly different speech. You may receive contradictory comments and some with which you flatly disagree. Reading or hearing those comments can be intimidating and frustrating. What should you do in such situations?

Key Points

Guidelines for Acting on Criticism

1. Focus on *what* your critics say, not *how* they say it.
2. Seek clear and specific feedback.
3. Evaluate the feedback you receive.
4. Develop a plan of action.

Most of us dislike receiving criticism, yet such feedback is important to our success as public speakers. If you want to communicate more effectively, you must seek feedback from your listeners. Ethical speakers respect their audiences. Consideration for the audience means, in part, trusting their opinions and advice. If you respect your listeners, you will value their questions and advice about your speech. The following suggestions will enable you to get the most out of this process.

Focus on *What* Your Critics Say, Not *How* They Say It

In other words, listen to the content of the feedback, not the way in which it was presented. Too often, we become defensive when someone critiques us. Remember that offering criticism is not easy, and your critic may not have mastered the suggestions we've presented in the previous section. Avoid reacting emotionally to feedback, even if it is poorly worded and insensitive. Instead, focus on the content of the suggestions you receive.

Seek Clear and Specific Feedback

To improve your speaking, you must be aware of specific areas for improvement. Suppose a critic says, "Your organization could be improved." That may be an honest and valid statement, but it isn't very helpful. Ask the critic to be more specific. Is the problem with the introduction, body, or conclusion of the speech? What specific strategies could you use to improve your organization? It may take some good interpersonal communication to elicit the feedback you need to become a better public speaker.

Sometimes you may receive conflicting feedback. Don't dismiss criticisms simply because they seem contradictory. For example, one critic may comment that your eye contact was good, another that it was poor. Both may be right. Perhaps you spoke only to those in the center of the room; they may have liked your eye contact, while others felt excluded. Perhaps some critics made their judgments early in your speech when you were interacting well with your listeners, and others reacted to the conclusion of your speech when you relied too much on your notes. Or a critic's reaction may have been based on cultural norms; some cultures value eye contact more than others. It's important to learn the reasons behind a critic's judgment before you can improve your public speaking. In other chapters, we will examine ways that critiquing applies to specific aspects of delivering and responding to speeches.

Evaluate the Feedback You Receive

It's not enough just to receive and understand feedback. You must use your critical thinking skills to analyze and evaluate that feedback. Repetition is one standard of judgment. If only one classmate thought your attention-getting step was weak, don't be too concerned. However, if your instructor and the majority of your classmates thought it deficient, you should target that as an area for improvement.

Develop a Plan of Action

After receiving feedback, summarize and record those comments. Then rank those areas needing improvement according to their importance. Rather than tackling every criticism, select a few to work on for your next speech. Write a plan of action that states your goals and the strategies you will use to achieve them.

Some of us are just generally thin skinned—easily hurt by anything that seems to be a negative criticism—and at times all of us can become defensive. But don't be too quick to dismiss the feedback others give you about your speeches. Remember that your goal as you move from one speech to the next in a public speaking classroom is not consistency but consistent improvement. So, rather than defending what you said or did in your speech, listen carefully and act on those suggestions for improvement that you receive most frequently. If you have doubts about the validity of suggestions your classmates are making, discuss the matter with your instructor. You will make the most accelerated improvement if you graciously accept the compliments of your peers and your instructor and then work quickly to eliminate problems that they bring to your attention.

We began this chapter by talking about the contract that we believe always binds public speakers and their audiences. Speech criticism is further recognition of that commitment between speaker and listener. The ultimate aim of speech criticism is not just to improve a speaker's skills or just to make a particular speech more enjoyable or instructive for an audience. Speech criticism should amplify and clarify the terms of the contract that any individual speaker will enter with all his or her future audiences.

Try This

Critiquing Yourself

Select a speech you've presented in this class. Using the guidelines discussed in this chapter, write a self-critique of your vocal and physical delivery, or other aspects identified by your instructor. Specifically, focus on your speaking rate, vocal variety, eye contact, gestures, and movement. You may want to review the delivery questions presented in the previous chapter (pages 55–56). Be sure to mention your strengths, as well as areas for improvement. Finally, write a plan of action for your next speaking assignment.

Summary

Poor listening costs American businesses billions of dollars yearly. The personal costs of poor listening include lost opportunities, embarrassment, financial losses, and, probably most important, lost time. We spend more time listening than we do involved in any other communication activity. Yet, ironically, we receive less instruction in listening than we do in reading, writing, or speaking. Luckily, we can teach and learn effective listening.

Listening differs from *hearing* in four ways. First, we listen only from time to time throughout the day, while hearing is continuous. Second, listening is a learned behavior, while hearing is a natural capacity for most people. Third, listening is active, hearing passive. Finally, listening implies doing something with the message received.

The complex act of listening contains six steps or phases. First, the listener *receives* sound stimuli from various senders or sources. Second, the listener *selects* particular parts of the total stimulus field for attention. Third, the listener *interprets* or decodes the message, attaching meanings to the various symbols received. The fourth step, *understanding,* involves matching the speaker's message with the listener's frame of reference. In the fifth step, the listener *evaluates* the reliability of the speaker and the speaker's message. Finally, after the reflection involved in the previous steps, the listener *resolves,* or decides what to do with, the information received.

Physical distractions from any part of the environment are one type of obstacle to effective listening. *Physiological distractions,* a second category, arise from conditions in the listener's body. A third obstacle is formed by *psychological distractions,* such as worry or preconceived attitudes toward the speaker or the message. *Factual distractions* are caused by our tendency to listen for small supporting details, even when we miss the main point the speaker is trying to make. Fifth and finally, listeners may be victims of *semantic distractions,* or confusion over the meanings of words.

Both speakers and listeners can contribute to effective listening in nine ways. First, listeners should develop a genuine desire to listen. Speakers promote this openness to listening by expressing a sincere desire to communicate. Second, they should focus on the speaker's message, rather than on distracting elements of delivery. Speakers assist listening when they minimize or eliminate distracting behaviors and employ forceful delivery to underscore their messages. Third, listeners should listen for the speaker's main ideas. Speakers make this task much easier by careful speech organization. Fourth, listeners should try to understand the speaker's point of view. Speakers ought to reveal their credentials and explain their reasons for speaking on a particular topic. Fifth, listeners should reinforce the speaker's message by using repetition, paraphrase, and summary. Sixth, effective listeners should provide the speaker with feedback. Speakers should adapt to those responses. Seventh, listeners should be ready to listen with the whole body. Eighth, listeners should withhold judgment about the speaker and the message until after hearing and considering both. Finally, though we have urged you to listen objectively to avoid prejudging speakers and their ideas, effective listening is ultimately critical listening. Gauging the credibility of the speaker's information is easier if the speaker has presented logically supported ideas and has cited credible sources.

You master public speaking faster and easier if you can rely on helpful criticism from your classmates and offer them helpful advice. Criticism consists of *judgments, reasons,* and *norms.* To be helpful, criticism must be balanced between positive and negative aspects of the speech, but it should begin and end with positive comments. Criticism should be well organized. Critics should reinforce positive aspects of the speech and problem-solve the negative. In addition, criticism should target a few key areas for improvement, be specific, be honest but tactful, be personalized, and should provide the speaker with a plan of action for future speeches.

To act effectively on the speech criticism you receive, you should focus on *what* your critics say rather than on *how* they say it. Seek clear, specific feedback about comments that seem vague. Evaluate the feedback you receive. Finally, target a few areas for improvement. Develop a plan of action that sets goals for your target areas and states the strategies you will use to make those improvements. Our years of teaching experience have convinced us that following these guidelines will pay big dividends as you give, receive, and act on constructive, beneficial speech criticism.

Exercises

1. Listen to a speech or lecture, paying particular attention to the five types of distractions discussed in this chapter. Give examples of distractions you encountered. What could you or the speaker have done to minimize these interferences? Discuss these options.

2. Select a speech you've seen on television or videotape, heard on radio, or read in print or electronic form. Using the guidelines presented in this chapter, write a one-paragraph critique of that speech's organization. You may want to review pages 52–53 in Chapter 3 to stimulate your thinking about clear organization.

3. Suppose you are asked to speak to a group of students at a local high school on the topic "What College Offers to You." Half of the audience plans to attend college; the rest does not. All the students have been requested to stay after school on the first sunny day this spring to attend the assembly. What are your listeners' likely psychological distractions with which you must contend? What strategies could you use to minimize them in your speech?

4. Sit in a different seat and next to a different classmate each class for the next two weeks. After this time period, analyze whether your location affected your listening attentiveness. If so, how?

5. If you've already had the opportunity to present a speech in this class, write a critique of your vocal and physical delivery. Be sure to mention your delivery strengths, as well as areas for improvement. Also, write a plan of action for your next speaking assignment.

Analyzing Your Audience

chapter

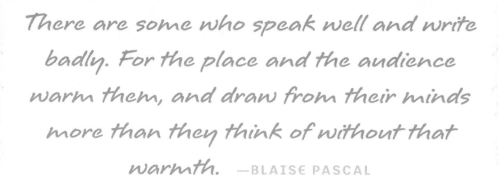

There are some who speak well and write badly. For the place and the audience warm them, and draw from their minds more than they think of without that warmth. —BLAISE PASCAL

Today we would call it an urban legend—the tale about Abraham Lincoln and how he wrote the Gettysburg Address. As the story goes, Lincoln was such a fine man and such a great thinker that he wrote his now-famous speech on some scraps of paper while on the train to Gettysburg, Pennsylvania.[1] Repeated for many, many years, the story seemed plausible because the speech is only 272 words long. Like many other stories that seem too good to be true, however, this one is false. Today, we have a better picture of how Lincoln composed the Gettysburg Address and why it is as brief as it is.

Lincoln was asked to speak at a ceremony dedicating a memorial cemetery for soldiers who had died in the Civil War battle at Gettysburg. He was not to be the main speaker on this occasion, however: Edward Everett, the most famous orator of his day, had top billing. Everett spoke for an hour and 57 minutes to an audience estimated at between 15,000 and 50,000 people seated and standing outdoors.[2] Afterward, Lincoln rose and, holding two pieces of paper, spoke ten sentences in less than three minutes.[3] Why were Lincoln's remarks so brief?

The answer is that Lincoln had done some excellent analysis of the audience and the speaking occasion. He knew, first, of Everett's reputation for making very long speeches. Lincoln undoubtedly knew that if he also delivered a long speech, he would lose either much of his audience's attention or even their presence. Remember, the speech was to be given outdoors, with audience members free to leave whenever they chose!

Second, Lincoln knew, as did his audience, that he was not the featured speaker on this occasion and was, therefore, not expected to make a major address. Even though he was president, Lincoln was losing popular support by 1863 and knew that a long speech would seem an inappropriate challenge to the importance of Everett's.

The third and final reason for the length of Lincoln's Gettysburg Address was that he had been anticipating for some time an occasion for an important speech on the same theme. The words of the speech began to take shape in his mind long before he wrote them on paper. For example, Lincoln began his speech at Gettysburg by saying,

> Four score and seven years ago our fathers brought forth on this continent a new nation, conceived in liberty and dedicated to the proposition that all men are created equal.

Yet Thomas Scheidel points out that, in informal remarks four months before delivering the Gettysburg Address, Lincoln had said:

> How long ago is it?—eighty-odd years since, on the Fourth of July for the first time in the history of the world a nation by its representatives, assembled and declared as a

Exploring Online

SPEECH TEXTS

http://douglassarchives.org

To compare the texts of Abraham Lincoln's and Edward Everett's speeches at Gettysburg, as well as many other speeches from the mid-1600s to the present, visit the Douglass Archives of American Public Address at Northwestern University. You can view the list of featured speeches chronologically, by speaker, by title, or by issue. Links at the side of each text will connect you to related speeches or study materials.

self-evident truth, that "all men are created equal." . . . Gentlemen, this is a glorious theme, and the occasion for a speech; but I am not prepared to make one worthy of the occasion.[4]

Lincoln's careful audience analysis helped him decide the topic, length, and scope of his remarks at Gettysburg. Making speeches "worthy of the occasion" requires meticulous audience analysis today, just as it did in Lincoln's time.

Recognize the Value of Audience Diversity

In interpersonal communication you adapt your message to one other person. The quantity and character of your communication depend on your relationship to that other individual. Your task as a public speaker is more challenging, however, for each added person compounds the dynamics of the communication event. Each additional person increases the diversity that is present in any audience. Each audience member is unique.

Today's college classroom, like most segments of American life, is increasingly diverse. Your classmates may differ from one another in terms of age, gender, ethnicity, educational background, beliefs, values, and numerous other characteristics. Talking *across* those differences *about* those differences can reveal what you have in common and build your sense of community. Your challenge as a public speaker is not only to recognize how your listeners differ from one another, but also to understand, respect, and adapt to this diversity as you develop and deliver your speeches. Evidence shows that it's a challenge worth taking.

Based on his research and his review of other scholars' studies, education professor Jeffrey Milem concludes that students benefit when they interact with peers of different backgrounds:

- They become more engaged in their own learning.
- They improve their critical thinking skills.
- They enhance their interpersonal and social competence.
- They are more satisfied with their college experience.
- They are more likely to engage in community service.
- They demonstrate greater acceptance of people from other cultures.

Research also suggests that students who have limited opportunities to interact with students from diverse cultural backgrounds can gain many of these benefits by taking classes with diversified course content. Milem argues that diverse environments provide students "opportunities to develop the skills and competencies they will need to function effectively as citizens of an increasingly diverse democracy."[5]

If you value your listeners and want to communicate successfully, then you must consider their diversity and view public speaking as an audience-centered activity. You can accomplish this in three ways. First, *recognize your own place as part of the audience.* You must be ready to admit that you are only one part of the total audience, a fact that should make you want to learn as much as possible about the other parts. Second, as we mentioned in discussing ethics in Chapter 2, *respect your listeners.* Respect and care for the audience means wanting to enhance their knowledge and understanding by providing interesting or useful information. To do this, you must recognize and appreciate their beliefs, values, and behaviors. This, in turn, leads to a third aspect of audience centeredness: *Recognize and act on feedback from your audience,* whether that feedback is verbal or nonverbal. Speakers who are attuned to their audience members will try to discover and cultivate interests their listeners already have, as well as challenge them with new, useful topics.

Ethical public speakers consider the diversity of their audiences and use appropriate channels to communicate with as many of them as possible. Here, an interpreter renders a message from spoken English to American Sign Language, making it accessible to members of the Deaf community.

> "*Reading America is like scanning a mosaic. If you look only at the big picture, you do not see its parts—the distinct glass tiles, each a different color. If you concentrate only on the tiles, you cannot see the picture.*"
>
> —ROBERT HUGHES[6]

To discover who your audience members are and what motivates them, you will exercise at least five critical thinking skills. You will engage in *information gathering* as you collect data to develop an increasingly clearer picture of who your listeners are. As you exercise the skill of *remembering*, you'll tap your memories of what you have heard your listeners say and do. You will *focus* on elements of the picture that seem most relevant to topic areas you are considering for your speeches. As you combine, summarize, and restructure pieces of information about your listeners, you will exercise the critical thinking skill of *integrating*. Finally, you will *analyze* the information you have collected by examining individual characteristics of your listeners and the relationships between those characteristics.

We believe audience analysis is a process that shapes and molds the preparation, delivery, and evaluation of any well-thought-out public speech. In other words, audience analysis occurs before, during, and after the act of speaking. Let's consider more closely how this process works.

Analyze Your Audience *before* the Speech

You will spend more time analyzing your audience before you speak than during or after your speech. Your speech may last only five or ten minutes, for example. Yet if you care about doing well, your audience analysis before the speech will take considerably more than five or ten minutes.

At the beginning of the semester or quarter, you may know few if any of your classmates. As with any general, unfamiliar audience you are preparing to address, you initially analyze your classroom audience by active sleuthing, as well as using your own common sense. Casual introductions students deliver at the beginning of the term can give you some information about who they are. Later, asking around about people's knowledge of or interest in a particular subject area is a good way to gauge your listeners' interest when you still don't know them well.

Audience analysis in a public speaking class you are taking on the Internet poses special challenges. You may or may not have a chance to meet some classmates at a face-to-face orientation session or at other scheduled meetings. Your instructor may invite you to post a message introducing yourself to the class listserv or bulletin board as the class begins. You may be able to administer an online questionnaire to collect student input on a topic area you are considering. Aside from those opportunities, you will have to analyze your classmates based on the messages you read or hear from them.

In contrast, a traditional face-to-face class provides you the rare opportunity to "live" with your audience for the duration of the course. From the comments they make in and outside class, from the questions they ask other student speakers or your instructor, and from their nonverbal feedback while listening to classroom speeches, you will gradually assemble an increasingly accurate portrait of this group of people. They will disclose, or you will deduce, information about their beliefs, values, interests, likes, and dislikes. Your audience analysis will be a semester- or quarter-long process, and by the time you deliver your final speech in the class, your audience analysis should be both easier and more accurate than it was at the beginning of the term.

Analyze Audience Demographics

Your first step as a speaker is to discover and evaluate as many specific characteristics of your audience as possible. **Demographics** is the term for those characteristics. Discovering the specifics about your audience will help you answer the question, "Who is my target audience?"

Demographic analysis helps you tailor a message to a specific audience. You will never know everything about your listeners, and so you will make generalizations from the information you do know. One note of caution, however: Be careful not to turn these generalizations into stereotypes about audience members. This will undermine your speech-making efforts.

Though some topics may be appropriate to only one type of audience, most subjects can have broader appeal. A speech on Third Wave Feminism is not just a women's topic—it could be informative to both men and women. The solvency of the social security system may be of immediate concern to someone approaching retirement, but with some creative thinking you can make it interesting to anyone who is a taxpayer or who plans to retire some day. The economic plight of the American farmer should interest not only the agriculture major but also anyone who eats.

Part of your audience analysis will involve discovering what you can about the various divisions, sections, or subgroups that constitute your listeners. Advertisers and public relations people call this process **audience segmentation.** You might then choose a topic that you believe you can relate to all segments of your audience. However, sometimes speakers choose to speak only to one or more segments of a larger audience, a strategy called **audience targeting.**

For example, if you know that some of your listeners love to travel but are on tight budgets, you could inform them about the option of becoming airline couriers. An informative speech on the dangers of heatstroke and heat exhaustion might be appropriate for athletes in your audience or for those who work outdoors. Of course, you must be sure that your target audience does exist and that it is sufficient in size to

Exploring *Online*

DEMOGRAPHIC PROFILING
www.ipl.org/div/subject/browse/ref24.00.00
Looking for a demographic profile of people in a particular country, state, county, city, or even zip code? The Internet Public Library's "Census Data & Demographics" list is a great place to start your search. It links to more than 40 other sites, with useful descriptions of the kinds of information you will find at each.

demographics: characteristics of the audience, such as age, gender, ethnicity, education, religion, economic status, and group membership.

audience segmentation: the strategy of dividing an audience into various subgroups based on their demographic and psychographic profiles.

audience targeting: the strategy of directing a speech primarily toward one or more portions of the entire audience.

Speaking with *Confidence*

Audience analysis is important for all public speakers. The more I learned about my classmates, the easier it was to choose a topic that would affect them, to avoid sensitive issues, and to relate to their life experiences. Although I did most of my analysis before my speech, it didn't stop there. I continued to analyze my audience as I spoke. Reading my listeners' expressions and body language helped me determine how my speech was going. For example, if students at the back of the room were having trouble hearing me, I would speak louder. If someone looked confused, I would give an example to clarify my point. If a couple of audience members seemed bored, I might use some humor or walk slightly toward them. And when my classmates smiled approvingly, I was confident that I was getting through to them. Audience analysis during a speech requires quick thinking, but it shows your listeners that you care about them.

—Krystal Graves, *West Texas A&M University*

> ❝ *Communicating with college students is always somewhat of a challenge. It is not that I have too much difficulty understanding your changing expressions and attitudes. It is that I forget what you never saw.* ❞

—TERRY SANFORD 7

justify giving them your primary focus. Generally, the more you know about your audience, the more secure you will be and the better speech you will deliver.

Seven of the most common characteristics you will want to analyze about your potential audience are age, gender, ethnicity, education, religion, economic status, and group membership. You will not always be able to learn this much information about your audience. Keep in mind, however, that the more you know, the better prepared you will be to present a successful speech.

Age. One of the most obvious concerns you have as you research your audience is their age. You may need to find out not only what the average age of your audience is, but also the age range. Your public speaking class may include first-year college students, people returning to college to change careers, and others pursuing interests after retirement. People who are 18 to 20 years old today relate to Watergate and the U.S. boycott of the 1980 Summer Olympics only as important topics of history. While that means that they may be eager to learn more about those topics, it also means they may not understand most casual references to them. Ask a college classroom audience today, "Do you remember where you were on January 28, 1986, when the space shuttle *Challenger* exploded?" and few if any of your listeners will have a positive answer. Most of your classmates were not yet born. To make a clear speech on any topic, you must use supporting materials that are familiar to your listeners, and age is one of the most obvious influences on the audience's frame of reference.

Gender. The next factor you need to consider is the gender of your listeners. It is obviously easier to determine gender than age. However, some students fall into the trap of stereotyping when they consider the gender of their audience. What seems to be sensitivity to gender turns out to be disguised sexism: "I'm going to inform you girls about the rules of football so you won't drive your boyfriends crazy with silly questions while they're trying to watch the game." Or "This recipe is so easy that even you guys should be able to fix it and avoid starving."

Effective speakers need to consider the individual life experiences of their audience members to avoid stereotyping and possibly offending some individuals.

Obviously, some speech topics will resonate more with listeners of one gender. An informative speech on the risks of estrogen replacement therapy has more immediate interest for women than for men; a speech on prostate cancer, more obvious importance for men than for women. But couldn't either of these topics benefit both male *and* female listeners?

Virtually every topic is or can be made relevant to both genders. If you are speaking to a group consisting of both men and women, focus on ways to make your topic relevant to everyone in the room. Rather than using the gender of your listeners to eliminate topics you don't think they would be interested in or, even worse, to select a topic you think they obviously *have* to be interested in because of their gender, approach any topic so that everyone can get something out of it. As society removes barriers based on gender, gender-specific topics will become fewer. Audience-centered speakers need to remember that.

Ethnicity. Ethnicity means the classification of a subgroup of people who have a common cultural heritage with shared customs, characteristics, language, history, and so on. Speakers appropriately tap these common experiences and feelings as they construct their speeches for audiences having similar ethnic backgrounds. For example, John Jacob, former president of the National Urban League, spoke to an audience of African Americans and observed: "Too often, we approach racial issues in a conceptual vacuum. We take a historical view. We forget that, while most Americans' forebears came to this nation seeking freedom and opportunity, ours came in chains and were enslaved and oppressed."[8] Jacob's statement was entirely appropriate for his audience, yet he would not have said the words "our forebears" were he speaking, for example, to listeners of diverse ethnic backgrounds.

As with the issue of gender, speakers should avoid ethnic stereotypes. Never assume that because individuals share the same ethnicity they also share similar experiences and attitudes. If you have a working-class Irish Catholic ancestry, do not assume that others having Irish surnames are working-class or Catholic. Two people of the same ethnicity may have diverse attitudes, interests, and experiences because of differences in their ages, education, income levels, and religion.

Education.   The educational level of your audience affects not only what subjects you can choose, but also how you approach those particular subjects. Students in your class probably have a variety of educational backgrounds. Some may have attended private schools, had home schooling, or earned graduate equivalency degrees after interruptions in their high school educations. Others may have lived and studied overseas. Smart speakers will find out as much as they can about the levels and types of education their listeners have.

Remember, also, that education can be informal as well as formal. Just as a high school diploma is unfortunately no guarantee of a solid educational background, listeners who have not completed high school or college are not necessarily uneducated. They may in fact have a wealth of "book" knowledge obtained through personal reading and study, as well as specialized practical knowledge and training. If you have the opportunity, find out not only what your audience knows about a potential speech topic, but also whether audience members have experience relevant to that topic.

Religion.   Your college public speaking class may contain members of various Protestant denominations, Catholics, Jews, Muslims, Hindus, Buddhists, and members of other religious groups, as well as agnostics and atheists. Students from other countries may also practice religions you do not know about, or they may practice familiar religions in a different way. Even among people who belong to the same denomination, religion will be very important to some and relatively unimportant to others.

> **"We must make room in our minds for one another."**
>
> —SR. MARY AQUIN O'NEILL[9]

Stereotyping people on the basis of what you know of their religious views is as potentially inaccurate and harmful as making generalizations based on other demographic characteristics. Do all Catholics oppose birth control and the ordination of women as priests? Do all Jews observe Hanukkah and Yom Kippur, or observe them in the same way? Do all Protestants interpret scripture in the same manner? Clearly, the answer is no, and this should remind you of the limitations of simply finding out the religious denominations represented in your audience. If your audience's religious views are truly important to a topic you are considering, you will need to find out more about the beliefs behind the denominational labels they prefer.

Economic Status.   Economic status is another key factor affecting audience attitudes and behaviors. If a family earns barely enough to subsist, they will probably be more concerned with filling basic life needs than with social or status needs. For that reason, they may readily relate to a speaker who advocates expanded health care benefits and automatic cost-of-living adjustments. Analyses of survey data and voting behavior suggest that, generally, the higher the income of a family, the more conservative their political attitudes. Even though many students in your class may not yet have significant incomes, their political attitudes are often similar to those of their parents. Just don't assume that all families who have substantial wealth hold conservative views.

Judging the range of incomes of your classmates' families may be difficult. Certainly, it would be impolite to ask. However, you can probably locate or construct several general profiles of the typical students at your college. Your school's Office of Institutional Research or Office of Student Life may compile and publish student fact books on their websites.

If you speak on significant national concerns, consult public opinion surveys on those issues. Such polls categorize responses according to several demographic characteristics, and one of them is often income.

Overall, be realistic, be fair, and be sensitive when choosing topics dealing with economic issues. We remember one student who was offended when a speaker said that students shouldn't go home for spring break but should travel with friends to different parts of the United States to expand their historical and cultural knowledge. The offended student argued that some students simply did not have that option. They needed to work in order to remain in college. Speeches that urge college students to consider investing in the stock market or in real estate usually ignore one important fact: Most college students do not have money to spend for these purposes. On the other hand, we have observed student speakers generate lively audience interest on topics such as summer employment opportunities at national parks and historic sites and how to negotiate the price of a new or used car. Although money may be of greater concern to some people than to others, few people want to spend money needlessly.

Group Membership. Today we join groups in order to spend time with others who enjoy our hobbies and pastimes, to learn more about subjects that can help us, or to further our political and social goals. Many of these groups are voluntary, such as the digital art club, the writer's guild, the karate club, Amnesty International, honor societies, and social fraternities or sororities. We may also belong to some groups—labor unions and professional associations, for example—because we are required to in order to get or keep jobs or special licenses.

Political parties are also important groups. Knowing your listeners' political affiliations can be particularly helpful as you prepare persuasive speeches. How you develop your persuasive appeal, as well as the supporting material you select, will reflect assumptions you have made about your audience. You can make an educated assumption, for example, that an audience composed mainly of Republicans will accept statements from Republican sources more readily than from Democratic ones. We usually identify with a political party because of its positions on significant issues, and it shouldn't be too hard for you to locate positions associated with key political parties. The major parties maintain websites and prepare position papers on key issues. Newspapers, magazines, and electronic media gather polling data. Special interest publications and a variety of websites may provide useful information as well.

You can also presume that audience members who belong to the Sierra Club, Greenpeace, the Nature Conservancy, or the Audubon Society have environmental concerns. Members of People for the Ethical Treatment of Animals, the World Wildlife Federation, and the Animal Liberation Front share a concern for animal welfare. Yet some of those groups have diverse goals and different methods of achieving them. If you are speaking to an organization—local, regional, or national—your audience analysis will require you to research the nature of that group as thoroughly as you can.

Analyze Audience Psychographics

Just as you should develop a demographic profile of your audience, you should also generate a psychological profile. **Psychographics** is a term for characteristics of the audience such as values, beliefs, attitudes, and behaviors. These elements help us understand how our listeners think, feel, and behave. If you look at Figure 5.1, you will see that, typically, our behavior is shaped by our attitudes, which are based on our beliefs, which are validated by our values. To understand better the interaction among these elements, we will look at each level of the pyramid, beginning with values and moving upward.

Values. We value something because we deem it to be desirable or to have some inherent goodness. A **value** expresses a judgment of what is desirable and undesirable,

Exploring *Online*

DEMOGRAPHIC PROFILING
www.census.gov
Want a profile of various demographic characteristics of people in the United States or in your specific geographic area? Need an estimate of the nation's or world's population at this minute? You have access to all this and much more on this site sponsored by the U.S. Census Bureau. Click on *Related Sites,* and you can access statistical information for all 50 states and more than 170 nations.

psychographics: characteristics of the audience, such as values, beliefs, attitudes, and behaviors.

value: judgment of what is right or wrong, desirable or undesirable, usually expressed as words or phrases.

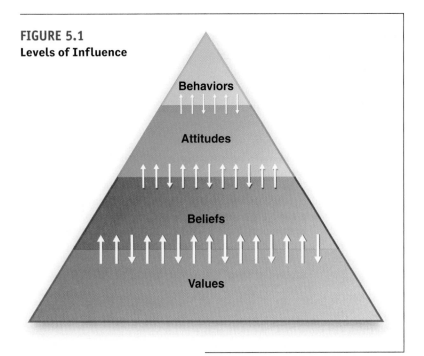

FIGURE 5.1
Levels of Influence

Behaviors

Attitudes

Beliefs

Values

right and wrong, or good and evil. Values are usually stated in the form of a word or phrase. For example, most of us probably share the values of equality, freedom, honesty, fairness, justice, good health, and family. These values compose the principles or standards we use to judge and develop our beliefs, attitudes, and behaviors.

If we value honesty, for example, we are probably offended when we learn that a political leader has lied to us. If we value equality and fairness, we will no doubt oppose employment practices that discriminate on the basis of gender, ethnicity, religion, or age. While our actions may not always be consistent with our values, those standards nevertheless guide what we believe and how we act. When we act contrary to our values, we may experience conflict or even guilt. That perceived inconsistency or dissonance will often motivate us either to change our behavior to match our beliefs and values or to change our beliefs by rationalizing our behavior.

Beliefs.   A **belief** is something you accept as true, and it is usually stated as a declarative sentence. We probably do not think about many of our beliefs because they are seldom challenged: Observing speed limits saves lives; sexual abuse is psychologically harmful to children; illiteracy in the United States undermines economic productivity; and so on.

Other beliefs are more controversial, and we often find ourselves defending them. Each of the statements below is debatable.

- Colleges place too much emphasis on athletics.
- The benefits of surveillance technology in the workplace outweigh its harms.
- Use of the Internet improves the quality of student research.

Those statements you accept as true are part of your beliefs.

Attitudes.   **Attitudes** are expressions of approval or disapproval. They are our likes and dislikes. A statement of an attitude makes a judgment about the desirability of an individual, object, idea, or action. Examples of statements of attitude include the following: I endorse Bob Estrada for Student Government Association president; I support capping enrollment at our college; I prefer classical music to jazz; I favor a pass–fail grading system for our school.

Attitudes usually evolve from our values and beliefs. Several values and beliefs may interact to complicate our decision making. When two values or two beliefs collide, the stronger one will generally predominate and determine attitudes. You may value both airline safety and the right to privacy. If a speaker convinces you that a proposed government action will diminish the right to privacy, you may oppose the action. If another speaker demonstrates that the plan is necessary to increase airline passenger safety, you may support the proposal. A single belief, then, in and of itself, is not a reliable predictor of a person's attitude. Again, when values collide, the stronger value usually takes precedence.

Behaviors.   A **behavior** is an overt action; in other words, it is how we act. Unlike values, beliefs, and attitudes, which are all psychological principles, behaviors are ob-

belief: a statement that people accept as true.

attitude: a statement expressing an individual's approval or disapproval, like or dislike.

behavior: an individual's observable action.

servable. You may feel that giving blood is important (attitude) because an adequate blood supply is necessary to save lives (belief) and because you respect human life (value). Your behavior as you participate in a blood drive and donate blood is a logical and observable extension of your outlook.

If you understand the foregoing components of psychology, you begin to understand the audience you intend to inform, persuade, or entertain. Your knowledge of those principles will help you analyze your audience and develop their psychological profile. How do you obtain information about your audience's values, beliefs, attitudes, and behaviors? You have two options, both requiring some work.

The first is to use your powers of observation and deduction. You can make educated guesses about people's values, beliefs, and attitudes by observing their behaviors. For example, what are your classmates talking about before and after class? What subjects have they chosen for classroom speeches? How do they respond to various speeches they hear? What do you guess their age range to be? How do they dress? What books do they carry with them to class? The answers to these and many other questions help you infer a psychological profile of your audience. The longer you are around your classmates, the less this profile will be based on stereotypes and the more accurate it will become.

The second way to gather information about your audience's values, beliefs, attitudes, and behaviors is to conduct interviews or administer questionnaires. Interviews and questionnaires may be informal or, if you have the time and resources, formal. You could interview classmates informally during conversation before or after class. Questionnaires administered during class may be as simple as asking for a show of hands to answer a question ("How many of you have broadband Internet access?") or as formal as asking classmates to answer a written questionnaire. (We will show you how to construct a questionnaire near the end of this chapter.) It's true that audience interviews and questionnaires are somewhat artificial; you don't often have the luxury of using them for presentations outside your college classroom. Still, if you are invited or required to address a group of strangers, you would be wise to ask your contact person lots of questions about the audience you will be facing.

Analyze Audience Needs

Demographic and psychographic analyses are not ends in themselves; you waste your time if you do not move beyond discovering these characteristics of your audience. Some of these factors may be irrelevant to the topic you choose for a classroom speech; others may be vital. Your task is to discover the significant items and then explore them more completely. Once you have considered your audience's demographic and psychographic profiles, you will be in a better position to determine your listeners' needs or what motivates them. Two particular models, Maslow's hierarchy and the VALS system, will get you thinking about audience needs in an organized way.

> "It is now a truism that American college graduates will live and work in a world where national borders are permeable; information and ideas flow at lightning speed; and communities and workplaces reflect a growing diversity of cultures, languages, attitudes, and values."
>
> —MADELEINE F. GREEN[10]

Exploring *Online*

ANALYZING PSYCHOGRAPHICS
http://people-press.org
www.gallup.com
What do *you* think? To find out what *others* think access these sites. The Pew Research Center and The Gallup Organization present the results of opinion polls they've conducted on a variety of political, social, educational, and other topic areas. Pew also provides a helpful link, "FYI Other Polls," reporting the results of recent surveys conducted by other organizations. Gallup gives you free access to some of their polls; unrestricted access requires a subscription fee, however.

©1982 Thaves. Reprinted with permission. Newspaper dist. by NEA, Inc.

Source: *Frank and Ernest.* Copyright © by Bob Thaves. Reprinted with permission of Bob Thaves.

Maslow's Hierarchy.   Sociologist and psychologist Abraham Maslow is best remembered for a model of human needs commonly referred to as **Maslow's hierarchy.**[11] A hierarchy is an arrangement of items according to their importance, power, or dominance. Maslow's thesis was that all human needs can be grouped into five categories, based on the order in which they are ordinarily filled.[12] As a public speaker, you should be aware of the needs dominating any particular audience you address. Maslow's categories, represented in Figure 5.2, are as follows.

1. *Physiological,* or physical, *needs*—basic human requirements for water, food, and sleep. As Maslow and others have observed, hungry people don't play.

2. *Safety needs*—everything that contributes to the "safe, orderly, predictable, lawful, organized world" on which we depend.[13] Having safe roofs over our heads and reliable transportation are typical safety needs.

3. *Belongingness and love needs*—our relationships with people around us, whether they are friends, spouses, parents, children, or others. Giving affection to and receiving affection from other people provides us a sense of community, of fitting in.

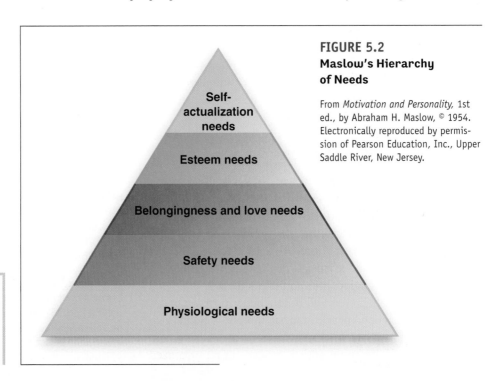

FIGURE 5.2
Maslow's Hierarchy of Needs

From *Motivation and Personality,* 1st ed., by Abraham H. Maslow, © 1954. Electronically reproduced by permission of Pearson Education, Inc., Upper Saddle River, New Jersey.

Maslow's hierarchy: a model of five basic human needs—physiological, safety, belongingness, esteem, and self-actualization—in an ordered arrangement.

4. *Esteem needs*—feelings of individual self-worth and reasonably high self-evaluation that other people confirm and validate as they recognize what we do well. Everyone has certain talents, and we all need a pat on the back from time to time.

5. *Self-actualization needs*—goals we need to achieve in order to feel that we have reached our potential or fulfilled our destiny. Highly individual, our cluster of self-actualization needs can change as we set long- and short-term goals at different points in our lives.

Note that we all fill our physiological needs in the same way (when it's possible to get those needs met): by taking nutrition and getting rest. The needs at the top of Maslow's model, in contrast, can be both personally distinctive and temporary.

VALS Typology. In 1978 the Stanford Research Institute built on Maslow's hierarchy of needs to develop a **VALS (Values and Lifestyle) typology** to categorize American consumers. In 1989 they introduced a slightly modified system that considers individuals' lifestyles, psychological characteristics, and consumption patterns. VALS is "the most recent refinement in psychographic segmentation."[14] The VALS model consists of eight categories of people, from those with the lowest resources to those with the highest.

Exploring *Online*

THE VALS SURVEY
www.sric-bi.com/VALS/presurvey.shtml
If you're interested in the VALS model and curious about the groups to which you belong, you can take the survey and get an immediate report of your primary and secondary "types." Just start from this address and click on the *Take the survey* box.

■ *Survivors* are poor, ill-educated, low-skilled, without strong social bonds, elderly, and passive. They feel powerless and avoid risk. Limited by the necessity of meeting the urgent needs of the present moment, their chief concerns are for security and safety.

■ *Makers* are practical people who have constructive skills, value self-sufficiency, and have enough income, skill, and energy to carry out their projects successfully. They live within a traditional context of family, practical work, and physical recreation. Makers are politically conservative, suspicious of new ideas, respectful of government authority, but resentful of government intrusion on individual rights.

■ *Strivers* seek motivation, self-definition, and approval from the world around them. They measure success by wealth and often feel that life has dealt them a bad hand because they have too little money. Strivers are impulsive, politically apathetic, and easily bored. Many of them seek to be stylish by copying those who own more impressive possessions.

■ *Believers* are conservative, deeply moral, conventional people with concrete beliefs based on traditional values. They follow established routines, organized in large part around home, family, and the social or religious organizations to which they belong. Their income, education, and energy are modest but sufficient to meet their needs.

■ *Experiencers* are young, enthusiastic, impulsive, and rebellious. They seek variety and excitement, but are politically uncommitted, uninformed, and highly ambivalent about what they believe. Their energy finds an outlet in exercise, sports, outdoor recreation, and social activities.

■ *Achievers* are successful career and work-oriented people who like to feel in control of their lives. They value consensus, predictability, and stability. Deeply committed to work and family, their personal and social lives center around family, church, and career. Achievers are politically conservative, and they respect authority and the status quo.

■ *Thinkers* are mature, well-educated, professional people with incomes that provide them satisfaction and comfort. They stay current with world and national events

VALS typology: a model that segments eight categories of people based on their lifestyles, psychological characteristics, and consumption patterns.

and are open to chances to increase their knowledge. Fulfilleds often seem calm and self-assured because they base their decisions on firmly held principles.

■ *Innovators* are successful, active people with high self-esteem and abundant resources. They are guided both by principle and by the desire to have an effect on the world around them. Independent, open to change, and socially conscious, they have a wide range of interests and tend to be leaders in government and business.[15]

The Importance of Audience Needs. But what do Maslow's hierarchy and the VALS system of categorizing individuals mean for you in your public speaking class? Do these models of needs apply to your listeners and, if so, how? We can suggest several ways to make these systems work for you.

First, the people sitting around you in class are not likely to be survivors. That is, they probably have most of their physiological and safety needs met. This does not mean that you cannot appeal to them on the physiological or safety needs levels. If you alert listeners to the harms of aggressive driving, dangerous food additives, or potentially deadly drug interactions, for example, you move them to focus on basic issues of survival. In fact, no matter how prosperous and healthy they are, everyone in class would likely be interested in a topic showing them how to save money or demonstrating the health hazards of certain products or practices.

Second, if many of your classmates entered college directly from high school, they are probably interested in being well liked and in fitting in. Consider some of the ways members of the Stanford Research Institute describe experiencers: "young"; fond of "the new, the offbeat, and the risky"; expending energy in "exercise, sports, outdoor recreation and social activities"; and spending a lot of their incomes on "clothing, fast food, music, movies, and video."[16] In other words, Maslow's third category, social needs, is extremely important at this point in such people's lives. If many or most of the people

People have different needs at different stages of their lives. Speakers need to identify those needs and to adapt their speech topics to address them.

in your class are in their first year of college, their self-esteem may depend partly on whether they succeed or fail in college, and speeches on scholastic success may easily hold their attention.

Finally, although many college students are unsure of the careers they will undertake upon graduation, most people have formed or are forming self-actualization needs by the time they are in their teens or twenties. Older students may be reassessing and reformulating their self-actualization needs. Those goals are changeable and will adapt as the individual discovers new talents, interests, and abilities. For that reason, a college-age audience is likely quite receptive to speeches showing how various topics can provide personal rewards or self-fulfillment.

It is critical for you to understand, however, that you cannot easily place all your listeners into a single VALS category or ascribe a specific set of Maslow's needs to all of them. In fact, as Maslow admits, all of us probably have unmet needs at each of the five levels of his hierarchy. We move from one level to another more frequently than we suspect. Whether you employ Maslow's model or the VALS system, *your challenge as a speaker is to identify and emphasize audience needs that are relevant to your topic.*

For example, if you feel secure in your surroundings, you may take your safety needs for granted. However, if you read in your school newspaper reports of several nighttime attacks on campus, your concern for your own and others' safety will increase. This concern for personal safety may not be on your mind as you walk to your classes during the day, but it may surface as you walk back to the dorm or to your car in the evening. If you choose to address this issue in a persuasive speech, you would want to stress this need for safety, bringing it to the front of your listeners' awareness. Once the situation is evident to your listeners, you can point out ways to satisfy that need. You might advocate better campus lighting, more security patrols, or personal escort services. Successful speakers identify the unmet needs of their listeners and respond appropriately in an informative, persuasive, or entertaining speech.

Using Maslow's hierarchy or the VALS typology can also help the speaker facing an unfamiliar audience outside the college classroom. Even though you may initially know little about such an audience, your goal will be to find out as much relevant information as possible about them before the speech. Knowing what motivates them, what they need or want to hear, is an excellent starting point in your audience analysis. It will also help you avoid unfortunate, unnecessary situations such as speaking on the joys of skydiving to a group of people barely able to provide food and clothing for themselves.

Analyze Specific Speaking Situations

Types of Audiences.   In terms of their reasons for attending a speech, audiences fall into two categories: voluntary and captive. A **voluntary audience** has assembled of its own free will. Most adults who attend a worship service or a political rally are there voluntarily. Similarly, you may be taking this class as an elective, just because you believe it will benefit you. The **captive audience**, in contrast, feels required to be present. Chances are that you have been part of a captive audience at many school assemblies during your education. You may even be taking this class to fulfill a requirement. You may attend a speech by someone visiting your campus because you are required to do so for this or some other course. Your reasons for attending a speech, a presentation, or a class may have a significant effect on your disposition as you listen.

Audience Disposition.   **Audience disposition** describes how listeners are inclined to react to a speaker and his or her ideas. Listeners may have any of three general attitudes toward speakers or their ideas: *favorable, unfavorable,* or *neutral.* They can be slightly, moderately, or strongly favorable or unfavorable toward your topic, and you

voluntary audience: a group of people who have assembled of their own free will to listen to a speaker.

captive audience: a group of people who are compelled or feel compelled to assemble to listen to a speaker.

audience disposition: listeners' feelings of like, dislike, or neutrality toward a speaker, the speaker's topic, or the occasion for a speech.

Ghosting 101

Politicians, especially national and state leaders, often do not write the speeches they deliver. Instead they rely on the words of speechwriters, sometimes called "ghostwriters." Journalist Ari Posner laments this tradition, observing, "If college or high school students relied on ghosts the way most public figures do, they'd be expelled on charges of plagiarism."[17] Is the practice of ghostwriting in politics ethical? What are the benefits and drawbacks of politicians' relying on speechwriters? Is it ever ethical for these leaders to deliver speeches they did not write? If so, what principles of audience analysis should guide the use of these speeches?

should try to determine this level of intensity. A listener who only slightly opposes your position that the amber alert system is a desirable way of apprehending suspected criminals will probably be easier to persuade than one who strongly opposes it.

If you sense that some of your listeners are neutral toward your topic, you should try to uncover the reasons for their neutrality. Some may be *uninterested* in your topic, and you will want to convince these listeners of its importance. Other listeners may be *uninformed* about your topic, and your strategy here should be to introduce your listeners to the data they need to understand and believe your ideas. Still other listeners may simply be *undecided* about your topic. They may be both interested and informed, aware of the pros and cons of your position. They may not have decided, however, which position they support. Your strategy in this instance should be to bolster your arguments and point out weaknesses in the opposition's case. As you can see, evaluating your audience's disposition is a complex activity. The more you know about your listeners, the easier this process becomes.

Listeners can be favorable, unfavorable, or neutral not only to speakers and their topics, but also to the reason for assembling to hear a speech. We are often tempted to view voluntary audiences as friendly and captive ones as hostile, and those situations certainly do occur. The connection between the audience's reasons for attending and their attitudes toward the speaker is not this simple and predictable, however.

An audience that has assembled freely may well be unfavorable to the speaker or the speaker's organization. As examples, consider the people who attend a political speech to protest or to heckle the speaker. Alternatively, a captive audience, instead of being hostile because they feel coerced into attending, may actually look forward to a speech. Even members of a captive audience initially unsympathetic to the speaker may find themselves becoming friendly as a result of the speaker's interesting message or engaging style of delivery.

Because attendance is a requirement of most college courses, you face a captive audience when you stand before your classmates. That shouldn't frighten you. However, the situation does pose an added challenge and makes your audience analysis especially important. You have a responsibility to choose novel, interesting topics for informative speeches, to choose significant topics for persuasive speeches, and to be thoroughly prepared for any speech you give. Classmates may develop an unfavorable impression of you if they perceive that you are taking your speech too lightly or exploiting the occasion to preach your own political or religious views. Remember that public speaking is an audience-centered activity; keep your listeners' needs and concerns in mind as you construct your message.

Size of the Audience.   In Chapter 1, we stated that the greater the number of people involved in speech communication, the less chance there is for verbal interaction

between the speaker and individual listeners. In speaking before a small group, a speaker may be frequently interrupted with questions. The situation may be so informal that the speaker sits in a chair or on the edge of a table during the presentation. A speaker in such a situation may use jargon and colloquial language, prepared presentational aids (as well as those devised on the spot with transparencies and chalkboards), and a relaxed, conversational style of delivery.

As the audience grows larger, however, the speaker will have to use greater volume and larger gestures. The language of the speech may become more formal, especially if the speaker knows that the speech will be published or videotaped. As the distance between the speaker and the last row of audience members increases, the speaker's volume must increase, gestures and facial expression must be exaggerated slightly, and presentational aids must be projected in order to be seen. Unless the audience is encouraged to ask questions after the speech, they will likely remain silent. As you can see, the size of your audience affects both the type of speech you deliver and your manner of presentation.

Occasion. The occasion, the reason for the speaking event, is a critical factor in determining what type of audience you will be facing. You need to ask yourself (and maybe even some members of the group), "Why is this audience gathering? What special circumstances bring them together?" A class, an annual convention, a banquet, a party, a competition, a reunion, and a regular meeting of an organization are all examples of occasions. Occasions can be formal or informal, serious or fun, planned or spontaneous, closed to the public or open to all.

In addition to a simple description of the occasion, you as a speaker may need to know about the history of the occasion or about the recent history of the group you will address. Say, for example, that the officers of an organization have invited you to speak to their entire organization. If there has been recent conflict between the members and the officers, the majority of your audience may look upon you and your speech skeptically. To understand any occasion, you must know both the purpose and the circumstances of the gathering.

Physical Environment. In previous chapters, we discussed the forms of noise that speakers and listeners must battle. Every physical environment or setting contains unique obstacles to communication. The size of the room itself may impede communication. You may be speaking as some audience members finish a meal. You may be speaking to a large audience through an inadequate or defective public address system. You may compete with a variety of physical noise: the sounds of another meeting next door, a room that is too warm, interruptions from caterers bringing in carts of ice water. Just as it makes good sense to practice a speech in the classroom where you will speak, you should always try to find out something about the physical location where you will be speaking.

Time. If you had your choice, would you rather take a college class at 9:00 A.M. or 1:00 P.M.? If you're typical, you'll choose the 9:00 A.M. class, even though you might not consider yourself a morning person. Both students and faculty seem to agree that classes at 1:00 P.M. are particularly difficult to attend and to teach because everyone's energy seems low.

The time at which you deliver your speech is an obvious part of your analysis of the speaking occasion. An address given at 4:00 P.M. on Friday will almost surely find an audience more fatigued and restless than will one given Tuesday at 9:30 A.M. If you are scheduled to speak first in a class that meets at 8:00 A.M., you may face an audience half asleep, so you may need to boost your own energy to enliven them.

Theory into Practice
TIPS
Using an Audience Questionnaire

If you're unable to learn enough about your listeners through informal means such as observation and discussion, you may have another option. If you need precise, measurable information and have the luxury of ample time and opportunity to collect it, you may want to administer a questionnaire.

A questionnaire is a set of written questions designed to elicit information about your listeners' knowledge, beliefs, attitudes, and/or behaviors regarding your specific speech topic.[18] The following guidelines will help you construct and administer a questionnaire and then interpret the results.

Construct a Questionnaire

First, determine what you need to know about your audience. What do they already know about your topic? If you're trying to persuade them, do they agree or disagree with you, or are they undecided? How strongly do they hold these positions?

Second, construct your questions depending on the type and amount of information you seek, how long respondents will have to complete your survey, and how you plan to compile and use the information you gather.

Closed questions, ideal for gathering demographic information, offer respondents a finite set of responses or a scale that asks people to place themselves along a continuum.

What is your gender?
       [ ] Female   [ ] Male
Are you currently employed?
       [ ] Yes   [ ] No
Smoking is bad for your health.
[ ] Agree   [ ] Disagree   [ ] Neutral
The honor code system at our school is too strict. *(Circle your answer.)*
       Strongly disagree
       Disagree
       Neutral
       Agree
       Strongly agree

Open questions invite respondents to answer in their own words. Though they take longer to answer, compile, and interpret, open questions often provide unexpected, helpful information or specific examples a speaker may include in a speech.

What do you think are the qualities of a good supervisor?

Why did you decide to attend this college? What are some activities that contribute to a healthy lifestyle?

Your questions, whether open or closed, should be clear, objective, and focused. Avoid emotional language that may "lead" respondents to a particular response. Pilot test your survey on friends who are similar to your intended audience, timing their completion rate and asking for feedback about the clarity and objectivity of your questions. See Figure 5.3 for an example of a clear, objective questionnaire.

Administer a Questionnaire

Because the information you gather will shape your speech, administer any questionnaire at least a week before your speech is due. Your written and oral directions should assure respondent anonymity. You have an ethical responsibility to consider your listeners' interests, respect their privacy, and not mislead them. Thank respondents for their participation, either orally or on your written questionnaire.

Analyze Questionnaire Responses

First, organize the responses to each question. For closed questions, simply count the number in each response category. Compiling responses to open questions is more subjective and time consuming. Summarizing responses on separate pieces of paper and then tabulating them according to common themes that emerge should speed the process.

Once you have organized the questionnaire responses, you are ready to answer the important question: *So, what does all this information tell me?* Do your listeners agree or disagree with your position on the topic, or are they neutral? Do their beliefs, attitudes, and behaviors vary widely? Do these differences vary according to age, gender, ethnicity, or academic classification? Are there well-worded answers to open questions that you can attribute to the anonymous respondent and use as supporting material? The payoff for all the work you put into constructing, administering, and analyzing the results of your questionnaire is that you have specific information about your audience to help you construct your speech for them.

FIGURE 5.3
Sample Audience
Questionnaire

Please take a few minutes to answer the following questions. The information gathered will be used to assist me in preparing for my persuasive speech. To maintain anonymity, do not include your name. Thank you for your assistance.

1. Please indicate your gender.   [ ] Female   [ ] Male

2. Do you live on or off campus?   [ ] On campus   [ ] Off campus

3. How would you describe your current state of health? (*Circle your answer.*)

    Very   Unhealthy   Neutral   Healthy   Very
    unhealthy   healthy

4. How would you describe your eating habits? (*Circle your answer.*)

    Very   Unhealthy   Neutral   Healthy   Very
    unhealthy   healthy

5. I believe that eating animals is unethical. (*Circle your answer.*)

    Strongly   Disagree   Neutral   Agree   Strongly
    disagree   agree

6. Would you consider changing your eating habits if it would improve your health?

    [ ] Yes   [ ] Maybe   [ ] No

7. A vegetarian diet is a healthy diet.   [ ] Agree   [ ] Neutral   [ ] Disagree

8. Are you a vegetarian?   [ ] Yes   [ ] No

9. What do you think are the benefits of a vegetarian diet? (*Please explain your answer.*)

    _____

10. What do you think are the drawbacks of a vegetarian diet? (*Please explain your answer.*)

    _____

Your speech's placement in a program may also affect how your audience receives it. If you follow several other speakers, you may need to work harder at getting and keeping the attention of your listeners. In short, if your listeners are not at their best, plan on working extra hard to enliven your delivery. Think about your class and when you will present your speech. The time factor may not cause you to change your topic, but it may affect how you deliver your speech.

When you use the techniques discussed in this chapter to analyze your audience's demographics, psychographics, and the specific speaking situation, you will be able to construct an **audience profile.** Keep in mind that your understanding of the audience will never be complete. You may have to make educated guesses based on incomplete data. Remember, too, that some information you may collect will be irrelevant to your speech topic. Finally, you must remind yourself that your audience is not a uniform mass, but a collection of individuals with varying experiences, values, beliefs, attitudes, behaviors, and personalities.

Analyze Your Audience *during* the Speech

Careful audience analysis before your speech will guide your topic selection, how you focus and develop your subject, and how you plan to deliver your speech. Even the most thorough, conscientious audience analysis will not guarantee a compelling, effective delivered speech, however. Speakers do not perform for audiences; they interact with them. The physical presence of listeners transforms and shapes each public speaking experience. To make that vital connection with your listeners, your audience

audience profile: a descriptive sketch of listeners' characteristics, values, beliefs, attitudes, and/or actions.

analysis must continue during the delivery of your speech. Communication scholars suggest that, as a speaker, you must be aware of three characteristics of your listeners as you speak.

First, you must be aware of the audience's *attention* or interest. Do their eye contact, posture, and other body language indicate to you that they are concentrating on you and your message? Are there physical distractions in the speech setting that are competing with you for the audience's attention? Do you seem to have the audience's attention throughout some parts of the speech, only to lose it during other parts? If you are concentrating on your message and on your listeners, rather than on how you sound and look, you will know the answers to these questions about the audience's attention.

If you detect a lapse of audience attention during your speech, how can you solve this problem? You could address some of your listeners by name. You could also make a connection between your speech and another one that the audience has already heard. You can also recapture your audience's attention with statements such as "The most important point to remember is. . . ." Recovering your listeners' attention might also be as simple as changing some aspect of your delivery: speaking more loudly or softly, for example, or moving away from the lectern for part of the speech so that you are closer to the audience. Any change in your established pattern of delivery will be likely to rekindle audience attention and interest. In addition, changing your usual style of delivery may be essential to overcome the distractions of a stuffy room, a noisy heater, or the coughs and other audience noise that occur whenever people assemble.

A second characteristic of your audience that you must try to assess is their *understanding* or comprehension of your message. If you have ever produced a false and hollow sounding laugh when you didn't really understand the joke that was just told, you know how difficult it is to fake comprehension. No matter how hard most of us try to cover up a lack of understanding, something about our voices or our bodies signals to others that we didn't really get it.

Of course, your audience may not try to hide their incomprehension. Members may deliberately tell you with puzzled expressions and other nonverbals that they are confused. The worst thing a speaker can do under either circumstance is to continue as if there were no problems. Clarifying something for the audience may be as simple as repeating or rephrasing the problem statement. If a particular word seems to be the source of confusion, defining the word or writing it on the board may solve the problem.

The third and final component of audience analysis during the speech is your listeners' *evaluation* of you and your message. Sensitive speakers attuned to their audiences are able to gauge the reactions of those listeners. Do members of the audience seem to agree with what you are saying? Do they approve of the suggestions you are making? Answers to these questions are particularly important when you are seeking to persuade your audience.

Sometimes the answer to such questions will be no. You may be delivering bad news or taking what you know will be an unpopular stand on an issue. Having the audience disagree with the content of your message doesn't necessarily mean that your speech has been a failure. Simply knowing that many listeners agree or disagree with you at the end of a persuasive speech shows that you are an audience-centered speaker, and that's an accomplishment in itself.

Analyze Your Audience *after* the Speech

Too often speakers assume that the speech-making process concludes as you utter your final statement and walk to your seat. Your influence on audience members can con-

Try This

Incorporating Questionnaire Results

Using the information presented in the Theory into Practice feature in this chapter, design a questionnaire to distribute to your classmates. Develop and ask demographic and psychographic questions to help you better understand your listeners' beliefs, attitudes, and behaviors related to the topic for an upcoming speech. Your questionnaire should include from five to ten questions. Be careful, however, not to ask too many open questions, so that you may gather information efficiently.

Distribute and collect your questionnaire at a time approved by your instructor. Analyze your classmates' responses. How did this information help you research and develop your speech?

If requested, provide your instructor a summary of your classmates' responses and a description of how you used this information to adapt your speech to your audience.

tinue for some time, however. We encourage you to add one additional step: *post-speech analysis*. Part of this step should be self-reflection as you analyze your performance. Did you accomplish what you hoped you would? What do you sense were the strongest aspects of your speech? What were the weakest? How would you rate the content, organization, and delivery of the speech? What can you do to improve these aspects of your next speech?

Your answers to these questions provide a very subjective evaluation of your speech efforts. You may be much more critical than your listeners were because only you know how you planned to deliver the speech. For that reason, you should also consider your audience's assessment of your speech content, organization, and delivery.

In this class, that information may come from oral or written critiques from your peers or from comments some of them give you after class. If you have given a good speech on an interesting topic, one pleasant reward in a college classroom is that audience members may have questions to ask you. The tone and content of those questions will tell you a great deal about how the audience received your message. You will also receive helpful suggestions from your instructor. If you expect to improve as a public speaker, pay attention to the feedback given you by all your listeners and act on the comments that are particularly relevant.

Summary

The best speeches are those that seem exactly right for the audience to whom they are delivered. They focus on interesting topics, use colorful but familiar language and supporting materials, are delivered with enthusiasm, and are the right length for the topic and the occasion. Such an accomplishment requires careful audience analysis before, during, and after delivery of the speech.

Before the speech, a speaker should consider audience demographics, audience psychographics, and audience needs. *Demographics* refers to characteristics of the audience, including age, gender, ethnicity, education, religion, economic status, and group membership. Information you gather about these characteristics can help you select a topic and then develop and support it for a particular group of listeners. Realize, however, that simply stereotyping listeners in terms of one or more of these characteristics may not only be incorrect, but may also cause a speaker to offend the audience.

Speakers can use information about audience demographics to analyze the way those listeners think. *Psychographics* is a term for audience psychology and how listeners' thoughts influence their actions. Four key components of audience psychology are values, beliefs, attitudes, and behaviors. *Values,* such as freedom and honesty, are expressions of worth or rightness. Our values are the basis for the development of beliefs and attitudes. *Beliefs* are statements we accept as true. They may be either provable or open to debate. *Attitudes* express our approval or disapproval of individuals, objects, ideas, or actions. Several values or beliefs may interact to form our attitudes. When these values or beliefs conflict, the stronger one usually predominates. A fourth element is *behavior,* an overt action that may reflect our values, beliefs, and attitudes.

Maslow's hierarchy of needs is a useful tool for analyzing audience motivation. That model ranks five human needs in terms of their predominance. The *physiological needs,* the most basic, include our needs for food, water, and rest. The *safety needs* include everything that contributes to a predictable, orderly existence—secure housing, reliable transportation, and freedom from civil unrest or war, for example. Once these needs are largely met, we begin to concentrate on our community of friends and associates and the ways that they fulfill our *love and belongingness needs.* Feeling that we fit in, that we give and receive affection from a group of people, contributes to our *esteem needs.* This fourth level is important, Maslow says, because we all need a pat on the back from time to time. The highest level of needs, the *self-actualization needs,* refers to our desire to fulfill our potential as human beings.

The VALS model provides a way of segmenting people into eight categories based on their lifestyles and psychological characteristics. In the VALS profiles, *survivors* are people working with very limited resources. *Makers* are traditional, practical people who possess skills that they use toward the goal of self-sufficiency. *Strivers* are people who lack confidence, measure success by wealth, and look to others for approval and validation. *Believers* are deeply moral, conservative people who feel most comfortable following established routines. *Experiencers* are young people, often rebellious, who seek variety and excitement in their lives. *Achievers* are successful, career-oriented people who enjoy feeling in control of their lives. *Thinkers* are mature, well-educated people with high incomes who value order and knowledge. *Innovators* are successful, active individuals with high self-esteem and abundant resources.

Audience analysis before the speech continues as you focus on the specific speaking situation. Will you be facing a *captive* or a *voluntary audience?* Are they likely to be favorable, unfavorable, or neutral to you and your topic? What is the nature of the speaking occasion? Where will the speech take place? What time is it to be delivered?

Gathering information about your audience's values, beliefs, and attitudes can be formal or informal. You can simply observe their behaviors and infer the thoughts behind them. Or you may need and have the opportunity to survey the audience by constructing and administering a questionnaire and analyzing its results.

During a speech, the speaker should pay attention to listeners' interest or *attention,* their *comprehension* or understanding of the message, and their *evaluation* of the speech. Speakers can influence each of these elements. Lively, sincere delivery helps generate audience interest in the topic. A speaker can help ensure the audience's comprehension of the message by defining unusual terms, slowing down the delivery of technical materials, and using repetition.

Finally, after delivering the speech, a speaker should continue to analyze the audience for signals about their evaluation of the message. What comments do audience members make about the speech, orally or in writing? What questions do they ask? What suggestions does the class instructor offer? Any student who is serious about improving as a public speaker must be aware of and act on audience feedback after the speech is over.

PracticeCritique

Evaluating a Speaker's Audience Analysis

Effective public speakers adapt their messages to specific audiences. Darla Goodrich sought to inform her classmates on "the physical and behavioral characteristics of four different age groups of whitetail buck." Read the transcript of her speech, "How Old Is He Anyway? Aging the Whitetail Buck," in the Appendix or watch the speech video. Write a critique to Darla assessing how well you think she incorporated audience analysis in developing her speech. What strategies did she use to help her audience, most of whom were not hunters, understand her key ideas? Suppose your instructor invited Darla to give her speech in your speech class. What suggestions would you give Darla for adapting her speech to you and your classmates?

Exercises

1. Select several topics that on first glance appear to be of interest primarily to people of one particular age group, gender, economic status, etc.—for example, the Lamaze method of childbirth, sports and male bonding, and expensive wines. Discuss how speakers could justify these topics as important to a broader audience.

2. Select a speech from *Vital Speeches* or some other published source or electronic database. Read the speech to discern how the speaker adapted, or failed to adapt, the message to the specific audience. Mark examples of audience adaptation strategies, writing in the margins of a copy of the speech the specific appeal or strategy used. Indicate where the speaker could better have adapted to the audience.

3. Using the speech you selected in Exercise 2, discuss how the speaker would need to adapt the purpose, content, organization, and language if he or she were speaking to your class.

4. Prepare an audience profile of your class using the seven demographic characteristics discussed in this chapter. After your analysis is done, answer the following questions: Which categories were easiest to determine? Which required more guesswork? Which characteristics do you think will be more important for most speeches given in this class?

5. Based on your analysis of students in this class, predict their opinions on the following questions.
   a. Should tax dollars be used to support men-only or women-only colleges and universities?
   b. Is a private college education superior to a public college education?
   c. Should women have the right to have an abortion?
   d. Do social fraternities and sororities do more harm than good?

   After you have made your predictions, poll the class to determine their responses to these questions. Were your predictions fairly accurate? Were you surprised at some of the answers? What factors caused you to predict as you did?

6. Listen to a broadcast debate or discussion on a controversial issue. You can usually find heated discussions on CNN's *Crossfire,* PBS's *NewsHour with Jim Lehrer,* and Sunday morning network talk shows. Discuss the differences in positions based on the values supporting each person's arguments.

7. Analyze your public speaking class using the VALS typology. What categories of people are represented in your class? Brainstorm some topics you think your classmates would find interesting and helpful. Select one of these topics, and discuss some of the needs and values you would tap in your audience.

8. Construct an audience questionnaire pertaining to the topic of an upcoming speech. Distribute it to your classmates, and then collect, compile, and interpret the results. Write an audience profile based on the results.

Selecting Your Speech Topic

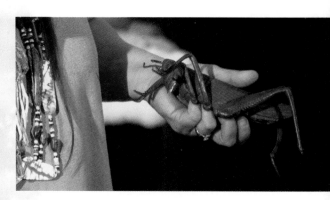

chapter

6

109

If I write what you know, I bore you;
if I write what I know, I bore
myself; therefore, I write what
I don't know. —ROBERT DUNCAN[1]

The successful writer begins with a blank sheet of paper or a clear computer screen. The successful director begins with an empty stage. To achieve a finished product—a book or a play—both must go through several complicated steps. Directors must study the literary form, understand its dynamics, research the script, generate ideas, focus and organize those ideas, and then translate them into performance. In so doing, they give the finished product their individual signatures. Writers follow a similar process to complete a project.

As a public speaker, you are both author *and* director, and you seek to fill two voids: a blank sheet of paper and an empty space before an audience. Speech making is an artistic process that needs the spark of creativity to live. You cannot use a template or other formula to produce an effective speech. As an artist, you will use your creativity as well as your research and organizational skills to transform your ideas into a living speech. However, before you can exercise your artistry with language, your persistence as a researcher, or any other talents you possess, you must have a topic. Selecting that topic with your audience, your own interests, and your speaking occasion in mind provides your first opportunity to exercise the creativity that will make the speech uniquely yours.

Choosing an excellent speech topic involves several steps. You should (1) generate a list of ideas for possible topics, (2) select a topic, (3) focus the topic, (4) determine your general purpose, (5) formulate your specific purpose, and (6) word your thesis statement. Depending on the specific speaking situation, you may also want or be asked to develop a speech title.

Generate Ideas

The first step in the process of selecting a speech topic is **brainstorming**. Brainstorming requires you to use the critical thinking skill of *generating*, discussed in Chapter 1. With this technique, you list all the ideas that come to your mind without evaluating or censoring any of them. Too often, a speaker spends insufficient time generating a list of potential topics. Yet, as Dr. Pauling suggests, in order to select a good topic you must generate many topics. Author John Steinbeck compared ideas to rabbits, saying, "You get a couple and learn how to handle them, and pretty soon you have a dozen." As a rule, the larger your list of possible topics, the better the topic you will finally select. Remember, do not evaluate or criticize your list as you brainstorm. What may seem silly to you at first can turn out to be an unusual speech subject with a lot of potential to interest your audience.

brainstorming: noncritical free association to generate as many ideas as possible in a short time.

For example, Angelita brainstormed topics for her informative speech by listing her interests and activities. She had played the saxophone in her high school band, so she

Thinking about your own hobbies and interests is one way to brainstorm for speech topics.

decided to inform her classmates how to play the saxophone. When she shared this idea with her instructor, however, the teacher cautioned her that such a goal was probably unrealistic in the five- to seven-minute time limits. Hadn't it taken her years to learn how to play the sax? Still interested in this topic area, Angelita consulted encyclopedias and found that this hybrid instrument was popular in military and American jazz bands. She began researching military bands and found the topic fascinating.

She learned that in the early 1600s, when European nations began to create standing armies, those troops started to need to march together. Musical composers wrote marches for this purpose. The military band played at outdoor celebrations and demonstrations, environments requiring instruments, such as the saxophone, that were louder than many string instruments. What began as a speech on how to play the saxophone eventually became a very interesting speech on the history of military bands. The topic expanded Angelita's knowledge in one of her fields of interest and also taught her listeners something new.

> *"You can't have good ideas if you don't have a lot of ideas."*
>
> —LINUS PAULING

You can turn brainstorming into productive work toward your speech by asking and then answering these four questions:

1. What topics interest *you*?
2. What topics interest your *listeners*?
3. What topics develop from the *occasion*?
4. What topics develop from your *research*?

Your answers will help you devise a list of many topics from which you can then select the most appropriate.

Self-Generated Topics

Self-generated topics come from you—your memory, your notes, your interests, your experiences, and your personal files. Take out a sheet of paper and jot down your hobbies, your favorite courses, books you have read, your pet peeves, names of people who intrigue you, and issues and events that excite you. What are your likes and dislikes? On what topics do you consider yourself knowledgeable? Review your list, writing beside each item possible speech topics. If you are irritated by people who are late, you could inform your audience about why people procrastinate or about how to set and meet goals. Are you uncomfortable in enclosed places? A speech on claustrophobia might interest you and your audience. If you are nearing graduation and have been reading books on how to land your first job, a speech on how to construct a résumé or dos and don'ts for the employment interview may be fitting.

Self-generated topics may also include subjects you *need* to know. If, for example, you expect to travel soon and will be making your own arrangements for the first time, you may find yourself riding in taxis, staying in hotels, and dining in some good restaurants. But are you familiar with tipping etiquette for cab drivers, baggage carriers, and waiters? Researching and delivering a speech on tipping will not only serve your needs, but can also be an interesting and informative topic for your listeners.

Consider the following topics generated by our students, using just their personal interests and knowledge:

Anger management	Parachuting, importance to the military
Black history in textbooks	Photograph restoration
Colleges of the future	Rappelling
Dream catchers	Study-abroad programs
Duncan, Isadora	Vertical ice climbing
Great Barrier Reef	Webtoon industry, evolution of
Music software	Wilderness therapy
Night terrors	Woods, Tiger

Use what you know as a starting point in your topic selection process. Don't worry that you don't know enough about each topic at this stage to construct a speech. Research will help you later in focusing, developing, and supporting your topic. *What is important is that you have a list of possible topics that interest you.* Because these topics come from *your* knowledge, experience, and interests, your commitment to them is usually strong. Your interest and knowledge will motivate you in preparing your speech. In addition, your enthusiasm for your topic will enliven and enhance your speech delivery.

As you can see, self-generated topics can provide you with interesting ideas. However, they can also pose some difficulties for a speaker. One potential pitfall of self-generated topics is the use of overly technical language and jargon. If your topic is technical, be especially attentive to the language you choose to convey your meaning. The speaker in the following example forgot that advice.

> Caryn, a pre-med student with a double major in biology and chemistry, found an interesting article that explained how some animals survive winter by freezing and then thawing in the spring. She chose this as an informative speech topic and did further research. She reasoned correctly that many of her classmates wouldn't know of this phenomenon or how it occurs.
>
> Yet most of her listeners knew they were in trouble when Caryn said in her introduction: "Today I want to explain how some animals such as the wood frog, the gray tree frog, painted turtles, and gallfly larvae use so-called antifreeze proteins, ice-

self-generated topics: speech subjects based on the speaker's interests, experiences, and knowledge.

Topic selection can be the most important step of the entire speech. When I brainstormed for topics, I would think about things that really interested me. If you choose something that doesn't excite you, you won't be comfortable speaking about it. Interesting topics, however, make the whole experience more enjoyable. During the past election, I really wanted my classmates to register and vote, so I made this my purpose for speaking. My com-

mitment to this topic motivated me to research and practice my speech. I wanted my audience to share my enthusiasm for voting. Public speaking doesn't have to be boring. You can be creative and have fun with your topic. Knowing that I had something important and interesting for my classmates to hear made me feel more confident delivering my speech.

—**Bryan McClure,** *Virginia Tech University*

nucleating proteins, trehalose, proline, and cryoprotectants to maintain the integrity of cells while their extracellular fluid freezes."

The audience never recovered. The remainder of her speech contained words and phrases such as *colligative cryoprotectants, polyhydroxyl alcohols, cytoplasm,* and *recrystallization.*

Caryn's problem was not with her topic; indeed, it's a fascinating subject. With simplified language and clear presentational aids, she could have made that topic accessible to her listeners and drawn them into the speech. But the technical vocabulary and jargon that she found understandable only confused and alienated most of her classmates who were not pre-med majors. Remember that your speech on any technical topic will lose its intended impact if you fail to define key terms clearly for listeners less knowledgeable about the subject. You will create semantic distractions, one of those major obstacles to listening that we discussed in Chapter 4.

A second potential problem with self-generated topics is the speaker's lack of objectivity about the subject. If you become too involved with a topic, you cannot always develop it objectively. Researching your subject is a process of discovery. When you begin with rigid preconceptions, you may disregard important information that doesn't match your preconceived ideas. Take the example of Ken and his proposed speech topic on the legal drinking age.

> When the time came to develop and deliver a persuasive speech for his public speaking class, Ken decided to try to persuade his classmates, most of them first-year students, that the legal drinking age should be lowered from 21 to 18. He was committed to this point of view. He had been mentally rehearsing his arguments since his eighteenth birthday: "If I'm old enough to register with Selective Service and defend my country, I'm old enough to drink if I care to." "If I'm old enough to marry without my parents' consent, I should be able to buy and consume any beverage I want."
>
> Yet two days before his speech was due, Ken asked his speech teacher for an extension. The reason, he explained, was that all of the published sources he had researched *supported* the increased legal drinking age. "Some of the sources even had graphs showing decreases in traffic fatalities among 18- to 21-year-olds or reductions in juvenile crimes since the drinking age was raised," he complained. Ken's instructor prodded him, "If all the evidence supports the higher drinking age, have you considered changing your view?" Ken's answer was no. He remained sure that, given more time, he could find the evidence that supported his position.

Ken's predicament is typical of people who form rigid expectations of what their research will reveal. If, after doing some research, he still supported lowering the drinking age, Ken probably should have abandoned the traffic safety and juvenile crime issues altogether. Instead, he could have pursued those philosophical arguments he believed strongly. His primary argument could have centered on the theme that society sends mixed messages by treating 18-year-olds as mature and responsible in many areas of life and irresponsible in others. To avoid following Ken's example, gather some good supporting data before you commit yourself to a specific focus for your topic.

Finally, lack of objectivity about a self-generated topic can take a second form: excessive devotion to the speech topic. You may choose as a topic an interest or hobby that has been a passion of yours for years. You are enthusiastic about the topic, you already have a wealth of information on it, and doing further research will seem a pleasure rather than a chore. What could possibly go wrong?

"The audience will love this topic," you think. Be careful. Your audience may not share your enthusiasm for aardvarks or restoring Studebaker cars. Your interest in a topic is just one criterion in the selection process. For most speech topics, you must also work to generate audience interest. We are not suggesting that you avoid self-generated topics of great interest to you. Just do not assume that your audience already has the same level of interest. They may not initially share your enthusiasm for aardvarks (or Bob Marley or the history of fireworks or optical illusions), but if you *work* at it, you can *make* them interested. Be prepared to work hard to do so.

In addition, be prepared to listen openly to others' speeches. Remember that ethical listeners do not prejudge either a speaker or that speaker's ideas. You may encounter some students who seem skeptical of any information that won't help them make the car payment. Granted, some topics seem so narrow or so offbeat that you can imagine thinking, "Who cares about aardvarks?" But can't you also imagine a *terrific* speech on aardvarks by a speaker who was genuinely interested in them and who had lots of vivid supporting material? Much of the value of education is that it makes you a better (smarter, happier, more well-rounded) person. Some information is intrinsically rewarding and just plain fun to know. Don't dismiss information presented in a speech (or anywhere else) just because it won't make you more money, save you time, or whiten your teeth.

Audience-Generated Topics

Pursuing **audience-generated topics** is a second way of triggering speech subjects. What topics are of interest or importance to your listeners? If you are asked to speak to a group, you are often asked because of your expertise in a particular area. Topic selection, in this case, may be predetermined.

On other occasions, such as in this class, you may not be provided with topics or topic areas. How can you find out what interests your classmates? There are three ways to do this. First, *ask them*. Ask some of your classmates in casual conversation about topics they would like to hear discussed. If allowed the opportunity, you could also use a questionnaire to seek topic suggestions from the entire class. When you speak outside class to an organization, ask the person who contacted you about issues of probable interest to the group.

Second, *listen and read*. What do your classmates discuss before and after class? Articles in your campus or local paper or letters to the editor may suggest issues of concern. Finally, *use the audience analysis strategies* detailed in Chapter 5 to generate topics.

> " ... [T]here is no such thing as a boring subject. ... [W]hether it's the plastics industry or the mating habits of a certain insect, you will always find that there are people out there who have devoted their entire lives to the subject. ... Well, if it can fascinate one person, then you can extract a kind of enthusiasm from that person and transfer it to others out there. "
>
> —TED KOPPEL

audience-generated topics: speech subjects geared to the interests and needs of a speaker's listeners.

Consider your listeners' needs. If your class is composed primarily of students just entering college, a speech on the history of your school would be interesting, informative, and appropriate. If your class is composed primarily of seniors, a speech on establishing a good credit history may be timely.

You may even find that most members of your audience seem to feel one way about a controversial topic while you take the opposite view. You may choose to use this situation to develop and deliver a persuasive speech aimed at winning support for your side of the issue.

The following topics were generated by our students using an audience-centered approach:

Coca-Cola, history of	Mnemonic (memory) devices
Critical incident stress	Networking home computers
Cruise vacations	Online scholarship searches
Cult movie classics	Palmistry (palm reading)
Ethereal music	Superwoman syndrome
Hazing on college campuses	Test anxiety, how to control
Horror movies, appeal of	TV reality shows, impact of
Interviews, dressing for	Used cars, how to buy

Occasion-Generated Topics

Occasion-generated topics constitute a third source of speech subjects. When and where a speech is given may guide you in selecting a topic. A speech on setting goals may benefit your classmates more at the beginning of the semester or quarter, whereas a speech on stress management may have more impact preceding midterm or final exams. A speech on "Office Pool Monday" will be particularly relevant if given near the Monday after NCAA "March Madness" basketball brackets are announced.

If you are scheduled to speak near a particular holiday, a speech on the history or importance of that holiday may be appropriate. If you have a speech scheduled on or near Victoria Day, for instance, you can take the opportunity to introduce your classmates to a part of Canadian history. To find examples of other holidays, look at your calendar, or examine different calendars at a bookstore. Specialty calendars or almanacs list unusual but interesting holidays, birth dates of notable and notorious people, or anniversaries of important historical events.

Online reference works can greatly aid your search for occasion-generated topics. For example, we accessed the AnyDay page (mentioned in the related Exploring Online sidebar) and typed the date April 23. We generated lists of 281 individuals who were born or died on this day, and 154 events that occurred. Many of these entries would make or lead you to excellent speech topics. For example, you could discuss the life and contributions of novelist Vladimir Nabokov, rockers Roy Orbison or Brent Muscat, or actors Jan Hooks or Melina Kanakaredes. You might describe the Shakespeare Memorial Theatre at Stratford-on-Avon that opened in 1932 or discuss how consumers reacted to the debut of New Coke in 1985.

We truly are a people who love to celebrate occasions, whether they are established national holidays or quirky, lesser-known ones. Many of these occasions can suggest possible speech topics. A speech detailing cable television's impact on the viewing habits of the American family would seem appropriately timed during National Cable Month.

Exploring *Online*

OCCASION-GENERATED TOPICS
www.scopesys.com/anyday
With three mouse clicks, you can search for occasion-generated speech topics at this site. The AnyDay page lets you see a list of events that occurred on any day and month you select. The almanac also lists names of people who were born or who died on that particular day, along with holidays or religious observances that mark the date.

Exploring *Online*

OCCASION-GENERATED TOPICS
www.festivals.com
Speaking near a particularly festive occasion, or wondering whether you are? This site is a worldwide guide to festivals. You can search by keyword, location, or subject, or just browse by clicking on culture, kids, motorsports, music, or sports.

occasion-generated topics: speech subjects derived from particular circumstances, seasons, holidays, or life events.

Rituals and special occasions can provide excellent speech topics. Here, guests arrive in traditional dress for a Lapp wedding.

Banned Book Month may be the ideal occasion for a speech on censorship. Consider some of the possible speech topics suggested by the following: Autism Awareness Month, Women's History Month, National Garlic Day, International Left-Handers Day, National Pasta Week, Straw Hat Day, National Relaxation Day, and American Chocolate Week. There are even months to celebrate ice cream, baked beans, and the hot dog.

Some of these lesser-known holidays can capture the interest of many people. For example, June 16, 1904, is the single day covered by James Joyce's novel *Ulysses*. Once banned, burned in protest, and even the object of a court case, the novel is now studied in many college courses. Each June 16 is also a holiday, Bloomsday, named for the novel's main character, Leopold Bloom. On this day in June, Joyce fans gather for public readings of sections of the massive novel. Others dress as characters in the novel. Certain Dubliners retrace parts of Bloom's journey around some of the still existent streets, shops, taverns, bridges, and public buildings mentioned in the book. Bloomsday is an occasion for a lot of literary, semi-literary, and strictly recreational activity "in at least sixty countries worldwide."[2] It could also be the subject of an interesting speech.

Our students generated the following topics as they focused on different occasions for speeches:

Bat mitzvah (female equivalent
  of bar mitzvah)
Charreada (Mexican rodeo)
Dia de los Muertos
Dragon Boat Festival in Hong Kong
Festival of the Lanterns
Fireworks, designing displays
Golden Globe Awards, history of
Hurricanes

Juneteenth
9/11
Papal conclaves
Papel picado (Mexican cut-paper art)
Ramadan
Running of the Bulls in Pamplona,
  Spain
Summer internships, finding
Superbowl commercials

Note that an occasion-generated topic can often lead you to other interesting topic possibilities. Drought conditions in your area may lead you to consider the subjects of cloud seeding or desalting sea water. The occasion of Memorial Day may get you thinking about The Wall, the Vietnam Veterans Memorial in Washington, D.C. You may then decide to focus on the competition for the design of the monument; on Maya Lin, whose design won that competition; or on the aesthetics of the wall and the stirring effect it has on visitors.

Research-Generated Topics

Research-generated topics, a fourth strategy for sparking speech ideas, require you to explore a variety of sources. First, you could consult some of the databases and indexes we list in Chapter 7. Look at the listing of subjects and jot down those that interest you. A second research strategy is to browse through magazines or journals in the current periodical section of your library, at a local newsstand, or online. Just remember that this exploration is the first step in selecting a speech topic. Don't leap at the first interesting topic you find. A third strategy for generating topics is to peruse book titles at a good bookstore, noting those that interest you. Bookstores are convenient places to discover speech topics because the books are grouped by general subject area and are arranged to catch your eye. By using these three research tools—databases and indexes, magazines and journals, and books—you can not only discover a speech topic, but you may also locate your first source of information.

Consider the following topics. You might not have thought of these on your own, but all have the potential to be excellent topics and they all came from resources our students found.

Adams, Ansel	Nanotechnology
Amish life	*Noh* (ancient Japanese) theater
Appalachian culture	Nuclear medicine, future of
Breed-specific dog legislation	Obsessive–compulsive disorder
Color's effects on moods	*Origami* (Japanese paper art)
Copyleft movement, the	Pet therapy
Curanderismo (Mexican folk healing)	Racial profiling
Fingerprints, features of	Stem cell research
Forensic hypnosis	Ties, history of
Insomnia, treatment of	Tomb sculptures
Jet lag, cures for	Travel abroad, post 9/11
Landscape design	Tuskeege Airmen, the
Marley, Bob	Video surveillance
Movies, how they are rated	Yoga techniques

It is important that you use all four of these strategies to generate possible speech topics. If you end your topic generation process too quickly, you limit your options. A substantive list of self-, audience-, occasion-, and research-generated topics gives you maximum flexibility in selecting a topic.

Once you have selected your topic area, we suggest that you use a technique called **visual brainstorming** to investigate the range of possibilities within that topic. Take out a sheet of paper and write your topic in the center. Now, think of how you might divide

research-generated topics: speech subjects discovered by investigating a variety of sources.

visual brainstorming: informal written outline achieved by free associating around a key word or idea.

and narrow that topic. It may help you to think of some generic categories such as "causes," "types," and "solutions" that are appropriate to numerous topics. As you think of subtopics, draw a line from the center in any direction and write the narrower topic.

As your thinking suggests additional topics, you will probably be surprised at the web of potential speech topics you have created just from your brainstorming. Figure 6.1 illustrates the end product of a visual brainstorming exercise on the topic of

FIGURE 6.1
Visual Brainstorming
This technique can reveal possible topic areas or clusters of subtopics for speeches.

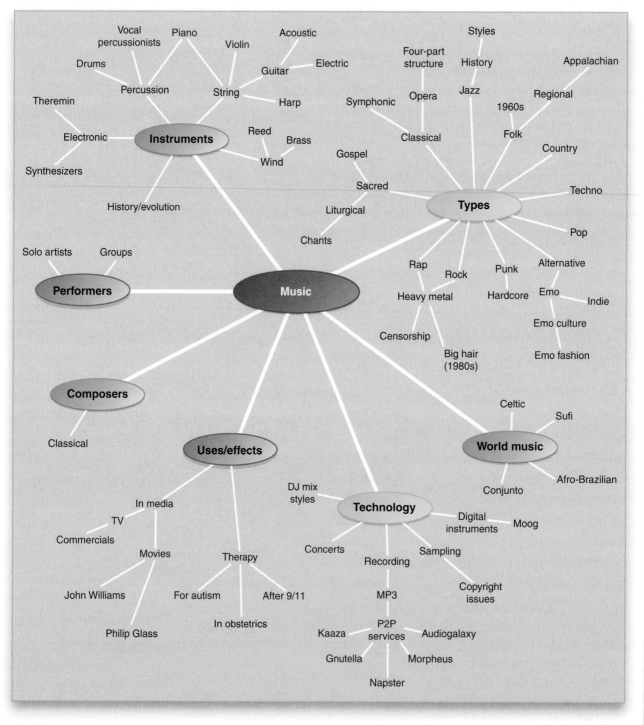

"music." Certainly, you can add to this list, but in just a few minutes our students were able to provide many options for focusing the subject of music. Some of these, such as the use of music in TV commercials, are excellent topics that would probably not have occurred to you without this brainstorming exercise.

You can incorporate research into your discovery and focusing process. For example, if you are really interested in indie music, your research would reveal the genre's

Theory into Practice
Tips
Selecting Your Topic

Once you have generated a list of possible speech topics, you must then select the best one. Determining what is best is an individual choice; neither a classmate, a friend, nor your instructor can make that choice. However, asking and answering four questions will help you make a wise decision.

1. **Am I interested in the topic?**

   The more enthusiastic you are about a topic, the greater the time and attention you will give to researching, constructing, and practicing your speech. When you enjoy learning, you learn better. As a result speakers motivated by their topics are almost always more productive than those bored with their topics.

2. **Is the topic of interest or importance to my audience?**

   This question helps you avoid choosing a topic that you love but that your audience will never care about. Speech making is easier when your listeners are potentially interested in what you have to say. When your audience is more attentive and receptive, you can relax and your delivery will be livelier. Sometimes, topics seem to be of little initial interest to audience members but may, nevertheless, be important to their personal or career success. As long as you can demonstrate the importance and relevance of the topic to them, you will motivate your audience to listen.

3. **Am I likely to find sufficient authoritative supporting material in the time allotted for researching and developing the speech?**

   Unless your topic is truly offbeat or brand new and assuming that you haven't waited until the last minute to start your research, the answer to this question will likely be yes. Even if the topic is so new that it has not yet appeared in articles, chances are good that you'll find information about it on the Internet. In that case you'll have to judge whether the information you find is authoritative. If your best sources are articles or transcripts that you have to purchase and download, can you afford the expense? Or if your top sources are going to be items you have to order through interlibrary loan or purchase and have mailed to you, do you have the time? You obviously cannot wait until the week before your speech to order such items. Remember the adage that if something can go wrong, it will. Build some flexibility into your schedule so that you can adapt to any crisis that may arise.

4. **Do I understand the topic enough to undertake and interpret my research?**

   A speaker arguing the merits of a tax increase must understand economics in order to assess research data. When you inform the audience about music therapy, you need some understanding of psychological treatment techniques and procedures. A speaker may misinterpret the reasons that violent crime in the United States is higher than in Japan if he or she does not understand Japanese culture. You don't need to know much about your topic as you begin your research, but you must know enough to be able to make sense of the data you discover.

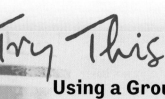

Using a Group to Select Your Topic

Review the assignment for your next graded speech. After conducting the necessary brainstorming and research, list a minimum of four self-generated, four audience-generated, four occasion-generated, and six research-generated topics on a sheet of paper. Be specific, and narrow your topics as much as possible.

On a separate sheet of paper, list the five topics that you think would make the best speeches. Bring both lists to class.

Meeting in small groups, share your first list with your classmates. They should select the five topics they like best, as well as scratch off the topics they like least. Compare their list(s) with yours. If possible, solicit more feedback on why they liked or didn't like certain topics.

Reevaluate your list in light of your classmates' input. Based on your analysis, peer comments, and the guidelines presented in this chapter, select the most appropriate topic for your next speaking assignment. Remember, however, that as you research and develop your topic, you will continue to focus and adapt it.

Key Points

Questions to Guide Topic Selection

1. Does this topic interest me?
2. Is this topic interesting or important to my listeners?
3. Am I likely to find sufficient supporting materials on this topic?
4. Do I know enough about this topic to start researching it and to interpret what I discover?

ancestry in fairly well-known groups such as Sonic Youth and Yo La Tengo. You would find that indie music has its own boy bands (Modest Mouse) and grrl [sic] bands (LeTigre, Sleater Kinney) and that it has branches such as emo (Promise Ring), alt country (Alejandro Escovedo), and trip-hop (Massive Attack, Portishead). In short, you would discover some talented musicians forming and then dissolving groups with quirky names, with the long-range goal of staying just off the pop radar screen. Any one or a combination of these subjects could provide the topic for an excellent informative speech.

Focus Your Topic

Once you have selected your topic, you must focus it. Even though we have heard students speak on topics that were too narrow, this is rare. More commonly, students tackle topics that are too broad, leaving too little time to develop their ideas. The result is a speech that is more surface than substance.

When you decide on a topic area, use visual brainstorming to determine some of its divisions, or subtopics. The subject of "loneliness," for example, could focus on any of the following topics: the causes of loneliness, the relationship between loneliness and depression, loneliness and the elderly, loneliness as a cause of teenage suicide, characteristics of the lonely person, the differences between being alone and being lonely, or strategies for coping with loneliness. You could never discuss all these topics meaningfully in a short speech. Narrowing the scope of your inquiry gives direction to your research and allows you sufficient time to support the limited ideas you will present to your audience.

Visual brainstorming is an excellent way of focusing your topic. A second way is through research. The more you read about your topic, the more you will likely discover its many aspects. Some may be too narrow for a complete speech, but others may be suitable for an entire speech or may be combined to form a speech.

For a five- to seven-minute informative speech assignment, Rob developed three main points in the body of his speech on baseball:

    I. The history of baseball
    II. How the game is played
    III. The uniform and equipment used

As you might guess, Rob found himself rushing through the speech, and he still did not finish it within the time limit. You probably noticed that each of his main points is too broad. Rob's problem was that he needed to focus his topic further.

One possibility for Rob was to concentrate on the history of baseball and maybe focus on a specific era that interested him. For example, he could have surprised and enlightened his listeners by discussing baseball during the Civil War. Or he could have focused on the all-black leagues operating from the 1920s until the integration of baseball during the 1950s. Rob could have spoken about the All-American Girls Professional Baseball League formed during World War II when many professional baseball players were being drafted. Each of these topics would probably have interested and informed Rob's listeners, regardless of their fondness for baseball. Notice, too, that each of these narrower topics also places baseball in a sociological context. Rob's speech on the history of baseball could have thus become a lesson in a particular period of American history, having appeal even for listeners not especially interested in baseball.

EthicalDecisions

Should Instructors Censor?

A colleague of ours had a long and distinguished career teaching communication. After class one day, she returned to her office visibly upset. When questioned by her colleagues, she said one of her students had announced in his speech introduction that his purpose was to teach the class how to make a lethal poison using ingredients people already had in their homes or could easily buy. "Moreover," she said, "to stress the significance of the topic, he assured us that this substance would kill any living animal, certainly even the heaviest human being."

"What did you do?" her colleagues asked. "I sat there thinking of the rash of teenage suicides, even copycat suicides, we've been hearing about lately, and all the other meanness in the world," she replied. "I wrestled with my conscience for about a minute and a half, and then, for the first time since I started teaching, I interrupted a speaker. I told the student I didn't think we needed to hear this information, and asked him to be seated."

Was this teacher's action justified? Did she violate the student's freedom of speech? Placed in that teacher's position, what would you have done?

Oral reports are one form of a speech to inform. Speakers impart information and understanding in an objective and unbiased manner.

Determine Your General Purpose

Broadly speaking, a speech may have one of three purposes: to inform, to persuade, or to entertain. The general purpose of your speech defines your relationship with the audience. You play the role of mentor when you provide information. You are an advocate when you seek to change beliefs, attitudes, values, or behaviors through a persuasive speech. Your speech to entertain is meant to amuse your audience. As the entertainer, you set a mood to relax your audience using your delivery style, tone, and content.

You may find it difficult at times to distinguish these purposes. Because information may affect both what we believe and how we act, the distinction between informative speaking and persuasive speaking is sometimes particularly blurred. A speech meant to entertain is frequently persuasive because it may make a serious point through the use of humor. Despite the overlap between these general purposes, you must be secure about your primary purpose any time you speak in public. A closer look at the objectives and intended outcomes of each general purpose will help you distinguish them.

Speeches to Inform

A **speech to inform** has as its objective to impart knowledge to an audience. You convey this information in an objective and unbiased manner. Your goal is not to alter the listeners' attitudes or behaviors, but to facilitate their understanding of your subject and their ability to retain this new information. We discuss the speech to inform in greater detail in Chapter 15. A speech on any of the following topics could be informative:

Art therapy	The middle child syndrome
Billboard liberation	Muralist movement in Mexican art
Hispanic film industry	Poetry slams
History of science fiction movies	Shopping addiction

speech to inform: a speech designed to convey new and/or useful information in a balanced, objective way.

Speeches to Persuade

A **speech to persuade** seeks to influence either beliefs or actions. The former, sometimes called a **speech to convince,** focuses on audience beliefs and attitudes. A speech designed to persuade audience members to embrace a belief stops short of advocating specific action. A speaker may argue, for example, that polygraph testing is unreliable without suggesting a plan of action. Another speaker may try to convince listeners that women have been neglected in medical research without offering a plan to solve the problem.

A speech designed to persuade to action, or a **speech to actuate,** attempts to change not only the listeners' beliefs and attitudes but also their behavior. A speech to actuate could move the audience to boycott a controversial art exhibit, to contribute money to a charity, to enroll in a specific course, or to urge their elected officials to increase funding for women's health research. In each case, the speaker's goal would be first to intensify or alter the audience's beliefs and then to show how easy and beneficial taking action could be. We discuss the speech to persuade in Chapters 16 and 17.

Speeches to Entertain

A third general purpose of speech is to entertain. A speech to entertain differs from speaking to entertain. *Speaking to entertain* is a general phrase covering several types of speaking. It includes humorous monologues, stand-up comedy routines, and storytelling, for example. When you tell your friends jokes or recount a humorous anecdote, you are trying to entertain them. You are probably not trying to develop a key point in an organized, methodical way.

A **speech to entertain** is more formal than simply speaking to entertain because it is more highly organized and its development is more detailed. Speeches to entertain are often delivered on occasions when people are in a festive mood, such as after a banquet or as part of an awards ceremony. For that reason, we discuss the speech to entertain in more detail in Chapter 18, Speaking on Special Occasions. Remember that all speeches, including those to entertain, should develop a central thought through organized supporting material and ideas. Though the ideas in a speech to entertain will be illustrated and highlighted by humor, a mere collection of jokes does not qualify as a speech. We agree with the communication scholars who contend that a speech to entertain is actually either a speech to inform or a speech to persuade, usually the latter.

Formulate Your Specific Purpose

When you are asked to state the **general purpose** of your speech, you will respond with two words from among the following: *to inform, to persuade* (or *to convince* or *to actuate*), or *to entertain.* When asked to state your specific purpose, however, you will need to be more descriptive. A **specific purpose** statement has three parts.

First, you begin with the general purpose of the speech, stated as an infinitive; for example, "to convince." Second, you name the individuals to whom the speech is addressed. This is usually phrased simply as "the audience" or "my listeners." Third, you state what you want your speech to accomplish. What should the audience know, believe, or do as a result of your speech? You may want to establish the belief that alcoholism is hereditary. In

---

speech to persuade: a speech designed to influence listeners' beliefs and/or actions.

speech to convince: a persuasive speech designed to influence audience beliefs and attitudes rather than behaviors.

speech to actuate: a persuasive speech designed to influence audience behaviors.

speech to entertain: a speech designed to make a point through the creative, organized use of humorous supporting materials.

general purpose: the broad goal of a speech, such as to inform, to persuade, or to entertain.

specific purpose: a statement of the general purpose of the speech, the speaker's intended audience, and the limited goal or outcome.

To Develop Your Specific Purpose Statement

1. State your general purpose.
2. Name your intended audience.
3. State the goal of your speech.

Key
Points

this case, then, your complete specific purpose statement would be: To convince the audience that alcoholism is hereditary. Other examples of specific purpose statements are:

- To inform the audience on how to communicate constructive criticism
- To inform the audience on celebrity worship syndrome
- To convince the audience that use of cellular phones while driving is a serious problem
- To convince the audience that publically funded professional sports stadiums are a misuse of taxpayers' money
- To move the audience to draft and sign a living will
- To move the audience to spend their spring break building a house for Habitat for Humanity

Word Your Thesis Statement

A **thesis statement** presents the central idea of the speech. It is a one-sentence synopsis of your speech. The thesis statement of a persuasive speech on compulsory national service could be this: "Compulsory national service would benefit the nation by promoting the national spirit, the national defense, and the national welfare." This statement is the central idea of the speech, a proposition the speaker will support with evidence and argument.

Notice that the process of topic selection has, up to this point, enabled you to focus your subject on something specific and manageable. You are now ready to construct a *working thesis:* a statement that, based on your current research and thinking, summarizes what you will say in your speech.[3] Although a thesis statement is designed to keep you focused, it may change as you continue to work on and develop your speech. It gives you a handle on your subject and, as you begin to develop your key ideas, you will be able to determine whether you can support your thesis statement. In organizing the body of the speech, you may realize that your ideas are not balanced or that two of your main points should be collapsed into one. As you research your speech, you may discover additional ideas that are more important than some you had planned to present. That was the experience of our student who spoke on compulsory national service.

Stuart was developing a persuasive speech advocating a system of compulsory national service (CNS). As he began his research, he planned to focus only on the national security that compulsory military service would provide. His working thesis was, "Compulsory national service would benefit the nation by ensuring its military readiness." Yet his research quickly revealed many other benefits of CNS: domestic conservation and recycling, rural health care, and in-home assistance to the elderly.

By the time he had completed his research, Stuart had broadened the focus of his speech and felt he had developed a much stronger case for instituting a CNS program. When he delivered his speech, he presented three main arguments:

I. CNS would promote the national spirit.
II. CNS would promote the national defense.
III. CNS would promote the national welfare.

Stuart made certain to revise his working thesis to reflect his new organization. (Remember, you will also need to modify your thesis statement any time you revise the content and structure of your speech.)

The following examples illustrate how you can narrow a topic's focus from a general area to the speech's thesis statement.

thesis statement: a one-sentence synopsis of a speaker's message.

Topic Area: Sculpture

Topic: Works by Andy Goldsworthy

General Purpose: To inform

Specific Purpose: To inform the audience about Andy Goldsworthy's sculptures

Thesis Statement: Andy Goldsworthy sculpts wood, ice, and leaves into intricate works in their natural settings.

Topic Area: Police oversight

Topic: Mandatory videotaping of police

General Purpose: To persuade

Specific Purpose: To persuade the audience that all police actions in police stations should be videotaped

Thesis Statement: Videotaping all police actions in police stations will deter police misconduct, deter false charges of police misconduct, and restore public confidence in police work.

Develop Your Speech Title

Some speeches don't require titles. Many public speaking instructors, for example, do not require titles for speeches delivered in class. In most formal public speaking situations, however, the audience knows the speaker and topic beforehand. The title is often included in a printed program or mentioned by the person introducing the speaker. Therefore, whenever you have the opportunity, you should title all your speeches, including your classroom speeches.

A well-crafted title accomplishes three purposes. First, it generates audience interest in your speech. By appealing to the needs and interests of your audience, a title can encourage active listening. Interesting titles may also enhance your image as a communicator. When you speak to an audience that does not know you, your title may generate the audience's first impression of you.

A second purpose of a title is to make your message more memorable. When you encapsulate the point of your speech in the title, you prepare the audience to listen for its development. Your title may even provide a reference point when a listener explains to others what you discussed.

If you study print advertisements, you will see that they usually use this strategy successfully. The headline usually contains a selling promise designed to capture the attention of those likely to buy the product or service. Speech titles such as "Converting Anger to Action" or "Making Your Anger Work for You" are clear and direct. Our student Christie titled her speech about online auctions "Sold on eBay!" That title is short, attention getting, and easy to remember and highlights Christie's enthusiasm for selling and buying online.

Our students developed the following titles for their classroom speeches. You probably have an idea of what each speech is about even though you have not heard or read it.

"Identity Protection 101"

"Unraveling the Mystery: Mummification Techniques of Ancient Egypt"

"The Need for Speed: The Unique World of Street Racing"

"Washing Away the Lies of Antibacterial Soaps"

If you get your listeners' attention and make your key ideas more memorable before you even utter your first word, you have gone a long way toward ensuring the success of your speech.

A third and final benefit of a good speech title is primarily for you, the speaker. When you give your speech a title, you are forced to state your point clearly and concisely. If you have difficulty constructing a title that distills your key ideas, your speech may lack a clear central thought, or you have strayed from your intended thesis. It is better to discover this before you speak so you have time to make proper adjustments.

There is no one best way to develop a title for a speech, but consider these three options. First, if your speech contains a key phrase or sentence that is used repeatedly, that statement may be your title. Martin Luther King, Jr., used the repeated theme *I have a dream* for the title of his "I Have a Dream" speech. (See the Appendix.) A speech arguing the harm of plastic surgery performed just to make a person feel more beautiful could be titled, "Making Stars, Leaving Scars." The use of rhyme makes the title easy to remember.

A second strategy for developing a good speech title is to promise your audience something beneficial in the title. A speech on the benefits of exercise could be titled "Living Longer, Feeling Better." Titles that begin with "How to" follow this strategy and are particularly appropriate when you know the audience is interested in acquiring a skill you can teach them. "How You Can Pass This Course without Spending Any More Time Studying" may not be the most creative title for a speech, but we bet you and your classmates would listen attentively.

Finally, a third strategy is to word your title as a question. A speech investigating laughter therapy could be titled "Is Laughter Really the Best Medicine?" Asking the question signals to the audience what they will know by the end of the speech. Keep in mind that your listeners will expect to be able to answer the question by the end of your speech. We remember one speech professor who titled a speech convention paper on the effects of humor "Can Humor Increase Persuasion, or Is It All a Joke?" The title used humor because the paper was *about* humor, and the fact that we still remember the title attests to its effectiveness.

Summary

By selecting topics for their speeches, students in public speaking classes determine the majority of what they will hear during the course. Six steps can simplify the important process of choosing an appropriate speech topic.

First, brainstorm a list of potential topics focused around your own interests, the needs and interests of your audience, and the occasion for your speech. Your research adds a fourth category of possible topics. Having a large list of subjects gives you the freedom and flexibility to make an appropriate selection.

The second step is to select your topic. Making this decision is easier if you ask yourself four questions while reviewing your topic list: "Am I interested in this topic?" "Is the topic already interesting or important to my audience, or can I interest them in it?" "Am I likely to find adequate, quality supporting materials on this topic in the time I have?" And "Do I know enough about the topic to start researching it and to interpret what I discover?"

The third step is to focus or narrow the subject you've selected. Two ways to accomplish this are *visual brainstorm-*

ing and initial research on the topic. Focusing the topic is important in guiding your research and helping you stay within the time limit for the speech.

The fourth step is to determine your *general purpose*: to inform, to persuade, or to entertain. The general purpose may be predetermined, as in most classroom speech assignments, or left to the judgment of the speaker. Whether you are determining the purpose or just reminding yourself of it, having that goal clearly in mind will keep you on target as you research and organize the speech.

The fifth step of selecting a topic is to formulate your *specific purpose*. That statement should specify three things: the general purpose in infinitive form ("to inform," for example), the intended audience, and what you want your listeners to know, believe, or do as a result of your speech.

The sixth step, wording your *thesis statement,* means distilling the message of the speech into one sentence. This step must come last, because it depends on your initial research and tentative organization of the speech. With the thesis statement in mind, a speaker is ready to conduct in-depth research and to proceed with the development of the speech.

A possible final step, not always required, is to title the speech. Creative, provocative titles achieve three goals. First, they intrigue the audience and make them want to listen to you. Second, they make your message more memorable. Third, they help speakers check to see that the speech has a central focus or thesis.

Practice Critique

Evaluating Titles

Read the transcript of Martin Luther King, Jr.'s speech in the Appendix. Discuss how "I Have a Dream" fulfills, or fails to fulfill, the three purposes of an effective title. (Using a key phrase that is repeated in the speech illustrates the first option for developing a speech title.) Think of alternative titles for Dr. King's speech using the other two strategies discussed in the chapter. Discuss the strengths and weaknesses of these alternative titles.

Exercises

1. Choose a broad subject area and write that topic in the middle of a blank page. Use the technique of visual brainstorming to generate a list of specific topics. Continue diagramming as long as it is productive. Review the topics you generated and identify the best topics for a speech in this class.

2. Using the following topic areas, narrow each subject and write a specific purpose statement for an informative speech and a persuasive speech on each topic.
   a. Attractiveness
   b. Class attendance
   c. Credit cards
   d. Diet and nutrition
   e. School mascots

3. Use any list in this chapter to help you learn more about what interests your classmates. You can do this by indicating the topics that interest or are important to you or your classmates and those topics that are not. What would a speaker have to do to generate interest in the topics not selected?

4. Select and read a speech in the Appendix. Determine its general purpose. Word its specific purpose and thesis statement.

5. Construct at least two titles for a speech on each of the specific purposes listed below. Word the title so that it attracts audience interest or captures the central ideas of the speech.
   a. To inform the audience on how to use AEDs (automated external defibrillators)
   b. To inform the audience on how to manage their time
   c. To inform the audience on the uses of light therapy to reduce depression
   d. To persuade the audience that the federal government should no longer mint the penny
   e. To persuade the audience that lotteries should be outlawed
   f. To persuade the audience that IQ tests are culturally biased

$\mathcal{R}$esearching Your Topic

chapter

7

> *Knowledge is of two kinds.*
> *We know a subject ourselves,*
> *or we know where we can find*
> *information upon it.* —SAMUEL JOHNSON

Whether you are headed toward pharmacy school, studying architecture, or majoring in economics, by the time you graduate, you will know about the history of pharmacology or architecture or will understand the interplay of forces that drive an economy. In Samuel Johnson's words, you will "know a subject." Yet your field of study will not stop evolving and developing on the day that you graduate from college. Learning information that becomes a part of who you are makes up only a fragment of your education. An "educated" college graduate in the 21st century "will no longer be defined as someone who has absorbed a certain body of factual information, but as one who knows how to find, evaluate, and apply needed information."[1]

> *If education is what you're left with after you forget everything you've learned, information literacy must be the best skill for . . . growing up in the information age.*
>
> —JENNY SINCLAIR[5]

If you do not already understand why information literacy is so important, consider these statistics. In 1993 there were 50 websites.[2] At the beginning of 2005, there were an estimated 11.5 billion individual web pages.[3] In the year 2000 alone, more than 100,000 books were published in the United States.[4] Add to this the information provided by millions of pages printed in newspapers, magazines, and other periodicals; volumes of public and private agency reports, hearings, and pamphlets; and countless hours of news and opinions broadcast through television and radio. Research scholar Patricia Breivik summarizes the snowballing accumulation of information as follows:

> The sum total of humankind's knowledge doubled from 1750–1900. It doubled again from 1900–1950. Again from 1960–1965. It has been estimated that the sum of humankind's knowledge has doubled at least once every 5 years since then.
>
> . . . It has been further projected that by the year 2020, knowledge will double every 73 days![6]

In light of these circumstances, it is surely smarter to think of being educated as *knowing how to access* information, rather than *possessing* it.

For public speakers the challenge is selecting from the wide range of available data the information most appropriate for their speeches. That requires knowing how to research, how to scratch "an intellectual itch."[7]

In Chapter 6, we discussed how to select a topic. In this chapter we consider the second step—how to research a topic. **Research** is the gathering of evidence and arguments you will need to understand, develop, and explain your subject. Research is not one step of the speech construction process, but should occur throughout that process. For example, we have already seen in Chapter 6 how research can help you select your topic. Once you have chosen your topic, additional research helps you focus it and de-

research: the process of gathering evidence and arguments to understand, develop, and explain a speech topic.

termine your specific purpose. As you move to the next step and begin to construct the body of your speech, you may need to develop some of your ideas further with additional research. Your research continues even as you consult dictionaries, thesauruses, and books of quotations to help you word the ideas of your speech before you deliver it in class.

Students often wonder how much research to conduct for a classroom speech. Obviously, there is no one answer to this question. Your instructor may specify a minimum number of sources you are to cite during your speech. Does that mean your research is finished when you reach that magic number? Not necessarily. Part of the joy of research is that it will likely reveal aspects of your subject that you had never considered. You may not collect enough information to support your working thesis, or the information you uncover may even contradict that thesis. If so, you need to keep researching to help you decide whether to shift your focus or even change topics. In short, research your topic until you have enough authoritative evidence to make an informative or persuasive statement to your listeners.

Research is not necessarily a linear process. As a result, you may be exercising and developing a number of your critical thinking skills simultaneously.

If you have some experience with or knowledge about the topic area you have chosen, you'll begin by *remembering* and assessing your knowledge. You'll be *information gathering* as you formulate questions you want your research to answer and then collect your data. You will use your *generating* skills as you develop new lines of inquiry based on the research you have completed. Throughout the process you'll be *analyzing* whether and how information from your different sources fits together. As you connect items of information, you'll be *integrating* and *organizing*. As you measure the quality and quantity of your research results, you'll be *evaluating*. And because you will often find more information than you can use, your entire research process will have you *focusing* your speech topic more and more narrowly.

If you are lucky, you may occasionally stumble onto one or two sources of great help as you craft your speech. But most of the time you will have to follow a research strategy that will depend on your particular topic and the available research facilities. The following general five-step sequence can assist you in generating excellent ideas and supporting material, regardless of your speech topic.

1. Assess your personal knowledge of the topic.
2. Develop your research plan.
3. Collect your information.
4. Record your information.
5. Conclude your search.

Let's look more closely at each phase of the research process.

Assess Your Personal Knowledge

The first question you should ask and answer is, "What do I know that will help me develop my topic?" When you begin your research, do not make the mistake of confining yourself only to published materials. Your personal memory has been shaped by what you have read, heard, observed, and experienced. Use that knowledge as a starting point for researching your topic.

The first step in the research process is to assess what you already know about your topic.

The concept of mastering public speaking we sketched in the preface to this book requires a public speaker to have an ongoing commitment to public communication. Establishing a personal information base is important for any speaker who wants to be informed and credible. You already have a great deal of personal knowledge. Don't be afraid to tap this resource as you select and develop your speech topic. For example, a student who worked as a plainclothes security guard for a major department store drew from personal experience in his speech on detecting and apprehending shoplifters. A student who assisted her father in administering polygraph tests chose as her speech topic the use and misuse of lie detectors. These speakers used their personal knowledge and experiences as starting points for their research. Each developed and delivered an interesting speech.

Winston Churchill was once asked how long he had prepared for one of his speeches. He replied, "For forty years." In discussing this incident, Robert Jeffrey and Owen Peterson observe, "In a sense, a speaker spends his or her entire life preparing for a speech. Everything we have learned and experienced, as well as the attitudes we have developed, shapes and influences our speech."[8] Your knowledge and personal files give you a head start in selecting and developing your topic.

Develop Your Research Plan

Your research plan begins as you answer several questions:

1. What information do I need?
2. Where am I most likely to find it?

Theory into Practice
Tips

Developing Personal Speech Resources

Throughout your life, you will occasionally, perhaps often, be called on to share your expertise, interests, and opinions with others in public speeches. We believe that you should consider developing personal files of information you can retrieve for these occasions. Three types of files can be particularly helpful:

- An **article file** includes informative items on topics that interest you. Whether you photocopy articles printed in magazines or journals, cut them from newspapers, or email online articles to yourself and print them later, be sure to record all relevant source information so that you can attribute material you use from these articles. You can save web pages as HTML files or print pages and place them in a labeled folder.
- A **quotation file** consists of memorable or provocative statements you have read or heard, along with the source for each. Quotations can be an excellent way to get an audience's attention at the beginning of a speech. They can also help you

explain and illustrate the ideas of your speech. Though there are many excellent books of quotations, a quotation file will contain only the ones that have some personal significance for you.

- A **speech file** contains materials you have used to prepare speeches you've already delivered or are preparing. These can be your speaking notes or manuscript, along with any research materials and notes about the delivery of the speech. Just make sure that your speech file remains your own, not used by someone else to prepare a speech on the same topic.

You may be a low-tech person who prefers pens, notecards, and file folders, or a high-tech individual who usually has a flash drive hanging around your neck on a lanyard. It doesn't matter. Getting organized by accumulating and saving potential and useful materials in these three types of files will make your life a lot easier when you get a chance to speak on that same topic, or a related one, for a different audience.

3. How can I obtain this information?
4. How will time constraints affect my research options?

Your topic and specific purpose clearly help determine your research plan. If you have seen a news report or read an interesting article about deep brain stimulation to treat Parkinson's disease and have selected that research-generated topic for a speech, you are obviously going to be finding and reading medical materials. If, on the other hand, you have decided to speak about the upcoming student activities-sponsored Octoberfest celebration on campus or about a brand new sleep clinic in your area, your best information may not be in print. You're going to be spending time talking to people. Different topics demand different research strategies; a good research plan accounts for these variations. Keep a running list of what you need and where you can obtain it.

You should also prepare a timetable for constructing your speech. If you will speak two weeks from now, you still have time for a lot of online or library research. You probably even have time to arrange some interviews, conduct them, and transcribe key quotations. However, two weeks is not enough time to order transcripts or videotapes to be mailed to you and be assured of their arrival in time to integrate them into your speech.

article file: a collection of articles, from print and electronic sources, that a speaker finds interesting or important.

quotation file: a collection of passages a speaker finds memorable or important, together with the source citation for each passage.

speech file: a personal collection of materials about the research, preparation, and delivery of speeches completed or initiated.

Collect Your Information

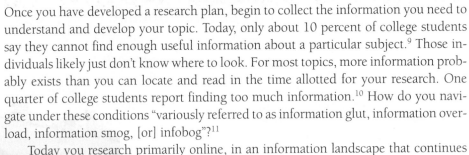

Once you have developed a research plan, begin to collect the information you need to understand and develop your topic. Today, only about 10 percent of college students say they cannot find enough useful information about a particular subject.[9] Those individuals likely just don't know where to look. For most topics, more information probably exists than you can locate and read in the time allotted for your research. One quarter of college students report finding too much information.[10] How do you navigate under these conditions "variously referred to as information glut, information overload, information smog, [or] infobog"?[11]

Today you research primarily online, in an information landscape that continues to undergo revolutionary changes. Partnerships between information providers form and dissolve, sometimes overnight, changing **URL (Uniform Resource Locator)** website addresses and the routes you use to retrieve information. Some such changes will no doubt occur between the time we write this and the time you use it, but we have taken great effort to provide accurate information about electronic sources in this chapter.

Most of the well-known **search engines** you probably use to research the Internet are now bundled together at one very useful search portal, MrSapo (mrsapo.com). Having celebrated its first anniversary as we write this, MrSapo may turn out to be an enduring web tool. We hope so. This site's truly useful feature is that it lets you type a search query just once and then utilize more than *forty* current search engines to search for web pages, images, audio and video files, reference tools, news sources, and blogs. The search engines you can select range from the familiar to the novel: Google, Yahoo, Netscape, Ask Jeeves, Lycos, AOL, Altavista, MSN, Mamma, MetaCrawler, DogPile, A9, Teoma, IceRocket, Looksmart, Wisenut, Alltheweb, Vivisimo, Exalead, Gigablast, DMOZ, Entireweb, Clusty, Search.com, Snap, SurfWax, ixquick. BananaPile, Alexa, ScrubtheWeb, Accoona, Kazazz, Uncover the Net, Genie Knows, blinkx, use, Splat, Hippo, hotsheet, FindForward, AlltheInternet, Don Busca, and iZito.

Any of these search engines can yield some excellent results quickly. They "spider" the Internet, locating relevant static web pages that are linked to other web pages. They often rank sites by popularity. You know, however, that they will often give you results that are too numerous to read. Even scrolling through the pages of results would take more time than you may feel you have. Those results will themselves be mixed, with quality sources alongside questionable ones. Sorting through them will use a number of your critical thinking skills.

For serious, targeted searches, choose an academic search engine that filters the extraneous from the essential. Here are a few academic search engines and their addresses:

Academic Info	www.academicinfo.net
Galaxy	www.galaxy.com
INFOMINE	infomine.ucr.edu
Librarians' Internet Index	lii.org
Resource Discovery Network	www.rdn.ac.uk

Information you retrieve by using academic search engines will be more focused and of higher quality than what you are likely to gather using a general, commercial search tool.

You may be unaware of the **deep web**, sometimes called the invisible web. These are rich databases of public, government, corporate, and private information. The "content in the deep web is massive—approximately 500 times greater than that visible to conventional search engines—with much higher quality throughout."[12] Deep web in-

---

URL (Uniform Resource Locator): the standard notation for each Internet website's unique address, often beginning with http://www.

search engine: a tool for locating information on the Internet by matching items in a search string with pages that the engine indexes.

deep web: huge databases of Internet information posted by public, government, corporate, and private agencies and available only by specific queries.

The modern college library provides computer terminals to help you research your speech topic. With a few keystrokes you can unlock a wealth of information in and beyond the library.

formation often exists in topic-specific databases as multimedia files, graphical files, or in Portable Document File (PDF) formats.[13] "A full ninety-five percent of the deep web is publicly accessible information—not subject to fees or subscriptions."[14] In contrast to static web pages, information in the deep web is "dynamic." That is, the "pages" form only in response to specific research queries.

If you're interested in exploring the deep web, check out the following portals:

- CompletePlanet   http://aip.completeplanet.com
  "70,000 searchable databases and specialty search engines."
- Invisible-Web   www.invisible-web.net
  "Select a category to drill-down through the database."
- ProFusion   www.profusion.com
  "Access hundreds of specialized vertical search engines."

ProFusion allows you to create your own personal search engine and has a feature that will even push web pages with new content to you through email alerts. Exploring the deep web is exciting and will, no doubt, become easier as more people begin to tap its content.

Though you will probably conduct much of your research online, your school library contains many resources that you can't find anywhere else. One of the most helpful sources of information is also one of the least often used: the library staff, particularly those who work in the reference section. A good reference librarian can (1) acquaint you with the library's services and holdings, (2) guide you to particularly helpful sources of information, and (3) instruct you in the use of library equipment. Although all libraries have much in common, each is organized to serve its specific constituency. Your

Exploring *Online*

MAXIMIZING YOUR SEARCH
www.accd.edu/sac/lrc/john/searchen.htm
Librarian John Deosdade of the San Antonio College Learning Resource Center has compiled a superb collection, "Search Engines for Quality Web Sites." From this one site you can find and use more than 400 academic and subject-specific search engines that cover everything from abbreviations to zoos.

> **"** *Good libraries are deeply conservative in that they guard and archive the culture's diverse wisdom and beauty, it's vast oddities and amusements. But they're also radical bastions of mutual aid. In a 'knowledge society' where information carries an ever-steeper price, where the rich get wealthier and the poor have less, libraries are one of the few ways still available for many to educate themselves— ideally, an American right.* **"**

—CHRIS DODGE[15]

database: a huge collection of information arranged for quick retrieval by computer using keywords stipulated by a researcher.

reference librarian can guide you to your library's areas of strength, making your research more efficient and your life easier.

In this chapter we cannot list all or even most of the resources available to you. Whether you are searching online from home, from a library computer, or browsing library shelves and periodical reading rooms, however, you are likely to be using magazines and journals, newspapers, government documents, books, reference works, television and radio. You may also be generating some original research by conducting interviews and contacting people and organizations for information.

Magazines and Journals

Magazine and journal articles are probably the most common source of information for student speeches. With more than 190,000 magazines from which to choose, however, how do you keep from being overwhelmed with information?[16] Using an index will help you filter useful from extraneous information. Hundreds of excellent indexes of periodicals exist, and many standard indexes are now available online. These indexes can guide you as you focus your search even more.

The true monster trucks of academic research in periodicals today are full-text **databases.** They are so powerful because each gives you access to articles in hundreds or even *thousands* of periodicals and scholarly journals. You can then print useful articles or email them to another address. Moreover, if you are a registered college or university student, you have already paid to be able to use these research tools from any computer with Internet access through your school's library website.

Your library's staff has subscribed to a select group of computer databases and indexes with your school's student body in mind. Some of the general full-text databases likely available to you are listed in Figure 7.1. In addition, specialized indexes exist for almost every academic field. Subject-specific computer databases include *Alternative Health Watch, Biography Resource Center, Contemporary Women's Issues,* and so on, through the alphabet. Similar print indexes in the reference section of your library may include titles such as *Education Index, Hispanic American Periodicals Index,* and *Music Index.* Remember that, because these indexes are so specialized, the periodicals and journals they lead you to will likely be written for a specific audience; they may use jargon and technical language familiar only to people in that field. Even if you understand these articles easily, you may have to simplify their language and ideas for the more diverse audience of your classroom.

If you have particular magazines and journals in mind at any stage in your research, you can also check the online versions of these publications directly. Some magazines provide full-text copies of current issues, along with searchable archives; others give

Database/Index	What It Provides
Academic Search Premier	Full-text database of nearly 3,000 peer-reviewed academic journals in arts and literature, computer sciences, education, engineering, ethnic studies, humanities, language and linguistics, and medical sciences. Updated monthly.
AccuNet/AP Multimedia Archive	Searchable archive of Associated Press (AP) photos, charts, logos, maps, and other graphics produced for AP, 19th century to present. Brief stories accompany most photos 48 hours after publication.
CQ Researcher	Articles on all sides of current, controversial issues. Archive of past articles is searchable by keyword, dates, and other criteria.
ERIC	Full text education research from over 2,200 *ERIC Digests;* citations and abstracts from nearly 1,000 education journals.
InfoTrac OneFile	Articles from more than 10,000 periodicals: refereed academic journals, newspapers, newswires, business and technology publications, general interest magazines, along with titles specializing in law, health care, and computers. InfoTrac OneFile now includes two long-popular databases, Expanded Academic ASAP and General Reference Center Gold.
LexisNexis Academic	International business, health, law, news, and reference articles, most in full text. Updated continually.
Opposing Viewpoints Resource Center	Pro–con essays on controversial topics. Includes text of reference works, magazine and newspaper articles, websites, statistics, and images.
Project Muse	Full-text articles from more than 200 scholarly journals published by more than 20 nonprofit, scholarly presses in the arts, humanities, social sciences, and mathematics.
Science Resource Center	Full-text articles from more than 200 magazines, scholarly journals, and links to quality websites. Includes biographies, experiment descriptions, pictures, illustrations, topic overviews, and news of recent scientific discoveries.

FIGURE 7.1
Subscription Databases and Indexes

Try This
Comparing Online Searches

Once you have chosen a topic for an informative or a persuasive speech, research the topic using Google, one of the subscription databases listed in Figure 7.1, and one of the deep web search portals listed on page 135. Compare your results. Are they quantitatively different? Qualitatively different? Which online tool would you say led you to the best quality sources in the least amount of time? Be prepared to discuss the results of your three searches in class.

you only sample articles and subscription information. Though browsing individual magazines is not an efficient use of limited research time, searchable online periodicals can be useful. To locate an online magazine, choose a search engine such as Google (www.google.com), type the magazine title or even a descriptive phrase ("magazines about horses"), and click the search button.

Newspapers

Including articles on topics from aardvarks to zoos, newspapers offer abundant information—local, national, or international in scope. Large newspapers, such as the *New York Times,* the *Washington Post,* and the *Christian Science Monitor* have been indexed individually in the past. The computer index to the *New York Times,* for example, provides full text of all articles from 1851 to the present.

Today, however, your campus library is more likely to subscribe to powerful databases such as *LexisNexis Academic* that contain full-text newspaper articles, in addition to other sources. Other newspaper databases that may be available from your library's homepage include those listed in Figure 7.2.

Most newspapers now have sites on the World Wide Web and provide indexes to their own archives. If you have selected a localized topic, you may want to research specific newspapers directly. To find a specific newspaper, search for its title using a search engine like Google. If you're unsure about newspaper titles, *Newslink* (http:// newslink.org) lets you browse lists of U.S. newspapers by state, as well as world newspapers by continent or country, and click on links to specific papers. Some newspapers allow free access to archived articles for only a certain period of time; you may have to pay to read or print older articles. If the source is important, however, it may be worth it to use a credit card and shop for materials from the comfort of home.

The newspapers to which your library subscribes are usually transferred to microfilm or microfiche. As a result, libraries can house in just a few file drawers many years' worth of newspapers. You will find citations and abstracts of newspaper articles in other electronic databases. If the full-text document is not available and the article seems important to your research, check the catalog to see whether your library subscribes to that newspaper. If so, you can access and print the article from microfilm.

FIGURE 7.2
Newspaper Databases

Ethnic Newswatch	Full-text articles on news, culture, and history from 200 ethnic, minority, and native publications. Searchable in English and Spanish. Updated monthly.
Factiva	Full-text access to top national and international newspapers (including full text of the *Wall Street Journal*), newswires, business journals, market research reports, analysts' reports, and websites. Contains more than 8,000 publications with content from 118 countries in 22 languages. Updated daily. Formerly called Dow Jones Interactive.
Historical Newspapers: New York Times	Fully searchable access to the newspaper, beginning with issue number one in 1851. Includes full-page PDF images for non-copyrighted years.
Info-Trac Custom Newspapers	Major newspapers in your state, plus the *New York Times,* the *Los Angeles Times,* the *Christian Science Monitor,* the *Times* (London), and others.
NewsBank	Mostly full-text articles from U.S. and international newspapers, wire services, broadcasts, and magazines. Includes *Business NewsBank, NewsBank Retrospective* (1979–1991), *Noticias en Español, StatBank,* and *AccessUN.*

Government Documents

The most prolific publisher in the United States is the federal government. Much of our bureaucracy is devoted to collecting, cataloguing, and disseminating information. Luckily, most of what's available is accessible online: presidential speeches and transcripts of press conferences, pending legislation, contact information for senators and representatives, agency reports, and ordering information for documents not available online in full text. Online, you can take a virtual tour of the White House, listen to audio files of unedited argument before the Supreme Court, and see digital photographs of historical documents. In short, almost every federal agency has a website.

Your library probably subscribes to several government databases, among them *LexisNexis Government Periodicals Index*, *Federal Register Online*, and *MarciveWeb DOCS*. Searchable by keyword, these databases save you time.

With just a couple of web addresses, however, you can access virtually any area of the government. The Library of Congress maintains *THOMAS: Legislative Information on the Internet* at http://thomas.loc.gov. The Government Printing Office maintains a two-page list of links to government information products at www.access.gpo.gov. At those two sites, you can get any information you need from the legislative, executive, or judicial branches of the government.

Exploring *Online*

GOVERNMENT DOCUMENTS

http://thomas.loc.gov

This Library of Congress website helps you obtain information from the U.S. Congress. You can download House and Senate committee reports, summaries of bills being considered and notes about their status, copies of laws enacted, and even remarks recorded in the *Congressional Record*. Especially helpful is the FAQ (frequently asked questions) feature that describes how to conduct a search in *THOMAS*, how to download a bill or committee report, how to contact your representative or senators, how to cite the documents you find, and other information that will enhance your research skills.

Books

Books, of course, are excellent sources of information. Because they are longer than magazine and newspaper articles, books allow authors to discuss topics in greater depth and often provide an index to key ideas and a bibliography of sources consulted. Recognize, however, that if your speech topic requires the most up-to-date data you can find, information in magazines may be more current and accessible than what you can find in books. Despite this limitation, books can be an integral part of your research plan.

Today the online catalog in most academic libraries permits you to search by subject, title, author, and keyword. Keyword searches are especially productive, and many librarians recommend them. If your library catalog has a "Search Tips" feature, read it to make the search you conduct and the list of sources you print especially productive.

The book you need may be available as an eBook that you can access—"check out"—in your choice of formats after you establish a library account. On the Internet, full-text literary works are also well represented by Literature Online (*LION*), a searchable subscription database of about 200,000 British and American books.

> *There are times when I think that the ideal library is composed solely of reference books. They are like understanding friends—always ready to meet your mood, always ready to change the subject when you have had enough of this or that.*
>
> —J. DONALD ADAMS

Reference Works

Perhaps the heart of any library is its reference section. These resources, usually available for use only in the library, include many types of collections to aid you in your research. Today many reference works have moved online. Your school library has probably purchased site licenses giving you and other registered students free access to various reference works from the library or from remote sites. Whether you are using hard-copy versions in the library, accessing databases through your library's web page, or logging on to the Internet, a few of the reference works you will find most helpful are dictionaries, encyclopedias, almanacs, yearbooks, and books of quotations.

Dictionaries.   Dictionaries help you clarify the meanings, spellings, and pronunciations of words. Many good general dictionaries exist, and you undoubtedly use these regularly. A number of more specialized dictionaries covering a wide range of topic areas are also available. A list of a few of these follows.

The Dictionary of Advertising	*A Dictionary of Slang and Unconventional English*
A Dictionary of Bad Manners	*A Dictionary of Statistical Terms*
Dictionary of Business and Economics	*A Feminist Dictionary*
A Dictionary of Color	

Thousands of dictionaries exist on the Internet. At *yourDictionary.com* alone, you can access 2,500 dictionaries, glossaries, and thesauruses in more than 300 languages. The following sites represent both the useful and quirky dictionaries on the Internet:

Biographical Dictionary	www.s9.com
Dictionary of Botanical Words	www.botany.com/index.16.htm
The English-to-American Dictionary	http://english2american.com
Symbols.Com	http://symbols.com/index/wordindex-a.html

Examining some of these dictionaries could both generate topics for future speeches and provide information about your current topic.

Encyclopedias.   You have, no doubt, used general encyclopedias, such as *Encyclopedia Americana, Encyclopædia Britannica,* and *World Book,* to prepare reports and papers in elementary and high school. These multivolume sets of books exist today along with their electronic counterparts, such as *Britannica Online,* the *Video Encyclopedia of the 20th Century,* and the *Encyberpedia.* Some electronic encyclopedias, such as *Encyclopedia.Com,* are free. Unless you access others from a library or through a library website, however, you may have to pay for a subscription.

Either in print or as electronic files, encyclopedias organize information on many branches of knowledge. However, you may be less familiar with encyclopedias such as the following, that focus on specific bodies of knowledge.

Encyclopedia of American Humorists	*Encyclopedia of Forensic Sciences*
Encyclopedia of American Shipwrecks	*Encyclopedia of Jazz*
Encyclopedia of Black America	*Encyclopedia of Medical History*

Your library's reference shelves contain many other types of specialized encyclopedias. Consult your college librarian for advice about subject-specific encyclopedias in the library or online.

Almanacs.   "Almanacs and Bibles were the first books to come to the United States," writes Lois Horowitz:

> At a time when there were few newspapers, the settlers used almanacs for a melange of valuable information and entertainment. Almanacs predicted the weather for the coming year; gave advice on crops and planting; listed home remedies, multiplication

tables, interest charts, and even stagecoach schedules. They also included inspirational verse and stories.[17]

Though they no longer publish stagecoach schedules, almanacs contain a wide range of specific and statistical information about topics including education, politics, sports, entertainment, and significant events of a particular year. Almanacs are excellent sources when you need specific facts and background information. What is the exact wording of Amendment II of the United States Constitution? In what year did Mother Teresa win the Nobel Peace Prize? A good almanac answers these questions and many others. If you selected the history of space flights as your speech topic, an almanac would be a ready reference for the dates, duration, and description of those flights.

General almanacs on library reference shelves include the *World Almanac and Book of Facts, Information Please Almanac, The New York Times Almanac,* the *New York Public Library Reference,* and the heavily used *Statistical Abstract of the United States.* Specialized print almanacs cover a wide range of subjects, as illustrated by these examples: *Almanac for Computers, Almanac for American Politics, Almanac of Higher Education,* and *Almanac of World Crime.*

Today you can find a host of searchable almanacs online. You can use the online version of the *Information Please Almanac* at www.infoplease.com. There you will find more than fifty almanacs grouped into categories ranging from sports to business to science and technology. The Internet Public Library (www.ipl.org/div/subject/browse/ref05.00.00) gives you access to four different almanacs, including the *Information Please Almanac.*

Yearbooks.   Yearbooks are usually published annually and include information pertinent to that year or the previous year. Encyclopedia publishers, for example, often offer yearbooks as supplements to their main set of books. Yearbooks enable researchers to update information on a particular topic. *Facts on File Yearbook,* for example, digests and catalogs world news originally published in the weekly publication *Facts on File.* Your library may also subscribe to *Facts.com,* a searchable database containing the complete content from *Facts on File World News Digest* from 1980 to the present. The diversity of topics covered in yearbooks is illustrated by the following titles: *Yearbook of Agriculture, Yearbook of Higher Education, Yearbook of Emergency Medicine, Yearbook of School Law,* and the *World Yearbook of Robotics Research and Development.*

Books of Quotations.   Captivating quotations, both serious and funny, can enliven the language of your speech. As we noted earlier, they are particularly appropriate in speech introductions and conclusions. Quoting another person also adds authority to your comments and thus can strengthen the development of your ideas. Fortunately, many excellent books of quotations are available in bookstores, libraries, and online. At www.bartleby.com/100, you can access not only the long-popular *Bartlett's Familiar Quotations,* but also *The Columbia World of Quotations* and *Simpson's Contemporary Quotations.* Some of our other favorite books of quotations include *The American Heritage Dictionary of American Quotations, Collins Quotation Finder, Famous Last Words, Famous Phrases from History, Respectfully Quoted: A Dictionary of Quotations from the Library of Congress,* and *The Quotable Woman.* In books or online, collections of quotations are organized alphabetically by author or subject, with handy indexes or search functions.

Television and Radio

You can find ideas for excellent speech topics and materials to support them among the investigative reports on television and radio. Many programs provide transcripts for

purchase, with ordering information given at the show's conclusion. Even better, transcripts of a number of these shows now appear on the networks' websites. You can print them or save them to a disk. If you require older transcripts, you may have to order them online and pay a charge. Many programs on National Public Radio are archived for downloading and listening after their initial broadcast. To check out television and radio websites, the following mostly searchable URLs should be helpful.

Network	URL
ABC	http://abcnews.go.com
CBS	www.cbsnews.com
CNN	www.cnn.com
CNN/SI	http://sportsillustrated.cnn.com
C-SPAN	www.c-span.org
Fox News	www.foxnews.com
MSNBC	www.msnbc.msn.com
NBC	www.nbc.com/News_&_Sports
NPR	www.npr.org
PBS	www.pbs.org

Your library and video rental stores may have copies of special televised broadcasts such as the PBS documentary series *Lewis and Clark* or Martin Scorsese's *Bob Dylan: No Direction Home*. Through videotapes, you can research topics such as military battles, McCarthyism, and space exploration, to name just a few. Informational videotapes (as well as websites) can take you on tours of museums such as the Louvre or the Museum of Modern Art and of distant places such as Australia and Italy. Instructional tapes can teach you how to garden, refinish furniture, and make a sales presentation.

Interviews

Depending on your topic, an interview may be the best source of firsthand information. Today you can interview people by email, instant messaging, or in electronic chat rooms, as well as by telephone or in person. The personal interview can aid you in four ways. First, if published sources are inaccessible, the personal interview may be your only option. The topic you have chosen may be so recent that sufficient information is not yet in print or online. Your topic may also be so localized as to receive little or no coverage by area media.

A second advantage of the personal interview is that it permits you to adapt your topic to your specific audience. Take, for example, the topic of recycling. If you interview the director of your school's physical plant to find out how much trash custodians collect and dispose of each day, you give your speech a personal touch. You could take your speech one step further by figuring out how much your college could contribute to resource conservation. What you have done is show your audience how this topic, recycling, affects them directly. You will grab their attention.

Third, personal interviews provide opportunities for you to secure expert evaluation of your research and suggestions for further research. The experts you interview may challenge some of your assumptions or data. If this happens, encourage their feedback and don't get defensive. Knowing all the angles can only help you give a more thoughtful speech. Near the end of your interview, ask your interviewee to suggest additional sources that will help you better research and understand your topic.

Finally, personal interviews can enhance your image as a speaker. Listeners are usually impressed that you went beyond library research in preparing your message for them.

Key Points

Preparing for the Interview

1. Determine whom you want to interview.
2. Decide the format for the interview.
3. Schedule the interview.
4. Research the person to be interviewed.
5. Prepare a list of questions.

Prepare for the Interview.   Once you decide to conduct a personal interview, you must take several steps in preparation. First, determine whom you want to interview. Your interviewee should be someone who is both knowledgeable on the topic and willing to speak with you.

Second, decide on the format for the interview. Will you conduct it face to face, by phone, or online? A face-to-face interview may give you the most information. People tend to open up more when they interact verbally and nonverbally. As a face-to-face interviewer, you can both listen to what the interviewee says and observe the nonverbal messages. An interview over the phone is another possibility when you cannot travel to the expert. A third option, conducting an interview by email or computer chat room, has both advantages and disadvantages. The email interview is time consuming because you must prepare a set of questions, send it to the interviewee, and wait for a response. It has the added disadvantage of not allowing for immediate follow-up questions. If something needs clarification, you must email another question. An interview in a chat room or by instant messaging eliminates this time lag. However, the email interview often results in more thoughtful and better worded responses than face-to-face, telephone, or chatroom interviews.

The third preparation step is to schedule the interview. When requesting an interview, identify yourself and the topic on which you seek information. Let the person know how you intend to use that information, the amount of time needed for the interview, and any special recording procedures you plan to use. Some people may object to being quoted or to having their comments recorded. If this is the case, it is best to find that out ahead of time rather than at the interview. You are likely to discover that most people you seek to interview are flattered that you selected them as experts and are therefore happy to cooperate.

Fourth, research the person to be interviewed before you show up at his or her doorstep. Obviously, your selection of the interviewee suggests that you already know something about him or her. In addition, read any articles the interviewee has published on your topic before the interview. This enables you to conduct the interview efficiently. You won't ask questions that the person has already answered in print, and your prior reading may prompt some specific questions on points you would like clarified. Also, your research will show that you are prepared. The interviewee will take you and the interview seriously.

Open questions, such as those that begin with the phrase, "How do you feel about," can elicit more substantive responses from interviewees than do closed yes or no questions.

Fifth, prepare a list of questions. Always have more questions than you think you will be able to ask, just in case you are mistaken. Mark those that are most important to your research, and make sure you ask them first. You may want to have some closed and some open questions, as Joel did when he interviewed a professor of recreation for his speech on how American adults spend their leisure time. *Closed questions* are those that can be answered with a yes, a no, or a short answer. For example, Joel asked, "Do American adults have more time for leisure activities today than they did a generation ago?" and "How many hours per week does the typical adult spend watching TV?" The first question can be answered by a yes or a no; the second, with a specific figure.

Open questions invite longer answers and can produce a great deal of information. Joel asked this open question: "How do American adults typically spend their leisure time?" When you ask open questions, sit back and prepare to listen for a while! The less time you have for the interview, the fewer open questions you should ask. Open questions can sometimes result in rambling, unnecessary information. At other times, the interviewee's rambling will trigger questions you would not have thought of otherwise. Joel was surprised to learn that American adults spend approximately two hours a week in adult education, a venture he had not included on his initial list of adult leisure activities. When you and the interviewee have plenty of time, and particularly if you are tape recording the interview, open questions can provide the richest information.

Conduct the Interview. The face-to-face interview is an excellent opportunity to practice your interpersonal communication skills. Specifically, you should follow these guidelines. First, introduce yourself when you arrive, thank the person for giving you time, and restate the purpose of the interview.

Second, conduct the interview in a professional manner. If you interview the president of the local savings and loan, don't show up in cut-off jeans, sandals, and your favorite flannel shirt. Make sure you arrive appropriately dressed, ready and able to set up and handle any recording equipment with a minimum of distractions. Try to relax the interviewee, establish a professional atmosphere, pose questions that are clear and direct, listen actively, take notes efficiently, and follow up when necessary. You should control the interview without appearing to be pushy or abrupt.

Third, thank the person again for the interview when you have finished.

Follow up on the Interview.   After the interview, review your notes or listen to your tape recording. Do this as soon as possible after the interview, when your memory is still fresh. If you are unclear about something that was said, do not use that information in your speech. You could call your subject to clarify the point if you think it will be important to the audience's understanding of the topic.

As a matter of courtesy, you should write to the people you interviewed, thanking them for the time and help they gave you. You may even want to send them a copy of your finished speech if it is in manuscript form.

Calling, Writing, and Emailing for Information

Some years ago, one of us taught a student, Lindahl, who wanted to develop an informative speech on the savant syndrome. This was before Dustin Hoffman's portrayal of Raymond in the film *Rain Man* made many people aware of the special talents and disabilities of savants. Lindahl had seen a *60 Minutes* segment on the syndrome, but could not find recent written sources. Her best source, she said, was an article from a three-year-old issue of *Time*. Others might have abandoned their research and switched topics, but Lindahl followed a hunch that paid off for her.

The *Time* article quoted several university professors and medical doctors who were engaged in ongoing research on the savant syndrome. Lindahl got their office telephone numbers through directory assistance. She called these experts to see if they could recommend new sources she had been unable to locate. Lindahl found that the people she called were all flattered by her attention and complimented her perseverance as a researcher. One psychologist mailed her a photocopy of a book chapter she had written on the savant syndrome; a medical doctor mailed Lindahl a packet of journal articles, including the galleys of an article of his that was about to be published; a psychology professor mailed her a tape of savants who had incredible musical talents playing piano concertos they had heard for the first time only moments before. In short, Lindahl received a gold mine of new, expert research as a result of her few long-distance calls. If Lindahl were to conduct such a search today, she might find that email would be a quicker, if less personal, way to contact the experts.

Lindahl was lucky that she began her research more than a month before her speech was due. To take advantage of pamphlets and brochures available through the mail, you will need to plan ahead as well. But thousands of organizations, such as the American Cancer Society and the United Way, publish their own informational literature. Political parties and lobbying groups prepare position papers on issues that affect them. Corporations distribute annual reports to their stockholders and will share these with people who request them. You can write to or email any of these organizations. Most have contact information posted on web pages. You can locate URLs for companies or groups through search indexes available online. Unfortunately, no index comprehensively catalogs the information available from such groups, so you must take the initiative in tracking down what you need. One source that can be helpful is the *Encyclopedia of Associations* (call number AS22.E5). This publication is divided into three volumes: National Organizations of the U.S.; International Organizations; and Regional, State, and Local Organizations. Each volume lists names, addresses, telephone numbers, email addresses, and URLs for websites, along with descriptions of the organizations. The information is also available through some libraries in *Associations Unlimited,* an electronic database of nonprofit organizations. Remember, this research source will not help you if you have five days left before your deadline. But if time permits and research warrants, writing, calling, or emailing these organizations to request information can add relevant primary research to your speech.

You may also want to use a listserv, a newsgroup, or even a live chat group to investigate your subject in more detail. Listservs are interest groups that use email to distribute messages among members. Your research librarian (or computer lab instructor) can show you how to locate and subscribe to a listserv on your topic. Once you have joined, you will receive all messages sent to the list, so you can read questions, responses, and ongoing discussions on your topic. Because most listserv members take a serious interest in their subject matter, it is probably best for you to "lurk" (simply read the group's exchanges for a while), before posting messages of your own. Some lists maintain a posting of frequently asked questions on their topic so that new members can catch up on background information. After you have read through these questions, if you decide to pursue the topic area for your speech, you can join in the ongoing conversation and ask targeted questions that should produce knowledgeable responses.

Newsgroups also focus on a topic of interest to all participants, but they are more like interactive bulletin boards. The group posts information—sometimes from professional news services—that readers can respond to with their own messages. Each time a new piece of information is posted, a "thread" of inquiry and debate begins to develop among users. Again, ask your librarian or computer lab instructor to help you locate a newsgroup on your topic; then read and study the group's posting of frequently asked questions before you contribute to an ongoing thread.

You may also want to participate in live chat sessions that you find on your topic. In these sessions, participants exchange messages instantaneously online, so chat resembles spontaneous conversation. However, many chats are unmonitored and somewhat unfocused, so they are likely to be less useful than newsgroup and listserv discussions. If you do begin exchanging ideas with other listserv or newsgroup participants, be sure to save on disk or print any information you may want to use in your speech.

Record Your Information

Once you have located information, you must determine what to record and how to record it.

What to Record

When in doubt, record more rather than less. Certainly, it is possible to copy too much information. If you find everything potentially important, your topic probably needs better focus. Without some focus, you run the risk of becoming so bogged down in research that you leave little time for organizing and practicing your speech.

On the other hand, if you are too selective, you may be inefficient. As you research your speech, you may shift your topic focus, and hence the supporting material you previously thought was irrelevant becomes important. Discarding unnecessary information is easier than trying to remember a source, retracing your steps, hoping that the information is still on the library shelves, or that the Internet source is still live, and then recording that information.

How to Record Information

Traditional advice to researchers is to record each piece of information on a separate notecard, along with the source citation, as you find it. With this strategy, you can organize your speech visually and experiment with different structures. The disadvantage of this method of recording information is that it consumes a great deal of library time that might be better devoted to searching for other sources. In addition, much of what you record on notecards may not be used in your speech at all.

Another, more common method is to photocopy material at the library or to print articles you find online and read them later. Sometimes the simplest and most thorough way to record research information is to photocopy pages from books, documents, reference works, or even entire articles. Later, at your leisure and in more comfortable surroundings, you can review, evaluate, and select from the photocopied materials. However, be aware that photocopies or printed articles may lull you into a false sense of accomplishment. What you have copied may later turn out to be of little or no use. How can you avoid this problem? Read your material before or very shortly after photocopying it. Do not wait until the night before your speech to read the pile of information you have been collecting on the role of women pilots in World War II.

Exploring *Online*

CITING ELECTRONIC SOURCES
www.mla.org
http://apastyle.org/elecref.html
Both the Modern Language Association and the American Psychological Association have websites, with examples of documentation that may be more current than those in their published style manuals. The only Internet guidelines for MLA documentation authorized by the MLA are available at their site. The APA site features their guidelines for citing information from the Internet and the World Wide Web.

Also, remember to note your sources on the copied pages. If the web page URL does not appear as a header or footer on printed pages, be sure to note it. You'd be wise to photocopy the table of contents of each magazine or journal from which you use an article. Copy the page or pages containing publication information for each book you use. If you follow these simple directions, photocopying and printing have two additional advantages over using notecards. First, you may not know what you want to use from an article at the time you first find it. If the focus of your speech changes, a different part of the article may become important. Indeed, sometimes your research forces you to refocus the speech topic. Second, if you are quoting from or paraphrasing one specific part of an article, you may need to check later to make sure that you are not quoting the author out of context. Having a photocopy or print of the book chapter, the journal article, or the encyclopedia entry lets you check the context and the accuracy of your quotation.

If you are gathering information from the Internet, be sure to print out the pages you will need or download the information to a disk. Remember that what appears on the Internet is ephemeral—it disappears quickly. If you do not capture it in print or store it in a file when you find it, you may have to forego using the information in your speech if you cannot locate it again. If you do not know how to create a storage file for Internet material, ask your librarian or computer lab instructor for help.

It is important to record full citations of sources you have consulted in your research in a bibliography at the end of your speech. Your **bibliography** is simply a list

bibliography: an orderly list of works consulted or cited during the preparation and delivery of a speech.

of works you have consulted in developing your speech. Most writer's handbooks will recommend a particular bibliographic form. Two popular forms are those presented in the *Modern Language Association Handbook for Writers of Research Papers* and the *Publication Manual of the American Psychological Association*. Be sure to check with your instructor, who may have a preference for one of these or some other bibliographic form.

Copies of the two style manuals we just listed are probably in your library's reference section. Figures 7.3 and 7.4 compare the bibliographic forms each presents. Whether you want to cite a segment of National Public Radio's *All Things Considered*, a stop-smoking videotape, or lecture notes you took in an anthropology class last week, the most recent editions of these reference books are likely to give you a pattern to follow.

Conclude Your Search

As you prepare your speech, you must make choices. Your goal is to support your ideas with the most compelling evidence and arguments you can find. The adage "Knowledge

FIGURE 7.3
MLA Form for Some Common Types of Sources

Book	Rivoli, Pietra. *The Travels of a T-Shirt in the Global Economy: An Economist Examines the Markets, Power, and Politics of World Trade.* Hoboken, NJ: Wiley, 2005.
Edited book	Ben-Joseph, Eran, and Terry S. Szold, eds. *Regulating Place: Standards and the Shaping of Urban America.* New York: Routledge-Taylor & Frances, 2005.
Article in weekly magazine	Kluger, Jeffrey. "When Gambling Becomes Obsessive." *Time* 1 Aug. 2005: 52–54.
Article in monthly magazine	Benchich, Elisabeth A. "What Happens When Galaxies Collide?" *Astronomy* Sept. 2005: 32–37.
Newspaper article	Wade, Nicholas. "Your Body Is Younger than You Think." *New York Times* 2 Aug. 2005, Washington ed.: D1+.
Article in online magazine	Kemper, Steve. "Shark." *Smithsonian* Aug. 2005. 9 Aug. 2005 <http://www.smithsonianmag.si.edu/smithsonian/issues05/aug05/shark.html>.
Article in online newspaper	O'Brien, Dennis. "Creation of First Cloned Dog Represents Medical Breakthrough, Ethical Dilemma." *Baltimore Sun* 4 Aug. 2005. 4 Aug. 2005 <http://www.baltimoresun.com/news/health/bal-te.cloning04aug04,1,5551158.story?coll=bal-health-headlines&ctrack=1&cset=true>.
Document available on university website	Ray, Benjamin C. *African Art: Aesthetics and Meaning.* 28 Oct. 2004. 9 Aug. 2005 <http://www.lib.virginia.edu/clemons/RMC/exhib/93.ray.aa/African.html>.
Organization website	StopHazing.org. "Hazing News." 9 Aug. 2005. 9 Aug. 2005 <http://www.stophazing.org/news/index.htm>.
Posting to online forum	Reeves, Thomas C. "Heretics Like Us Need Tenure." Online posting. 15 June 2005. NAS Online Forum. 9 Aug. 2005 <http://www.nas.org/forum.html>.

Book	Rivoli, P. (2005). *The travels of a t-shirt in the global economy: An economist examines the markets, power, and politics of world trade.* Hoboken, NJ: Wiley.	**FIGURE 7.4** **APA Form for Some Common Types of Sources**
Edited book	Ben-Joseph, E., & Szold, T. S. (Eds.). (2005). *Regulating place: Standards and the shaping of urban America.* New York: Routledge.	
Article in weekly magazine	Kluger, J. (2005, August 1). When gambling becomes obsessive. *Time,* 52–54.	
Article in monthly magazine	Benchich, E. A. (2005, September). What happens when galaxies collide? *Astronomy,* 32–37.	
Newspaper article	Wade, N. (2005, August 2). Your body is younger than you think. *The New York Times,* pp. D1, D4.	
Article in online magazine	Kemper, S. (2005, August). Shark. *Smithsonian.* Retrieved August 9, 2005, from http://www.smithsonianmag.si.edu/smithsonian/issues05/aug05/shark.html	
Article in online newspaper	O'Brien, D. (2005, August 4). Creation of first cloned dog represents medical breakthrough, ethical dilemma. *Baltimore Sun.* Retrieved August 4, 2005, from http://www.baltimoresun.com/news/health/bal-te.cloning.04aug,5551158.story?coll=bal-health-headlines&ctrack=1&cset=true	
Document available on university website	Ray, B. C. (2004, October 28). *African art: Aesthetics and meaning.* Retrieved August 9, 2005, from Bayly Art Museum, University of Virginia website: http://www.lib.virginia.edu/clemons/RMC/exhib/93.ray.aa/African.html	
Organization website	StopHazing.org. (2005, August 9). Hazing News. Retrieved August 9, 2005, from http://www.stophazing.org/news/index.htm	
Posting to online forum	Reeves, T. C. (2005, June 15). Heretics like us need tenure. Message posted to http://www.nas.org/forum.html	

is power" certainly applies to speech making; the more you know about your topic, the greater your flexibility in determining its content and, subsequently, its impact. This concept of choice may make your task more complex, but it will also produce a more effective speech.

There is a limit, however, to the time you can spend researching. An important part of effective research is knowing when to stop accumulating materials and when to start using them. In his book *Finding Facts Fast,* Alden Todd provides the following guideline for research projects:

> If the last 10 percent of your planned research time has brought excellent results, you are doubtless on a productive new track and should extend the project. But if the last 25 percent of your scheduled time has brought greatly diminished results, this fact is a signal to wind up your research.[18]

"If we would have knowledge, we must get a world of new questions."

—SUSANNE K. LANGER

Although Todd's 10/25 formula may not be wholly applicable to your researching a speech for this class, it does highlight an important issue: At some point you must stop researching and start structuring your speech.

In the next chapter, we discuss the purposes and types of supporting material. Understanding these topics will help you evaluate your research and select the best information to support the ideas of your speech.

Summary

Research is the process of gathering information and evidence to understand, develop, and explain your topic. Learning to research is fundamental to mastering public speaking. Even if you are not required to use outside sources for a particular speech, knowing your subject thoroughly greatly reduces your speech anxiety. An agenda for thorough research of a subject involves five steps.

First, assess your knowledge of the subject and begin to organize that knowledge. Chances are good that you chose the topic because you were interested in it or already knew something about it. Keeping an *article file* and a *quotation file* on subjects that interest you gives you a head start in your research. As you prepare the speech and after you deliver it, keep your research notes and speaking notes or manuscript in a *speech file*.

Second, develop a research plan for your topic. What information do you need? Where can you find it? How can you get it in the time you have? Your topic may lead you to interview people or collect printed information from businesses and organizations. Sooner or later, however, you will probably need to search online or use a local library efficiently. Reference librarians can teach you the strengths and limitations of the library you select.

The third step in research is to collect information from a variety of sources. Potential sources include magazines and journals, newspapers, government documents, books, and reference works, including dictionaries, encyclopedias, almanacs, yearbooks, and books of quotations. Many of these sources are also available online. Productive online research requires you to be able to use available databases or to launch out onto the Internet using popular, academic, and rating search engines. Sources outside the library include interviews and electronic media resources such as radio, television, and videotape. Interviews allow you to collect authoritative, unpublished information on your subject, but they require special planning and preparation. You must select the best interviewee, decide on the format, schedule the interview, research the interviewee you have selected, and prepare a list of questions. After conducting the interview in a competent, professional manner and promptly recording the information you have gathered from it, you should send a note of thanks to the person you interviewed.

The fourth step in research is to record the information you consider important and useful. You may choose to take notes on notecards or to photocopy or print your information. In either case, be sure to record the source of the information—author, title, and publication information—using a current *bibliography* form.

The fifth and final step in research is to conclude your search. The quality and quantity of the information you collect will not only help you focus and organize the subject, but should also signal you when you have exhausted your research efforts.

Practice Critique

Evaluating Research

Suppose that the International Olympic Committee just declared public speaking to be a new event for the Olympic Games. You've been hired as a coach for the U.S. Olympic Public Speaking Team. Suppose, further, that Susan Chontos has entered her speech "The Amish: Seeking to Lose the Self" in the competition. Read the transcript of this speech in Chapter 15. Then write Susan a letter to help her develop a research plan for revising her speech. What information should remain in her speech? What information needs to be updated, clarified, and/or improved? Where could she search for this information?

Exercises

1. Select a topic for one of your speeches; then answer the following questions:
   a. What information do I need?
   b. Where am I most likely to find this information?
   c. How can I obtain the information?
   d. How will time constraints affect my research options?

2. Using any magazine or journal index listed in this chapter, construct a bibliography of at least seven sources for an upcoming speech. Locate at least three of these articles.

3. Using a print or an online newspaper index, construct a bibliography of at least five sources for an upcoming speech. Locate at least three of these articles.

4. Which of the reference works discussed in this chapter could you consult to answer the following questions?
   a. What is the derivation of the word *boycott*?
   b. What is the per capita personal income in your state?
   c. Gordon Matthew Sumner is the real name of what music icon? How did this artist obtain his nickname?
   d. The first Earth Day was celebrated on what date?
   e. What is the preferred pronunciation of the word *data*? In how many other ways can it be pronounced correctly?
   f. The swallows return to San Juan Capistrano on or around St. Joseph's Day. What is this date?
   g. What is the history of tiramisu?
   h. In what year and what city was the first Super Bowl played? Who won the game?

5. Using books of quotations, such as those listed in this chapter, prepare a list of at least two quotations on each of the following topics:
   a. Making a Good First Impression
   b. The Importance of Friendship
   c. The Dangers of Student Apathy
   d. Appreciating Diversity
   Bring your list to class and be prepared to discuss how you could use some of the quotations in a speech. Which would contribute to an effective introduction or conclusion? Which could be used to illustrate an idea in the body of a speech?

6. Select an expert to interview for an upcoming speech. Using suggestions in the chapter, arrange, prepare for, and conduct an interview, and follow up on it.

Supporting Your Speech

chapter

8

> *A fact in itself is nothing. It is valuable only for the idea attached to it, or for the proof which it furnishes.* —CLAUDE BERNARD

Solo rock climbing is a sport for serious-minded, physically fit people. Before tackling the face of a cliff, climbers study their routes and gather the proper equipment for the conditions they are likely to encounter. All this helps them proceed more safely from one particular point to another on the face of the rock. Just as rock climbers use their planning, strength, and equipment to secure themselves to points on the face of a cliff, you will use the supporting materials in your speech to provide specific points of reference for your audience. Your goal is to present a clear, memorable, and believable message to your audience. Effective supporting materials help you anchor your ideas in the minds of your listeners.

When you think of argument, you likely think of two people trying to persuade each other. In a real sense, however, all public speaking is argument. We should speak and accept ideas only if they are supported with sufficient evidence and reasoning. Speakers must prove what they assert in informative speeches, as well as in persuasive ones. For example, when Susan Chontos tells her audience in her speech in Chapter 15, "The second major tenet of the Amish faith is the desire to be simple, or plain," she introduces an idea that they may accept or reject. Listeners should think critically and evaluate the merits of that statement based on the evidence Susan offers for its support.

Toward the end of Chapter 3, we recommended a formula for structuring each major idea in your speech. This pattern, called the "4 S's," consists of *signposting, stating, supporting,* and *summarizing* each of your key ideas. In Chapter 9, we will explain this pattern in detail and show examples of how to use it. In this chapter, however, we focus on the third of these four S's: *supporting* your major ideas. You will learn more about the purposes of supporting materials. We will also discuss and show you examples of seven types of supporting materials you can use. Finally, we'll suggest ways to evaluate your evidence and how to cite it to ensure that you communicate your ideas clearly, memorably, and authoritatively.

Purposes of Supporting Materials

Supporting materials in a speech serve a variety of purposes. They help give your ideas clarity, vividness, and credibility.

Clarity

A sign in an Austrian ski hotel says, "Not to perambulate the corridors in the hours of repose in the boots of ascension."[1] Translation (we assume): Don't tramp down the halls in ski boots while guests are sleeping. You have no doubt seen other examples of what happens when well-meaning people translate English. Yet even people whose first language is English can send unclear messages in that language. Thus we have an advertisement on a bag of chips: "You may be a winner! Details inside! No purchase necessary."

As a speaker, your first goal is to communicate clearly. *Clarity* refers to the exactness of a message. The clarity of any message you send results partly from your language, as we discuss in Chapter 12. In addition, the supporting material you choose should make your message clear. As you develop a speech, ask yourself, "Does my supporting material really explain, amplify, or illustrate the point I'm trying to make?" If it does not, disregard it and continue your search for relevant material. Clear supporting materials help listeners better understand your ideas.

Vividness

Suppose that someone wanted to compare the number of deaths resulting from the terrorist attacks on the World Trade Center in New York City in September 2001 with the bombing of the Murrah Federal Building in Oklahoma City in April 1995. Which of the following statements makes a stronger impression?

> Considerably more people died in the New York City terrorist attacks than in Oklahoma City.

or

> At the anniversary of the Oklahoma City blast, people traditionally stand in silence one second for each victim—168 seconds, or nearly three minutes, which feels excruciating. To do the same in New York City would take almost an hour and a half.[2]

The first comment is something that Amanda Ripley, social issues commentator for *Time* magazine, could have said. The second is what she actually wrote to demonstrate the enormity of the loss in New York City. Which statement do you think is more vivid? Most people would choose the second statement as more vivid and memorable. Why? The first remark is general; the second, specific.

In this chapter, we use several excerpts from speeches to illustrate various types of supporting materials. Once you finish reading the chapter, you will no doubt remember some of the examples and forget others. Those you remember will be ones you found particularly vivid. *Vivid* supporting materials are striking, graphic, intense, and memorable. A major purpose of supporting materials, then, is to help your audience remember the key points in your speech. You will accomplish this best by using vivid forms of support chosen with your unique audience in mind.

Credibility

You gasp as you see the headline "Scientists Discover Microbial Life on Mars." Would it make a difference whether you saw this on the cover of *Scientific American* or the *National Enquirer*? Of course it would. "Microbial life" is nothing to the folks who write for the tabloids; they've shown photographic evidence of human faces carved into the Martian landscape! On the other hand, a scientific article reviewed and selected for publication by a panel of experts is significantly more believable than an article from any weekly tabloid. **Credibility** refers to the dependability or believability of a speaker or that speaker's sources.

Many ideas in the speeches you prepare will require simple supporting materials: short definitions, brief examples, or quick comparisons, for example. In other instances, you may present complex or controversial ideas that require several types of supporting materials. A speech with all its ideas and support taken from a single source is too limited. Using several sources to corroborate your ideas and facts can be a valuable and persuasive tool. Your main points will be more credible if you present evidence that these ideas are shared by several experts.

credibility: the believability or dependability of speakers and their sources.

You establish clarity by explaining your idea so that listeners *understand* it. You establish vividness by presenting your idea so that listeners will *remember* it. Finally, you establish credibility by presenting the idea so that listeners *believe* it. If the supporting materials in your speech make the audience understand, remember, and believe what you say, you have done a good job selecting them.

Accomplishing these goals will require you to use four critical thinking skills. You will *focus* and *evaluate* as you select specific pieces of information and measure their quality. You will *analyze* as you examine different supporting materials to see how they fit together to clarify your message. Finally, you will *integrate* as you combine and restructure your information in a way that is both appropriate to your listeners and uniquely your own.

You know that you want to present clear, vivid, and believable supporting materials. But how do you make sure people understand, remember, and believe your message? You have a wide range to choose from as you organize your supporting materials. Next we discuss the most common types of supporting materials and show you how they can work effectively in your speech.

Types of Supporting Materials

To help you achieve clarity, vividness, and credibility in your speaking, consider seven types of supporting material available to you: examples, definition, narration, comparison, contrast, statistics, and testimony. Keep in mind that there is no one best type of support for your ideas. Select what is most appropriate to your topic, your audience, and yourself.

Examples

An **example** is a specific illustration of a category of people, places, objects, actions, experiences, or conditions. In other words, examples are specimens or representations of a general group. The sound of the word itself gives perhaps the easiest definition to remember, however: An *example* is a *sample* of something. Measles, mumps, and chicken pox are examples of common childhood illnesses. *Schindler's List, Saving Private Ryan,* and *War of the Worlds* are examples of Steven Spielberg movies. Using examples that are familiar to listeners is an excellent way to make your points more clear and memorable. This, of course, requires you to have done some good audience analysis.

Brief Examples.   In your speech you can use either brief examples, such as those just noted, or extended ones. Brief examples are short, specific instances of the general category you are discussing. They may be used individually, but are often grouped together. Notice how Jocelyn combined a number of brief examples early in her speech on the attractions of New York City:

> Your walking tour of midtown Manhattan could take you to places as diverse as St. Patrick's Cathedral, Rockefeller Center, the Gotham Book Mart, and the Museum of Modern Art. Try not to gawk as you look at some of the most famous architecture in the world—the Chrysler Building, the Empire State Building, and Grand Central Station. Tired of pounding the pavement? Slip into a chair in the Algonquin Hotel's dim lobby, soak up the literary history, ring the bell on your table, and order something to drink. Hungry? You've got the world's table to choose from—everything from four-star restaurants to little holes in the wall serving the best ethnic dishes: Chinese, Vietnamese, Indian, Mexican, Thai.

example: a sample or illustration of a category of people, places, objects, actions, experiences, or conditions.

Supporting materials clarify, enliven, and add credibility to your speech. When you prepare for delivery, ensure accuracy by recording in complete form any quotations or definitions you plan to use.

Extended Examples. Extended examples are lengthier and more elaborate than brief examples. They allow you to create more detailed pictures of a person, place, object, experience, or condition. Later in her speech, Jocelyn developed an extended example of one of her favorite New York City attractions:

> Beginning with my second visit to New York, one of my first stops has usually been the Museum of Modern Art. If you're like me, you'll need to give yourself at least a couple of hours here, because for a small admission price you're going to get a chance to see up close art that you've only seen before as photographs in books. Upstairs on my last visit, I saw works such as Vincent Van Gogh's *Starry Night* and Roy Lichtenstein's huge pop art paintings of comic strip panels. My favorite Lichtenstein was one called *Oh, Jeff, I Love You Too, But. . . .* On a wall with a number of other paintings was a canvas so small that I almost missed it. I'm glad I didn't. It was Salvador Dali's famous surrealist work, *The Persistence of Memory,* with its melting clock and watch faces. Then over in a corner is a special room that holds only one painting. As you walk in, you see an expanse of gray carpet and several upholstered benches. One wall is glass, two others are white and bare, but the fourth one holds the three panels of Claude Monet's massive painting, *Waterlilies.*

Notice how vividly this extended example suggests a scene and re-creates an experience. But whether your examples are brief or extended, they can be of two further types: actual and hypothetical.

Actual Examples. An **actual example** is real or true. Each of the examples we've used so far is an actual example. Steven Spielberg did direct the three films listed. The Chrysler Building and the Empire State Building are famous New York landmarks.

Notice how Ali tells a real story in her speech on binge drinking on college campuses:

> A skier since age five, Scott Kreuger knew he had a good shot at becoming the next captain of his university's ski team. Thrilled at the possibility, Scott braced himself. According to the *Christian Science Monitor* of May 8, 2000, on the day of the competition he

actual example: a true instance or illustration.

had an early pasta lunch to settle his stomach, and then he went for it. Scott and twelve other members of his ski team gathered that night around a keg in his basement while friends and girlfriends stood by. At countdown, they began chugging one beer a minute. The last one to throw-up would become captain. Finally, with an alcohol blood level of .22, Scott lost it at twelve beers. He didn't even make junior captain.[3]

Later in this chapter we'll show how Ali combined this one example with statistics, another type of supporting materials, to develop a compelling case against binge drinking.

Hypothetical Examples.   A **hypothetical example**, on the other hand, is imaginary or fictitious. A speaker often signals hypothetical examples with phrases such as, "Suppose that," "Imagine yourself," or "What if." Hypothetical examples clarify and vivify the point you are making, but they do not prove the point.

Notice how the following introduction mentions actual products but places them in a hypothetical situation. The speaker chose this method knowing that not all listeners would have all the products listed. The speaker then generalizes from these examples to support the claim that we live in an electronic world.

> We wake up in the morning to soothing music coming from our AM/FM digital clock radio equipped with a gentle wake-up feature. We stumble downstairs, enticed by the aroma of coffee brewed by a preset coffee maker with 24-hour digital clock timer and automatic shut-off function. We zap on our 34-inch wide-screen HDTV with on-screen display of current time and channel. As we sit in our six-way action recliner, we use our 26-function wireless remote to perform the ritual of the morning channel check. Finding nothing that captures our interest, we decide instead to watch the video of last week's family reunion recorded with our 12X power zoom, fully automatic digital camcorder with self-timer, electronic viewfinder, and "flying erase head for 'rainbow'-free edits." Oh dear! What would our grandparents think? Certainly, we live in an electronic world!

Definition

A **definition** tells us the meaning of a word, a phrase, or a concept. Definitions are essential if your audience is unfamiliar with the vocabulary you use or if there are multiple definitions of a particular term. You want to clarify terms early in your speech so you don't confuse your listeners and lose their attention.

Definitions can take several forms. Four of the most common are definition by synonym, definition by etymology, definition by example, and definition by operation. Choose the form most appropriate to your audience and to the term you want to clarify, and your audience will remember it.

Definition by Synonym.   The first type of definition is **definition by synonym**. Synonyms are words that have similar meanings. You have probably used a thesaurus when writing a term paper or report. A thesaurus is simply a dictionary of synonyms. Consider these pairs of words:

mendacity and *dishonesty*	*pariah* and *outcast*
plethora and *excess*	*anathema* and *curse*
mitigate and *lessen*	*surreptitious* and *secret*

Each word is coupled with one of its synonyms. The first word of each pair is probably not a part of your listeners' working vocabulary. As a speaker, you would want to use the second word in each pair; those words are more familiar and thus more vivid. The second word of each pair communicates more clearly. As the joke goes, never use a big word when a diminutive one will do.

hypothetical example: an imaginary or fictitious instance or illustration.

definition: an explanation of the meaning of a word, phrase, or concept.

definition by synonym: substituting a word having similar meaning for the word being defined.

A student in one of our introductory public speaking classes used definition by synonym in his speech on the ritual of bullfighting. After introducing each Spanish term, he provided its English translation. Notice how unobtrusively he defines terms in the following excerpt describing the parade to the bullfighting ring: "The *matadores* enter the ring as the band strikes up a *paso doble*, or two-step. Each matador is followed by a *guardia*, or a team of helpers. . . ." By using two languages, the speaker gave his speech a Spanish flavor, yet his English-speaking audience understood his description clearly.

Definition by Etymology.   A second type of definition is **definition by etymology.** Etymology is the study of word origins. You may find that describing how a word has developed clarifies its meaning. For example, the word *decimate* means "to destroy a large portion of," as in, "The hailstorm decimated the soybean crop." You may not know that *decimate* comes from the Latin word for *ten* or *tenth*. The word *decim* was a common military term used by the ancient Romans. If soldiers mutinied against their generals, the entire group was punished. The troops were lined up and every tenth soldier was killed, whether guilty or innocent. This arbitrary punishment made others think twice before trying similar action against their leaders. Not only a word's origin but also the history of a word's use can be fascinating.

Most of the time we use definitions to make an unfamiliar term familiar. However, you can also use definition by etymology to highlight the unusual nature of a familiar term. The following etymological definition of the word *debate* is from John Ciardi's *A Browser's Dictionary*. Notice how Ciardi captures both the meaning and the flavor of the word as he traces its historical evolution:

> **debate:** Now signifies a formal presentation of arguments and counterarguments within parliamentary guidelines and time limits. As the formal rules of debate are lost, the discussion descends to wrangling. [Yet wrangling is the root sense. <L. *de-*, down (also functions as an intensive); *battere*, to beat (BATTERY, ABATE). This root sense is nicely expressed by the colorful It. word *battibecco*, hot argument; lit. "a beating of beaks" (as if two birds are fencing).][4]

That image of birds fighting with their beaks certainly enlivens this definition. The reference section of your library and a variety of websites will have a number of dictionaries of word origins and histories of word usage. We enjoy browsing in them, and in Chapter 17 we use definition by etymology to explain the red herring and bandwagon fallacies of reasoning (see pages 354–355, 356–357).

Definition by Example.   An example is a specific instance or illustration of a larger group or classification. **Definition by example** uses a specific instance to clarify a general category or concept. In his informative speech on violent crimes, Jacob presented two definitions to help his audience understand the distinction between "assault" and "battery."

> Of course, different jurisdictions define crimes in slightly different ways. But, according to the Chicago Police Department website, accessed last Saturday, "In Illinois assault is a threat, while battery is an actual attack." The *New York Public Library Desk Reference* provides a more vivid explanation. Their 2002 calendar draws this distinction: "If you angrily shake your fist at someone, it's legally considered assault. If you follow up your actions by punching the person in the nose, the offense is assault and battery."

definition by etymology: explaining the origin of the word being defined.

definition by example: providing an instance or illustration of the word being defined.

Jacob used, first, definition by synonym and then definition by example to clarify the distinction between these two terms.

You need not confine your definitions by example to language, however. Often audible and visual examples can be your quickest and most vivid ways to define a term or concept.

Audible examples are those you let your audience hear. Speeches on types of music, voice patterns, or speech dialects could define key terms by audible examples. For example, if you were using the word *scat* in a speech on jazz, you could offer a dictionary definition of the term: "jazz singing that uses nonsense syllables."[5] But wouldn't a taped example of Ella Fitzgerald, Al Jarreau, or Bobby McFerrin singing scat be more memorable to your audience? Other terms appropriate for audible definitions include Boston Brahmin dialect, industrial music, straight-ahead jazz, and vocalese.

Visual examples define a term by letting the audience see a form of it. If you're using the term *krumping* in a speech on contemporary dance, you could offer the *Wikipedia* definition: a style of dance involving "elaborate face-painting and freestyle dance moves usually performed in competition with other crews."[6] But a more vivid way to define the term would be to show a clip from a Missy Elliott or a Chemical Brothers' video. Speeches on styles of architecture or painting could also benefit from visual definition, as could any of the following terms: abstract expressionism, concrete poetry, embedded messages, emoticon [:-o], optical illusion, and photorealism.

Definition by Operation.   Sometimes the quickest and liveliest way to define a term is to explain how it is used. **Definition by operation** clarifies a word or phrase by explaining how an object or concept works, what it does, or what it was designed to do. The terms *radar detector, MP3 player,* and *laser scalpel* are but a few of the physical objects best defined by explaining their operation.

You can also define concepts, actions, or processes by operation. To define magnetic resonance imaging, you would have to explain how that technology operates. Notice how George Lawton defines "cookies" by explaining their functions:

> Cookies are an early example of technology that lets outside parties access users' computers. Cookies are code that a Web site's server can send to individuals' browsers and store on their hard drives. Users can provide information such as a password for a cookie to store, or a cookie can record information on its own, such as user activities while visiting the Web site. . . . Some cookies can even track user activity across multiple Web sites.[7]

Definition by operation is often livelier and more complete than most dictionary definitions. And, as this example illustrates, it is especially useful in the case of new technologies whose dictionary definitions have yet to be written.

Narration

Narration is storytelling, the process of describing an action or a series of occurrences. If you come to school on Monday and tell a friend about something you did during the weekend, you are narrating those events.

Personal Narrative.   As a participant in the events, you will probably speak in first person at least part of the time, using the pronouns *I* or *we*. Such a story is called a **personal narrative.** We have suggested that you draw on your own experiences as you select and develop a speech topic, and personal narratives can be rich and interesting supporting materials.

Sultana, a student whose husband is Muslim and who had herself converted to the Muslim religion, used a personal narrative effectively. She told the story of her first ex-

definition by operation: explaining how the object or concept being defined works, what it does, or what it was designed to do.

narration: the process of describing an action or series of occurrences; storytelling.

personal narrative: a story told from the point of view of a participant in the action and using the pronouns *I* or *we*.

perience with the celebration of Ramadan, a period of daylight fasting during the ninth month of the Muslim year:

> My first Ramadan I was a bit nervous. I had just become a Muslim, and I thought, "There is no way I can go from sunup to sunset without food. It's not even logical." I like to eat, as some of you may have noticed. And I thought, "There's no way that I can do this." Also, I was a student at the time, and it was finals. I honestly believe that you can't function if you don't eat. I mean, how can you think and pass a final? But I was determined at least to begin Ramadan; it goes for thirty days. So I set out and the first few days were a bit difficult. You can get hungry; there's no denying that. Your stomach growls out loud in class. But after about three days, the body adjusts. You don't really need as much food as most of us consume. You can live a long time on that stored up fat we have and survive quite well. But the experience provides a lot of self-confidence, because if you can spend thirty days fasting, you can do just about anything.

Her classmates laughed along with Sultana as she poked fun at students' eating habits during the stress of final exams, as well as at her own tendency to be finishing a snack as her speech class started. In addition to creating interest in the topic, Sultana's story reinforced her credibility to speak on the topic of Ramadan. We tend to believe the accounts of people who have experienced events firsthand. That is an important reason for using personal narratives.

Third-Person Narrative.   Narratives, of course, need not be personal, but may relate a series of incidents in the lives of others. When you speak from the point of view of a witness and use the pronouns *he, she,* or *they,* you are telling a **third-person narrative.**

In the following example, notice how Kimberly used third-person narrative to illustrate the danger of running red lights:

> Michael approached the intersection and noticed it [the light] turn red. He was so late for his appointment that he decided to run right through, hoping no one was coming. There was someone, though, and Michael got broadsided as he ran the light. His car was shoved sideways, narrowly missing a 10-year-old boy riding through the intersection on his bicycle. This scenario may seem like fiction, but in fact, situations like this occur every day, when drivers race to beat the light.[8]

Comparison

Comparison is the process of depicting one item—person, place, object, or concept—by pointing out its similarities to another, more familiar item. Just as examples can be actual or hypothetical, comparisons can be literal or figurative.

Literal Comparison.   A **literal comparison** associates items that share actual similarities. Bill Gates used the following literal comparison in a 2005 speech critiquing contemporary high school education:

> Training the workforce of tomorrow with the high schools of today is like trying to teach kids about today's computers on a 50-year-old mainframe. It's the wrong tool for the times. Our high schools were designed fifty years ago to meet the needs of another age. Until we design them to meet the needs of the 21st century, we will keep limiting—even ruining—the lives of millions of Americans every year.[9]

Figurative Comparison.   When you draw a **figurative comparison**, you associate two items that do not necessarily share any actual similarities. The purpose of figurative comparisons is to surprise the listener into seeing or considering one person, place, object, or concept in a new way.

third-person narrative: a story told from the point of view of a witness and using the pronouns *he, she,* or *they.*

comparison: the process of associating two items by pointing out their similarities.

literal comparison: associations between two items that share actual similarities.

figurative comparison: associations between two items that do not share actual similarities.

In his persuasive speech on bacterial meningitis Ben used the following figurative comparison to explain why college students have a greater risk of contracting such diseases:

> Everybody comes to school bringing with them their own strain of influenza, like ingredients for a stew. We're all dumped into this crock pot called a campus, put on simmer for one or two weeks, and it's no wonder it occasionally boils over into something very serious. Have you noticed most campus flu outbreaks occur shortly after summer vacation and around Christmas break? This is because people leave and bring back more than the tinker toys they bargained for. And so the crock pot cycle continues.[10]

Effective figurative comparisons must contain an element of surprise, as well as a spark of recognition. One student, describing the density of a neutron star, quoted from *Sky & Telescope* magazine that "your bathroom sink could hold the Great Lakes if the water were compressed to the density of a neutron star."

Contrast

Contrast links two items by showing their differences. A **literal contrast** distinguishes items that do share some similarities. A **figurative contrast**, on the other hand, distinguishes items that share no similarities. In a persuasive speech on the dangers of overexposure to the sun, our student Patricia effectively used the following literal contrast:

> Sunblocks are either chemical or physical. Oils, lotions, and creams that claim a certain SPF factor all contain chemical blocks. On the other hand, zinc oxide, the white or colored clay-looking material you see some people wearing, usually on their noses, is a physical block.

You can use comparison and contrast together in your speech. If you clarify a term by showing how it is similar to something the audience knows, you can often make the term even clearer by showing how it differs from something the audience also knows.

Statistics

Statistics are collections of data. Broadly speaking, any number used as supporting material is a statistic. Used appropriately, statistics, too, can make your ideas clear and vivid, increase your credibility, and prove your point.

We place a great deal of trust in statistics that we feel have been accurately gathered and interpreted. Think of how much trust politicians as well as the general public put in preference polls gathered before elections. Statistics can predict certain events in our daily lives, such as price increases or decreases on certain goods and services. When you use statistics in your speech, you can demonstrate trends or compare a situation today with one in the past.

Used inappropriately, however, statistics may baffle or even bore your audience. The following five suggestions should guide you in presenting statistical material.

Do Not Rely Exclusively on Statistics.   If statistics are your only form of supporting material, your audience will likely feel bombarded by numbers. Remember, your listening audience has only one chance to hear and assimilate your statistics. As a speaker, then, use statistics judiciously and in combination with other forms of support. A few key statistics combined with examples can be quite powerful. Too many statistics will confuse your audience.

Remember Ali's speech on binge drinking? She used a real example, Scott Kreuger, to illustrate the deadly consequences of this behavior and tap listeners' emotions. Ali then introduced statistics to demonstrate the breadth of this problem.

---

contrast: the process of distinguishing two items by pointing out their differences.

literal contrast: distinctions between two items that share actual differences.

figurative contrast: distinctions between two items that do not have actual differences.

statistics: data collected in the form of numbers.

Supporting materials, such as the visual aids this speaker is using, can help make a complicated concept clearer and easier for an audience to grasp.

If Scott Kreuger were the only student to die from overdrinking, his story would be an isolated incident of lost potential. But in fact, college binge drinking is more of an issue than ever. Yet the fact is that at least two out of every five U.S. college students binge drink, and according to the *New York Times* of March 24, 2002, this results each year in approximately fourteen hundred student deaths, a distressing number of assaults and rapes, and a shameful amount of vandalism, and countless cases of suicide."[11]

Round off Statistics. A statistic of 74.6 percent has less impact and is more difficult for your audience to remember than "nearly three-fourths." No one in your audience will remember the statistic of $1,497,568.42; many, however, may be able to remember "a million and a half dollars." Rounding off statistics for your listeners is neither deceptive nor unethical. Instead, it reflects your concern for helping your audience understand and retain key statistical information.

Use Units of Measure That Are Familiar to Your Audience. In her speech on worker incomes in China, Kim cited the example of the Yue Yuen company, which makes sports shoes for Adidas, Nike, and Reebok.

> According to an August 1996 issue of *Far Eastern Economic Review,* junior high school graduates are paid, on average, 600 renminbi a month. That's approximately $72 in U.S. dollars and is a typical wage for that region.

Six hundred renminbi would probably have been a meaningless figure to most of her listeners. Kim helped her audience to understand that statistic by translating it to U.S. dollars and by indicating how it compared with other salaries in the region.

LOCATING STATISTICS
www.fedstats.gov
Need a statistic to document the extent of a condition or problem? The Federal Interagency Council on Statistical Policy maintains this website containing information and statistics provided by more than 100 hundred U.S. federal agencies. You can search agencies alphabetically or by subject area.

Use Presentational Aids to Represent or Clarify Relationships among Statistics. In his first informative speech of the semester, Alec discussed U.S. college study-abroad programs. Researching on the Internet, he accessed a report by the

Institute of International Education listing the percentages of students studying in various host countries: 20.4 percent in the United Kingdom, 9.7 percent in Spain, 9.0 percent in Italy, 8.3 percent in France, and so forth. Alec decided that his classmates would remember more of this information if he presented it orally and visually. So he constructed a chart that ranked these nations according to the percentage of U.S. students studying there. Listeners were able to see the rankings as Alec discussed his topic and focus on the particular countries where they would like to study.

Stress the Impact of Large Numbers.   Former Surgeon General C. Everett Koop used statistics effectively to make his point that tobacco-related diseases cause significant deaths. Notice how he used repetition and helped his audience visualize the enormity of these deaths.

> Let's start with a factual description of the problem. Based on the calculations of the finest statistical minds in the world and the World Health Organization, they have predicted that by 2025, . . . 500 million people worldwide will die of tobacco-related disease. That's a numbing figure. It is too large to take in, so let me put it in other terms for you. That's a Vietnam War every day for 27 years. That's a Bhopal every two hours for 27 years. That's a Titanic every 43 minutes for 27 years.
>
> If we were to build for those tobacco victims a memorial such as the Vietnam Wall, it would stretch from here [Washington, D.C.] 1,000 miles across seven states to Kansas City. And, if you want to put it in terms per minute, there's a death [every] 1.7 seconds, or about 250 to 300 people since I began to speak to you this afternoon.[12]

Testimony

Examples, definition, narration, comparison, contrast, and statistics are discrete types of supporting materials. Each is a different strategy for validating the ideas of a speech. Speakers sometimes generate these types of support themselves. Other times, they glean them from their research, citing their sources, but justifying the point in their own words. Still other times, speakers find the words and structure of the original source so compelling that they quote directly or paraphrase the source. This latter strategy is known as **testimony**. Testimony, sometimes called quotation, is another method of presenting types of supporting material. When you quote or paraphrase the words and ideas of others, you use testimony.

In his speech, "Ribbons: Function or Fashion," Tony discussed how awareness ribbons can inform and connect communities. To give his ideas credibility, he used the testimony of a communication professor and an animal welfare website.

> Dr. Judith Trent, a communication professor at the University of Cincinnati, states in the *Cincinnati Enquirer* of September 18, 2001, that wearing a ribbon "shows you're a part of something that's larger than yourself. It helps to unify and support the cause. It's a public signal about a private thought." By wearing ribbons, people can easily give support and find comfort in people around them. The Purple Ribbon Campaign website, last updated July 15, 2003, states, "Wearing a ribbon allows a person to represent their hopes and drive for a better day to come. It also provides support to others in letting them know that they are not suffering alone."[13]

Tony clearly identified two sources and quoted them directly, trusting their credibility and their words to persuade his listeners. Testimony relies largely on the reputation of the source being quoted or paraphrased.

Expert testimony is not limited to the statements of other people, however. As a speaker, you use *personal testimony* when you support your ideas with your own experiences and observations. Many students select a speech topic because they have some

testimony: quotations or paraphrases of an authoritative source to clarify or prove a point.

special knowledge or experience with the subject. One of our students, for example, gave a speech comparing retail prices at large supermarkets to those at convenience stores. He was careful to explain his credentials and establish his expertise in the subject. Not only did he wear his store apron and manager's name tag, but he also said early in his introduction, "As a former receiving control manager, I was in charge of purchasing products for the store, so I have some knowledge of how wholesale prices are translated into the retail prices you and I pay." The speaker enhanced his credibility both verbally and nonverbally.

Tests of Evidence

Speakers should choose supporting materials, summarized in Figure 8.1, carefully and ethically. The positions you develop in your speech will be only as strong as the evidence supporting them. Seven guidelines will help you evaluate the validity and strength of your supporting materials. These suggestions will also help you evaluate evidence you hear others present in their speeches.

Is the Evidence Quoted in Context?

Evidence is quoted *in context* if it accurately reflects the source's statement of the topic. Evidence is quoted *out of context* if it distorts the source's position on the topic.

For example, suppose Joyce was preparing a speech on the topic of hate crimes on campus. She has read in the campus paper the following statement by the president of her college:

> **Tests of Evidence**
>
> 1. Is the evidence quoted in context?
> 2. Is the source of the evidence an expert?
> 3. Is the source of the evidence unbiased?
> 4. Is the evidence relevant to the point being made?
> 5. Is the evidence specific?
> 6. Is the evidence sufficient to prove the point?
> 7. Is the evidence timely?

> We've been fortunate that our campus has been relatively free of bias-motivated crimes. In fact, last year, only two such incidents were reported—the lowest figure in the past five years. Yet, no matter how small the number is, any hate crime constitutes a serious problem on this campus. We will not be satisfied until our campus is completely free from all bias-motivated intimidation.

Now, suppose Joyce used the following statement to support her position that hate crimes are prevalent on campus:

> We need to be concerned about a widespread and growing problem on our campus: the prevalence of hate crimes. Just this past week, for example, our president argued that hate crimes constitute, and I quote, "a serious problem on this campus."

The president did say those words, but Joyce failed to mention the president's position that hate crimes on campus are few and decreasing. By omitting this fact, she has distorted the president's message. Joyce has presented the evidence out of context. The evidence you cite in your speech should accurately represent each source's position on the topic.

Is the Source of the Evidence an Expert?

If you delivered a speech advocating the licensing of law clerks to draft wills and conduct other routine legal business, would you rather quote a first-year lawyer or a

FIGURE 8.1
Supporting Materials:
Types and Uses

TYPE OF SUPPORT	USE
Example	Provides instances or samples of people, places, objects, actions, conditions, or experiences.
Actual example	Provides clarification and proof.
Hypothetical example	Provides clarification, but does not alone provide proof.
Definition	Clarifies an unfamiliar word or phrase.
Definition by synonym	Substitutes a familiar word for the one defined.
Definition by etymology	Explains the origin of the word defined.
Definition by example	Provides an illustration or sample of the word defined.
Audible example	Lets listeners hear sample of the term defined.
Visual example	Lets listeners see sample of the term defined.
Definition by operation	Explains use, function, or purpose of the object or concept defined.
Narration	Describes action or event.
Personal narrative	Describes action from participant's point of view; uses *I* and *we*.
Third-person narrative	Describes action from witness's point of view; uses *he, she,* and *they*.
Comparison	Clarifies term by showing its similarity to a more familiar term.
Literal comparison	Associates items having actual similarities.
Figurative comparison	Associates items not having actual similarities.
Contrast	Clarifies term by showing its difference from a more familiar term.
Literal contrast	Distinguishes items having actual differences.
Figurative contrast	Distinguishes items not having actual differences.
Statistics	Clarify or prove a point with numbers.
Testimony	Clarifies or proves a point using the speaker's words or those of an expert.

senior law partner of a major legal corporation? Of course it would depend on the specific individuals and what they said, but you would probably place more trust in the latter, more experienced person.

An expert is a person qualified to speak on a particular topic. We trust the opinions and observations of others based on their position, education, training, or experience. The chairperson of a committee that has just completed a study on the effects of a community-based sentencing program is knowledgeable about the facts concerning that issue. A person completing graduate study on the effects of a local Head Start program on literacy has also developed an area of expertise. As a speaker, select the most qualified sources to support your position.

Our student who compared the pricing policies of large supermarkets and convenience stores was careful to establish his own credibility both verbally and nonverbally. When you as a speaker fail to present your qualifications or the qualifications of those you quote, you give listeners little reason to believe you.

Is the Source of the Evidence Unbiased?

When Markdown Marty of Marty's Used Cars tells you he has the best deals in town, do you accept that claim without questioning it? Probably not. Marty may be an expert on used cars, but he's understandably biased. When individuals have a vested interest in a product, a service, or an issue, they are often less objective.

You expect representatives of political parties, special-interest groups, business corporations, labor unions, and so forth, to make statements advancing their interests. It will probably not surprise you, for example, that the supermarket receiving control manager we quoted earlier concluded his speech by stating that it is more economical to shop at large supermarkets than at convenience stores. When you include testimony and quotations in your speeches, try to rely on objective experts who do not have a vested interest in sustaining the positions they voice.

Is the Evidence Relevant to the Point Being Made?

Evidence should relate to the speaker's claim. Sounds pretty obvious, doesn't it? However, both speakers and listeners often fail to apply this guideline in evaluating evidence. A speaker who contends that amateur boxing is dangerous, but presents only evidence of injuries to professional boxers, has clearly violated the relevance criterion. But many times irrelevant evidence is more difficult to detect.

Ryan's speech called for increased funding of medical trauma centers. Throughout his speech, he cited the need for the specialized care provided in these facilities. Yet, when he estimated the demand for this care, he used statistics of emergency room use. Trauma centers are not the same as emergency rooms. Therefore, Ryan's evidence was irrelevant to his argument. As you construct your speech, identify your key points and make certain your evidence relates specifically to them.

Is the Evidence Specific?

Which of the following statements is more informative?

The new convention center will increase tourism a lot.

The new convention center will increase tourism by 40 percent.

What does "a lot" mean in the first statement? Twenty percent? Fifty percent? Eighty percent? We don't know. The second statement is more precise. Because it is more specific, we are better able to assess the impact of the new convention center. Words such as *lots, many, numerous,* and *very* are vague. When possible, replace them with more specific words or phrases.

In his persuasive speech, Travis asserted that commercial truck drivers who drive fatigued pose a serious problem. If he had stopped there, his audience might have asked, "Is the problem really that serious? How many of these truckers actually fall asleep and get in accidents? Are others hurt in these crashes?" Travis wisely continued:

The October 15, 1998, *New England Journal of Medicine* cites driver fatigue as the leading cause of truck crashes. A *Journal of the American Medical Association* survey found that half of commercial drivers have driven drowsy, one in four has fallen asleep at the wheel, and one in twenty has crashed while drowsy. Worse, the National Transportation Safety Board estimates that for every commercial driver who dies behind the wheel four other victims also perish.[14]

Is the Evidence Sufficient to Prove the Point?

In her speech on rap music, Lea played excerpts from two rap songs, one of which she characterized as antiwoman and the other as antipolice. She encouraged her listeners to boycott rap music because "it demeans women and law enforcement officers." Lea did not apply this sixth guideline to her evidence. Two examples do not justify a blanket indictment of rap music.

When considering the guideline of sufficiency, ask yourself, "Is there enough evidence to prove the point?" Three examples of college athletes graduating without acquiring basic writing skills are insufficient to prove that athletes are failing to get a good education. One example may illustrate a claim, but it will rarely prove it. Make certain you have sufficient evidence to support your points.

Is the Evidence Timely?

If you were preparing a travel budget for a trip overseas, which would you find more helpful: an airline ticket pricing schedule you had from last year or one you printed from a travel website this week? Of course, you would want to rely on your more recent information. The timeliness of information is especially important if you are speaking about constantly changing issues, conditions, or events. What you read today may already be dated by the time you give your speech.

Some speech topics, however, are timeless. If you speak about the gods of Mount Olympus, no one would question your use of Robert Graves's *Greek Gods and Heroes*, published in 1960. As a scholar of mythology, Graves earned a reputation that time is not likely to diminish. Similarly, if you deliver a speech on the ancient Olympic Games,

Ethical Decisions

Biased Sources: To Use or Not to Use

You probably wouldn't be surprised that a Gallup study sponsored by Motorola found that people who use cellular phones are more successful in business than those who don't, or that a Gallup poll sponsored by the zinc industry revealed that 62 percent of Americans want to keep the penny. These are just two examples that *Wall Street Journal* writer and editor Cynthia Crossen uses in her book, *Tainted Truth: The Manipulation of Fact in America*, to illustrate the difficulty of distinguishing between neutral research and commercially sponsored studies.

Assume that you are preparing to give a speech on hormone replacement therapy to counteract the effects of aging. Through an electronic database search, you find a study that shows the substance melatonin prevents cancer, boosts the immune system, and improves the quality of sleep. When you look for the source, you see that the study was sponsored by a pharmaceutical company that produces melatonin. What course of action should you follow? Should you disregard the findings because the study was commercially sponsored, use the findings without mentioning the study's sponsor, mention the findings and acknowledge the study's commercial sponsorship, or treat the findings in some other way?

your most authoritative sources may be history textbooks. If, however, your topic concerns current drug-testing procedures in Olympic competition, it would be vital for you to use the most recent sources of the best quality you can find. The date of your evidence must be appropriate to your specific argument.

Evaluating Electronic Information

Testing the quality of your evidence using the preceding questions exercises a number of your critical thinking skills. When you use the Internet for research, however, those skills may get not just exercise, but a full-tilt workout. This is because anything can get posted and quickly communicated to millions of people online. Some messages posted on websites may just be nutty hoaxes (stories about expensive cookie recipes or fictitious computer virus alerts, for example). Other Internet sites, however, spread dangerous information; fan suspicion, fear, and prejudice; or just lie with other malicious intent. For all the convenience that it provides, the Internet forces us to take on a lot of the evaluation of information that other people used to do for us.

Traditionally, materials that appeared first in print often had fact checkers, expert reviewers, or editorial boards who had to be convinced of the truth and value of an article before publishing it. Today the online versions of magazines and newspapers, as well as government documents, are regarded on a par with their print counterparts. Most educational, governmental, or organizational sites also have a review process for materials published under their sponsorship. Yet many sites you access on any topic have never been edited, fact-checked, or reviewed. In addition, they may appear today and disappear tomorrow.

A real advantage of the Internet is that so many sites are interesting to look at and fun to navigate. Aside from issues of design and aesthetics, however, what do you need to ask yourself about sites that you are considering using to support your speech? Hundreds of college and university library websites now have links to guidelines for evaluating Internet sources. Basic questions you may need to ask are listed below.

Exploring *Online*

EVALUATING INTERNET SOURCES
www.library.jhu.edu/researchhelp/general/evaluating/index.html
This site, one of many library sites on the topic "Evaluating Information Found on the Internet," provides a particularly thorough checklist of criteria. Maintained by Elizabeth E. Kirk of Johns Hopkins University, it includes links to related subtopics.

Purpose

- What seems to be the purpose of this site: to provide information? to promote a position? to sell a product or service?
- What type of site is it: aviation (.aero), commercial (.com, .coop, or .biz), educational (.edu), governmental (.gov), information business (.info), military (.mil), nonprofit organization (.org), personal (.name), or professional (.pro), for example?
- Is there an institution, agency, or organization identified as sponsoring the site?
- Does the site contain advertising? If so, by whom?
- Who is the author's apparent audience, as reflected by the vocabulary, writing style, and point of view? Students? Professionals? Consumers? Advocates?

Expertise

- Is the author, compiler, or web master identified?
- Does the author have apparent expertise on the subject?

- Are the author's or compiler's credentials provided?

  Do you know the author's occupation?
  Do you know the author's educational background?
  Do you know the author's organizational affiliation?

- Does the author provide contact information, such as email address, phone number, or mailing address?
- If the site is a compilation, are sources and authors of individual works identified?
- If the site is a research project, does the author explain data, methodology, and interpretation of results?
- If the site is a research project, does the author refer to other works? Provide notes?
- If links to other works are provided, are they evaluated in any way?
- Is the site linked to another site that you already trust or value?
- Are sources or viewpoints missing that you would expect to be present?
- What does this page offer that you could not find elsewhere?

Objectivity

- Does the author's affiliation with an organization, institution, or agency suggest a bias?
- Does the site's sponsorship by an organization or institution suggest an inherent bias?
- Are opposing views represented or acknowledged?
- Are editorial comments or opinions clearly distinguished from facts?

Accuracy

- Can you corroborate the facts using either other Internet sources or library resources (reference works or indexed publications)?
- Is the site inward-focused (providing only links to other parts of the site) or outward-focused (providing links to other websites)?
- Has the author expended the effort to write well, with correct spelling and proper grammar?
- Does the author solicit corrections or updates by email?

Try This

Evaluating Internet Sources

Select a topic appropriate for your next speaking assignment. On the World Wide Web, locate and print two pieces of information on that topic, one from an authoritative source and one whose validity you doubt. Evaluate each source by answering the seven "Tests of Evidence" questions presented in this chapter. What criteria made you trust the first source and doubt the second? Use these seven guidelines to assess the credibility and validity of all supporting materials you consider using in your speeches. As an ethical listener, remember to use these same questions as you evaluate the speeches of others.

Timeliness

- Is the date of publication important to this subject matter?
- Can you tell when the site was created?
- Can you tell when the site was last updated?
- Are links from this site current or broken?[15]

Citing Your Sources

A bibliography of quality sources you consulted in researching your speech will build your credibility with your instructor. In Chapter 7 we directed you to sources that will help you compile a correct bibliography. However, most of your listeners will not have an opportunity to see that bibliography. To acknowledge your sources and take credit for the research you have done, you will need to provide "oral footnotes" for ideas and supporting materials in your speech that are not your own. Doing so accomplishes two goals. First, clear source citations enhance the credibility of what you say by demonstrating that experts and data support your position. Second, clear source citations help interested listeners find published sources that they might wish to read or study.

How do you "orally footnote" sources as you deliver your speech? Your instructor may require more or less information in oral source citations than we do, so be sure to check. Our rule of thumb is this: Give only the information necessary to build the credibility of the source, but enough information to help listeners find your source if they wish to do so.

Do you need to include *all* the information that was in your bibliographic entry for the source? No. Only the most active listener would remember the title and page numbers of a journal article or the publisher of a book that you cite, for example. Is there any information not in your bibliography that you *should* mention as you cite a source? Yes.

To establish the credibility of any source you name, you need to explain at least briefly that individual's qualifications. You can usually find such information somewhere in the book, magazine, journal, or website you are using. If not, check a biographical database.

If the author is a newspaper or magazine staff writer, however, you do not need to name that individual. If the publication has a corporate author (a group, committee, or organization), just mentioning the name of the group or organization is probably sufficient. The date of publication may be extremely important to building credibility on a current topic. For periodicals published weekly or for online magazines that are frequently updated, specify the date, month, and year that the material was published or that you accessed it.

Orally footnoting Internet sources poses special challenges. Though it is never acceptable to say just, "I found a web page that said . . ." or "I found this on Yahoo," most listeners will not remember a long URL that you mention. If the URL is simple and easily recognizable, mention it: "pbs.org," "cnn.com," or "espn.com," for example. Identifying the sponsor of a website is important. If you cannot identify the group or individual who published and maintains the site, you may need to look for a better source.

"Who is the fairest one of all, and state your sources!"

Speaking with *Confidence*

When I first started citing my sources in my speeches, I found it difficult to do so without sounding too formal and unnatural. I thought detailed citations were unnecessary. However, after listening to classmates' speeches and practicing my own, I now realize how important it is to have good supporting evidence from quality sources. Determining if information is biased or unbiased, outdated or recent, from an uninformed source or from an expert is vital to both researching a speech and listening to one. Listening with a critical mind has helped me in figuring out what position I should take on vital issues. In the same manner, researching has helped me to spread true, legitimate knowledge to my listeners. Being able to recognize a bad source hidden in seemingly good information has helped cultivate my beliefs according to what is true, rather than what sounds good.

—Elisabeth Pallante, *Radford University*

Compare the following source citations:

Instead of saying:	**Say this:**
"Studs Terkel says in his book *Will the Circle be Unbroken?* . . ."	Studs Terkel, Pulitzer Prize-winning oral historian, says in his 2001 book *Will the Circle be Unbroken?* . . ."
"According to an article I found on the Lexis/Nexis Academic database . . ."	"According to an article in the July 18, 2005, issue of the *Roanoke Times and World News* . . ."
"Leigh T. Hollins says in his article in the journal *Fire Engineering* . . ."	"Leigh T. Hollins, a certified EMT and battalion chief in the Manatee County, Florida, fire department, says in his article in the June 2005 issue of the journal *Fire Engineering* . . ."
"According to statistics from the Bureau of Labor Statistics . . ."	"According to figures I found on the U.S. Department of Labor's Bureau of Labor Statistics website on March 3, 2005, . . ."
"I found an article at memory.loc.gov/ ammem/ jrhtml/jr1940.html . . ."	"On March 12th of this year, I found an article entitled 'Breaking the Color Line: 1940–1946.' It's a link from the Recreation and Sports collection of the Library of Congress's website *American Memory* . . ."

In each case, the oral footnote that takes a few more words identifies the source more clearly and more specifically, and would reinforce the speaker's credibility. The Theory into Practice feature in this chapter summarizes our advice for citing books, articles, and other types of sources.

Theory into Practice

Tips

Information for Oral Footnotes

If you are citing:	Tell us:
A magazine/journal article	That it is an article, the title of the magazine or journal, the author's name and credentials (if other than a staff writer), and the date of publication
A newspaper article	That it is an article, the name of the newspaper, the author's name and credentials (if other than a staff writer), and the date of the issue you are citing
A website	The title of the web page; the name of the individual, agency, association, group, or company sponsoring the site; and the date of publication, last update, or the date you accessed it
A book	That it is a book, the author's name(s) and credentials, the title of the book, and the date of publication
An interview you conducted	That you interviewed the person, the person's name, and his or her position or title
A television or radio program	The title of the show, the channel or network airing it, and the date of broadcast
A videotape or DVD	The title of the tape or disk
A reference work	The title of the work and the date of publication
A government document	The title of the document, the name of the agency or government branch that published it, and the date of publication
A brochure or pamphlet	That it is a brochure; its title; the name of the agency, association, group, or company that published it; and the date of publication (if available)

Summary

We use supporting materials in a speech to achieve three purposes: *clarity, vividness,* and *credibility.* Clarity helps the audience understand your ideas. Vividness assists them in remembering your ideas. Credible supporting materials make your ideas believable.

Types of material you can use to support the main ideas of your speech include examples, definition, narration, comparison, contrast, statistics, and testimony. *Examples* are samples or illustrations of a category. Those categories may be people, places, objects, actions, experiences, or conditions. Examples may be *brief* or *extended* and actual or hypothetical. *Actual examples* are real or factual. *Hypothetical examples* are imaginary or fictitious. Both types of examples make a general or abstract term more specific and vivid for the audience.

Definitions are explanations of an unfamiliar term or of a word having several possible meanings. We can define terms by synonym, etymology, example, or operation. *Definition by synonym* offers a word or phrase that is the rough equivalent of the word being defined. *Definition by etymology* shows the origin of the word being defined. *Definition by example* gives an illustration or sample of the word in question. *Definition by operation* explains how something works or what it was designed to do. Definitions are crucial if you are using words you suspect your audience will not know or if you want them to adopt one particular meaning for a term.

Narration is storytelling. Narratives may be personal or third person. *Personal narratives* originate from the speaker's experience; they use the first-person pronouns *I* or *we*. *Third-person narratives* are stories about other people, and they are delivered using either people's names or the third-person pronouns *she, he,* or *they.*

Comparisons associate two or more items to show the similarities between or among them. Comparisons can be either literal or figurative. A *literal comparison* links two items that share actual similarities. A *figurative comparison* associates items that do not share any actual similarities.

Contrasts function like comparisons except that their purpose is to distinguish or show differences between two or more items.

Statistics are data collected in the form of numbers. Used properly, statistics can bolster a speaker's credibility and lend vivid support to the ideas of the speech. To ensure your proper use of statistics, you should follow five guidelines. First, don't rely exclusively on statistics, but combine them with other supporting materials. Second, round off statistics to help your listeners remember them. Third, use units of measure familiar to your audience. Fourth, use visual aids to clarify the relationships among various statistics. Fifth, stress the impact of large numbers.

The final form of support is testimony. You use *testimony* when you cite, quote, or paraphrase authoritative sources. The authorities you cite may employ examples, definitions, narration, comparison, contrast, or statistics.

To help ensure that your supporting materials are credible, you should ask seven questions about each piece of evidence you consider using: Is the evidence quoted in context? Is the source of the evidence an expert? Is the source of the evidence unbiased? Is the evidence relevant to the point you are making? Is the evidence specific? Is the evidence sufficient to prove your point? Is the evidence timely?

Evaluating information you collect from the Internet or the World Wide Web requires you to ask and answer additional questions. What is the apparent *purpose* of the website providing the information? What evidence of the author's *expertise* do you find? What evidence of the author's *objectivity* do you find? Can you confirm the *accuracy* of the site's information? Is the information *timely*? Based on your answers to these questions, is the information appropriate for your purposes?

If you use supporting materials that others have developed, you must cite them in your speech by providing "oral footnotes." You should offer enough information to establish the credibility of the source without overwhelming the listener. Your citation should be specific enough to help interested listeners locate the source in question. For most printed sources, you should provide the author's name and credentials, the title of the work, and the publication date. The credibility of electronic sources may hinge on your ability to identify the website sponsor and the date its material was published or was last updated or that you accessed it.

Practice Critique

Evaluating Evidence

The Appendix includes a transcript of a speech by Gene Fox. After reading this speech, write a critique to Gene evaluating the evidence he uses to support his ideas. What types of material does he use to support his assertions? Are there better choices he could have made to support these ideas? Use the tests suggested in this chapter for evaluating evidence. Does Gene include assertions for which he offers inadequate support? If so, what other types of evidence should he provide to make his arguments more convincing?

Exercises

1. Rewrite the following sentences to make them more vivid.
   a. The food at the Cozy Café is very good.
   b. I have a lot of homework to do.
   c. The students in my speech class are interesting people.
   d. We have a good time at the beach.

2. Locate a transcript of a speech in *Vital Speeches of the Day* or in some other publication or electronic database. Read it and note in the margins the different types of supporting materials the speaker used. Discuss the materials used most effectively, and account for their effectiveness. Discuss those used least effectively, and suggest ways the speaker could improve them.

3. Read the five statements below, indicating those with which you agree or disagree. Discuss the type(s) of supporting materials you would likely use to support your positions.
   a. European soccer is a more popular sport than American football.
   b. The fear of giving a speech can be reduced.
   c. Art is more important than science.
   d. Life in the country is more fun than life in the city.
   e. This state is an excellent place to visit.

4. Think of someone who is known to you but unknown to your classmates. Describe this person (personality traits, physical features, attitudes, etc.) by comparing and contrasting him or her with people in your class.

5. Discuss a method of definition you could use for each of the following terms:
   a. Deep web
   b. Aphorism
   c. Contralto
   d. Palpable
   e. Ballistic fingerprinting
   f. Autocad drafting
   g. Pandemic
   h. Global positioning system

Organizing the Body of Your Speech

Formulate an Organizing Question

Divide the Speech into Key Ideas
Topical Division
Chronological Division
Spatial Division
Causal Division
Pro–Con Division
Mnemonic or Gimmick Division
Problem–Solution Division
Need–Plan Division

Develop the Key Ideas
Signpost the Idea
State the Idea
Support the Idea
Summarize the Idea

■ **THEORY INTO PRACTICE:** Applying the "4S's"

Connect the Key Ideas

■ **TRY THIS:** Developing One Key Idea

chapter

If you want me to talk for ten minutes, I'll come next week. If you want me to talk for an hour, I'll come tonight. —WOODROW WILSON

I have made this letter longer than usual, because I lack the time to make it short. —PASCAL[1]

Have you ever furiously written several pages to answer an essay question on an exam only to discover that the answer requires just one brief paragraph? Or perhaps you have given a driver long-winded directions for getting to a particular location, then remembered a shortcut. If you have had experiences similar to these, Pascal's and Wilson's comments probably make a great deal of sense to you. It takes time to organize your thoughts to write a coherent letter, give a succinct answer to an essay question, or give clear directions. Spending the time to organize, however, simplifies the task in the end. Getting organized will also simplify your speech preparation and make your speech more vivid and memorable for your listeners

A coherent speech is similar to a written essay because it also has a beginning, a middle, and an end—what we call the introduction, body, and conclusion. Many speech textbooks and instructors summarize the overall strategy of a speech as follows: *"Tell us what you are going to tell us. Tell us. Then, tell us what you told us."* Use this organizational perspective in every speech.

Clear organization arranges ideas so that your listeners can remember them. It also maximizes your information so that listeners have more than one chance to "get" your point. Effective delivery provides visual and vocal clues that help you further emphasize your message, and we'll discuss the elements of speech delivery in Chapter 13.

In this chapter we will teach you how to organize the body of your speech. In Chapter 10 you will learn how to organize the introduction and the conclusion. You may find this an unusual order in which to organize the parts of a speech. Be assured that by the end of Chapter 10 you will see the logic of this sequence.

Although you deliver it after the introduction, organize the body of your speech first, for in order to "tell us what you are going to tell us," you must first determine what to tell us. In constructing the body of a speech, your best strategy is to formulate an organizing question, to divide the speech into key ideas, and then develop each idea.

Exploring *Online*

ORGANIZATION: WHY AND HOW
http://grammar.ccc.commnet.edu/grammar/composition/organization.htm
This essay, "Principles of Organization," by Prof. John Friedlander of Southwest Tennessee Community College is an excellent explanation of the importance of organization to effective writing, thinking, and speaking. Friedlander also discusses various patterns of organization.

Formulate an Organizing Question

If your research is productive, you'll gather more information than you can use in your speech. Some of that information will be relevant to your topic; some of it will not. You may also be missing some information that you need to develop your topic fully. Deciding what is relevant, irrelevant, or missing requires you to use your critical thinking skill of *analyzing* as you examine items of information and the relationships among them. You will also be *integrating* as you combine and restructure the different pieces of information and *organizing* as you arrange your information so that you can present it effectively, in a way your listeners can understand.

How can you start assessing the information you have, how it fits together, and what you still need? Begin by constructing an organizing question. An **organizing question** is one that, when answered, indicates the ideas and information necessary to develop your topic. The way your question is worded will shape the structure of your speech. For example, if you wanted to speak on the process of selecting a baby's gender, you could ask any of the following organizing questions:

- What issues are involved in gender selection?
- What are the different methods of gender selection?
- What are the benefits of gender selection?
- What are the problems with gender selection?

Each of these questions will lead you to a different set of answers and, thus, a different speech. The first two questions are appropriate for an informative speech; the latter two, for persuasive speeches.

Suppose you selected the first organizing question: What issues are involved in gender selection? To answer this question, you would probably study the opinions and research of ethicists and medical experts, among others. From the information you collected, you might construct the following thesis statement: Before deciding on the process of gender selection, parents should consider the ethical, medical, and social issues involved. Constructing, researching, and answering your organizing question helps you focus your speech and determine what information you will need to support it.

Keep sight of your organizing question as you research and develop your speech. Write the question on a notecard or sheet of paper, and keep it in view as you sift through your research. Ask yourself periodically, "What information helps answer that question?" As you continue working, you may change your organizing question; usually it will become more specific, helping you focus your speech further.

You should find that your organizing question suggests a pattern, perhaps several possible patterns, of organization. Consider these examples:

- What does it take to brew a great cup of coffee?
- What does the U.S. National Holocaust Memorial Museum contain?
- Why do some people favor and others oppose the medical use of marijuana for terminally ill patients?

Answering the first question will probably require you to discover a formula or procedure. The second question calls for a description of the different areas of the museum, based on your memory, your research, or both. Answering the third question will require you to study and organize the arguments for and against the medical use of marijuana.

Divide the Speech into Key Ideas

In the body of the speech, you develop your key ideas according to a specific organizational pattern. Public speakers employ a wide variety of organizational structures. We will discuss eight patterns most commonly used: topical, chronological, spatial, causal,

organizing question: a question that, when answered, indicates the ideas and information necessary to develop your topic.

Key Points

Patterns for Dividing Your Speech into Key Ideas

1. Topical division
2. Chronological division
3. Spatial division
4. Causal division
5. Pro–con division
6. Mnemonic or gimmick division
7. Problem–solution division
8. Need–plan division

pro–con, mnemonic or gimmick, problem–solution, and need–plan. The first six of these patterns are appropriate for either informative or persuasive speeches. Problem–solution and need–plan patterns, however, are appropriate only for persuasive speeches.

Keep in mind as you consider these patterns that no one of them is best. To be effective, you must select a structure that accomplishes the purpose of your speech. In other words, fit the organization to your topic, rather than your topic to the organization.

Topical Division

The **topical division** is the most common organizational pattern for public speeches. This strategy creates subtopics, categories that constitute the larger topic. For example, a speech on graffiti is divided topically if it focuses on graffiti as artistic expression, as political expression, and as vandalism. A speech on the American Indian tribal colleges is arranged topically if the speaker's main points include the history of the tribal colleges, examples of the tribal colleges, and success of the tribal colleges.

As a further example of topical organization, consider this students' experience. Rowena enjoyed a good cup of coffee. Waiting at the airport for a connecting flight, she sipped a Starbuck's coffee and read some of their brochures about coffee. She found them interesting and thought coffee would make a good topic for an informative speech. When she returned to campus, she did some additional research and organized her speech to cover the following points:

Specific Purpose: To inform the audience on the types and tastes of coffee
Key Ideas: I. Types of coffee
    A. Dark roasts
    B. Blends
    C. Decaffeinated
    D. Specialties
  II. Tastes of coffee
    A. Acidity
    B. Aroma
    C. Body
    D. Flavor

An example of topical division for a persuasive speech is as follows:

Specific Purpose: To persuade the audience to adopt a pet
Key Ideas: I. Caring for a pet reduces anxiety and stress.
  II. Caring for a pet increases exercise and physical health.
  III. Caring for a pet decreases loneliness and depression.
  IV. Caring for a pet enhances empathy and self-esteem.

As these examples suggest, topical organization is particularly appropriate as a method of narrowing broad topics, and that may explain its popularity and widespread use. In addition to helping you stay within your time limits, the topical pattern is also attractive because it lets you select subtopics to match your own interests and the interests and needs of your audience.

topical division: organizes a speech according to aspects, or subtopics, of the subject.

Chronological Division

The **chronological division** pattern follows a time sequence. Topics that begin with phrases such as "the steps to" or "the history of" are especially appropriate to this organization. Examples of such topics include the history of your university, the biography of author Toni Morrison, the stages of intoxication, steps to getting your first job, and how a product is marketed.

The following ideas are developed chronologically:

Specific Purpose: To inform the audience of Elisabeth Kübler-Ross's five stages of dying
Key Ideas: I. Denial
              II. Anger
             III. Bargaining
              IV. Depression
               V. Acceptance

Specific Purpose: To inform the audience about the history of garage rock
Key Ideas: I. The 1960s: The British Invasion inspiration
              II. The 1980s: The Garage Rock Revival
             III. Today: The Neo-Garage Movement

Chronological organization works best if you are explaining procedures or processes. A simple and familiar example of chronological organization is a recipe. Any well-written recipe is organized in a time sequence: First, make sure that you have these ingredients; second, preheat the oven; and so forth. For her speech on coffee, used earlier as an example of topical organization, Rowena could have organized her ideas chronologically if her main points were (1) selecting the coffee, (2) grinding the coffee, (3) brewing the coffee, (4) serving the coffee, and (5) storing unused coffee.

Spatial Division

You use **spatial division** when your main points are organized according to their physical proximity or geography. This pattern is appropriate for a speech discussing the parts of an object or a place. For example, a speech on the Mazda Miata might discuss the engine, the interior, and the body exterior.

Other examples of spatial division are the following:

Specific Purpose: To inform the audience about the halls and palaces of the Forbidden City in Beijing, China
Key Ideas: I. The Halls of Harmony
              II. The Palace of Heavenly Purity
             III. The Palace of Earthly Tranquility
              IV. The Hall of the Cultivation of the Mind

Specific Purpose: To inform the audience of the parts of the U.S. National Holocaust Memorial Museum
Key Ideas: I. Four classrooms, two auditoriums, and two galleries for temporary exhibits occupy the lower level.
              II. The permanent exhibit occupies four floors of the main building.
             III. The library and archives of the U.S. Holocaust Research Institute occupy the top floor.

chronological division: organizes a speech according to a time sequence.

spatial division: organizes a speech according to the geography or physical structure of the subject.

Causal Division

You would choose a **causal division** pattern when you want to trace a condition or action from its causes to its effects, or from effects back to causes. Medical topics, in which a speaker discusses the symptoms and causes of a disease, can be easily organized using this method of division. Informative speeches on topics such as hurricanes, lightning, earthquakes, and other natural phenomena may also use this pattern. The following speech outline illustrates the causal pattern:

Specific Purpose: To inform the audience about the effects and causes of sports-victory riots

Key Ideas:
  I. Effects
    A. Death and injuries
    B. Vandalism
    C. Law enforcement costs
  II. Causes
    A. The competitive nature of sports
    B. Mob psychology
    C. Unfavorable economic conditions
    D. Inadequate police presence

Because the causal pattern may be used any time a speaker attributes causes for a particular condition, it is suitable for persuasive as well as informative speeches. A speaker could attempt to prove that certain prescription drugs are, in part, responsible for violent behavior among those who use them; that televising executions would lead to a call for an end to capital punishment; or that new antibiotic-resistant bacteria are increasing infections once thought to be under control. The causal pattern would work well for speeches on any of these topics.

Pro–Con Division

The **pro–con division** presents both sides of an issue. You explain the arguments for a position and the arguments against. Because it is balanced in perspective, this pattern is more appropriate for an informative speech than a persuasive one. After discussing each side of an issue, however, you could choose to defend the stronger position. In this case, your division becomes *pro–con–assessment,* a pattern appropriate for a speech to persuade.

Brian decided to inform his classmates on "snapping." Also known as "cracking," "dissing," and "playing the dozens," this game of insults is part of African American his-

causal division: organizes a speech from cause to effect, or from effect to cause.

pro–con division: organizes a speech according to arguments for and against some policy, position, or action.

Effective speakers use a combination of facial expressions, eye contact, and gestures to emphasize key points for their listeners.

tory and culture. In the book *Snaps,* Brian found examples of this war of words, such as Quincy Jones's snap: "Your house is so small, you have to go outside to change your mind."

At first, Brian thought he would use a topical division and discuss (1) the history of snaps, (2) how the game is played, (3) common topics, and (4) sample snaps. As he continued to research his topic, however, he discovered that there is a lively debate as to whether snapping is constructive or destructive. Brian decided to use a pro–con division to tell his listeners about the debate:

I. Snapping should be encouraged.
   A. It is part of African-American history and culture.
   B. It is a nonviolent way of expressing hostility.
   C. It encourages imagination and creative wordplay.
II. Snapping should be discouraged.
   A. It is demeaning.
   B. It can provoke violence.
   C. There are better ways of expressing anger.

The following outline also demonstrates a pro–con analysis of a controversial issue:

Specific Purpose: To inform the audience of the arguments for and against an increase in the minimum wage

Key Ideas: I. Increasing the minimum wage would be beneficial.
   A. The number of poor would decrease.
   B. The number of people on welfare would decrease.

C. The concept of social justice would be affirmed.
II. Increasing the minimum wage would be harmful.
   A. Unemployment would increase.
   B. Inflation would increase.
   C. Business bankruptcies would increase.

An advantage of the pro–con pattern is that it sets an issue in its broader context and provides balance and objectivity. A disadvantage, however, is the time required to do this. You need plenty of time to discuss both sides of an issue in sufficient detail. Therefore, you will probably want to use this strategy only in one of your longer speeches for this class. If you do not devote sufficient time to each idea, a pro–con or pro–con–assessment development may seem simplistic or superficial to your audience.

Mnemonic or Gimmick Division

A final organizational strategy you can consider for a speech to inform is **mnemonic or gimmick division.** The most common use of this strategy develops and words the key ideas in such a way that the first letter of each key idea forms a word. As a student, you have been using gimmicks for years to help you retain information you need to know. In a science class, for example, you may have memorized the order of colors in the visible spectrum by remembering the name Roy G. Biv: **r**ed-**o**range-**y**ellow-**g**reen-**b**lue-**i**ndigo-**v**iolet.

Gimmicks work so well as memory devices that even advertisers and public service groups occasionally use them. If you can recall what the "four C's" of diamond grading refer to, you probably memorized that information according to a gimmick. The four C's stand for **c**ut, **c**olor, **c**larity, and **c**arat weight. We have heard several students use this gimmick to organize informative speeches on diamonds.

Our student Debra applied mnemonic or gimmick division only to one of the main points in her speech on skin cancer. After answering the questions "Who is at greatest risk for developing skin cancer?" and "What are the three types of skin cancer?" her third point was "What are the warning signs of skin cancer?" To answer that important question, she cited and used the Skin Cancer Foundation's ABCDs of skin cancer: **A**symmetry, **B**order irregularities, **C**olor variations, and **D**iameters larger than typical moles. The brilliance of this mnemonic is that once you hear it explained as clearly as Debra did you will retain it for a long time.

Exploring Online

APPLYING MNEMONICS

www.mindtools.com/memory.html

To learn more about memory techniques and a variety of mnemonic devices that you could use to organize a speech or to study, visit this site. Its links to brief articles give you access to methods of improving your memory.

If you were giving a speech explaining how to improve listening, you could use the gimmick developed by Robert Montgomery (giving him credit in your speech, of course).[2] Montgomery suggests six guidelines for better listening:

L — Look at the other person.

A — Ask questions.

D — Don't interrupt.

D — Don't change the subject.

E — Express emotions with control.

R — Responsively listen.

mnemonic or gimmick division: organizes a speech according to a special memory device, such as alliteration, rhyme, or initial letters that spell a word.

No doubt, the word *ladder* would help you remember your major points as you prepared and delivered such a speech. More important, though, the gimmick would help your listeners retain what you had said.

At times, the gimmick pattern of organizing a speech may seem corny or trivial to you. If you feel that way about this pattern, you probably should avoid it, as your speech delivery may seem self-conscious. When used well and with confidence, however, the gimmick helps your audience remember not only what points you have covered, but also the order in which you have covered them. That is a major accomplishment! In the next section of this chapter, we use a gimmick as we introduce you to our "4 S's" of developing the ideas of the speech. See if it helps you remember these important points.

Problem–Solution Division

The **problem–solution division** is a simple, rigid, organizational approach for a persuasive speech. In this approach the major divisions of your speech and their order are predetermined: You first establish a compelling problem and then present a convincing solution. Because you advocate a plan of action, this pattern is by nature persuasive.

A speaker discussing rape prevention could divide the problem area into physical and psychological effects of rape. The solution phase could include a six-step plan to prevent rape. Speeches that call for a law or some action often use a problem–solution format, as in the next example:

Specific Purpose: To persuade the audience to support reform of our national park system

Key Ideas: I. Our national parks are threatened.
     A. Political influence is a threat.
     B. Environmental pollution is a threat.
     C. Inadequate staffing is a threat.
   II. Our national parks can be saved.
     A. The National Park Service should have greater independence.
     B. Environmental laws should be stricter.
     C. Funding should be increased.

A common alternative to the problem–solution division is to divide the speech into a discussion of problems, causes, and solutions. Notice how Matthew uses this approach:

Specific Purpose: To persuade the audience that involuntary psychiatric commitment laws should be reformed

Key Ideas: I. The problems caused by involuntary commitment laws are serious.
     A. Many are potential victims of being wrongfully committed.
       1. The elderly are especially at risk.
       2. The poor are at risk.
       3. All of us are at risk.
     B. Victims face physical and financial dangers.
   II. Two factors perpetuate these problems.
     A. Medicare policies indirectly encourage hospitals to commit patients regardless of their actual health.
     B. Involuntary commitment laws are too vague.
  III. To remedy this problem, we must act on three levels.
     A. The federal government must reform involuntary commitment procedures.
     B. The psychiatric industry must establish greater control over mental hospitals.
     C. We, as individuals, must take action as well.[3]

Need–Plan Division

The **need–plan division** is a variation of the problem–solution division. This four-fold approach (1) establishes a need or deficiency in the present system, (2) presents a

problem–solution division: a rigid organizational pattern that establishes a compelling problem and offers one or more convincing solutions.

need–plan division: a variation of problem–solution organization that (1) establishes a need or deficiency, (2) offers a proposal to meet the need, (3) shows how the plan satisfies the need, and (4) suggests a plan for implementing the proposal.

proposal to meet the need, (3) demonstrates how the proposal satisfies the need, and (4) suggests a plan for implementing the proposal. Business executives and managers often intuitively employ the need–plan organizational strategy. For example, a company president informs the board of directors of the problem of being located in a town not having an airport. Documenting a loss of sales due to unnecessary driving time, the president proposes relocating company headquarters to a city having a major airport. This would permit the company to cover more territory without expanding its sales force. Finally, the president distributes to the board a detailed plan of action for selecting the appropriate city for relocation.

Salespeople also use the need–plan strategy. They demonstrate or create a need, supply the product or service to meet that need, demonstrate or describe how well it will work, and often even arrange an easy payment plan to help guarantee your purchase. This fundamental sales approach is prevalent for one simple reason: It works! You can use this strategy when you want to prompt an audience to action.

Suppose the specific purpose of your speech is to persuade your audience that employers should provide health promotion programs for their employees. Using the need–plan pattern, you could make four arguments. First, employee illness results in absenteeism, lost productivity, and increased health care costs. Second, employers should establish on-site health and fitness centers for their employees. Third, when health promotion programs have been tried, they have reduced absenteeism, increased productivity, and capped health care costs. As your final step, you could suggest an implementation strategy to include exercise and conditioning programs, alcohol- and drug-awareness education, stress-management workshops, antismoking clinics, and health status testing and evaluation.

Develop the Key Ideas

Assume that your speech is divided into the key ideas, that you have selected the most appropriate pattern to organize them, and that you have decided their order in the speech. Now you need to develop each major point. Obviously, the number of major points you can develop in a speech depends on the time you have been allocated to speak, the complexity of the topic, and the audience's level of education and knowledge of the subject. There is no fixed rule, but most speech instructors recommend that you develop at least two but not more than five main points. Many speakers find that a three-point structure works best.

Regardless of the number of points you select, your responsibility is to explain and support each one sufficiently. The organizational strategy we suggest is one we call the "4 S's." Your listeners will better comprehend and remember your speech if you *signpost, state, support,* and *summarize* each idea.

> **Key Points**
>
> **The "4 S" Strategy of Developing Key Ideas**
>
> 1. Signpost the idea.
> 2. State the idea.
> 3. Support the idea.
> 4. Summarize the idea.

Signpost the Idea

It's Monday morning and you're sitting in your introductory psychology class. You take notes as Dr. Potter lectures on factors that influence interpersonal attraction. In which scenario will you likely understand and remember more of what she says?

Dynamic speakers combine words and gestures to provide signposts that guide listeners through their speeches.

1. Dr. Potter presents her material using words and phrases such as "also," "another factor," and "moving on to similarity."
2. Dr. Potter introduces her ideas with statements such as "a third factor of attraction is proximity" and "similarity is a fourth component of attraction."

If you're like most students, you chose the second scenario. In fact, one experiment tested this and found that "students are able to process information more effectively when lecturers use obvious organizational cues." The researcher's advice to teachers is: "Incorporating organizational cues appears to pay substantial dividends. . . ."[4]

That same advice is equally important for public speakers. Because your audience may not be comprised of note-takers, your task is even more challenging. One of those "obvious organizational cues" you can use is signposting. A **signpost** is a word such as *initially, first, second,* and *finally.* Just as a highway signpost tells travelers where they are in their journey, so a signpost in a speech tells the audience where they are in the speaker's message. Signposts help listeners follow your organizational pattern and increase the likelihood that they will remember your key ideas.

State the Idea

Each major idea needs to be worded precisely and with impact. In her persuasive speech, Esperanza argued the benefits of a multicultural college experience. Her specific purpose was to persuade the audience that ethnic studies (ES) courses should be required for all students. Her organizing question was, "Why should all students be required to

signpost: numbers (*one*) or words (*initially, second,* or *finally*) that signal the listener of the speaker's place in the speech.

take ES courses?" Using a topical organization, Esperanza presented three reasons to support her proposal. Before we tell you how she actually worded those ideas, let's take a look at how a less experienced student might have stated them:

1. ES courses promote cultural awareness.
2. I would like to discuss ES courses and what research and expert opinion say about the way they affect conflict that may be ethnic or racial.
3. Third, social skills.

Do these points seem related to each other? Are they easy to remember? No, they're a mess!

To avoid clutter, keep the following suggestions in mind when wording your key ideas.

1. *Main headings should clearly state the point you will develop.* The first statement ("ES courses promote cultural awareness") does that; the others do not.

2. *Main headings should usually be worded as complete sentences.* Think of the main heading as a statement that you will prove with your supporting materials. Listeners would probably remember the wording of statement 1 in the previous list. As a result, they would remember the point of the speaker's evidence. That is not true of either of the other two statements.

3. *Main headings should be concise.* You want listeners to remember your key ideas. The first statement is easier to remember than the second. The third statement is the shortest, but it isn't a complete sentence. Remembering it doesn't help you understand the point the speaker made.

4. *Main ideas should be parallel to other main ideas.* Parallel wording gives your speech rhythm and repetition, two qualities that help listeners remember your points.

5. *Main ideas should summarize the speech.* When you state your main points, listeners should see how those points answer the organizing question and achieve your specific purpose.

Now let's see how Esperanza worded each of her key ideas:

Specific Purpose: To persuade the audience that ES courses should be required for all students
Key Ideas: I. ES courses promote cultural awareness.
II. ES courses reduce ethnic and racial conflict.
III. ES courses improve social skills.

Each of these main headings clearly states a distinct point that Esperanza will argue. Each statement is a concise, complete sentence. All three sentences are grammatically parallel. Notice, too, that each of the three key ideas directly answers Esperanza's organizing question: Why should ES courses be required for all students?

An alternative to introducing your key idea as a declarative sentence is to ask a question. For example, the specific purpose of Elly's speech was "to persuade the audience that the U.S. should continue to fund the space station *Freedom*." She organized her supporting materials to answer three questions: (1) What will we gain scientifically? (2) What will we gain technologically? (3) What will we gain economically? She introduced each of these ideas with a signpost, for example: "A *third* question we must answer to determine the merits of the space station is: What do we have to gain economically?" She was then ready to answer that question using various types of supporting materials.

You can usually accomplish the first two S's, signposting and stating your idea, in one sentence. For an informative speech assignment requiring the use of visual aids, our student Jennifer decided to speak about Victorian homes, America's "painted ladies." Using spatial organization, she focused her speech on interior details and decoration, taking her listeners on a virtual tour of a Victorian home she called Conglomeration House. Jennifer introduced her first key idea as follows: "The first room we will visit on our tour of a Victorian home is the parlor, the woman's domain."

Support the Idea

This third S is the meat of the "4 S's". Once you have signposted and stated the idea, you must support it. Several categories of supporting materials are at your disposal, limited only by the amount of research you have done and by time limits on your speech. Some of those categories of supporting materials, discussed in detail in Chapter 8, are examples, definitions, comparisons, and statistics.

In her speech on Victorian homes, Jennifer combined specific language with visual aids to depict a different style of each room. For example, as part of her "support" for the first room, the parlor, she stated:

> The parlor in Conglomeration House is done in the Rococo revival style, which is almost exclusively used in interior design. In their book *The Secret Lives of Victorian Homes,* Elan and Susan Zingman-Leith, who restore Victorian houses, give us this wonderful example of this style. [Jennifer showed an enlarged photograph.] Typical of the Rococo theme, the walls are painted white or a pastel color and are broken into panels decorated with wooden molding or even artwork painted directly onto the wall. Around the windows and ceiling are intricately carved wooden details that are influenced by botanical or seashell designs. These are painted to match the color of the walls, but are heavily accented with gilt, or gold-colored paint. Following the pale color scheme, the mantle is made of marble. It is also intricately carved in a botanically inspired design and has cherubs worked into it as well.

Summarize the Idea

A summary at the end of each major division helps wrap up the discussion and refocus attention on the key idea. These periodic summaries may be as brief as one sentence. Avoid "Forrest Gump" summaries, however: "That's all I have to say about that." Early in the course our students sometimes summarize a point by saying, "So I've told you a little about ____." What you say in these summaries within the body needs to be more substantial and more varied than that. An effective summary should reinforce the point you have just developed and also provide a note of closure for that key idea.

If you introduced your idea as a question, your summary should provide the answer. Remember, your point is lost if the audience remembers only your question; they must remember your answer. Elly summarized her point this way: "So the answer to our third question is clear and convincing. What do we have to gain economically from continued funding of the space station? A brighter economic future for American workers, American communities, and the American economy."

Jennifer summarized her first key idea with the following statement: "So the parlor gives us a wonderful example of the Rococo revival architectural style: very feminine, very ornate, and very French." Such a summary not only clued her audience that she had finished discussing this first room, but alerted them that they were about to move to the second room on the tour.

We believe that use of the "4 S's" is fundamental to effective organization within the body of any speech. As you begin to master and apply this four-step strategy, it may seem to be a cookie-cutter approach to public speaking. It *is* exactly that. The "4 S's" are to speech organization what the required movements are to gymnastics—basics that

Theory into Practice
Tips

Applying the "4 S's"

Assigned to deliver an informative speech about something that originated or that exists outside of the United States, our student Alex developed the first main point in the body of his speech as follows:

Signpost of key idea — *First,* I'd like to *describe the Itsukushima Shrine's Grand O-Torii Gate* as I experienced it for the first time. Along the way I'll give you some specific details about the structure. During 1991 and halfway into 1992, I was still in the military and living in Japan. On one of our off weekends, we decided to visit the Shrine in Miyajima-guchi, a small town south of the military base where we were stationed. We boarded a train and enjoyed the 30–45-minute ride to the small town. From the train station, we walked a short distance to a pier. There we boarded a ferry that took us to Miyajima Island, where the shrine was located. We got off the ferry and walked toward the shrine location, not knowing that it was really close. The tide was in. Suddenly, there appeared this big red Japanese gate in the water about half a football field away from where we were standing near the shore.

Statement of key idea

Support for key idea

(narration)

(comparison) I was already excited from the train ride and the ferry ride. Seeing the Grand O-Torii Gate was kind of like seeing Sleeping Beauty's Castle at Disneyland for the first time. You see it in pictures and movies all the time. But seeing it for real, well, if you've been to Disneyland you know the feeling. This is what the Grand O-Torii Gate looks like when the tide is in. [Alex shows the photograph.] It really looks like it's floating in the water, especially if you have never seen it when the tide is out.

(visual example)

(citation)
(source)
(statistics) I promised you some specific details about the structure and I won't let you down. On the 3rd of June 2005, I found a website, www.hiroshima-cdas.or.jp, sponsored by a Japanese Internet service provider. The site mentions that the gate is almost 52½ feet tall and that each pillar is about 44 feet tall and at least 24½ feet around. The gate is constructed entirely of wood from the camphor tree, which is native to the area. Concrete beams and pillars support the O-Torii gate, and it's covered with vermillion, or deep red, lacquer. Because it is out at sea, partially submerged in the water, shipworms and barnacles encrust and slowly deteriorate the wood at the base. I've seen the barnacles but I had no clue of the damage that was going on. Fortunately, plastic resin has been found to be effective in preserving the wood.

(definition)

Summary of key idea You can now imagine the impression the Grand O-Torii gate made on me even from a distance, but it can be even more awe-inspiring when you get a chance to stand as close to it as I did.

Transition to second key idea Japan is, unfortunately, subject to destructive typhoons. That's why governments and organizations have banded together to help preserve this shrine for future generations. So, second, let's examine some of the work required to preserve the gate.

To clarify the look of the Grand O-Torii Gate for his listeners, Alex showed them this view he had seen as he stood on the shore of Miyajima Island at high tide looking out at the Sea of Japan.

you must learn before you are able to develop your own style or flair. As you master the "4 S's" and gain confidence in public speaking, clear organization will become almost a reflex reaction performed without conscious effort. As your ability to organize ideas clearly becomes second nature to you, you will find that the structure of your thinking, writing, and speaking has greatly improved.

Connect the Key Ideas

A speech is composed of key ideas, and you have just seen how to develop each according to the "4 S" approach. Those key ideas form the building blocks of your speech. For your speech to hang together, however, you must connect those ideas, just as a mason joins bricks and stones with mortar. A speaker moves from one idea to the next—puts mortar between the units—with the aid of a transition. A **transition** is a statement connecting one thought to another. Without transitions, the ideas of a speech are introduced abruptly. As a result, the speech lacks a smooth flow of ideas and sounds choppy.

A transition not only connects two ideas, but also indicates the nature of the connection between the ideas. Transitions are usually indicated by *markers*, words or phrases near the beginning of a sentence that indicate how that sentence relates to the previous one.[5] You will use some transitions *within* each of your main points to offer illustrations (*for example*), indicate place or position (*above, nearby*), or make concessions (*although, of course*).[6] However, the transitions you use *between* the main points of your speech will indicate four basic types of connections: complementary, causal, contrasting, and chronological.

A **complementary transition** adds one idea to another, thus reinforcing the major point of the speech. Typical transitional markers for complementary transitions include *also, and, in addition, just as important, likewise, next,* and *not only.*

Each of the following transitions uses the complementary approach to reinforce the speaker's thesis:

transition: a statement that connects parts of the speech and indicates the nature of their connection.

complementary transition: adds one idea to another.

It is clear, then, that golf courses have sociological effects on communities where they are located. Just as important, however, are their environmental effects.

Vocal cues, however, are not the only source of information that may help you determine if someone is lying. You may also look for body cues.

A **causal transition** emphasizes a cause-and-effect relation between two ideas. Words and phrases that mark a causal relationship include *as a result, because, consequently,* and *therefore.*

In his speech, Victor documented problems resulting from excessive noise. As he shifted his focus from cause to effect, he used the following transition:

> We can see, then, that we live, work, and play in a noisy world. An unfortunate result of this clamor and cacophony is illustrated in my second point: Excessive noise harms interpersonal interaction.

A **contrasting transition** shows how two ideas differ. These transitions often use markers such as *although, but, in contrast, in spite of, nevertheless, on the contrary,* and *on the other hand.*

In her tour of Conglomeration House, Jennifer moved her audience from her first to her second main idea with the following clear contrasting transition:

> In sharp contrast to the parlor is the library, the man's retreat in the home. This is the second room we will visit on our tour.

A **chronological transition** shows the time relationships between ideas, and uses words or phrases such as *after, as soon as, at last, at the same time, before, later,* and *while.*

Will informed his classmates on the SQ3R system of studying and remembering written material. He organized his five main points around five key words: survey, question, read, recite, and review. His transitions emphasized the natural sequence of these stages, as in:

> After surveying, or overviewing, what you are about to read, you are ready for the second stage of the SQ3R system: to question.

A second example of a chronological transition is the following:

> If thorough preparation is the first step in a successful job interview, the second step is to arrive on time.

A good transition serves as a bridge, highlighting the idea you have just presented and preparing your listeners for the one to come. It smooths the rough edges of the speech and enhances the cohesiveness of your ideas. Note, however, that transitions alone cannot impose order on a speech. The main ideas and their natural links must already exist before you can underscore their connections with transitions.[7] Developing and pursuing an organizing question can help ensure that you know your main ideas and their connections in the first place.

Effective transitions require more than just inserting a word or phrase between two ideas. If you find yourself always using a single word such as *now, next,* or *OK* to introduce your ideas, you need to work on your transitions. Avoid using weak and pedestrian phrases as transitions, such as "Moving on to my next point" or "The next thing I would like to discuss." Instead, work on composing smooth, functional transition statements as Bonnie, one of our students, did in the following example.

In her persuasive speech, Bonnie advocated voluntary school uniforms for students in kindergarten through high school. She previewed her ideas in her introduction by stating that pilot programs demonstrate that "voluntary uniforms would help create a safer school environment, enhance academic achievement, and promote a positive

causal transition: establishes a cause–effect relation between two ideas.

contrasting transition: shows how two ideas differ.

chronological transition: shows how one idea precedes or follows another in time.

social climate." In the body of her speech, Bonnie explained and supported each of these points, connecting them by using smooth transitions. Bonnie used the following excellent transition as she moved from her first to her second idea:

> Every student has a right to learn in a safe environment, and school uniforms help eliminate one cause of school violence. But schools should do more than ensure safety, they should promote learning. A second benefit of school uniforms is that they enhance academic achievement.

If you follow the guidelines and examples in this chapter, the body of your speech will be well organized. You should now know how to generate an organizing question and use it to select an organizational pattern that is appropriate to your topic, your

Try This

Developing One Key Idea

Select a topic appropriate for an informative or a persuasive speech in this class. Brainstorm several key ideas and an appropriate organizational pattern for the body of your speech. Using the "4 S" strategy discussed in this chapter, develop *one* key point. Signpost and state the idea. Support it with at least two types of supporting materials, citing at least two quality sources. After stating your internal summary, include a transition that guides listeners to your next key idea. Remember, you are developing just one compelling argument, so you should be able to deliver this point within two or three minutes.

purpose, and your audience. You should also know how to develop each main idea in the body of your speech according to the "4 S's" and how to connect those main ideas with appropriate transitions. In Chapter 10 you will learn how to extend this excellent organization to the introduction and conclusion of your speech.

Summary

Being sure of your speech organization gives you confidence as a speaker; communicating your information in a well-organized manner makes it much easier for the audience to remember what you have said. The chief goal of speech organization is to assist your listeners in understanding and retaining your information.

The three parts of a speech are the *introduction, body,* and *conclusion.* You should organize the body first because it is the most substantial part of the speech and because its content determines the content of the introduction and the conclusion.

To help you evaluate the information you have researched and select an appropriate organizational pattern, you should formulate an *organizing question.* Answering this question will tell you what main ideas and information you need in order to develop your topic for your listeners. Your answer should also suggest possible ways of organizing the body of your speech.

Depending on your purpose in speaking, you may select any of eight organizational patterns for the body of the speech. *Topical division* narrows a broad topic by limiting it to certain subtopics chosen by the speaker. *Chronological division* organizes a historical topic or a speech explaining a process into a time sequence. *Spatial division* lets the geography or physical structure of a place or thing organize the speech for you. *Causal division* allows a speaker to explore a condition or action from its causes to its effects or from effects back to causes.

Pro–con division presents the arguments for and against some policy, position, or action, and with the addition of a final assessment step becomes a persuasive speech pattern. *Mnemonic or gimmick division* uses a memory device such as the letters of a word to organize key points in the speech and help the audience recall them.

Two final organizational patterns are appropriate only for persuasive speeches. *Problem–solution division* presents a compelling issue and then advocates a course of action to resolve it. *Need–plan division,* a variation of problem–solution division, establishes a need, presents a proposal for satisfying that need, demonstrates how the proposal satisfies the need, and then suggests a plan for implementing the proposal.

After choosing a general organizational pattern and establishing your main points, you are ready to organize the presentation of each major idea in the body of your speech. To do this, we recommend a memory device we call the "4 S's": *signpost* the idea, *state* the idea, *support* the idea, and *summarize* the idea. Apply these four steps to each major idea in the speech.

Each of the main points you develop needs to be connected to the others by *transitions.* Effective transitions indicate the nature of the relation between the ideas: *complementary, causal, contrasting,* or *chronological.*

Practice Critique

Evaluating Organization

Read the transcript of Tiffanie Petrin's speech on steganography in the Appendix. Write her a critique evaluating the organization of the body of her speech. Does she focus on a few key ideas? Does she develop each idea using the "4 S" strategy? Are these ideas connected with smooth transitions? What suggestions can you offer to improve Tiffanie's speech in any of these areas? Provide specific examples from her speech to support your comments.

Exercises

1. Read the student speeches in the Appendix, and formulate organizing questions each speaker might have used.

2. Look at the list of self-generated topics in Chapter 6, and select several that would lend themselves to topical organization. What subtopics could each include?

3. Look at the list of self-generated topics in Chapter 6, and select a topic that would lend itself to spatial division. What are some subtopics a speech on this topic could include?

4. Brainstorm for possible topics about processes of which you have a working knowledge (how to conduct a library computer search, the best way to study for an exam, etc.). Select one of these topics, and develop three to five key ideas, organizing them according to a time sequence.

5. Select one topic and show how it could be developed using three different organizational patterns. Which do you think would make the best speech? Why?

6. What memory devices or gimmicks have you used recently to help you remember materials in this or another class? For example, you may have used "IRS" to help you remember the elements of the triangle of meaning in Chapter 1.

7. Brainstorm some speech topics that could be developed according to a pro–con division. Select one, and write a specific purpose statement. List the divisions you could use in the body of the speech.

8. Select an organizational pattern you think would be appropriate for speeches with the specific purposes listed below. Could the specific purpose be achieved using other patterns? Are there some patterns that would clearly be inappropriate?
   a. To inform the audience about relaxation techniques
   b. To inform the audience about the history of Groundhog Day
   c. To inform the audience about the advantages and disadvantages of raising money for charitable causes by telethons
   d. To inform the audience about marriage rituals in various cultures
   e. To persuade the audience that illiteracy is seriously harming national productivity
   f. To persuade the audience that the health benefits from one exercise program are greater than those from another

Introducing and Concluding Your Speech

chapter

197

I think the end is implicit in the beginning. It must be. If that isn't there in the beginning, you don't know what you're working toward. You should have a sense of a story's shape and form and its destination, all of which is like a flower inside a seed. —EUDORA WELTY

Consider some good beginnings: the first notes of a favorite piece of music; the opening shots of a favorite film; a cool early morning start for a long, summer road trip. Each of these beginnings marks a boundary between what you've been doing or paying attention to and some new activity. Each refocuses your energy or concentration. Whether you are the speaker or a listener, the opening of a speech has the potential to achieve these same effects.

Famed Southern writer Eudora Welty was talking specifically about beginning and ending a short story or novel in the quotation at the beginning of this chapter. However, other writers and speakers share her concerns. Your first words allow you to make a positive impression on your audience, capture their attention, prepare them to listen more effectively, and enlist their support. Those first words are crucial, of course, because they can occur only once in a given speech.

In Chapter 9 you learned how to organize the most substantial part of your speech, the body. In this chapter we examine how you frame the body by discussing the objectives of speech introductions and conclusions, as well as specific strategies you can use at these important points.

Exploring *Online*

INTRODUCTIONS AND CONCLUSIONS
http://wps.ablongman.com/ab_public_speaking_2/
0,9651,1593275-,00.html
"Starting a Talk with an Introduction" from this Allyn & Bacon/Longman website offers a list of attention-getting devices for beginning a speech effectively. It also provides links to federal statistics and daily quotations that may be useful at the start of a speech.

Organize the Introduction of the Speech

After you work on the body of your speech, you are ready to turn your attention to the introduction and conclusion. An introduction should be constructed to achieve five objectives: (1) get the attention of your audience; (2) state your topic; (3) establish the importance of your topic; (4) establish your credibility to speak on your topic; and (5) preview the key ideas of your speech. Studying these objectives and the ways to achieve them will enable you to get your speech off to a clear, interesting start.

Key Points

Functions of a Speech Introduction

1. Get the attention of your audience.
2. State your topic.
3. Establish the importance of your topic.
4. Establish your credibility to speak on your topic.
5. Preview the key ideas of your speech.

Get the Attention of Your Audience

Your first objective as a speaker is to secure the audience's attention. If you are fortunate enough to have a reputation as a powerful, captivating speaker, you may already have the attention of your listeners before you utter your first word. Most of us, however, have not yet achieved such reputations. Consequently, it is important to get the audience quickly involved in your speech. The strategy you select will depend on your personality, your purpose, your topic, your audience, and the occasion. Your options include the following seven possible techniques for getting the audience's attention.

Strategies for Getting Your Audience's Attention

1. Question your audience.
2. Arouse curiosity.
3. Stimulate imagination.
4. Promise something beneficial.
5. Amuse your audience.
6. Energize your audience.
7. Acknowledge and compliment your audience.

Question Your Audience.   A speaker can get an audience involved with the speech through the use of questions, either rhetorical or direct. A **rhetorical question** stimulates thought but is not intended to elicit an overt response. For example, consider the following opening questions:

- How did you spend last weekend? Watching television? Going to a movie? Sleeping late?
- What would you do if you saw your best friend copying another student's answers during a test?
- Do you remember when you first suspected that there really wasn't a Santa Claus?

A speaker who asks any of the above questions does not expect an overt audience response. In fact, it would probably disrupt the rhythm of the presentation if someone answered orally. A question is rhetorical if it is designed to get the audience thinking about the topic.

A **direct question** seeks a public response. Audience members may be asked to respond vocally or physically. For example, the following questions could all be answered by a show of hands:

- How many people have worked as a volunteer for some charitable group within the last year? The last six months?
- Last week the Student Government Association sponsored a blood drive. Who in this class donated blood?

Like the rhetorical question, a direct question gets the audience thinking about your topic. But the direct question has the additional advantage of getting your listeners physically involved in your speech and, consequently, making them more alert. This strategy may be especially appropriate if your class meets at 8:00 A.M. and you are the first speaker, or if you have an evening class and are the last speaker, or if you give your speech during midterm week when your classmates are especially tired.

Sometimes a direct question may invite an oral response. In his speech urging classmates to volunteer their efforts at charitable agencies, Lou discovered by a show of hands that only a few people volunteered regularly. He then asked the rest of the class why they did not. Several complained of lack of time. One person said she did not know how to locate groups that need volunteers. Lou continued, incorporating these excuses into his speech and refuting them.

When you ask a direct question and you want oral responses, you need to pause, look at your listeners, and give them sufficient time to respond. If you want your direct question answered by a show of hands, raise your hand as you end the question.

rhetorical question: a question designed to stimulate thought without demanding an overt response.

direct question: a question that asks for an overt response from listeners.

"I didn't answer No. 11, because I thought it was a *rhetorical* question."

© 2002. Reprinted courtesy of Bunny Hoest and *Parade* Magazine.

In this way you indicate nonverbally how you want the question answered. If you seek and get oral responses, however, make sure that you neither lose control nor turn your public speech into a group discussion. Practice this technique as you rehearse in front of friends before making it part of your speech.

A few final cautions about using a question to get the audience's attention. First, avoid asking embarrassing questions of your listeners. "How many of you are on scholastic probation?" "Has anyone in here ever spent a night in jail?" Common sense should tell you that most people would be reluctant to answer direct questions such as these. Second, don't use a question without first considering its usefulness to your speech. Many questions are creative and intriguing. Remember, asking a valid question that listeners answer either openly or to themselves gets them immediately involved and thinking about your speech topic. Just don't rely on a question because you have not developed or found a more creative attention-getter.

Arouse Your Audience's Curiosity. A lively way to engage the minds of your listeners is the technique of suspense. Get them wondering what is to come. Consider the combination of humor and suspense our student David used at the beginning of the following introduction:

> "You what? . . . When? . . . Why? . . . Here, talk to your father!"
>
> "Hey, what the hell's the matter with you, you nuts or what? . . . A perfectly good airplane for no reason at all? . . . What, are you crazy?"
>
> These were the initial responses I received from my mother and father when I called to tell them that I had just gone skydiving for the first time. Growing up I always said that you couldn't pay me to jump out of an airplane. Well, as it turned out, I ended up paying to jump out of one. This morning I would like to share with you three of the things I paid for: a three-hour class, a fifteen-minute airplane ride, and a five-minute fall to Earth.

His mother's comments made us wonder what David's subject was. By the end of his father's questions, we had an inkling, which David confirms in the final part of his introduction.

Speaking with Confidence

Knowing that my speech had a solid introduction made me feel a lot more confident. I used the guidelines presented in this chapter as I constructed the introduction to my informative speech about anthrax. First, I asked how many people in my audience had heard about anthrax before September 11, 2001. The majority had not. Asking this direct question not only got the attention of the audience, but it also told the class and me that most of us had little knowledge on this topic. That gave me added confidence, knowing that my information would benefit my listeners. Next I told them that I would be discussing the history of anthrax and explaining how anthrax attacks a person's body. To reinforce the importance of this topic, I reminded the audience that anthrax had been used as a terrorist weapon. I knew this would stir up some feelings and that added to my confidence that the audience was motivated to listen. By using the guidelines for an effective introduction, I was able to get the attention of my audience, introduce my topic, preview what I would discuss in the body of the speech, and keep them motivated to listen.

—Jacquine Stenz, *Montana State University*

Jake chose to keep his audience in suspense in his attention-getting step. Notice, also, how he incorporated rhetorical questions in his introduction to heighten his listeners' curiosity:

> A 76-year-old mother of four slices bread at her kitchen counter. In a moment, her life will be over—cut down by a culprit who has been lying quietly in wait for almost two decades. In a way, she's lucky. This culprit frequently strikes women far younger than she. But nevertheless, in a moment a family will begin to mourn. But who was this stealthy assassin? Some rare and untreatable virus? No. An incredibly patient serial killer? Uh-uh. The truth is this villain is not only far deadlier than both of these, but also the most preventable.[1]

Jake resolved the suspense when he introduced his topic: heart disease in women.

You can also arouse curiosity by what you do as well as what you say. Our student David began one speech by carrying a small ice chest to a table holding a portable CD player at the front of the room. Without saying a word, he placed a folded towel on the table, opened the chest, and lifted a Bose speaker from the water in which it had been soaking. His classmates were completely silent. David's first words were, "I put this in here to soak last night, so it will take a few seconds to drain."

Exploring Online

QUOTATIONS
www.theotherpages.org/quote.html
The "Quotations Home Page," established in 1994, touts approximately 25,000 entries in 30 categories. Use the "Alpha by Topic" link to get to specific subjects quickly. If you're looking for ideas, browse "Recent Quotes," "Great Leaders," "Definitions," or even more than 150 quotations from "Steven Wright."

By the end of his speech on outdoor speaker technology, he had hooked the speaker up to his portable CD player and played a few seconds of crystal clear music by Candy Dulfer.

Stimulate Your Audience's Imagination.   Another way to engage the minds of your listeners is to stimulate their imaginations. To do this, you must know what referents they share, and this requires some good audience analysis on your part. Notice in the following example how Jennifer began her speech by relating a personal experience that many in her audience probably found familiar:

> The year was 1984. Saturday morning had finally arrived, and I was in my Strawberry Shortcake nightgown, complete with Strawberry Shortcake necklace and watch, humming along with the theme to *The Smurfs*. I can still hear it in my head. [She hums part of the show's theme song.] My sister sat beside me with her Optimus Prime Transformer in hand. My younger brother was quietly awaiting *Teenage Mutant Ninja Turtles* to come on. All was right with the world.

In the rest of her speech Jennifer discussed "retro toys" such as Transformers and Strawberry Shortcake and the reasons for their return to store shelves.

Our student Lori introduced one of her speeches in the following way:

> Imagine yourself on a beach, at night. Through the moonlight you see the palm trees swaying as the warm tropical breeze comes in from the sea. There's an undercurrent of excitement as you all load into the boat. Moonlight shimmers off the waves as you approach your unmarked destination. The boat stops. Backward, with gear intact, you fall into the pitch black water. There are no words to express the sensation of your first night dive. You hear only the sounds of your own breathing. You see only the brilliantly colored marine life that swim in and out of the scope of your flashlight; all else is a black abyss.

In spite of what she says, we would argue that Lori did find some words to express the sensation of night scuba diving. Notice her strong appeals to our senses of sight and hearing in this example. In Chapter 12, we discuss the use of language to create these and other sensory impressions in your audience.

Promise Your Audience Something Beneficial.   We listen more carefully to messages that are in our self-interest. In Chapter 5, we recommended that you consider your listeners' needs using Maslow's hierarchy or the VALS typology. If you can promise your audience something that meets one or more of their needs, you secure their attention very quickly. For example, beginning your speech with the statement "Every person in this room can find a satisfying summer internship related to your major field of study" immediately secures the attention of your listeners—at least those not currently working in their dream jobs. Other effective examples are ones in which a speaker promises that her information can save audience members hundreds of dollars in income tax next April, or in which a speaker says, "The information I will give you in the next ten minutes will help you buy an excellent used car with complete confidence." Job satisfaction, savings, and consumer confidence—the promises of these three attention-getters—are directly related to the interests of many audience members.

Exploring *Online*

QUOTATIONS
www.bartleby.com/quotations
If you're searching for a profound or funny quotation to get your listeners' attention, this site offers a searchable database that provides more than 87,000 entries from multiple sources, including the venerable *Bartlett's Familiar Quotations*.

In addition to promising a benefit that meets your listeners' self-interests, you can also appeal to their selflessness. Notice how David tapped his audience's altruism in the following speech attention-getter:

> When Tricia Matthews decided to undergo a simple medical procedure, she had no idea what impact it could have on her life. But more than a year later, when she saw five-year-old Tommy and his younger brother Daniel walk across the stage of *The Oprah Winfrey Show,* she realized that the short amount of time it took her to donate her bone marrow was well worth it. Tricia is not related to the boys who suffered from a rare immune deficiency disorder treated by a transplant of her bone marrow. Tricia and the boys found each other through the National Marrow Donor Program, or NMDP, a national network that strives to bring willing donors and needy patients together. Though the efforts Tricia made were minimal, few Americans make the strides she did. Few of us would deny anyone the gift of life, but sadly, few know how easily we can help.[2]

Amuse Your Audience.   The use of humor can be one of a speaker's most effective attention-getting strategies. Getting the audience to laugh with you makes them alert and relaxed. You can use humor to emphasize key ideas in your speech, to show a favorable self-image, or to defuse audience hostility. However, any humor you use should be tasteful and relevant to your topic or the speaking occasion. As a speaker, you must be able to make a smooth and logical transition between your humorous opening and the topic of your speech. Telling a joke or a funny story and then switching abruptly to a serious topic trivializes the topic and may offend your listeners.

Carl Wayne Hensley, professor of speech communication at Bethel College, used humor to introduce his speech on effective communication:

> A woman went to an attorney and said, "I want to divorce my husband." Lawyer: "Do you have any grounds?" Woman: "About 10 acres." Lawyer: "Do you have a grudge?" Woman: "No, just a carport." Lawyer: "Does your husband beat you up?" Woman: "No, I get up about an hour before he does every morning." Lawyer: "Why do you want a divorce?" Woman: "We just can't seem to communicate."
>
> This woman's problem is not unique. Many husbands and wives, many parents and children, many managers and employees, many professionals and clients can't seem to communicate.[3]

Notice how the speaker used humor to provide a smooth transition to the main topic of the speech.

At the 53rd annual Emmy Awards, host Ellen DeGeneres finally appeared, briefly, in a dress. In her typical self-deprecating way, Ellen and her Bjork-style dress not only caused the audience to howl in laughter, but also commented on the superficiality of fashion, the cult of celebrity, and even on the trap of gender role stereotyping.

Similarly, Stacey encouraged her classmates to study a foreign language, introducing her classroom speech with the following attention-getting riddle:

> What do you call someone who is fluent in many languages? A polylingual. What do you call someone who is fluent in two languages? A bilingual. What do you call someone who is fluent in only one language? An American!
>
> This is a joke commonly told among the Japanese. Behind the apparent humor of this joke are some embarrassing truths.

Stacey combined humor and rhetorical questions to get her listeners' attention. She then discussed those "embarrassing truths" and the price we pay for speaking only one language.

Energize Your Audience. Sometimes speakers can command attention simply by their "presence." Martin Luther King, Jr., had that ability. Today speakers as diverse as Tony Blair, Rudy Giuliani, and Oprah Winfrey bring to their audiences an expectation that excites listeners. Although few people can achieve such dynamism, most speakers can work to enliven their delivery. A positive attitude, appropriate dress, a confident walk to the platform, direct eye contact, a friendly smile, erect posture, a strong voice, and forceful gestures give an introduction as much impact as any of the preceding strategies. Conversely, the absence of these elements can destroy the effect of even the best-worded opening statement. Remember, though, that an energized delivery is not a stand-alone strategy. It cannot substitute for a well-worded opening statement, but rather it is best used in combination with one of the other attention-getting strategies.

The advantages of an "energized" presence extend far beyond a speech introduction, however. In Chapter 13, we'll give you specific suggestions for achieving dynamic delivery throughout your speech.

Acknowledge and Compliment Your Audience.   At some point in your life, you will probably be called on to deliver a formal, public speech to an assembled group. Perhaps you will be the keynote speaker for a convention, or maybe you will accept an award from a civic group. The group inviting you to speak may even be paying you, anything from a small honorarium to a substantial fee. Such an occasion usually requires that you begin by acknowledging the audience and key dignitaries.

On February 26, 2005, Bill Gates, chairman of Microsoft Corporation, addressed the National Education Summit on High Schools. He was introduced by Mark Warner, chair of the National Governors Association. Notice how Gates included and complimented his audience in his introduction:

> Thank you for that kind introduction. I also want to thank you, Governor Warner, and your fellow governors, for your leadership in hosting this education summit on America's high schools. It is rare to bring together people with such broad responsibilities and focus their attention on one single issue. But if there is one single issue worth your focused attention, it is the state of American high schools.
>
> Many of us here have stories about how we came to embrace high schools as an urgent cause. Let me tell you ours.

Gates then stated a goal of the Bill and Melinda Gates Foundation: "to promote equity through education."[4] This shared commitment for educational reform connected Gates with his audience.

In this class, your classmates make up your audience. You have interacted with them and, by now, probably know them pretty well. To begin your speech formally by acknowledging and complimenting them would seem stiff and insincere. You should not have to compliment fellow classmates; in fact, if you have prepared well, they should be thanking you for providing excellent information. For your assigned speeches, therefore, you should probably choose one of the other attention-getting strategies.

State Your Topic

Once you have the attention of your audience, state the topic or purpose of your speech directly and succinctly. For an informative speech, your statement of purpose typically takes the form of a simple declarative sentence. "Today, I will show you how you can improve your study skills" clearly informs the audience of your topic.

This second goal of a speech introduction is vitally important, even though the actual statement of purpose will take only a few seconds for you to say. Consider the following beginning section of a speech introduction:

> How many of you have had a cholesterol count taken in the last year? Do you know what your numbers are and what they mean? It seems like we have all recently become much more aware of good cholesterol and bad, high-density lipoproteins and low-density ones, the dangers of high-fat diets and how difficult they can be to avoid in these fast-food, nuke-it-till-it's-hot times. People who never really considered exercising are spending a lot of money to join health clubs and work out. They know that a high cholesterol count can mean you are in danger of developing arteriosclerosis and finding yourself a candidate for surgery. Even if you don't have a heart attack, you may be hospitalized for one of several new procedures to clean out arteries clogged with plaque.

Now answer the following question: This speaker's purpose was to

(a) discuss the interpretation of cholesterol tests.
(b) explain sources of cholesterol in popular foods.
(c) encourage exercise as a key to reducing serum cholesterol.
(d) explain new nonsurgical procedures for opening clogged arteries.
(e) I can't tell what the speaker's purpose was.

Unfortunately, in this case, the correct answer is e. What went wrong? The speaker started off well enough by using two legitimate questions—the first direct, the second rhetorical—as an attention-getter. But then things got out of control; for almost a minute of speaking time, the speaker lapsed into a series of generalizations without ever stating the purpose of the speech. This excerpt represents a minute of wasted time! In a five- to seven-minute speech, that minute represents one-fifth to one-seventh of total speaking time. The speaker has confused the audience with vague statements and has lost their confidence. The real shame is that any of the four purposes just listed could be the goal of a good speech. Prepare properly and you will know your purpose. Then, state that purpose clearly as the second step of your introduction.

Establish the Importance of Your Topic

This third goal in organizing the introduction to your speech should convince the listeners that the topic is important to them. You want to motivate them to listen further. In his speech on unsafe water used in dental procedures, Brian used expert testimony and statistics to show his listeners that they were at risk:

> Professor Robert Staat, a microbiologist with the University of Louisville Dental School, reported to *20/20* the results of his research testing water samples from more than 60 dental offices across the country. His investigation revealed that almost 90 percent of water used in dental procedures does not meet federal drinking water standards, and two-thirds of the samples contained saliva from previous patients. After comparing dental water with water collected from public toilets, he discovered that in nearly every case the water from the toilets was cleaner than the water going into our mouths. His conclusion: The water used in most dental procedures is dangerously unsanitary, and we must act to protect ourselves.[5]

Remember the way Jake tapped his listeners' curiosity before introducing his topic of heart disease in women? He then provided statistics and examples to establish the importance of his topic for the women and men in his audience:

> "[T]he truth," as stated in the *Pittsburgh Post Gazette* of December 12, 2000, "is that heart disease kills more women every year than all forms of cancer, chronic lung disease, pneumonia, diabetes, accidents, and AIDS combined." Whereas one in twenty-eight women will die of breast cancer, one in five will die of heart disease. And guys, before you take the next nine minutes to decide what you'll eat for lunch, ask yourself one question: What would my life be like if the women who make it meaningful are not there? Clearly, this is an issue that concerns us all.[6]

Establish Your Credibility to Speak on Your Topic

The fourth goal of a speech introduction is to establish your credibility to speak on your topic. Your listeners should understand why you selected your topic and should believe that you are qualified to speak on it. Establishing your credibility begins in the introduction and should continue throughout the rest of your speech. Introducing relevant supporting materials and citing their sources are two ways to demonstrate that you have carefully researched and considered your topic. You can also enhance your credibility by drawing on your own experience with your topic. Our student Liz mentioned her nursing degree and her work as a nurse in the introduction to her speech on physician-assisted suicide. In the body of her speech she also mentioned sources that she had studied in a bioethics class. Our student Humberto mentioned in the introduction of his speech on computer scams how he had once almost been victimized. In the final point of his speech body, he explained how he detected the fake money order he had received to pay for a boat he was selling.

Preview Your Key Ideas

A final objective in organizing your introduction is the **preview,** in which you "tell us what you're going to tell us." The preview, working like a map, shows a final destination and reveals how the speaker intends to get there. As a result, the audience can travel more easily through the body of the speech. A person discussing the political, economic, and medical implications of national health insurance should inform the audience of these three divisions. A speaker addressing the issue of urban decay could preview her speech by saying, "To better understand the scope of this problem, we must look at four measurable conditions: the unemployment rate, housing starts, the poverty level, and the crime rate." That preview lists the four topics to be covered in the body of the speech and prepares the audience to listen more intelligently.

Preview statements are usually from one to three sentences in length. Rarely do they need to be longer. Each of the following examples is appropriately brief and specific in preparing the audience for the key ideas and the organizational pattern of the speech:

> Assuming that you have the necessary materials, the three steps to constructing a piece of stained glass are, first, selecting or creating a design; second, cutting the glass; and third, assembling and fixing the individual pieces.

> An enhanced self-concept benefits us in at least three ways. Specifically, it improves our social interaction, our academic achievement, and our chances for career success.

> Having a *quinceañera* serves two main functions for a young girl and her family. The first is to mark the transition from adolescence to adulthood. The second is to allow the parents to present their daughter to society.

preview: a statement that orients the audience by revealing how the speaker has organized the body of a speech.

A person suffering from narcolepsy, then, experiences unexpected attacks of deep sleep. This little-known sleep disorder is better understood if we know its symptoms, its causes, and its treatment.

Today the *charreada* often draws both participants dressed in their traditional costumes and protestors carrying signs. To understand both sides of this issue, we'll look at those who say that the *charreada* is a valid sport that deserves to be practiced and at those who insist that the *charreada* is cruel and inhumane.

If you have written a thesis statement for your speech, you'll have no trouble constructing a preview statement. Preview statements, however, are often bland and predictable. Use your creativity to accent the ideas that will follow. For example, Jayme could have used the following preview statement in her speech on e-paper: "To understand the potential impact of e-paper, we must look first at what it is and how it works; next, at its advantages and disadvantages; and finally, at its future." Although this statement previews the key ideas of the speech, it conveys little creativity. Instead, Jayme opted for a longer statement to reinforce the ideas of her speech:

> In order to understand why the impact of e-paper could be of Gutenberg proportions, we must first start with a blank sheet as we explore what e-paper is and how it works; next, fill up the page with its advantages and disadvantages; and finally, widen the margins to discuss future directions of this amazing new technology.[7]

Put It All Together

How does the introduction sound when all five of its functions are working together? Our student Rose showed us that she certainly knows how to develop a complete and effective introduction:

> According to an old Indian saying, every person dies three times. The first time is the moment your life ends. The second is when your body is lowered into the ground. The third is when there is no one around to remember you. I'm going to talk to you today about death, or rather the celebration of death. This is a special celebration that comes from a Mexican tradition called *Dia de los Muertos,* or Day of the Dead. Now it may seem strange and morbid to speak of celebration and death in the same breath, but in the Mexican culture, death is embraced and worshipped just as much as life is. After I give you a little background on *Dia de los Muertos,* I'll explain the different ways this holiday is celebrated and show you some of the traditional objects used in the celebration.

Our student Shannon began one of his speeches in this way:

> *Scene one:* It's late at night. You've been up since 6:00 A.M. Your roommate has the thermostat set on 102 degrees, and you need to start reading that stack of materials you copied at the library for your upcoming persuasive speech. Exhausted, you start to reach for that ice-cold bottle of Jolt Cola™ for a quick infusion of caffeine. Hold it! There may be a better alternative.
>
> *Scene two:* It's the day of your persuasive speech. As you walk to class, the stress builds. With each step, your heart beats more rapidly. By the time you arrive at your classroom, those butterflies have taken flight in your stomach. Before reaching for that bottle of Inderal™ or some other drug, stop! Just say no! There may be a better alternative.
>
> What is this better alternative? Is it a new, just-discovered miracle drug? Well, actually, this remedy has been around for more than 5,000 years and is still used among many cultures. This alternative form of medicine is known as aromatherapy. In its precise definition, aromatherapy is treatment by smelling some odor. *Aromatherapy*

Shannon uses visualization, taps common experiences, and arouses curiosity to involve his audience.

Shannon satisfies his listener's curiosity when he introduces his topic of aromatherapy.

Shannon previews the ideas
he will develop in the body
of his speech.

Quarterly defines this treatment as "the skillful use of essential plant oils for medical, psychological, and spiritual applications."

In this speech, I will discuss three personal benefits of aromatherapy: increased alertness, reduced stress, and even weight control.

Throughout his introduction, Shannon tried to establish his credibility to speak on the topic by demonstrating (1) preparation—he followed the steps of an introduction outlined in his textbook; (2) concern for his audience—he did not rely on his notes but interacted with his listeners and tapped experiences that were important to them; and (3) accuracy—he referred to history and quoted from a source.

If you achieve the five objectives we have outlined for a speech introduction, your audience should be attentive, know the purpose of your speech, be motivated to listen, trust your qualifications to speak on the topic, and know the major ideas you will discuss. The only remaining part of the speech is the conclusion. Although it is often briefer than the introduction, your conclusion is vitally important to achieving your desired response. The conclusion is the last section your listeners hear and see and must be well planned and carefully organized.

Organize the Conclusion of the Speech

In John Guare's play *Six Degrees of Separation,* the character Flan, a high-stakes New York art dealer, recalls learning something about art in an unexpected place:

> When the kids were little, we went to a parents' meeting at their school and I asked the teacher why all her students were geniuses in the second grade. Look at the first grade. Blotches of green and black. Look at the third grade. Camouflage. But the second grade—your grade. Matisses everyone. You've made my child a Matisse. Let me study with you. Let me into second grade! What is your secret? And this is what she said, "Secret? I don't have any secret. I just know when to take their drawings away from them."[8]

Knowing when and how to conclude your speech is an art you must master without the luxury of having someone watching over your shoulder. This last division of a speech will be easier to develop, however, if you work to achieve three goals: summarize your

Try This

Developing Introductions

Once you've decided on the key points for the body of your next speech, write your preview and summary statements. Then, draft two different introductions for the speech, using a different type of attention-getting strategy in each.

"Test" both introductions by presenting them to friends, family members, or a few classmates. Ask for their feedback. Did each introduction capture your listeners' attention, introduce the topic, establish the importance of the subject, and build your credibility? Overall, which introduction did they prefer and why?

Evaluate their feedback as well as your perceptions of the strengths and deficiencies of both introductions. Select the one that more effectively introduces the topic to your specific audience, or continue to brainstorm and develop other approaches. Creating a powerful first impression benefits your listeners and helps build your confidence.

key ideas, activate audience response to your speech, and provide closure.

Key Points

Functions of a Speech Conclusion

1. Summarize your key ideas.
2. Activate audience response.
3. Provide closure.

Summarize Your Key Ideas

In the **summary** you "tell us what you told us." Of all the steps in the process of organization, this should be the easiest to construct. You have already organized the body of the speech and, from it, constructed a preview statement. The summary parallels your preview. If your speech develops three key ideas, you reiterate them. If your speech is on self-concept enhancement, for example, you may simply say, "A good self-concept, therefore, benefits us in three ways. It enhances our social interaction, our academic achievement, and our career success." A speech on dying might be summarized: "Denial. Anger. Bargaining. Depression. Acceptance. These are the five stages of dying as described by Kübler-Ross."

An excellent summary step, however, does more than just repeat your key ideas. It also shows how those ideas support the goal of your speech. Remember Stacey's humorous attention-getter to her speech encouraging her classmates to study a foreign language? In the speech she discussed three harms from the nation's failure to promote bilingualism: "First, we lose economically . . . Second, we lose scholastically . . . Third, we lose culturally." Notice how Stacey reiterates and reinforces these points in the summary step of her conclusion:

> Clearly, these three points show us that by being monolingual we lose *economically, scholastically,* and *culturally.* Becoming proficient in another language and its culture may help us reduce our deficit and increase our competitiveness in world trade by recognizing possible problems in marketing campaigns. We will gain intellectually by increasing our vocabulary and expanding our minds. We will gain culturally by breaking barriers and possibly eliminating misunderstandings that occur as a result of being unfamiliar with another language, its people, and its culture.

The summary step gives the listener one last chance to hear and remember the main points of your presentation. Thus, the summary step reinforces the ideas of the speech and brings it to a logical conclusion.

Activate Audience Response

What do you want your audience to do with the information you have provided or the arguments you have proved? The second function of a speech conclusion is to activate an audience response by letting your listeners know whether you want them to accept, remember, use, believe, or act on the content of your speech. Whether your speech is informative or persuasive, you want the audience to have been involved with your information and ideas. The conclusion is your last opportunity to ensure your audience's involvement. If you have provided practical information that can make your listeners smarter, healthier, happier, or wealthier, challenge them to remember and use what they learned. If you have educated them about a problem and proposed a solution to it, remind them of the significance of not acting. If you have spoken on a topic that you find inherently interesting, hoping to generate audience interest by communicating your enthusiasm as well as your information, this is your last opportunity to invigorate or animate your listeners about the subject. Speechwriter and consultant Elinor Donahue echoes this advice:

> Be sure to wrap up with feelings as well as fact. . . . If you charge an audience with a sense of elevated purpose, if you show them possibilities for growth and new perspective, you will magnify the effect of your speech—and maybe make a difference in some lives.[9]

summary: a statement or statements reviewing the major ideas of a speech.

This second function of a conclusion should certainly do something other than say, "I hope you enjoyed my speech" or "I hope you'll find this information about Gutzon Borglum, the sculptor of Mount Rushmore, useful." Rather than saying, "I hope you'll find what I've said about the film scores of Philip Glass useful," you might say something like this: "The next time you find your attention drawn to a movie's soundtrack because you like the music or feel that it could stand on its own, think about the painstaking process of matching sight and sound that an acclaimed composer like Philip Glass has to go through."

In her speech, Kimberly discussed an often overlooked problem: motorists who run red lights. Using vivid examples, expert testimony, and compelling statistics, she documented the problem: More than "200,000 people are injured and more than 800 people die every year in the United States due to motorists running red lights."[10] She called for individual, community, and government action to combat the problem. After reiterating her key ideas in the conclusion of the speech, Kimberly sought to activate personal responsibility in her listeners:

> On your way home tonight, when you approach that traffic light, think of the facts we have talked about today. These facts apply to you every time you approach a traffic signal. Don't run red lights! When we take an extra minute or two to stop for the light, we are helping to protect hundreds of innocent people. The lives you save could be your neighbor's, your mother's, or your own.[11]

Provide Closure

While a final summary of your key ideas is important, ending a speech on the summary step is unsatisfying. Such a strategy is what we call, to borrow from Porky Pig, the "b'dee, b'dee, b'dee, that's all folks" conclusion. You should not have to tell your listeners that the speech is finished. Your wording, as well as your delivery, should make this clear.

If your summary concludes your speech *logically*, your activation and closure statements end the speech *psychologically*. An effective final statement ties the speech together and provides a strong note of finality or closure. The audience should know that you are about to finish, and they should have the feeling that you have said exactly as much as you need to say. Without resorting to saying, "In conclusion," or "To conclude," you should mark the end of your speech by slowing your rate, maintaining direct eye contact with your listeners, and pausing briefly before and after your final sentence.

Sometimes a speaker employs what is called a **circular conclusion**, in which the final statement echoes or refers to the attention-getting step of the introduction. Remember Jennifer, the grown-up Strawberry Shortcake who spoke about retro toys? At the end of her speech, she brought her listeners back to the familiar scene she had created at the start of her introduction:

> Toy comebacks seem to run in twenty- to thirty-year cycles; I wonder how many different Elmos there will be in 20 years. For now, on Saturday morning, the Disney Channel delights us with *The Wiggles, Stanley,* and the *Higgleytown Heroes.* The little girl in the Strawberry Shortcake nightgown is my four-year-old, Maddie. She and her baby sister hold their Care Bear dolls and sing along with the programs. Strawberry Shortcake still brings me joy, only now the joy comes from watching how happy Strawberry and her gang make my little girl.

Your final statement does not have to allude to your attention-getting step. Any of the specific techniques we discussed for gaining audience attention can help bring your speech to a strong, clear, psychologically satisfying conclusion. You can ask a question, even the same one you began with or a variation of it. Or you can answer the question you initially asked. Once you arouse your audience's curiosity in your speech, you must satisfy it in order to provide closure. You could stimulate their imaginations through vivid imagery or promise them that the information you have provided can bring them

circular conclusion: a conclusion that repeats or refers to material used in the attention-getting step of the introduction.

Providing closure means moving beyond your summary to present a satisfying conclusion to ideas or issues you have raised. Referring to your speech introduction, calling for action, or posing a provocative question are all effective strategies for ending a speech.

benefits. You could conclude with a joke or humorous story relevant to your topic. Through lively delivery, you could energize the audience to act on the information you have provided them. In a speech presented on more formal occasions than a classroom assignment, you may end by complimenting and thanking the audience.

Put It All Together

All three functions of the conclusion are important. The summary step reinforces the *ideas* of the speech, while the final two functions reinforce the *impact* of the speech. Consider how Jake accomplished these three functions at the end of his persuasive speech. His use of words such as *we* and *ourselves* involved his listeners, and he used a circular conclusion, revealing the identity of the 76-year-old mother of four he mentioned in his attention-getting step:

> So today, we have learned about the problems of heart disease in women, traced its cause, and put forth some answers.
>
> As with anything, these solutions aren't perfect—and it's unlikely we'll be able to change society or stop this virulent disease in its tracks. We can, however, change ourselves. Through controlling risk on a personal level, lives will be saved. Not every life, but many.
>
> And that 76-year-old mother of four? She was my grandmother. She died last August. But the tragedy was not in the years we have lost with her. It isn't even in the fact that those years could've been saved through different habits and greater understanding. The tragedy will only be if others do not learn from her example. Regret—that's the real tragedy.[12]

Jake restates his key ideas.

Jake requests audience action.

Jake provides closure.

A diagram of the individual steps in a well-organized speech would contain the following:

1. Attention-getting step
2. Statement of topic
3. Emphasis on importance of topic
4. Emphasis on speaker credibility
5. Preview
6. Body of speech
7. Summary
8. Activation of audience response
9. Closure

This is the correct sequence to follow as you *deliver* a speech. In your *preparation*, however, you will follow the sequence we discussed in Chapter 9 and in this chapter. You should prepare the body of your speech first. Some instructors recommend that you develop your introduction next and your conclusion last. Others suggest that you prepare your introduction last. Remember, there is no one correct way of constructing a speech. Select the method that works best for you.

We suggest an alternative strategy (see the Theory into Practice feature). Speakers who begin preparing speeches by starting with the introduction often end up trying to fit the rest of their speech to the introduction. Speakers who develop their introduction, body, and conclusion separately often produce three parts, rather than a unified whole. The outward method of development we suggest helps you avoid these pitfalls and enables you to present your ideas clearly, cohesively, and convincingly.

Summary

The introduction and conclusion are brief parts of the speech, but they must be well organized and practiced since they are, respectively, your first and last chances to create a favorable impression for yourself or your topic. The introduction should achieve five goals: (1) get the attention of your audience; (2) state your topic or purpose; (3) stress the importance or relevance of your topic; (4) establish your credibility to speak on your topic; and (5) preview the key ideas you will be developing in the body of the speech. To get your audience's attention, you can question your listeners, arouse their curiosity, stimulate their imaginations, promise them something beneficial, amuse them, energize them, or acknowledge and compliment them. An effective conclusion must do three things: (1) summarize your key ideas, or bring your speech to a logical conclusion; (2) secure your listeners' commitment to your information and ideas; and (3) provide closure, or bring the speech to a satisfying psychological conclusion.

Rather than organizing the introduction, body, and conclusion of your speech separately, we recommend that you organize the body first and then work outward from that center. Once you have determined the main ideas of the body, you can easily construct your preview statement for the introduction and your summary statement for the conclusion. Next, amplify your introduction by stating your purpose clearly, emphasizing the significance of your topic, and building your credibility to speak on your topic. Decide how to activate an audience response in your conclusion. Finally, work on your attention-getter and your closure statement simultaneously to help ensure that your speech holds together as a satisfying, cohesive unit.

If you follow the suggestions in Chapters 9 and 10, your speech should be well organized. That clear organization will, in turn, make your information easier for the audience to remember, and that's a major goal of public speaking.

Practice Critique

Evaluating Introductions

You have just been appointed judge for a public speaking contest. Your task is to present the award for "best introduction" from among the five student speeches in the Appendix. Read these speeches and evaluate their introductions using the guidelines presented in this chapter. Select the introduction you think is best and explain the reasons for your selection.

Exercises

1. Evaluate the openings of chapters you have read thus far in this book. Which are most and least successful at getting your attention? What made them effective or ineffective?

2. Select a magazine and examine the various ways journalists begin their stories. Which of the seven attention-getting devices discussed in this chapter do the stories employ? Are there other attention-getting techniques you can identify?

3. Examine the attention-getting step of Susan Chontos's speech in Chapter 15. Rewrite the attention-getter using two strategies other than the one Chantos uses.

Theory into Practice

Outward Method of Speech Development

Using the "outward method" of developing a speech, construct the body of your speech first, determining the key ideas and developing them using the "4 S's." Then move outward, working simultaneously on your introduction and conclusion. Word your preview and summary statements that highlight your key ideas. Next, decide how you will state your topic, explain its importance, build your credibility, and activate audience response. Finally, develop the attention-getter and the final statement at the same time to increase the total unity of your speech.

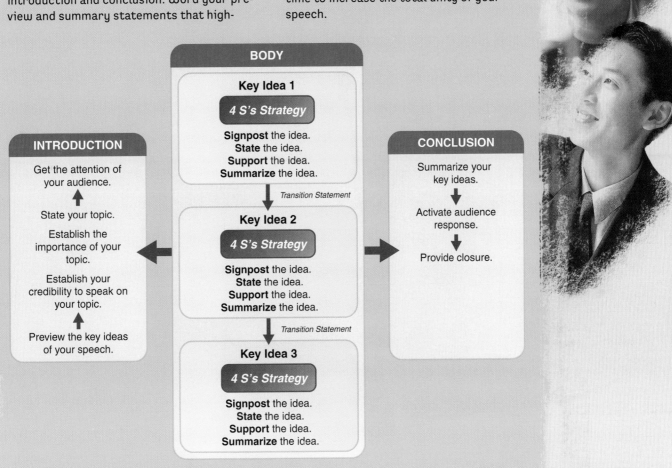

INTRODUCTION

Get the attention of your audience.

↑

State your topic.

Establish the importance of your topic.

Establish your credibility to speak on your topic.

↑

Preview the key ideas of your speech.

BODY

Key Idea 1

4 S's Strategy

Signpost the idea.
State the idea.
Support the idea.
Summarize the idea.

Transition Statement

Key Idea 2

4 S's Strategy

Signpost the idea.
State the idea.
Support the idea.
Summarize the idea.

Transition Statement

Key Idea 3

4 S's Strategy

Signpost the idea.
State the idea.
Support the idea.
Summarize the idea.

CONCLUSION

Summarize your key ideas.

↓

Activate audience response.

↓

Provide closure.

---

4. Suppose the specific purpose of a speech is to persuade an audience to contribute money for needed playground equipment for a local elementary school. Write a statement establishing the importance and relevance of the topic for each of the following audiences:
   a. Parents of children who attend the school
   b. Senior citizens on limited, fixed incomes whose children and grandchildren no longer attend the school
   c. Traditional-age college students

5. Locate the preview statements in the introductions of the student speeches in the Appendix.

6. Rewrite the closure statement of Susan Chontos's speech in Chapter 15 using two strategies other than the one Chontos uses. Discuss the strengths and weaknesses of each closure statement. Which closure strategy do you prefer? Why?

7. Prepare three conclusions for the same body of content. Discuss the advantages and disadvantages of each. Select the one you think is best and explain why.

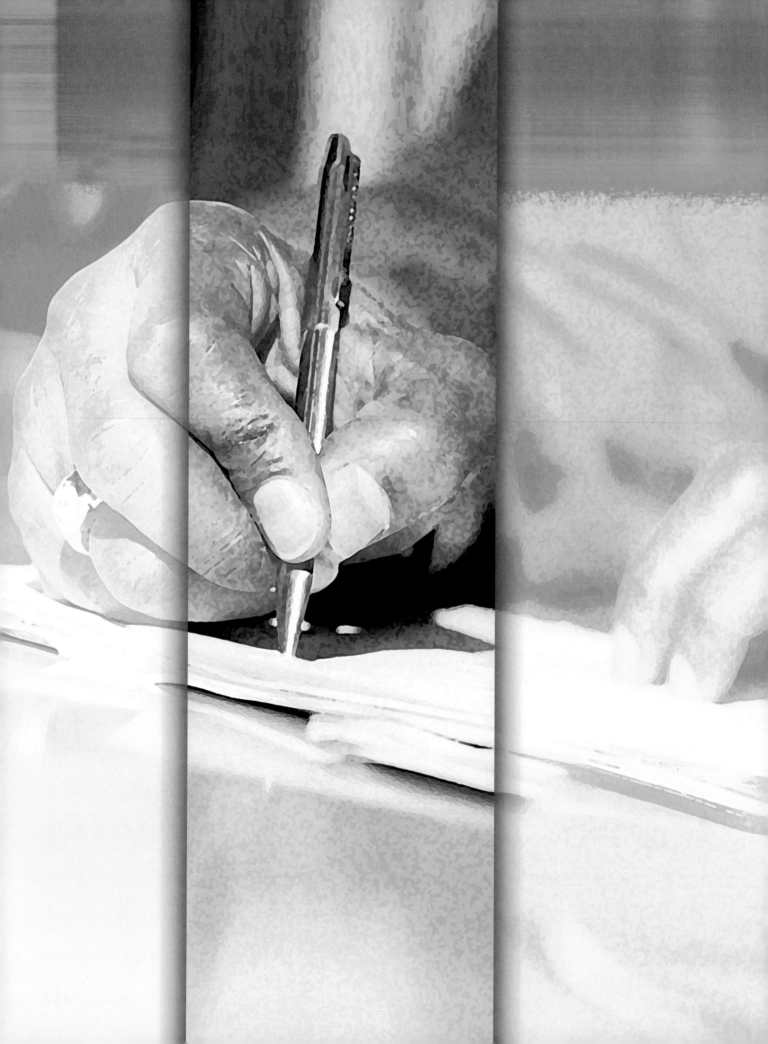

Outlining Your Speech

chapter

11

*Order and simplification
are the first steps toward the
mastery of a subject.* —THOMAS MANN

How long would it take you to memorize and be able to repeat the following 26 letters: *c-p-s-y-n-i-r-t-y-m-v-i-e-m-r-t-o-i-p-o-e-m-o-m-e-m*? A typical learner would need a good deal of practice to remember more than the first four to seven letters you just read.[1] Would it help you if the letters were rearranged as follows: *y-m-c-o-i-t-p-s-i-p-t-y-m-m-v-e-n-e-o-i-r-r-m-e-o-m*? Unless you have an eidetic or photographic memory, such a shuffling of letters is likely no help at all. But what if the letters were scrambled again: *m-y-t-o-p-i-c-i-s-p-t-y-m-m-v-e-n-e-o-i-r-r-m-e-o-m*? Those first nine letters are now recognizable as the English words *my, topic,* and *is,* and you can easily repeat them in correct sequence. Those three words would be even more obvious if we eliminated the dashes and used a familiar pattern of grouping and spacing: *my topic is.* If the last seventeen letters were also reorganized as *m-e-m-o-r-y-i-m-p-r-o-v-e-m-e-n-t,* or *memory improvement,* you could master the entire sequence of 26 letters in correct order, orally or in writing, without much effort.

Notice that we did not add or delete any letters. We merely reorganized them until they formed a pattern that is easy to recognize and repeat. When you outline, you perform essentially the same task. You organize and reorganize material into a pattern easy to recognize and remember.

In Chapters 9 and 10, we discussed the importance of organization to the delivered speech and suggested some ways of achieving a well-organized presentation. Outlining your speech is the preliminary written work necessary to foster clear organization of your oral message. In this chapter, you will learn why outlines are important to your speech, examine some different types of outlines, and, finally, study how to write an excellent outline.

Functions of Outlining

A well-prepared outline serves five important functions for a speaker:

1. It tests the scope of the speaker's content.
2. It tests the logical relations among parts of the speech.
3. It tests the relevance of supporting ideas.
4. It checks the balance or proportion of the speech.
5. It serves as notes during the delivery of the speech.

Tests Scope of Content

The first purpose of outlining is to test the scope of the speaker's content. Have you narrowed the topic sufficiently to cover your key ideas in some depth? Or are you trying to cover too much material, so that you will merely skim the surface of the subject, repeating things your audience already knows? In Chapter 9, we stated that a speaker should ordinarily have no more than two to five main points in a speech. Outlining allows you to use paper and pen to organize your main ideas and then add, delete, regroup, shuffle, condense, or expand these ideas so you approach your topic in a manageable way. In other words, outlining is a process of setting goals for the speech.

Tests Logical Relation of Parts

Second, outlining allows speakers to test the logical relations among the various parts of the speech. Does one idea in the outline lead to the next in a meaningful way? Do the arguments or subtopics under each of your main points really develop that point? To answer these questions, you must understand the concepts of coordination and subordination. **Coordinate ideas** are those of equal value or importance in the overall pattern of the speech. The following hypothetical example illustrates the relation between coordinate and subordinate ideas.

If you delivered an informative speech on the functions of service dogs, you might arrange your speech topically and focus on just these two areas:

I. Search functions
II. Protection functions

These two topics are coordinate because they seem to be of equal value. You might have more information on one of them than on the other and thus spend more time in the speech discussing that topic, but neither is a subtopic of the other. Under that first main topic, you would then list **subordinate ideas,** subtopics that support it:

I. Search functions
   A. Narcotics detection
   B. Bomb detection
   C. Arson detection
   D. Cadaver location
   E. Disease detection

Notice that points A through E are not only subordinate to the main idea, search functions, but are also coordinate with each other since they seem to be equally important. Subordinate points for the second main point could include the following:

II. Protection functions
   A. Seeing eye dogs
   B. Guard dogs
   C. Attack dogs
   D. Seizure alert dogs

Your outline is not yet complete, but you can begin to ask yourself the following questions: Are my main points different enough to qualify as separate points? Do my subordinate points really support the main ideas? At this stage, the answers to both of these questions seem to be yes. In this way, the visual form of the outline helps you test the logical connections among parts of your speech. You continue this process to further refine and add to the outline.

Tests Relevance of Supporting Ideas

Third, an outline helps the speaker test the relevance of supporting ideas. To understand how this works, assume that you had written the following portion of an outline for a speech on roller coasters:

I. Famous roller coasters
   A. Coney Island's "Cyclone"

coordinate ideas: ideas that have equal value in a speech.

subordinate ideas: ideas that support more general or more important points in a speech.

B. Montreal's "Le Monstre"

C. Busch Gardens's "Kumba"

D. New design technology

Notice that the fourth subpoint, "new design technology," is out of place because it is irrelevant to the main point. How do you solve this problem? One option is to make "new design technology" a separate main point if you can gather adequate supporting material on it; if you can't, eliminate it.

Checks Balance of Speech

A fourth function of outlining is to check the balance or proportion of the speech. If you look back to the outline on functions of service dogs, you will notice that the first main point has five subpoints and the second has four. As a result, the speech looks balanced, even though a speaker might actually spend more time on one of those main points than on the other. Yet if the main point "search functions" had five subpoints and "protection functions" had only two, the outline might not be balanced. This lack of balance could be reflected in the speech.

How can you fix such an imbalance? In the speech on the functions of service dogs, the speaker might focus just on those five search functions by making the subpoints into main points:

I. Narcotics detection

II. Bomb detection

III. Arson detection

IV. Cadaver location

V. Disease detection

As you can see, by testing the balance of your speech an outline can even lead you to alter your specific purpose.

Serves as Delivery Notes

Fifth, and finally, a special type of abbreviated outline can serve as notes for the speaker during the actual delivery of the speech. This outline, called a speaking outline and discussed later in this chapter, has only one rule: It must be brief. If you have prepared adequately for your speech, you should need only key words and phrases to remind you of each point you want to discuss. Moreover, having your notes in outline form rather than arranged randomly on notecards or sheets of paper will constantly remind you of the importance of clear organization as you are delivering the speech.

Principles of Outlining

complete sentence outline: an outline in which all numbers and letters introduce complete sentences.

key word or phrase outline: an outline in which all numbers and letters introduce words or groups of words.

Correct outlines take one of two possible forms: the **complete sentence outline** and the **key word or phrase outline.** In a complete sentence outline, each item is a sentence; each item in a key word or phrase outline is a word or group of words. These two forms of outlines should be kept consistent and distinct. Combine them only in the speaker's outline from which you deliver your speech. So far in this chapter, we have used only phrase outlines. More word or phrase outlines and an example of a complete sentence outline will follow.

Principles of Outlining

1. Each number or letter in the outline should represent only one idea.
2. Coordinate and subordinate points in the outline should be represented by a consistent system of numbers and letters.
3. If any point has subpoints under it, there must be at least two subpoints.
4. Each symbol in a sentence outline should introduce a complete sentence. Each symbol in a word or phrase outline should introduce a word or phrase.
5. Coordinate points throughout the outline should have parallel grammatical construction.

As you construct your outline, you will work more efficiently and produce a clearer outline if you follow a few rules, or principles.

Singularity

First, each number or letter in the outline should represent only one idea. A chief goal of outlining is to achieve a clear visual representation of the connections among parts of the speech. This is possible only if you separate the ideas. For example, suppose a speaker preparing a speech on color blindness has worded a key idea as "causes of and tests for color blindness." The phrase contains two distinct ideas, each requiring separate discussion and development. Instead, the speaker should divide the statement into two coordinate points: "causes of color blindness" and "tests for color blindness."

Consistency

Second, coordinate and subordinate points in the outline should be represented by a consistent system of numbers and letters. Main ideas are typically represented by Roman numerals: I, II, III, and so forth. Label subpoints under the main points with indented capital letters: A, B, C, and so forth. Beneath those, identify your supporting points with indented Arabic numerals: 1, 2, 3, and so on. Identify ideas subordinate to those with indented lowercase letters: a, b, c, and so on. Using this notation system, the labeling and indentation of a typical outline would appear as follows:

I. Main point
  A. Subpoint
    1. Sub-subpoint
    2. Sub-subpoint
    3. Sub-subpoint
  B. Subpoint
    1. Sub-subpoint
    2. Sub-subpoint
      a. Sub-sub-subpoint
      b. Sub-sub-subpoint
II. Main point
  A. Subpoint
  B. Subpoint
    1. Sub-subpoint
    2. Sub-subpoint
  C. Subpoint

Adequacy

A third principle is that if any point has subpoints under it, there must be at least two subpoints. A basic law of physics is that you cannot divide something into only one part. If you have an A, you must also have a B. (You may, of course, also have subpoints C, D, and E.) If you have a 1, you must also have at least a 2.

Uniformity

Fourth, each symbol in a sentence outline should introduce a complete sentence. Each symbol in a word or phrase outline should introduce a word or phrase. Keep the form of the outline consistent. Sentences and phrases should be mixed only in your speaking outline.

Parallelism

Finally, coordinate points throughout the outline should have parallel grammatical construction. For example, a key phrase outline of a speech on how to write a résumé begins with a first main point labeled "Things to include." The second point should be "Things to omit," rather than "Leaving out unnecessary information." The first point is worded as a noun phrase and, therefore, you must follow it with another noun phrase ("Things to omit"), rather than a predicate phrase ("Leaving out unnecessary information"). This does not mean that you must choose noun phrases over verb phrases, but rather that all points must match grammatically. In this next example, all coordinate points have parallel grammatical construction.

    I. Including essential information
       A. Address
       B. Career objective
       C. Educational background
       D. Employment history
       E. References
    II. Omitting unnecessary information
       A. Marital status
       B. Religious denomination
       C. Political affiliation

As you can see, coordinate main points I and II are verb phrases, while the coordinate subpoints are all nouns or noun phrases.

Stages of Outlining

If you have difficulty generating or discovering the main points for a speech topic you have chosen, don't worry; you are not alone. Many people are intimidated by the prospect of selecting and organizing ideas, particularly for a first speech. We especially worry if an organization plan doesn't come to us quickly. When we get a plan, we worry that it is not the right organizational pattern to use. You can avoid these self-defeating lines of thinking if you keep in mind four guidelines to organizing and outlining.

First, organization is not something that comes to you, but rather it is something that you must go after. Structuring a speech requires you to invest time and thought, investments whose dividends may not be apparent until you deliver the speech. Second, there is no one right way of organizing all speeches on a particular topic. True, some topics logically lend themselves to certain patterns of organization. As you learned in Chapter 9, speeches about processes often almost organize themselves according to a chronological pattern. Speeches about people may be arranged chronologically or topically. Persuasive speeches on social issues are perhaps most logically organized according to a problem–solution format. Yet different speakers may use different structures. You have to determine what works best for you, your topic, and your audience.

Third, the early stages of organizing and outlining a speech are filled with uncertainty. You may find yourself asking, Do I have enough main points, too many, or too few? Can I find adequate information to support all those main points? Am I overlooking other main points the audience would be interested in hearing me discuss? Rather than feeling pressured by such questions, look on the early stages of outlining as a period of flexibility. The early, informal versions of your working outline are all provisional—temporary and open to change. Don't be afraid to experiment a little. Fourth, and finally, identifying the main points in a speech is also easier than many people imagine. In the remainder of this chapter we will guide you through the process of outlining, from those first tentative ideas you put on paper to the final outline you use as speaking notes.

Exploring Online

DEVELOPING AN OUTLINE
http://owl.english.purdue.edu/handouts/print/general/gl_outlin.html
www.writingonyourpalm.net/column030310.htm
As it does so well with many topics, the Online Writing Lab at Purdue University presents an excellent rationale for outlining and provides a sample word/phrase outline. At the second site, writer and mobile technology consultant Jeff Kirvin discusses alternatives to traditional outlines, including mindmapping on paper or on a computer.

The Working Outline

The first step in preparing an outline is to construct a **working outline**, a list of aspects of your chosen topic. Such a list may result from research you have already conducted, or it may simply be a result of some productive brainstorming. Once you have spent significant time researching the subject, you will notice topics that are repeated in different sources on the subject. If, for example, you had selected the so-called super staph—methicillin-resistant *Staphylococcus aureus* (MRSA)—as the topic for an informative speech and had conducted adequate research, your list of possible aspects of the topic would include:

Cause	Diagnosis	Prevention
Symptoms	Treatment	

Notice that these same topics could be applied to any disease, physical illness, or mental condition.

You can also generate topic areas through brainstorming and visual brainstorming, techniques we discussed in Chapter 6. Not only can brainstorming help you generate topics, it can also help you explore areas of the topic you finally select.[2] Your creative

working outline: an informal, initial outline recording a speaker's process of narrowing, focusing, and balancing a topic.

brainstorming might even reveal interesting areas of your topic that have not been adequately treated in the existing research. This discovery provides you an opportunity to conduct original research or experimentation.

As you can see, at this stage the term *outline* is very loose; the list of key ideas you are developing does not have any numbers or letters attached to it. That's fine, since these notes are for your benefit alone. This working outline is not so much a finished product as it is a record of the process you go through in thinking about a speech topic.

To illustrate these first steps in preparing an outline, consider the experience of a speaker, Chris, who came up with a speech topic in the following manner:

I like simple things; the simpler, the better. My watch doesn't have any numbers on the dial; I know where those numbers would be and what they are. I drive a car that's strictly no frills. The few gauges and buttons that you need to drive and maintain it are exactly where you would expect them to be. In the same way, if I find myself on a website and can't navigate around in it intuitively, I know there's a problem with the site design.

As an art major with a brother who's an architect, I'm always interested in stories about important structures. And, there too, the designs that usually impress me the most are simple—so clear and straightforward that you end up thinking, "Of course, how else could that building be put together? It's just right."

I first learned about the Gateshead Millennium Bridge when I saw a story about it in *Newsweek*. Later I remembered the story when I read that the bridge had won some design award. That got me interested in researching the structure, and I soon learned that it has won a number of awards and has webcams where you can see live views of the bridge any time you want.

Then, in the summer of 2003, I got the chance to travel around England with a group of artists and activists. We eventually went to Newcastle in northeastern England, and I got to see the bridge and walk across it. I thought it was pretty amazing.

At this point, Chris knew that he wanted to talk about this one bridge. He also knew from his preliminary research that he would have no trouble finding enough information about it. Just by brainstorming topics that might apply to any bridge, Chris developed the following working outline:

History of the project

Design

Impact

As he researched the bridge further, Chris read several articles about its engineering. He added that topic to his working outline. Then, adding subtopics as he thought of them or encountered them in his research, he developed the visual brainstorming example shown in the Theory into Practice feature.

After completing his research on the bridge, Chris realized that the information he had about its engineering was too technical to interest most of his listeners. He also had a great deal of interesting information about the history of the area and efforts to revive it economically. Including all of this information would have made him exceed the time limit for his speech. As a result, he decided to focus on just three main points. Chris's working outline was as follows:

I. Design challenges
II. Specific features of the bridge
III. Impact of the bridge

So was all of that time spent reading the engineering and history articles wasted? "Not at all," Chris says. "Even though I'm not going to have the time to discuss the me-

Theory into Practice
Visual Brainstorming

Subject: The Gateshead Millennium Bridge

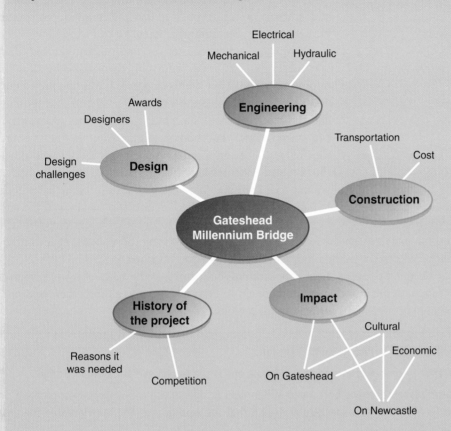

chanical and electrical engineering or the hydraulics of the bridge, I know those topics better and have more confidence. If someone asks me a technical question about how the bridge operates or why it was built as it was, I feel sure I will either know the answer or remember where to find the answer."

Try This
Developing a Working Outline

Once you have chosen a topic for an upcoming speech, and before you research it (or research it further), brainstorm ideas that you could include in such a speech. Prepare a keyword or phrase outline developing at least two coordinate main points with at least two subordinate points under each one. Use the five principles of outlining discussed in this chapter to check the clarity and uniformity of your main points and subpoints.

The Formal Outline

Your **formal outline** is a complete sentence outline reflecting the full content and organization of your speech. In its final form, it is the finished product of your research and planning for your speech. A stranger, picking up your formal outline, should be able to read how you have organized and supported all your main points. If you keep that goal in mind, you should have no trouble deciding what needs to be included.

If your instructor requires you to turn in an outline when you speak, make sure you know whether it is to be a formal outline or can be in key words or phrases. Your instructor may also require you to include any or all of the following items above the outline: your speech title, a statement of your specific purpose, and your thesis statement. Your instructor is also the final authority on whether you are to write out your introduction and conclusion or just to outline them and whether your speech requires a bibliography or not. The actual outline should follow the accepted pattern of symbols and indentation that we showed you earlier in this chapter. Some instructors also ask students to label the superstructure of the speech—introduction, body, and conclusion—by inserting those words at the appropriate places in the outline, but without any symbols attached to them.

We asked Chris to show you a formal outline of just the body of his informative speech, with the introduction and conclusion written out, and all the other "options." The final version of his formal outline looked like this:

> **formal outline:** a complete sentence outline written in sufficient detail that a person other than the speaker could understand it.

> Chris's simple title not only gets attention but also hints at his topic. To check the goals of the speech, Chris then states his specific purpose and thesis.

Speech title: Perfect(ly Simple) Design

Specific purpose: To inform the audience about the Gateshead Millennium Bridge

Thesis statement: The Gateshead Millennium Bridge solved a transportation problem on the Tyne River with a spectacular design that has won awards and reinvigorated the area where it is located.

Introduction

I've read and heard the phrase "carrying coals to Newcastle," but I never knew what it meant. According to the third edition of *The New Dictionary of Cultural Literacy,* which I accessed at Bartleby.com on May 28, 2005, "carrying coals to Newcastle" means doing something that's completely useless. Newcastle, England, was a rich coal mining area, so no one would need to carry coals to Newcastle. I mention this because Newcastle is the site of what I want to inform you about today: the Gateshead Millennium Bridge. If you're looking for spectacular design and an active arts community, you don't need to carry anything with you—just head to Newcastle.

As an art major, I'm always interested in stories about important structures. I first learned about the bridge when I saw a story about it in *Newsweek.* Later I read that the bridge had won a design award that's usually given to a building. That got me interested in researching the structure. Then, in the summer of 2003, I got to visit England. We went to Newcastle and I walked across this famous structure. The bridge has a lot to teach us about great design that seems perfectly matched to its function. It's not only great to look at, but surprising to watch in operation. From personal experience crossing it, I can say that the bridge inspires a feeling of weightlessness because you can feel the bridge flexing with each step. The effect is a combination of fear and reassurance. You know that the bridge will hold you but you're not sure how, because the structure seems to defy the laws of physics.

> Note that Chris writes out his entire introduction, gaining audience attention by arousing their curiosity. He builds his credibility by mentioning that he has walked across the bridge, the subject of his speech.

To appreciate the Gateshead Millennium Bridge more fully, it's useful to know the main challenges its designers faced, specific features of the bridge, and the impact that it's had on the area where it's located.

His introduction ends with a clear preview of three main points Chris plans to discuss.

I. The site of the proposed bridge posed several design challenges.
   A. The industrial towns of Newcastle and Gateshead have faced each other across the River Tyne since Roman times.
      1. The area flourished during the Industrial Revolution.
         a. The territory was rich in coal.
         b. The territory was commercially important because of its port.
      2. Gateshead on the south was in economic shambles by the 1990s.
         a. Industries along the river had closed.
         b. Warehouses and plants were empty.
         c. People moved south in search of work.
      3. Newcastle on the north was better off.
      4. Gateshead wanted to encourage some of Newcastle's prosperity to cross the river.
   B. Construction of the bridge could not stop river traffic for an extended time.
   C. The bridge had to allow both foot traffic on it and navigation beneath it.
   D. Once planners chose the design, the bridge developed quickly.
      1. The winning design was announced in 1997.
      2. Construction began in 1999.
      3. The bridge was positioned in November of 2000.
      4. The bridge's opening mechanism was tested for the first time in June of 2001.

II. The Gateshead Millennium Bridge design is so simple that it is revolutionary.
   A. Two parabolic steel arches form the bridge.
      1. The architectural engineering firm of Guilford and Partners and Wilkinson Eyre Architects collaborated on the design of the pedestrian walkway.
      2. The deck contains separate paths for foot and cycle traffic.
         a. The outer bicycle path is almost one foot lower than the inner footway.
         b. The bicycle passageway joins two cross-country riverside paths, part of a nationwide network.
      3. The deck was built in thirteen separate sections.
      4. The supporting arch was built in nine separate sections.
      5. Eighteen cables connect the supporting arch to the deck.
   B. Specific details about the bridge are impressive.
      1. The bridge cost $32 million.
      2. The bridge weighs more than 850 tons.
      3. Its total span is 413 feet.
      4. The supporting arch rises 164 feet above the river level.
      5. The foundation extends down ninety-eight feet to anchor in the river bed.
      6. Constructed off-site some six miles downstream, the completed bridge was carried upstream by the world's second largest floating crane, Hercules II.
      7. The bridge has a striking appearance.
         a. In daylight it looks white with a hint of blue.
         b. At night, changing multicolored lights beneath the pedestrian walkway reflect on the water below.
   C. The design of the bridge created the world's first tilting bridge in order to accommodate boat traffic underneath it.
      1. The entire bridge rotates 40 degrees when it opens.
      2. People have nicknamed it the "blinking eye."
      3. The cables connecting the pedestrian path to the supporting arch are horizontal when the bridge is raised.

The outline's three main points match Chris's thesis and preview statements. Each item in the outline is a complete sentence. Each level of the outline has at least two headings, and many subordinate points are grammatically parallel.

4. A series of electric motors and hydraulic rams moves the bridge.

5. Opening or closing the bridge takes only four minutes.

6. Each opening or closing costs just a little more than $6.50 currently.

7. Any litter dropped on the bridge rolls into special traps each time it opens.

    D. To date, the structure has received more than thirty-seven design awards.

1. In 2002 the structure won the most prestigious award for British architecture, the RIBA (Royal Institute of British Architects) Stirling Prize.

2. In 2005 the structure won the International Association for Bridge and Structural Engineering's Outstanding Structure Award.

III. The Gateshead Millennium Bridge has exceeded expectations of its impact on the reinvigoration of the area.

    A. In its first year, 2002, the bridge had over a million visitors, four times the number expected.

1. The same number visited the nearby Baltic Center.

2. The new Biscuit Factory is now England's largest commercial art space.

    B. The Sage Gateshead Music Center opened in 2004.

    C. People are now staying in the area in greater numbers.

1. Forty-six percent of graduates from universities in the area now remain in the area.

2. The Gateshead-Newcastle area is now one of the top six centers of culture in Great Britain.

3. The quays are now home to large, new, luxury residential complexes.

4. The area is now a popular tourist destination and convention hub.

Conclusion

An article in *Tech Directions,* December 2001, reminds us that American architect Louis Sullivan, who created early versions of what we later called skyscrapers, is credited with the saying that "form follows function." In the case of the Gateshead Millennium Bridge, form *is* function. The bridge had to permit river traffic and had to be built offsite so that it didn't stop traffic during its construction. Gateshead Millennium did that. The fact that it was so novel and so great to look at that it attracted a lot of foot traffic was just icing on the cake. It's generated so much traffic, been the subject of so much commentary, and won so many awards that it has helped reinvigorate the towns that it joins.

If you can't get to Newcastle in the near future, you can at least take a virtual stroll across the Gateshead Millennium Bridge. Just do a Google image search to see any of more than 2,000 photos of it. Or go to www.tynebridgewebcam.com to see live pictures that refresh often around the clock from a variety of webcams. If you're lucky, you might get to see the bridge opening or closing. As Chee Pearlman, one of the RIBA Stirling Award jurors, put it: "It's such a stunning move in terms of engineering. And yet so simple. It's a simple motion, and yet it takes your breath away when you watch it happen."

Chris's conclusion begins with a clear summary of his three main points. He then activates audience response by mentioning sources where listeners can see numerous images of the bridge. His final quotation provides a strong sense of closure to the speech.

Bibliography

Booth, Robert. "Stirling Win Is 'Dream Ticket.'" *Building Design* 18 Oct. 2002: 1.

"Bow of Hope: Wilkinson Eyre's Elegant and Dramatic Contribution to Neglected Gateshead Is a Symbol of Hope and Regeneration." *The Architectural Review* Dec. 2002: 58–59.

"Bridge on the River Tyne." *The America's Intelligence Wire* 4 Nov. 2002: n.p.

Cattermole, Howard. "*ISR* Editorial." *Interdisciplinary Science Reviews* 2004: 113.

Engelbrecht, Gavin. "The Jewel in the Region's Cultural Crown." *European Intelligence Wire* 17 Dec. 2004: n.p.

"Gigantic Floating Crane Places Pedestrian Bridge over River." *Civil Engineering* Feb. 2001: 13.

Johnson, John. "The Gateshead Millennium Bridge." *Physics Review* Apr. 2003: 29–32.

Lewis, Gareth. "Gifford Grabs Glory for Design of Iconic Bridge." *UK Newsquest Regional Press—This Is Hampshire* 19 Apr. 2005: n.p.

A formal outline should include a complete bibliography; it's an important resource for interested listeners, including your instructor.

McAllister, J. F. O. "From Coal to Culture: This Old Mining Town in the Northeast of England Used to be a Grimy Industrial Wasteland. Now It's Becoming a Gleaming Cultural Center and—Who Would Have Thought It?—Tourist Destination." *Time International (European Edition)* 30 Aug. 2004: 32.

"Millennium Bridge—Fact Sheet." 5 June 2005 <http://www.gateshead.gov.uk/bridge/facts.htm>.

"News in Brief: Gateshead Wins." *Professional Engineering* 27 Apr. 2005: 4.

Phillips, Tom. "Ornament on Trial." *The Architectural Review* Apr. 2003: 79–87.

Pierce, Alan. "Gateshead Millennium Bridge." *Tech Directions* Dec. 2001: 9.

Pope, Chris. "Raising Eyebrows." *Professional Engineering* 28 Nov. 2001: 23.

"Tyneside's Twin Cities of Culture Are Where the Art Is." *Europe Intelligence Wire* 10 Feb. 2003: n.p.

The Speaking Outline

The **speaking outline,** the one you actually use to deliver your speech, is a pared-down version of your full formal outline. You construct the formal outline for an interested reader having no necessary prior knowledge of your topic. However, you write the speaking outline for yourself as a unique speaker. The only rule for the speaking outline is that it be brief.

Why is the speaking outline briefer than the formal outline? Chances are that your instructor will want most or all of your speeches delivered from notes, rather than from a written manuscript. Your brief speaking outline, made up of essential words and phrases, meets the requirements of the assignment while also serving as your speaking notes. But more important, if you spoke from a complete sentence outline, you might be tempted to read the speech, sacrificing eye contact and other vital interaction with your audience. Alternatively, you might try to memorize the formal outline, another dangerous tactic because you then face the prospect of forgetting part of the speech. If, instead, you speak using the outline having just key words and phrases to jog your memory, your delivery will seem more natural and conversational, and you will find yourself freer to interact with your audience.

> *Outlining never hurt; how helpful it is depends on what kind of thinker you are.* [4]

Though the speaking outline leaves out a lot of what the formal outline includes, it also contains some important items not found in the formal outline. For example, you can include directions to yourself about the delivery of the speech. A speaker with a tendency to speak too softly could write reminders in the margins, such as "volume" or "Speak up!" You might also want to note in your speaking outline places where you want to pause, to slow down, or to use presentational aids. Some speakers find it particularly helpful to make these delivery notes in a color of ink different from the rest of the outline.

Second, most speaking outlines include any supporting material you plan to use. Quotations and definitions should be written in complete sentences, even though the rest of the outline is in words and phrases. When you quote others, you must be exact. For that reason, you'll also want to insert notes about the exact sources you want to cite. Examples, illustrations, and statistics could be noted in only a few words or numbers. Any symbols or abbreviations you are comfortable with are likely appropriate in your speaking outline.

For his speech on the Gateshead Millennium Bridge, Chris condensed his formal outline and added the following notations for the actual delivery of the speech:

speaking outline: a brief outline for the speaker's use alone and containing source citations and delivery prompts.

I. Design challenges
   A. Newcastle & Gateshead face across River Tyne
      1. Area flourished during Industrial Revolution
         a. Coal
         b. Port
      2. Gateshead, on south, in economic shambles by 1990s
         a. Industries closed
         b. Warehouses, plants empty
         c. People went south for work
      3. Newcastle, on north, better off
      4. Gateshead wanted to attract Newcastle's prosperity
   B. Construction could not stop river traffic
   C. Had to allow foot traffic on it, navigation beneath it
   D. Developed quickly
      1. Winning design, 1997
      2. Construction began, 1999
      3. Bridge positioned, November 2000
      4. Bridge's opening mechanism tested, June 2001
         PAUSE

   (GMB centerpiece . . . why? . . . specific features unique)

II. GMB design: so simple it's revolutionary
   A. 2 parabolic steel arches
      1. Architectural engineers Guilford and Partners, Wilkinson Eyre Architects collaborated on pedestrian walkway design
      2. Deck → separate paths for foot, cycle traffic
         a. Outer bicycle path → almost 1 ft. lower than the inner footway
         b. Bicycle passageway joins 2 cross-country paths, part of national network (*MB Fact Sheet*)
      3. Deck built in 13 sections
      4. Supporting arch built in 9 sections
      5. 18 cables connect 2 arches (*Physics Review,* April 2003)

   Artist Tom Phillips in *The Architectural Review,* April 2003: "At the Gateshead Millennium Bridge, exposed technology becomes ornament in itself. . . .
      SHOW PHOTO

   B. Specific details of bridge → impressive
      1. $32 million cost

Delivery prompts are in capital letters so Chris can see them at a glance and not confuse them with content prompts.

In its closed position, the Gateshead Millennium Bridge allows pedestrian and bicycle traffic between Newcastle and Gateshead across the River Tyne.

Opened to allow a tall ship to pass, the bridge reveals its deck supports and its suspension cables stand out against the sky. The silvery, undulating structure on the far shore is the Sage Music Center, part of the local arts community that has sprung up to revitalize the area.

    2. 850+ tons weight
    3. Span = 413 feet
    4. Supporting arch 164 feet
    5. Foundation → 98 feet into river bed
    6. Constructed off-site, completed bridge carried 6 mi. upstream by Hercules II, world's 2nd largest floating crane (*Civil Engineering,* Feb. 2001)
    7. Striking appearance
        a. Daylight: white, hint blue
        b. Night: changing multicolored lights beneath walkway reflect on water (*MB Fact Sheet*)

Howard Cattermole (strategy manager for Transpower, the New Zealand power grid) said in a 2004 *Interdisciplinary Science Review* editorial: "It has the excitement of a truly great design. An exquisitely slender, slanting, shining white arch supports a sweeping deck with separate pedestrian and cycle lanes." . . . [W]ith seagulls circling and squawking overhead, the feeling is of a pier more than of a bridge."

C. World's 1st tilting bridge to allow boat traffic underneath
    1. Entire bridge rotates 40 degrees
    2. "Blinking eye"
    3. Cables horizontal when bridge raised (*Physics Review,* April 2003)
    4. Electric motors, hydraulic rams move bridge

        SHOW PHOTO

    5. 4 minutes
    6. Costs $6.50 +
    7. Litter → special traps when bridge opens (*Prof. Engineering,* Nov. 28, 2001)
D. 37 design awards so far
    1. 2002 → most prestigious, RIBA Stirling Prize
    2. 2005 → Int. Assoc. for Bridge & Structural Engineering's Outstanding Structure Award (*Prof. Engineering,* April 27, 2005)

        PAUSE

(Worth seeing, but effect on area?)

III. GMB exceeded expectations

"Nick Henry, the leader of the Gateshead Council, said: 'It is easy to underestimate the social impact of the project. This is one of the most deprived areas of the UK.'" (Booth article)

Although Chris's speaking outline entries are abbreviated, many are parallel in structure.

Chris's speaking outline contains specific supporting materials such as statistics and quotations, along with information about each source he needs to cite.

A. 1st year, 2002 → 1+ million visitors, 4 x number expected
   1. Same no. visited Baltic Center
   2. Biscuit Factory now England's largest comm. art space
B. Sage Gateshead Music Center opened 2004
C. People now staying in area
   1. 46% of area univ. graduates remain in vicinity
   2. Gateshead-Newcastle now 1 of top 6 centers of culture in GB
   3. Quays home to large, new, luxury residential complexes
   4. Popular tourist destination, convention hub

Someone who knew nothing of the subject and had not seen Chris's formal outline might not be able to make much sense of his speaking outline. That's OK. As long as your notes make sense to you, you're fine. For example, no one would realize that Chris's note in parentheses, "GMB centerpiece . . . why? . . . specific features unique" was his prompt to say, "It was clear that the Gateshead Millennium Bridge was going to be the centerpiece of a special place, but why? We can understand that better if we know some of the specific features that make it unique." If you plan and practice your transitions as carefully as Chris did, you too should need only a few words to remind you of what you planned to say in those important sections of your speech.

We believe that keeping your speaking notes in outline form will remind you of the importance of clear organization in the speech you deliver. Ultimately, though, they are *your* notes. As long as they assist you without drawing attention to themselves, they are doing their job. If you tend to forget things under pressure, you may need a few more words in notes than some other people do. Resist the temptation to write out too much of the speech, however. If you write it, you'll want to read it. Instead, try the following suggestions.

Use keywords or phrases to remind you of each step in your introduction and conclusion. Then try to deliver those crucial parts of the speech without referring to your notes. In the body of the speech, your main ideas need to be worded precisely and powerfully. Either write those ideas in complete sentences or use a keyword or phrase to remind you of the wording you practiced. Just don't read those main ideas when you actually deliver the speech. Use keywords also to remind yourself of supporting material and transitions; use numbers to remind you of statistics. Include just enough information to be able to cite each of your sources clearly. Write out any material you want to quote, using complete sentences. Using words, colors, or any other symbols that will jog your memory, insert delivery prompts. We have even had students with two or three main points in the bodies of their speeches use notecards of two or three different colors—one color for each main idea. It's an idea we might never have thought of, but it obviously reinforced the organization of the students' speeches. And that's what outlining and preparing speaking notes should do.

Summary

Outlining serves five main purposes for a speaker preparing a speech. First, it allows the speaker to check the scope of the topic. Is the topic too broad? Are you trying to cover too much or too little? Second, the outline permits a speaker to test the logical relations between main points and subpoints. Are the points related and yet distinctive enough to qualify as separate ideas? Third, outlining provides a check of the relevance of subpoints. Supporting ideas should all be related to the main idea under which they are listed. Fourth, a speaker can use an outline to gauge the balance of the speech. Does it look as though you will be spending too much time on one of your points and too little on others? Should you eliminate the points that have little support and reorganize those with a great deal of support? Finally, an outline can function as speaking notes, jogging the speaker's memory with keywords in correct order.

Outlines can take one of two possible forms: the *complete sentence outline* or the *keyword or phrase outline*. In the first of these outlines, each item introduced by a number or letter is a complete sentence. The keyword or phrase outline avoids complete sentences. The two forms of outlines should generally not be combined.

Effective outlining is greatly simplified if the speaker keeps in mind these traditional principles or rules. First, each symbol—number or letter—in the outline should represent only one idea. Second, coordination and subordination should be represented by a consistent system of letters and numbers properly indented. Third, any point divided into subpoints must have at least two subpoints. Fourth, complete sentences and keywords should be mixed only in the speaking outline. Finally, coordinate points throughout the outline should have simple, parallel grammatical construction.

The first phase of outlining is a *working outline*, an informal list of different aspects of the selected speech topic. From there, the speaker should develop a complete sentence outline, or *formal outline*, that is clear and thorough enough to communicate the essence of the speech to any reader. Having checked the scope of the topic and the logical connections, relevance, and balance of the subpoints, the speaker can then select keywords and phrases for a *speaking outline*. That outline may also include transitions, quotations, and source citations, as well as personal directions or prompts for the delivery of the speech.

A speaking outline provides a visual test of the organization of a speech. While effective outlining does not guarantee clear organization in the delivered speech, chances are good that any well-organized speech has been carefully outlined at some stage in its development.

Practice Critique

Evaluating a Speech Outline

Read the transcript of Susan Chontos's speech, "The Amish: Seeking to Lose the Self," which appears in Chapter 15. As you read, write down an outline of the three main ideas that she develops, including the subpoints. Then, using this outline, write brief answers to the following questions and be prepared to discuss them with your classmates: (1) Did Susan narrow the topic sufficiently to develop her key ideas in some depth? (2) Does one idea in the outline lead to the next in a meaningful way? (3) Do the subtopics under each main idea develop that point? (4) Are the three ideas balanced? In summary, does the outline reveal a well-organized speech? If you were advising Susan, would you offer any suggestions to help her present her ideas more clearly and support them more effectively?

Exercises

1. Test your understanding of coordination and subordination by outlining the following statements:
   a. Blind artists draw objects from a single perspective.
   b. Blind artists use lines to represent surfaces.
   c. Blind artists draw distant objects smaller than close ones.
   d. Blind artists use many of the same visual devices as sighted artists.
   Which of the above statements is the key idea? Which statements are subordinate to it? Which statements are coordinate?[5]

2. Select one of the speeches in the Appendix, and prepare a keyword or phrase outline of the speech. Identify three ways the outline reveals whether the speech was well organized, whether the ideas are balanced, and whether each point directly relates to the specific purpose of the speech.

3. Using the outline you constructed in Exercise 2, reword it as a complete sentence outline. When is it better to develop a keyword or phrase outline? When is a complete sentence outline preferred?

4. Listen to a speech in person or on radio, television, or videotape, and outline its main and supporting ideas. Review the outline. Did the speaker try to cover too many points? Are the main points and subpoints relevant, balanced, and logically sequenced? Based on the outline, what suggestions could you give the speaker to improve the speech?

5. Using the entries below, construct an outline of four major points on the topic of "Latin music." The major headings are included in the list:

mariachi	Ruben Blades
small folk band	countries
Cuba	*merengue*
styles	Jennifer Lopez
Marc Anthony	*salsa*
artists	*mariachi* band
Puerto Rico	Mexico
rumba	Enrique Iglesias
Latin big band	Elvis Crespo
instrumentation	Brazil
Spain	*mambo*

We originally got this information from two websites: www.latinmusicspecialists.com and www.dj.net.

Wording Your Speech

Functions of Language
Communicate Ideas
Send Messages about User
Strengthen Social Bonds
Serve as Instrument of Play
Check Language Use

Principles of Effective Language Use
Use Language Correctly
Use Language Clearly
Use Language Vividly
Use Language Inclusively

■ **TRY THIS:** Becoming an Inclusive Speaker

Use Oral Style

■ **THEORY INTO PRACTICE:** Keys to Effective Oral Style

chapter

12

Socrates was a famous Greek teacher who went around giving people advice. They killed him. Socrates died from an overdose of wedlock. After his death, his career suffered a dramatic decline. —FROM A STUDENT PAPER[1]

Sisters Reunited after 18 Years in Checkout Line at Supermarket —NEWSPAPER HEADLINE[2]

A congressman was concerned about the costs of unnecessary medical tests and warned his constituents, "They might take you in there and perform a C-SPAN." —JEFFREY MCQUAIN[3]

Speakers of English have access to the richest vocabulary on Earth, largely because we have adopted words so freely from other languages. In fact, three out of five words in English come from a foreign tongue.[4] As a result, the revised *Oxford English Dictionary* is huge, containing 615,000 words. That is more than three times as many words as the German language contains and more than six times the number of words available to the French.[5] People who speak English can achieve degrees of subtlety and nuance that are impossible in most languages. So you would think we could manage to be clearer than the speakers and writers in the examples above.

Socrates died of an overdose of hemlock, not wedlock. We doubt that those sisters had to wait in the supermarket checkout line for 18 years, even if there were lots of double-coupon days! As for the final example, we assume the congressman meant to say "CAT scan." C-SPAN is a cable television network.

Examples of language abuse, both spoken and written, are all around us. Their effects can be comic or serious. More important for our purposes are examples of words used correctly, clearly, vividly, inclusively, and in an oral style. How we use words makes us stand out from others. Language empowers us, and we can employ it to serve both ethical and unethical purposes.

In this chapter you will learn five functions language serves for us. We will also discuss five principles of effective language use and offer suggestions for adhering to them.

Functions of Language

Studying language is important, because the more you know about it, the greater influence you will have as you communicate in public. The language we use fulfills at least five functions.[6]

Communicate Ideas

"Humans are alone on the planet in their use of language to communicate."[7] Our language can communicate an infinite number of ideas because it has a structure of separate words. Unlike the sounds most animals make to signal danger, for example, our language allows us to specify the type of threat, the immediacy of the danger, and any number of other characteristics of the situation.[8] However, a speaker's language is effective only if it communicates to listeners. As we mentioned in Chapter 1 in discussing the "triangle of meaning," as long as the speaker and the listener attach similar referents to the words they use, the two can communicate indefinitely.

Send Messages about User

Our vocabulary reveals aspects of our educational background, our age, and even what area of the country we call home. Consider the following exchange from the award-winning sitcom *Frasier:*

> **Frasier, to his brother Niles:** "If you were stranded on an island, what would you choose as your favorite meal, aria, and wine?
>
> **Niles:** The Coulibiac of Salmon at Guy Savoy. "Vissa d'arte" from *Tosca.* And the Cotes du Rhone, Chateau Neuf du Pape, '47.
>
> **Frasier:** You're so predictable."[9]

Even if you've never seen the TV show, you probably form a vivid picture of who these brothers are—or think they are.

In addition, language expresses the feelings or emotions of the speaker. The words we select communicate how we feel about both our listeners and the subject under discussion. Which of these terms suggests the strongest emotion, for example?

crisis   dilemma   problem

Crisis suggests a more powerful feeling than do the other terms. Language can carry considerable emotional impact, and the words you select carry messages—sometimes obvious, sometimes subtle—about your background and the nature and strength of your emotions.

Strengthen Social Bonds

Precisely because it communicates ideas and emotions between people, language serves a social function. For example, we often use language to identify ourselves as part of a particular group. Think of the slang expressions you used around friends when you were younger to signal that you were a member of a certain group and in the know. Many of these utterances are fun and harmless. In 2005 *Merriam-Webster Online* asked readers to submit favorite words that are not yet in the dictionary. Fourth on the list was the verb *chillax,* a term used by many teenagers. Those who understood the slang knew that it meant to calm down or relax, as in: "Stop stressing. Just chillax."[10] Outsiders, however, were often puzzled when they heard the word.

Nelson Mandela carefully crafts his language to urge his listeners to work toward a day when "we shall, together, rejoice in a common victory over racism."

Other language serves a social function when spoken in unison. A group of kindergarten students reciting the alphabet or counting from 1 to 20 strengthen their group identity and celebrate the group's accomplishment. Adults repeating a pledge or prayer experience similar group feelings. Or consider the words we use to greet one another. The exchange, "Hi, how are you?" and, "Fine, how are you doing?" may be a hollow, automatic social ritual. Nevertheless, such rituals acknowledge the social bond that exists even between strangers.

Serve as Instrument of Play

You have to love the name The Wailin' Jennys, three talented Canadian singer–songwriters (none named Jenny). Our language not only works, it also entertains. Movie history buffs tell the story of the famed gossip columnist of the 1950s, Hedda Hopper. As part of her research on him, Hopper sent Cary Grant the following telegram: "How old Cary Grant?" Grant responded by telegram: "Old Cary Grant fine. How old Hedda Hopper?"

We use language not only for such verbal dueling, but also for the pleasure of its sounds. Many linguists believe we all vocalize as children partly because it just feels and sounds good. Luckily, we do not entirely lose that capacity for play as we mature. The jump-rope chant, the forced rhyme of much rap music, and the rapid-fire lyrics of a hit single used in a car commercial are all examples of language used mainly for the sheer fun of its sounds.

Speaking with Confidence

Wording my speeches properly was a very high priority for me. I knew that if I did not effectively communicate my ideas, they would fall on deaf ears. I found it extremely important in my persuasive speech on college binge drinking deaths. Since I was delivering this speech to an audience in a city that ranked in the Top 10 for binge drinkers, I had to be sure that the language I used would grab their attention and keep it for the duration of the speech.

I used four techniques that aided in my success in this speech. First, I used language that appealed to the audience's emotions by painting vivid imagery. Second, when delivering quotes and statistics, I tried to use appropriate voice qualities to give them dramatic impact and to stress their logic. Third, I established my credibility by using my personal experiences and education in my field of study for an ethical appeal, while speaking on the audience's level and not using technical jargon. Finally, I imagined that I was speaking to each listener as "a friend." I just conversationally stated the facts and explained how I felt.

By employing these techniques and rehearsing several times, I felt more comfortable and confident in this speech and its delivery than I ever had before.

—**Suzanne L. Hamilton,** *San Antonio College*

Check Language Use

When in doubt, we as speakers will sometimes check with our listeners to see whether they are decoding a message similar to the one we intended: "Do you understand?" "Get it?" As listeners during interpersonal communication, we may even interrupt a speaker to signal our misunderstanding: "Wait a minute. I don't follow you."

These five functions of language should be obvious to you by this point in your public speaking class. The fact that most of your classmates understood the speeches you have given so far testifies to the power of language to carry a speaker's ideas. Yet your listeners have learned more about you than the ideas you communicated. From your language during your speeches and while commenting on others' speeches, they have learned about your likes and dislikes. They may have even made accurate guesses about aspects of your background. During the semester or quarter, the language you used in your speeches and in class discussion has also established and strengthened the social bonds between you and your classmates. Anytime speakers used humor or showed any verbal virtuosity, they invited you to play with language. Whenever you used an interjection such as "Get this" or "This is important" or whenever you questioned a speaker after a speech, you used language to check and measure your understanding.

Language has many registers, from chatty and confidential to simple and direct, complex and technical, lofty and formal. You speak differently to different people, depending on the environment, the subject under discussion, and your relationship with your listeners. Though public speaking is generally more formal than casual conversation, the precise level of language you use will depend on what you want your speech to accomplish.

At times, we want our language to be "transparent," almost to disappear. In these instances, we focus on getting our meaning across to our listeners quickly and clearly. If you were reporting a fire, a gas leak, or some other emergency to a group of people and advising them to vacate their building, you would try to communicate that information directly, simply, and quickly, without causing panic. You would not waste time mentally editing and practicing the message to make it more clever or more memorable. In giving instructions or issuing a warning, you would never want to use language your audience did not know. Because your goal in these circumstances is getting your message across to a listener, you would use language with clear denotations. **Denotation** is the dictionary definition of a word.

On other occasions, you speak to get a message across, but also to convey it in an especially vivid way. At such times, you pay particular attention to the way you encode the message, choosing your words carefully. When your purpose is to signal your feelings about a subject, to strengthen the social bonds between you and your listeners, or to engage them in verbal play, you will likely use language that is "opaque" and has strong connotations.[11] **Connotation** is the emotional association that a particular word has for an individual listener. The word *fire* may have pleasant connotations for you if you spent some time around a campfire recently. The same word will have negative connotations for someone whose home has burned down.

Your choice of language depends on the purpose of your speech. Usually, you will use a combination of denotative and connotative language registers. Whether the wording of your speech is straightforward or evocative, direct or highly embroidered, however, you must use language carefully. The following section offers guidelines for using language that is correct, clear, vivid, inclusive, and in an oral style.

Principles of Effective Language Use

Words are sometimes compared to tools and weapons, and, in a sense, you draw from that arsenal every time you speak. The words you choose help determine your success in informing, persuading, and entertaining your audience. Five principles should guide your use of language and make you a more effective speaker.

Key Points

Principles of Effective Language Use

1. Use language correctly.
2. Use language clearly.
3. Use language vividly.
4. Use language inclusively.
5. Use oral style.

Use Language Correctly

When you use language incorrectly in your speech, you run the risk of sending unintended messages, as well as of undermining your credibility and the causes you support. Poorly worded ideas are sometimes evaluated as poor ideas, although this may not be the case. For example, one student, concerned about the increase of sexually transmitted diseases, encouraged her listeners to commit to "long-term monotonous relationships." We hope she meant to use the word *monogamous*.

If you hear examples of incorrect language in your class, they will likely be more subtle than the example given above. Nevertheless, it is important for speakers to rid their speeches of all unnecessary intrusions. Speakers perceived to care about how they state their ideas are also perceived to care about what they say.

The following examples illustrate some common language errors we have heard in student speeches:

1. The first criteria for selecting a good wine is to experience its bouquet. (The speaker should use the singular noun *criterion*.)

2. If our school is to remain financially solvent, we must choose between three options. (*Among* is the correct word when more than two options are included.)

3. Because she failed to wear her seat belt, she was hurt bad: a broken leg, fractured ribs, and a mild concussion. (She was *badly* hurt.)

Exploring *Online*

GRAMMAR CHECK

www.trh.bc.ca/grammar/grammar.html

This funny site maintained by Tim Hicks of British Columbia is a grammar hall of shame. You can browse lists of words and phrases that are often misused, misunderstood, and misspelled; or contact Hicks to nominate a word you find menacing.

denotation: the literal meaning or dictionary definition of a word or phrase.

connotation: the emotional associations that a word or phrase may evoke in individual listeners.

4. Because they conduct most of their missions at night, a drug trafficker often alludes our understaffed border patrol. (*They* is plural, so the speaker should use *drug traffickers*. Also, the correct word is *elude*, not *allude*.)

5. Less than twenty students attended the lecture given by Dr. Hinojosa last Wednesday. (Use *fewer* for people or items that can be counted. Yes, those supermarket check-out lane signs that say "10 Items or Less" are wrong!)

Some of these errors may seem less severe to you than others. Remember, though, that your language is an important part of the delivery of your speech. Your language, like your physical and vocal delivery, should be free of all distractions. Errors in subject–verb agreement, misplaced modifiers, and incorrect word choice immediately attract the attention of everyone who recognizes these errors. You won't upset anyone if your language is grammatically correct, but even small errors run the risk of monopolizing some people's attention. In turn, they stop listening carefully to *what* you say because they are paying attention to *how* you speak.

You can speak correctly if you follow a few simple guidelines. First, make a note of grammatical mistakes you hear yourself and other people make in casual conversation. Attentive listening is a first step to improving your use of language. Second, when you are unsure of a word's meaning, consult a dictionary. Third, if you have a question about proper grammar, refer to a handbook for writers. Fourth, when practicing your speech, record it and play it back, listening for mistakes you may not have noticed as you were practicing. Fifth, practice your speech in front of friends and ask them to point out mistakes. These strategies will help you detect and correct errors. Not only will your speaking improve, but you may also save yourself some embarrassment. As Mark Twain noted, "The difference between the right word and the almost right word is the difference between lightning and the lightning bug."

> "Remember the word "choice." Every speaker, every writer, every user of language, chooses the words that he or she wants to use. . . . Imprecise or weak words detract from the meaning of the message, while the choice of exact words empowers language. Stronger English comes from making stronger choices, and exact wording, when it becomes a habit, can become fun as well as fascinating."
>
> —JEFFREY MCQUAIN[12]

Use Language Clearly

Language use must not only be correct, it must also be clear. To achieve clarity, a speaker should use language that is specific and familiar. If you sacrifice either criterion, your language may confuse your listeners.

Use Specific Language. In Chapter 1, we mentioned that many of our communication problems spring from the fact that there are always two messages involved whenever two people are communicating. There is, first, the message that the speaker intends. In addition, there is the message that the listener infers or interprets. If you tell your instructor that you missed an assignment deadline because you were "having some problems," you leave yourself open to a wide range of possible interpretations. Do you have health problems, family troubles, or stress from a personal relationship? You could be having trouble juggling a work schedule with your study time or having car problems. You could be grieving over the loss of a loved one or struggling with one particularly difficult course. These and other interpretations are possible because *problem* is an abstract term.

To clarify your ideas, use the lowest level of abstraction possible. Words are not *either* abstract or concrete, but take on these qualities in relation to other words. Look at the following list of terms, for example.

class

college class

college communication class

Comm 110: Introduction to Public Communication

Comm 110 at Montana State University

Comm 110 with David McLaughlin at Montana State University

The term at the top of this list is more abstract than the one at the bottom. As we add those limiting, descriptive words, or *qualifiers,* the referent becomes increasingly specific. The lower the level of abstraction used, the more clearly the listener will understand the speaker.

Suppose you were giving a speech on how citizens can protect their homes from burglaries, and you made the following statement:

> Crime is rampant in our city. Burglary alone has gone way up in the past year or so. So you can see that having the right kind of lock on your door is essential to your safety.

What is wrong with this statement? The language is vague. What does "rampant" mean? How much of an increase is "way up"—15 percent, 50 percent, 400 percent? Is "the past year or so" one year, two years, or more? What is "the right kind of lock"? As a speaker you should help your audience by making these ideas more concrete. After some research, you might rephrase your argument like this:

> Last week I spoke with Captain James Winton, head of our City Police Department's Records Division. He told me that crime in our city has increased by 54 percent in the last year, and the number of burglaries has doubled. We can help deter crime by making our homes burglar-proof, and one way of doing this is to make sure that all doors have solid locks. I brought one such lock with me: It's a double-keyed deadbolt lock.

Notice the improvement in the second paragraph. Your message is clearer, and with that clarity you would gain added credibility as a speaker.

Use Familiar Language. Your language may be specific but still not be clear. If listeners are not familiar with your words, communication is impaired.

Occasionally, we hear speeches in which students try to impress listeners with their vocabularies. We suspect they drafted their remarks with a pen in one hand and a thesaurus in the other, or that they used the thesaurus in their word processing program too frequently while typing. Phrases such as "a plethora of regulations," "this obviates the need for," "the apotheosis of deceit," and "the anathema of censorship" detract from rather than enhance the speaker's message. "We must ever be mindful to eschew verbosity and deprecate tautology" is good advice and fun to say. But if you are trying to communicate with another person, it's probably better simply to say, "Avoid wordiness."

The use of jargon can also undermine clarity. **Jargon** is the special language of a particular activity, business, or group of people. What, for example, are the meanings

> " *The chief virtue that language can have is clearness, and nothing detracts from it so much as the use of unfamiliar words.* "
>
> —HIPPOCRATES

jargon: the special language used by people in a particular activity, business, or group.

of the following acronyms: BRB, ROFL, FWIW, and GAL? If you participate in Internet chatrooms, message boards, or instant messaging (IM), you probably quickly interpreted these letters as the phrases "be right back," "rolling on the floor laughing," "for what it's worth," and "get a life." If you lack much online experience, however, this unfamiliar jargon thwarted effective communication. If you inform your classmates on the development of maglev trains, you will probably also need to tell them that *maglev* is short for "magnetic levitation" and then explain what that means.

If you are certain that the people you are addressing know such terms, jargon presents no problem. In fact, it is usually quite specific and can save a lot of time. Jargon can even increase your credibility by indicating that you are familiar with the subject matter. If you have any doubts about whether your listeners know the jargon, however, either avoid such terms or define each one the first time you use it.

Use Language Vividly

In addition to selecting language that is correct and clear, speakers should choose language that is colorful and picturesque. Vivid language engages the audience and makes the task of listening easier. Read the following critiques of the speeches of our twenty-ninth president, Warren Harding:

1. Warren Harding was not an effective public speaker. His speeches often were confusing and uninspired. He did not make his points well.

2. "His speeches left the impression of an army of pompous phrases moving over the landscape in search of an idea; sometimes these meandering words would actually capture a straggling thought and bear it triumphantly a prisoner in their midst, until it died of servitude and overwork." William G. McAdoo, Democratic party leader[13]

Which of these two statements did you enjoy reading more? Which characterization of Harding's speaking did you find more colorful? Which paragraph contains the more vivid images? Which would you like to read again? We're fairly certain that you selected the second statement. Why?

The language of the first critique communicates an idea as simply and economically as possible without calling attention to itself. To use a term we introduced earlier

Writers and poets such as Maya Angelou make the written word come alive through vivid and picturesque language. Successful speakers use these same techniques to make the spoken word evoke vivid images.

in this chapter, its language is transparent. It is also drab and colorless and displays little creativity. The language style is not nearly as lively as the second example. The language of the second statement is opaque; it calls attention to its sounds, textures, and rhythms. Vivid language helps listeners remember both your message and you.

One of the fiercest enemies of vivid language is the **cliché**, a once-colorful expression that has lost most of its impact through overuse. Many clichés involve comparisons. For example, complete the following phrases:

Cute as a _____.

Dead as a _____.

Between a rock and a _____.

Did you have any trouble completing those expressions? Probably not. In fact, *button, doornail,* and *hard place* most likely popped into your mind without much thought. Each of these sayings is a cliché, an overworked expression that doesn't require (or stimulate) much thinking. Clichés are bland and hackneyed. Avoid them!

Now that you have seen some of the effects of dull wording, what techniques can you use to make your language more vivid? The answer to this question may be limited only by your imagination. We offer three strategies for your consideration: (1) use active language; (2) appeal to your listeners' senses; and (3) use figures and structures of speech. Following these suggestions will give you a good start on making your speeches more colorful and, thus, more memorable.

Use Active Language.   Which of the following statements is more forceful?

It was decided by the Student Government Association that the election would be delayed for one week.

The Student Government Association decided to delay the election for one week.

The second one, right? The first sentence uses passive voice; the second active. Active voice is always more direct because it identifies the agent producing the action and places it first in the sentence. In addition, active voice is more economical than passive voice; the second sentence is shorter than the first by five words.

Active language, however, involves more than active voice. Active language is language that works. It has energy, vitality, and drive. It is not bogged down by filler

cliché: a once-colorful figure of speech that has lost impact from overuse.

phrases such as "you know," "like," and "stuff like that." Rather than being cliché-ridden, it may convert the commonplace into the unexpected. Language that is lively and active has impact. Notice how the following student twisted a familiar expression to achieve more dramatic results in her speech conclusion.

> Cherie spoke of injuries, even deaths, children suffer from playing baseball. After detailing some ways the game could be made safer, she concluded, "[C]hildren may be dying to play baseball, but they should never die because of it."[14]

Exploring *Online*

WRITING RESOURCES ONLINE
www.garbl.com/writing
Garbl's Writing Resources provide speech writers with lots of practical information, from basic grammar to style and usage. Especially helpful to persuasive speakers is the action writing link, which provides information on how to write persuasively. The links to reference sources are also helpful, as well as the option of contacting an online expert for answers to writing questions.

Coining a word or phrase is another way of making your language work for you. The widespread popularity of email has led us to distinguish it from "snail mail." A well-turned phrase also actively engages the minds of your listeners as they hear the interplay of words and ideas. Indian nationalist leader Mohandas Gandhi, for example, urged his listeners to "live simply so others might simply live."

Appeal to Your Listeners' Senses.   Another way you can achieve impact with language is by appealing to your listeners' senses. The obvious and familiar senses are sight, hearing, touch, taste, and smell. To these we can add the sense of motion or movement and the sense of muscular tension. Colorful language can create vivid images that appeal to each of these various senses. Those sharp images in turn heighten audience involvement in the speech, inviting listeners to participate with their feelings and thereby increasing their retention of what you have said.

Assume that you are a roller coaster enthusiast and have decided to deliver an informative speech on roller coasters. Such a topic certainly begs for language to create or re-create the various sensations of a coaster ride for your audience. But what if you are not confident about your ability to appeal to your audience's various senses in your speech? You can always do some research on this topic and use the words of others, as long as you accurately attribute your quotations. We easily found four magazine articles on roller coasters. Figure 12.1 lists and defines the different kinds of sensory images and provides examples from two of these articles.[15] Notice how many of these examples of sensory impressions are not only evocative, but also funny and fun to say. Active language and appeals to the senses are not your only techniques for enlivening your speech language, however. Public speaking gives you an opportunity to use some special language structures and to devise some of the figures of speech you may have studied before in English classes.

Use Figures of Speech.   Important ideas are easier to remember if they are memorably worded. Drawing attention to the way you phrase your thoughts—making your language "opaque"—can produce memorable effects in your listeners. To enliven your language, you can use various figures and structures of speech. Some of the most common figures of speech are simile, metaphor, and personification. Common structures of speech are alliteration, parallelism, repetition, and antithesis.

Simile and **metaphor** are comparisons of two seemingly dissimilar things. In simile the comparison is explicitly stated using the words *as* or *like* for example, "Trying to pin the Senator down on the issue is like trying to nail a poached egg to a tree." In her persuasive speech Kristin sought to heighten audience awareness that recent laws designed to protect the United States were actually threatening individual freedoms. She began her speech with a simile:

> "Just like the frog in a pot of water that doesn't realize it's being boiled to death because the temperature is raised so gradually, so too can a populace fail to appreciate the erosion of its freedom." So states the October 20, 2002, *St. Petersburg Times.*[16]

simile: a comparison of two things using the words *as* or *like.*

metaphor: an implied comparison of two things without the use of *as* or *like.*

FIGURE 12.1
Types of Sensory Images

This sensory impression:	Achieves this effect:	Example:
Visual image	Recreates the sight of something.	"The Cyclone differs from other roller coasters in being (a) a work of art and (b) old, . . . decrepit, rusting in its metal parts and peeling in its more numerous wooden parts."
Auditory image	Suggests the sound of something.	"Yes it may be anguishing initially . . . terrifying, even, the first time or two the train is hauled upward with groans and creaks and with you in it. At the top then—where there is a sudden strange quiet but for the fluttering of two tattered flags. . . ."
Tactile image	Recreates the feel of something.	"I should mention that a heavy, cushioned restraining bar locks down snugly into your lap and is very reassuring, although, like everything upholstered in the cars, it may be cracked or slashed. . . ."
Thermal image	Creates impressions of heat or cold.	"It was an awful moment, with a sickening sense of betrayal and icy-fingered doubt."
Gustatory image	Recreates the taste of something.	Nothing matches the faint metallic taste of fear as you feel the train set free to begin falling from the top of that first hill.
Kinetic image	Creates feelings of motion or movement.	"At nearly 65 mph, the train shot into a tunnel and spun 540 degrees around a banked helix. . . ."
Kinesthetic image	Suggests states of muscular tension or relaxation.	"My teeth clenched and my knuckles locked bone-white around the lap bar."
Olfactory image	Suggests the smell of something.	We are brought to a "quick, pillowy deceleration in the shed, smelling of dirty machine oil. . . ."
Synesthesia	Combines two or more sensory impressions.	Riding a coaster is "like driving your car with your head out the window at 70 miles per hour. But to get the full effect, you have to drive it off a cliff."

In metaphor, the comparison is not explicitly stated but is implied, without using *as* or *like*. Metaphor making is an ancient activity. Scholars who have studied the earliest language that gave rise to English and dozens of other languages have discovered the phrase *wekwom texos*, or "weaver of words." This title distinguished the tribal poets who preserved stories and legends by weaving them into sung or chanted verse.[17] Some of the earliest metaphors probably originated as speakers extended human physiology, as in "the mouth of the river" and "the bowels of the earth."[18] Today our language is full of metaphorical comparisons.

Metaphor helps us accommodate the new in terms of the familiar. As a nation, we have moved from being "couch potatoes" to "channel surfers." At the same time, television executives and advertisers may conceive of us, remote controls in hand, as a nation of "grazers."

If we think of ourselves as channel surfers, perhaps we are compensating heavily for sitting in front of the television actually doing nothing. If the industry calls us grazers, perhaps they don't have too high an opinion of us. The metaphors people use give us insights into their conceptual and fantasy worlds. More than that, the metaphors shape how we perceive our "real world," and what we are doing in it.[19]

The difference between simile and metaphor is greater than just the presence or absence of *as* or *like,* however. While simile makes a comparison that can sometimes be fairly ordinary and reasonable, metaphor achieves a "qualitative leap . . . to an identification or fusion of two objects" with the characteristics of both.[20] To produce metaphors is to extend meanings, to improvise, to let your imagination go.[21]

Fresh metaphors have the power to surprise us into new ways of seeing things. Theodore Roosevelt created a memorable metaphor when he made the following comparison: "A good political speech is a poster, not an etching."[22] Peter Schjeldahl, author of one of the articles on Coney Island's Cyclone, uses metaphor when he compares that roller coaster to a poem:

> The coaster is basically an ornate means of falling and a poem about physics in parts or stanzas, with jokes. The special quality of the Cyclone is how different, how *articulated,* all the components of its poem are, the whole of which lasts a minute and thirty-some seconds—exactly the right length, composed of distinct and perfect moments. By my fifth ride, my heart was leaping at the onset of each segment as at the approach of a dear old friend, and melting with instantaneous nostalgia for each at its finish.[23]

> *"A word is not crystal, transparent and unchanged; it is the skin of a living thought and may vary greatly in color and content according to the circumstances and time in which it is used."*
>
> —OLIVER WENDELL HOLMES, JR.

Notice that near the end of the description the roller coaster begins to take on human characteristics.

Personification gives human qualities to objects, ideas, or organizations. Blind justice, the angry sea, and jealousy raising its ugly head are all examples of personification. Our student Amanda used personification in her speech on drummers. Notice how the drum beat takes on human qualities as she introduces her topic:

> It's the catalyst to any gut wrenching rock song, the groove behind any rapper's flow, and the driving force behind any marching band. It's a drum beat. No matter where or when you hear it, a drum beat grabs you by the lapels, screams in your face, and then slams you back into your seat for the ride of your life.

Another student, Phillip, began his speech, "Nearly eight years ago, a new neighbor moved to East Liverpool, Ohio. But residents of this low-income, minority town didn't greet the newcomer with welcoming signs." This "Unwanted Neighbor," the title of Phillip's speech, was just "400 yards from an elementary school site." The neighbor? A toxic waste incinerator. Using personification, Phillip made the incinerator an enemy, someone who needed to be turned away. [24]

Use Structures of Speech. In addition to these figures of speech, you can also employ language structures, such as alliteration, parallelism, repetition, and antithesis. **Alliteration** is the repetition of beginning sounds in adjacent or nearby words. A speaker who asks us "to dream, to dare, and to do" uses alliteration. The sounds of words give your speech impact. A student speaking on the topic of child abuse described the victims as "badly bruised and beaten." Not only did these words themselves convey a severe problem, but the repetition of the stern, forceful *b* sound vocally accentuated the violence of the act.

In his "I Have a Dream" speech in the Appendix, Martin Luther King, Jr., used alliteration to describe his dream of a nation where people "will not be judged by the color

personification: a figure of speech that attributes human qualities to a concept or inanimate object.

alliteration: the repetition of beginning sounds in words that are adjacent, or near one another.

of their skin but by the content of their character." Holocaust survivor Elie Wiesel used alliteration in a speech entitled "The Shame of Hunger" when he spoke of "faith in the future," "complacency if not complicity," and "hunger and humiliation."[25]

Speakers use **parallelism** when they express two or more ideas in similar language structure. When they restate words, phrases, or sentences, they use **repetition**. Parallelism and repetition work in concert to emphasize an idea or a call for action. For example, Travis used an alarm clock image to summarize his persuasive speech on the dangers of sleep deprivation. He then used parallelism and repetition in his call to action and closure steps:

> Today, we've sounded the alarm about the harms of sleep deprivation, opened our eyes to the reasons this situation has developed, and finally awakened to the steps we must take to end this nightmare. Before we are all, literally, dead on our feet, let's take the easiest solution step of all. Tonight, turn off your alarm, turn down your covers, and turn in for a good night's sleep.[26]

Another excellent example of the use of parallel construction is Martin Luther King, Jr.'s, "I Have a Dream" speech. King repeats the phrase "one hundred years later" to dramatize the "shameful condition" of inequality. He prefaces his hopes for the future with the phrase "I have a dream." And near the end of his speech he uses parallelism and repetition to create a dramatic climax:

> So *let freedom ring* from the prodigious hilltops of New Hampshire. *Let freedom ring* from the mighty mountains of New York. *Let freedom ring* from the heightening Alleghenies of Pennsylvania! *Let freedom ring* from the snowcapped Rockies of Colorado!
> But not only that. *Let freedom ring* from Stone Mountain of Georgia! *Let freedom ring* from Lookout Mountain of Tennessee! *Let freedom ring* from every hill and molehill of Mississippi. From every mountainside, *let freedom ring.*
> And when this happens . . . we will be able to join hands and sing, in the words of the old Negro spiritual, *"Free at last! Free at last!* Thank God almighty, we are *free at last!"* [italics added][27]

Antithesis uses parallel construction to contrast ideas. You can probably quote from memory John Kennedy's statement: "Ask not what your country can do for you, ask what you can do for your country." Dedicating a memorial for soldiers who had died in the Civil War battle at Gettysburg, Abraham Lincoln proclaimed, "The world will little note nor long remember what we say here, but it can never forget what they did here." The fact that we *do* remember both of these statements attests to the power of antithesis. Notice also that each speaker places what he wants the audience to do or remember at the end of the comparison. Antitheses are usually more powerful if they end positively. Mario Cuomo, an accomplished speaker and former governor of New York, used this strategy when he constructed his keynote address to the 1984 Democratic National Convention:

> We must get the American public to look past the glitter, beyond the showmanship—to reality, to the hard substance of things. And we will do that not so much with speeches that sound good as with speeches that are good and sound. Not so much with speeches that bring people to their feet as with speeches that bring people to their senses.[28]

Sarah Meinen of Bradley University won the national speech tournament of the Interstate Oratorical Association in 1999 with her speech "The Forgotten Four-Letter Word." She carefully researched and organized her speech on the problem of compassion fatigue, "the inability to care anymore about social issues." She crafted her language carefully, using the figures and structures of speech we have just discussed. Sarah's work

parallelism: the expression of ideas using similar grammatical structures.

repetition: restating words, phrases, or sentences for emphasis.

antithesis: the use of parallel construction to contrast ideas.

paid off. She captured the attention and tapped the concern of her listeners, encouraging them to rekindle a passion for AIDS awareness and activism.

> With statistics and expert opinions, Sarah reminded her listeners of the "savage spread" of this "vicious virus" [alliteration]. "AIDS has been too grim, too overwhelming, and it's been around too long" [parallelism and repetition]. She lamented that "despite our exposure to death and destruction, facts and figures, names and Quilt squares, AIDS has slowly faded from our national consciousness . . . " [alliteration and antithesis]. Sarah concluded, "Our well of compassion has run dry . . . " [metaphor].
>
> Sarah urged her listeners to become advocates for change on a national and personal level. "[C]losing our eyes won't make a monster of this magnitude go away" [personification]. "We may be over AIDS, but AIDS is not over . . . [antithesis]. "We may be immune to the stories and statistics, but none of us is safe from the reality of AIDS" [alliteration and antithesis]. Sarah exhorted her audience to do "whatever you have to do to be shocked, to be scared, to be involved, to be compassionate, and to keep this pandemic from being ignored, dismissed, and forgotten" [parallelism].[29]

Simile, metaphor, personification, alliteration, parallelism, repetition, and antithesis enable speakers to create vivid language and images. One note of caution, however: Always remember that your objective as a speaker is not to impress your listeners with your ability to create vivid language. Vivid language is not an end in itself, but rather a means of achieving the larger objectives of the speech. As language expert William Safire notes, "A good speech is not a collection of crisp one-liners, workable metaphors, and effective rhetorical devices; a good speech truly reflects the thoughts and emotions of the speaker. . ."[30]

Use Language Inclusively

Exploring Online

INCLUSIVE LANGUAGE
www.apastyle.org/styletips.html
The American Psychological Association offers excellent suggestions for removing bias in language. Scroll down to "Style Topics" and click on "Disabilities," "Race & Ethnicity," or "Sexuality" for guidelines to ensure inclusive, unbiased language. Especially helpful are the lists of problematic and preferred ways of referring to others.

In Chapter 2 we argued that ethics is a working philosophy that we apply to daily life and bring to all speaking situations. Nowhere is this more evident than in the words we select to address and describe others. Ethical communicators neither exclude nor demean others on the basis of their race, ethnicity, gender, sexual orientation, disability, age, or other characteristics. Their language is inclusive, unbiased, and respectful.

At least three principles should guide you as you become a more inclusive communicator.[31] First, *when referring to individuals and groups of people, use the names they wish to be called.* Yes, ethical public speakers are audience centered. Acceptable terms when referring to race or ethnicity include African American or black; Asian or Asian American; Native American or American Indian; white or Caucasian; and Hispanic, Latino, or Chicano. Refer to individuals' sexual orientations, not their sexual preferences. Lesbians, gay men, and bisexual women and men are acceptable terms. Address females and males who are 18 years or older as women and men, not girls and boys. Not everyone with these characteristics favors the terms listed, and you should consider those preferences as you address a specific audience. Your goal, though, should be to respect individuals' rights to choose what they wish to be called.

A second principle is to *use the "people first" rule when referring to individuals who have disabilities.* As the name implies, we should place people before their disabilities. Avoid calling someone a disabled person, an epileptic, or an AIDS victim. Instead, refer to a person with disabilities, a person with epilepsy, or a person who has AIDS.

Finally, *avoid using language that is gender biased.* The issue of gender bias is particularly pervasive and problematic. Language is sexist if it "promotes and maintains attitudes that stereotype people according to gender. It [**sexist language**] assumes that the

sexist language: language that excludes one gender, creates special categories for one gender, or assigns roles based solely on gender.

male is the norm—the significant gender. **Nonsexist language** treats all people equally and either does not refer to a person's sex when it is irrelevant or refers to men and women in symmetrical ways when their gender is relevant."[32]

Gender bias occurs when language creates special categories for one gender, with no corresponding parallel category for the other gender. *Man* and *wife,* for example, are not parallel terms. *Man* and *woman* or *husband* and *wife* are parallel. Other examples of nonparallel language are *nurse* and *male nurse, chairman* and *chairperson,* and athletic team names such as *The Tigers* (the men's team) and *The Lady Tigers* (the women's team).

Perhaps the most common display of gender-biased language comes from the inappropriate use of a simple two-letter word: *he.* Sometimes called the "generic he," this word is used to refer to men and women alike, usually with the fallacious justification that there aren't acceptable alternatives without cluttering speech with intrusive phrases such as "he and she" and "him and her." Fortunately, this assumption is false.

Consider the following sentence: "A coach must be concerned with his players' motivation." Sexist, right, since both women and men are coaches? Now, consider how simple it is to remove this gender bias without changing the meaning of the sentence. First, use the plural form: "Coaches must be concerned with their players' motivation." Second, eliminate the pronoun: "A coach must be concerned with player motivation." A third way to avoid gender bias is to include both pronouns: "A coach must be concerned with his or her players' motivation." Although the use of "he and she" may seem wordy and intrusive, speakers sometimes use this double-pronoun construction strategically to remind listeners that both women and men perform the role being discussed.

Speakers exhibit fairness when they express their ideas and examples in language that treats others equally and fairly. The strategies discussed in this section should help you design, develop, and deliver a speech that uses inclusive language and respects your audience. If you'd like to learn more about how to use bias-free language, read the excellent sources we have listed in endnote 30, or consult a dictionary such as *The Bias-Free Word Finder: A Dictionary of Nondiscriminatory Language,* by Rosalie Maggio.

Speaking inclusively is an ethical obligation for those who value civil discourse. Maggio highlights both the limitations and possibilities of the role language can play in achieving tolerance, acceptance, and change:

> There can certainly be no solution to the problem of discrimination in society on the level of language alone. Replacing *handicap* with *disability* does not mean a person with disabilities will find a job more easily. Using *secretary* inclusively does not change the fact that fewer than 2 percent of U.S. secretaries are men. Replacing *black-and-white* in our vocabularies will not dislodge racism. However, research indicates that language powerfully influences attitudes, behavior, and perceptions. To ignore this factor in social change would be to hobble all other efforts.[33]

Use Oral Style

To speak appropriately, you must recognize that your oral style differs from your written style. Unless your instructor asks you to deliver some speeches from a manuscript, we believe that you will be better off if you think of "developing" speeches rather than "writing" them. Avoid writing your speeches for two reasons. First, you will likely try to memorize what you have written, and the fear of forgetting part of the speech will add to your nervousness and make your delivery seem stiff and wooden.

Exploring *Online*

NONSEXIST LANGUAGE

http://owl.english.purdue.edu/handouts/general/gl_nonsex.html

www.rpi.edu/dept/llc/writecenter/web/genderfair.html

These two sites provide useful information on how to make your language nonsexist. The Purdue University Online Writing Lab provides guidelines endorsed by the National Council of Teachers of English for using pronouns and references to various occupations. The Writing Center at Rensselaer Polytechnic Institute offers information on how to use "gender-fair" language. This article, written by Jenny Redfern, presents specific ways to avoid the sexist use of *he* and *man.*

nonsexist language: language that treats both genders fairly and avoids stereotyping either one.

Try This

Becoming an Inclusive Speaker

The best way to ensure that you communicate inclusively is to monitor what you say and write. Rosalie Maggio, author of *Talking about People: A Guide to Fair and Accurate Language,* offers an interesting test to see if you've succeeded in incorporating unbiased language in your speaking and writing:

> Too often, language makes assumptions about people—that everyone is male, heterosexual, able-bodied, white, married, between the ages of 26 and 54, of western European extraction. Until it becomes second nature to write without bias, reread your material as though you were: a

gay man, someone who uses a wheelchair, a Japanese American woman, someone over 80 or under 16, or other "individuals" of your own creation. If you do not feel left out, discounted, and ignored, but instead can read [or listen] without being stopped by some incongruence, you have probably avoided hidden bias.[34]

As you prepare your speech, apply Maggio's test for becoming more audience-centered. Review your notes and listen to yourself as you practice. Does your language exclude some people who might be in your audience? If so, how much effort would it really take to include everyone?

The second and more important reason for not writing out a speech is that the act of writing itself often affects the tone of the communication. **Tone** is the relationship established by language and grammar between a writer or speaker and that person's readers or listeners. Many of us think of writing as something formal and correct. In fact, many of us are intimidated by writing specifically because we think it must be formal and correct. For that reason, we tend not to write the way that we speak. Novelist and screenwriter Richard Price speaks from his own experience about the crucial difference between the written and the spoken word:

> It's amazing how much stuff looks dazzlingly authentic and true and beautiful on the page, but dies in someone's mouth. That's the importance of a read through for the writer and the director. Because when the actors at a big round table read all the parts of a script, what doesn't work is going to pop up so obviously. And there's no substitute for that. There's no other way you can learn that except to hear it in somebody's mouth.[35]

If you compose parts of a speech on paper, make certain that you read what's on the page out loud to see if it sounds oral rather than written. How can you tell the difference?

Our oral style differs from our written style in at least four important ways. First, *in speaking we tend to use shorter sentences than we write.* Speakers who write out their speeches often find themselves gasping for air when they try to deliver a long sentence in one breath.

Second, *when we communicate orally, we tend to use more contractions, colloquial expressions, and slang.* Our speaking vocabulary is smaller than our writing vocabulary, so we tend to speak a simpler language than we write. Speakers who write out their speeches often draw from their larger written vocabularies. As a result, their

tone: the relation established by language and grammar between speakers and their listeners.

presentational style seems formal and often creates a barrier between them and their listeners.

Third, *oral style makes greater use of personal pronouns and references than written style does.* Speakers must acknowledge the presence of their listeners, and one way of doing this is by including them in the speech. Using the pronouns *I, we,* and *you* makes your speech more immediate and enhances your rapport with your listeners. You may even want to mention specific audience members by name: "Last week John told us how to construct a power résumé. I'm going to tell you what to do once your résumé gets you a job interview." Notice how the name of the student, coupled with several personal pronouns, brings the speaker and audience together and sets up the possibility for lively interaction.

A fourth difference is that *oral style uses more repetition.* As we discussed in Chapter 4, readers can slow down and reread the material in front of them. They control the pace. Listeners don't have that luxury. Speakers must take special care to reinforce their messages, and one way of accomplishing this is by using repetition. The Theory into Practice feature illustrates some of the key differences between written and oral styles.

No matter which of the world's roughly 6,800 languages you speak, the words you choose telegraph messages about your background, your involvement with your topic, and your relationship with your listeners.[36] Like the unique voice and body you use to deliver your speeches, your language is an extremely important part of your delivery.

Theory into Practice

Tips

Keys to Effective Oral Style

Oral Style Checklist	Instead of this:	Say this:
Use Active Voice	A tuition increase was enacted by our college last year.	Last year, our college increased our tuition.
Use Familiar Language	Such an action would not be prudent at this juncture.	I don't think we should do that.
Use Personal Pronouns	People need to stand up and say, "Enough is enough."	We must stand up and say, "Enough is enough."
Use Contractions	You will not find him in a library on a weekend if his personal computer is working.	You won't find him in a library on a weekend if his computer's working.
Use Short Sentences	According to Nigel Hawkes in his book *Structures: The Way Things Are Built,* an accidental discovery by well diggers in 1974 has led archaeologists in central China to unearth an army of possibly 8,000 terracotta figures of warriors and horses in the tomb of China's first emperor.	According to Nigel Hawkes in his book *Structures: The Way Things Are Built,* well diggers in central China discovered pieces of broken terracotta in 1974. Since then, archaeologists have unearthed what may be a total of 8,000 figures. They are terracotta figures of warriors and horses guarding the tomb of China's first emperor.

If you are conscientious, you must know when to speak simply and directly and when to embellish your language with sensory images, figures of speech, and unusual structural devices. In short, you don't have to be a poet to agree with poet Robert Frost, "All the fun's in how you say a thing."[37]

Summary

Language is a distinctly human instrument, no less important than any other tool we have developed for building and creating. Although other animals produce sounds and noises, the human language alone is articulated into words and is capable of expressing an infinite variety of thoughts.

Language serves five functions. First, it communicates ideas between speaker and listener. Second, language sends messages, either intentional or unintentional, about the person who uses it. Your choice of language may reveal your age, your background, and your attitudes about the subjects you discuss. Third, language establishes and strengthens social bonds between groups of people. Fourth, language is an instrument of play because it is the arena for joking and battles of wits. Fifth, we use language to monitor and check our use of language.

As a speaker you use different language on different occasions, depending on the environment, the topic, and your relationship with your listeners. Five principles should guide your use of language: (1) use language correctly, (2) use language clearly, (3) use language vividly, (4) use language inclusively, and (5) use oral style.

As a speaker, your first obligation is to use language *correctly*. Select the right word for the thought you wish to convey, and then phrase the thought correctly. Incorrect language may communicate unintended messages as well as undermine a speaker's credibility. Five guidelines will help you detect and correct language errors. First, listen to the language you and others use, and focus on how it can be improved. Second, consult a dictionary when you are unsure of the meaning of a word. Third, refer to a writing handbook when you have a question about proper grammar. Fourth, use a tape recorder to detect incorrect language use. Fifth, practice your speech in front of friends, and ask them to point out your mistakes.

A second principle of language use is to use language *clearly*. You achieve clarity when you use specific and familiar language. The more concrete your language, the more closely your referents will match those of your listeners. In addition to being specific, language must also be familiar. Listeners must know the meanings of the words you use. One type of language that may undermine clarity is *jargon,* a special language of a particular activity, business, or group of people. If you doubt that your listeners know the jargon, either avoid such terms or else define each the first time you use it.

A third guideline is to use language *vividly*. Colorful language makes the task of listening easier and the message more memorable. Three strategies for making your language more vivid are to use active language, appeal to your listeners' senses, and use figures and structures of speech. Active language avoids *clichés* and filler phrases, using instead active voice, coined words, and well-turned phrases.

A speaker can use any of eight types of sensory images to appeal to listeners' senses. *Visual images* appeal to the sense of sight. *Auditory images* suggest sounds. *Tactile images* recreate the feel of an object. *Thermal images* suggest temperatures. *Gustatory images* appeal to the sense of taste. *Kinetic images* suggest movement or motion. *Kinesthetic images* recreate states of muscular tension or relaxation. *Olfactory images* appeal to the sense of smell. *Synesthesia* is the combination of two or more sensory appeals in a single image.

A third way to achieve vividness is to use figures and structures of speech. *Simile* and *metaphor* are figures of speech comparing two dissimilar things. In simile the comparison is explicit, using words such as *like* and *as*. These words are omitted in metaphors because the comparison is implied. *Personification* attributes human qualities to objects, ideas, or organizations. *Alliteration* is the repetition of beginning sounds. *Parallelism* expresses two or more ideas in similar language structure. *Repetition* is the restatement of words, phrases, or sentences. Like parallelism, *antithesis* uses parallel construction, but it does so to contrast ideas.

A fourth criterion is to use language *inclusively*. Inclusive language incorporates audience diversity and avoids stereotypes about people based on characteristics such as race, ethnicity, age, and gender. Nonsexist language, for example, treats both genders symmetrically and fairly. It does not create special categories or assign roles based solely on gender. Speakers who have difficulty selecting inclusive language should consult a dictionary of bias-free terms.

A final criterion for effective language use is to use *oral style*. Oral style differs from written style in at least four important ways. First, in speaking we tend to use shorter sentences. Second, when we communicate orally we use more contractions, colloquial expressions, and slang. Third, oral style makes greater use of personal pronouns and references. Fourth and finally, we use more repetition when we speak than when we write.

Practice Critique

Analyzing Language Use in a Powerful Speech

Speech experts consider Martin Luther King, Jr.'s, "I Have a Dream" to be one of the most powerful speeches of the twentieth century. Dr. King combined the integrity of his ideas with strong imagery and a masterful delivery to create a memorable speech. Read the transcript of the speech in the Appendix, and then write a brief analysis of the language he used to express his ideas and arouse emotions. Note examples of how Dr. King appealed to his listeners' senses and how he used alliteration, parallelism, repetition, antithesis, and metaphor. Comment on Dr. King's use of gender-specific language. If the speech were being delivered today, how might it be rewritten to make the language more inclusive?

Exercises

1. Generate examples of words and phrases that identify a speaker as being from a particular region of the country. Examples could include the pronoun *y'all*, the salutation *yo!*, or the use of *pop* for carbonated soft drinks. Do these examples also suggest stereotypes about the educational levels of the speakers?

2. Linguists believe that Shakespeare invented one-tenth of the words he used. According to Richard Saul Wurman in *Information Anxiety*, the Stanford University admissions form asks applicants to invent and explain a new word. Invent, define, and illustrate the use of a new word in a one- to two-minute practice speech.

3. Select a one- or two-paragraph passage from a book or magazine. Using the guidelines listed in this chapter, rewrite the passage for a speech, incorporating elements of oral style.

4. Decide on nonsexist words that could be substituted for each of the following examples:
   a. Policeman
   b. Salesmanship
   c. Mother country
   d. Old wives' tale
   e. Clothes make the man.
   f. Man's best friend
   g. All men are created equal.
   h. Brotherly love

5. Listen to an album, cassette tape, or compact disc of your favorite vocal recording artist or group. Try to identify at least one example of each of the following language devices in the song lyrics:
   a. Alliteration
   b. Metaphor
   c. Simile
   d. Personification
   e. Visual image
   f. Tactile image
   g. Olfactory image
   h. Gustatory image
   i. Auditory image
   j. Kinesthetic image
   k. Kinetic image

6. Select a speech from *Vital Speeches of the Day* or another published source. Identify examples of as many types of the language devices listed in Exercise 5 as possible.

7. Test your understanding of principles discussed in this chapter by answering the following questions:
   a. What sensory appeal is featured in paragraph 18 of Martin Luther King, Jr.'s, "I Have a Dream" speech in the Appendix?
   b. What are the first two examples of alliteration in paragraph 1 of the student preface to this book?

c. What figure of speech does William McAdoo develop in the second quotation under the heading "Use Language Vividly" in this chapter?

d. What extended figure of speech did Martin Luther King, Jr., develop in paragraphs 4 through 6 of his "I Have a Dream" speech in the Appendix?

$\mathcal{D}$elivering Your Speech

chapter

13

A printed speech is like a dried flower: the substance, indeed, is there, but the color is faded and the perfume gone. —PAUL LORAIN

In Chapter 1 we quoted communication scholar Karlyn Kohrs Campbell: "Ideas do not walk by themselves; they must be carried—expressed and voiced—by someone." Each of us has a unique voice, body, and way of wording ideas. Your manner of presenting a speech—through your voice, body, and language together—forms your style of delivery. In other words, *what* you say is your speech content and *how* you say it is your **delivery.** If you and a classmate presented a speech with the same words arranged in the same order (something we don't recommend), your listeners would still receive two different messages. This is because your delivery not only shapes your image as a speaker, but also changes your message in subtle ways. Having expended the energy and effort necessary to choose, research, organize, and word your message, on most occasions your goal should be delivery that seems effortless.

Sometimes events seem to conspire to make your effort glaringly obvious: The room is too hot and you begin to perspire; distracted for a moment by some noise, you lose your train of thought; allergens in the air have made your voice sound forced or nasal. No one is immune to such incidents, not even people with extensive public speaking experience.

Speech delivery is so important that one criticism of televised presidential debates is that they turn into "beauty contests," emphasizing looks, poise, and personality, while minimizing the importance of what the candidates say. Strong delivery can no doubt mask weak content for some listeners. More important, though, effective delivery can bolster important, well-organized ideas, and poor delivery can diminish the impact of those same ideas.

As the Paul Lorain quotation suggests, your delivery gives color and fragrance to your words. To help you understand how that invigoration occurs, we discuss the qualities and various elements of effective delivery in this chapter. Before we examine the individual elements that constitute physical and vocal delivery, let's first consider some rules that apply to all nonverbal communication and four possible methods of delivering a speech.

Exploring Online

DELIVERY ADVICE FOR ACADEMICS

www.si.umich.edu/~pne/acadtalk.htm

Visit this website to see the delivery suggestions one insider gives other academics to improve their "talks." A link to a PDF file will let you download a six-page article by Paul N. Edwards of the University of Michigan's School of Information. See his "Usually Better–Usually Worse" chart for a delivery checklist, with explanations that follow.

delivery: the way a speaker presents a speech, through voice qualities, bodily actions, and language.

Principles of Nonverbal Communication

Your nonverbal behavior communicates a great deal of information concerning your feelings about what you say. In particular, four principles of nonverbal communication help account for the importance of speech delivery. These principles provide a framework we will use later to evaluate the specific elements of vocal and physical delivery.

1. *Part of our nonverbal communication is deliberate, while another part is unintentional.* You do certain things deliberately to make other people feel comfortable

Speaking with *Confidence*

Delivery is one of the most important aspects of public speaking, but it can also be intimidating: looking at your audience, wondering if you should move, trying to figure out what to do with your hands. All this requires some planning and work. To improve my delivery, I practiced my entire speech in my room while visualizing my audience. As I spoke, I concentrated on my hand gestures, the amount of eye contact I was making, and the tone and level of my voice. I always timed my speech and made sure I wasn't rushing my delivery, adding pauses where necessary. The more I practiced, the less nervous and more confident I became. My delivery not only made me look more professional, but it also kept my classmates involved in my speech and interested in what I was saying.

—**Michael Gino,** *Suffolk County Community College, Selden, New York*

around you or attracted to you. You dress in colors and fabrics that flatter you or make you feel comfortable. When speaking or listening to others, you look them directly in the eyes. You smile when they tell you good news and show concern when they share a problem.

On the other hand, you may have habits of which you are unaware. You fold your arms, assuming a closed and defensive body position, or jingle your keys when nervous. You tap your fingers on the lectern when anxious or look down at the floor when embarrassed. You can control only those things you know about. Therefore, the first step toward improving your speech delivery is to identify and isolate any distracting nonverbal behaviors you exhibit.

In this chapter, we discuss fourteen nonverbal elements of speech delivery. Of these elements, only one—vocal quality—is difficult to change or control. The others are much easier to modify. But how can you learn whether you have annoying and distracting habits? Feedback from your instructor and your classmates can show you areas in which you need to improve. If you have access to voice recording software or a cassette recorder, you can listen to your voice as you practice your speech; a video camera or webcam will enable you to observe and assess your physical delivery. Keep in mind that discovering and improving your delivery weaknesses is not a quick, one-shot event, but continues with each successive speech you deliver in class.

2. *Few nonverbal signals have universal meaning.* Standing at a bakery in Paris, France, you can't resist the aroma of long, golden loaves of bread hot from the oven. Unable to speak French, you get the clerk's attention, point to the loaves, and hold up two fingers, as in a V for victory. The clerk nods, hands you three loaves, and charges you for all three. Why? The French count from the thumb, whether it is extended or not.

Just as the meanings of gestures and movements can change from one culture to the next, nonverbal delivery that is appropriate and effective in one speaking situation may be inappropriate and ineffective in another. Though this chapter focuses on improving delivery of your classroom speeches, you can adapt many of our suggestions to your delivery in other speaking situations.

3. *When a speaker's verbal and nonverbal channels send conflicting messages, we tend to trust the nonverbal message.* A supervisor at work tells you privately that she is impressed with your work, but then doesn't allow you to speak at staff meetings. A person keeps saying, "I love you," but never does anything to show consideration for you. Would you doubt the sincerity of these people? If you are typical, you certainly would.

We have each been interpreting and responding to other people's nonverbal communication for so long that we lose sight of its significance. But we are reminded of the importance of nonverbal communication when someone breaks a nonverbal rule. One of those rules demands that a person's words and actions match. Suppose Doris walks reluctantly to the front of the classroom, clutches the lectern, stands motionless, frowns, and says, "I'm absolutely delighted to be speaking to you today." Do you believe her? No. Why? Doris's speech began not with her first words, but with the multiple nonverbal messages that signaled her reluctance to speak. Nonverbal messages should complement and reinforce verbal ones. When they do not, as in Doris's case, actions speak louder than words. We tend to trust the nonverbal message to help us answer the question, "What's really going on here?" As a result of this, one final principle of nonverbal communication becomes extremely important.

4. *The message you intend may be overridden by other meanings people attach to your nonverbal communication.* You stare out the window while delivering your speech because you feel too nervous to make eye contact with your listeners. The audience, however, assumes that you are bored and not really interested in speaking to them. Even though it may be far from the truth, your audience's perception that you are disinterested is the more important one in this case. Eliminate distracting behaviors that mask your good intentions if you care about presenting the best speech you can.

This chapter is about the process of presenting your speech vocally and physically. Before we survey the individual elements that make up delivery, it's important to know the possible methods of delivering a speech and the qualities that should mark the method you choose or are assigned.

Methods of Delivery

The four basic ways you can deliver your public speech are (1) impromptu, or without advance preparation; (2) from memory; (3) from a manuscript; or (4) extemporaneously, or from notes. The impromptu and the memorized methods have very limited applications, particularly for an important speech, but they deserve at least brief attention.

Exploring *Online*

DELIVERING YOUR SPEECH
http://wps.ablongman.com/ab_public_speaking_2
Click on "Deliver" at this Allyn & Bacon site to read information on topics such as modes of delivery, developing dynamism, interacting with your audience, and managing nervousness. You can even take a short quiz about your perception of some of your delivery habits. Upon submitting the questionnaire, you get advice based on your answers.

Speaking Impromptu

We engage in **impromptu speaking** whenever a teacher, a colleague, or a boss calls on us to express an opinion on some issue or whenever someone unexpectedly asks us to "say a few words" to a group. We deal with those special occasions and offer specific guidelines for impromptu speaking in Chapter 18 (see pages 379–380). In those informal situations, other people do not necessarily expect us to be forceful or well organized, and we are probably more or less comfortable speaking without any preparation. Yet the more important the speech is, the more inappropriate the impromptu method of delivery. Although impromptu speaking is excellent practice for anyone, no conscientious person will risk a grade, an important proposal, or professional advancement on an unprepared speech.

Speaking from Memory

impromptu speaking: speaking without advance preparation.

speaking from memory: delivering a speech that is recalled word for word from a written text.

Speaking from memory is similarly appropriate only on rare occasions. We speak from memory when we prepare a written text and then memorize it word for word. At its best, the memorized speech allows a smooth, almost effortless-looking delivery because the speaker has neither notes nor a manuscript and can concentrate on interacting with the audience. For most of us, however, memorizing takes a long time. Our concentration on the memory work we've done and our fear of forgetting part of the speech can also make us sound mechanical or programmed when reciting. For these reasons, the memorized method of delivery is usually appropriate only for brief speeches, such as those introducing another speaker or presenting or accepting an award.

Speaking from Manuscript

Speaking from manuscript, or delivering a speech from a complete text prepared in advance, not only ensures that the speaker will not be at a loss for words, but is also essential in some situations. An address that will be quoted or later published in its entirety is typically delivered from a manuscript. Major foreign policy speeches or State of the Union addresses by U.S. presidents are always delivered from manuscript, because the premium is not just on being understood, but on not being misunderstood. Speeches of tribute and commencement addresses are also often scripted. Any speaking situation calling for precise, well-worded communication may be appropriate for manuscript delivery.

Having every word of your speech scripted should boost your confidence, but it does not ensure your effective delivery. When you write the manuscript, you must take care to write in an oral style. In other words, the manuscript must sound like something you would say in conversation. The text of your speech thus requires a good deal of time to prepare, edit, revise, and type for final delivery. In addition, if you do not also take time to practice delivering the manuscript in a fluent, conversational manner and with appropriate emphasis, well-placed pauses, and adequate eye contact, you are preparing to fail as an effective speaker.

If a speech were a style of dress, it would be somewhere between a tuxedo and a flannel shirt. Not stiff. Not sloppy. . . . A speech is more like conversation than formal writing. Its phrasing is loose—but without the extremes of slang, the incomplete thoughts, the interruptions that flavor everyday speech.

—ELINOR DONAHUE[1]

Speaking Extemporaneously

The final method of delivery, and by far the most popular, is **speaking extemporaneously,** or from notes. Assuming that you have researched and organized your materials carefully and that you have adequately practiced the speech, speaking from notes offers several advantages over other methods of delivery. You don't have to worry about one particular way of wording your ideas, because you have not scripted the speech. Neither do you have to worry that you will forget something you have memorized. With your notes before you, you are free to interact with the audience in a natural, conversational manner. If something you say confuses the audience, you can repeat it, explain it using other words, or think of a better example to clarify it. Your language may not be as forceful or colorful as with a carefully prepared manuscript or a memorized speech, but speaking from notes helps ensure that you will be natural and spontaneous.

The freedom, naturalness, and spontaneity of extemporaneous speaking make this method of delivery particularly attractive. John Kao, professor of entrepreneurship and creativity at Harvard Business School, compares an effective presentation to a successfully performed piece of music. Your content and organization provide the "reference

speaking from manuscript: delivering a speech from a text written word for word and practiced in advance.

speaking extemporaneously: delivering a speech from notes or from a memorized outline.

point from which the presentation is going to spring." Your outline and speaking notes are therefore like sheet music. Just as a piece of music can be played in a variety of styles, skillful extemporaneous speaking always involves a degree of improvisation. Perhaps jazz music and extemporaneous speaking have the clearest similarities. Kao notes that

> . . . improvisation in music has a lot to do with keeping to certain themes that are reinforced. If there isn't that sense of form even through the improvisation, the music won't sound good. . . . And the more one knows the tune, the more one feels comfortable with an audience, the more one feels free to experiment.[2]

You can't experience the freedom that extemporaneous speaking permits unless you have taken the time to develop your speech content and organization and to know your audience. In the words of the great jazz trumpeter Harry "Sweets" Edison, "If you don't know the tune, you can't improvise."[3]

Former New York governor Mario Cuomo, skilled in various methods of delivery, reveals that he speaks extemporaneously whenever possible because of its advantages:

> Spontaneity is one. Audience contact is another. Because you're not tied to a text, your eyes scan the audience and you can detect signs of agreement that encourage you to elaborate effective points. Or you see impatient fidgeting, the sidelong glances of disapproval, and occasionally, the sure sign of abject failure—eyes closed, chin on chest, a customer not only declaring "no sale," but making it clear he or she is no longer shopping. Alerted, the speaker can then change pace, improvise, move on to a more interesting proposition. It's easier to engage the audience when you have both eyes in direct contact with the people you're addressing, both arms drawing pictures in the air, adding punctuation, fighting off the glaze. It's more fun, too. It has an adventurous quality that one misses when the assignment is just to read a prepared text.[4]

When speaking either from notes or a manuscript, keep several practical points in mind:

1. *Practice with the notes or manuscript you will actually use in delivering the speech.* If you use sheets of paper, use a weight slightly heavier than bond, so that it's easier to handle. Double- or even triple-space a speech manuscript and format text in a font size that's easy for you to see. Both of these strategies will make your words easier to read and help you keep your place. Type sentences on the upper two-thirds of each sheet of paper to help ensure better eye contact. You need to know where things are on the page so that you have to glance down only briefly.

2. *Number your notecards or the pages of your manuscript.* Check their order before you speak.

3. *Determine when you should and should not look at your notes.* Looking at your notes when you quote an authority or present statistics is acceptable. In fact, doing so may even convey to your audience your concern for getting supporting materials exactly right. However, do not look down while previewing, stating, or summarizing your key ideas. If you cannot remember your key points, what hope is there for your audience? Also, avoid looking down when you use personal pronouns such as *I, you,* and *we* or when you address audience members by name. A break in your eye contact at these points suddenly distances you from the audience and creates the impression that the speech is coming from a script rather than from you.

4. *Slide your notes or the pages of your manuscript rather than turning them.* So that you won't have to pick them up and turn them over, avoid writing on the backs of notecards or sheets of paper that you use as notes. As a rule, if you use a lectern, do not let the audience see your notes after you place them in front of you. The less the audience is aware of your notes, the more direct and personal your communication with them will be.

5. *Devote extra practice time to your conclusion.* The last thing you say can make a deep impression, but not if you rush through it or deliver it while gathering your notes and walking back to your seat. Your goal at this critical point in the speech is the same as your goal for all your delivery: to eliminate distractions and to reinforce your message through your body, voice, and language.

The most satisfactory way of delivering your classroom speeches combines all four of the methods we have discussed. We have advised you not to look at your notes during the preview of your introduction or the summary step of your conclusion. We stressed the importance of the introduction and conclusion in Chapter 10. To demonstrate that you are well prepared and to ensure contact with your audience, you may even want to have your introduction and conclusion memorized. That won't be difficult, because they are brief sections. You may decide or be assigned to deliver the body of your speech extemporaneously, looking at your notes occasionally. Just don't look at your notes while you are stating or summarizing each main point. If you quote sources at different points in your speech, you are, in effect, briefly using a manuscript. Finally, as an audience-centered speaker, you should be flexible enough to improvise a bit. You speak impromptu whenever you repeat an idea or think of a clearer or more persuasive example. If you are well prepared, this combination of delivery methods should look natural to your audience and feel comfortable to you.

Qualities of Effective Delivery

As you begin to think about the way you deliver a speech, keep in mind three characteristics of effective delivery. First, *effective delivery helps both listeners and speakers.* If you are well prepared for a particular speech, you have probably spent a good deal of time formulating and rehearsing it. You know what you want to say, but your audience does not. Your audience has only one chance to receive your message. Just as clear organization makes your ideas easier to remember, effective delivery can underscore your key points, sell your ideas, or communicate your concern for the topic.

Second, understand that *the best delivery looks and feels natural, comfortable, and spontaneous.* No one should notice how hard you are working to deliver your speech effectively. Some occasions and audiences require you to be more formal than others, of course. Speaking to a large audience through a stationary microphone, for example, will naturally restrict your movement. For a speech in this class, on the other hand, you may find yourself moving, gesturing, and using presentational aids extensively. You want to orchestrate all these elements so that your presentation looks and feels relaxed and natural, not strained or awkward. You achieve spontaneous delivery such as this only through practice.

Third, and finally, *delivery is best when the audience is not aware of it at all.* Your goal should be delivery that reinforces your ideas and is free of distractions. When the audience begins to notice how you twist your ring, to count the number of times you say "um," or to categorize the types of grammatical mistakes you make, your delivery is momentarily distracting them from what you are saying. Your delivery has now become a liability rather than an asset.

How can you help ensure effective delivery? Concentrate on your ideas and how the audience is receiving them, rather than on how you look or sound. If you are really interacting with your listeners, you will pay attention to their interest in your speech, their understanding of your message, and their acceptance or rejection of what you are saying. If you notice listeners checking their watches, reading papers, whispering to friends, or snoozing, they are probably bored. At this point you can enliven your

A natural and confident delivery style comes with practice. Record and view yourself on video or rehearse in front of friends to try out gestures and movements that will enhance your effectiveness.

delivery with movement and changes in your volume. Such relatively simple changes in your delivery may revive their interest.

But what if you notice looks of confusion on your audience's faces? You want to make certain your listeners understand the point you are making. Slow down your rate of delivery, and use descriptive gestures to reinforce your ideas. If you observe frowns or heads shaking from side to side, you've encountered a hostile audience! There are ways to help break down the resistance of even an antagonistic group. Look directly at such listeners, establish a conversational tone, incorporate friendly facial expressions, and use your body to demonstrate involvement with your topic. These helpful tips take practice. Start with the basics. Once you have mastered the essentials of speech delivery, you will be flexible and able to adapt to various audiences. Your delivery will complement your message, not detract from it.

Any prescription for effective delivery will include three basic elements: the *voice,* or vocal delivery; the *body,* or physical delivery; and *language.* In Chapter 12, we discussed how your language contributes to your delivery style. In the remainder of this chapter we focus on vocal and physical delivery. Vocal delivery includes rate, pause, volume, pitch, inflection, voice quality, articulation, and pronunciation. The elements of physical delivery are appearance, posture, facial expression, eye contact, movement, and gestures. Let's consider, first, how vocal delivery can enhance your speech.

Elements of Vocal Delivery

Rate and Pause

You have probably heard the warning, "Look out for him; he's a fast talker," or words to that effect. Such a statement implies that someone who talks fast may be trying to put something over on us. At the other end of the spectrum, we often grow impatient with people who talk much slower than we do, even labeling them uncertain, dull, or dense. Though these stereotypes may be inaccurate, we have already noted that the impressions people form based on our nonverbal communication can become more important than anything we intend to communicate.

Key Points

Elements of Vocal Delivery

1. Rate and pause
2. Volume
3. Pitch and inflection
4. Voice quality
5. Articulation and pronunciation

Your **rate** or speed of speaking can communicate something, intentionally or unintentionally, about your motives in speaking, your disposition, or your involvement with the topic. Your goal in a speech, therefore, should be to avoid extremely fast or slow delivery; you should instead use a variety of rates. Your various rates should, in turn, reinforce your purpose in speaking and make you seem conversational.

In Chapter 4, you learned that the typical American speaker talks at a rate between 125 and 190 words per minute. Although we can process information at rates faster than people speak, our comprehension depends on the type of material we are hearing. You should slow down, for example, when presenting detailed, highly complex information, particularly to a group that knows little about your subject. Our student René did just that in his informative speech, detailing the history of political and religious conflict in the Middle East. Not only did he speak slower than he had in other speeches, but he also used a clearly labeled map of the area and a timeline showing the splintering of groups into smaller factions. His reduced rate of delivery and his repetition of information in visual form showed his concern for his audience's comprehension. This can work both ways, however. In other situations, speaking slightly faster than the rate of normal conversation may actually increase your persuasiveness by carrying the message that you know exactly what you want to say.

Pauses or silences are an important element in your rate of delivery. You pause to allow the audience time to reflect on something you have just said or to heighten suspense about something you are going to say. Pauses also mark important transitions in your speech, helping you and your audience shift gears. World-renowned violinist Isaac Stern was once asked why some violinists were considered gifted and others merely proficient or competent when they all played the correct notes in the proper order. "The important thing is not the notes. It's the intervals between the notes," he responded.

To test the importance of pauses, let's look at four sentences from a commencement address that Steve Jobs delivered. The co-founder and chief executive officer of Apple Computer issued a challenge to the 2005 graduating class at Stanford University. Try reading this passage without any internal punctuation or pauses, ignoring even the periods:

> Your time is limited so don't waste it living someone else's life. Don't be trapped by dogma which is living the results of other people's thinking. Don't let the noise of others' opinions drown out your own inner voice. And most important have the courage to follow your heart and intuition.

The sentences make sense only if you insert appropriate pauses. Speakers reading from a written text sometimes mark their manuscripts to help them pause appropriately. Now try reading Jobs's sentences again, pausing a beat when you see one slash (/) and pausing a bit longer when you encounter two (//).

Exploring *Online*

ASSESSING VOCAL DELIVERY
www.historychannel.com/speeches/speeches.html
The History Channel's rich index of more than 500 speeches and verbal messages that changed the world gives you a chance to appreciate the vocal deliveries of historical and contemporary figures. Just click on "Great Speeches" for a complete listing of speeches.

rate: the speed at which a speech is delivered.

pause: an intentional or unintentional period of silence in a speaker's vocal delivery.

Your time is limited / so don't waste it living someone else's life. / / Don't be trapped by dogma / which is living the results of other people's thinking. / / Don't let the noise of others' opinions / drown out your own inner voice. / / And most important / / have the courage to follow your heart and intuition.[5]

If the pauses marked were meaningful for you, the statement should have gained power. You may even disagree with the placement and length of the pauses we chose. You might say the sentences differently, and that's fine. Public speaking is, after all, a creative and individual process. Remember, though, that to be effective in a speech, pauses must be used intentionally and selectively. If your speech is filled with too many awkwardly placed pauses or too many vocalized pauses, such as "um" and "uh," you will seem hesitant or unprepared, and your credibility will erode quickly.

Volume

Your audience must be able to hear you before they can listen to your ideas. **Volume** is simply how loudly or softly you speak. A person who speaks too loudly in a classroom speech may be considered boisterous or obnoxious. In contrast, we often label the inaudible speaker unsure, timid, "wimpy." The truth could be that you speak too loudly because of a hearing loss, and you are not aware that your volume is uncomfortable to your listeners. The frustratingly quiet speaker may have grown up in a household with six other children and parents who were constantly yelling "Quiet!" But your audience will not know about your history. What they will know is that you are shouting or whispering your speech, and they will judge you by that behavior. Remember that hearing is the first step in listening. If you frustrate your audience or divert their attention with inappropriate volume, your chances of getting them to listen carefully to your message are slim.

Make sure you adapt your volume to the size of the room where you speak. In your classroom, you can probably use a volume just slightly louder than your usual conversational level. When you speak before a large group, a microphone may be helpful or even essential. If possible, practice beforehand so that the sound of your amplified voice does not startle you. You may even be called on to speak before a large audience without a microphone. This is not as difficult as it sounds. In fact, your voice will carry well if you support your breath from your diaphragm. To test your breathing, place your hand on your abdomen while repeating the sentence "Those old boats don't float" louder and louder. If you are breathing from the diaphragm, you should feel your abdominal muscles tightening. Without that support, you are probably trying to increase your volume from your throat, a mistake that could strain your voice.

At times, you may have to conquer not only a large space but also external noise, such as the chattering of people in a hallway, the roar of nearby traffic, or the whoosh of the air conditioning system. That may require hard work. If you can, use a microphone in such a situation, speak at normal volume, and let the public address system do the work for you. If a microphone is unnecessary, don't use it; in a small room, a microphone distances you from the audience. We discuss the use of two different types of microphones in more detail in Chapter 18 (see pages 383–384).

> "Pauses are a powerful and essential part of any presentation. A pause allows the listener to make a personal connection to the words she just heard. A pause invites the listener to relax into a presentation. A pause makes it possible for the speaker to sense the response of an audience to a presentation. Pauses are those beautiful moments when meaning happens and common ground emerges."
>
> —ACHIM NOWAK[6]

volume: the relative loudness or softness of a speaker's voice.

When you speak to a large audience, it is especially important to articulate clearly and adapt your volume to ensure that everyone in your audience can catch every word. If you are using a microphone, try to listen to your amplified voice before delivering your speech.

Pitch and Inflection

Pitch is a musical term, and when we talk about vocal pitch, we are referring to the highness or lowness of vocal tones, similar to the notes on a musical staff. Every speaker has an optimal pitch range, or key. This is the range in which you are most comfortable speaking, and chances are good that in this range your voice is also pleasant to hear. People who speak in unusually high or low voices are rare, and in these cases work with speech therapists helps them to achieve a flexible, useful pitch range.

Speakers who are unusually nervous sometimes raise their pitch. Other speakers think that if they lower their pitch they will seem more authoritative. In truth, speakers who do not use their normal pitch usually sound artificial.

The following practice technique may help you retain or recapture a natural, conversational tone in your delivery. Begin some of your practice sessions seated. Imagine a good friend sitting across from you, and pretend that she asks you what your speech is about. Answer her question by summarizing and paraphrasing your speech: "Mary, I'm going to talk about the advantages of mandatory school uniforms in elementary and middle schools. I've divided my speech into three main arguments. School uniforms will enhance student self-esteem; they will reduce discipline problems; and they will save parents money." Listen closely to the tone of your voice as you speak. You are having a conversation with a friend. You're not tense; you feel comfortable.

Now, keeping this natural, conversational tone in mind, stand up, walk to the front of the room, and begin your speech. Your words will change, but the tone of your speech should be comfortable and conversational, as it was before. In a sense, you are merely having a conversation with a larger audience. We have found this technique helpful for students whose vocal delivery sounds artificial or mechanical. Not only do they find their natural pitch range, but they also incorporate more meaningful pauses.

A problem more typical than an unusually high- or low-pitched voice is vocal delivery that lacks adequate **inflection**, or changes in pitch. Someone who speaks without changing pitch delivers sentences in a flat, uniform pitch pattern that becomes monotonous. Indeed, the word *monotone* means "one tone," and you may have had instructors whose monotonous droning invited you to doze. People whose voices sound monotonous are usually actually using three tones: one in the middle, one slightly higher, and one lower. That's still too little vocal variety, however. Your inflection is an essential tool for conveying meaning accurately. You can give a simple four-word sentence

pitch: the highness or lowness of a speaker's voice.

inflection: patterns of change in a person's pitch level while speaking.

such as "She is my friend" four distinct meanings by raising the pitch and volume of one word at a time:

"**She** is my friend." (Not the young woman standing with her.)

"She **is** my friend." (Don't try to tell me she isn't!)

"She is **my** friend." (Not yours.)

"She is my **friend.**" (There's nothing more to our relationship than that.)

In public speaking, women can generally make wider use of their pitch ranges than men can without sounding affected or unnatural. For this reason, men often find that they need to vary other vocal and physical elements of delivery—volume, rate, and gestures, for example—to compensate for a limited pitch range.

Voice Quality

Voice quality or **timbre,** the least flexible of the vocal elements discussed here, is the characteristic that distinguishes your voice from other voices. You may have called a friend on the phone and had difficulty telling him from his father or her from her mother or sisters. Most of the time, however, even through the telephone, an instrument causing a lot of distortion, you recognize the voices of friends easily. In general, our individual voices are easily recognized as distinct. In fact, police investigators often use voice prints to identify and distinguish individual voices on tape recordings.

Sometimes the clarity and resonance of your voice can be temporarily affected by colds, allergies, or strain after you spend hours screaming support for a favorite team. That temporary change should not cause alarm. However, if many people describe your voice as strident, harsh, nasal, breathy, or hoarse over a long period of time, you may want to consult a speech therapist.

Articulation and Pronunciation

The final elements of vocal delivery we will discuss are articulation and pronunciation. **Articulation** is the mechanical process of forming the sounds necessary to communicate in a particular language. Most articulation errors are made from habit. You tell your parents that you're going to the "libary," for example. Even though you know how to spell the word and would say it correctly if pressed to do so, you have fallen into a habit of misarticulating it. Sometimes our articulation errors are reinforced by people around us who make the same mistakes. Sometimes illness or fatigue affect our articulation temporarily.

Articulation errors take four principal forms: deletion, addition, substitution, and transposition. One of these, represented by the example of "libary," is the *deletion* or leaving out of sounds. Saying "goverment" for "government" is another example of a deletion error. If you have heard someone say "athalete" for "athlete," you've heard an example of an articulation error caused by the *addition* of a sound. Examples of errors caused by the *substitution* of one sound for another are "kin" for "can" and "git" for "get." The final type of articulation error is one of *transposition,* or the reversal of two sounds that are close together. This error is the vocal equivalent of transposing two letters in a typed word. Saying "lectren" for "lectern" or "hunderd" for "hundred" are examples of transposition errors.

Articulation errors made as a result of habit may be so ingrained that you can no longer identify your mistakes. Your speech instructor, friends, and classmates can help you significantly by pointing out articulation problems. You may need to listen to tape recordings of your speeches to locate problems and then practice the problem words or sounds to correct your articulation.

voice quality or **timbre:** the unique characteristics that distinguish one person's voice from others.

articulation: the mechanical process of forming the sounds necessary to communicate in a particular language.

Pronunciation, in contrast to articulation, is simply a matter of knowing how the letters of a word sound and where the stress falls when that word is spoken. We all have two vocabularies: a speaking vocabulary and a reading vocabulary. Your speaking vocabulary—the group of words you use in day-to-day conversation—is much smaller than your reading vocabulary. To test this, think of the times you have been reading something and encountered a word you have never spoken or even heard spoken: "Her *vitriolic* parting words stung him," for example. You may have seen the word before in print. Even though you may have never looked up its pronunciation or meaning in a dictionary, you probably feel that you know more or less what it means in the context of the sentence. Such a word is part of your reading vocabulary.

Most of us make errors in pronunciation primarily when we try to move a word from our reading vocabulary to our speaking vocabulary without consulting the dictionary. In a public speech, the resulting pronunciation error can be a minor distraction or a major disaster, depending on how far off your mispronunciation is and how many times you make the error. If you have any doubt about the pronunciation of a word you plan to use in a speech, look it up in a current dictionary and then practice the correct pronunciation out loud before the speech. Apply this rule to every word you select, including those in quotations. If you follow this simple rule, you will avoid embarrassing errors of pronunciation.

Pronunciation of proper nouns, the names of specific people, places, and things, can also pose difficulties. Suppose that for your speech on mountain climbing you want to quote from a fine book entitled *Flow: The Psychology of Optimal Experience.*[7] You copy an excellent passage about the psychology of dangerous sports onto a notecard. Then you turn to the title page to find the author's name: Mihaly Csikszentmihalyi! Don't tear up the notecard.

Obviously, proper nouns should be pronounced the way that the people who have the name (or who live in the place or who named the thing) pronounce them. The large city on the Texas Gulf Coast is pronounced "HEW stun"; the street in New York City spelled the same way is pronounced "HOW stun." When you see the name Schroeder, you may think of the *Peanuts* character and mentally pronounce the word with a long *o* sound. Yet the late William Schroeder, world's first artificial heart recipient, pronounced his family's name as though the *oe* were a long *a.*

If you refer to people who are well known, make sure that your pronunciation corresponds to common usage. If you quote or refer to a person who is unfamiliar to your audience—as Csikszentmihalyi may well be—your listeners will not know that you have mispronounced the name unless you appear to stumble uncertainly over it. You could be lucky enough to read an article that tells how the person pronounces his or her name; *Psychology Today* says Csikszentmihalyi is pronounced Chick-sent-me-HIGH.[8] The only other way to confirm your pronunciation of a name like "Csikszentmihalyi" would be to locate the person, e-mail or place a long-distance call, and ask. No one expects you to do that. Instead, decide on a reasonable pronunciation, practice it, and deliver it with confidence in your speech. For names of places, consult the *Pronouncing Gazetteer* or list of geographical names found at the back of many dictionaries.

Once you have mastered these elements of vocal delivery, your speech will be free of articulation errors and mispronounced words. Your unique voice quality will be pleasant to hear. Your voice will be well modulated, with enough inflection to communicate your ideas clearly. You will speak loudly enough that all your listeners can hear you easily. You will adapt your rate to the content of your message, and you will pause to punctuate key ideas and major transitions. In short, your sound will be coming through loud and clear. Now let's consider the picture your listeners will see by examining the aspects of physical delivery.

Exploring *Online*

CHECKING PRONUNCIATION

www.m-w.com

Use this website to check the pronunciations of unfamiliar words. Enter your query term and click the "Go" button. To hear the word pronounced correctly, just click the loudspeaker icon near the definition.

pronunciation: how the sounds of a word are to be said and which parts are to be stressed.

Elements of Physical Delivery

Key Points

Elements of Physical Delivery

1. Appearance	4. Eye contact
2. Posture	5. Movement
3. Facial expression	6. Gestures

Appearance

We all form quick impressions of people we meet based on subtle nonverbal signals. **Appearance**, in particular our grooming and the way we dress, is an important nonverbal signal that helps people judge us. Why is appearance so important? Does it really come down to "it's not who you are but what you wear"? Of course, that is not the case. But you would be foolish to underestimate the power of first impressions and the initial reactions people have to your appearance.

Studies demonstrate that people we consider attractive can persuade us much more easily than can those we find unattractive. In addition, high-status clothing carries more authority than does low-status clothing. For example, studies show we are more likely to jaywalk behind a person dressed in a dark blue suit, a crisp white shirt, and a dark tie, and carrying an expensive black-leather briefcase than we would behind a person dressed in rags or even in jeans. We will also take orders more easily from that well-dressed person than we would from someone poorly dressed. These studies reinforce the adage that "clothes make the person," a saying any public speaker would do well to remember.

Since John T. Molloy's first book, *Dress for Success,* came out in 1975, we have all been getting plenty of advice about the best colors, fabrics, and styles of clothing for the business office. Dressing for success has become big business. Today, "image consultants" across the country teach men and women how to dress for increased productivity and influence. Some of this may seem unrealistic or inappropriate for you as a public speaker. But some commonsense tips will help you choose clothing that eliminates problems and adds impact to your speech.

The safest advice we can offer the public speaker on appearance is to avoid extremes in dress and grooming. Use clothes to reinforce your purpose in speaking, not to draw too much attention to themselves. Every moment that the audience spends admiring your European-cut navy blue suit or wondering why you wore the torn Old Navy

appearance: a speaker's physical features, including dress and grooming.

When it comes to public speaking, think about "dressing for address" rather than "dressing for success." This speaker chose clothing suited to her topic, audience, speaking occasion, and the image she wanted to project.

Theory into Practice
Tips
Dressing for Address

Consider the Occasion
The speaking occasion dictates, in part, how formally or informally you can dress. A student delivering a valedictory would dress differently from one delivering an impromptu campaign speech outside the campus student center. A speech in your classroom probably permits you to be more informal than you'd be delivering a business presentation to a board of directors or an acceptance speech at an awards ceremony.

Consider Your Audience
Some of your listeners dress more casually than others. In any audience, there is a range of attire. As a rule, dress at or near the top of that range. For speeches outside the classroom, traditional, tasteful, and subdued clothing is your wisest choice. You should appear as nicely dressed as the best dressed people in your audience.

In other words, when in doubt, dress "up" a little. An audience is more easily insulted if you appear to treat the speaking occasion too casually than if you treat it too formally. Remember, your listeners will make judgments based on your appearance before you even open your mouth.

Consider Your Topic
Though a public speech is not a costumed performance, your clothing can underscore or undermine the impact you want your speech to have. A hot pink dress or a lime green shirt would be entirely appropriate for a speech on Mardi Gras, but not for one on the high cost of funerals. On the other hand, you would look and feel silly demonstrating basic poses in heated power yoga dressed in a business suit.

Consider Your Image
The clothing you select can shape—or even change—the image you want to create as a speaker. Darker colors convey authority and seriousness; lighter colors establish a friendlier image. A student perceived as the class clown should dress more formally to help dispel this image.

T-shirt is a moment they are distracted from your message. In selecting your clothes, consider the guidelines we discuss in the Theory into Practice feature: "Dressing for Address."

Clothing not only influences our perceptions of others but also shapes our self-perception. Just think of your own experiences. You probably have certain clothes that give you a sense of confidence or make you feel especially assertive or powerful. You feel differently about yourself when you wear them. Dressing "up" conveys your seriousness of purpose to your listeners. It also establishes this same positive attitude in your own mind.

As a practical matter, we suggest that you decide what you will wear before the day of your speech and that you practice, at least once, in those clothes. One of our students complained that she was distracted during her presentation because every time she moved her arms to gesture her coat made a rustling sound. She could have eliminated this distraction had she practiced in that suit coat before the day of her speech. Whatever the problems, it's best to encounter and fix them before the speech. You can then concentrate fully on the speech itself.

Posture

A public speaker should look comfortable, confident, and prepared to speak. You have the appropriate attire. Your next concern is your **posture**, the position or bearing of your body. In posture, the two extremes to avoid are rigidity and sloppiness. Don't hang

posture: the position or bearing of a speaker's body while delivering a speech.

on to or drape yourself across the lectern, if you are using one. Keep your weight balanced on both legs, and avoid shifting your weight back and forth in a nervous swaying pattern. Equally distracting is standing on one leg and shuffling or tapping the other foot. You may not realize that you do those things. Other people will have to point them out to you. Remember that before your delivery can reinforce your message, it must be free of annoying mannerisms.

Facial Expression

Estimates of the number of possible human facial expressions range from 5,000 to 250,000.[9] Even if the actual number is closer to 5,000, that's still a significant amount of communication potential. Yet, ironically, many people giving a speech for the first time put on a blank mask, reducing their **facial expression** to one neutral look. We have often seen our students do this, and we know why it occurs. Inexperienced speakers are understandably nervous and may be more concerned with the way they look and sound than they are with the ideas they are trying to communicate.

Exploring *Online*

STUDYING FACIAL EXPRESSION

http://mambo.ucsc.edu/psl/fanl.html

This graphics-heavy page links to a number of sites with bibliographies, annotated bibliographies, and images on research in facial expression. Many of these sites use computer modeling to measure facial movements or to teach speech recognition.

However, your facial expression must match what you are saying. The speaker who smiles and blushes self-consciously through a speech on date rape will simply not be taken seriously by the audience and may offend many listeners. If you detail the plight of earthquake victims, make sure your face reflects your concern. If you tell a joke and your listeners can't stop chuckling, you certainly should break into a smile rather than a frown. In other words, your face should register the thoughts and feelings that motivate your words.

The way to use facial expression appropriately to bolster your message is simple: Concentrate as much as possible on the ideas you present and the way your audience receives and responds to them. Try not to be overly conscious of how you look and sound. This takes practice, but your classroom speeches provide a good forum for such rehearsal. You will learn to interact with the audience, maintain eye contact, and respond with them to your own message. Chances are that, if you do those things, your facial expression will be varied and appropriate and will reinforce your spoken words.

Eye Contact

We've all heard the challenge, "Look me in the eye and say that." We use direct eye contact as one gauge of a person's truthfulness. **Eye contact** can also carry many other messages: confidence, concern, sincerity, interest, and enthusiasm. Lack of eye contact, on the other hand, may signal deceit, disinterest, or insecurity.

Your face is the most important source of nonverbal cues as you deliver your speech, and your eyes carry more information than any other facial feature. As you speak, you will probably look occasionally at your notes or manuscript. You may even glance away from the audience briefly as you try to put your thoughts into words. Yet you must keep coming back to the eyes of your listeners to check their understanding, interest, and evaluation of your message.

As a public speaker, your goal is to make eye contact with as much of the audience as much of the time as possible. The way to do this is to make sure that you take in your entire audience, from front to back and from left to right. Include all those boundaries in the scope of your eye contact, and make contact especially with those individuals who seem to be listening carefully and responding positively to your message. Whether you actually make eye contact with each member of the audience is immaterial. You must, however, create that impression. Again, this takes practice before you feel comfortable.

facial expression: the tension and movement of various parts of a speaker's face.

eye contact: gaze behavior in which a speaker looks at listeners' eyes.

Movement

Effective **movement** benefits you, the speaker, your audience, and your speech. First, place-to-place movement can actually help you relax. Moving to a visual aid, for example, can help you energize and loosen up physically. From the audience's perspective, movement adds visual variety to your speech, and appropriate movement can arouse or rekindle the listeners' interest. Most important, though, physical movement serves your speech by guiding the audience's attention. Through movement, you can underscore key ideas, mark major transitions, or intensify an appeal for belief or action.

Remember that your speech starts the moment you enter the presence of your audience. Your behavior, including your movement, sends signals about your attitudes toward the audience and your speech topic. When your time to speak arrives, approach your speaking position confidently, knowing that you have something important to say. Addressing a large audience through a microphone mounted on the lectern will naturally restrict your movement. If the lectern is there as a matter of convenience and particularly if you are speaking to a relatively small audience, don't automatically box yourself into one position behind the lectern. Remember that even the smallest lectern puts a physical barrier between you and your audience. Moving to the side or the front of it reduces both the physical and the psychological distance between you and your listeners and may be especially helpful whenever you conclude your speech with a persuasive appeal.

Make certain that your movement is selective and that it serves a purpose. Avoid random pacing. Movement to mark a transition should occur at the beginning or the end of a sentence, not in the middle. Finally, bring the speech to a satisfying psychological conclusion, and pause for a second or two before gathering your materials and moving toward your seat in the audience.

Gestures

Gestures, movements of a speaker's hands, arms, and head, seem to be as natural a part of human communication as spoken language. Deaf communities throughout the world spontaneously develop various sign languages. "Indeed, children exposed from an early age only to sign language go through the same basic stages of acquisition as children learning to speak, including a stage when they 'babble' silently in sign!"[10] Among adults, gestures not only punctuate and emphasize verbal messages for the benefit of listeners, but apparently also ease the process of encoding those messages for speakers. Various studies show that people asked to communicate without gestures produce labored speech marked by increased hesitations and pauses. Such speakers also demonstrate decreased fluency, inflection, and stress, and they use fewer high-imagery words.[11] Hand gestures, then, seem to help speakers retrieve elusive words from their memories.[12]

Gestures are important adjuncts to our verbal messages; at times, they can even replace words altogether. As a public speaker, you can use gestures to draw a picture of an object, to indicate the size of objects or the relationships between them, to re-create some bodily motion, to emphasize or underscore key ideas, to point to things such as presentational aids, or to trace the flow of your ideas. If you don't normally gesture in conversation, force yourself to include some gestures as you practice your speech. At first you may feel self-conscious about gesturing. Keep practicing. Gestures that seem natural and spontaneous are well worth whatever time you spend practicing them. Not only do they reinforce your ideas and make you seem more confident and dynamic, but gestures, like movement, can also help you relax.

To be effective, then, gestures must be coordinated with your words and must appear natural and spontaneous. In addition, any gesture should be large enough for the audience to see it clearly. The speaker who gestures below the waist or whose gestures

movement: a speaker's motion from place to place during speech delivery.

gestures: movements of a speaker's hands, arms, and head while delivering a speech.

are barely visible over the top of a lectern may appear timid, unsure, or nervous. Speakers who gesture too much—who talk with their hands—may be perceived as nervous, flighty, or excitable. The two extremes to avoid, therefore, are the absence of gestures (hands clenched in a death grip on the sides of the lectern) and excessive gestures (gestures emphasizing everything, with the result that nothing stands out). Remember, if your audience is waiting for you to gesture or counting your many gestures, they are distracted from your message.

The following two generalizations from research on gestures are particularly helpful for the public speaker. First, people who are confident, relaxed, and have high status tend to expand into the space around them and use gestures that are wider than those of other people. Speakers who wish to emphasize their authority can do so by increasing the width of their gestures. Second, a wide, palm-up gesture with both hands creates an openness that is entirely appropriate when a speaker is appealing for a certain belief or urging the audience to some action. A palm-down gesture with one or both hands carries more force and authority and can be used to command an audience into action or to exhort them to a certain belief.

As a speaker, adapt the size of your gestures to the size of your audience. On stage before a crowd of several thousand, your gestures should be more expansive than when you stand at the front of a small classroom. In a cavernous auditorium, you must adjust your gestures, as well as your facial expression and eye contact, so that they will be clear to those in the back rows.

These, then, are the tools of vocal and physical speech delivery, from rate of speaking to hand gestures. Your goal throughout this class and in your future public speaking experience will be to eliminate any distracting elements and then work toward delivery that is conversational, forceful, and as formal or informal as your audience and subject require.

One traditional saying is "If it's worth doing, it's worth doing well." That's wise counsel for the public speaker. Your gestures, rate of delivery, and grammar may seem trivial until they begin to interfere with your communication, undermine your credibility, and erode your persuasiveness. Delivery is a vital part of your public speech, and effective delivery is an asset worth cultivating.

Try This

Practicing Your Delivery

After a few practice sessions, record your speech on video. First, listen to the playback without viewing it. Analyze your vocal delivery: your use of rate, pauses, volume, pitch, inflection, articulation, and pronunciation. Identify both strengths and weaknesses. Construct a list of specific suggestions to improve your vocal delivery.

Now listen to and watch the video, this time focusing primarily on the elements of physical delivery discussed in this chapter. What are your strengths? What are areas for improvement?

Develop some strategies to improve your physical delivery.

Before each subsequent practice session, review both lists. Concentrate on using a few of your suggestions each time you rehearse your speech. After several practices, record your speech on video again. Compare your first and second recorded versions. Do you hear and see improvement in your delivery? What additional suggestions might you incorporate to ensure delivery that's natural and forceful and that reinforces the message of your speech?

Summary

Speech *delivery* is composed of a speaker's voice qualities, bodily actions, and language. This chapter focused on vocal and physical delivery, aspects of a speech presentation that are subject to four principles of nonverbal communication. First, part of our nonverbal communication is intentional, while another part is unconscious and unintentional. Second, few if any nonverbal signals have universal meaning. Third, when a speaker's verbal and nonverbal channels send conflicting messages, we tend to trust the nonverbal message. These three principles contribute to a fourth: The message you intend may be overridden by other messages people attach to your nonverbal communication.

As a speaker, you can select any of four methods of delivery: *impromptu speaking*, or speaking without advance preparation; *speaking from memory; speaking from manuscript; and speaking extemporaneously*, or from notes. While each type of delivery is appropriate under certain public speaking circumstances, impromptu speaking and speaking from memory should almost certainly be avoided for prepared, graded classroom speeches. Speeches from a manuscript and, particularly, from notes have far fewer limitations and more applications than the other two methods of delivery. Those who can speak clearly and emphatically from a few notes after the necessary period of practice have gone a long way toward ensuring success, not only in the public speaking classroom, but also in any future public speaking situations.

The nonverbal elements of delivery include everything about your speech that could not be captured and recorded in a manuscript of the speech. *Vocal delivery* is comprised of your rate, use of pauses, volume, pitch and inflection, voice quality, articulation, and pronunciation. Your appearance, posture, facial expression, eye contact, movement, and gestures make up the elements of your *physical delivery*. With each of these elements, your goal as a speaker should be to eliminate distractions and to work for variety so that you look and sound natural. Once you are aware of unconscious mannerisms you may have and of the characteristics of effective delivery that you should have, you can make significant improvements in the way you deliver a speech.

You exercise a good deal of control over most of these physical and vocal elements of delivery. With the confidence that comes from practice, you should be able to adapt your delivery to different speaking situations and audience sizes. Though this chapter examined several different elements of delivery, speech delivery is best when none of those elements makes an impression on the audience. Instead, delivery should reinforce the clear, forceful communication of your ideas.

Practice Critique

Pairing Gestures and Movements with Words

Read the transcript of Melissa Janoske's speech on Renaissance fairs in the Appendix. Focusing on Melissa's use of language, suggest places in the speech where she might incorporate movement and gestures to enhance her delivery. Describe the types of gestures and movements you recommend. Also, using the markings discussed on pages 263–264, note where Melissa could incorporate meaningful pauses to emphasize her ideas.

Exercises

1. Make a list of famous people you think are exciting speakers and ones you find boring. Or list instructors who have reputations for being exciting or boring lecturers. How do these individuals' vocal and physical deliveries add to or detract from their ideas? Which of these techniques could you adapt to make your own speaking more dynamic?

2. Using the guidelines discussed in the "Rate and Pause" section of this chapter, mark pauses for paragraphs 15–19 of Martin Luther King, Jr.'s "I Have a Dream" speech in the Appendix. Practice reading this excerpt aloud to convey its meaning with the greatest impact.

3. Select a short passage from a novel, short story, speech, or other prose selection and photocopy it. Study the meaning and emotion of the excerpt. After marking the copied text, read the passage aloud, emphasizing key words and phrases and using pauses to enhance the message's impact.

4. Attend a speech and analyze the speaker's vocal and physical delivery. Was the message delivered effectively? What nonverbal elements enhanced and what detracted from the speech? What suggestions could you give the speaker to improve the delivery of the speech?

*U*sing Presentational Aids

chapter

14

*A space shuttle exploding
in a cloudless azure sky . . .*

*A young man standing motionless
in a street in front of four tanks . . .*

*A bloody teenaged boy dropping from
a second-story window into the
arms of EMTs standing on the roof
of an ambulance . . .*

*Coal dust–blackened miners
lifted into the glare of TV and
emergency work lights . . .*

*A Boeing 767 disappearing
into the glass and steel frame
of a 100-story building . . .*

*A wall of ocean water racing toward
a tropical coastline . . .*

If you form a vivid mental image at the description of any of these events, you prove the haunting power of pictures.[1] We have all grown up in a visually oriented society. Even our language reflects the power of the visual message:

"A picture is worth a thousand words."

"I wouldn't have believed it if I hadn't seen it with my own eyes."

Today, television and film are our primary entertainment media. Our newspapers, magazines, and computer screens are filled with pictures, black and white or color. When the news is bad, we expect to see pictures or video of the airplane wreckage, the flooding, or the aftermath of the earthquake. When the news is good, we expect to see pictures of the winning team or the heroic rescue. We are, indeed, people for whom "seeing is believing."

Because pictures are such an important part of life, delivering a public speech without even considering using presentational aids is a little like playing tennis with your racquet hand tied behind your back. As a speaker, you need not rely only on words to communicate your ideas precisely and powerfully. You can add force and impact to many messages by incorporating a visual dimension as well.

The Importance of Using Presentational Aids

A well-designed, appropriate presentational aid can add significantly to the effectiveness of the speech and the speaker. Such aids serve four important functions. First, they add clarity to a speaker's message. Second, they reinforce the impact of the message. Third, they can increase the dynamism of a speaker's delivery. Finally, effective presentational aids used well can enhance a speaker's confidence. Consider these four functions as you determine whether to include presentational aids in a particular speech.

Increases Message Clarity

First, presentational aids give your speech greater clarity. They can specify the demographic breakdown of voters in the past presidential election, illustrate the structure of an online course, or explain the process of monitoring and controlling air traffic. You can convey detailed statistical information more clearly in a simplified line graph than by simply reciting the data. Speeches using a spatial organizational pattern in particular often benefit from visual reinforcement.

Reinforces Message Impact

Second, presentational aids give your speech greater impact. Seeing may encourage believing; certainly, it aids remembering. Duncan Anderson asserts the dramatic power of visual elements to capture an audience's attention. Others have concluded that adding visual aids to a presentation "has been shown to increase audience retention *at least fivefold*."[2] And a University of Minnesota study found that a presenter using computer-generated transparencies or slides "was perceived to be 43 percent more persuasive than in meetings with unaided presentations."[3]

Remember: It is ten times harder to command the ear than to catch the eye.

—DUNCAN MAXWELL ANDERSON

Studies draw different conclusions as to the degree of impact presentational aids give to a speech. They all conclude, however, that a well-constructed presentational aid helps listeners remember more of your speech for a longer period of time. Because they both hear and see the message, listeners are more fully involved in the speech. This greater sensory involvement with the message lessens the opportunity for outside distractions and increases retention.

Increases Speaker Dynamism

Third, presentational aids make you seem more dynamic. In Chapter 13, we discussed the importance of gestures as part of your delivery. Most speakers, unfortunately, have difficulty incorporating meaningful gestures into their delivery. They remain behind a lectern, their hands resting on, or clutching, their notes. Consequently, they may

appear uninvolved, perhaps even bored, with their speech. Using presentational aids forces you to move, to point, to become physically involved with your speech. Your gestures become motivated and meaningful, and, consequently, you appear more dynamic and forceful.

Enhances Speaker Confidence

A fourth benefit of using presentational aids in your speech is that it can increase your confidence as a public speaker. Clear, attractive presentational aids that you have practiced using can help you relax in three ways. First, knowing that your presentational aids will enhance the clarity and impact of your message should increase your confidence. Second, revealing your presentational aids gives purpose to your movement and gestures, and this will help burn off some of your nervous energy. Finally, if you become nervous when you see the listeners' eyes focused on you, you can use your presentational aids to divert their attention to your speech content. Just remember that the primary purpose of your presentational aids should not be to divert attention from you, but to enhance the impact of your message.

Before you plan presentational aids to clarify and enliven your speech, ask yourself, "Will such aids make my presentation more effective?" This question is important because any presentational aid, no matter how well designed and planned, involves some distractions for both speaker and audience. It may require setup time, for example. When you uncover the aid for audience view and cover it later, you create a visual break in the speech. In addition, presentational aids remove part of a listener's focus from the speaker. "Quite simply," as one professional speech coach notes, "the moment a visual appears on a screen, the audience will focus on the visual rather than listen to what you, the speaker, is saying. . . . [T]he visual always wins."[4] So *use presentational aids only if they are necessary to the speech,* and be prepared for possible distractions.

Remember, too, that presentational aids are supplements to, not replacements for, your spoken words. As a speaker, you communicate; your presentational aids simply illustrate. "Whether your presentation hinges on flipping a few charts or running a multimedia computer, the three secrets to effective presentations remain: communication, communication, communication."[5] To test what you are actually going to be communicating, ask yourself:

> How would the presentation "play" if it were stripped of visual tools and presented in a face-to-face meeting across a bare wooden desk? Looking at a presentation this way

Speaking with Confidence

As a mother of three (two teenage boys) returning to school after 20 years, I selected a topic very important to me and our youth culture: drunk driving. I decided that visual aids would give my message greater impact. I work full time at our local police department and was able to borrow photographs taken at some of our fatal motor vehicle accidents. These photos were graphic, so before passing around the folder with my visual aids, I explained to my classmates that what they were about to view might be quite disturbing. Using such graphic visual aids really grabbed my audience's attention and concern, and generated conversations that filled the room when my speech was over. After delivering my speech, I felt very confident that my speech, with the help of my visual aids, touched my listeners and made them think about what can happen if you drink and drive.

—**Joanie Klingel,** *Suffolk County Community College, Selden, New York*

strips away the decoration and focuses on content. It may also serve as contingency planning in disguise—preparation for a mechanical failure or a collapsed schedule.[6]

The requirement for a presentational aid should guide your topic selection, research, and practice of the speech. Don't incorporate a visual aid just to show that you know how to use the technology, to demonstrate your artistic skills, or to add length to a presentation that you fear is too short. Would Martin Luther King, Jr.'s "I Have a Dream" speech, reprinted in the Appendix, really have required a slide show if that technology had been available to him? More importantly, how different would the effect of that historic speech have been with slides projected on some jumbo screen for his thousands of listeners?

Now that you understand how presentational aids can enhance your speech, some of the problems they may pose, and some of the circumstances in which you should not use them, let's examine the various types of aids you might consider using in a speech.

Types of Presentational Aids

Once you have decided to use presentational aids, you need to determine the type most appropriate to your presentation. Presentational aids come in many forms, but they can generally be divided into five classifications: objects, graphics, film and video, handouts, and audio aids.

Objects

Objects may be either actual, such as a digital camera, or scaled, such as an architect's model. Other three-dimensional presentational aids are, for instance, a scuba diver's oxygen tank and breathing regulator, a deck of tarot cards, a replica of the Statue of Liberty, or an MP3 player.

Also included under the category of objects are people or animals you employ in delivering a speech. You might enlist a volunteer to help you demonstrate tests for color blindness or, with your instructor's permission, bring in a Jack Russell terrier for a speech on that breed of dog. Objects used effectively give your speech immediacy and carry a great deal of impact.

Graphics

The term **graphics** includes a variety of two-dimensional presentational aids used to clarify or illustrate a point being made orally. Five types of graphics to consider are pictures, diagrams, graphs, charts, and maps.

Pictures can make a speaker's oral presentation more concrete and vivid. It is difficult to imagine how a speech on the artistic styles of Georgia O'Keeffe or Edward Hopper could be effective without pictures or prints of some of their paintings. A speaker trying to persuade the audience that subliminal messages are common in advertising without showing some actual examples would be both vague and unconvincing.

> "Before you start stressing over what kinds of visual aids you might want, relax and take a moment to think. What do you want your visual aid to do? Aid. Exactly. Whatever visual support you choose, remember that the operative word is "support." Slides, overheads, video, audio, computer-generated presentations, or flip charts should support and enhance your message, not duplicate or dominate it. Use them only to add color and life to the point you make."
>
> —JUDE WESTERFIELD[7]

object: an actual item or three-dimensional model of an item used during the delivery of a speech.

graphic: a two-dimensional visual aid, including pictures, diagrams, graphs, charts, and maps, used during the delivery of a speech.

picture: a photograph, painting, drawing, or print used to make a point more vivid or convincing.

Exploring *Online*

USING AUDIOVISUAL AIDS
www.2myprofessor.com/Common/guidelines_for_using_
audiovisual.htm
Dr. Mernoush Banton of Florida International University's
College of Business Administration maintains this page of
practical tips for planning and choosing appropriate presentational aids. Her list of "dos" and "don'ts" and her
criteria for judging audiovisuals are especially helpful.

Speakers can also use pictures to dramatize a point. Our student Dora delivered an informative speech on crop circles. She used several photographs scanned, enlarged, and printed from a book she had purchased.[8] Some of Dora's photos showed crop circles whose creators were known. In one case, a groom had commissioned a crop circle to mark his wedding. Other crop circles had appeared quickly and without a known creator. Dora effectively explored this controversial topic by showing the range of crop circles, from relatively simple (Figure 14.1a) to highly complex (Figure 14.1b). By citing her source and using enlarged photographs that were easy to see, she gave her classmates a clear and vivid glimpse of the phenomenon.

If you are not using your own photographs, you can locate pictures on the Internet in three different ways.[9] First, you can choose a search engine and just enter the term you want followed by the file format extension that you prefer (Eiffel Tower.jpg or roller coaster.gif, for example). Second, all popular search engines have either a toolbar icon or radio button to let you limit your search to pictures, photos, or images. Third, you can use the photograph databases at special websites such as the ones mentioned in the Exploring Online feature below. Be sure to record information about the source of any photograph so that you can cite it appropriately in your speech and in a written bibliography.

Exploring *Online*

LOCATING PHOTOGRAPHS
www.ditto.com
www.freefoto.com
www.picsearch.com
Search any of these sites to find photographs for noncommercial use. You can search each site by category
or keyword.

When you use pictures, make sure that you select them with size and clarity in mind. A small snapshot of the Palace of Versailles or a picture from an encyclopedia held up for audience view detracts from, rather than reinforces, the speaker's purpose. Pictures used as visual aids often must be enlarged. You can use a color copier at a copy shop or at your campus multimedia center to enlarge your pictures. If your classroom has a visual presenter, such as Elmo, you can project small pictures on a screen for easy audience viewing. You can also scan or copy your picture and save it to a disk, a CD, or a USB flash drive. Then project your visual aid from a computer.

Diagrams are graphics, typically designed on a computer or drawn on posterboard, showing the parts of an object or organization or the steps in a process. A diagram could show the features of a commercial spacecraft design, the organizational structure of the U.S. judicial system, or the steps in the lost-wax method of casting jewelry. The best diagrams achieve their impact by simplifying and exaggerating key points. For example, no diagram of manageable size could illustrate all the parts of a hybrid, gas-electric car engine. A carefully constructed diagram, whether drawn on posterboard or projected from the latest high-tech storage device, could isolate and label key parts of that engine design, however.

Graphs can take several familiar forms and can be used as presentational aids to illustrate some condition or progress. A **line graph** is useful in depicting trends and developments over time. A speaker might convincingly use a line graph to illustrate the rising cost of a college education over the past twenty years. Some line graphs trace two or more variables—income and expenditures, for example—in contrasting colors.

A **bar graph** is useful in comparing quantities or amounts. We can measure the economic health of an institution, a company, or a nation, for example, by learning whether it is "in the red" or "in the black." A bar graph contrasting deficits and profits, showing their relative size, provides a clear, visual indication of economic health, particularly when income is represented in black and deficits in red.

diagram: a graphic, usually designed on a computer or drawn on posterboard, showing the parts of an object or organization or the steps in a process.

line graph: a diagram used to depict changes among variables over time.

bar graph: a diagram used to show quantitative comparisons among variables.

FIGURE 14.1
Crop Circles

Crop circles, from relatively simple to more complex.

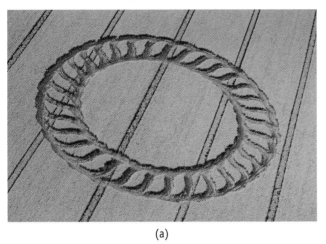

(a)

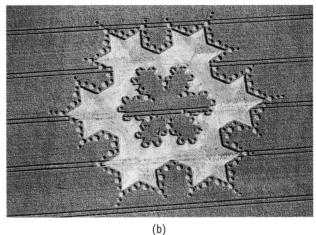

(b)

Curtis found an interesting bar graph to inform his audience about grade inflation at representative U.S. colleges and universities. Notice how the graph (Figure 14.2) clearly shows increases of grade point averages at both public and private schools.

A third type of graph, the **pie** or **circle graph**, is helpful when you want to show relative proportions of the various parts of a whole. If you are analyzing the federal budget, for example, a pie graph could illustrate the percentage of the budget allocated for defense. Pie graphs can show proportions of how people spend their time in a typical day, the causes of cancer deaths, and the composition of your university according to declared majors. When using a pie graph, emphasize the pertinent "slice" of the pie graph with a contrasting color.

pie or **circle graph:** a diagram used to show the relative proportions of a whole.

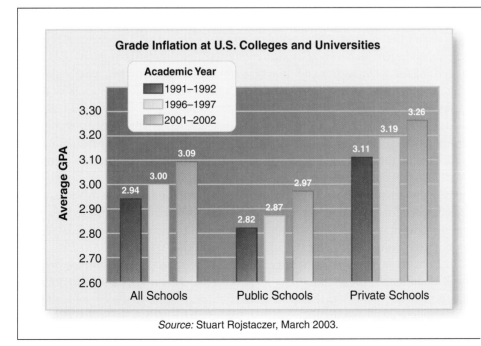

Source: Stuart Rojstaczer, March 2003.

FIGURE 14.2
Bar Graph: Grade Inflation at U.S. Colleges & Universities

FIGURE 14.3
Pie Graph:
Percentages
of a Population

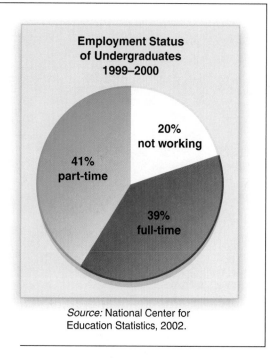

Employment Status
of Undergraduates
1999–2000

20%
not working

41%
part-time

39%
full-time

Source: National Center for
Education Statistics, 2002.

Cheryl informed her classmates on how college students spend their time outside class. One of her main points described the employment status of students. In her research, Cheryl found that 39.3 percent of students worked full-time, 40.8 percent worked part-time, and 19.9 percent were not employed. She rounded her statistics to the nearest percentage point and then constructed a pie graph (Figure 14.3). Notice that she used color for the slices representing students who worked either full- or part-time to emphasize that approximately 80 percent of all college undergraduates work to pay for part or all of their education.

Similar to diagrams and graphs, **charts** condense a large amount of information into a small space. Speakers introducing an audience to new terms will sometimes list those words on a chart. This strategy is particularly effective if the words can be uncovered one at a time in the order they are discussed. Using charts, you could list the top ten states in per capita lottery ticket sales or rank professional sports according to players' average salaries. Charts are particularly appropriate for medical and other technical topics. A speaker detailing the solution phase of a problem–solution speech could list steps advocated on a chart and introduce them in the order they are discussed.

As a speaker, you can either prepare charts in advance or draw them during the speech. For example, charts could show how regular investment in an Individual Retirement Account can lead to financial security in later life, and those calculations could be done ahead of time or during the course of the presentation. If you plan to draw one or more charts during your speech, rehearse the drawing. Make sure that you can continue to speak as you draw, so that your speech is not marred by long gaps of silence. If a chart is so complex that you cannot draw it as you speak, prepare it in advance.

Paige thought her classmates would be interested in learning more about where they spent much of their time: on the Internet. She researched this topic and located an excellent source that discussed how people used their time online.[10] Paige adapted one of her source's charts into a series of slides. In the spirit of a David Letterman top ten list, she revealed the activities from tenth to first. On the day she gave her speech, she projected ten slides from a disk. Her final slide (Figure 14.4) revealed the ten most popular uses of the Internet.

Maps, the final type of graphic presentational aid, lend themselves especially well to speeches discussing or referring to unfamiliar geographic areas. Speakers informing an audience on the islands of Hawaii, the Battle of Gettysburg, or threats to the Alaskan wildlife refuge would do well to include maps to illustrate their ideas. Although commercial maps are professionally prepared and look good, they may be either too small or too detailed for a speaker's purpose. If you cannot isolate and project a section of the map for a larger audience, you will probably want to prepare a simplified, large-scale map of the territory in question.

Colleen became interested in the geography of cyberspace after a guest lecturer presented a multimedia presentation on this topic in her computer class. Colleen wanted to learn more about these virtual geographies and, with some guidance from her computer professor, began researching the topic. She accessed a website that displayed maps of cyberspaces. There, she learned that Emmanuel Frécon had developed a tool called

chart: a graphic used to condense a large amount of information, to list the steps in a process, or to introduce new terms.

map: a graphic representing a real or imaginary geographic area.

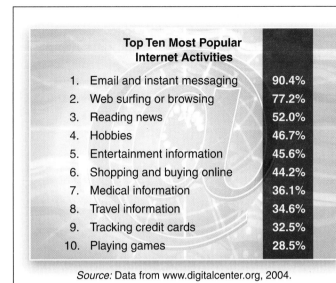

FIGURE 14.4
Chart: Top Ten Most Popular Internet Activities

Top Ten Most Popular Internet Activities	
1. Email and instant messaging	90.4%
2. Web surfing or browsing	77.2%
3. Reading news	52.0%
4. Hobbies	46.7%
5. Entertainment information	45.6%
6. Shopping and buying online	44.2%
7. Medical information	36.1%
8. Travel information	34.6%
9. Tracking credit cards	32.5%
10. Playing games	28.5%

Source: Data from www.digitalcenter.org, 2004.

WebPath that visually maps users' trails as they browse the Web.[11] She downloaded and printed a color copy of one of these Surf maps. She took it to the library's Media Resource Center, where she had the map enlarged (see Figure 14.5). Colleen had a challenging task of making a technical topic understandable for her listeners, but her presentational aid made her goal easier. After the speech her classmates and the instructor seemed genuinely interested in her topic and asked several questions. Several students even stayed after class to look at her visual aid.

Any of the graphics we have mentioned—pictures, diagrams, graphs, charts, or maps—can be drawn on posterboard or projected onto a screen. **Projections** refer not so much to a type of presentational aid as to a manner of presentation. This option is

projection: a manner of presenting visual aids by casting their images onto a screen or other background.

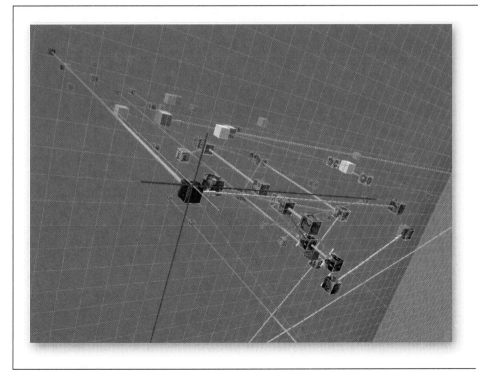

FIGURE 14.5
Map: Surf Map of Web Browsing

> *"You should use PowerPoint . . . sparingly. Don't think of it as wallpaper that's always there behind you, but a discrete moment in your talk when you turn to an illustration because it's too difficult to put the idea into mere words."*
>
> —NICK MORGAN[12]

Exploring Online

USING POWERPOINT
http://office.microsoft.com/en-us/FX010857971033.aspx
This site contains numerous links for both novice and experienced users of PowerPoint™. Step-by-step instructions will help you design slides and incorporate appropriate color, sound, graphics, and animations.

slide: a small transparency mounted in a frame or computer file designed for projection.

transparency: a sheet of clear or tinted plastic with drawn or printed images projected using an overhead projector.

opaque projection: an image cast directly from a sheet of paper by use of an opaque projector.

especially appropriate when your audience is too large to see the presentational aid easily and clearly. In such a case, you may want to use projections, such as slides, transparencies, or opaque projections. For convenience, we can group projections into two categories: *still projections* (slides, transparencies, and opaque projections) and *moving projections* (film and video).

Projections can be critical to business and other public presentations. They may not, however, always serve the purpose of the public speaker and, particularly, the student of this class. Two notes of caution are in order: As a beginning public speaker, you need to control and be the primary focus of the public speaking event. When you stand at the back of the room and narrate a slide show, you get little experience in speaking before an audience. For this reason, your instructor may not allow you to give a slide show, although you may be able to present a few relevant slides. Presentational aids must always support, not become, your speech.

We discuss moving projections in the next section; here, we discuss three types of still projections. **Slides** are small mounted transparencies or computer files designed specifically for projection, and usually shown one at a time. Most of us associate slides with photographs or pictures. Yet any of the graphics we discussed earlier can be photographed and developed into slides. Whereas maps, charts, graphs, and diagrams may be cumbersome and subject to wear, slides of those graphic presentational aids are easily transported and easily reproduced. However, you should be aware of two disadvantages. One, slides require projection equipment that is frequently noisy and intrusive. The second disadvantage is that slides must be projected in darkness to be easily visible, and this, of course, takes the focus away from you, the speaker.

Transparencies are clear or tinted sheets of plastic with words or images drawn or printed on them. Shown with an overhead projector, the transparency may be either prepared in advance or drawn with a felt-tip marker during the presentation. Many computer graphics programs can generate professional-looking transparencies. Overhead transparencies allow you to work through a problem, for example, without turning your back to the audience, thus helping you maintain audience involvement and interaction. If you plan to use transparencies in your very first speech, prepare them beforehand. You will be nervous enough without having to worry about drawing your presentational aid as you speak.

The **opaque projection** is an image that can be projected directly from a sheet of paper. Noisy, cumbersome opaque projectors of the past are rapidly being replaced by high-tech visual presenters such as the Elmo. This equipment offers the advantage of enlarging and projecting visual aids without the work of preparing transparencies. However, such systems can also project transparencies, video, computer slide shows and computer animation, and images of three-dimensional objects. Many models feature autofocus and power zoom magnification controlled by wireless remotes.

Each of these types of still projections can visually enhance a presentation. They help ensure that the images are big enough for even the largest audiences to see clearly. All require special projection equipment, however. Practice with the equipment so that you know how to operate it and how to minimize any noise it makes. On the day of

Theory into Practice
TIPS
Designing Transparencies and Slides

Computer technology has revolutionized the production and display of presentational aids. If you know how, you can use the computer to design and display professional-looking visual aids. Whether you are preparing transparencies or a slide show to project from a computer, your presentational aids will have a positive impact only if they are clear and readable. Consider the following guidelines before preparing any visuals.

Focus

- *Focus on a few key points.* Resist the temptation to present all your information visually. Select ideas that are the most important or that can best be made through the use of presentational aids.
- *Present ideas one at a time.* Don't let the audience get ahead of you. If you are discussing the first of five solutions for road rage, keep steps 2 through 5 covered. If you have those steps on a transparency, cover the ones you have not yet discussed with a sheet of paper, revealing each step when you get to it. If you are using PowerPoint, build your list through a series of slides.

Layout

- *Use a landscape (horizontal) page format rather than a portrait (vertical) format.* Text displayed horizontally is easier to read and gives you a better chance of expressing an idea in a single line.
- *Compose your text in the top half or two-thirds of your transparency or slide.* This ensures better viewing by those in the back of the classroom.
- *Use left-margin alignment.* It is easier to read than full- or right-margin justification.

Highlighting

- *Use bullets or numbers to highlight your key points.* If you have several key ideas, number them. Listeners can more readily focus on the appropriate part of the visual aid if they see a number when they hear you say, "My third suggestion . . ."

- *Use no more than six words per line.* Longer sentences are more difficult to read and remember. Learning how to condense and simplify your message also hones your speaking skills.
- *Use no more than six lines per page.* Listeners in the back of the room may have difficulty seeing the lower portion of a transparency projection or a posterboard.

Fonts

- *Use strong, straight fonts.* Ariel, Helvetica, and Times New Roman are good choices. Ornate fonts are more difficult to read.
- *Use no more than two fonts per transparency or screen.* Too many fonts can make your presentational aid more difficult to read.
- *Select a font size large enough to be read easily from the back row.* Minimum font size will vary according to the size of the classroom and the distance between the projector and the screen. Check out the font size prior to the time of your presentation.

Color and Art

- *Use color to enhance your presentational aids.* Research suggests that color can increase the audience's understanding and retention of information. Select colors that highlight the ideas you present. For example, a red line may reinforce a line graph showing a decline in student contributions to charitable organizations. Color can also complement the mood of a speech. A presentational aid for an informative speech on the celebration of Mardi Gras could use bright colors.
- *Limit the number of colors in your presentational aid.* Too many colors make reading a visual aid more difficult. Use no more than six colors per presentational aid and even fewer if the aid contains only text.
- *Avoid "chartjunk."*[13] Irrelevant graphics and art clutter and detract from your visual aid. An effective presentational aid draws the reader's attention to key points you are making in your speech.[14]

your speech, you will need to be extremely well organized and punctual because projection equipment requires time for setup and focusing and is subject to mechanical failure. Your diligence can pay off handsomely, however. If you are sure that the visual aid is important enough to project, its contribution to your speech will probably outweigh these potential disadvantages and reward your extra effort.

Rapid innovations in the field of computer graphics are exciting. But be sure that any presentational aids you produce this way enhance your message, rather than just showcase what the software can do. Avoid the temptations to overload or complicate your computer-generated visual by using all the bells and whistles of the program you choose. The same qualities that we've discussed for freehand presentational aids—clarity, simplicity, and contrast—should be evident in any computer graphic you use.

Film and Video

Moving projections include **films** and **videos,** and they are appropriate whenever action will enhance a visual presentation. Moreover, with the widespread popularity of DVDs and video cassettes, this type of presentational aid is becoming easier and cheaper to use. The choice between film and video is dictated both by the projection equipment available to you and by the size of the audience. You can project larger images from film than from video, making film a wise choice for presentations to large groups. Videotapes and DVDs are entirely appropriate for presentations to small audiences or before larger groups that have multiple viewing monitors. However, films and videos are lengthy, and their organization is predetermined. It is important that you, not a presentational aid, organize and present the ideas of your speech. Use only short video clips to illustrate your key ideas.

Videos have one obvious advantage over films: They do not require you to darken the room for projection. Though both film and video carry with them possible distractions, their potential impact is undeniable. Many speeches on social problems are significantly more compelling if the audience not only hears about but also sees graphic evidence of the problem. Luckily, you can find numerous video clips on the Internet using most search engines. Be sure to note the source of any that you plan to save for multimedia display in your speech so that you can cite them accurately.

Video and film can also introduce viewers to aspects of various cultures. One of our students, Henry, delivered an informative speech on the topic of Sufism, an Islamic tradition that is both mystical and multicultural. He informed his listeners how this tradition combines dance and music to express spiritual ecstasy. He played a videotape of

film and **video:** moving projections used to enhance a speaker's point.

the dance of the "whirling dervishes" of the Mevlevi Order, pointing out the religious significance of the dancers' gestures and movements.

Handouts

A final method of presenting material visually is the **handout.** Copies of any graphic presentational aid—pictures, diagrams, graphs, charts, or maps—may be handed out to individual audience members.

Handouts are appropriately used under two conditions: (1) when the information cannot be effectively displayed or projected or (2) when the audience needs to study or refer to the information after the speech. Gwen, a student presenting a speech on "The Power Résumé," used a handout to great benefit. She distributed a sample power résumé and referred to it at key intervals in her speech: "If you look at line fifteen, you will see . . ." She had numbered the lines of the résumé in the margin so that the audience could find the references without fumbling. Not only could the audience refer to the résumé as Gwen discussed its key features, but many also probably saved it to use later as they prepared to enter the career world upon graduation. Gwen's speech and her presentational aid made a convincing argument for the importance of the power résumé. In a similar way, if you try to persuade your audience to contribute time and money to local charities, you will more likely achieve your goal if you distribute a handout with the name, address, telephone number, and brief description of each charity.

If you are distributing handouts to listeners who are likely to receive handouts from other speakers on the same day you speak, use colored paper to distinguish your materials. If you are the only speaker and are distributing several handouts, consider putting each one on a different color. It's easier to identify which handout you want your listeners to look at if you can say, "On the blue sheet . . . ," for example.

Audio and Other Aids

Audio aids include records, tapes, compact discs, and MP3 files, and certainly there is an audio dimension to films and videos. Certain speech topics lend themselves to audio reinforcement of the message. A speech on Janis Joplin, for example, would be more vivid and informative if the audience could see and hear a videotaped clip of one of her performances. Lindahl, a student whose research we mentioned in Chapter 7, began her speech on the savant syndrome by playing half a minute of a taped piano performance of Chopin's Polonaise no. 6 in A-Flat Major. Her first words were, "The person who was playing that music is considered handicapped, but he heard this piece of music for the first time only minutes before sitting down to play it." The audiotape was a compelling example of one form of the savant syndrome. A speech comparing the jazz styles of Branford and Wynton Marsalis could hardly be effective without letting listeners hear examples from each of those artists.

Audio aids need not be confined to music topics, however. An audience listening to a speech on Winston Churchill could benefit from hearing his quiet eloquence as he addressed Great Britain's House of Commons and declared, "I have nothing to offer but blood, toil, tears, and sweat." A speaker analyzing the persuasive appeals of radio and television advertisements could play pertinent examples.

You may want to appeal to senses other than sight and hearing. For example, a student of ours gave each audience member an envelope before her speech on aromatherapy. When she discussed the effects of certain scents on behavior, she had students open the envelopes and remove strips of lavender- and vanilla-scented paper, two of the scents she discussed. Think creatively as well as critically as you consider ways of supporting what you say.

handout: any graphic visual aid distributed to individual audience members.

audio aid: a cassette tape, compact disc, or record used to clarify or prove a point by letting listeners hear an example.

We have discussed the importance and major types of presentational aids. Remember, though, that even the most brilliant presentational aid cannot salvage a poorly planned, poorly delivered speech. Visuals can aid, but they cannot resuscitate a weak speech. On the other hand, even the most carefully designed and professionally executed visual aid can be spoiled by clumsy handling during a presentation. The effect of public speaking is cumulative, with each element contributing toward one final effect. If you use presentational aids, you cannot afford to use them poorly. The following section offers some practical guidelines on how to use presentational aids in your public speech.

Strategies for Using Presentational Aids

Key Points

Strategies for Using Presentational Aids

Before the Speech

1. Determine the information to be presented visually.
2. Select the type of aid best suited to your resources and speech.
3. Ensure easy viewing by all audience members.
4. Make sure that the aid communicates the information clearly.
5. Construct an aid that is professional in appearance.
6. Practice using your aid.
7. Arrange for safe transportation of your aids.
8. Carry backup supplies with you.
9. Properly position the aid.
10. Test your presentational aid.

During the Speech

1. Reveal the aid only when you are ready for it.
2. Talk to your audience—not to the aid.
3. Refer to the aid.
4. Keep your aid in view until the audience understands your point.
5. Conceal the aid after you have made your point.
6. Use handouts with caution.

Before the Speech

Determine the Information to Be Presented Visually.   Sections of a presentation that are complex or detailed may be particularly appropriate for visualization. Be careful, however, not to use too many visual aids. The premium in a speech is on the spoken word. Multimedia presentations can be exciting; they may also be extremely difficult to coordinate. Handling too many objects or charts quickly becomes cumbersome and distracting.

Select the Type of Presentational Aid Best Suited to Your Resources and Speech.   The information you need to present, the amount of preparation time you have, your technical expertise at producing the aid, and the cost involved will all influence the visual aid you select. If preparing quality presentational aids to illustrate your speech will take more time, money, or expertise than you have, you are probably better off without them. A presentational aid that calls attention to its poor production is a handicap, no matter how important the information it contains.

Ensure Easy Viewing by All Audience Members.   A speaker addressing an audience of 500 would not want to use a videotaped presentation displayed on a single television or computer monitor. A bar graph on posterboard should be visible to more than just the first four rows of the audience. If possible, practice with your presentational aids in the room where you will speak. Position or project the aid and then sit in the seat of

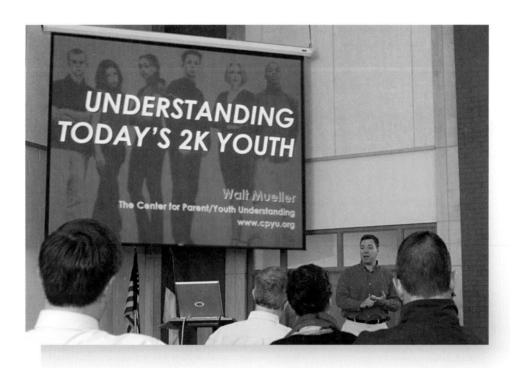

Presentational aids help listeners see as well as hear your message. Well-designed PowerPoint graphics, for example, can enhance the impact of your ideas.

your farthest possible audience member. (In an auditorium, make it the back row; people will not move forward unless forced to.) If you can read your presentational aid from that distance, it is sufficient in size. If you cannot, you must either enlarge or eliminate it.

Make Sure That the Presentational Aid Communicates the Information Clearly.   Simplicity should be your guiding principle in constructing your visual aid. Michael Talman, a graphics design consultant, compares a graphic in a presentation to "going by a highway billboard at 55 miles per hour. Its effectiveness can be judged by how quickly the viewer sees and understands its message."[15] Speakers sometimes construct posters or slides in technicolor to make them lively and interesting. However, too much color, like too much information, clutters and confuses. Limiting the range of colors, as well as muting secondary visual elements such as frames, grids, arrows, rules, and boxes, can clarify the primary information you want to convey.[16] Remember that the chief purpose of visual aids is to inform, not to impress, the audience. You can use red to indicate a budget deficit, but, as a rule, black or dark blue on white is the most visually distinct color combination for graphics.

Construct a Presentational Aid That Is Professional in Appearance.   In the business and professional world, a hand-lettered poster, no matter how neatly done, is inappropriate. Professionals understand the importance of a good impression and are willing to pay graphics designers to help them create polished presentational aids. Today, however, the computer puts a galaxy of inexpensive, professional-looking design options at the fingertips of anyone willing to learn the programs. If you are familiar with a computer graphics program that meets your needs, by all means use it. If you can't use a computer and doubt your freehand skills, hiring an art student to draw and letter a presentational aid you have designed is another alternative.

If you throw together a chart or graph the night before your speech, that is exactly what it will look like. Your hastily prepared work will undermine an image of careful and thorough preparation.

Exploring *Online*

USING PRESENTATIONAL AIDS
www.presentersuniversity.com/Courses.php
The InFocus Corporation sponsors this site, called Presenters University, to help business and professional people present their ideas more effectively. Click on "Visual Aids" to read their suggestions for choosing, designing, and using visual aids.

Practice Using Your Presentational Aid. A conscientious speaker will spend hours preparing a speech; presentational aids are a part of that presentation. Just as you rehearse the words of your speech, you should rehearse referring to your aid, uncovering and covering charts, advancing slides, and writing on overhead transparencies. In short, if you plan to use presentational aids, learn how *before* your speech; no audience will be impressed by how much you learn during the course of your presentation.

Arrange for Safe Transportation of Your Presentational Aids. Aids worth using are worth transporting safely. The laptop computer you've bought or borrowed needs obvious care. Posterboards should be protected from moisture and bending. Cover your presentational aid with plastic to protect it from that freak rainstorm you encounter just before speech class. Do not roll up paper or posterboard charts, carrying them to different classes or leaving them in a car trunk throughout the day, and then expect them to lay flat when you speak. You will have a cylinder, not an effective presentational aid.

Carry Backup Supplies with You. An exciting and informative presentation can be ruined when a projector bulb blows as you are preparing to speak. Make an inventory of equipment you may need, such as extension cords, bulbs, and batteries, and then take them with you.

Properly Position the Presentational Aid. Get to the place where you will give your speech *before* the audience arrives. Check out the equipment you will use. Check the height of the easel if you are using a flip-chart or posterboards. If you are using an overhead projector or a multimedia computer system, make sure that the equipment works. Position or project your presentational aid in the most desirable location. Make sure that the maximum number of people will see it and that nothing obstructs the audience's view. If you are not to be the first speaker, have your presentational aid and any necessary equipment out of the way, but located so that you can set up quickly and with little disruption.

Test Your Presentational Aid. Finally, if you are using transparencies or slides, make sure that they are in focus, in the correct order, and that any remote control you plan to use works. Use a test transparency. If there are people already in the room, you may not want to "give away" your topic by displaying one of your presentational aids. Some speakers use a transparency with the words *Test Transparency* on it. Although this keeps the audience from seeing part of the speech before you deliver it, it reveals little thought or creativity. A transparency or slide with a creative title for your speech can create interest in your topic without revealing key information. In fact, it could motivate your audience to listen even before you utter your first word.

During the Speech

Not even the most careful preparation of a presentational aid guarantees that it will work for you as you deliver your speech. Keep the following commonsense guidelines in mind as you practice incorporating the aid into your delivery.

Reveal the Presentational Aid Only When You Are Ready for It. A presentational aid is designed to attract attention and convey information. If it is visible at the beginning of the speech, the audience may focus on it, rather than on what you are saying. Your aid should be seen only when you are ready to discuss the point it illustrates.

If your presentational aid is on posterboard, cover it with a blank posterboard, or turn the blank side to the audience. At the appropriate time, expose the visual aid. If you are using projections, have someone cued to turn the lights off and the projector on at the appropriate time.

Planning Presentational Aids for the Classroom

If you have a speech assignment that requires or encourages you to use presentational aids, take the time necessary to visit your campus multimedia center. If you have not yet developed the visual aids you will eventually use, design a rudimentary graphic and save it to a disk or other storage device. Then use your time in the lab to explore the different ways of delivering that image. What are the advantages of projecting your aid from different devices or of printing your aid in various formats? Which will be best for your classroom setting? Practice using the equipment. Which are you most comfortable using? Be sure to check the availability of the equipment you prefer for your classroom.

Occasionally, a speaker will stop speaking, uncover a presentational aid, and then continue. This is where rehearsal can really help you. You want to avoid creating unnecessary breaks in the flow of your speech. With practice you will be able to keep talking as you uncover or project your aid.

Talk to Your Audience—Not to the Presentational Aid.   Remember, eye contact is a speaker's most important nonverbal tool. Sustained visual interaction with your audience keeps their attention on you and allows you to monitor their feedback regarding your speech. Turning your back to your listeners undermines your impact. For this reason, use prepared graphics, rather than a dry erase board.

Refer to the Presentational Aid.   Speakers sometimes stand at the lectern using their notes or reading their manuscript, relatively far from their aid. This creates two lines of vision and can confuse your audience. It may also give the impression that you must rely on your notes because you do not fully understand what the presentational aid conveys.

Other speakers carry their notes with them as they move to the aid, referring to them as they point out key concepts. This is cumbersome and again reinforces the image of a speaker unsure of what he or she wants to say.

A well-constructed presentational aid should function as a set of notes. The key ideas represented on the aid should trigger the explanation you will provide. You should not need to refer to anything else as you discuss the point your visual aid illustrates. When you practice using your presentational aid, use your aid as your notes.

If you use a metal, wooden, or light-beam pointer to refer to the aid, have it easily accessible, use it only when pointing to the presentational aid, and set it down immediately after you are finished with it. Too many speakers pick up a pen to use when referring to their aid and end up playing with the pen during the rest of the speech.

Finally, point to your presentational aid with the hand closer to it. This keeps your body open and makes communication physically more direct with your audience.

Keep Your Presentational Aid in View Until the Audience Understands Your Point.   Remember that you are more familiar with your speech than is your audience. Too often, a speaker hurries through an explanation and covers or removes an aid before the audience fully comprehends its significance or the point it makes. Just as you should not reveal your aid too soon, do not cover it up too quickly. You will have invested time and effort in preparing the aid. Give your audience the time necessary to digest the information it conveys. As you discuss and describe the presentational aid, check your audience response. Many will likely signal their understanding of the presentational aid by nodding their heads or changing their posture.

Conceal the Presentational Aid After You Have Made Your Point. Once you proceed to the next section of your speech, you do not want the audience to continue thinking about the presentational aid. If the aid is an object or posterboard, cover it. If you are using projections, turn off the projector or clear the computer screen.

Use Handouts with Caution. Of all the forms of presentational aids, the handout may be the most troublesome. If you distribute handouts before your remarks, the audience is already ahead of you. Passing out information during a presentation can be distracting, especially if you stop talking as you do so. In addition, the rustling of paper can distract the speaker and other audience members. Disseminating material after the presentation eliminates distractions, but does not allow the listener to refer to the printed information as you are explaining it. In general, then, use handouts in a public speech only if that is the best way to clarify and give impact to your ideas.

You will encounter some speaking situations, such as the business presentation, that not only benefit from but may also demand handout material. Those audiences are often decision-making groups. During an especially technical presentation, they may need to take notes. Afterward, they may need to study the information presented. Handouts provide a record of the presenter's remarks and supplementary information the speaker did not have time to explain.

Presentational aids—objects, graphics, film and video, handouts, and audio aids—can make your speech more effective. By seeing as well as hearing your message, the audience becomes more involved with your speech and more responsive to your appeals.

Summary

We live in a visually oriented world, expecting not only to hear about events around the globe, but also to see color pictures and videos of them. Various studies show that presentational aids complement the spoken word by increasing audience involvement with a speech and aiding listeners' retention of the information presented. Presentational aids can contribute to the clarity and impact of a speaker's message and, when handled well, can make a speaker's delivery seem more dynamic.

The five categories of presentational aids discussed in this chapter are objects, graphics, film and video, handouts, and audio and other aids. *Objects* are three-dimensional and may be either actual items or models of large or small items. *Graphics* refers to a large group of two-dimensional presentational aids, including pictures, diagrams, graphs (line, bar, or pie graphs), charts, and maps. If you know any of the wide range of computer graphics programs, you can produce electronically generated graphics. Any type of graphic may be shown by a still projection: a slide, a transparency, or an opaque projection. Moving projections include *film* and *video*. *Handouts* of any type of graphic may be given to audience members when no other method of presentation is possible. In addition to these strictly visual supports, a speaker may choose *audio aids* such as records, tapes, compact discs, or MP3 files of music, spoken words, and other sounds.

To design graphics that have maximum impact, a speaker should *focus* on just a few key points and should present these points one at a time. For graphics that contain text, the *layout* should be horizontal, with text placed in the top half or two-thirds and left-margin aligned. Graphics should have no more than six words per line, no more than six lines per page, with bullets or numbers *highlighting* key points. A speaker should use strong, straight *fonts,* with no more than two different fonts on each graphic. Finally, a speaker should select *color and art* that amplify the impact of the graphic without cluttering it.

To use these graphics or other presentational aids for maximum impact, a speaker needs to prepare them carefully using the following steps as guidelines: (1) Determine the amount of information to be presented; (2) select the type of aid best suited to the speaker's resources and topic; (3) ensure easy viewing by all audience members; (4) ensure that the aid communicates its information clearly; (5) construct an aid that appears carefully or professionally done; (6) practice using the aid; (7) arrange for safe transportation of the aid;

(8) carry backup supplies in case of equipment failure; (9) properly position the aid before beginning the speech; and (10) test the aid before using it.

During the actual delivery of the speech, the speaker using presentational aids needs to remember the following: (1) Reveal the aid only when ready to use it; (2) talk to the audience, not to the aid; (3) refer to the aid; (4) keep the aid in view until the audience understands the point it makes;

(5) conceal the aid after making your point with it; and (6) use handouts with caution.

Presentational aids can greatly enhance many speeches, and some speeches would be difficult to deliver without appropriate audio or visual aids. Effective use of those aids, however, requires careful planning and practice to integrate them into your speech delivery without distraction.

Practice Critique

Evaluating Presentational Aids

Tiffanie Petrin delivered her speech on steganography using visual aids. Because we were unable to determine who controls the copyright of those photographs, we could not reprint them. You may be able to view them if you do a Google image search using "steganography Pentagon" as your query. As you read her speech in the Appendix, look at the visuals Tiffanie used or identify places where presentational aids would make her speech clearer, more vivid, or more credible. Are there other points in Tiffanie's speech that would have benefited from visual support? If so, what are those points, and what types of visuals could she have used to illustrate them?

Exercises

1. Select a graph, diagram, or chart that you find in a magazine article or on an Internet website. Describe how you would adapt it as a presentational aid for a speech.

2. Compile a list of memorable television advertisements. Discuss the visual elements of the ads. What strategies do they use to reinforce the message? Can some of these techniques be adapted to a speech? Are there elements in any of the ads that detract from viewers' remembering the product or brand name? How can a public speaker avoid this pitfall when designing and presenting a presentational aid?

3. Using information you obtain from the Department of Transportation's National Highway Traffic Safety Administration website (www.nhtsa.dot.gov) or from a site linked to it, prepare one PowerPoint slide that illustrates the "Guidelines for Preparing Presentational Aids" discussed in this chapter and one slide that violates one or more of those guidelines. Be sure to include a source line indicating where you got this information. Save the slides to a disk, or print them in color. Display your printed slides in class, or project them if multimedia equipment is available, showing the problem slide first. After classmates correctly identify the problems you have illustrated, show the improvements you made on the second slide.

4. Select a statistical table from an almanac, a government report, the *Gallup Poll Monthly, American Demographics,* or some other source. Decide how you could convert the information to a line, bar, or pie graph. Construct the graph on a sheet of paper, posterboard, or transparency film.

5. Sketch a presentational aid you could construct for one of the speeches in the Appendix. Describe how the aid would make the message of the speech clearer and more memorable.

6. Describe at least two different types of presentational aids you could use for a speech having the following specific purposes:
   a. To inform the audience about techniques of handwriting analysis
   b. To inform the audience about "the look" of a Quentin Tarantino film
   c. To inform the audience about the process of photograph restoration
   d. To persuade the audience that federal funding for Parkinson's disease research should be increased
   e. To persuade the audience that [name of building on campus] should be razed and replaced with another facility

Speaking to Inform

chapter

15

We are drowning in information and starving for knowledge. —JOHN NAISBITT

Our thirst for knowledge and stimulation seems insatiable. It has also never been easier to satisfy. "On a typical day at the end of 2004, some 70 million American adults logged onto the Internet to use email, get news, access government information, check out health and medical information, participate in auctions, book travel reservations, research their genealogy, gamble, seek out romantic partners, and engage in countless other activities."[1] The "always-on" function ensures that subscribers lucky enough to have broadband and DSL have the Internet always at hand.[2] For many of us, "iPod, therefore I Am."[3] We choose our own play lists rather than just living to the soundtracks commercial radio stations offer. We subscribe to weblogs, audioblogs, and videoblogs, often receiving them on our cell phones. Of course, we send text, pictures, and video from those same cell phones. Many who want to be connected—"plugged in"—find it amazingly easy to do so.

Why is it, then, that when asked to speak about what we consider interesting or important, so many of us feel all dressed up with nowhere to go? Perhaps we lack the sense of community that people experienced more easily when almost everyone watched the same few network TV news reports, read the same newspapers, and listened to the same radio stations. "Technology has given us finally a universe entirely for ourselves— where the serendipity of meeting a new stranger, or hearing a piece of music we would never choose for ourselves, or an opinion that might actually force us to change our mind about something are all effectively banished." That's the assessment of Andrew Sullivan, long-time member of iPod nation, who catalogs some of the things we miss by focusing solely on our own diversions:

> That hilarious shard of an over-heard conversation that stays with you all day; the child whose chatter on the sidewalk takes you back to your own early memories; birdsong; weather; accents; the laughter of others; and those thoughts that come not by filling your head with selected diversion, but by allowing your mind to wander aimlessly through the regular background noise of human and mechanical life.[4]

An informative speech assignment challenges you to take a small step toward building a sense of community within your classroom. Such an assignment also poses at least three challenges:

1. Choosing a topic you find personally interesting and that your listeners will find interesting or relevant
2. Finding adequate information to make you well informed about the topic
3. Organizing your information in the most fitting manner

These three tasks form the essence of informative speaking, the subject of this chapter.

Characteristics of a Speech to Inform

Dr. Jones, your geology professor, enters the classroom, takes out a folder of notes, puts up the first of a series of slides, and begins to lecture on the differences between active and inactive volcanoes. At the morning staff meeting, Dr. Mendez explains how the hospital will implement its new policy to secure the confidentiality of patient records. Scott, a classmate in your business communication class, spends half the period summarizing his outside reading on factors that shape a company's corporate culture. The lecture, briefing, and oral report these people deliver are three of the forms informative speeches can take. In this chapter we focus on the variety of subject areas for a **speech to inform.**

At the most fundamental level, we seek knowledge for three reasons: We want to *know, understand,* and *use* information. The goals of any informative speaker, in turn, are to impart knowledge, enhance understanding, or permit application. Suppose you decided to prepare an informative speech on the general subject of advertising. You could select as your specific purpose to inform the audience about advertising in ancient times. Your listeners probably know little about this topic, and you can readily assume that your speech would add to their knowledge. Alternatively, you could inform the audience about how effective advertising succeeds. Using examples your audience already knows, you could deepen their understanding of advertising strategies and principles. A third specific purpose could be to inform your listeners about how they can prepare effective, low-cost advertisements when they want to promote a charity fund-raising project or a garage sale. In this instance you would help the audience apply basic advertising principles.

Speakers inform us, then, when they provide us with new information, when they help us understand better some information we already possess, or when they enable us to apply information. When you prepare an informative speech, however, you must make sure that you don't slip into giving a persuasive speech. How can you avoid this problem? After all, a persuasive speech also conveys information. In fact, the best persuasive speeches usually include supporting material that is both expository and compelling.

Some topics, of course, are easy to classify as informative or persuasive. A speaker urging audience members not to use a cell phone while driving is clearly trying to persuade; the speaker is attempting to intensify beliefs and either change or reinforce behavior. On the other hand, a speech charting the most recent options in cell phone technology is a speech to inform. A speech describing different forms of alcohol addiction is informative, whereas a speech advocating the Alcoholics Anonymous program to overcome addiction would be persuasive.

Sometimes speakers, both beginning and experienced, begin preparing a speech with the intention to inform, only to discover that somewhere during the speech construction process their objective has become persuasion. In other instances, speakers deliver what they intended to be an informative speech only to find that their listeners received it as a persuasive message. How can this happen? Let's look at the experience of one speaker, Sarah.

> Sarah designed a speech with the specific purpose of informing the audience of the arguments for and against allowing women to serve in military combat. In her speech, she took care to represent each side's arguments accurately and objectively. After her speech, however, Sarah discovered that some listeners previously undecided on the issue found the pro arguments more persuasive and now supported permitting women to serve in combat roles. But Sarah also learned that others in the audience became more convinced that women should be excluded from such roles. Did Sarah's speech persuade? Apparently for some audience members the answer is yes; they changed their attitudes because of this speech. Yet Sarah's objective was to inform, not to persuade.

In determining the general purpose of your speech, remember that both speakers and listeners are active participants in the communication process. Listeners will interpret what they hear and integrate it into their frames of reference. Your objectivity as a speaker will not stop the listener from hearing with subjectivity. As a speaker, though, you determine *your* motive for speaking. It is not to advocate specific beliefs, attitudes, and behaviors on controversial issues. Your objective is to assist your hearers as they

speech to inform: a speech to impart knowledge, enhance understanding, or facilitate application of information.

come to know, understand, or apply an idea or issue. As you word the specific purpose of your speech, you should be able to determine whether your general purpose is to persuade or to inform.

Informative Speech Topics

Experts identify several ways of classifying informative speeches. We have chosen a topical pattern that we think will work well for you. This approach is based on the types of topics you can choose for your speech. As you read about these topic categories, keep two guidelines in mind. First, approach each category of topics with the broadest possible perspective. Second, recognize that the categories overlap; the boundaries between them are not distinct. Whether you consider the Great Pyramid of Cheops an object or a place, for example, is much less important than the fact that it's a fascinating informative speech topic. The purpose of our categories is to stimulate, not to limit, your topic selection and development. As you begin brainstorming, consider information you could provide your listeners regarding people, objects, places, activities and events, processes, concepts, conditions, and issues. In the following sections, we discuss these eight major topic areas for informative speeches and the patterns of organization appropriate for each.

Key Points

Topic Categories for Informative Speeches

1. Speeches about people
2. Speeches about objects
3. Speeches about places
4. Speeches about activities and events

5. Speeches about processes
6. Speeches about concepts
7. Speeches about conditions
8. Speeches about issues

Speeches about People

Activities and accomplishments of other people fascinate us. We gravitate toward books, magazine articles, television programs, films, and even supermarket tabloids that reveal the lives of celebrities. We are interested in the lives of the rich and the famous. We are also interested in the lives of the poor and the not-so-famous. Lifetime TV's

We read about, listen to, and watch people who fascinate us. Many of them have unique, interesting stories. Sharing this information with an audience can make an excellent speech.

Intimate Portrait series features the lives of influential women. Bravo's *Profiles* explores the lives of creative people. A&E's *Biography* has been so popular and so critically acclaimed that it has spawned its own cable channel.

People, then, are an obvious and abundant resource of topics for your informative speech. You can be as historical or as contemporary as you wish. A speech about a person allows you the opportunity to expand your knowledge in a field that interests you while sharing those interests with your listeners. If you're a fan of animated films, you may be disappointed that Disney has abandoned freehand animation. An informative speech assignment gives you the option to discuss J. Stuart Blackton, one of the pioneers of American animation, or contemporary Japanese animator Hayao Miyazaki, creator of *Spirited Away* and *Howl's Moving Castle*. If you're an avid photographer, you could discover and communicate something about the life and accomplishments of Ansel Adams, Diane Arbus, Alfred Stieglitz, or Annie Leibovitz, for example.

Exploring *Online*

ONLINE BIOGRAPHIES
www.biography.com
http://lifetimetv.com/shows/ip
Visit these sites for thousands of ideas for speeches about people. At Biography.com you can search paragraph-length biographies of more than 25,000 people. At Lifetime's Intimate Portrait page you can search alphabetically for longer biographies of hundreds of influential women.

Of course, you don't need to confine your topic to individuals associated with your major or areas of interest. You could interest and inform audiences by discussing the lives and contributions of people such as:

Lance Armstrong	Sally Hemings	M. Night Shyamalan
Ray Charles	Jimi Hendrix	Patrick Tilman
Cesar Chavez	Margaret Mead	Andy Warhol
Johnny Depp	Jackie Robinson	Prince William of Wales

You may choose to discuss not one person but a group of people, such as the Marx Brothers, the Four Horsemen of Notre Dame, or the Red Hat Society. You could even compare and contrast two or more individuals to highlight their philosophies and contributions. The following pairs of noted figures could generate lively exposition: Rachel Carson and Ralph Nader, Britney Spears and Avril Lavigne, Thurgood Marshall and Clarence Thomas, or Malcolm X and Martin Luther King, Jr.

In considering an informative speech about a person, you must decide not only what is important but also what the audience will remember. Too often, students organize

Speaking with *Confidence*

Though informative speaking sounds like a simple concept, it is more complicated than it may first appear. It is all too easy to fall into the trap of biased speaking. I selected the hotly debated topic of standardized testing for my informative speech. I then began my research. Throughout the process I would write down notes, only to realize that the information could be interpreted as leaning toward one side of the debate. In order to remain objective, I made an outline to plot the main points that needed to be discussed. I carefully chose ideas that were purely informative, such as "What exactly is standardized testing?" and "When did standardized testing become widely used?" As I constructed my speech, I made sure to use reliable, objective websites that were not gung-ho for either side of the debate. Also, if I had a piece of information that had the slightest inclination of bias, I took it out and saved it for my persuasive speech. Researching an informative speech proved to be more challenging than I anticipated, because it's human nature to be biased in any hotly debated issue. But all this work kept me focused. When I delivered my speech, I felt confident that it was strictly informative.

—**Patty Pak,** *Virginia Tech University*

speeches about people so that the speeches resemble biographical listings in an encyclopedia. The speech amounts to a seemingly limitless compendium of dates. This is a mistake. Even the most attentive listener will remember few of the details in such a speech.

Speeches about people are often organized chronologically or topically. Cary used a chronological pattern to trace the life and legacy of Christopher Reeve. She presented three main points:

   I. The actor
  II. The accident victim
 III. The activist

In her second key idea, Cary discussed the equestrian accident that left Reeve paralyzed in 1995. Using acting metaphors, she described how this event transformed him. Reeve moved from the roles he had portrayed as an actor to a more important role as an activist. His final performance would be not on a Broadway stage or a movie screen, but on an international stage as an advocate for medical research to discover cures for spinal cord injuries.

Speeches about Objects

A second resource of informative topics is objects. Speeches about objects focus on what is concrete, rather than on what is abstract. Again, consider objects from the broadest perspective possible so that you can generate a maximum number of topic ideas. Topics for this type of speech could include the following:

Exploring *Online*

RESEARCHING HISTORICAL TOPICS
http://memory.loc.gov/ammem/index.html
If you're interested in discussing an informative topic from a historical perspective, check out *American Memory,* historical collections maintained by the Library of Congress. The site contains more than 125 collections, with topics including the African American odyssey, early baseball cards (1887–1914), Civil War photographs, Hispanic music and culture, historic buildings, and sound recordings of speeches from World War I.

crocodiles	performance clothing
electric cars	smart roads
the Great Wall of China	volcanoes
"nanny cams"	

Speeches about objects can use any of several organizational patterns. A speech on the Cathedral of Notre Dame or the Statue of Liberty could be organized spatially. A speech tracing the development of cyclones and anticyclones evolves chronologically. A speaker discussing the origins, types, and uses of pasta also uses a topical division. If the speech focused only on the history of pasta, however, it may best be structured chronologically.

Kevin used a topical organization for his speech on genetically modified (GM) animals, sometimes called designer animals:

   I. The process of designing animals
  II. Benefits of GM animals
     A. Medical uses
     B. Commercial uses
 III. Problems of GM animals
     A. Animal health issues
     B. Ethical issues

Speeches about Places

Places are an easily tapped resource for informative speech topics. These speeches introduce listeners to new locales or expand their knowledge of familiar places. Topics may include real places, such as historic sites, emerging nations, national parks, famous

A visit to a museum, a historic site, a natural attraction, or even a mural painted on the side of a building might provide inspiration for an informative speech topic.

prisons, and planets. Topics may also include fictitious places, such as the Land of Oz or the Island of the Lord of the Flies. Speeches about places challenge speakers to select words that create vivid images.

To organize your speech about places, you would typically use one of three organizational patterns: spatial, chronological, or topical. A speech about the Nile, the world's longest river, is organized spatially if it discusses the upper, middle, and lower Nile. A presentation about your college could trace its development chronologically. A speech on Poplar Forest, Thomas Jefferson's getaway home, could use a topical pattern discussing Jefferson's architectural style.

Suppose you selected as your informative speech topic Ellis Island, the site of the chief U.S. immigration center from 1892 to 1954. You could choose any of the following patterns of development:

Pattern: Spatial

Specific Purpose: To inform the audience about Ellis Island's Main Building

Key Ideas: I.   The Registry Room
 II. The Baggage Room
 III. The Oral History Studio

Pattern: Chronological

Specific Purpose: To inform the audience of the history of Ellis Island

Key Ideas: I.   Years of Immigration, 1892–1954
 II. Years of Dormancy, 1954–1984
 III. Years of Remembrance, 1984–present

Pattern: Topical

Specific Purpose: To inform the audience of the history of Ellis Island

Key Ideas   I.   The Process of Immigration
 II. The Place of Immigration
 III. The People Who Immigrated

Notice that each of these outlines is organized according to a distinct pattern. The key ideas in the first outline are organized spatially. Although the specific purposes of the second and third speeches are identical, the former is organized chronologically and the latter topically.

If you choose to speak about a place, be aware of a couple of common pitfalls. First, avoid making your speech sound like a travelogue. The speaking occasion is not an opportunity to show a captive audience slides you took during your last vacation ("And here are my cousins Lois and Louie. If you look closely, you can see part of Berkeley Plantation, the site of the first Thanksgiving and the birthplace of William Henry Harrison and Benjamin Harrison."). Your speech should identify and develop ideas that contribute to the general education of your listeners.

A second pitfall to avoid is inappropriate presentational aids. We have too often seen speakers illustrate their ideas visually by holding up postcards or books and magazines containing pictures of places. This strategy is a mistake. These pictures are too small to be seen. Use presentational aids that are large enough for all audience members to see easily. On other occasions, students speaking about places have distributed photographs or postcards to be passed among audience members during the speech. Although listeners could see the presentational aids clearly as they held them, they often became preoccupied with the pictures and missed much of what the speaker was saying at the time. Reviewing the guidelines you learned in Chapter 14 will help you design and display visual aids that reinforce your speaking goals. Remember, your presentational aids should not distract your audience from the main attraction: you, speaking to inform.

Exploring *Online*

TOURING MUSEUMS ONLINE
www.virtualfreesites.com/museums.museums.html
Virtual Tours of Museums is an excellent resource for speeches about places. You can read text, view pictures, and, occasionally, listen to audio or see a short movie as you enjoy online guided tours of nearly 50 museums. From this site you can also access "Virtual Tours of Exhibits" and "Virtual Tours of Special Interest."

Speeches about Activities and Events

Activities are things you do at home, work, or school; by yourself or with friends; to learn, relax, or accomplish a required task. You may shop, play video games, deliver meals to shut-ins, collect baseball cards, cook, knit, design websites, socialize with friends, or engage in countless other activities. In Chapter 6 we suggested that one source of speech topics is your hobbies, your interests, and your experiences. Topics that you already know well, and are willing to explore more fully, often enhance your credibility and energize your delivery.

If your purpose is to inform your audience about aerial sports, you could discuss (1) gliding, (2) ballooning, and (3) skydiving. If you're interested in dancing, a speech on krumping, sometimes called street dancing or clown dancing, could be lively and informative. You could use a topical pattern, informing your audience on these key points:

   I. The origins of krumping
  II. The purposes of krumping
 III. The style of krumping
 IV. The face-painting of krumping

Events are important or interesting occurrences. Examples of topics for this type of speech include 9/11, the sinking of the *Titanic,* and the Woodstock festival. For a speech assignment that does not require you to conduct research, you could speak about an event in your life you consider important, funny, or instructive, for example: "the day I registered for my first semester in college," "the day my first child was born," or "my most embarrassing moment."

Speeches about events typically use a chronological or topical pattern. For example, if your topic is the daring Great Train Robbery that took place in Britain in 1963, you could organize your speech chronologically, describing what happened before, during, and after those famous fifteen minutes. Lisa used a topical organization in her speech on the "World's Longest Yardsale." She excited her audience with an enthusiastic discussion of this four-day event. More than 5,000 vendors spanned 450 scenic miles from Kentucky through Tennessee and into Alabama. Lisa divided her topic into two key ideas:

   I. Shopping
     A. Antiques
     B. Collectibles
     C. Furniture
     D. Food
  II. Scenery
     A. Lookout Mountain Parkway
     B. Big South Fork National River
     C. Little River Canyon National Preserve

Speeches about Processes

A process is a series of steps producing an outcome. Your informative speech about a process could explain or demonstrate how something works, functions, or is accomplished. Our students have given informative speeches on such how-to topics as reading a food packaging label, suiting up and entering a "clean room," and using an automated external defibrillator. Informative topics such as how Doppler radar works and how to make children "waterproof" (a speech on the process of teaching water safety) are both process speeches. Speeches on global positioning systems, high pressure processing of juices, nuclear medicine, and cryptography (encoding and decoding messages in a code known only to those who understand) are also potentially good informative topics about processes.

Because a process is by definition a time-ordered sequence, speeches about processes commonly use chronological organization. For example, if your specific purpose is to inform your audience of the steps to a successful job interview, you could present these key ideas:

    I. Prepare thoroughly
   II. Arrive promptly
  III. Enter confidently
  IV. Communicate effectively
   V. Follow up immediately

Speeches about processes, however, are not confined to a chronological pattern. As we have argued earlier, the best organization is the one that achieves the purpose of the speech. A student presenting a how-to speech on podcasting would likely choose a chronological pattern if the specific purpose is to explain the steps in the process. Another student might examine the process of podcasting more generally, using a topical pattern to discuss the equipment needed, the most popular file formats, the rapid growth of podcasts, or their effects on traditional broadcasters. Both speeches concern a process, but each uses an organizational pattern that's suitable for the speaker's specific purpose.

Speeches about Concepts

Speeches about concepts, or ideas, focus on what is abstract, rather than on what is concrete. Whereas a speech about an object such as the Statue of Liberty may focus on the history or physical attributes of the statue itself, a speech about an idea may focus on the concept of liberty. Other topics suitable for informative speeches about concepts include ecotourism, concrete poetry, pirate radio, traumatic obsessions, antique software, and endangered languages.

Speeches about concepts challenge you to make specific something that is abstract. These speeches typically rely on definitions and examples to support their explanations. Appropriate organizational patterns vary. A speech on Norse mythology could use a topical division and focus on key figures. Speeches about theories, particularly if they are controversial, sometimes use a pro–con division.

Drew, a student of ours, entertained all his listeners with a speech on onomastics, or the study of names. Notice how his introduction personalizes his speech and quickly involves his listeners. You can also see from his preview statement that he, too, used a topical organization for this speech about a concept:

> These are some actual names reported by John Train in his books *Remarkable Names of Real People* and *Even More Remarkable Names*. Let me repeat: These are actual names found in bureaus of vital statistics, public health services, newspaper articles, and hospital, church, and school records: E. Pluribus Eubanks, Loch Ness Hontas, Golden Pancake, Halloween Buggage, Odious Champagne, and Memory Leake.
>
> Train says in *Even More Remarkable Names* that "what one might call the free-form nutty name—Oldmouse Waltz, Cashmere Tango Obedience, Eucalyptus Yoho—is the one indigenous American art form."
>
> We're lucky. No one in here has a name as colorful as any of those. But we all have at least two names—a personal and a family name. Today, I'll tell you, first, why personal names developed, and second, the legal status of names. Finally, I have something to tell each of you about the origin of your names.

Speeches about Conditions

Conditions are particular situations: living conditions in a third-world country or social and political climates that give rise to movements such as witchcraft hysteria in Salem, McCarthyism, the women's movement, the civil rights movement, jihad, and national independence movements.

The word *condition* can also refer to a state of fitness or health. Speeches about conditions can focus on a person's health and, indeed, medical topics are a popular source of student speeches. Informative speeches about crush syndrome, obsessive–compulsive disorder, and pre-eclampsia, for example, can educate listeners about these interesting conditions. A speaker could choose as a specific purpose "to inform the audience about the causes and treatment of repetitive stress injuries." Topical organization is appropriate for many speeches about specific diseases or other health conditions.

Jean became interested in the topic of autism. She gathered information from several organizations that conducted research and provided information on this developmental disability. Reviewing the FAQ links on several Internet websites, Jean selected four questions to organize the body of her speech:

    I. What is autism?
    II. What causes autism?
   III. How do you treat autism?
   IV. Is there a cure for autism?

Though the fourth question is closed, requiring only a yes or no answer, Jean used it as an opportunity to discuss types of research being conducted in search of a cure. At the conclusion of her speech, she gave her audience the URLs for the Autism Society of America and the Center for the Study of Autism websites, so that they could continue to learn more about this important topic.

States of health also characterize the economy, individual communities, and specific institutions. Recession, depression, and full employment are terms economists use to describe the health of the economy. Speakers inform their listeners about conditions when they describe the state of the arts in their communities, assess the financial situation of most college students, or illustrate how catch limits have affected the whale population, for example.

Speeches about Issues

Speeches about issues deal with controversial ideas and policies. Topics appropriate for informative speeches on issues include the use of polygraphs as a condition for employment; uniform sentencing of criminals; freedom of expression versus freedom from pornography; stem cell research; and eliminating sugared soft drinks from school vending machines. Any issue being debated in your school, community, state, or nation can be a fruitful topic for your informative speech.

You may be thinking that controversial issues are better topics for persuasive speeches, but they can also be appropriate for speeches to inform. Just remember that an informative speech on a controversial topic must be researched and developed so that you present the issue objectively.

Two common organizational patterns for speeches about issues are the topical and pro–con divisions. If you use a topical pattern of organization for your speech about issues, it will be easier for you to maintain your objectivity. If you choose the pro–con pattern, you may run the risk of moving toward a persuasive speech. A pro–con strategy—presenting both sides of an issue—lets the listener decide which is stronger. If your informative speech on an issue is organized pro–con, guard against two pitfalls: lack of objectivity and lack of perspective.

Speakers predisposed toward one side of an issue sometimes have difficulty presenting both sides objectively:

> Carl presented a speech on the increasingly popular practice of adopting uniforms for public schools. He presented four good reasons for the practice: (1) uniforms are more economical for parents; (2) uniforms reduce student bickering and fighting over designer clothes; (3) uniforms increase student attentiveness in the classroom; and (4) uniforms identify various schools and promote school spirit. Carl's only argument against public school uniforms was that they limit students' freedom of expression. His speech seemed out of balance, and most of his classmates thought Carl favored school uniforms. Though the assignment was an informative speech, Carl's pro–con approach was ultimately persuasive. If, like Carl, you feel strongly committed to one side of an issue, save that topic for a persuasive speech.

A second pitfall that sometimes surfaces in the pro–con approach is lack of perspective. Sometimes a speaker will characterize an issue as two-sided when, in reality, it is many-sided. For example, one of our students spoke on the issue of child care. He mentioned the state family leave laws that permit mothers of newborn infants to take paid leaves of absence from work and fathers to take unpaid leaves while their jobs are protected. The speaker characterized advocates of such bills as pro-family and opponents as pro-business. He failed to consider that some people oppose such laws because they feel the laws don't go far enough; many state laws exempt small companies with fewer than 50 employees. If you fail to recognize and acknowledge the many facets of an issue in this way, you lose perspective and polarize your topic.

Exploring *Online*

DISCOVERING ISSUES
www.aldaily.com
Arts & Letters Daily is an invaluable resource for locating issues in art, criticism, culture, history, literature, music, and philosophy. Updated each weekday and once for each weekend, it features current articles, book reviews, essays, and opinions. The site also contains extensive links to newspapers, news and radio services, journals, magazines, weblogs, music sites, columnists, amusements, and a virtual reference desk.

In the preceding sections, we have discussed eight types of informative speeches. As you begin working on your own informative speech, remember to select a topic that will benefit your listeners and then communicate your information clearly and memorably. Use these eight subject categories to narrow and focus your topic. As you go through each category, use the self-, audience-, occasion-, and research-generated strategies we discussed in Chapter 6 on pages 112–120 to come up with many topics to consider for your informative speech.

As you review this list you will, no doubt, find several persuasive topics. Before excluding them, see if there are related topics suitable for an informative speech. For example, you may have some strong feelings about intercollegiate athletic programs and their role in colleges and universities. To argue their merits or to suggest that they be scaled back would make your speech persuasive rather than informative. However, you could change your focus to a more informative topic related to the issue of intercollegiate athletics. You could inform the audience of the history and intent of Proposition 48, the National Collegiate Athletic Association's statement of academic entrance requirements for college athletes.

As you go about selecting your topic, keep in mind this question: "How will the audience benefit from my topic?" Remember, your informative speech must help your audience know, understand, or apply information you provide. A speech detailing what employers look for in an employment résumé, for example, is clearly relevant to a class of students ready to enter the job market.

What about topics such as the golden age of vaudeville, the origins of superstitions, the history of aviation, the effect of music on livestock production, or the psychological aspects of aging? Maybe you think that these topics are not relevant to your audience. But part of the process of becoming an educated individual is learning more about the world around you. We are committed to this perspective and believe it is one you should encourage in your listeners.

Exploring *Online*

CHOOSING AND RESEARCHING INFORMATIVE TOPICS

http://vos.ucsb.edu

Whether you are generating ideas for informative speeches or researching a topic you've already chosen, you ought to look at this site if your subject is in the area of the humanities. *The Voice of the Shuttle: Web Site for Humanities Research* contains numerous links in areas from anthropology to science, technology, and culture. Use the Search VOS option to access this site's database of links on your topic.

Try This

Targeting an Informative Topic

Using the techniques of brainstorming and research, generate a list of two informative topics for each of the eight speech categories discussed in this chapter. Evaluate the suitability of each topic by asking and answering the following questions:

1. Does the topic interest me?
2. Is the topic likely to interest my audience?
3. Will I be able to find sufficient supporting materials on this topic?
4. Can I develop a speech that is clearly informative, rather than persuasive?
5. Does this topic meet all the criteria for the assigned speech?

Place an asterisk (*) by each topic that received five yes answers. Continue to assess and narrow this short list until you've decided on the most appropriate topic for your informative speech.

Once you have selected a topic that meets the criteria discussed in Chapter 6, ask yourself the following three questions: (1) What does the audience already know about my topic? (2) What does the audience need to know to understand the topic? (3) Can I present this information in a way that is easy for the audience to understand and remember in the time allotted? If you are satisfied with your answers to these questions, your next step is to begin developing the most effective strategy for conveying that information. Use the Theory into Practice feature below as you select an appropriate organizational pattern.

Theory into Practice

Organizing Informative Speeches

Speeches about	Use	If your purpose is to
People	Topical organization	Explain various aspects of the person's life
	Chronological organization	Survey events in the person's life
Objects	Topical organization	Explain various uses for the object
	Chronological organization	Explain how the object was created or made
	Spatial organization	Describe various parts of the object
Places	Topical organization	Emphasize various aspects of the place
	Chronological organization	Chart the history of or developments in the place
	Spatial organization	Describe the elements or parts of the place
Activities and Events	Topical organization	Explain the significance of the activity or event
	Chronological organization	Explain the sequence of the activity or event
	Causal organization	Explain how one event produced or resulted from another
Processes	Topical organization	Explain aspects of the process
	Chronological organization	Explain how something is done
	Pro–Con organization	Explore the arguments for and against the procedure
	Causal organization	Discuss the causes and effects of the process
Concepts	Topical organization	Discuss aspects, definitions, or applications of the concept
Conditions	Topical organization	Explain aspects of the condition
	Chronological organization	Trace the stages or phases of the condition
	Causal organization	Show the causes and effects of the condition
Issues	Topical organization	Discuss aspects of the issue's significance
	Chronological organization	Show how the issue evolved over time
	Pro–Con organization	Present opposing viewpoints on the issue

Guidelines for Speaking to Inform

In the remainder of this chapter, we offer ten guidelines for the informative speech. Use them as a checklist during your speech preparation, and you will deliver an excellent informative speech.

Stress Your Informative Purpose

The primary objective of your informative speech is to inform. It is important for you to be clear about this, especially if your topic is controversial or related to other topics that are controversial. For example, if you are discussing U.S. immigration policy, political correctness, or the role of women in religion, you must realize that some in your audience may already have some very strong feelings about your topic. Stress that your goal is to give additional information, not to try to change anyone's beliefs.

Be Objective

One of the most important criteria for an informative speech is objectivity. If you take a stand, you become a persuader. Informative speakers are committed to presenting a balanced view. People representing political parties, charitable organizations, business associations, and special interest groups are understandably committed to the objectives and policies of their groups. Your research should take into account all perspectives. If, as you develop and practice your speech, you find yourself becoming a proponent of a particular viewpoint, you may need to step back and assess whether your orientation has shifted from information to persuasion. If you do not think you can make your speech objective, save the topic for a persuasive speech.

Tour guides have clear, informative purposes as they describe objects and places to their audiences.

In Chapter 12, we discussed the use of language. Nothing betrays the image of objectivity that is essential in an informative speech as quickly as the inappropriate use of language. For example, in an informative speech on the pros and cons of juvenile curfew laws, one of our students used language that telegraphed his personal opinion on the issue. Even when explaining the arguments for such laws, he described them as "silly," "costly," and "unenforceable." In an informative speech, your language should be descriptive, rather than evaluative or judgmental.

Be Specific

At times we have had students tell us they will deliver a brief informative speech on "sports." This topic is far too broad and reflects little or no planning. Many of us know a little about a lot of subjects. An informative speech gives you the perfect opportunity to fill in the gaps by telling your audience a lot about a little. Narrow your topic. To help you do that, we have suggested in this chapter that you focus on specific people, objects, places, activities and events, processes, concepts, conditions, and issues. Your "sports" topic could be narrowed to sports commentators; the history of AstroTurf; Forest Hills, former home of the U.S. Open Tennis Championships; competitive team sports and male bonding; and so on. The more specific you are about your topic, your purpose, and the materials you use to support your speech, the more time you will save during your research. Your specific focus will also make your speech easier for the audience to remember.

Be Clear

If you choose your topic carefully and explain it thoroughly, your message should be clear. Do not choose a topic that is too complex. If your speech topic is Boolean polynomials or the biochemistry of bovine growth hormone, you run the risk of being too technical for most audiences. You would never be able to give your audience the background knowledge necessary to understand your presentation in the limited time you have. At the same time, be careful about using jargon. Impressing the audience with your vocabulary is counterproductive if they cannot understand your message. The purpose of informative speaking is not to impress the audience with complex data, but to communicate information clearly.

Be Accurate

Information that is inaccurate does not inform; it misinforms and has two negative consequences. First, inaccuracies can hurt your credibility as a speaker. If listeners recognize misstatements, they may begin to question the speaker's credibility: "If the speaker's wrong about that, could there be other inaccuracies in the speech?" Accurate statements help you develop a positive image or protect one you have established earlier.

Second, inaccurate information can do potential harm to listeners. Such harm can be mental or physical. For example, you give an informative speech on the life-threatening reactions some people have to sulfites, a common ingredient in certain food preservatives. Your audience leaves the class worried about their health and the damage they may have suffered. You neglected to mention that these reactions are rare. Your misinformation has harmed your audience. If audience members are unaware of factual errors, they may form beliefs that are not valid or make decisions that are not wise.

Not only should your information be accurate, but you must accurately cite the sources you used to develop your speech. Some speakers assume that because they do not take a controversial stand in an informative speech, they need not cite sources. An informative topic may require fewer sources than you would use to establish your side of a debatable point. Demonstrating the truth of your ideas and information is nevertheless important. Also, you must cite the sources for any quotations.

Limit Your Ideas and Supporting Materials

Perhaps the most common mistake speakers make in developing the content of their speeches is including too much information. Do not make the mistake of thinking that the more information you put into a speech, the more informative it is. Listeners cannot process all, or even most, of what you present. If you overload your audience with too much information, they will stop listening. Remember the adage that "less is more." To spend more time explaining and developing a few ideas will probably result in greater retention of these ideas by your listeners than the "speed and spread" approach.

Be Relevant

As you research your topic, you will no doubt discover information that is interesting but not central to your thesis. Because it is so interesting, you may be tempted to include it. Don't. If it is not relevant, leave it out.

> One student, Larry, delivered an intriguing informative speech on the Jains, a tribe of monks in India whose daily life is shaped by reverence for all living things. As you might guess, the Jains are vegetarians. But they don't eat vegetables that develop underground because harvesting them may kill insects in the soil. Larry had done a good deal of research on this fascinating topic, including his own travels in India. His firsthand knowledge was both a blessing and a curse. Listening to a speaker who had visited the Jains's monasteries certainly made the topic immediate and compelling. But because he knew so much about the country, Larry included a lot of information about India that was interesting but irrelevant to his main point. His speech became much too long.

To avoid this problem and to keep yourself on track, write out your central thesis and refer to it periodically. When you digress from your topic, you waste valuable preparation time, distort the focus of your speech, and confuse your audience.

Use Appropriate Organization

There is no one best organizational pattern for informative speeches. You choose the pattern that is most appropriate to your topic and specific purpose. However, some patterns are inappropriate for an informative speech. While a pro–con approach is appropriate, a pro–con-assessment strategy moves the speech into persuasion. Problem–solution and need–plan patterns are also inherently persuasive. The motivated sequence strategy, to be discussed in Chapter 17, is also traditionally used for persuasive, not informative, speeches. Again, this chapter's Theory into Practice feature offers suggestions for selecting an appropriate organizational pattern. If you have any doubt that your organization is informative rather than persuasive, check with your instructor.

Use Appropriate Forms of Support

As with persuasive speeches, speeches to inform require appropriate supporting materials, such as those we discussed in Chapter 8. These materials should come from sources that are authoritative and free from bias. If you discuss a controversial issue, you must represent each side fairly. For example, if your specific purpose is to inform your audience on the effects of bilingual education, you must research and present information from both its proponents and its critics.

Use Effective Delivery

Some speakers have a misconception that delivery is more important for a persuasive speech than for an informative speech. Regardless of the type of speech, show your involvement in your speech through your physical and vocal delivery. The suggestions offered in Chapter 13 are appropriate for the speaker who informs as well as the speaker who persuades. Your voice and body should reinforce your interest in and enthusiasm for your topic. Your delivery should also reinforce your objectivity. If you find your gestures, body tension, or voice conveying an emotional urgency, you have likely slipped into persuasion.

Key Points

Guidelines for Informative Speaking

1. Stress your informative purpose.
2. Be objective.
3. Be specific.
4. Be clear.
5. Be accurate.
6. Limit your ideas and supporting materials.
7. Be relevant.
8. Use appropriate organization.
9. Use appropriate forms of support.
10. Use effective delivery.

After reading this chapter you should know the principles and characteristics of informative speaking, understand how they contribute to effective speaking, and be able to apply them as you prepare your speeches. Our student Susan Chontos understood and used these principles when she delivered the following speech to her classmates. Notice how her supporting materials and her organization of the introduction, body, and conclusion contributed to a seamless, organic whole. In the marginal annotations we have indicated the major strengths of Susan's speech, as well as some improvements she might make.

Annotated Sample Speech

The Amish: Seeking to Lose the Self [5]
Susan Chontos, San Antonio College, San Antonio

1 Our society is one that caters to the individual. We have seminars on how to be assertive, books on how to better your self-image, and countless articles on how to take control of your life. It seems that everyone today is in a great rush to find themselves. There

Susan's topic is apparent by the end of her first paragraph.

is, however, a small group of people in our country who are seeking rather to lose themselves. They are the Amish.

2 The Amish were a small group of persecuted immigrants who came to this country 250 years ago seeking religious freedoms. They quietly settled along the northeastern coast of the United States, primarily in Pennsylvania. Last summer, I visited this Pennsylvania settlement and toured an Amish home. So, this morning, I would like to briefly examine the three major tenets of the Amish faith. They are based on Biblical scriptures. They are separation from the world, simplicity in the world, and a strong dedication to their group.

3 The first major tenet of the Amish faith is a desire to be separate from this world. 2 Corinthians 6:17 states, "Therefore come out from them and be ye separate, says the Lord." You can see how the Amish separate themselves from society in many ways. First, they are an endogamous people. That is, they marry within their group. Marriage to non-Amish outsiders is strictly forbidden. Also, they separate themselves in that they speak a Germanic dialect among themselves, and this further distances them from their non-Amish neighbors. In addition, the Amish are separate from what would be considered the public life of most Americans. They don't seek public office. They don't participate in local sports teams or any other community organizations. Most recently, the Amish have separated themselves from our public school system. The Amish believe in attending school only from elementary up through the eighth grade, which they feel is adequate time to learn the basic skills necessary to succeed in Amish culture. In the 1950s, however, states began requiring attendance up through high school. The Amish parents and children protested this and were fined and even imprisoned. According to the *Encyclopedia of World Cultures,* this controversy was finally resolved in 1972, when the Supreme Court unanimously ruled in favor of the Amish separating themselves on the basis of their religious beliefs.

4 This Amish desire to remain separate from our world—to be in our world but not of our world—has required them to strike many compromises with the rise of modern technology around them. Don Kraybill, in his book *The Puzzles of Amish Life,* describes some of these compromises. For example, the primary mode of transportation for the Amish is the horse and buggy. Today, however, they are permitted to ride in automobiles, although they can't own one. Similarly, they may use a telephone, but they can't have one in their home. In addition, they may use modern farm equipment, but only if it's pulled by their plow horses. Certainly, it is becoming more and more difficult for the Amish to separate themselves from our modern world and its conveniences.

5 The second major tenet of the Amish faith is the desire to be simple, or plain. 1 Peter 3:3–4 states, "Your beauty should not come from outward adornment, such as braided hair or the wearing of gold jewelry or fine clothes. Rather, it should be that of your inner self." Therefore, the Amish don't seek any material possessions at all. Rather, they strive to be plain and simple. Nicknamed "the plain people," nowhere is this plainness more evident than in their dress. In their dress, the Amish don't allow anything that represents style: no buttons, belts, bright colors, or pockets. Instead, they use hooks and ties and straight pins to fasten their clothes. As you can see in this picture [presentational aid], the Amish men are restricted to wearing only black and white. They must always have a wide-brimmed hat to cover their head, and you can tell that this man is married since he has a beard but no mustache. The Amish women are allowed a little more variation in their clothing, and they can wear different combinations of dark solids—dark purples or blues or browns. The Amish women must also wear bonnets to cover their hair, and they must never cut or curl their hair.

6 Not only do the Amish have simple ways of dressing, but they also provide very simple toys for their children to play with. I have here an example of a wooden bear toy [presentational aid]. This toy is very popular among Amish boys, since it has fun marbles and moving parts. The Amish girls, however, as you might expect, like to play with dolls.

This section of the introduction establishes Susan's credibility and previews the three key ideas she will develop in the body of the speech.

Here Susan begins to apply the "4 S's" to her first point. She signposts ("first") and states her idea (separation from the world). She supports her point using testimony, definition, and examples.

In her fourth paragraph Susan reiterates her point, provides support using contrast, and briefly summarizes her key idea. She does not include a transition statement.

Susan signposts her second key idea and again uses a Biblical quotation to explain the Amish tenet of simplicity. She uses several examples and five presentational aids in paragraphs 5 through 7 to illustrate both this simplicity and the exceptions the Amish allow themselves.

And here is a traditional Amish doll [presentational aid]. There are two things I'd like for you to notice about this doll. First, her simple dress. Notice again the dark colors and the ties and hooks instead of buttons. The second thing I'd like for you to notice is that she doesn't have a face. The Amish don't believe in putting the human face on any object, or even having their pictures taken. They feel that this represents a graven image and is a sign of personal pride.

7 There are two exceptions to this rule of simplicity for the Amish people, and these are the only two things that they may wear, or hang, or display in their homes. The first exception to the rule of being a simple people is their quilts [presentational aid]. Notice again the dark colors and the simple patterns. John Ruth, in his book *A Quiet and Peaceable Life,* states that quilts began as a way for frugal housewives to use leftover scraps of cloth. Now quilts have grown into a beautiful expression of the artistry and creativity of the Amish women. A second exception to this rule of being a simple people is what's known as *Fraktur* art [presentational aid]. And this dates back to the Middle Ages and is characterized by calligraphy writing and bright colors, with hearts or birds or flowers. What the Amish will do is they will write scripture verses in this *Fraktur* style and they will hang these plaques in their homes to remind them to be humble. We can see how this inner desire of the Amish to be a simple people is reflected outwardly in such tangibles as their dress and their toys.

8 The third and final tenet of the Amish faith is a strong commitment to the group. 1 John 3:16 states, "This is how we know what love is. Jesus Christ laid down his life for us, and we ought to lay down our lives for our brothers." John Hostetler, in his book *Amish Society,* describes some of the ways the Amish care for and are committed to their brothers. Perhaps the most vivid example of this is what would be known as the barn-raising day. If any of you have seen the movie *Witness,* you will recall the barn-raising scene, where the entire community of twenty to thirty families came together to join forces and build a barn. Barn-raising day is a very common occurrence among Amish communities, and they use it to provide new barns, either for newlyweds who are just starting out, or for families whose original barns have been destroyed by fire or rains. And this barn is actually a gift from the entire community to that family, since all of the builders of the barn share in the cost of the materials.

9 A second way we can see how the Amish are dedicated to their group is in times of hardship. For example, if there is a birth in the family or a death in the family, the neighbors of that family will come together and they will cook for the family, care for their children, tend their crops, and do everything necessary until that family is able to emotionally and physically recuperate.

10 Lastly, we can see how the Amish are dedicated to their group in the way they care for their elderly. The Amish elderly are treated with the greatest respect, and they hold all of the authority and leadership positions in the community. Instead of sending their elderly to nursing homes, they build additions onto their farmhouses, where the elderly grandparents can live comfortably and have their needs provided for. Certainly, this strong dedication to the group has its benefits. John Ruth, in *A Quiet and Peaceable Life,* describes one of these benefits as "a powerful deliverance: to sense the blending of your thoughts and prayers with those who would give their lives for you."

11 This morning we have briefly reviewed the three major tenets of the Amish faith. That is separation from this world, simplicity in the world, and strong dedication to their group. Clearly, the Amish have chosen a different path in life than have most of us: one that is not so fancy, not so modern, not so fast-paced, and, perhaps, one that is not so bad after all.

Reprinted with permission of the speaker.

Susan could speak more economically near the end of this paragraph by saying, "Second, notice that she doesn't have a face."

Throughout her speech Susan mentions Don Kraybill, John Ruth, and John Hostetler without stating their qualifications regarding the topic. She concludes with a summary of her second point, but again does not include a transition statement to her final idea.

Susan signposts and states her third idea clearly. She divides this main point into three subpoints, which she discusses in these three paragraphs. Her example of barn-raising is particularly vivid, as is her discussion of how the Amish treat elderly people in paragraph 10.

In her final paragraph Susan summarizes her key ideas and uses repetition in her closure statement. Involving the audience more actively could have enhanced her psychological closure.

Summary

As part of your work in this class, you will present at least one *speech to inform*. An informative speech assignment provides you with the opportunity to be the sender rather than the receiver of information; it requires you to research a subject of your choice, synthesize data from various sources, and pass it on to your listeners. Your goals as an informative speaker are to expand listeners' knowledge, assist their understanding, or help them apply the information you communicate.

Classifying informative speeches by subject gives you an idea of the range of possible topics and the patterns of organization each subject typically uses. Speeches about *people* are often arranged chronologically, but may explore subtopics, such as aspects of the subject's life. Speeches about *objects* use spatial organization if your purpose is to describe various parts of the object, chronological organization if your purpose is to explain how the object was created, and topical organization if your purpose is to explain how the object is used. Speeches about *places* use chronological organization if your purpose is to explain the history or stages of development of the place, topical organization if you want to emphasize various aspects of the place, and spatial organization if your purpose is to describe the parts of the place. Speeches about *activities* and *events* also use one of three methods of organization: chronological organization to explain a sequence of events, topical organization to explain the significance of events, and causal organization to show how one event produced or led to another.

Speeches about *processes* can use chronological organization to tell listeners how to do something or how something is done, pro–con organization to explore the arguments for and against the process, or causal organization to discuss what caused or causes some process and the effects that result. Speeches about *concepts* typically use topical organization as the speaker discusses various aspects, definitions, or applications of the concept.

Speeches about *conditions* may use topical organization to discuss various aspects of the condition, chronological organization to trace the stages or phases of a condition, or causal organization to show the causes of the condition and the effects that the condition has. Finally, speeches about controversial *issues* may use a pro–con organization if your purpose is to explore opposing viewpoints on the issue, topical organization if your purpose is to discuss the significance of the issue, or chronological organization if your purpose is to discuss how the issue has evolved.

As you begin to prepare an informative speech on a subject from one of these categories, ask yourself three questions: (1) How much does the audience already know about this topic? (2) What does the audience need to know in order to understand this topic? (3) Can I present this information in the allotted time so that the audience will understand and remember it? When you answer these questions, you can be sure that your topic is sufficiently narrow and appropriate to your listeners.

Finally, we offer ten guidelines to help you develop and deliver an effective informative speech. (1) Begin with an overall picture; let your audience know that your purpose is to inform. (2) Be objective in your approach to the topic and the language you use. (3) Be specific; narrow the topic you have chosen. (4) Be clear; remember that your audience probably knows much less about this topic than you do. (5) Be accurate; misinformation can harm your listeners. (6) Limit the ideas and supporting material that you try to include. Covering a few ideas in depth is usually more informative than discussing many ideas superficially. (7) Be relevant; do not be sidetracked by interesting but irrelevant information. (8) Use the pattern of organization best suited to achieving your specific purpose. (9) Use appropriate forms of support. (10) Use lively, effective speech delivery.

Practice Critique

Evaluating and Comparing Two Informative Student Speeches

Melissa Janoske's and Darla Goodrich's speeches in the Appendix are examples of informative speeches delivered in two different introductory public speaking classes. Read the transcripts or watch the videos. Then, using the guidelines you have learned in this and previous chapters, compile a list of strengths and weaknesses in each speech. Suppose you were judging these speeches in a competition. Which speech would you select for the first-place award? In writing, provide the reasons for your decisions.

Exercises

1. Write and bring to class five specific purpose statements for speeches on any topics you choose. Do not identify the general purpose (to inform or to persuade) in these statements, for example: "To _____ the audience on the effects of fragrance on personal health, worker productivity, and product sales." Two or three of these statements should be for informative speech topics; the remainder for persuasive topics. Be prepared to exchange your paper with another classmate. Each person should write "inform" or "persuade" in the blank provided in each specific purpose statement. Return the papers and discuss the answers.

2. Using the list you generated in this chapter's Try This feature, select one topic from each of four categories, and write a specific purpose statement for each. Think about how you could develop each specific purpose, and then discuss what organizational pattern you think would be most appropriate.

3. Suppose you are asked to speak to a group of incoming students on the topic "Using the Campus Library." Your objective is to familiarize new students with the physical layout of the library so that they can research more efficiently. Outline the key ideas you would develop in your speech. What types of presentational aids would you use to reinforce your message?

4. Select an emotionally charged issue (political correctness, Internet filtering in public libraries, or legaliza-tion of drugs, for example). Brainstorm aspects of the issue that would be appropriate for an informative speech. State the specific purpose of the speech and briefly describe what you could discuss. In discussing your topic, point out what makes the speech informative rather than persuasive.

5. Select an informative speech from *Vital Speeches of the Day*, some other published source, or the Internet. Analyze the speech to see if it adheres to the guidelines discussed in this chapter. If it does, show specifically how it fulfills the goals of each guideline. If it does not, list the guidelines violated, and give examples of where this occurs in the speech. Suggest how the speaker could revise the speech to meet the guidelines.

6. Using the speech you selected in Exercise 5, identify and write down the specific purpose of the speech. Does it meet the characteristics of a speech to inform? Why or why not? What method of organization did the speaker use? Do you think this is the best pattern to achieve the speech's specific purpose? Why or why not?

7. Analyze a lecture by one of your instructors to see if it adheres to the guidelines listed in this chapter. Which guidelines for informative speeches do you think also apply to class lectures? Which do not apply? If the instructor violated any guidelines you think apply to lecturing, how might the instructor remedy this?

*T*he Strategy of Persuasion

chapter

16

> *The only reason to give a speech*
> *is to change the world.* —NICK MORGAN

M edia specialist Tony Schwartz, producer of political commercials for presidential and other political candidates, combined the words *manipulation* and *participation* to create a new word—

partipulation. He argues that voters are not simply manipulated by campaign and advertising strategists. Voters do, after all, have the option of rejecting the messages politicians present to them. So Schwartz contends, "You have to participate in your own manipulation."[1]

Persuasion is similar to Schwartz's concept of partipulation. The persuasive speaker tries to move the audience to his or her side of an issue. But, as we discussed in Chapter 2, you, the critical listener, have a right and an ethical responsibility to choose whether you are persuaded. Speakers should view listeners as active participants in the communication process. As a speaker, your goal should be to establish a common perspective and tap values your listeners share, not to manipulate or trick your audience. Charles Larson echoes this speaker–listener orientation:

> [T]he focus of persuasion is not on the source, the message, or the receiver, but on *all* of them equally. They all *cooperate* to make a persuasive process. The idea of *co-creation* means that what is inside the receiver is just as important as the source's intent or the content of messages. In one sense, *all* persuasion is *self-persuasion*—we are rarely persuaded unless we participate in the process.[2]

In this chapter and in Chapter 17, we examine the three elements Larson mentions—source, message, and receiver—that interact to co-create persuasion.

We began this chapter with a quotation by educator and author Nick Morgan. He credits that statement to an old friend, a speechwriter, who "meant it as a challenge. It was his way of saying that, if you're going to take all the trouble to prepare and deliver a speech, make it worthwhile. Change the world. Otherwise, why bother?"[3] Today, Morgan gives this advice at workshops for leaders of corporations, colleges, and government. Though changing the world may seem unrealistic and intimidating at this stage of your life, you do have the opportunity to help shape the values, beliefs, and behaviors of those around you and in this class. As Henry Ward Beecher stated, "The humblest individual exerts some influence, either for good or evil, upon others." Ethical and effective communicators can make a permanent, positive difference in the lives of others.

In this chapter we introduce you first to the *strategy* of persuasion. Why is persuasive speaking important? How does the persuasive process work? What are some principles and strategies you can use as you prepare your message? The answers to these questions provide a blueprint for your speech. In the next chapter, we introduce you to the *structure* of persuasion. You will use your blueprint as you build your persuasive speech. You will study how to organize and test the arguments of your speech. You will then discover how to integrate those arguments into a clear and convincing message.

The Importance of Persuasion

It is impossible to isolate yourself from persuasive messages, either as a receiver or as a sender. Each day, we are bombarded by appeals from political, business, education, and

Dana Reeve, a persuasive voice on behalf of people affected by paralysis, bases many of her arguments on factual information as well as personal experience. She is seen here speaking on "Caregivers and Health Policy: Lessons for the Future from Ten Years with Chris."

religious leaders, among others, who try to enlist our support, sell us products or services, and change our behaviors. Persuasive speaking is both inescapable and consequential. While we can all cite examples of messages that are intentionally misleading and patently unethical, we can also list persuasive messages that benefit us as senders and receivers.

In this public speaking course, you will probably be asked to deliver a persuasive message to your classmates, and that will challenge and benefit you in several ways. First, it will require you to select an issue you think is important and to communicate your concern to your audience. Voicing your beliefs will demand that you confront their logic and support; in other words, you must test your ideas for their validity. That process, in turn, will require that you gather supporting materials and draw valid inferences from them as you develop your arguments. Approached seriously and researched energetically, a persuasive speech assignment can develop both your critical thinking and speech-making skills. Finally, you may also use it as an opportunity to improve your school or community. Change can occur when people speak and audiences are moved. You can be an instrument of constructive social and political change.

As a listener, you also benefit by participating in the persuasive process. A speaker can make you aware of problems around you and show how you can help solve them. You hear other points of view and, consequently, may better understand why others have beliefs different from yours. A speech that challenges your beliefs often forces you to reevaluate your position. Your "partipulation" can correct erroneous beliefs or confirm valid beliefs you hold. Regardless, participating as a listener also heightens your critical thinking and improves your ability to explain and defend your beliefs. Finally, as a listener you have an opportunity to judge how others use persuasive speaking techniques, thus enabling you to improve your own persuasive speaking.

A Definition of Persuasion

Persuasion is the *process of influencing another person's values, beliefs, attitudes, or behaviors.* Key to understanding persuasion is the concept of influence. Too often, we equate persuasion with power, but, as you will learn, persuasion does not necessarily require power. Power implies authority or control over another. For example, employers who want you to be on time will state that policy and then issue reprimands, withhold

persuasion: the process of influencing another person's values, beliefs, attitudes, or behaviors.

promotions, and even terminate your employment to ensure that you obey the policy. They do not need to persuade you. Likewise, in this class, you probably speak on the days assigned because failing to do so would hurt your grade. In each instance the power residing in some other person's position shapes your behavior, at least in part.

Persuasion, however, is more accurately equated with influence than with power. As a speaker you try to influence the audience to adopt your position. You probably have little power over your listeners, and they have the freedom to reject your intended message. Suppose, for example, that your speech instructor wants your class to attend a lecture given on campus by author Tom Wolfe. You are not required to attend, and there is no penalty or reward. To influence you, however, your instructor emphasizes the importance of this opportunity by telling you about Wolfe's background. To make certain that you know who Wolfe is, your instructor lists some of Wolfe's best-known books: *A Man in Full, The Bonfire of the Vanities,* and *The Right Stuff.* Your instructor also mentions Wolfe's reputation as a lively, entertaining speaker, quoting some of Wolfe's controversial views of modern novels.

In this case, your instructor is using influence rather than power to persuade. The concept of persuasion as influence means that you can bring about change whether or not you are the more powerful party in a relationship. You can also see that, compared to power, influence requires more effort, creativity, and sensitivity, but in the long run is probably more effective. If persuasion is our attempt to influence others, let's look more closely at the types of influence we can achieve.

Types of Influence

Our definition of persuasion suggests three types of influence. You can change, instill, or intensify your listeners' values, beliefs, attitudes, and behaviors. Your goal is to move your listeners closer to your position. It may help you to think of this process as a continuum:

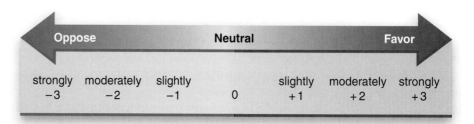

Remember, when you speak to persuade, you are speaking to listeners who may oppose, be indifferent to, or support your position. What strategy will you adopt to reach them? The information you gather and the assumptions you make about your audience before your speech determine the strategy you use as you develop your remarks.

Many students preparing persuasive speeches make the mistake of thinking that they must change their audiences' opinions from "oppose" to "favor," or vice versa. Take the example of Chris, who argued in his persuasive speech that the National Collegiate Athletic Association should adopt a playoff system to determine each year's college football champion. After his speech, only one classmate who opposed a playoff system said that Chris had persuaded her to support the proposal. Chris thought he had failed to persuade. Further class discussion, however, proved him wrong. A few listeners said they had changed their position from strong opposition to mild opposition. In addition, several who already supported the playoff system said that Chris's arguments had strengthened their opinion. And several listeners who were neutral before the speech found that Chris persuaded them to agree with him. As you can see, even though Chris persuaded only one audience member to move from "oppose" to "favor," his speech was quite successful. Persuasion occurs any time you move a listener's opinion in the direction you advocate, even if that movement is slight.

Change

The most dramatic response you can request of your listeners is that they *change* a value, belief, attitude, or behavior. The response you seek is dramatic because you attempt to change opposition to support, or support to opposition. For example, if you discover that the majority of your listeners eat foods high in cholesterol, you could give a persuasive speech encouraging them to alter their diets. You would be trying to change your audience's behaviors.

Instill

Second, you can attempt to *instill* a value, an attitude, a belief, or a behavior. You instill when you address a particular problem about which your listeners are unaware or undecided. If you persuade your audience that a problem exists, you have instilled a belief. A speaker trying to persuade an audience that Intensive Care Unit psychosis is a serious health problem would first need to define that term for listeners unfamiliar with it. Then, by documenting cases of "psychotic activity occurring specifically in the intensive care unit among patients . . . which can cause them to fall out of bed, pull out breathing tubes, or . . . pull out central [arterial] lines," the speaker could instill a belief in the audience.[4]

Intensify

Finally, you may try to *intensify* values, beliefs, attitudes, or behaviors. In this case you must know before your speech that audience members agree with your position or behave as you will advocate. Your goal is to strengthen your listeners' positions and actions. For example, your audience may already believe that recycling is desirable and may even do it occasionally. If your persuasive speech causes your listeners to recycle more frequently, you have intensified their behavior. Your persuasive speech may even encourage them to persuade family and friends to adopt similar behavior. When you change believers into advocates and advocates into activists, you have intensified their attitudes and behavior.

Your persuasive speech will target your audience's thoughts and actions. It's true that we sometimes act without fully considering the consequences of our actions; we also sometimes think about taking certain actions without ever acting. For this reason, your persuasive speech may aim to change your listeners' thoughts, actions, or both. Your goal determines the type of persuasive speech you will be giving, so let's consider your options in more detail.

Types of Persuasive Speeches

Persuasive speeches are generally classified according to their objectives. An effective persuasive speech may change what people believe, what people do, or how people feel. Persuasive speeches, then, may be divided into speeches to convince, to actuate,

Theory into Practice
TIPS

The Pyramid of Persuasion

You can't know *how* to change your listeners until you know *what* you want to change. Do you want to influence what they believe, how they feel, how they act, or some combination of these?

- The upward arrows in the figure below reflect a traditional view of how we effect change. You know that your listeners appreciate economic prosperity (value). If you convince them that a new convention center would help revive your city's economy (belief), they may favor its construction (attitude), and vote for the necessary bond issue to pay for it (behavior).

- The arrows in the model point down as well. Behaviors may filter down to influence audience attitudes, beliefs, and values. You might persuade listeners to volunteer their time at a community adult literacy program (behavior), knowing that the experience will show such volunteers how helpful they can be (attitude) and how hard adult learners work to improve themselves (belief). The first-hand experience your speech induces can thus lead to beliefs that are more permanent than a speech alone can achieve.

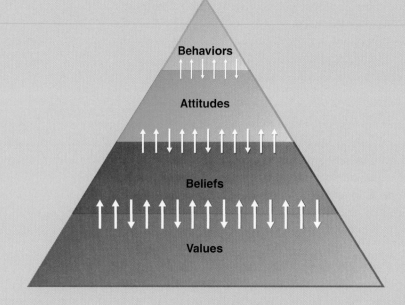

or to inspire. Understanding these divisions can help you determine your primary objective as you work on your speech, but keep in mind that persuasive speeches often include two or more objectives. For example, if your purpose is to get your audience to boycott fur products, you must first convince them of the rightness of your cause. We usually act or become inspired after we are convinced.

Speeches to Convince

speech to convince: a persuasive speech designed to influence listeners' beliefs or attitudes.

In a **speech to convince**, your objective is to affect your listeners' beliefs or attitudes. Each of the following specific purpose statements expresses a belief the speaker wants the audience to accept:

To convince the audience that "hate speech" is constitutionally protected

To convince the audience that hybrid cars are commercially feasible

To convince the audience that there is a constitutional right to privacy

To convince the audience that sealed adoption is preferable to open adoption

The speaker's purpose in each of these speeches is to establish belief. While a speech to convince does not require listeners to act, action may be a natural outgrowth of their belief. So be aware that you may need an action step in your speech. For example, if you convince your audience that exit polling harms democracy, but you suggest no remedy for the problem, you may leave your audience frustrated. In this case, you can suggest a simple action step, such as urging your listeners to express their views to their elected representatives. When a speech includes this step, it becomes a speech to actuate.

Speeches to Actuate

A **speech to actuate** may establish beliefs, but it always calls for the audience to act. The specific purpose statements listed here illustrate calls for action:

To move, or actuate, the audience to donate nonperishable food to a local food bank

To move the audience to spay or neuter pet cats and dogs

To move the audience to begin a low-impact aerobic workout program

To move the audience to sign a petition banning smoking in all public places on campus

Speeches to Inspire

A third type of persuasive speech is the **speech to inspire.** The speech to inspire attempts to change how listeners feel. Examples include commencement addresses, commemorative speeches, eulogies, and pep talks. Some specific purposes of speeches to inspire are these:

To inspire the audience to honor the service of fallen fire fighters

To inspire the audience to appreciate those who made their education possible

To inspire audience members to give their best efforts to all college courses they take

The purposes of inspiration are usually noble and uplifting. These speeches typically have neither the detailed supporting material nor the complex arguments characteristic of speeches to convince or actuate.

Thus far, we have seen the importance of audience involvement in the important process of persuasion. We have provided a definition of persuasion and discussed the various goals that persuasive speakers can have. In the following section we will discuss six important strategies that apply to all persuasive speeches.

Persuasive Speaking Strategies

As far back as the era of Ancient Greece, we can find evidence of people giving advice on how to be an effective persuasive speaker. Aristotle, for example, devoted much space in his classic work *The Rhetoric* to the subject. Aristotle discussed three modes of persuasion speakers have at their disposal: *ethos, logos,* and *pathos.*[5] These three modes

speech to actuate: a persuasive speech designed to influence listeners' behaviors.

speech to inspire: a persuasive speech designed to influence listeners' feelings.

Leaders in business, government, religion, education, and other areas need to know when and how to convince, actuate, and inspire their audiences.

remain an important foundation today for our understanding of persuasive speaking. What do these terms mean and how can they help you as you prepare a persuasive speech?

Ethos, or speaker credibility, derives from the character and reputation of the speaker. *Logos,* or logical appeal, relies on the form and substance of an argument. *Pathos,* or emotional appeal, taps the values and feelings of the audience. Like Aristotle, we have emphasized throughout this text that any speech is shaped by the speaker, the message, and the audience. Each of these variables affects the finished product. After all, no two people will give the same speech on the same topic to the same audience. Therefore, no person can give you a simple formula to make your persuasive speech effective. Your strategy for each speech must be based on your unique situation and on your own creativity. Nevertheless, we can give you some strategies, or guidelines, to follow as you prepare your persuasive speech.

Key Points

Persuasive Speaking Strategies

1. Establish your credibility.
2. Focus your goals.
3. Connect with your listeners.
4. Organize your arguments.
5. Support your ideas.
6. Enhance your emotional appeals.

Establish Your Credibility

As a speaker, your first available source of persuasion is your own credibility, or *ethos.* **Credibility** is simply your reputation, and it helps determine how your listeners evaluate what you say. Research confirms what you already probably believe: The higher your perceived credibility, the more likely the audience is to believe you.[6]

Speaker credibility is fluid, varying according to your listeners. You possess only the credibility your listeners grant you. If you pepper your speaking with humor, for example, some listeners may see you as lively and interesting, while others may think you frivolous. You probably have as many different images as you have audience members.

ethos: speaker credibility.

logos: logical appeal.

pathos: emotional appeal.

credibility: the degree to which listeners believe a speaker.

Credibility also varies according to time. Your credibility before, during, and after your speech may change. These chronological divisions are sometimes referred to as initial, derived, and terminal credibility.[7] Your image or reputation prior to speaking comprises your **initial credibility.** The more the audience knows about you, the firmer your image.

But what if your listeners do not know you personally? Even in this case, you still bring varying images to the speaking occasion. For example, if you are a spokesperson for an organization, you may assume the image of that organization in the minds of your audience. What if someone asked you to describe the kind of person who belongs to the Democratic Party, the Republican Party, the Sierra Club, or the National Rifle Association? An image probably comes to your mind for each group. If a representative from one of those associations were to speak to you, you would make certain assumptions about the individual based on what you know about that organization. Just as you do with strangers, you form impressions of your classmates based on what they say in class, how they dress, whether they arrive at class on time, their age and appearance, and any organization to which they belong. They have also formed impressions of you, of course. Such images constitute your initial credibility.

Derived credibility is the image the audience develops of you as you speak. The moment you enter the presence of your listeners, you provide stimuli from which the audience can evaluate you. As you begin your speech, the number of stimuli multiplies quickly. If you begin your speech with an offensive joke, listeners' images of you will become more negative. When you appeal to your listeners' values and present reasoned arguments to advance your position, you enhance your image. Your information obviously helps your audience judge your credibility. They will also judge your nonverbal behaviors, such as gestures, posture, eye contact, and appearance. If you convey confidence, authority, and a genuine concern for your listeners, you will enhance your credibility.

Terminal credibility is the image the audience has of you after your speech. Even this credibility is subject to change. The listener may be caught up in the excitement and emotion of your speech and end up with an elevated opinion of you. As time passes, that evaluation may moderate. As you can see, the process of generating and maintaining credibility is ongoing. In this class, for example, your credibility at the conclusion of one speech will shape your initial credibility for your next speech.

Studies demonstrate that a speaker having high credibility can more successfully persuade than a speaker having low credibility. Clearly, you need to pay careful attention to your credibility at each stage in order to deliver a successful persuasive speech. How do you enhance your image? Communication theorists agree that speakers who appear competent, trustworthy, and dynamic are viewed as credible speakers.[9] If your audience believes that you possess these qualities, you can be effective in persuading them.

Convey Competence. In this class you are among peers, and so your audience probably considers you a fellow student, rather than an expert on your chosen topic. How

> *"One can stand as the greatest orator the world has known, possess the quickest mind, employ the cleverest psychology, and have mastered all the technical devices of argument, but if one is not credible, one might just as well preach to the pelicans."*
>
> —GERRY SPENCE[8]

Exploring Online

READINGS ON RHETORIC
www.rpi.edu/dept/llc/webclass/web/project1/group4/index.html
Visit this student-generated website for easily understood explanations of the concepts of *ethos, logos,* and *pathos.* The site includes links to examples and dictionary definitions of each rhetorical form.

initial credibility: a speaker's image or reputation before speaking to a particular audience.

derived credibility: the image listeners develop of a speaker as he or she speaks.

terminal credibility: the image listeners develop of a speaker by the end of a speech and for a period of time after it.

My persuasive speech argued for banning or regulating realistic toy guns, in particular realistic-looking pellet guns. Being a police officer, I knew I had the credibility to speak on the topic. But how was I going to establish it for my audience, who knew nothing about me? I remembered that one way was to acknowledge my personal involvement and experience with the topic. I had experienced a heart-stopping incident one night about a year ago. It was the deciding factor for choosing my topic, and I decided to relate it in my introduction. To develop emotional appeals, I focused part of my research on statistical information about injuries to children. Nothing angers any of us more than a child needlessly dying or being seriously injured. After my speech, one of my classmates, a mother herself, stated she had no idea these "toys" were so dangerous. She was so moved that she was actually thinking about getting more involved in this issue. I know that if I hadn't obtained a better understanding of *ethos, logos,* and *pathos,* I would never have had such strong speech content nor would I have felt so confident in giving my speech.

—Gene Fox, *San Antonio College*

Key Points
Guidelines for Enhancing Your Image of Competence

1. Know your subject.
2. Document your ideas.
3. Cite your sources.
4. Acknowledge personal involvement.

can you get them to see you as knowledgeable and worthy of their trust? Your task is to establish an image of **competence** on your subject. Four strategies will help you do that.

First, the obvious: *Know your subject.* From which of these people would you be more likely to buy a new PDA: a salesperson who can answer all your questions about the product or someone who doesn't know the answers and doesn't care to find out? The answer is obvious, isn't it? In a persuasive speaking situation, you as speaker are a salesperson, and your audience members are consumers. To speak ethically, you must be well informed about your subject. You will discover that the more you read and listen, the easier it is to construct a message that is both credible and compelling.

Not only should you know your specific topic, but you should also understand how it interacts with related topics. Just as the salesperson must know the PDA and how easy it is to operate, you should comprehend both the content and the context of your persuasive message. Persuading your classmates to begin recycling low-density plastics (LDPs) does you little good if your area has no processing plant for LDPs and thus recyclers will not accept them. In addition, you will feel foolish if an audience member asks after your speech, "Did you know that no recycling center will accept those plastics?" This is where your research helps you by enhancing your expertise on your subject. A well-researched speech increases persuasion by contributing to your image as a well-informed individual. In a public speaking course such as this, the image building you do is cumulative. Thorough, quality research not only enhances your credibility on the immediate topic, but also generates positive initial credibility for your next appearance before the same group.

Second, you can bolster your image of competence if you *document your ideas.* You document ideas by using clear, vivid, and credible supporting materials to illustrate them, as we discussed in Chapter 8. Unsupported ideas are mere assertions. Though your listeners don't expect you to be an expert on your topic, they need assurance that what you say is corroborated by facts or experts. Providing documentation supports your statements and increases your believability.

A third strategy for enhancing your credibility is to *cite your sources.* Simply presenting the data on which your conclusions are based is insufficient. Remember, your

competence: listeners' views of a speaker's qualifications to speak on a particular topic.

Combining personal credibility with logic and emotion, Michael J. Fox advocates funding cutting-edge research to find a cure for Parkinson's disease.

audience is not going to have the opportunity to read your bibliography. You need to tell your listeners the sources of your information. Citing sources enhances the credibility of your ideas by demonstrating that experts support your position. It also requires that your sources be unbiased and of good quality.

Fourth, *acknowledge any personal involvement* or experience with your subject. Listeners will probably assume that you have an edge in understanding color blindness if you let them know you are color-blind. They will probably make the same positive assumption if you have diabetes and are speaking on diabetes. If you have worked with terminally ill patients and are speaking on hospice care, mentioning your experience will similarly add authority to your ideas.

Convey Trustworthiness. A second criterion of speaker credibility is **trustworthiness,** and it should tell us two things about you. First, we should trust you as an individual: You are honest in what you say. Second, we should trust you with your topic: You are unbiased in what you say. A speaker can demonstrate trustworthiness in two ways:

1. *Establish common ground with your audience.* If listeners know that you understand their values, experiences, and aspirations, they will be more receptive to your arguments. When you let them know you identify with those values, experiences, and aspirations, you increase your persuasiveness.

2. *Demonstrate your objectivity in approaching the topic.* The information and sources you include in your speech should demonstrate thorough, unbiased research. One student gave his speech on cigarette smoking, arguing that its harmful effects were greatly exaggerated. He relied on studies sponsored by the tobacco industry. Few in the

trustworthiness: listeners' views of a speaker's honesty and objectivity.

audience were persuaded by his evidence. He undermined his image of trustworthiness because he limited his research to sources the audience considered biased on the topic, sources that had a financial interest in supporting one side of the issue. The same fate befell a student who tried to enlist contributions of time and money to the American Red Cross using only Red Cross promotional literature as her sources.

Convey Dynamism.   A third element of credibility is **dynamism.** Competence and trustworthiness are obviously legitimate criteria used to determine speaker credibility, but you may wonder why we include personal dynamism on this list. Dynamism is more closely associated with delivery than with content. We enjoy listening to speakers who are energetic, vigorous, exciting, inspiring, spirited, and stimulating. But should speakers whose delivery is static, timid, and unexciting be considered less credible than their more exuberant counterparts? Perhaps not, and the ethical listener will focus more on the content than on the form of the message. Yet you should know that studies continue to document dynamism as an element of speaker credibility, and it would be wise for you to develop this attribute.

Dynamism contributes to persuasion because it conveys both confidence and concern. You show confidence largely through your speech delivery. If you appear tentative or unsure of yourself, the audience may doubt your conviction. To the extent that you can strengthen your verbal, vocal, and physical delivery, you can enhance your image of confidence and, hence, your credibility. No one expects you to give a professional-level performance. Remember that mastering public speaking is a process that involves study and practice. If you take yourself and your speech seriously, you will do fine.

Dynamism also demonstrates a concern for the audience and a desire to communicate with them. If your delivery seems flippant, distracted, or detached from the audience, your listeners will assume that you are not concerned about the topic or about them. On the other hand, conveying enthusiasm for your topic and your listeners communicates a strong positive message.

> **dynamism:** listeners' views of a speaker's confidence, energy, and enthusiasm for communicating.

As a speaker, then, present a well-researched and documented message and communicate it in an honest and unbiased manner. Your verbal, vocal, and physical

Try This

Assessing and Building Your Credibility

Write a self-profile that describes how you think your audience views you as an advocate of the position you plan to take in an upcoming persuasive speech. Consider their perceptions of your competence and trustworthiness on the topic, as well as the dynamism you'll convey as you deliver your message. Include both positive statements (e.g., "My classmates probably re- spect my willingness to consider diverse opinions based on my previous speeches.") and equivocal statements (e.g., "My audience has no reason to believe that I have any special expertise on this specific topic."). Develop a plan of action for constructing and delivering your speech that will help overcome any negative perceptions and build your speaker credibility.

delivery should show you to be a fluent, forceful, and friendly individual serious about the issue you address. If listeners perceive you to be competent, trustworthy, and dynamic, you will have high source credibility and, hence, be an effective persuader.

Focus Your Goals

Limit Your Goals.   A common mistake many beginning speakers make is to seek dramatic change in the values, beliefs, attitudes, and behaviors of their listeners. In our experience, the speaker who can accomplish this is rare, particularly if he or she seeks change on highly emotional and controversial issues such as abortion, gun control, capital punishment, religion, or politics. Keep in mind that the more firmly your audience is anchored to a position, the less likely you are to change their attitudes. It is unrealistic for you to expect dramatic change in a person's beliefs and values in a one-shot, five- to ten-minute speech. Instant conversions occur, but they are rare. Rather than try to convince your audience to support (or oppose) the death penalty, try to convince them of a limited goal, a smaller aspect of the topic; for example, argue that capital punishment deters crime (or does not). Once a listener accepts that belief, you or another speaker can build on it and focus on a successive objective: support for (or opposition to) the death penalty.

Which specific purpose statement in the following pairs is the more limited and reasonable goal?

> To persuade the audience that exposure to violent video games promotes aggression, *or*

> To persuade the audience that habitual exposure to violent video games promotes aggression in children

> To persuade the audience that actively involving students in classroom learning is desirable, *or*

> To persuade the audience that team learning is a cost-effective way to promote student learning

In both cases, the second statement is the more limited and potentially more persuasive. To be successful as a persuasive speaker, you must view persuasion as a process of moving a listener incrementally through a range of positions. Your speech may be only one part of this process. Select a realistic goal and channel your efforts toward achieving it. Remember the persuasive principle: *Persuasion is more likely if your goals as a speaker are limited, rather than global.*

Argue Incrementally.   A second principle builds on the first one: *Persuasion is more permanent if you achieve it incrementally.* To be effective and long-lasting, persuasion should occur incrementally, or one step at a time. This principle becomes more important if your audience is likely to hear counterarguments to your argument. In any speech, you speak for a fixed amount of time. The greater the number of points you must prove, the less time you have to support and explain each. Because you must move through several steps, your limited time may force you to abbreviate your support of some of these steps. When your listeners hear another speaker attack one of those steps later, they may lack sufficient evidence to counter those attacks; as a result, what you accomplished may be only temporary. Your goal should be to "inoculate" your listeners to possible counterarguments. The stronger your arguments, the greater the likelihood that you will bring about enduring change in the opinions of your audience. If you know your audience has been exposed to counterarguments, you may need to address those arguments before introducing your own.

Connect with Your Listeners

Which source advising you to "take Carolyn DeLecour for public speaking; she's a great teacher" would you find more persuasive: a friend who is also a college student or a counselor at your school? If you are typical, your answer is "my friend," particularly if that friend has already taken a public speaking class with Professor DeLecour. The counselor may have taken DeLecour's public speaking class, may know DeLecour personally, or may have heard many complimentary remarks about DeLecour from her former students. But the counselor may also just be trying to fill a class that other students are avoiding.

PRIMER OF PRACTICAL PERSUASION

www.as.wvu.edu/~sbb/comm221/primer.htm

For an excellent discussion of persuasion theories, visit this website authored by Dr. Steven Booth-Butterfield of West Virginia University. Of particular interest is his explanation of "Message Characteristics" and how organization, evidence, repetition, examples, and other strategies affect message effectiveness.

Persuasion is more likely if a speaker establishes common ground with the audience. The example above illustrates this concept. You are probably more easily persuaded by people similar to you than by those who are different. Your friends, for example, are credible sources not because they possess special expertise, but because they share your values and interests. We all reason that individuals having backgrounds like ours will view situations and problems as we would. Furthermore, we believe that people who share our beliefs will investigate an issue and arrive at a judgment in the same manner we would if we had the time and the opportunity.

One way to increase your persuasion, then, is to identify with your listeners. Sonja, a weekend news anchor for a local television station, was asked to speak to a college television production class on employment opportunities in television. Notice how Sonja used the strategy of identification in her introduction as she focused on experiences she shared with her listeners.

> Seven years ago a timid freshman girl sat in a college classroom much like this. Just like you, she was taking a TV production class. And like some of you, I suspect, she dreamed of being in front of a camera someday, sitting at an anchor desk, reporting the news to thousands of families who would let her come into their homes through the magic of television.
>
> There was little reason to predict that this girl would achieve her dreams. In many ways she was rather ordinary. She didn't come from a wealthy family. She didn't have any connections that would get her a job in broadcasting. She was a B student who worked part-time in the university food service to help pay for her education. But she had a goal and was determined to attain it. And then one day, it happened. An instructor announced that a local TV station had an opening for a student intern. The instructor said the internship would involve long hours, menial work, and no pay. Hardly the opportunity of a lifetime! Nevertheless, after class, she approached the instructor, uncertain of what she was getting into. With her instructor's help, she applied for and received the internship. It is because of that decision that I am now the weekend anchor of the city's largest television station.

The rest of Sonja's speech focused on the importance of student internships in learning about the reality of the broadcast media and making contacts for future references and employment. Her opening comments made Sonja a more believable speaker by bridging the gap between her and her listeners. Sonja's suggestions had more impact on her audience because she had established common ground with them.

Four principles of persuasion should guide how you establish common ground with your audience. Each of these principles requires you to understand your listeners as a result of some careful audience analysis.

Assess Listeners' Knowledge of Your Topic. Persuasion is more likely if the audience lacks information on the topic. In the absence of information, a single fact can be compelling. The more information your listeners possess about an issue, the less likely you are to alter their perceptions.

Arturo applied this principle in a speech to persuade his audience that auto insurance companies should not be allowed to set rates based on drivers' credit ratings. Few of his listeners knew that the practice occurred. Yet, by citing just a handful of credible sources, Arturo proved that the practice increased beginning in the mid-1990s, had been adopted by 92 percent of insurers by 2001, and was "nearly universal" by March 2002. As a result, drivers with the worst credit ratings paid rates that were, in some cases, 40 percent higher than those with the best ratings.

New and surprising information such as this can have great persuasive impact. Of course, this principle also has significant ethical implications. Ethical speakers will not exploit their listeners' lack of knowledge to advance positions they know are not logically supported.

Assess How Important Your Audience Considers Your Topic.

Ken, Andrea, and Brad gave their persuasive speeches on the same day. Ken's purpose was to persuade the audience to support the school's newly formed lacrosse team by attending the next home game. Andrea's topic concerned the increasing number of homeless adults and children in the city. She told the class about Project Hope, sponsored by the Student Government Association, and asked everyone to donate either a can of food or a dollar at designated collection centers in campus dining halls or in the Student Center. Finally, Brad advocated legalization of marijuana, citing the drug's medical and economic potential.

Which speaker do you think had the most difficult challenge? In answering this question you must consider the audience. A significant factor is how important the audience considers the topic.

The importance of a topic can increase the likelihood of persuasion. Audience members in the above example probably agreed with both Ken and Andrea, and both may have been successful persuaders. Listeners who viewed combating hunger as a more important goal than supporting the lacrosse team were probably more persuaded by Andrea and may have contributed to Project Hope.

Just as the importance of a topic can work for you as a persuasive speaker, it can also work against you and decrease the likelihood of persuasion. It is surely easier, for example, for someone to persuade you to change brands of toothpaste than to change your religion. The reason is simple: Your religion is more important to you. Brad probably had a tougher time persuading his listeners than did either Ken or Andrea. Legalizing marijuana probably ran counter to some deeply held audience opinions, and the intensity of those beliefs and values may have made them more resistant to Brad's persuasive appeals. The importance of an issue will vary according to each audience member, and you need to take this into account as you prepare your persuasive appeal.

Motivate Your Listeners.   A third principle of persuasion is that persuasion is more likely if the audience is self-motivated in the direction of the message. People change their values, beliefs, attitudes, and behaviors because they are motivated to do so. To be an effective persuader, you must discover what motivates your listeners. This requires an understanding of their needs and desires. How can you do this? You can enhance your persuasive appeal by following three steps. First, identify as many of the needs and desires of your listeners as possible. Second, review your list, and select those that your speech satisfies. Third, as you prepare your speech, explain how the action you advocate fulfills audience needs. If you discover that your speech does not fulfill the needs or desires of your listeners, then you have probably failed to connect with these

listeners. They may receive your speech with interest, but such listeners will probably not act on your message. What you intended as a persuasive speech may in fact be received as informative.

Relate Your Message to Listeners' Values.   Finally, persuasion is more likely if the speaker's message is consistent with listeners' values, beliefs, attitudes, and behaviors. We have discussed the importance of consistency elsewhere in this text, but we think it important enough to mention here. People want to establish consistency in their lives. We expect coherence between our beliefs and actions, for example. In fact, we will call someone a hypocrite who professes one set of values, but acts according to another. Your ability to persuade is thus enhanced if you request an action that is consistent with your audience's values.

Use this principle of consistency in constructing your persuasive appeal. For example, we have had students who persuaded their classroom audience to oppose the use of animals in nonmedical product testing. They first identified the beliefs that would cause a person to challenge such tests—for example, product testing harms animals and is unnecessary. Next they showed their audience that they share these beliefs. Once they accomplished that, the speakers then asked their listeners to act in accordance with their beliefs and boycott companies that continue to test cosmetics on animals, because continuing to buy such products would be inconsistent with their beliefs.

Organize Your Arguments

In Chapter 3 you learned that most of us are inefficient listeners. Immediately after your speech, chances are that your classmates will remember only 50 percent of what they heard. Two days later that figure drops to only 25 percent. And a speech that is poorly organized in the first place has even less of a chance of surviving in the minds of audience members. Using the organizational strategies presented in Chapters 9 and 10 can increase your listeners' retention of your message. This is especially important if you seek long-term changes in your audience's attitudes and behaviors or if you want your listeners to deliver your message to a larger audience.

In addition to what you've already learned about structuring your speech, we offer one more organizing principle: *Persuasion is more likely if arguments are placed appropriately.* Once you have determined the key arguments in your speech, you must decide their order. To do that, you must know which of your arguments is the strongest. Assume for a moment that your persuasive speech argues that the public defender system needs to be reformed. Assume, too, that you are using a problem–solution organization, discussed in Chapter 9. Your first main point and the arguments supporting it could be:

1. The public defender system is stacked against the defendant.
   A. Public defenders' caseloads are too heavy.
   B. Public defenders have too little experience.
   C. Public defenders have inadequate investigative staffs.

One of these three arguments will probably be stronger than the other two. You may have more evidence on one; you may have more recent evidence on it; or you may feel that one argument will be more compelling than the other two for your particular audience. Assume that you decide point B is your strongest. Where should you place it? Two theories of argument placement are the primacy and recency theories.

primacy theory: the assumption that a speaker should place the strongest argument at the beginning of the body of a speech.

Primacy Theory.   **Primacy theory** recommends that you put your strongest argument first in the body of your speech to establish a strong first impression. Because you are most likely to win over your listeners with your strongest argument, this theory suggests that you should win your listeners to your side as early as possible. Primacy theorists tell you to move your strongest argument to the position of point A.

Recency Theory.   Recency theory, on the other hand, maintains that you should present your strongest argument last, thus leaving your listeners with your best argument. They would have you build up to your strongest argument by making it point C.

If your listeners oppose what you advocate, you may want to present your strongest argument first. Moving them toward your position early in the speech may make them more receptive to your other ideas. If your audience already shares your beliefs and attitudes and your goal is to motivate them to action, you may want to end with your most compelling argument. Both the primacy and recency theorists generally agree that the middle position is the weakest. If you have three or more arguments, therefore, do not place your strongest argument in a middle position. When you sandwich a strong argument between weaker ones, you reduce its impact.

Support Your Ideas

Well-supported ideas benefit your speech in two ways. First, they provide an ethical underpinning for your position. Ethical speakers test their ideas for validity and support and share that support with their listeners. Second, as we mentioned in discussing credibility, well-supported ideas enhance your *ethos*. Research demonstrates that using quality evidence, citing your sources, and employing valid reasoning increase your credibility as a speaker.[10]

Two sections of this book will help you construct a convincing case for your position. In Chapter 8, we discussed the types of supporting material and tests of evidence that you can use to prove your arguments. You can use examples, definitions, narration, comparison and contrast, statistics, and testimony to give your ideas credibility. In Chapter 17, we will introduce you to the elements of an argument, describe five types of arguments you can use in your persuasive speaking, and define several categories of faulty reasoning you should avoid.

recency theory: the assumption that a speaker should place the strongest argument at the end of the body of a speech.

Ethical Decisions

Dynamism: Masking or Making Credibility

In this chapter, we noted that a speaker's ability to influence an audience depends, in part, on his or her credibility. Credibility, in turn, is a function of an audience's perception of the speaker's competence, trustworthiness, and dynamism. Dynamic speakers convey confidence; they also communicate a sense of concern for their audiences, a desire to make a connection with their listeners.

Unfortunately, dynamism sometimes masks a speaker's questionable motives. Both Hitler and Mussolini, for example, were dynamic speakers. So were many other leaders throughout the ages who led their followers into battle for unjust causes. How can listeners separate a speaker's dynamism from his or her trustworthiness and competence? If a dynamic speaker *seems* to care about the audience, how do listeners determine whether the speaker's feelings are sincere? Moreover, what ethical responsibility do listeners have to evaluate the credibility of speakers whose delivery is timid and unexciting? Is it legitimate to tune out a speaker's message if he or she is not effective at making an emotional connection with the audience? In general, what guidelines should listeners follow when they evaluate a speaker's dynamism and credibility? Write your answers to the questions above, and be prepared to discuss them in class.

Enhance Your Emotional Appeals

As we indicated near the beginning of this chapter, *pathos* is the appeal to emotions. Among the emotions speakers can arouse are your anger, envy, fear, hate, jealousy, joy, love, or pride. When speakers use these feelings to try to get you to believe something or act in a particular way, they are using emotional appeals.

Many of the feelings listed above seem negative—anger, fear, hate, and jealousy, for example. Consequently, you may consider emotional appeals as unacceptable or inferior types of proof. Perhaps you have even heard someone say, "Don't be so emotional; use your head!" It is certainly possible to be emotional and illogical, but keep in mind that it is also possible to be both emotional and logical. Is it wrong, for example, to be angered by child abuse, to hate racism, or to fear chemical warfare? We don't think so. The strongest arguments combine reason with passion. *Logos* and *pathos* should not conflict but complement each other.

Jessica began her persuasive speech by relating a personal narrative she remembered from her childhood:

> I was four years old; my sister was only two. It was not long after we reached my grandma's house that the phone rang. I could hear ambulance and police sirens head toward the highway as tears were forming in my mom's eyes. There had been a car accident. My dad was rushed to the hospital; his little Fiesta car was totaled. He had been hit on the passenger side by a man driving a station wagon, and, fortunately, both my dad and the other driver survived. Because the other driver fell asleep at the wheel, my dad went to the hospital instead of coming home that night to his family.

Jessica quoted several sources with examples and statistics related to driver fatigue, including these powerful statistics:

> Drowsy driving is estimated to cause about 20 percent of [all vehicle] accidents, 1.2 million a year, more than drugs and alcohol combined. It accounts for an astonishing five percent of all fatal crashes, and 30 percent of fatal crashes in rural areas.[11]

Did the speaker construct a logical argument? Yes. She presented examples and statistics to support her position. Did Jessica construct an emotional argument? Again, yes. She tapped her listeners' need for safety and their compassion for those who have suffered because of drowsy drivers. *Logos* and *pathos* coalesced to form a compelling argument.

As you can see, when properly constructed, emotional appeals make your listeners active participants in the development of your message. By tapping their feelings, you involve them psychologically and physiologically. Use the following four guidelines to develop and enhance the *pathos* of your persuasive speech.

Tap Audience Values. The first, and probably most important, guideline for developing emotional appeals is to *tap audience values*. As we have mentioned repeatedly, you must conduct careful audience analysis before you can deliver an effective speech. Demonstrate in your speech how your audience's values support your position. In Chapter 5, we discussed how you can relate your topic to audience needs (see pages 96–99). Try some of the strategies discussed in that section. The more attached listeners are to the values a speaker promotes, the more emotional is the appeal. Part of your responsibility as a speaker is to make that connection evident to your listeners.

Use Vivid Examples. A second strategy for enhancing emotional appeals is to *use vivid, emotionally toned examples*. An example may not be sufficient to prove your point, but it should illustrate the concept and generate a strong audience feeling. Notice how the following student used visual examples to enhance the *pathos* of his speech.

Duncan selected as the specific purpose of his speech to persuade the audience to become members of Amnesty International. He had joined the organization because he felt that, as an individual, he could do little to help end torture and executions of prisoners of conscience throughout the world. As part of a concerted worldwide effort, however, he saw the opportunity to further social and political justice. His speech included ample testimony of persecution coupled with statistical estimates of the extent of the problem.

Duncan wanted to infuse his speech with convincing emotional appeals to support the data. After presenting the facts, he paused and spoke these words to his listeners:

> In the last four minutes you've heard about the anguish, the pain, the suffering, and the persecution experienced by thousands of people, simply because they want to be free and follow their consciences. I want you not only to *hear* of their plight, but also to *see* it.

Duncan pushed the remote control button of a slide projector and proceeded to show five slides of people brutalized by their own governments. He did not speak, but simply showed each slide for ten seconds. After the last slide, he spoke again:

> They say a picture is worth a thousand words. Well, these pictures speak volumes about man's inhumanity to man. But these pictures should also speak to *our consciences*. Can we stand back, detached, and do nothing, knowing what fate befalls these individuals?

Duncan then told the audience how they could become involved in Amnesty International and begin to make a difference. Duncan's speech had a powerful effect because he touched his audience's emotions with vivid examples.

Use Emotive Language. Duncan also employed *pathos* by using a third technique: he *used emotive language*, such as "the anguish, the pain, the suffering, and the persecution . . ." In Chapter 12, we discussed the power of words. Nowhere can words be more powerful than when they work to generate emotional appeals. Notice how former President Bill Clinton begins with fairly neutral language and builds to a crescendo with increasingly emotive words in the following example:

> The divide of race has been America's constant curse. Each new wave of immigrants gives new targets to old prejudices. Prejudice and contempt, cloaked in the pretense of religious or political conviction, are no different. They have nearly destroyed us in the past. They plague us still. They fuel the fanaticism of terror. They torment the lives of millions in fractured nations around the world.[12]

Destroyed, plague, fuel, fanaticism, terror, torment, and *fractured* are all words carefully chosen to evoke strong feelings among the audience.

Use Effective Delivery. Finally, you should *use effective delivery* to enhance emotional appeals. As we discussed in Chapter 13, when a speaker's verbal and nonverbal messages conflict, we tend to trust the nonverbal message. For that reason, speakers who show little physical and vocal involvement with their speeches usually come across as uninterested or even insincere. When you display emotion yourself, you can sometimes generate audience emotion.

Before leaving the subject of *pathos,* a few parting comments are in order. Emotional appeals are powerful persuasive tools. They can stir passions, intensify beliefs, and impel actions. Speakers have an ethical responsibility to use emotional appeals wisely. Emotional appeals are never in order if the speaker disregards the logical basis of the speech. Emotion and logic are best used in concert with each other.

It is important to remember that these three modes of persuasion—*ethos, logos,* and *pathos*—all work to enhance your persuasive appeal. The best persuasive speeches combine all three. Effective persuaders are credible, present logically constructed and supported arguments, and tap the values of their listeners.

Summary

Persuasion is a dynamic activity requiring the participation of a speaker, a message, and at least one listener. Politicians, educators, businesspeople, and religious leaders flood us with persuasive appeals daily. To benefit from sound persuasion and avoid the pitfalls of flawed or unethical persuasion, speakers and listeners must understand what persuasion involves.

Persuasion is the process of influencing another person's values, beliefs, attitudes, or behaviors. *Influencing* can mean changing attitudes or actions, instilling new beliefs, or simply intensifying people's feelings about their existing beliefs or behaviors. The Pyramid of Persuasion helps you determine the specific purpose of your speech and generate arguments you can use to achieve that purpose. A persuasive speech aimed at changing beliefs and attitudes, but not requesting any overt behavior of listeners, is called a *speech to convince.* A *speech to actuate* seeks to change behaviors. A *speech to inspire* encourages positive changes in the way listeners feel about their beliefs or actions.

Three modes of persuasion, discussed at least as early as the time of Aristotle, are *ethos, logos,* and *pathos. Ethos,* the first source of persuasion available to speakers, is their credibility or believability. *Logos* is a logical appeal based on the form and substance of the message. It appeals to the listener's intellect and reasoning. *Pathos,* or emotional appeal, relies on the audience's feelings for its persuasive impact.

Whether you target values, beliefs, attitudes, behaviors, or a combination of these, your job as an effective persuader will be easier if you are aware of some persuasive strategies. First, the higher your perceived credibility, the more likely the audience is to believe you. A starting point for persuasion, then, is to establish your credibility. Some speakers have *initial credibility* with a particular audience, based on the listeners' prior knowledge of the speaker. An unknown speaker may take on the credibility of the organization he or she represents. All speakers have *derived credibility,* developed from the ideas they present in their speech and their speech delivery, and *terminal credibility,* based on the audience's evaluation of speaker and message after the speech.

Competence, trustworthiness, and *dynamism* are three components of a speaker's credibility. To build images of competence, speakers should know their speech subjects, document their ideas, cite their sources, and mention any special experience or involvement that they have with their topics. To demonstrate trustworthiness, speakers should establish common ground with their audiences and show evidence of objectivity through thorough, unbiased research. Because listeners associate dynamism with the energy, vigor, and friendliness of a speaker's delivery, developing a dynamic image requires showing confidence about speaking and concern for the well-being of the audience.

A second persuasive strategy deals with your goals as a speaker. You are more likely to persuade if your goals are limited, rather than global. In addition, your persuasiveness with an audience will be more permanent if you achieve it incrementally, or step by step.

A third strategy is that persuasion is more likely if a speaker establishes common ground with the audience. Connecting with your listeners requires careful analysis of your audience's knowledge, values, and motivation. You are more likely to persuade an audience if your listeners lack information on your subject. Persuasion is also related to how important the audience considers your topic. Its importance (or relative unimportance) can boost your persuasiveness for listeners who are self-motivated in the direction of your message. Persuasion is also more likely if your message is consistent with listeners' values, beliefs, attitudes, and behaviors.

A fourth persuasive strategy deals with the organization of your message. Persuasion is more likely if the speaker's arguments are appropriately placed within the speech. *Primacy theory* asserts that you should place your strongest argument first in the body of your speech. *Recency theory* maintains that you should build up to your strongest argument, placing it last in the body of your speech. The lesson for public speakers is to avoid placing a strong argument between weaker ones.

A fifth persuasive strategy is to provide solid support for the ideas you present. Well-supported ideas provide an ethical underpinning for your speech and enhance your *ethos* for the audience. Use a variety of quality supporting materials, cite your sources, and reason logically to increase your persuasiveness.

Finally, you can increase your persuasiveness by enhancing the emotional appeals of your message. To develop powerful emotional appeals, a speaker should tap audience values; use vivid, emotionally toned examples; use emotive language; and display emotion in the physical and vocal delivery of the speech. *Pathos* should complement, rather than replace, the logical structure of a speech.

Practice Critique

Analyzing Persuasive Appeals in a Powerful Speech

Martin Luther King, Jr., delivered his "I Have a Dream" speech on August 28, 1963. The speech helped elevate a national debate on equal access to employment opportunities, public accommodations, home ownership, and voting rights. In 1964, 1965, and 1968, the Congress and President Lyndon Johnson approved legislation that prohibited racial discrimination in these areas. Some historians claim that Dr. King's powerfully persuasive speech spurred creation of a coalition to support this legislation.

As you read the transcript of Dr. King's speech in the Appendix or watch the video, note how he directed his arguments to several diverse audiences: black and white; rich and poor; powerful and powerless; nonviolent and militant. Identify appeals that are designed to convince, actuate, and inspire listeners. What values and beliefs did Dr. King tap to influence his listeners' attitudes and behaviors? How did he seek to establish common ground with such diverse audiences?

Exercises

1. List on a sheet of paper the messages aimed at persuading you that you have heard, read, or seen during the past 24 hours. These messages may come from friends, family members, politicians, religious leaders, advertisers, newspaper or magazine columnists, television commentators, and so forth.

2. Select three print, broadcast, or Internet advertisements for the same kind of product (soft drinks, insurance, automobiles, and so on). Discuss the persuasive appeals of each ad. Which one do you think is the most effective? Why? Could any of these strategies of persuasion be incorporated in a speech? Provide some examples.

3. Select a copy of an editorial from your campus newspaper, a local or national paper, or *Editorials on File*. Identify the beliefs, attitudes, and values implicit in the editorial, as well as any behaviors the writer advocates.

4. Select a topic, and write a specific purpose statement that seeks dramatic change in the behavior or attitude of your audience. Divide the change you seek into several incremental steps. Discuss what you would need

to prove to achieve each step. Could any of these steps be the basis for a speech by itself?

5. Listen to a speaker on C-SPAN, *The NewsHour with Jim Lehrer*, a news interview show, or some other broadcast. Keep a chronology of the speaker's initial, derived, and terminal credibility. What changes occurred in your impression of the speaker? What accounted for those changes? What might the speaker have done to improve his or her credibility?

6. Brainstorm a list of values you think the majority of your class holds. You might use the PERSIA framework (political, economic, religious, social, intellectual, and artistic) to get you thinking about a broad range of values. Refer to this list as you discuss how you could develop an audience-centered persuasive speech for an upcoming assignment.

7. Locate a speech that you feel includes examples of unethical emotional appeals. Many political campaign speeches are a good source of these examples. Explain why the emotional appeals are questionable.

*T*he Structure of Persuasion

chapter

17

> *Good argument, like good architecture, reveals its structural elements so that what is being said and how it is being supported lie open to the consideration of all.* —PERRY WEDDLE

Structuring sound arguments and detecting flawed reasoning are important skills for the public speaker. Thomas Gilovich, professor of psychology at Cornell University, explains:

> Thinking straight about the world is a precious and difficult process that must be carefully nurtured. . . . In the words of Stephen Jay Gould, "When people learn no tools of judgment and merely follow their hopes, the seeds of political manipulation are sown." As individuals and as society, we should be less accepting of superstition and sloppy thinking, and should strive to develop those "habits of mind" that promote a more accurate view of the world.[1]

Developing your own persuasive arguments and responding to others' persuasive appeals exercises all your critical thinking skills. Your research involves *information gathering* as you formulate questions and collect data to answer them. As you develop new lines of inquiry based on the research you have conducted, you will use your *generating* skills. As you develop your arguments from various sources, you'll be *remembering, integrating,* and *organizing.* Throughout the process you'll be *analyzing* and *evaluating* your evidence, discarding weaker sources, and *focusing* your speech more sharply.

In the previous chapter we discussed the *strategy* of persuasion. You learned what persuasion is and also some strategies you can use to develop a convincing message. In this chapter we discuss the *structure* of persuasion. We will show you how to construct an argument and how to detect faulty arguments. In addition, you will study characteristics and types of persuasive propositions and special organizational patterns you can use in your persuasive speeches.

Exploring *Online*

CONSTRUCTING ARGUMENTS

http://owl.english.purdue.edu/handouts/general/gl_logic.html

This section of the Purdue University Online Writing Lab website provides both examples and exercises to help you understand logic and to practice constructing arguments. It also includes information on various types of fallacies.

Making and Refuting Arguments

Aristotle's description of the effective persuasive speech sounds simple, doesn't it? Before you can prove your case, however, you must understand the structure of arguments and how those arguments are organized in your speech. In the previous chapter, we referred to this type of persuasive appeal as *logos.* Let's see how all this works.

> **"** *A speech has two parts. Necessarily, you state your case, and you prove it.* **"**
>
> —ARISTOTLE[2]

Steps of an Argument

Suppose you make the following statement: "I am more confident about public speaking now than I was at the beginning of this course." If someone asked you to justify your statement, you could respond in this way:

> Well, I experience fewer symptoms of nervousness. I seem to worry less about facing an audience. The night before my speech, I sleep better than I used to. I establish eye contact with my audience now, rather than avoiding looking directly at them, as I did in my first speech. I no longer nervously shift my weight from foot to foot, and I've stopped playing with my high school class ring and have started gesturing.

Together, your statement and response constitute an argument. You have made a claim ("I am more confident about public speaking now") and then supported it with evidence—in this case, examples from personal observation. Aristotle would be pleased!

At its simplest level, an argument includes three steps:

1. You make a claim.
2. You offer evidence.
3. You show how the evidence proves the claim.[3]

The *claim* is the conclusion of your argument. It is a statement you want your listeners to accept. Some examples of claims are:

The influence of race undermines the accuracy of eyewitness testimony.

Textbook prices are too high.

The most important thing you can learn in college is how to learn.

Visual aids make ideas easier to remember.

The validity of any claim depends on the evidence supporting it. **Evidence** is the supporting material you use to prove a point. As an advocate, you have an obligation to support your position with valid arguments. In other words, you must offer your listeners reasons to accept your conclusion.

Speakers may introduce a claim and then present supporting materials, or they may introduce evidence and show how that information leads to an inescapable claim. In her persuasive speech on the need to reform the organ donation system, Ali's first key idea was that an organ shortage existed. Notice how she gently introduced her claim, and then presented statistical evidence and cited her sources. She let the evidence build to a more compelling claim, that "the demand for organs far outweighs the supply":

> First, let us examine the extent of the organ shortage in the United States.
>
> Every patient waiting for an organ transplant in the United States is registered with the United Network for Organ Sharing or UNOS. The UNOS is a non-profit organization established by Congress in 1984 that seeks to encourage organ donation. *US News & World Report* of January 13, 2003, reports that every morning more than 83,000 people awaiting a new heart, liver, kidney, or other organ wake up to a brutal imbalance of supply and demand.
>
> During the next 24 hours, while it is likely that 66 of them will receive a transplant, 17 will die. And by the way, another 115 new names will be added to the waiting lists. Day by day, the human toll and the organ deficit grow. For example, the *Tulsa World* of August 18, 2003, reports that one of the most common organ transplants is the kidney. Approximately 13,000 kidney transplants are done each year in the United States, but there are almost 50,000 patients waiting for kidneys. There are also approximately 5,000 liver transplants done in the U.S. every year, but the waiting list for these organs is still about 15,000.

Exploring *Online*

THE TOULMIN MODEL OF ARGUMENT
www.unl.edu/speech/comm109/Toulmin
The Toulmin Project Home Page, created by Charles Soukup and Scott Titsworth of the University of Nebraska at Lincoln, offers a substantial introduction to Stephen Toulmin's popular model of argumentation. Designed specifically for students enrolled in communication classes, this website provides a thorough explanation of the model with examples and practice test questions.

Makes a claim.

Offers evidence.

evidence: supporting material a speaker uses to prove a point.

Shows how the evidence proves the claim.

Clearly the demand for organs is due to the low number of actual registered donors and a system unable to meet the exponentially growing demand for organ transplants in this country.[4]

Refuting an Argument

In Chapter 9 we offered the "4 S" strategy for developing your key ideas in a speech. In a persuasive speech you signpost your claim, state your claim, support your claim with quality evidence, and summarize, showing how your evidence proves your claim. That's how you develop and present a persuasive argument. But how do you refute, or dispute, another's argument? The question is relevant because topics you and your classmates select for your persuasive speeches will involve a spark of controversy. There is always another side, perhaps several sides, in addition to the one the speaker presents. You may even select a topic because you read or heard a statement with which you disagreed. Persuasive speakers and critical thinkers must know both how to prove arguments and how to refute them. For each argument you **refute**, you may want to use the following four-step **refutational strategy**:

1. State the position you are refuting.
2. State your position.
3. Support your position.
4. Show how your position undermines the opposing argument.

refute: to dispute; to counter one argument with another.

refutational strategy: a pattern of disputing an argument by (1) stating the position you are refuting, (2) stating your position, (3) supporting your position, and (4) showing how your position undermines the opposing argument.

States position to be refuted.

Seth selected his topic, the importance of language skills for career advancement, after hearing a comment by his roommate. He presented the following argument in his speech. Notice the marginal comments that show how Seth used each of the four steps of refutation:

Last week, my roommate stormed into the dorm room shaking a paper he just got back from his English composition teacher. He threw the paper on his bed and screamed, "I can't wait until I get out of college, away from teachers who are obsessed with grammar, and into the real world where people judge you on what you say, not how you say it!" Sound familiar? I bet many of us have felt the same way after getting back a paper with all those picky corrections marked in red ink. As my roommate says, "In the real world, you're not judged on your grammar."

Speaking with Confidence

I began drafting a persuasive speech on business ethics, targeting my peers as the next generation of business leaders. It quickly became clear, however, that I failed to research my audience. Many of them intended to pursue professions other than business, so I decided to show why it's important for *all* students to take ethics courses. I supported my claims with evidence from expert and unbiased sources. I gave examples of recent business scandals to show some of the problems created by unethical behavior. I shared what I learned in my ethical leadership class and quoted from the textbook. I argued that a better understanding of ethics would give all of us guidelines to use when we faced unexpected and difficult decisions in the future. Near the end of my speech, I provided my audience with specific ethics courses for all the majors in our class, and asked them to look into these classes for fall registration. Knowing that I had supported my claims well, I was confident that I had persuaded my audience to consider taking these ethics courses.

—**Brian Davis**, *Virginia Tech University*

Well, my roommate's wrong. Grammar is important in the business world just as it is here in the classroom. How we express our ideas *is* important to our success. At least that's the conclusion of Camille Wright Miller, and she ought to know. She's a Ph.D. and a consultant on workplace issues. In her January 13, 2002, *Roanoke Times* column, she told about a candidate who was interviewed for an important position in a company, one that would pay more than $100,000. After the interview, one of the owners said, "How many times did he say 'I seen.'"? Those two words cost him the job. And this isn't an isolated example. Dr. Miller says, "Many . . . organizations recognize the power of language and the negative impact of grammatically flawed language on their customers and employees." Employers evaluate grammar "in determining an individual's intelligence, capabilities, and fitness to be a manager."

States speaker's position.

Supports speaker's position.

Shows how speaker's position undermines opposing argument.

Using incorrect language can keep us from landing a good job or getting promoted once we're hired. So, I'm going to tell my roommate that he probably should listen to what his English composition teacher says. And all of us should read those picky comments written in red on the papers we get back, too. Because there's some truth in the cliché "Good grammar never goes out of style."

Statesman and diplomat Adlai Stevenson proclaimed, "Freedom rings where opinions clash." Democracy and education are about making and testing arguments. The quality of our decisions—indeed, the quality of our lives—depends on what we know and how we use that information. You can use five types of argument as you select and develop the ideas for your speech and refute arguments you encounter. Knowing how to construct and test arguments will also help you as you listen to the speeches of others.

Types of Argument

Speakers can justify their claims by using any of five types of argument. You may offer proof by arguing from example, analogy, cause, deduction, or authority. The type of argument you select will depend on your topic, the available evidence, and your listeners. You may combine several types of argument in a single persuasive speech. In fact, the best speeches usually do combine types of argument. Let's look in more detail at these five basic types of argument available to you as a persuasive speaker.

Argument by Example

Argument by example is an inductive form of proof. **Inductive argument** uses a few instances to assert a broader claim. For example, if you have struggled through calculus and analytic geometry, you may conclude that math is a difficult subject for you. You arrive at this conclusion by generalizing from the few specific math classes you have taken.

We form many of our opinions through proofs provided from argument by example. We hear a few friends complain of electrical problems with a particular make of car and decide not to buy that model. A speaker relates several examples of corruption in city hall, and we conclude that political corruption is widespread. Those are both examples of inductive reasoning.

Kateri argued that a teacher shortage had forced school districts throughout the nation to lower their standards for substitute teachers. She used examples of eight states to suggest a larger trend.

According to the March 19, 2000, *Denver Rocky Mountain News,* with thousands of openings and no substitutes "school districts are being forced to hire more substitute

argument by example or **inductive argument:** says that what is true of a few instances is true generally.

Trial lawyers know that cases—and arguments—cannot be won by eloquent language alone. The validity of any claim depends on the quality of the evidence supporting that claim.

teachers with less experience and education." In Colorado, a teacher can obtain a one-year emergency substitute license without earning even a bachelor's degree or passing the state's teacher tests. According to the November 7, 2000, *Telegraph Herald,* "Illinois, South Dakota, Kansas, and Nebraska do not . . . require a teaching license." The previously cited *Press Enterprise* states that "in some districts of Maryland, Kentucky, and Idaho, only a high school diploma is required to substitute teach."[5]

How can you test whether an argument by example is sound? Its validity hinges on the quality of the examples a speaker chooses. Ask yourself the following four questions to test the validity of argument by example. Keep in mind that argument by example is valid only if you can answer yes to each of four tests of argument:

1. *Are the examples true?* The first test of argument by example is to determine whether the examples are true. In Chapter 8, we noted that hypothetical or imaginary examples can clarify a point, but they do not prove it. Only when true examples are presented should you proceed to the next question.

2. *Are the examples relevant?* Suppose Susan presents the following evidence in her speech on homelessness: "According to police reports published in yesterday's *News Journal,* city police picked up three individuals who were found sleeping on downtown streets and in the park this past weekend. So, you can see that even in our city homelessness is a serious problem." Do these examples really support the claim? Did these individuals not have homes? Had they passed out? Were they there for other reasons? Until you can answer these questions, you cannot assume that they were homeless. The examples must relate to the specific claim.

3. *Are the examples sufficient?* In Chapter 8 we stated that "one example may illustrate a claim, but it will rarely prove it." Susan must present enough examples to prove her assertion. In general, the greater the population for which you generalize, the more examples you need. Three examples of homelessness may be statistically significant in a small town, but, even though tragic, that number is actually far below average for many large cities.

4. *Are the examples representative?* Was this weekend Susan reported typical? How did it compare with other weekends, weekdays, or seasons? To prove her argument, Susan must present examples that are true, relevant, sufficient, and representative.

Argument by Analogy

An analogy is a comparison. **Argument by analogy** links two objects or concepts and asserts that what is true of one will be true of the other. Arguing that online registration would work at your college because it works at State U is an example of reasoning by analogy.

Argument by analogy is appropriate when the program you advocate or oppose has been tried elsewhere. Some states have lotteries, no-fault insurance, and the line-item veto; others do not. Some school systems allow corporal punishment, offer magnet programs, and require a passing grade for participation in extracurricular activities; others do not. A speech defending or disputing one of these programs could demonstrate success or failure elsewhere to establish its position.

Marcus wanted to persuade his classmates that Virginia should reform its welfare system. He researched experimental programs that other states had tried and found several articles describing Wisconsin's program. In his speech, he explained some of the facets of that program: investments in job training, job placement, and child care for welfare recipients. He argued that this approach to welfare reform had reduced Wisconsin's caseload by nearly 45 percent compared to a decade ago. Marcus then argued that, because the states have similar welfare populations and total populations, with Virginia the twelfth largest and Wisconsin the sixteenth largest state, Wisconsin's program had a good chance of achieving similar beneficial results in Virginia.

The preceding example illustrates the persuasive appeal of argument by analogy. You introduce a situation that is familiar to the audience and explain why we respond to it as we do. You then assert that your idea or proposal is analogous and, therefore, deserves a similar response. The key to this pattern of argument is the similarity between the two entities. In testing the validity of your argument by analogy, you need to answer this question: "Are the two entities sufficiently similar to justify my conclusion that what is true of one will be true of the other?" If not, your reasoning is faulty. This question can best be answered by dividing it into two questions:

1. *Are the similarities between the two cases relevant?* For example, suppose you used argument by analogy to advocate adopting an online registration system similar to the one used at State U. The facts that both schools have similar library facilities and the same mascot would be irrelevant. Equivalent student enrollments, advising procedures, and periods for registration are highly relevant and can be forceful evidence as you build your case.

2. *Are any of the differences between the two cases relevant?* If so, how do those differences affect your claim? If you discover that, unlike State, your college has neither an integrated computer network nor the technical staff to program it, these differences are relevant to your topic and will undermine the validity of your claim.

Argument by Cause

Argument by cause connects two elements or events and claims that one is produced by the other. Causal reasoning takes two forms—reasoning from effect to cause and from cause to effect. The difference between the two is their chronological order. An *effect-to-cause argument* begins at a point of time (when the effects are evident) and moves back in time (to when the cause occurred). When you feel ill and go to the doctor, the doctor will usually identify the symptoms (the effects) of the problem and then diagnose the cause. The doctor is problem solving by reasoning from effect to cause. In contrast, *cause-to-effect argument* begins at a point of time (when the cause occurred) and moves forward (to when the effects occurred or will occur). Doctors reason from cause

argument by analogy: says that what is true in one case is or will be true in another.

argument by cause: says that one action or condition caused or will cause another.

to effect when they tell their patients who smoke that this habit may result in emphysema or lung cancer.

In his persuasive speech, "The Death of Reading," Nicholas used a book metaphor to organize and phrase his message. He previewed his key ideas: "Chapter One: The Death of Reading; Chapter Two: The Autopsy; and Chapter 3: The Resurrection." Before presenting his solutions, Nicholas argued from effect to cause to explain why children today read less:

Effect

Reading leisurely, whether newspapers, magazines, or books, has decreased over 50 percent in today's families since 1975. The American Psychological Association on December 17, 2003, argued that reading is essential to childhood imaginative growth. Modern entertainment such as television and movies leaves little room for creative interpretations. "A lack of reading invites big brother, preventing our children from being able to create the world themselves. When reading, the children are in control of the reality, not the films."

Cause

Now that we have looked at the symptoms, we must next crack open the spine of today's books and run an autopsy to discuss the inherent causes of the death of reading. To children the answer is simple: reading isn't fun any more. The December 28, 2003, *St. Petersburg Times* tell us that many children believe that the only motivation that they have to read is to pass tests. In 2002 alone, over 85,000 third graders were not allowed into the fourth grade due to an inability to pass their FCAT reading scores, and over 43,000 were forced into summer reading to pass. This form of education is known as "Extrinsic Motivation." This means that America's schools rely on external rewards, such as grades and test scores. Extrinsic motivation does not teach our children to think independently and critically about situations. Reading, it seems, has fallen prey to this school of thought, because children are taught to read to get good test scores, not because reading is entertaining and intellectual.[6]

The following speech excerpt demonstrates cause-to-effect argument. Ellen Wartella, executive vice chancellor at the University of California, Riverside, spoke on the context of television violence:

Cause

In the past fifteen or so years, a remarkably cavalier, vicious, wanton, and senseless pattern of violence entered society and the American psyche. Drive-by shootings and gangbanger crimes, fueled by a trade in handguns and crack cocaine, ushered in fears of an epidemic of violence we may not fully comprehend. The violence panic of this time, unlike that of the 1960s, seems much more to surround children and youth, as both the victims and the perpetrators of violence. . . .

Effect

[This] cycle of violence has helped us become the most violent industrialized nation on earth. A lot of numbers gird that conclusion. But the numbers that tell the most tragic story concern children and adolescents:

- Among young people in the age group from 15 to 24 years old, homicide is the second leading cause of death and for African American youth is number one.
- Adolescents account for 24 percent of all violent crimes leading to arrest. The rate has increased over time for those in the 12 to 19 year old age group, while it is down in the 35 and older age group.
- Every five minutes a child is arrested in America for committing a violent crime; gun-related violence takes the life of an American child every three hours.[7]

When you argue by cause, test your reasoning to make certain it is sound. To do this, ask yourself the following three questions:

1. *Does a causal relationship exist?* For an argument from cause to effect or effect to cause to be valid, a causal relationship must exist between the two elements. As we will discuss later in this chapter, just because one event precedes another does not mean that the first caused the second. One of our students argued that the scholastic decline of American education began with, and was caused by, the Supreme Court's decision outlawing mandatory school prayer. We doubt the connection.

2. *Could the presumed cause produce the effect?* During the highly inflationary times of the late 1970s, one of our students gave a speech in which she argued that various price hikes had contributed to the high inflation rate. She provided three examples of price increases: The cost of postage stamps had increased 87.5 percent, chewing gum 100 percent, and downtown parking meter fees 150 percent. While she was able to document the dramatic percentage increase in the prices of each of these products, her examples had more interest than impact. Her examples did not convince her audience or her instructor that these increases by themselves could produce a significant influence on the inflation rate.

3. *Could the effect result from other causes?* A number of causes can converge to produce one effect. A student who argues that next year's increased tuition and fees are a result of the college president's fiscal mismanagement may have a point. But a number of other factors may have made the tuition increase necessary: state revenue shortfalls, decreased enrollment, cutbacks in federal aid, major spending on campus building projects, and so on. Speakers strengthen their arguments when they are able to prove the following: that the alleged cause contributed substantively to producing the effect and that without the cause the effect would not have occurred or the problem would have been much less severe.

Argument by Deduction

Ben began his speech on time management with the following statement:

> All of us are taking courses that require us to be in class and to study outside class. In addition, many of us are members of social, academic, religious, or career-oriented clubs and organizations. Some of us work. All of us like to party! Crowded into our school and work schedules are our responsibilities to friends and family members. In short, we're busy!
>
> College is a hectic time in our lives. Sometimes it seems that we're trying to cram 34 hours of activity into a 24-hour day. In order to survive this schedule and beat the stress, college students need to develop effective time-management skills. You are no exception! If you listen to my speech today, you will learn how to set realistic goals, meet them, and still have time to socialize with friends and get a good night's sleep. Sound impossible? Just listen closely for the next eight minutes.

Ben used two types of arguments in his introduction. He opened by arguing from example, providing several instances to make his case that college life is busy. He then used deductive reasoning to make the speech relevant to each member of the audience. A **deductive argument** moves from a general category to a specific instance. In this sense, deductive arguments are the reverse of argument by example. To see why that's true, consider the structure of a deductive argument.

Deductive arguments consist of a pattern of three statements: a major premise, a minor premise, and a conclusion. This pattern of deductive argument is called a **syllogism.** The **major premise** is a claim about a general group of people, events, or conditions. Ben's major premise was this: "College students need to develop effective time-management skills." The **minor premise** places a person, event, or condition into a general class. Ben's minor premise could be phrased like this: "You are a college student." The **conclusion** argues that what is true of the general class is true of the

deductive argument: says that what is true generally is or will be true in a specific instance.

syllogism: the pattern of a deductive argument, consisting of a major premise, a minor premise, and a conclusion.

major premise: a claim about a general group of people, events, or conditions.

minor premise: a statement placing a person, an event, or a condition into a general class.

conclusion: the deductive argument that what is true of the general class is true of the specific instance.

Participants in a political debate are judged on the quality of their arguments as well as their manner of presentation.

specific instance or individual. Ben concluded that each college student in his audience needed to develop effective time-management skills.

Use the following steps to check the structure of your deductive argument:

1. State your major premise.
2. Say "because," and then state your minor premise.
3. Say "therefore," and then state your conclusion.

The resulting two sentences should flow together easily and make sense. This strategy tests the interconnectedness of the parts of your deductive argument. Ben could have tested the clarity of his argument by saying the following: "College students need to develop effective time-management skills. *Because* you are a college student, *therefore* you need to develop effective time-management skills." Notice that if the two premises are true and relate to each other, the conclusion must also be true.

Major premises sometimes embody principles that shape our beliefs and guide our actions. A speaker who makes the following statement is using deductive reasoning: "Judge Shady committed an ethical violation when she accepted a campaign contribution from the defendant in a case scheduled for her court." A diagram of this argument is as follows:

Major premise: It is unethical for judges to accept campaign contributions from individuals involved in cases in their courts.

Minor premise: Judge I. M. Shady accepted a contribution from the defendant in a case scheduled for her court.

Conclusion: Judge Shady is guilty of unethical judicial conduct.

For deductive arguments to be valid, they must meet certain tests. Whether you are listening to others' arguments or evaluating arguments in your own speech, keep in mind three questions:

1. *Do the premises relate to each other?* "All men are created equal. Equal is an artificial sweetener. Therefore, all men are artificial sweeteners." This statement doesn't make much sense, does it? The first sentence uses the word *equal* to mean "equivalent." The second uses *Equal* as a product name for a sugar substitute. For an argument to be valid, the premises must relate to each other. In this case they clearly do not.

Let's construct another example. Suppose John prepares a speech trying to persuade his classmates to apply for a new academic scholarship named after his father, James Burke. In his speech, John makes the following statement:

> Any student enrolled in State U who is a U.S. citizen can apply for the Burke Scholarship. That includes everyone in this class. Just think, next year you could have your entire tuition and fees paid, and you can spend your money for something you've been wanting but were unable to afford. Maybe even that new computer!

Before John convinces his classmates to apply for the scholarship, he first tells them that they are eligible. His argument may be depicted as follows:

Major premise: Any State U student who is a U.S. citizen can apply for the Burke Scholarship.

Minor premise: Every student in this class is a State U student who is a citizen of the United States.

Conclusion: Therefore, every student in this class can apply for the Burke Scholarship.

The terms in the minor premise fall within the scope of the major premise. Both premises relate to each other, and the conclusion seems logical.

2. *Is the major premise true?* Before John's classmates head to the financial aid office to begin filling out a scholarship application form, they should ask the question, "Is the major premise of the argument true?" Suppose two prerequisites for application are full-time student status and good academic standing. The statement "any State U student who is a U.S. citizen can apply for the Burke Scholarship" is then false. Part-time and probationary students cannot apply. The conclusion of the argument ("every student in this class can apply for the Burke Scholarship") would therefore not necessarily be true. You must be able to prove your major premises before you draw conclusions.

3. *Is the minor premise true?* A false minor premise is just as damaging to an argument as a false major premise. Let's suppose that John's major premise is true and that any State U student who is a U.S. citizen can apply for the Burke Scholarship. What if his class includes some foreign students? His minor premise ("every student in this class is a State U student who is a citizen of the United States") is then false. Those students are not eligible for the scholarship, and John's conclusion is false. Arguing a position entails ethical considerations. You must know your facts and reason logically from them.

Argument by Authority

Argument by authority differs from the four other forms of argument we have discussed. To see how it is different, consider the following example from Lynn's speech:

> I believe that every student should be allowed to vote for Outstanding Professor on Campus, rather than having the award determined by a select committee of the faculty. And I'm not alone in my opinion. Last year's recipient of the award, Dr. Linda Carter, agrees. The President of the Faculty Senate spoke out in favor of this proposal at last week's forum, and the Student Government Association passed a resolution supporting it.

Argument from authority uses testimony from an expert source to prove a speaker's claim; its validity depends on the credibility the authority has for the audience. In this example, Lynn did not offer arguments based on example, analogy, cause, or

argument by authority: uses testimony from an expert source to prove a speaker's claim.

deduction to explain the validity of her position. Instead, she asserted that two distinguished professors and the SGA agreed with her. She asked her audience to believe her position based on the credentials of the authority figures who endorsed her claim. Her rationale was that her sources had access to sufficient information and had the expertise to interpret it accurately; thus, we should trust their conclusions.

An argument based on authority is only as valid as the source's credibility. To test your argument, ask and answer two questions: (1) *Is the source an expert?* (2) *Is the source unbiased?* Our discussion of these questions, as well as other tests of evidence in Chapter 8, will help you select the best authority for your claim.

In this section, we have identified and discussed five types of argument. You will want to select as many of these forms as are appropriate to your topic and audience. We have also illustrated how to test these arguments so that they work to make your speech more believable.

Testing the arguments you use and hear others use is crucial to effective, ethical speaking and listening. When you analyze the arguments you use, you strengthen them and can save yourself the embarrassment of being caught using illogical or invalid proof. It is just as important to check the validity of persuasive arguments you hear, however. By doing this, you avoid being duped into misguided thoughts and actions.

In spite of these tests, persuasive speakers sometimes incorporate certain errors of proof into their speeches. These errors are so widely used that they have been named and studied. In the following section, we take a look at some of these mirages of persuasion—arguments that appear, but only appear, to say something authoritative. We want you to be able to identify these errors so you can avoid them.

Theory into Practice
Tips
Testing Your Arguments

Mario Cuomo, noted speaker and former governor of New York, encouraged leaders to persuade others "not so much with speeches that sound good, as with speeches that are good and sound."[8] As you select and develop the arguments for your speeches, ask and answer these questions that we discussed in this chapter. Remember to use these same guidelines when you listen to the speeches of others.

Argument by Example
- Are the examples true?
- Are the examples relevant?
- Are the examples sufficient?
- Are the examples representative?

Argument by Analogy
- Are the similarities between the two cases relevant?

- Are any of the differences between the two cases relevant?

Argument by Cause
- Does a causal relationship exist?
- Could the presumed cause produce the effect?
- Could the effect result from other causes?

Argument by Deduction
- Do the premises relate to each other?
- Is the major premise true?
- Is the minor premise true?

Argument by Authority
- Is the source an expert?
- Is the source unbiased?

Fallacies of Argument

Does Twain's argument seem convincing to you? Does it strike you as more humorous than persuasive? If so, you've just detected a fallacy. A **fallacy** is "any defect in reasoning which destroys its validity."[9] Twain assumed that what had occurred in the past 176-year history of the Mississippi River could be projected farther back in time. The example is humorous because of its obvious distortion of figures. Unfortunately, not all distortions of logic we hear are so obvious, nor are they always used for humorous effect. In fact, fallacies are often persuasive and dangerous for the same reason: Because they resemble valid reasoning, we often accept them as legitimate. They can produce bad decisions leading to harmful consequences.

We want to stress that fallacies are flawed patterns of reasoning that you will want to avoid as both speaker and listener. As you construct your persuasive speech, make sure that the arguments you encounter in your research are valid. Then, use your research to develop sound arguments to support the ideas in your speech. As a listener, you have an ethical responsibility to evaluate critically the ideas other persuasive speakers present to you. Be alert for those arguments based on sound reasoning and for those based on flawed reasoning. Consider the valid arguments, and reject fallacious ones. How can you tell the difference?

Fallacies come in many different varieties. In fact, *The New York Public Library Desk Reference* notes that "there are now over 125 separate fallacies, most with their own impressive-sounding names, many of them in Latin."[11] For our purposes, we will discuss ten of the most common fallacies. Some you will readily recognize, while others may be new to you. As you read them, notice how many of them resemble the patterns of argument we have just discussed.

> " *In the space of one hundred and seventy-six years the Lower Mississippi has shortened itself two hundred and forty-two miles. That is an average of a trifle over one mile and a third per year. Therefore, any calm person, who is not blind or idiotic, can see that... just a million years ago next November, the Lower Mississippi River was upwards of one million three hundred thousand miles long.* "
>
> —MARK TWAIN[10]

Fallacies of Argument

1. Hasty generalization
2. False analogy
3. *Post hoc ergo propter hoc*
4. Slippery slope
5. Red herring
6. Appeal to tradition
7. False dilemma
8. False authority
9. Bandwagon
10. *Ad hominem*

Hasty Generalization

People who jump to conclusions commit the fallacy of **hasty generalization,** a faulty form of argument by example. What distinguishes valid from fallacious inductive proof is the quantity and quality of examples. When speakers make claims based on

fallacy: a flaw in the logic of an argument.

hasty generalization: a fallacy that makes claims from insufficient or unrepresentative examples.

The power of persuasion can mobilize students to debate issues, combining logic with passion.

insufficient or unrepresentative instances, their reasoning is usually flawed. For example, a speaker uses examples of two students convicted of plagiarism and concludes that cheating is widespread on campus. An advertisement shows a dentist recommending a particular brand of toothbrush, and the consumer assumes that it carries the endorsement of dentists in general. A student concludes that a public speaking course will not be helpful based on a hectic first class meeting. People who rely too much on first impressions, who do not read widely, or who spend little time researching are prime candidates for reasoning from hasty generalization. They often develop beliefs and opinions that later prove erroneous. Just as dangerous, such people will often reason from hasty generalization in the speeches they deliver.

False Analogy

Speakers argue by analogy when they link two items and assert that what is true of one will be true of the other. If the two items are sufficiently similar, the speaker's claim may be valid. However, if the items differ in critical ways, the persuader may be guilty of using a **false analogy,** and the claim may be fallacious. You've probably heard someone respond to an argument by saying, "That's like comparing apples and oranges." That person just detected a faulty comparison. Read some of the arguments we've heard in students' speeches and see if you can detect some faulty reasoning:

> We license drivers; why shouldn't we license parents? You can't take to the road until you learn how to drive and pass a test. Aren't children more important than cars?

> Part of being an adult includes the right to make choices and accept the consequences of your actions. If it's legal to purchase tobacco, shouldn't it also be legal to buy marijuana?

> We prohibit cigarette advertising on television, why shouldn't we prohibit ads for beer?

false analogy: a fallacy that occurs when an argument by analogy compares entities that have critical differences.

What do you think of these arguments? Which comparisons are valid arguments by analogy? Which are fallacies? Your answers may differ from your friends' and classmates'; detecting fallacies is not always easy. Researchers are careful about making claims that a diet that reduced cancer in laboratory animals will produce the same result in humans. Policy makers are cautious about assuming that traffic laws appropriate for New York City are suitable for those living in the plains of Montana. You need to exercise your critical thinking skills as you read, listen to, and develop arguments by analogy.

Post Hoc Ergo Propter Hoc

This fallacy uses the Latin title and literally means "after this, therefore because of this." A chronological fallacy, **post hoc** (as it is usually called) assumes that because one event preceded another, the first caused the second. Perhaps you have heard a friend comment, "I should have known it would rain; I just washed my car!" Your friend is probably making a joke based on the *post hoc* fallacy. People exhibit *post hoc* reasoning when they expect something good to happen if they carry a lucky charm while gambling in a Las Vegas casino, wear a lucky shirt to a football game, or cross their fingers as a teacher returns a graded exam.

Science News Online reports this truly bizarre theory of false causation:

> The Super Bowl "theory" links U.S. stock market performance to the results of the championship football game, held each January since 1967. It holds that, if a team from the original National Football League wins the title, the stock market increases for the rest of the year, and if a team from the old American Football League wins, the stock market goes down.[12]

Although this "theory" seemed to be remarkably accurate (82 percent correct) in predicting stock market performance during the early years of the Super Bowl, its reliability has declined significantly in recent years. Economist Paul Sommers, who has developed a mathematical model to analyze the relationship between Super Bowl wins and stock market performance, has a simple explanation for the alleged causality: "statistical fluke."

These examples may seem absurd, with obvious defects in reasoning. Yet other examples of confusing coincidence with causation are more subtle and potentially more damaging. For example, a person rejects medical treatment, relying instead on an unresearched cure because someone else tried it and subsequently got well. An individual refuses to exercise and diet, citing the example of his Uncle Bert who "drank like a fish, smoked like a chimney, ate anything he wanted, never worked a day in his life, and lived to be 93!" An incumbent mayor takes credit for every city improvement that occurred since she took office; her opponent blames her for everything bad that happened during this time. An event may have more than one cause. It is also preceded by occurrences having no effect on it whatsoever. As a result, determining the relationship between two events or conditions is often difficult. But you must examine that relation if you are to avoid the *post hoc ergo propter hoc* fallacy.

Exploring *Online*

FALLACIES OF REASONING
www.datanation.com/fallacies
For an explanation of the ten fallacies of reasoning discussed here and many others, visit Stephen's Guide to Logical Fallacies. This site provides definitions, examples, and explanations of the missing proof of more than 50 fallacies.

Slippery Slope

Envision yourself at the top of a hill on a wintry day. You take one step, slip on a patch of ice, lose your footing, and begin sliding down the hill. You try to regain your balance, but you continue your slide, stopping only when you reach the bottom of the hill. This visual image depicts the slippery slope fallacy. A fallacy of causation, **slippery slope** asserts that one action inevitably sets in motion a chain of events or indicates a trend. This defect in reasoning is exemplified in the following two arguments:

post hoc: a chronological fallacy that says that a prior event caused a subsequent event.

slippery slope: a fallacy of causation that says that one action inevitably sets a chain of events in motion.

If you amend the Constitution to prohibit flag burning, you open the door to other amendments to our Bill of Rights. Ultimately, you destroy the freedoms upon which our nation is based.

If we begin to control the sale of guns by restricting the purchase of handguns, where will it end? Will shotguns be next? And then hunting rifles? Soon the right to bear arms will disappear from the Constitution, and sportsmen and -women will be denied one of their basic freedoms.

These speakers' arguments imply that a single act will set in motion a series of events that no one will be able to stop, but that is not necessarily the case. Just because legislators support one constitutional amendment or one law doesn't necessarily mean that they must support subsequent reforms. Most of the time, a slide down the slope is preventable. Each journey involves a series of decisions, and it is possible to retain or regain your footing.

Red Herring

The name of the **red herring** fallacy apparently originated with the English fox hunt. When the hunt was over, the hunt master would drag a red herring—a type of fish that is smoked and salted—across the path of the hounds. The pungent scent would divert the dogs from their pursuit of the fox, and they could then be rounded up. This diversionary tactic was also supposedly used by escaping criminals to throw dogs off their trails. If you love to read murder mysteries, you may have trained yourself to be on guard for some incidental twist in the plot that seems to be there just to throw less attentive readers off track. Such devices have come to be called red herrings.

A red herring fallacy is an example of a faulty argument by deduction. An arguer makes a claim based on an irrelevant premise. How does the red herring fallacy work in a speech? Bruce Waller provides a vivid example and analysis of this defect in reasoning using the issue of gun control:

> If the debate is over whether handguns should be banned, it is relevant to consider how many people have been killed in handgun accidents. But suppose someone asserts, "Everybody talks about handgun accidents! But think of how many people are killed each year in auto accidents! Why don't we ban automobiles?" You must hold your breath and cover your nose and stay on the trail, for a red herring has just been dragged across the argument. The danger of auto accidents is certainly serious, and perhaps on another occasion we should discuss how to reduce that danger—but that has nothing to do with the question of banning handguns. Whether there are other unacceptable dangers in society is not the issue; the question is instead whether handguns pose an unacceptable risk. Perhaps they do, perhaps they do not, but no progress will be made on that issue if the arguers are distracted by irrelevant reasons.[13]

In essence, then, a speaker guilty of the red herring fallacy introduces an irrelevant issue to deflect attention from the subject under discussion. The following speakers each attempted to divert discussion from germane issues to irrelevant concerns:

A politician answers charges that she accepted illegal campaign contributions by noting her service on the state's ethics advisory board.

When asked about rumors of excessive drinking, a legislator declares, "Madam, my father was a Methodist minister. That should answer your question."

A student responds to a charge of plagiarism with the statement, "I was a Boy Scout throughout high school."

When you present a persuasive speech, you are an advocate for the position you present. As such, you have an ethical responsibility to defend your arguments. Answer

red herring: a fallacy that introduces irrelevant issues to deflect attention from the subject under discussion.

criticisms of your argument with evidence and logic; don't deflect criticism by diverting your audience to another track.

Appeal to Tradition

This fallacy is grounded in a respect for traditional ways of doing things. On the surface, respect for tradition seems reasonable. But the fallacy commonly called **appeal to tradition** defends the status quo and opposes change by arguing that old ways are always superior to new ways. A speaker who argues against admitting men to her college because of the school's history as a women's school commits this fallacy unless she offers additional support for the claim. Its most common form of expression—"We've always done it that way"—is merely descriptive. It discourages discussion and reevaluation of our traditions.

PROPAGANDA
www.propagandacritic.com
Why should we study propaganda? You can find a discussion of that question on this excellent website constructed by Dr. Aaron Delwiche. Drawing from the work of the Institute for Propaganda Analysis, this communication professor discusses eight common techniques of propagandistic messages and offers numerous examples of faulty logic.

As important as many traditions are to us, they should not be used to thwart needed change. Our nation's founders created a glorious document that gave us many of the freedoms we enjoy. Yet that document also precluded non-European Americans and women from full participation in our society. The fight to secure the right to vote for all citizens challenged that tradition. Keep in mind that the old ways are not always the best ways.

False Dilemma

When forced to choose between alternatives, you face a dilemma. Dilemmas can be actual or false. In an actual dilemma, the alternatives you face are real; there is no room for compromise. For example, suppose you are asked to choose between going to a movie with friends and attending a review session for an upcoming test. If the review and theater hours coincide, your dilemma is real and you must forfeit either entertainment or study.

A **false dilemma** exists when you have more than the two options presented. For example, if there is a late showing of the movie, perhaps you can convince your friends to meet you at the theater after you attend the review. In this instance, the dilemma is false because you do not have to choose between studying and seeing the movie; you can do both. Woody Allen's quotation is an example of a false dilemma. Certainly, humans face alternatives other than utter hopelessness and total extinction.

The fallacy of false dilemma, sometimes called the either–or fallacy, presents the listener with two choices when, in reality, there are more. Characterized by a "bumper sticker" mentality, the dilemma usually polarizes issues into two mutually exclusive categories, such as "Stand with America or stand for terrorism" and "When guns are outlawed, only outlaws will have guns!" Neither of those slogans allows for middle-ground positions.

Listeners should be especially attentive to all "either–or" and "if–then" statements they hear. These grammatical constructions lend themselves to the fallacy of false dilemma, as in the following examples:

> A person is either a Republican or a Democrat. Because I know Carolyn isn't a Republican, she must be a Democrat.

> *More than at any time in history, mankind faces a crossroads. One path leads to despair and utter hopelessness, the other to total extinction. Let us pray we have the wisdom to choose correctly.*
>
> —WOODY ALLEN

appeal to tradition: a fallacy that opposes change by arguing that old ways are always superior to new ways.

false dilemma: a fallacy that confronts listeners with two choices when, in reality, more options exist.

The issue is very simple: Either you support the Constitution on which this nation was founded, or you're not a patriotic American.

I don't support a cutback in defense spending. I don't want to see a weakening of America's strength.

Each of these examples presents the listener with only two choices. However, they disregard other legitimate options: Carolyn may be a Libertarian, a Socialist, a member of the Green Party or some other political party, or an independent. We can exhibit patriotism and still question a nation's laws and policies. Eliminating unnecessary defense spending does not necessarily weaken the country. Using that money for other important projects—like major road and bridge repair—may actually make America stronger.

During the heat of the 2004 elections, Barack Obama, then a candidate for the U.S. Senate, cautioned media pundits against thinking in terms of rigid either–or categories:

> The pundits like to slice-and-dice our country into Red States and Blue States: Red States for Republicans, Blue States for Democrats. But I've got news for them, too. We worship an awesome God in the Blue States, and we don't like federal agents poking around our libraries in the Red States. We coach Little League in the Blue States and have gay friends in the Red States. There are patriots who opposed the war in Iraq and patriots who supported it. We are one people, all of us pledging allegiance to the stars and stripes, all of us defending the United States of America.[14]

That's pretty good advice. When we focus only on our differences, we fail to discover what we have in common. Bridging differences and creating acceptable, alternative solutions are important goals of any serious persuader.

False Authority

The fallacy of **false authority** is an invalid form of argument by authority. This fallacy occurs when advocates support their ideas with the testimony of people who have apparent but not real expertise. Before deciding to accept someone's opinion or testimony, ask the question, "Is the person an objective expert on this topic?" Celebrity endorsements of commercial products frequently illustrate this fallacy. The famous sports personality who urges you to buy that 260-horsepower sedan with an all-aluminum, high-output, 3.5-liter, 24-valve, V6 engine may know only what she's reading from a script. Celebrities are often used more for their popularity or status than for their credibility.

It is important to exercise your critical thinking skills to avoid using the fallacy of false authority. If you cite information from a website without checking its authority and accuracy or if you quote from authors of books and articles without knowing their credentials, you have used the fallacy of false authority, most likely unintentionally. The statement "I couldn't find any information about the author" is a recipe for irresponsibility. You can avoid the fallacy of false authority by using only information you believe to be expert and credible.

Bandwagon

In the 1800s and early 1900s, political candidates held parades to meet the people. A band rode on a wagon leading the parade through town. As the wagon passed, local leaders would jump on the bandwagon to show their support. The number of people on board was considered a barometer of the candidate's popularity and political strength.

The **bandwagon** fallacy is also a faulty argument by authority. It assumes that popular opinion is an accurate measure of truth and wisdom. The Latin name for this appeal to popular opinion is *argumentum ad populum*. Frequently referred to as the

false authority: a fallacy that uses testimony from sources who have no real expertise on the topic in question.

bandwagon: a fallacy that determines truth, goodness, or wisdom by popular opinion.

"everybody's doing it" fallacy, bandwagon arguments commonly use phrases such as "everyone knows" or "most people agree." Door-to-door salespeople or intrusive phone solicitors who tell you that all your friends and neighbors are purchasing their encyclopedia or portrait package use the bandwagon appeal. They base their sales pitch on the product's popularity, not on its merits.

Speakers who defend the rightness of their positions by pointing to polls showing popular support similarly exploit the bandwagon fallacy. While agreement regarding a belief or action may be reassuring, it is no guarantee of accuracy or truth. "Truth is not always democratic."[15] History is cluttered with popularly held misconceptions. Remember, most people once believed that the world was flat; that the sun revolved around Earth; and that leeching, or bleeding, patients was state-of-the-art medical treatment. You should decide the validity of an argument by its form and substance, not merely by how many people agree on it.

Ad Hominem

Ad hominem, literally meaning "to the man," arguments ask listeners to reject an idea because of the allegedly poor character of the person voicing it. Political speeches, especially those delivered at national conventions, are peppered with *ad hominem* arguments. These statements often evoke applause, cheers, and laughter, but they provide little insight into issues. When Rush Limbaugh refers to feminists as "feminazis," he is making an *ad hominem* attack rather than engaging in reasoned discourse. A club member commits this fallacy when he argues that Bryan's proposal for an alcohol-free party should not be taken seriously because Bryan has two DUI (driving under the influence) convictions.

In its most obvious form, this fallacy is name calling. For some people, simply knowing that a speaker is liberal, conservative, feminist, or fundamentalist is sufficient to close their minds. They disregard the merits of an idea because of the person giving the message. But, as we stated in Chapter 2, an ethical listener has a responsibility to give all ideas a fair hearing.

> *If you can't answer a man's argument, all is not lost; you can still call him vile names.*
>
> —ELBERT HUBBARD

To be an effective and ethical persuader, you must know how to construct valid arguments and avoid defective ones such as those we have just discussed. Once you have mastered this ability, you can use your arguments to achieve the overall goal of your speech. In the remainder of this chapter, we will show you how to develop a persuasive proposition and how you can effectively organize your arguments.

Selecting Propositions for Persuasive Speeches

In Chapter 6, we explained that your first steps in constructing a speech are to select your topic, focus or narrow it, determine your general purpose, formulate your specific purpose, and construct a thesis statement. In persuasive speaking, you can add one additional step: State your proposition. Let's make sure that we understand the difference between a proposition and a thesis statement.

For example, if you speak on the topic of improving education, you may narrow this broad subject and select as your specific purpose to persuade the audience that teacher salaries should be increased. Your basic position—"teacher salaries should be

ad hominem: a fallacy that urges listeners to reject an idea because of the allegedly poor character of the person voicing it; name calling.

increased"—can be thought of as a proposition. A **proposition** is a declarative sentence expressing a judgment you want the audience to accept. Notice that this proposition *expresses a judgment* that *is debatable* and that *requires proof*. We will discuss these three characteristics of propositions in the next section.

Your thesis statement, in contrast, lists the reasons you offer to prove your proposition. In the preceding example, your thesis statement could be this: Higher teacher salaries would recruit better teachers, retain better teachers, and improve student learning. The following example illustrates the similarities and differences among the proposition, specific purpose, thesis statement, and key ideas of speech:

Proposition: The new campus classroom building should be named Richter Hall.

Specific Purpose: To persuade the audience that the new classroom building should be named for Louise Richter

Thesis Statement: The new classroom building should be named for Louise Richter, an outstanding teacher, advisor, and friend.

Key Ideas: I. The name of the new classroom building should honor an outstanding educator.
            II. Louise Richter deserves this recognition.
               A. She was an outstanding teacher.
               B. She was an outstanding advisor to student organizations.
               C. She was a cherished friend.

Notice that this proposition expresses a judgment, while the thesis statement includes the reasons the speaker will offer to prove the proposition.

Characteristics of Propositions

If you formulate a well-worded proposition early in preparing your persuasive speech, you will be sure of your persuasive goal and can keep it firmly in mind. Your proposition also helps you to focus your persuasive speech and test the relevance of supporting ideas as you develop them. Devising your proposition can be relatively easy. As we suggested before, propositions are marked by three characteristics.

Key Points

Requirements of Propositions

1. Propositions express a judgment.
2. Propositions are debatable.
3. Propositions require proof.

Propositions Express a Judgment.   A proposition for a persuasive speech states the position you will defend. Consequently, it should be worded as a declarative sentence expressing your position. If you advocate statehood for Puerto Rico, you could word your proposition like this: The United States should grant Puerto Rico statehood. This simple declarative sentence clearly states your position on the issue.

Sometimes, however, you may be interested in a topic, but lack enough information to have developed a position on it. In this case, you may first want to phrase a question to guide your research. Once you answer the question, you can then develop your proposition.

Mark was a criminal justice student interested in the issue of the death penalty. He had read an article discussing the pros and cons of capital punishment for juveniles convicted of capital crimes, but he had not developed his own position on the issue. To guide his research, Mark worded the following question: Is the death penalty for juveniles cruel and unusual punishment? He researched the topic, reading articles by scholars and jurists on both sides of the issue. He made a list of arguments for and against capital punishment for juveniles. Although Mark supported capital punishment for

proposition: a declarative sentence expressing a judgment a speaker wants listeners to accept.

adult offenders, his research convinced him to oppose it for juveniles. The proposition he subsequently decided to defend was "The death penalty for juveniles is cruel and unusual punishment." By phrasing his position statement, writing it out, and keeping it in front of him as he continued researching and assembling his arguments, Mark was able to keep his speech focused on arguments against capital punishment for juveniles.

Propositions Are Debatable. Propositions are appropriate for persuasive speeches only if they are debatable. In other words, the judgment must include some degree of controversy. The proposition "Earth revolves around the sun" is not a good proposition for a persuasive speech because you are unlikely to find any qualified authority today opposing that statement. We now accept it as fact. Once we accept a proposition as fact, it ceases to be an appropriate topic for persuasive speeches. However, in the sixteenth century, when Copernicus's heliocentric theory opposed governmental and religious teaching as well as popular opinion, the topic was debatable. It was then a proposition appropriate for persuasive speaking.

Propositions Require Proof. Finally, propositions require proof. A proposition is an assertion, and assertions are statements that have not yet been proved. Your objective as a persuasive speaker is to offer compelling reasons for listeners to accept your proposition. As we discussed earlier in this chapter, you may support your proposition with arguments from example, analogy, cause, deduction, or authority.

Types of Propositions

Propositions for persuasive speeches are of three types: fact, value, and policy. The type of organization and support materials you will use depends on the type of proposition you defend.

Propositions of Fact. A proposition of fact focuses on belief. You ask the audience to affirm the truth or falsity of a statement. The following are examples of propositions of fact:

Electric automobiles are commercially feasible.

Access to math tutors increases students' grades in mathematics courses.

Gun control laws violate the second amendment of the U.S. Constitution.

An aspirin a day can reduce the risk of heart disease.

Jennifer's speech on random drug testing was a speech on a proposition of fact. Jennifer defended this proposition: Random drug testing on the job decreases workplace drug use. Her specific purpose and key ideas were as follows:

Specific Purpose: To convince the audience that random drug testing (RDT) decreases workplace drug use
Key Ideas: I. RDT deters casual drug use.
              II. RDT helps decrease drug addiction.
                   A. RDT identifies users.
                   B. RDT encourages users to seek therapy.

Propositions of Value. A proposition of value requires a judgment on the worth of an idea or action. You ask the audience to determine the "goodness" or "badness" of something, as in this proposition: "Corporal punishment in schools is wrong." Remember Mark's speech defending the proposition "The death penalty for juveniles is

proposition of fact: an assertion about the truth or falsity of a statement.

proposition of value: an assertion about the relative worth of an idea or action.

cruel and unusual punishment"? That too was a proposition of value. Propositions of value can also ask you to compare two items and determine which is better, as in Sir William Blackstone's statement, "It is better that ten guilty persons escape than one innocent suffer." Other propositions of value include:

Censorship is a greater evil than pornography.

Retribution is a more important goal of criminal justice than rehabilitation.

Civil disobedience is justifiable in a democracy.

Educational tracking of students by ability perpetuates social and racial inequality.

Suppose you decided to persuade your audience that free agency is bad for professional sports. You could develop your speech on this value proposition as follows:

Specific Purpose: To persuade the audience that free agency is hurting professional sports

Key Ideas: I. It destroys the competitive balance of teams.
              II. It undermines the financial solvency of teams.
             III. It creates bad role models for kids.

Propositions of Policy.   A proposition of policy advocates a course of action. You ask the audience to endorse a policy or to commit themselves to some action. These statements usually include the word *should*. Here are some examples of policy propositions:

College athletes should be paid.

Nonviolent offenders should be excluded from "three strikes and you're out" sentencing.

Students should be able to repay student loans through community service.

Canned hunting should be banned.

Duane wanted to persuade his classmates and instructor to support the student government association's proposal to change from a quarter to a semester academic calendar. Organizing his speech topically, he presented three benefits to a semester system.

Specific Purpose: To persuade the audience that this college should adopt a semester calendar

proposition of policy: a statement requesting support for a course of action.

Try This

Formulating Your Persuasive Proposition

Early in your preparation for an upcoming persuasive speech, word the proposition you plan to argue and identify it as a proposition of fact, value, or policy. Then revise the proposition to make it a clear example of the other two types of propositions. How does your job as a persuader change with each revision to a different type of proposition? Select the wording that matches your goals as you begin researching and developing your speech. Keep your written proposition at hand as you research, paying special attention to evidence that forces—or even nudges—you to revise the wording further.

Key Ideas: I. Semesters allow more time for research in theory courses.

          II. Semesters allow more time for skill development in performance courses.

        III. Semester credits are easier to transfer to other institutions.

Monroe's Motivated Sequence

In Chapters 9 and 10 we discussed how to organize the introduction, body, and conclusion of a speech. Those guidelines apply to the organization of persuasive, as well as informative, speeches. One type of persuasive speech, the speech to actuate, provides an interesting challenge to speakers. They must move their listeners to action using a progression of motivated steps. One of the most popular patterns for organizing the superstructure of a speech to actuate was developed by Alan Monroe in the 1930s.[16] Called "the motivated sequence," this pattern uses strategies you've already studied and applied in your speeches. The motivated sequence is particularly appropriate when you discuss a well-known or easily established problem. Monroe drew from the conclusions of educator and philosopher John Dewey that persuasion is best accomplished if a speaker moves a listener sequentially through a series of steps.[17] **Monroe's motivated sequence,** then, includes the following five steps, or stages: attention, need, satisfaction, visualization, and action.

Monroe argued that speakers must first command the *attention* of their listeners. Suppose your geographic area is experiencing a summer drought. You could begin your speech with a description of the landscape as you approached your campus a year ago, describing in detail the green grass, the verdant foliage, and the colorful, fragrant flowers. You then contrast the landscape of a year ago with its look now: bland, brown, and blossomless. With these contrasting visual images, you try to capture the attention and interest of your audience.

A speaker's second objective is to establish a *need.* This step is similar to the problem and need steps in the problem–solution and need–plan patterns of organizing a speech. For example, your speech on the drought situation could illustrate how an inadequate water supply hurts not only the beauty of the landscape, but also agricultural production, certain industrial processes, and, ultimately, the economy of the entire region.

When you dramatize a problem, you create an urgency to redress it. In the *satisfaction* step of the motivated sequence, you propose a way to solve, or at least minimize, the problem. You may suggest voluntary or mandatory conservation as a short-term solution to the water shortage crisis in your area. As a longer-range solution, you might ask your audience to consider the merits of planting grasses, shrubs, and other plants requiring less water. You could advocate that the city adopt and enforce stricter regulations of water use by businesses or that it develop alternative water sources.

However, Monroe argued that simply proposing a solution is seldom sufficient to bring about change. Through *visualization,* Monroe's fourth step, a speaker seeks to intensify an audience's desire to adopt and implement the proposed solution. You could direct the audience to look out the window at their campus and then ask if that is the scenery they want. More often, though, you create word pictures for the audience to visualize. Without adequate water, you could argue, crops will die, family farms will be foreclosed on, industries will not relocate to the area, and the quality of life for everyone in the area will be depressed. In contrast, you could refer to the landscape of a year ago, the image you depicted as you began your speech. The future can be colored in green, red, yellow, and blue, and it can represent growth and vitality.

The final step of the motivated sequence is the *action* you request of your listeners. It is not enough to know that something must be done; the audience must know what

> **Monroe's motivated sequence:** a persuasive pattern composed of (1) getting the audience's attention, (2) establishing a need, (3) offering a proposal to satisfy the need, (4) inviting listeners to visualize the results, and (5) requesting action.

you want them to do, and your request must be within their power to act. Do you want them to join you in voluntary conservation by watering their lawns in the evening when less water will evaporate or by washing their cars less frequently? Are you asking them to sign petitions pressuring the city council to adopt mandatory conservation measures when the water table sinks to a designated level? Conclude your speech with a strong appeal for specific, reasonable action.

Dolly decided that her final speech would be a speech to actuate; she wanted her classmates to decide to study a foreign language. She researched articles she found in the library and on the Internet. She interviewed a professor in the foreign languages department and borrowed some brochures published by the Modern Language Association. After taking extensive notes, she opened a new computer file and typed five phrases: Attention Step, Need Step, Satisfaction Step, Visualization Step, and Action Step. She then began to draft the framework for her speech. Using the motivated sequence helped Dolly move her listeners step-by-step to her final request for action:

Attention Step

In January 1997 Diane Crispell, executive editor of *American Demographics,* observed that "America is a linguistic paradox. Even as it boasts a richly diverse population speaking a host of languages, it encourages immigrants to forsake their mother tongues and doesn't encourage native English speakers to acquire foreign-language skills." Those who reject opportunities to connect with other cultures do so at their personal and professional peril. Studying a foreign language can give you a competitive edge. Learning a foreign language develops your communication skills, your analytical skills, and your employment opportunities.

Need Step

College students need a variety of competencies for personal, academic, and career success.
  A. Communication skills are essential in each of these areas.
  B. Problem-solving skills are necessary to function successfully in life.
  C. An understanding of other cultures is increasingly important in a global society.

Satisfaction Step

Studying a foreign language can give you a competitive edge.
  A. It improves your communication skills.
  B. It develops your analytical skills.
  C. It provides employment advantages.

Visualization Step

Wouldn't it be nice to take a friend to a romantic French movie and be able to understand the dialogue without having to read the translation? Or, when visiting another country, to be able to pick up a newspaper and to read the headlines? Or, when you land that dream job, to be able to negotiate an important business deal with that client from another country, in part because you spoke her language and understood the customs of her culture?

Action Step

Before the semester is over, I want you to take that step that will give you a competitive edge in your personal, academic, and professional life.
  A. Enroll in a foreign language class while you are in college.
  B. Visit the International Programs Office, and sign up for a study abroad program.
  C. Buy some foreign language self-study learning tapes.
  D. Begin learning a foreign language from a friend from another culture.

Annotated Sample Speech

James Chang delivered the following persuasive speech and placed first at the 2003 Interstate Oratorical Association National Speech Contest. As you read his speech, notice how he used Monroe's motivated sequence to frame his problem–solution discussion of contributing to sustainable charity programs.

Sustainable Giving[18]

James Chang, Cypress College

1 Beatrice Biira, a nine-year-old girl in Uganda, lives in abject poverty. Living in a shanty home where the rain seeps through the roof every night, neither she nor any of her siblings has ever stepped foot in a school. Her story, sadly, is not unique. The World Bank in 2001 concluded that nearly three billion people live on less than two dollars a day. We hear this and we want to help, so we write checks to groups who claim that they will make a difference by donating food, clothing, and other short-term essentials, and we feel like we have helped make a difference in Beatrice's life, and, indeed, we probably have.

2 But what happens after the food runs out? Despite our best intentions, by donating to charities that offer short-term aid, we inadvertently perpetuate the cycle of poverty. Thus, I am advocating today that potential donors to charities should give to organizations that provide solutions that are sustainable in nature and that, furthermore, we change our very conception of the role of charities in fighting poverty. First, we will evaluate the problems caused by traditional conceptions of charitable giving, and then we will take a look at two examples of the solution—sustainable charity programs. Finally, we will see how we can personally take steps to implement these solutions.

3 The American Association of Fundraising Counsel reports that Americans gave $212 billion to charity in 2001, and while that money was certainly donated with good intentions, much of it went to short-term causes that don't solve for poverty in the big picture. Certainly, charities that fight poverty see those horrors on a daily basis. The UN Food and Agricultural Organization reports in their 2002 assessment of the State of Food Insecurity in the World that more than 840 million people in the world are malnourished and more than 150 million of them are under the age of five. Six million children die every year as a result of hunger. The nonprofit almanac *In Brief* reported in July 2001 that there are more than 700,000 nonprofit charities registered in the United States. Many of these organizations are like the Children's Hunger Fund and Food for Life Global, which provide care packages of food to needy families. These programs certainly fulfill an immediate and important need in emergency situations like the aftermath of natural disasters or armed conflict.

4 Outside of these emergency situations, however, there is still massive poverty, and it is here where many of these programs fall short. The unfortunate result of this type of giving is that the families remain dependent on the charities as their very source of livelihood. Because no sustainable solution is ever given, recipients become trapped in a cycle of dependency. This problem is not caused by a lack of giving, for the Independent Sector Coalition reports that 89 percent of American households gave to charity in 2000. It is because of a lack of public awareness of the distinction between traditional charitable giving, as I have just described, and sustainable giving. Andrew Natsios, administrator of the United States Agency for International Development, puts this problem best in a speech delivered on May 31, 2001, when he said, referring to the term *sustainable development,* "it is just not a term that makes it easy for other people to understand what we do. If you explain that we do economic growth, . . . agriculture, . . . environmental program[s], . . . micro-enterprise programs, we perform all of these different functions, people intuitively know what we do."

Attention
In his introduction (paragraphs 1 and 2), James focuses his audience's *attention* on the pervasive problem of poverty. He appeals to his listeners' self-interest (values) by suggesting that they are, unintentionally, part of the problem.

Need
James discusses the problems of traditional charitable giving in paragraphs 3 and 4. He establishes a *need* for reform by demonstrating that traditional giving is not reducing poverty, but actually trapping millions in a cycle of poverty.

Satisfaction
In paragraphs 5 and 6, James seeks to *satisfy* the need for a change by explaining the merits of sustainable development.

5 In order to fight poverty successfully, then, we must learn what sustainable development means and its ramifications for solving the problems of poverty. There are some charities that already realize the importance of providing sustainable development measures. Unfortunately, these organizations do not receive the support that they need, still taking a back seat to traditional conceptions of giving. These organizations take different forms, but all share the common denominator of promoting self-reliance and sustainable, long-term solutions, powerful ends that they can only advance with your support.

6 The old adage goes, "Give a man a fish, and you feed him for a day; teach a man to fish, and you feed him for a lifetime." It was the belief of the founder in the simple premise that people should have the ability to feed themselves that was the foundation for the Heifer Project. Heifer International operates Animals to Families as sustainable gifts. The families raise the animals, benefiting from the products of those animals and selling them as a source of revenue. For example, beehives are given to many families for the sale of honey and beeswax. Of course, the Heifer Project also provides heifers—young female cows that provide up to four gallons of milk a day. The families benefit from the much-needed vitamins and protein in milk, and sell the surplus.

Visualization
After introducing the solution to the problem, James asks his audience (in paragraphs 7 and 8) to *visualize* how sustainable giving can make a difference for those living in poverty. To intensify the desire to contribute, he describes specific success stories, using the examples of Beatrice, Oliverio, and Irma. James returns to that visualization in paragraph 10.

7 The effects of the Heifer Project on these families are very real indeed. Beatrice Biira was able to afford the $60 needed to go to school after the Heifer Project donated a goat to her family in 1994, as documented by *ABC News* in March 2001. Oliverio was a fifteen-year-old young man in Guatemala when the Heifer Project first helped him. Heifer International trained Oliverio to use rabbit droppings as manure on farms, and because rabbits have over 40 offspring a year, they also provided much needed protein and food. Oliverio was then able to likewise train other members of his own village, selling the rabbits to them to raise enough money to pay for his and his sister's tuition. According to Heifer International's 2002 annual report, the Heifer Project has donated 28 different kinds of livestock, helping millions of families in 125 countries.

8 Programs like the Heifer Project are unique in providing permanent solutions. While other organizations continue to provide short-term aid and entrench dependency, sustainable programs make a long-term difference. Just as the Heifer Project donates animals to help its recipients, another organization, the Grameen Foundation, or the Grameen Bank, operates by issuing micro-credit loans that are interest- and collateral-free. The beneficiaries use the money to start businesses to become permanent sources of revenue. The foundation trains and supervises their recipients and organizes them into support groups. For example, Irma Hernandez, a woman from Honduras, joined with four other women in taking out a loan for $120 from the Adelante Foundation, a program supported by and modeled on Grameen. Her husband worked full-time as a farm laborer, but because work was not always available, the income was simply too low and too unstable to support the five children that they had. With the money that Irma borrowed, she was able to buy the necessary tools to start a clothes-making business that brought a steady second income to the family. Micro-credit loans are not a new concept—in fact, governments have used them effectively to spur development. *The Economist* of April 19, 2003, reports that the Thai government is now endowing each village in the country with a micro-credit fund worth about $23,000 each. Despite the success of sustainable programs where implemented, we as donors continue to choose the quick fix, contributing to organizations that provide short-term aid when in fact it is sustainable programs that are needed.

Action
In paragraph 9, James tells his listeners how they can *act* to implement the solution on an institutional and an individual level. He encourages his audience to contribute to two organizations, and he provides the URLs for their websites.

9 The most important question that should then remain is how you personally can help out. On an institutional level, the United States Agency for International Development, US-AID, is one of the leaders in fighting global poverty and should be encouraged to strengthen and increase its sustainable programs. Information about US-AID and the ability to contact the agency can be found on its website at usaid.org. On an individual level, the two private organizations I've talked about today provide detailed information about

their on-going operations as well as the opportunity to contribute on their websites. The Heifer Project, donating animals as sustainable gifts and having directly improved the lives of Beatrice and Oliverio, has a website at heifer.org. The Grameen Bank, issuing micro-credit loans and having directly helped Irma Hernandez and her family, has a website at gfusa.org. These are only two of a small but growing number of sustainable charities. Earlier, we learned that 89 percent of American households give regularly and that $212 billion was given in 2001. Clearly, we want to give, so the question is not whether or not we give, but to what we give.

10 Today, we've looked at the problems of poverty in the developing world and seen how the traditional conception of giving only traps recipients in a cycle of dependency and poverty. We then evaluated two examples of the solution—sustainable charities—and discussed action steps that we can all take. Sustainable charities empower people to help themselves. It is these organizations that give the needy people of the world not only a better today, but the opportunity for a better tomorrow—created by and for themselves.

Summary

Persuasion is the art of affecting other people's values, beliefs, attitudes, or behaviors. The logical impact of a persuasive speech springs from a speaker's *evidence* and reasoning. To be an effective persuader, you must know how to structure a valid argument, how to detect flaws in reasoning, and how to word propositions. If you are delivering a speech to actuate, you also need to have a clear grasp of the motivational super-structure of your message. The three steps of structuring an argument are (1) to make a claim you want the audience to accept, (2) to supply evidence supporting that claim, and (3) to explain how the evidence proves the claim. The validity of any claim ultimately depends on the quality of the evidence supporting it.

Speakers sometimes select a particular persuasive topic because they hear or read an argument they wish to oppose. The act of countering one argument with another is called refutation. To refute an argument, follow this four-step *refutational strategy:* First, state the position you are refuting. Second, state your own position. Third, support your position with evidence. And fourth, show how your position undermines the argument you oppose.

To give listeners a reason to accept a persuasive claim, speakers may use any of five types of arguments. First, *argument by example* uses specific instances to support a general claim. For an argument by example to be valid, the speaker must use examples that are true, relevant to the claim, sufficient in number, and representative. Second, *argument by analogy* links two concepts, conditions, or experiences and claims that what is true of one will be true of the other. The validity of argument by analogy depends on the quality of the comparison a speaker develops. To test that analogy, ask two questions: (1) Are the similarities between the cases relevant? and (2) Are any differences between the two cases relevant?

Argument by cause, the third type of argument, links two concepts, conditions, or experiences and claims that one causes the other. A speaker arguing by cause can move listeners' attention forward from cause to effect or can trace effects back to their causes. To test the validity of the cause–effect relationship, speakers and listeners should consider three questions: (1) Does a causal relationship exist? (2) Could the presumed cause produce the effect? and (3) Could the effect result from other causes?

A fourth type of argument, *deductive argument,* employs a pattern called a *syllogism,* consisting of three parts. The major premise is a claim about a general group of people, events, or conditions. The minor premise places a person, event, or condition into that general class. And the conclusion argues that what is true of the general class is also true of the specific instance. For an argument by deduction to be valid, both the major and minor premises must be true and they must be related.

Finally, *argument by authority* uses testimony from an expert source to prove a speaker's claim. The validity of this type of argument depends on the credibility the authority has with the audience. To be credible, the source should be both competent and unbiased.

Both speakers and listeners must watch out for logical flaws or *fallacies* in persuasive arguments. Fallacious arguments are particularly dangerous because they may resemble sound reasoning as we read or listen to them. Unfortunately, ten fallacies of argument are common. The fallacy of *hasty generalization* involves making claims on the basis of insufficient or unrepresentative examples. *False analogy* occurs when an argument by analogy compares entities that have critical differences. *Post hoc ergo propter hoc* falsely argues that, because event A preceded event B, A caused B. It confuses chronology with causation. The *slippery slope* fallacy asserts that one event inevitably unleashes a series of events. The *red herring* fallacy introduces irrelevant issues to deflect attention from the true question under discussion. The fallacy called *appeal to tradition* asserts that old ways of doing things are correct or best, simply because they are traditional. A *false dilemma* argues that we must choose between two alternatives, when in reality we may have a range of options. The fallacy of *false authority* uses testimony from sources who have no real expertise on the topic in question. The *bandwagon* fallacy argues that we should behave or think a particular way because most people do. Finally, the *ad hominem* fallacy urges listeners to reject an idea because of allegations about the character, politics, religion, or lifestyle of the person voicing the idea.

All persuasive speeches advocate *propositions*, position statements the speaker wants listeners to accept. Persuasive propositions must be stated as a declarative sentence expressing a judgment, must be debatable, and require proof in order to be accepted. The three types of persuasive propositions are propositions of fact, value, and policy. *Propositions of fact* ask the audience to accept the truth or falsity of a statement. *Propositions of value* ask the audience to determine the relative worth of an idea or action. *Propositions of policy* ask the audience to support a course of action.

A persuasive speech must move listeners through a series of steps. *Monroe's motivated sequence* is a formal, five-step pattern for moving listeners to belief or action: (1) get the attention of your listeners, (2) clarify the need, (3) show how to satisfy that need, (4) visualize the solution, and (5) request action.

Practice Critique

Identifying a Claim and Evaluating Evidence

Read the transcript of James Chang's speech, "Sustainable Giving," in this chapter. Before offering a solution, James discusses barriers of traditional charitable giving to combating long-term poverty. As you read his speech, make a list of the problems and causes he presents, and then analyze how he develops each. What is the claim? What supporting material does James offer to support that claim? Does the evidence prove the point? Why or why not? Write a few suggestions you could offer James to make his arguments stronger and more persuasive.

Exercises

1. You have been asked to visit your former high school to speak to a group of college-bound students. The school's counselor has asked you to speak on the topic "College Years Are the Best Years of Your Life!" Construct three arguments that support this position. Give an example of how your speech could use each type of argument: example, analogy, cause, deduction, and authority.

2. Using argument by analogy, construct a short speech on one or more of the following topics. What similarities between the two entities make your analogy credible? What differences undermine the believability of each statement?
   a. Being in college is like being in a demolition derby.
   b. Life is like an athletic contest.
   c. Studying for an exam is like tying your shoe.
   d. Marriage is like gardening.
   e. A job interview is like an audition for a role in a film.

3. Determine whether each of the following statements is a proposition of fact, value, or policy.
   a. The university should build a new library.
   b. A new library would cost the university seven million dollars.
   c. It is more important to build a new library than to expand our athletic facilities.
   d. Sex education encourages sexual activity among schoolchildren.
   e. The FDA should reduce required testing for experimental drugs to fight life-threatening illnesses.
   f. It is more important for a country to do good than to feel good.

4. Identify the major premise, minor premise, and conclusion in each of the following groups of statements:
   a. *Inquiring Minds* should be aired on the Trashy Cable Network.
   Inquiring Minds is a fluffy news show.

All fluffy news shows should be aired on the Trashy Cable Network.
   b. A high grade-point average is important to Charlotte. Today's college students value high grade-point averages.
   Charlotte is a college student.

5. Find an editorial from a recent campus, local, or national newspaper. Identify the different types of arguments used.

6. Locate examples of each fallacy discussed in this chapter. Examine advertisements in newspapers and in magazines and on radio, television, and the Internet. Read editorials, letters to the editor, and transcripts of speeches.

7. Apply the three criteria for well-worded propositions by writing specific propositions on the following topics:
   a. Hate crimes
   b. Lotteries
   c. Minimum legal drinking age
   d. Feminism
   e. Living wills

8. Write a proposition analysis thinkpiece on the topic you have selected for a persuasive speech.
   a. Write the proposition you intend to support or oppose.

   b. Define key or ambiguous terms.
   c. Determine the important debatable issues.
   d. Suggest types of supporting materials necessary to prove your points.

9. Write a proposition of fact, value, and policy for each of the following topic areas.
   a. Electric cars
   b. A foreign language requirement for all college students
   c. Competency tests for teachers
   d. Funding for cancer research

10. Consider the topic "This college should use only a pass–fail grading system." Prepare an argument for this topic using the "4 S" structure. Then refute your argument using the four-step refutational strategy.

11. Select a topic not discussed in this chapter, and describe how you might go about developing it using each step of Monroe's motivated sequence.

12. If there will be a question–answer period following your persuasive speech, read the "Try This" assignment on page 382 in Chapter 18.

Speaking on
Special Occasions

chapter

18

> *If we use common words on a great occasion, they are the most striking, because they are felt at once to have a particular meaning, like old banners, or everyday clothes, hung up in a sacred place.* —GEORGE ELIOT

On June 18, 2004, celebrities including B. B. King, Stevie Wonder, Willie Nelson, and Clint Eastwood gathered to memorialize and celebrate the life of musician Ray Charles. Reverend Jesse Jackson began his remarks by declaring, "Now heaven has a maestro."[1]

On July 25, 2004, the first year he was eligible for the honor, Major League pitcher Dennis Eckerseley was inducted into the Baseball Hall of Fame in Cooperstown, New York. "I never envisioned myself standing next to my childhood idols, Juan Marichal and Willie Mays," Eckersley said at the beginning of his speech.[2]

In April 1993, Elie Wiesel, 1986 winner of the Nobel Prize for Peace, spoke at ceremonies to dedicate the United States Holocaust Memorial Museum in Washington, D.C. He described a Jewish woman from the Carpathian mountains who was confused when she read about the Warsaw Ghetto uprising. "Treblinka, Ponar, Belzec, Chelmno, Birkenau; she had never heard of these places. One year later, together with her entire family, she was in a cattle-car traveling to the black-hole of history named Auschwitz." Many in the audience were quietly weeping as Wiesel revealed at the end of his speech, "She was my mother."[3]

Exploring *Online*

COMMENCEMENT SPEECHES
www.heraldnet.com/grads
Since 1997 *The Herald* newspaper in Everett, Washington, has collected complete text speeches given by students at area high school and college graduation ceremonies. Browse this collection, organized by year, to read and analyze how students developed their speeches for these occasions.

Though none of us has the celebrity or visibility of talk show host and entrepreneur Oprah Winfrey, inducted into the NAACP Hall of Fame in the spring of 2005, we can all count on being called on to deliver a speech on some special occasion: introducing a guest speaker at a club meeting, accepting an award from a civic group, or delivering a eulogy at the funeral or memorial service of a relative or friend. In addition to these common occasions, remember some of the unique occasions we mentioned in Chapter 1: speaking to accept a Heisman Trophy, a Tony, or an Academy Award or to present important research findings to a national convention and the media.

To speak your best on any of these occasions, you must consider the customs and audience expectations in each case. In this chapter, we will discuss eight special occasions or special circumstances for public speeches: the speech of introduction, the speech of presentation, the acceptance speech, the speech of tribute, the speech to entertain, the impromptu speech, the question–answer period, and the videotaped speech. You will learn guidelines for each of these types of speeches and read examples of many of them. This information can serve you well beyond the classroom and prepare you for any occasion when you are requested, invited, or expected to speak.

The Speech of Introduction

One of the most common types of special-occasion speeches is the **speech of introduction.** Some people use that phrase to indicate speeches by people introducing themselves to an audience. As we use the phrase in this chapter, however, we mean a speech introducing a featured speaker. The following guidelines will help you prepare such a speech of introduction.

Guidelines for the Speech of Introduction

1. Focus on the featured speaker.
2. Be brief.
3. Establish the speaker's credibility.
4. Create realistic expectations.
5. Set the tone for the speech.

The first guideline to remember is to *keep the focus on the person being introduced.* The audience has not gathered to hear you, so don't upstage the featured speaker. Keep your remarks short, simple, and sincere.

To achieve the first guideline, you will want to follow the second: *Be brief.* If you can, request and get a copy of the speaker's résumé. This will give you a body of information to select from when preparing your introductory remarks. The key word in that last sentence is *select.* Your listeners will tune out quickly if your introduction is a lengthy chronology of jobs or events in a person's life. Highlight key information only.

A third guideline is to *establish the speaker's credibility on the topic.* You do this by presenting the speaker's credentials. As you prepare your speech of introduction, ask and answer questions such as these: What makes the speaker qualified to speak on the subject? What education and experiences make the speaker's insights worthy of our belief?

Fourth, remember to *create realistic expectations.* Genuine praise is commendable, just be careful not to oversell the speaker. Can you imagine walking to the microphone after the following introduction: "Our speaker tonight is one of the great speakers in this country. I heard her last year, and she had us laughing until our sides hurt. She will keep you spellbound from her first word to her last. Get ready for the best speech you've heard in your entire life!"

Finally, you should phrase your remarks to *establish a tone consistent with the speaker's presentation.* Would you give a humorous introduction for a speaker whose topic is "The Grieving Process: What to Do When a Loved One Dies"? Of course not. On the other hand, if the evening is designed for merriment, your introduction should help set that mood.

Communication professors should certainly know how to introduce a featured speaker. In the following example, Professor Don Ochs of the University of Iowa did an exemplary job of introducing his longtime colleague, Professor Samuel L. Becker. Becker was the keynote speaker at a Central States Communication Association convention. You'll see that Ochs uses some communication jargon because he is speaking to a group of communication professionals. Notice, though, how Ochs's brief, cordial remarks focus on Becker, establishing his credibility and setting the tone for Becker's informative and inspirational speech:

> Thirty years ago I walked out of an Iowa City store onto the main street and noticed Sam Becker walking about twenty feet ahead of me. His youngest daughter was alongside Sam but she was terribly upset about something; crying, and obviously hurt about something. Sam put his arm around his daughter and, in the space of two blocks, said something that comforted and fixed the problem. She was smiling when they parted company.
>
> I share this snapshot of Sam with you because, for me, it captures Sam's approach to life, higher education, scholarship, and our profession.

speech of introduction: a speech introducing a featured speaker to an audience.

Sam Becker has figuratively put his arm around difficulties and problems for his entire career. He's made all of us as teachers and scholars better persons and better professionals with his intellect, his vision, his energy, and his instinctive willingness to help.

As a rhetorician I would much prefer to introduce Sam with figures and tropes, with synechdoche, litotes, and hyperbole. But Sam is a social scientist, so I will be quantitative instead.

How much has Sam helped us? Sam has taught at four universities; written six books; been active in eight professional associations; authored ten monographs; served on twelve editorial boards; worked on evaluation teams for thirty-two colleges and universities; served on thirty-six university committees; lectured at fifty colleges and universities; directed fifty-five PhDs; and authored 105 articles. Without doubt, he has helped and assisted and supported all of us. Our speaker today, Sam Becker.[4]

The Speech of Presentation

The **speech of presentation** confers an award, a prize, or some other form of special recognition on an individual or a group. Such speeches are typically made on special occasions: after banquets or parties; as parts of business meetings or sessions of a convention; or at awards ceremonies such as the Tony Awards, the Academy Awards, or the Grammy Awards, during which many people will be recognized.

We will restrict our discussion of the speech of presentation to prepared statements commenting on and presenting an award to an individual or group. Thus, remarks made by a presenter about an actor honored with the American Film Institute's Lifetime Achievement Award would qualify as a speech of presentation; opening the envelope and reading the winner of the Grammy Award for Song of the Year is really an announcement, rather than a prepared speech. When you give a speech of presentation, let the nature and importance of the award being presented, as well as the occasion on which it is being presented, shape your remarks. The following guidelines will help you plan this special-occasion speech.

Key Points

Guidelines for the Speech of Presentation

1. State the purpose of the award or recognition.
2. State the recipient's qualifications.
3. Adapt your speech's organization to audience knowledge.
4. Compliment finalists for the award.

First, as a presenter, you should *state the purpose of the award or recognition.* If the audience is unfamiliar with the award—if it is a new or special award—or if they know nothing about the organization making the award, you will probably want to begin by briefly explaining the nature of the award or the rationale for presenting it. This is especially important if you, as the speaker, represent the organization making the award. In contrast, an award having a long history probably needs little if any explanation.

A second guideline is to *focus your speech on the achievements for which the award is being made;* don't attempt a detailed biography of the recipient. Because you are merely highlighting the honoree's accomplishments, the speech of presentation will be brief, rarely more than five minutes long and frequently much shorter.

Third, *organize a speech of presentation primarily according to whether your listeners know the name of the recipient in advance.* If they do not know the name of the individual you are honoring, capitalize on their curiosity. If you begin by announcing the name of the recipient and then explaining why that person was selected, the bulk of your speech will be anticlimactic. Instead, let ambiguity about who will receive the honor propel the speech and maintain the audience's attention. Begin by making general comments that could refer to several or many people; as the speech progresses, let your

speech of presentation: a speech conferring an award, a prize, or some other recognition on an individual or group.

Following a speech of presentation, the recipient of the award or honor often delivers a brief, gracious acceptance speech.

comments get more specific. If the person receiving your award is from a group containing both men and women, use gender-neutral descriptions ("this person" or "our honoree"), rather than using "he" or "she." In this way, you keep your audience guessing and allow them the pleasure of solving a puzzle. If the audience knows in advance the name of the person being recognized, your strategy changes. In this case, begin the speech with specifics and end with more general statements that summarize the reasons for the presentation.

Finally, if a group of individuals has been nominated and you are announcing the winner with your speech of presentation, briefly *compliment the entire group of people who have been nominated for the award.*

We asked Josh McNair, a graduate teaching assistant, to create and present an award for the graduate student selected to follow him. Notice how he focuses on the reasons for the award and the honoree's qualifications. Josh also uses imagery and quotations appropriate to the occasion.

Exploring *Online*

SAMPLE SPEECHES
http://gos.sbc.edu
"Gifts of Speech" is an ongoing project from Sweet Briar College in Virginia. This site offers access to texts of speeches by influential women from around the world. You can search this collection alphabetically by particular speakers or chronologically by year. The site also lists the "Top 100 American Speeches of the 20th Century," with transcripts of the speeches by women.

> Laurent A. Daloz, a 20th-century educator, once observed, "In the end, good teaching lies in a willingness to attend and care for what happens in our students, ourselves, and the space between us." I couldn't agree more. Teaching is the dynamic process of filling the space between teacher and student through authentic and open communication.
>
> As part of a new tradition at Radford University, graduate students who have completed their teaching responsibilities are given the opportunity to recognize Graduate Teaching Fellows (GTFs), who will soon begin their teaching journey as communication instructors. The Great Teaching Future Award recognizes graduate students in the Department of Communication who have demonstrated academic excellence, teaching aptitude, and commitment to higher education. This year's honoree has shown all these qualities and now begins his journey to fill the space between himself and his students with knowledge, skills, and the desire for learning. It is both a privilege and pleasure to present the first Great Teaching Future Award to Mr. Zach Henning.
>
> This year's award recipient has demonstrated a unique commitment to teaching speech communication. This past year he independently sought out academic and

Josh states the purpose of the award.

He announces the name of the award recipient.

The Speech of Presentation **373**

applied opportunities for training as a college instructor. Last fall he successfully designed and delivered a public speaking teaching module in a graduate seminar in communication education. As an intern in Dr. George Grice's undergraduate persuasion class, Zach used multimedia and email to actively engage students in learning both in and out of the classroom. He completed his instructor training over the summer when, on a volunteer basis, he assisted Dr. Bill Kennan in teaching two sections of public speaking. Under Dr. Kennan's tutelage, Zach listened to and critiqued more than a hundred student speeches.

Josh states the recipient's qualifications.

Those of us who know Zach have witnessed his commitment to filling the space between himself and his students. First, Zach fills the space with knowledge of *what* to teach. The public speaking teaching module he developed includes clear teaching objectives that emphasize both the critical thinking and experiential components of constructing and delivering speeches. Second, Zach fills the space with skills on *how* to teach. In Dr. Grice's persuasion class, he successfully incorporated communication technology, traditional lecture, and small-group formats to motivate students. Finally, Zach fills the space with humor and his unique wit to foster in his students a desire for learning.

He reinforces the purpose of the award and presents it to the recipient.

As our teaching mentor, Dr. Grice, states in his teaching philosophy, "Understanding and applying knowledge comes from discovering relationships through communication, imagination, and invention." The Great Teaching Future Award follows this teaching philosophy and recognizes Graduate Teaching Fellows who have demonstrated excellence in attending to and caring for the space between themselves and their students. It is with great pleasure, then, that I present Zach Henning with this year's Great Teaching Future Award.[5]

The Acceptance Speech

At some point in your life, you may be commended publicly for service you have given to a cause or an organization. You may be presented a farewell or retirement gift from your friends or co-workers. You may receive an award for winning a sporting event, an essay contest, or a speech contest. Although these are different occasions, they have at

Ethical Decisions

How (and Whether) to Polish a Bad Apple

King is president of the Porridge Players, an organization that stages musical comedies on his campus. This season, the Players have performed *South Pacific,* and the actress who played Nelly Forbush is Maria MacIntosh, an enormously talented singer, dancer, and actress with a horrible temper and an insufferably arrogant attitude. As president of the Players, King has been called on time after time to mediate disputes between this woman and other members of the cast and crew. By the time the season is over, he has little respect for her, despite her considerable talents.

At the end of each season, the faculty advisory board for the Players votes on awards for the best performers, director, technical people, and so forth. No one is very surprised when Maria is chosen to receive the award for best actress. King, however, is dismayed to learn that he has to present it, along with a short introductory speech. He wonders what to do. Should he simply praise Maria's performance and not mention the difficulties she caused, or is it his responsibility to make the faculty board aware of her flaws and negative impact on the company? What kind of information do you think King should include in his speech? Be prepared to discuss your answer with the class.

least one thing in common—each requires a response. To accept a gift or an award without expressing appreciation is socially unacceptable. An **acceptance speech**, then, is a response to a speech of presentation. When a recipient acknowledges the award or tribute, he or she provides closure to the process. A gracious acceptance speech usually includes four steps.

First, *thank the person or organization bestowing the award.* You may wish to name not only the group sponsoring the award, but also the person who made the speech of presentation. In addition, you may want to commend what the award represents. Your respect for the award and its donor authenticates your statement of appreciation.

Second, if you are accepting a competitively selected award, and especially if your competitors are in the audience, acknowledge their qualifications and compliment them. This step need not be lengthy; you can *compliment your peers* as a group rather than individually.

Third, *thank those who helped you achieve the honor.* Seldom do we achieve things by ourselves. Whether you are an accomplished pianist, vocalist, artist, athlete, or writer, you have usually had someone—parents, teachers, or coaches—who invested time, money, and expertise to help you achieve your best.

Finally, *accept your award graciously.* In response to Josh's speech of presentation, graduate student Zach Henning delivered the following acceptance speech. Notice how he incorporates all the guidelines we've discussed:

Guidelines for the Acceptance Speech

1. Thank those who bestowed the award.
2. Compliment the competition.
3. Thank those who helped you attain the award.
4. Accept the award graciously.

Exploring *Online*

SAMPLE ACCEPTANCE SPEECH
www.eliewieselfoundation.org/ElieWiesel/
speech.html
Visit this site for an excellent example of an acceptance speech that was both inspirational and persuasive. On December 10, 1986, Elie Wiesel graciously accepted the Nobel Peace Prize. In this famous speech he blended examples and evocative language to remind his audience of suffering and injustice and to call them to action, "the only remedy to indifference."

Thank you, Josh, for your kind words and for your support. It is with great honor that I accept this award. I realize that I have big shoes to fill and I will do my best to follow your example.

When I think about teaching, I'm reminded of what the great philosopher Aristotle said, "Teaching is the highest form of understanding." Through my internship and volunteer work with the communication department, I've learned more about who I am and how I can help others succeed. My understanding started with the feelings I experienced when I noticed 34 students looking up and paying attention to my words and thoughts. Their eagerness to learn inspired me to be the best instructor I can.

I know many qualified candidates who share my beliefs and feelings about teaching. Each could easily take my place with the experiences they bring to this department. I'm sure they would agree that teaching is more than a chore or an occupation. Instead, it's an art that is mastered through experience and guidance.

For that guidance, I turned to Dr. George Grice and Dr. William Kennan. They taught me about classroom logistics, lesson plans, and practical knowledge about the mechanics of teaching. More importantly, however, they taught me how to be passionate about what I am doing and how to positively influence the lives of students beyond the textbook and lecture material. For this I thank you both for your patience and generosity in offering me the opportunity to share in that passion.

I would also like to thank Dr. Gwen Brown, the director of our graduate program. Last year, new to the program and this university, I came to her wanting to know how I could become a graduate teaching fellow. Though there were no positions available at that time, Dr. Brown guided me to curricular and extracurricular opportunities that

Zach thanks the presenter and accepts the award.

He compliments the competition.

Zach thanks those who helped him attain the award.

acceptance speech: a speech responding to a speech of presentation by acknowledging an award, a tribute, or recognition.

would heighten my interest in teaching. Her advice gave me the opportunity to reapply and accept this honor today.

And, most importantly, I would like to thank my students for their hard work and dedication. It is my goal not only to teach you about how to succeed in the classroom, but also to teach you about how to succeed in life. I am a firm believer in Dr. Martin Luther King, Jr.'s challenge that "the function of education is to teach one to think intensively and to think critically." I share this goal of education to teach both knowledge and character to prepare you for the challenges and opportunities you will encounter in your professional lives.

I hope that I never stop learning and understanding. There are always new challenges and new ways of thinking and teaching. I hope to continue to grow and change as I gain more experience and knowledge. Thank you for this first step to a lifetime of teaching and learning.[6]

He accepts the award graciously.

The Speech of Tribute

A **speech of tribute** honors a person, a group, or an event, and it can be one of the most moving forms of public address. A special form of the speech of tribute is the **eulogy**, a speech given for those who have recently died. "Though perceived as ponderous, weepy, and weighted with sadness, the eulogy is actually a vibrant and adaptable art whose best examples shine down the ages, from Pericles's funeral oration to Lincoln's Gettysburg Address to Reagan's eulogy for the *Challenger* astronauts."[7]

Peggy Noonan, presidential speechwriter, captures the power of eulogies:

They are the most moving kind of speech because they attempt to pluck meaning from the fog, and on short order, when the emotions are still ragged and raw and susceptible to leaps. It is a challenge to look at a life and organize our thoughts about it and try to explain to ourselves what it meant, and the most moving part is the element of implicit celebration. Most people aren't appreciated enough, and the bravest things we do in our lives are usually known only to ourselves. No one throws ticker tape on the man who chose to be faithful to his wife, on the lawyer who didn't take the drug money, or the daughter who held her tongue again and again. All this anonymous heroism. A eulogy gives us a chance to celebrate it.[8]

Five guidelines will help you write a eulogy or any other speech of tribute.

First, *establish noble themes*. As you begin developing the eulogy, ask "Why is this person worthy of my respect and praise?" Answer this question by developing themes you want the audience to remember. Remember to focus on the positive. A speech of tribute celebrates what is good about a person; it is not an occasion for a warts-and-all biography. You must be careful, however, not to exaggerate a person's accomplishments. To do so may undermine your speech by making it seem insincere or unbelievable.

Our student Stuart delivered a speech of tribute for one of his childhood heroes: Hall of Fame baseball player, Ted Williams. He avoided the trap of organizing his speech as a biographical listing in an encyclopedia. Instead, he highlighted three lessons that all audience members, whether baseball fans or not, could learn from studying Williams's life. Stuart introduced these themes as he previewed his key ideas:

He was given many eloquent nicknames by his teammates and the news media: The Splendid Splinter, The Kid, and Teddy Ballgame. All portray his amazing baseball tal-

Key Points

Guidelines for the Speech of Tribute

1. Establish noble themes.
2. Provide vivid examples.
3. Express audience feelings.
4. Create a memorable image.
5. Be genuine.

speech of tribute: a speech honoring a person, group, or event.

eulogy: a speech of tribute praising a person who has recently died.

ent, but all fail to capture the values that directed his life. Ted Williams taught us a lesson in *patriotism,* a lesson in *perseverance,* and a lesson in *charity.* And he did so not by lecturing or preaching, but by powerfully leading by example.

Second, *develop the themes of your speech with vivid examples.* Anecdotes, stories, and personal testimony are excellent ways of making your speech more vivid, humane, and memorable.

Third, *express the feelings of the audience assembled* or those whom you represent. The audience needs to be a part of the occasion for any speech of tribute. If you are honoring a former teacher, you may speak for yourself, but you can also speak for your class or even all students who studied under Mr. Crenshaw. The honoree should feel that the tribute expresses more than one person's view.

Your use of noble themes, vivid examples, and audience feelings should combine to *create a memorable image of the person being honored.* Your speech not only honors someone, it also helps audience members focus on that person's importance to them.

Finally, *be genuine.* If you are asked to deliver a speech of tribute about someone you do not know, you may want to decline respectfully. The personal bond and interaction you develop in getting to know someone well is essential for a speech of tribute. Also, the person being honored may find the tribute more meaningful if it comes from a person he or she knows well.

> *A great eulogy is both art and architecture—a bridge between the living and the dead, memory and eternity.*
>
> —CYRUS M. COPELAND[9]

The Speech to Entertain

The three main purposes of speaking are to inform, to persuade, and to entertain. Although many informative and persuasive speeches contain elements of humor, the speech designed specifically to entertain is a special case because it is often difficult to do well.

The **speech to entertain** seeks to make a point through the creative, organized use of the speaker's humor. The distinguishing characteristic of a speech to entertain is the entertainment value of its supporting materials. It is usually delivered on an occasion when people are in a light mood: after a banquet, as part of an awards ceremony, and on other festive occasions.

A *speech to entertain* is different from *speaking to entertain.* In their opening monologues, Jay Leno and David Letterman are both speaking to entertain. Their purpose is to relax the audience, establish some interaction with them, and set the mood for the rest of the show. Their remarks are not organized around a central theme, something essential to a speech to entertain. If you combine the following five guidelines with what you already know about developing a public speech, you will discover that a speech to entertain is both challenging and fun to present.

The first requirement for a speech to entertain is that it *makes a point,* or communicates a thesis, no less than does the most carefully crafted informative or persuasive speech. Frequently, the person delivering a speech to entertain is trying to make the audience aware of conditions, experiences, or habits that they take for granted. Here are

Key Points

Guidelines for the Speech to Entertain

1. Make a point.
2. Be creative.
3. Be organized.
4. Use appropriate humor.
5. Use spirited delivery.

speech to entertain: a speech used to make a point through the creative, organized use of the speaker's humor.

examples of topics on which we have heard students present successful speeches to entertain:

The imprecision and incorrectness of language, especially that used in some advertisements

Many doctors' failure to speak language that their patients can understand and many patients' failure to ask their doctors the right questions

Our interest in or curiosity about tabloid news stories

The routine, expensive date versus creative, less expensive dating options

In some of these speeches, the speaker had stated the main point fairly bluntly by the end of the speech: Take a careful look at the language used to sell you things; you owe it to your health to ask questions of your doctor; you do not have to spend a fortune to have an interesting time on a date. In other speeches, speakers simply implied their thesis. Each of these speeches did make a point, however.

Second, *a speech to entertain is creative.* To be creative you must make sure that your speech to entertain is your product, and not simply a replay of a Bernie Mac or an Ellen DeGeneres monologue. A replay like this is not creative, no matter how great a job you think you do delivering the other person's lines. Moreover, if you copy Bernie's or Ellen's words and don't credit them, you are plagiarizing. Your speech to entertain should be original and creative. It should give your audience a glimpse of your unique view of the world.

Third, *a speech to entertain is organized.* It must have an introduction, body, and conclusion, just as informative and persuasive speeches do. In other words, the speech to entertain must convey a sense of moving toward some logical point and achieving closure after adequately developing that point. Failure to organize your materials will cause you to ramble, embarrassing both you and your audience. You will feel, quite literally, like the novice comic caught without a finish, a sure-fire joke that makes a good exit line. The audience will sense that you are struggling and will have trouble relaxing and enjoying your humor.

Use of appropriate humor is the fourth guideline for a speech to entertain. The speech to entertain is difficult to do well for a simple reason: Most people associate entertainment with lots of laughter and feel that if the audience is not laughing a good deal they are not responding favorably to the speech. But stop to consider for a moment the range of things that entertain you, from outrageous antics to quiet, pointed barbs. Your humor should be adapted to your topic, your audience, the occasion, and your own personal style. The following four suggestions should guide your use of humor:

1. *Be relevant.* Good humor is relevant to your general purpose and makes the main ideas of your speech memorable. Humor not related to the point you are making should still be relevant to your general purpose: to entertain. Michael's speech to entertain discussed the ways we label products and people. One of his points was that the product warnings printed on packaging tell us about various companies' views of their customers. His examples at this point in the speech were relevant to that main idea and added humor to his speech by helping him show the absurdity of many product labels.

For example, the first thing I saw on the box my toaster came in was a warning. Warning—do not submerge in water, especially when the plug is connected to an electrical outlet. Now just at a practical level, I'm pretty sure that almost anyone should be able to figure out that the chances of getting your Pop Tart to turn brown at the bottom of a Jacuzzi are pretty slim to begin with. But as far as this whole electrocution thing is concerned, I'm not entirely sure how much damage 500 volts could do to these people. I mean let's face it, if you're going to plug in your toaster just so you can take it into the shower with you, a little shock there may not be such a bad idea.[10]

2. *Be tasteful.* Important to any speech, audience analysis is vital for a speech to entertain. Taste is subjective. What delights some listeners may offend others. Do the best job you can in analyzing your audience, but when in doubt, err on the side of caution. Remember, humor that is off-color is off-limits.

3. *Be tactful.* Avoid humor that generates laughter at the expense of others. There may be times when good-natured ribbing is appropriate, but humor intended to belittle or demean a person or group is unethical and unacceptable. For that reason, most sexist or ethnic humor should also be off-limits.

4. *Be positive.* The tone for most occasions featuring speeches to entertain should be festive. People have come together to relax and enjoy each other's company. Dark, negative humor is usually inappropriate as it casts a somber tone on the situation.

Finally, *a speech to entertain benefits from spirited delivery.* We have often heard good speeches to entertain and looked forward to reading transcripts of them later. We were usually disappointed. The personality, timing, and interaction with the audience that made the speech lively and unforgettable could not be captured on paper. We have also read manuscripts of speeches to entertain that promised to be dynamic when presented, only to see them diminished by a monotonous, colorless, and lifeless delivery.

The Impromptu Speech

You are standing in the back of a crowded orientation session when, to your surprise, your supervisor introduces you and says, "Come up here and say a few words to these folks." Or you receive an award you didn't know you were being considered for. As people begin to applaud and whistle, you start walking to the front of the room to accept an attractive plaque. These are but two situations in which you would deliver an impromptu speech.

The **impromptu speech,** one with limited or no advance preparation, can be intimidating. You have not had time to think about the ideas you want to communicate. You begin speaking without knowing the exact words you will use. You have not practiced delivering your speech. Don't panic! All is not lost. By now you have a pretty good understanding of how to organize, support, and deliver a speech. You have practiced these skills in prepared classroom speeches. All this practice will help you in your impromptu speech. With experience comes confidence. You already know what it feels like to stand before an audience. "But this is different," you might be saying right about now. "In those cases I had time to prepare." Well, if you follow these four guidelines, you should be ready for almost any impromptu speech that comes along.

> **Key Points**
>
> **Guidelines for the Impromptu Speech**
>
> 1. Speak on a topic you know well.
> 2. Make the most of the preparation time you have.
> 3. Focus on a single or a few key points.
> 4. Be brief.

First, if you have a choice, *speak on a topic you know well.* The more you know about your topic, the better you will be able to select relevant ideas, organize them, and explain them as you speak. You will also be more comfortable talking about a subject you know, and your confidence will show in your delivery.

impromptu speech: a speech delivered with little or no advance preparation.

By the end of this course, you should learn enough public speaking skills to comfortably and confidently offer your impromptu thoughts about a subject you know.

Even though your preparation time is limited or nonexistent, *make the most of the time you have.* Don't waste "walking time" from your seat to the front of the room worrying. Instead, ask yourself, "What do I want the audience to remember when I sit down? What two or three points will help them remember this?"

Third, *focus on a single or a few key points.* This may be easier if you think a bit like the character Charlie Fox in David Mamet's play *Speed-the-Plow.* As a movie producer, Charlie's test of a screenplay is whether he can condense it to one sentence so that *TV Guide* can print a blurb about it. As silly as it may seem, this strategy could help you focus on the few ideas you want to get across to your listeners. If you have been asked to explain why you support building a new library instead of renovating the existing facility, think of the two or three most important reasons underlying your position. And remember to use the "4 S's" as you present those reasons to your audience.

Finally, *be brief.* One public speaking axiom is, "Stand up! Speak up! Shut up!" Although this can be carried to an extreme, it is probably good advice for the impromptu speaker. An impromptu speech is not the occasion for a long, rambling discourse. Say what you need to say, and then be seated.

The Question–Answer Period

Guidelines to Answering Questions

1. Restate or clarify the question.
2. Compliment the question.
3. Answer the question.
4. Check the response with the questioner.

question–answer period: a time set aside at the end of a speech for audience questions of the speaker.

If time permits, seize the opportunity to answer your listeners' questions. Holding a **question–answer period** following your speech offers you an opportunity to interact directly with your audience. This usually results in a natural, lively delivery and makes for better speaker–listener rapport.

Almost any question asked can help you. If questions are friendly, that is a high compliment: The audience is genuinely interested in you and your topic. If questions stem from audience confusion about your presentation, you have an opportunity to clarify. If someone asks you a combative and contentious question, you've just been given a second chance to win this person over to your point of view.

Before tackling the Q–A period, study the guidelines in the Key Points box. You will find them helpful when you stand in front of an audience and ask, "Are there any questions?"

The first step, *restating or clarifying the question,* is important for three reasons. First, repetition makes sure that the entire audience has heard the question. Second, repeating the question allows the questioner the opportunity to correct you if you misstate it, saving you the embarrassment of beginning to answer a different question. Third, if the question seems confusing to you or somehow misses the point, you can rephrase the question to make it clearer, more focused, and more relevant. Never answer a question you don't understand.

A second step in answering a question is to *compliment the question* whenever possible. We have all heard speakers say, "I'm glad you asked that." Of course, you cannot repeat that same remark after each question. But without seeming insincere you can say, "That's a good (or perceptive or interesting) question" or "I was hoping someone would ask that."

This applies even to hostile questions. Sincerely complimenting a hostile question or questioner can defuse a tense situation and focus attention on issues, rather than on personal antagonism.

You are now ready for the third step: *answering the question.* Of course, the content and the form of your answers depend on the specific questions; nevertheless, the following suggestions may be helpful:

1. *Know your topic thoroughly.* Your success during the Q–A period will depend, in large part, on your research and preparation for your speech. You should always know more than you included in your speech. Most of the time, poor answers reflect poor preparation.

2. *Be as brief as possible.* Obviously, some questions require longer, more thoughtful answers than others. The question, "How much did you say it will cost to complete Phase II of the new library?" can be answered simply, "Two and a half million dollars." The question, "What will that $2.5 million provide?" will require a much longer answer. There are two reasons for making your answers as succinct as possible. First, short answers are easier to remember than lengthy ones. Second, the shorter each answer, the greater the number of questions you can field.

3. *Be methodical when giving lengthy answers.* When you need to give a detailed answer, use the "frame it, state it, and explain it" approach. Suppose you were asked the question, "How will the $2.5 million budgeted for Phase II of the new library be spent?" You could answer as follows:

> To answer that question, we need to look at three categories of costs: construction, furniture and equipment, and instructional materials.
>
> Mike Phillips, the director of buildings and grounds, estimates cost breakdowns as follows: $1.7 million for construction, $300,000 for furniture and equipment, and $500,000 for instructional materials.
>
> Unlike many institutions, we're fortunate that we can provide a sizable amount of money—half a million dollars—in addition to our regular annual budget of $200,000 for instructional resources. This is a one-time infusion of money. You should also know, however, what these figures do not include. Not included are personnel costs, energy costs, and costs for purchases of materials and equipment beyond the first year.

4. *If you don't know an answer, admit it.* Making up an answer is unethical. Fabricated answers can not only undermine your credibility, but the audience may also act on incorrect information you have provided. There is nothing wrong with saying,

Anticipating and Answering Listeners' Questions

After constructing a persuasive speech for this class, brainstorm a list of questions you think listeners might ask. Be sure to include tough questions that challenge what you advocate. Also, practice your speech in front of a few friends and solicit their questions. Write each question on a notecard, and develop well-reasoned responses. Shuffle those cards, and randomly draw questions. Using the guidelines we suggest in this chapter, practice delivering your answers. Even if you don't have the opportunity for a question–answer period following your speech, this exercise is still valuable. Are there ways that you can develop your message so that these questions are answered in your speech?

"I don't know" or "I don't know, but I'll check on it and let you know." If you give the second response, make sure you follow up promptly.

5. *Be careful about what you say publicly.* Remember that in a public gathering there is no such thing as an off-the-record statement. Don't say, "It's not official and I would not want it reported yet, but we expect that the governor will be our commencement speaker." You will probably read the following headline in the next issue of your school paper: "Governor Possible Commencement Speaker." If the press is present, what you say may indeed be reported. As a rule, never say anything that would embarrass you or slander others if it were to appear in the next morning's paper.

The fourth and final step in answering a question is to *check the response with the questioner.* Did you answer the question to his or her satisfaction? Is there a follow-up question? Remember two drawbacks to this approach, however. If each person is allowed a question and a follow-up, you will be able to answer fewer people's questions. Second, if questioners are argumentative, asking them if you answered the question to their satisfaction gives them an opportunity to keep the floor and turn the Q–A period into a debate.

The Videotaped Speech

In Chapter 1, we introduced you to the components of the communication process: speaker, message, listener, feedback, channel, environment, and noise. Channel, you remember, refers to the way the message is sent. Messages may be written or spoken. If spoken, they may be delivered in person or transmitted electronically. Video is an increasingly popular electronic medium. Even though you still see and hear the speaker, video introduces a new dynamic to the public speech, and that dynamic affects how audience members receive the message.

The **videotaped speech** is increasingly common, for both practice and presentation. If you have access to a camcorder or webcam, you may want to use it as you practice your speeches for this class. If you are nervous about your speech and self-conscious

videotaped speech: a speech taped during practice for the speaker's review or during actual delivery for viewing by another audience.

practicing in front of another person, just set up a camera, turn it on, walk to the front of the room, and deliver your speech. You can then watch yourself on the videotape or video file and note what you do well and what still needs work. After viewing yourself, you may even ask some friends to look at the video with you and offer their comments and suggestions. If you use video, keep a copy of your final practice tape or file for each of your speeches in this class. After you have a few examples, review them. You will probably be surprised to see how much you have improved since your first effort.

Videotaping actual presentations is also increasingly common. Speeches given to community groups or before governmental bodies are often taped for possible broadcast on local news. Speakers can now include digital video in multimedia peripherals. Your instructor may have played tapes of great speeches for you or speeches other students gave when they took a public speaking class. These examples may have been particularly helpful, because videotape re-creates the event better than a lifeless manuscript does. In this section we discuss videotaping an entire speech for playback, and we offer three guidelines to help you meet this challenge.

Key Points

Guidelines for the Videotaped Speech

1. Adapt your delivery to your audience(s).
2. Adapt your delivery to your microphone.
3. Adapt your delivery to your camera shots.

Your first consideration in preparing for a videotaped or filmed speech is your *audience*. Are you speaking primarily to the immediate group assembled or to those who will view the videotape later? Which is your primary audience and which your secondary? Or are both equally important? Unlike traditional speaking situations requiring analysis of one audience, the videotaped speech often requires you to analyze several audiences. If these audiences differ in significant ways, the task of constructing your speech is more difficult.

The audience you expect to view your videotape should also guide the way you respond to the camera. If you are videotaping your speech for your own analysis, you want the camera to see what any audience member in the camera's location would see. In that case, don't look directly into the camera during your entire speech. Make eye contact with all parts of your audience as you practice, treating the camera as just another audience member. If you are speaking only to an external audience, as the president does when speaking to the public from a desk in the Oval Office, you will want to make eye contact only with the camera, treating it as your only listener. As a rule, if audience members viewing a videotape see another audience in the speaker's presence, they will expect the speaker to be interacting with those people. If audience members watching a videotape believe themselves to be the speaker's only audience, they will expect to receive the full measure of the speaker's eye contact.

A second concern is the *microphone* you will use. A lapel microphone clips to your shirt, blouse, tie, dress, or jacket. It moves with you. A fixed, or stationary, microphone is often fastened to the lectern or held in place by a microphone stand. You may or may not be given a choice of microphones. What are the advantages and drawbacks of each?

A *lapel microphone* allows you freedom of movement. You can walk and keep the same voice level. This mike is also unobtrusive, as it is not easily seen by you or your audience. Speakers who experience "mike fright" usually prefer the lapel to the fixed microphone because it is out of their sight. However, if you use a lapel mike, you will want to select your clothing carefully. If your jacket and shirt or blouse rustle as you move, the mike will pick up distracting noise.

Even a *fixed microphone* attached to the lectern sometimes picks up distracting noises, such as nervous tapping of fingers on the lectern or shuffling of paper as you move your speaking notes. To do your best job as a speaker, you need to be aware of all that the audience hears. A disadvantage of the fixed microphone is that it restricts movement. As you walk away from the mike, your volume may fade. Most fixed microphones today, however, are multidirectional, or able to pick up sound from many directions. You do not need to stand rigidly twelve inches away from the fixed mike, speaking without turning your head from side to side. You may (and should) move your head as you make eye contact with various sections of your audience. Avoid looking at the mike and becoming preoccupied with its presence.

A third factor you should consider when planning and practicing your speech is the *camera*. Where is it positioned? What is its angle of vision? Will it record close-up or long shots? What the camera sees should help determine your delivery. If the camera takes only head shots, your facial expressions become more important and gesturing less so. Glancing down at your notes will be more noticeable. In a full-body shot, you will be able to gesture and move about more freely. If the camera sees you from chest up, you will want to ensure that your gestures are high enough to convey your dynamism visibly. Someone videotaping your speech rehearsal or actual presentation may use the camera's zoom lens to get a variety of shots. If possible, find out this person's plans before you speak.

In summary, try to determine what the viewing audience will see. If possible, find out how your speech will be taped beforehand so that you can practice accordingly. If this is not possible, be prepared to adapt during the event. Arrive early and talk to the camera operator; you may even want to suggest how you would like the speech recorded. Let the camera operator know if and when you will use a visual aid so that he or she can zoom in on it at the appropriate time. If your primary audience is the tape-viewing audience and if you are given a choice, request many close-up shots. Remember, your eyes and face are the most expressive parts of your body. Emphasizing those aspects of your physical delivery can make the speaker–viewer relationship more personal.

As with any speech, practice is the key to effective delivery. Videotaping adds another dynamic to that delivery. You must be concerned not only with how your body and voice carry your message, but also with how the medium of transmission affects the message your listeners receive.

Summary

The *speech of introduction* presents a featured speaker to an audience. If you are called on to introduce another speaker, your speech should not compete with the one you are introducing. Be brief, focus your remarks on the featured speaker, establish that person's credibility, create positive but realistic audience expectations, and match the tone of the featured speech.

The *speech of presentation* confers an award, prize, or special recognition on an individual or group. Such a speech should state the purpose of the award or recognition, particularly if it is new or unfamiliar to the audience. The speaker should state the recipient's qualifications to reveal why the person deserves the award. If the audience does not know the name of the recipient in advance, the speech of presentation should create suspense, revealing the recipient's name only late in the speech. If the person being honored

has been selected from nominees known to the audience, the speech of presentation should compliment those other individuals.

The *acceptance speech* is an honoree's response to a speech of presentation. Social custom dictates that you thank at least briefly any group presenting you an award, prize, or other recognition. When accepting an award, you should thank the people bestowing the award, compliment your competitors if you know them, and thank those who helped you attain the award. Your acceptance speech gives you a chance to say thanks humbly and sincerely.

The *speech of tribute* honors an individual, a group, or a significant event. A *eulogy*, spoken to honor a person who has recently died, is one of the most familiar speeches of tribute. In delivering a speech of tribute, you should establish noble or lofty themes built on vivid examples from the subject's life.

Theory into Practice

Appearing on Video

Historically, speeches existed only for a specific moment in a specific place and for a specific audience. Recording equipment, however, changed that. Actual speeches, not just their manuscripts, have become part of the permanent record. Today, political, business, religious, and social leaders address not just immediate audiences but future audiences through videotapes and DVDs. You may have taped some of your speeches for this class for your own viewing and practice; however, it's likely that you'll give videotaped presentations in your career and on other occasions. Your instructor may even want to record your speech to show in future public speaking classes.

In addition to all the suggestions we hope you've learned about how to construct and deliver an excellent speech, here are some tips to follow specifically related to being videotaped:

1. *Avoid wearing predominantly white or black clothing.* Pastel clothing is usually preferred. Men often look best in blue, grey, or beige, using ties, if worn, as accent pieces. Women can wear brighter colors.

2. *Avoid wearing finely striped clothing or other busy patterns.* Solid colors are more appropriate for larger pieces, such as suits, jackets, slacks, and skirts.

3. *Don't fade into the background.* Before selecting your clothing, consider the walls or backdrop where you'll be videotaped. Wear a color that will stand out from the backdrop and focus attention on your face, shoulders, arms, and hands.

4. *Avoid wearing large or excessive jewelry.* Keep the focus on you, not on the light show or sound effects your jewelry may create.

5. *Keep makeup simple and natural.* Treat shiny facial and head areas with powdered makeup matched to your skin tone. Men who have "5 o'clock shadows" should shave or use corrective makeup before they speak.

6. *Request a wireless microphone, if possible.* You'll soon forget about the mike and relax, and you won't trip over the cord. Do a sound check before you get up to speak, but remember not to tap or blow into the microphone.

7. *Make eye contact with the camera, without staring at it.* Think of it as an audience member. Media coaches agree: connect with the camera, and you'll likely connect with the viewer.

8. *Don't make exaggerated movements in front of the camera.* Gestures that look natural to the audience in the room where you speak may appear exaggerated in a close-up shot.

9. *Exercise caution in projecting your visual aids.* Overhead projectors, slides, and other types of projections may require the lights to be dimmed. Not only may insufficient lighting affect how you look on tape, the camera may not be able to videotape your projections efficiently.

10. *Remain poised after you've completed your speech.* Remember, the camera may be running and the microphone still on, even though your speech and the event are finished.

As a speaker, you should attempt to express the collective feelings of the audience. You should create a memorable image of the subject, and you should be genuine.

The *speech to entertain* seeks to make a point through the creative, organized use of the speaker's humor. Usually delivered on a light, festive occasion, your speech to entertain should make a point, be creative, be well organized, use appropriate humor, and be delivered in a spirited manner. The humor you use in a speech to entertain should be relevant to your point, tasteful, tactful, and positive.

An *impromptu speech* is one delivered with little or no advance preparation. You speak impromptu whenever someone asks you a question or calls on you to speak with only a moment's notice. Under these circumstances, speak on a subject you know well, if possible, and use your limited preparation time in a positive way. Ask, "What do I want the audience to remember from what I say?" Then focus your remarks to achieve that goal. Cover only a few key points and be brief. To improve your impromptu speaking, reflect on each speech to see how you could have improved its content, organization, and delivery.

The *question–answer period* after your speech gives you the opportunity to interact with your audience. Answering questions from audience members will be easier if you follow four steps. First, restate or clarify the question. Second, compliment the question or the questioner. Third, answer the question. Finally, check your response with the person who asked the question.

The *videotaped speech* is becoming increasingly common, both for practice and for actual presentation of the speech. Videotaping requires speakers to adapt their delivery to their various audiences, to the microphone, and to the camera. The presence of a video camera will influence your eye contact, movement, gestures, and other elements of your vocal and physical delivery.

Practice Critique

Evaluating a Speech of Tribute

In 2001, in the U.S. Capitol Rotunda, the family and friends of Charles M. Schulz gathered to celebrate the life of the cartoonist and creator of the *Peanuts* comic strip. Edwin Anderson delivered a moving speech of tribute about his longtime friend who had died the previous year. Read the transcript of Anderson's speech in the Appendix. Then, using the five guidelines discussed on pages 376–377 in this chapter, write a brief critique of the speech, noting places where the speaker did or did not follow each guideline.

Exercises

1. Pair up with another member of the class. Discuss each other's speech topics and relevant personal background. Following the guidelines discussed in this chapter, prepare a speech introducing your partner on the day of his or her speech. Your partner will introduce you when you speak.

2. Pair up with someone and discuss what each of you does well. Create an award that one of you will receive. One of you will give a speech of presentation and the other a speech of acceptance.

3. Watch all or a portion of an awards ceremony (the Oscars, Grammys, or the Tony awards, for example).

Select the best and worst acceptance speeches; justify your choices.

4. Prepare and deliver a speech of tribute for someone you admire who is known to the class. This person may be a campus, local, national, or international figure.

5. Select a humorous magazine article or newspaper column. Discuss how you might edit, revise, and adapt the article for a speech to entertain, as well as how you would cite the source. Write a thesis statement, outline the key ideas, and develop entertaining examples to support those points.

6. Listen to or read a transcript of a question–answer period following a speech or at a press conference. Sources may include network broadcasts of presidential press conferences; C-SPAN broadcasts of interviews, National Press Club addresses, conference proceedings, news briefings, and call-in shows; and transcripts of presidential press conferences published in *Weekly Compilation of Presidential Documents* and *Public Papers of the Presidents of the United States.* Analyze the speaker's strategies and effectiveness in responding to audience questions.

Speaking in and as a Group

chapter

19

Never doubt that a small group of thoughtful, committed citizens can change the world. Indeed, it's the only thing that ever has. —MARGARET MEAD

Take out a sheet of paper and start listing all the small groups to which you belong. Think of committees, boards, and councils on which you serve. Include your network of close friends. Add your family to the list. What about athletic teams, honor societies, fraternities or sororities, the debating society, the arts council, study groups, and other groups? After a few minutes of this brainstorming, you will probably be surprised at the length of your list. Groups are so prevalent in our society that it is estimated that there are more groups in America than there are people.[1]

Not only are groups plentiful, they are also influential. They shape our society and our behavior. Government, businesses, educational institutions, and other organizations depend on groups to gather information, assess data, and propose courses of action. Our families and our close friends give us counsel and support in times of need. We do so much planning, problem solving, and recreating in small groups that we can all relate to the humorist's remark that "there are no great people, only great committees."

Because groups significantly influence our lives, it is essential that groups communicate effectively. Unfortunately, small-group communication seems not to be a skill most of us master easily. Estimates are that professionals lose thirty-one hours a month—nearly four workdays—in unproductive meetings.[2] Clearly, poor group communication can be costly. You will work more effectively in groups if you understand the subjects covered in this chapter: the relationship between small-group communication and public speaking, the characteristics of a group, the types of groups, the principles of group decision making, the responsibilities of group leaders and members, and the most frequently used formats for group presentations.

Small-Group Communication and Public Speaking

Why study group work as an adjunct to public speaking? The answer is twofold: (1) Groups of people often make presentations, either internally or to the public; and (2) the quality of those presentations depends on how well group members have functioned together.

For most of your work in your public speaking class, you have operated alone. You selected your speech topics. You researched as much as you wanted and at your own convenience. You organized your speeches as you thought best and practiced them as much as you thought necessary. Your individual work continues in a group. You must still present, support, and defend your ideas. As you'll see in this chapter, group communication involves a variety of speeches, from the chairperson's orientation speech, to internal reports to other group members, to public presentations about the group's work. Each time you share your ideas and opinions with other group members, you will, in effect, be giving an impromptu speech. The more you know about effective speech content, organization, and delivery, the better your individual speeches within the group will be.

As part of a group solving a problem and preparing a presentation, your work is more complex, however. On-the-spot interaction in a group elevates the importance of listening and critiquing. You will need to utilize all the critical thinking skills we discussed in Chapter 1. You'll also be challenged to provide feedback to other group members. Using the guidelines for critiquing that we discussed in Chapter 4 will help you do your part to create and maintain a constructive, supportive communication environment. Group processes will truly test your ability to work productively and congenially with other people.

Small Groups Defined

A **small group** is a collection of three or more individuals who interact with and influence each other in pursuit of a common goal. This definition includes four important concepts: individuals, interaction, influence, and goal.

The number of *individuals* in a group may vary. There must be at least three. Two people are not a group but rather an interpersonal unit, sometimes called a dyad. The addition of a third person adds a new dynamic, a new perspective. Paul Nelson describes the new relationship in the following way:

> Something happens to communication when it involves more than two people: It becomes much more complex. For example, imagine two people, A and B, having a conversation. There is only *one* possible conversation, A-B. Add one more person, C, however: Now there are *four* possible interactions, A-B, A-C, B-C, and A-B-C. Add another person, D, and there are *eleven* possible interactions. And so on.[3]

Although we can all agree that three is the minimum number for a small group, we do not always agree on the maximum number. Even communication experts disagree, with some using seven as a workable maximum and others stretching the range to twenty. What characterizes a small group is not a specific number of participants, but the *type* of communication they undertake. A group that is too large cannot maintain meaningful interaction among members and may have to be divided into smaller working groups.

A group's size, then, affects a second characteristic of a small group: *interaction*. A small group offers each participant an opportunity to interact with all other members of the group. A group cannot function if its participants fail to interact, and it functions ineffectively when a few members dominate. Generally, the larger the group, the fewer opportunities for any one member to participate and the greater the likelihood that a few members will dominate the flow of communication, making certain that meaningful interaction does not take place.

A third characteristic of small groups is *influence*. Members of a group interact in order to influence others. Groups function best when members express differences of opinions openly and try to persuade others with data and arguments.

Finally, a group has a purpose. As we noted in Chapter 1, a group is more than simply a collection of individuals who interact; it exists for a reason. Members interact and influence each other over a period of time in order to achieve a *goal*. The group process fails when members are unsure of their goal or when they fail to resolve conflicting perceptions of that goal.

> **“When all think alike, no one thinks very much.”**
>
> —WALTER LIPPMAN

small group: a collection of three or more people influencing and interacting with one another in pursuit of a common goal.

Types of Groups

People form groups for two reasons: because they enjoy interacting with each other or because they need to accomplish a task. Therefore, we can classify groups into two general types: socially oriented and task oriented. A **socially oriented group** is one that exists primarily because its members enjoy interacting with one another. Group members may not have a major task in mind, but rather are concerned mainly with relationships, enjoying time spent with other members of the group. A **task-oriented group** is more formal. Members interact having a specific goal in mind. For example, you and a few classmates may form a study group to review for examinations and to be an audience for each other as you practice your speeches.

The objectives of socially and task-oriented groups often intermingle. Say you and your friends decide to go to a movie. Clearly, this is a social occasion, but you still must accomplish certain tasks: What movie does the group want to see? When is the best time for everyone to see it? Will you go together or just meet at the theater? At times you have probably been frustrated when your social group was unable to make some of these "easy" task decisions.

While socially oriented groups may have task objectives, the converse is also true. You form a study group to accomplish certain tasks, but as you get to know the others in the group you discover that you enjoy their company. As social objectives emerge, the group meets more frequently and functions more effectively. If social purposes predominate, however, you may find that your group sacrifices studying for socializing. Even though most groups have both social and task objectives, one purpose usually takes precedence according to the situation. That purpose determines the structure of your group and the nature of the communication among its members.

In this chapter, we will focus on task-oriented groups, sometimes called working groups. These include study groups, problem-solving groups, and action groups. The objective of a **study group** is to learn about a topic. It gathers, processes, and evaluates information. When you and your classmates work together to prepare for an exam, you are a study group. A **problem-solving group** decides on courses of action. This type of group explores a problem, suggesting solutions to remedy it. The objective of an **action group** is, as its name implies, to act. It has the power to implement proposals. These categories may overlap. In fact, you may be a member of a group that studies a situation, devises a solution, *and* implements it.

Successful athletic teams recognize the importance of working together as a group of individuals to accomplish their goals. They rely on individual responsibility and shared leadership. A pitcher's role is uniquely different from that of the second baseman, but both are critical to team success. Being able to strike out a power hitter is no less important than the ability to turn a flawless 6-4-3 double play. Business and professional organizations are increasingly using **work teams** to accomplish their objectives. Communication scholars Thomas Harris and John Sherblom argue, "Teams differ substantially from many small groups, because the teams themselves, rather than the leader, control the group process."[4] The sport analogy is particularly apt because team leaders gradually assume the role of coach, similar to the athletic coach.

A type of action group becoming increasingly common in the business world is the **self-directed work team.** Such work teams manage themselves, in addition to getting work done. Responsibilities and characteristics of self-directed work teams include:

- sharing management and leadership roles;
- planning, controlling, and improving their own work;

Exploring *Online*

GROUP DEVELOPMENT
www.abacon.com/commstudies/groups/devgroup.html
This Allyn and Bacon website presents several models that describe how groups develop. It also includes an interactive activity, a self-graded quiz, and links to pages that discuss other aspects of group communication.

socially oriented group: a small group that exists primarily because its members enjoy interacting with one another.

task-oriented group: a small group that exists primarily to accomplish some goal.

study group: a task-oriented group devoted to researching and learning about a topic.

problem-solving group: a task-oriented group devoted to deciding on courses of action to correct a problem.

action group: a task-oriented group devoted to implementing proposals for action.

work team: a team or group of people who perform all activities needed to produce the product, service, or other goal specified by an outside leader, supervisor, or manager.

self-directed work team: a group of people who manage themselves by identifying, conducting, and monitoring all activities needed to produce a product or service.

Although a task-oriented group functions more effectively if members enjoy one another's company, social interactions should not take precedence over the group's basic objective: to accomplish the task.

- setting team goals, creating schedules, and reviewing group performance;
- identifying and securing necessary training;
- hiring and disciplining team members; and
- assuming responsibility for products and services produced.[5]

Work teams obviously require that traditional leadership responsibilities gradually shift to team members. Many teams rotate the role of team leader, with members occupying the position for a designated length of time.

As you go through this chapter, you will find that participating in task groups and delivering public speeches are similar in several ways. Both usually involve research, analysis of information and ideas, and the presentation of that information to others. Yet despite these similarities, there are notable differences between public speaking and group communication. The effective communicator will seek to master both sets of skills.

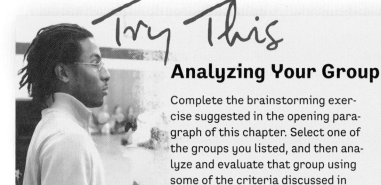

Try This

Analyzing Your Group

Complete the brainstorming exercise suggested in the opening paragraph of this chapter. Select one of the groups you listed, and then analyze and evaluate that group using some of the criteria discussed in this chapter: (1) Describe the group according to four characteristics: individuals, interaction, influence, and goal. (2) Classify the group. Is it primarily a socially oriented group, a task-oriented group, or a group that balances both goals? As you continue to read this chapter, think about the various roles and responsibilities you and other group members assumed.

Group Discussion and Decision Making

Principles of Group Decision Making

1. Group decision making is a shared responsibility.
2. Group decision making requires a clear understanding of goals.
3. Group decision making benefits from a clear but flexible agenda.
4. Group decision making is enhanced by open communication.
5. Group decision making requires adequate information.

One of the most important reasons we form groups is to make decisions. We may seek a friend's guidance because we believe that two heads are better than one. The philosophy behind this decision is the foundation of group decision making. You may have heard the expression that in communication "the whole is greater than the sum of its parts." This is particularly true in group communication. What this means is that, if a group of five functions effectively, its product will be qualitatively or quantitatively superior to the total product of five people working individually. But a group is able to work most effectively only when members follow certain principles of group decision making.

Principles of Group Decision Making

Group Decision Making Is a Shared Responsibility.   It's true that the group leader plays a special role in the group. As a matter of fact, we include separate sections in this chapter about the responsibilities of the group leader, as well as of members. The presence of a group leader does not necessarily establish a leader–follower or even an active–passive association. In fact, this relationship is usually better represented as a partnership. Group decision making requires the active participation of all members performing mutually reinforcing responsibilities.

Group Decision Making Requires a Clear Understanding of Goals.   Every group has a goal. Sometimes that goal is predetermined. Your instructor may, for example, divide your class into small groups, assigning each group to generate a list of 25 topics suitable for a speech to inform. In your career, you may be part of a small group having the task of studying specific job-related problems and proposing workable solutions. In both instances, the group has a clear statement of its objective. In other situations, the goal of your group may be less clear. If that is the case, you will have to clarify, specify, or even determine your goals.

Group Decision Making Benefits from a Clear but Flexible Agenda.   Every group needs a plan of action. Because a group's process affects its product, it is vital that members spend sufficient time generating an action plan. The leader can facilitate this process by suggesting procedures that the group may adopt, modify, or reject. The best plan, or agenda, however, is one not dictated by the leader, but rather one developed by both the leader and the members of the group.

A group's agenda should be both specific and flexible. Group participants must know what is expected of them and how they will go about accomplishing the task at hand. Raising $1,000 for charity could be accomplished by dividing the membership into five teams, each having the responsibility for generating $200. These teams would need to communicate and coordinate to avoid unnecessary overlap as they decided on their fund-raising projects. Groups also need to be flexible as they pursue their goals. Unexpected obstacles may require revising the agenda. The group needs a backup plan, for example, if its car wash is canceled because of rain.

Group Decision Making Is Enhanced by Open Communication. If all members of a group think alike, there is no need for the group. One person can simply make the decision. Diversity encourages alternative perspectives. Both the group leader and individual members should protect and encourage the expression of minority views.

Groups should avoid *groupthink*, a term coined by Irving Janis. **Groupthink** occurs when group members come to care more about conforming and not making waves than they do about exercising the critical evaluation necessary to weed out bad ideas.[6] Groupthink reduces open communication and adversely affects the quality of decision making. To be effective, a group must encourage each member to exercise independent judgment.

Group Decision Making Requires Adequate Information. Access to information that is sufficient and relevant is extremely important. A group suffers if its information is based on the research of only one or two of its members. To avoid this problem, a group should follow a few simple steps. First, the leader should provide essential information to the group as a starting point. Second, each member of the group should contribute critical knowledge to the group. Third, the group should divide the gathering of information in a way that is efficient and yet provides some overlap. Later in this chapter, we provide suggestions for gathering information. Now that we understand the principles of group decision making, let's take a look at how the group makes decisions.

Exploring *Online*

GROUPTHINK
http://changingminds.org/explanations/theories/groupthink.htm
www.valuebasedmanagement.net/methods_janis_groupthink.html
These websites discuss Irving Janis's concept of *groupthink*. You can learn eight symptoms of groupthink, as well as suggestions for enhancing effective group decision making.

The Process of Group Decision Making

In his celebrated book *How We Think,* published in 1910, John Dewey argued that decision making should be a logical, orderly process.[7] His "Steps to Reflective Thinking" have provided one of the most useful, and we think one of the best, approaches to problem solving. Authors and theorists differ in their adaptations of the reflective thinking model, organizing it around five, six, or seven steps. We prefer a seven-step approach.

If you are a member of a problem-solving discussion group or a task-oriented group and you have not been assigned a topic, the group will need to select a topic and word it. A good discussion topic is current and controversial and has a body of data and opinion from which to construct and refute positions. Once you select a topic meeting these criteria, you must word the topic according to the following guidelines.

First, it should be worded as a question the group will seek to answer. "The campus parking problem" fails to meet this criterion and, consequently, does not direct participants in the discussion toward a goal. Better wordings are evident in the examples presented in the second criterion.

Second, the question should be open rather than closed. Open wording might include "What can be done to alleviate the parking problem on campus?" or "How should this college solve the campus parking problem?" These questions are open because they do not direct the group to one particular solution. They invite a variety of solutions and can generate lively and productive discussion. The question "Should the campus build a multistory parking facility to solve the campus parking problem?" is an example of a closed question, because it focuses attention on only one solution. This yes-or-no question limits discussion of alternative proposals. Because it forces individuals to choose sides, a closed question is probably more appropriate for a debate than for a discussion format.

After members have agreed on a topic question, the group should begin answering it in a logical, methodical manner. The following seven-step process, based on Dewey's model, will aid your group. It is important that you go through these steps chronologically and

groupthink: excessive agreement among group members who value conformity more than critical evaluation.

The Steps to Problem Solving

1. Define the problem.
2. Analyze the problem.
3. Determine the criteria for the optimal solution.
4. Propose solutions.
5. Evaluate proposed solutions.
6. Select a solution.
7. Suggest strategies for implementing the solution.

not jump ahead in your discussion. Solutions are best discussed and evaluated only after a problem is thoroughly defined and analyzed.

Define the Problem. Before you can solve a problem, you must first define it. By defining the key terms of the question, group members decide how they will focus the topic, enabling them to keep on track and to avoid extraneous discussion. Suppose your college asks you to be part of a student advisory committee to address the issue "What can be done to alleviate the parking problem on campus?" To answer the question, members must agree on what constitutes "the parking problem." Are there too few parking spaces? If there are sufficient spaces, are they not geographically located to serve the campus best? Is there congestion only during certain times of the day or week? Is the problem how the spaces are designated—for example, is there adequate parking for faculty, but not for students? Is the problem not the number of spaces, but the condition of the parking lots? How your group defines the problem determines, to a large extent, how you will solve it. If there is no problem with the condition of the lots or the number of spaces for faculty, you can safely delete these considerations from your discussion agenda.

Analyze the Problem. In analyzing any problem, a group looks at both its symptoms and causes. We gauge the severity of a problem by examining its *symptoms*. For example, the group needs to know not only the approximate number of students unable to find parking spaces, but also why that is detrimental. Students may be late for class or may avoid using computer labs because of parking congestion; accidents may occur as cars crowd into small spaces; the college may spark resentment from students who pay to attend, but have no place to park; students walking to dimly lit and distant parking spaces after an evening class may worry about physical attacks. These symptoms point to the magnitude of the problem. Certainly, some symptoms are more serious than others, and group members must identify those needing immediate action.

However, the group is still not ready to propose remedies. The group must now consider the *causes* of the problem. By examining how a difficulty developed, a group may find its solution. The parking problem may stem from a variety of causes, including increased enrollment, parking spaces converted to other uses, lack of funds to build new parking lots, too many classes scheduled at certain times, inadequate use of distant parking lots, and some student parking spaces earmarked for faculty and administrators.

Determine the Criteria for the Optimal Solution. Decision-making criteria are the standards we use to judge the merits of proposed solutions. It is wise to state these criteria before discussing solutions. Why select an action plan only to discover later that sufficient funding is unavailable? The group studying campus parking worked to avoid this pitfall. Some of the criteria they considered were as follows:

Criteria	Explanation
Economics	The proposal should be cost effective.
Aesthetics	The proposal should not spoil the beauty of the campus.
Legality	The proposal cannot force residents and businesses adjacent to campus to sell their land to the college.
Growth	The proposal should account for future increases in enrollment.
Security	Students should be safe as they go to and from parking lots.

The group could also have considered ranking parking privileges according to student seniority or giving students parking status equal to faculty.

Propose Solutions. Only after completing the first three steps is the group ready to propose solutions. This is essentially a brainstorming step with emphasis on the quantity, not quality, of suggestions. At this stage, the group should not worry about evaluating any suggested solutions, no matter how farfetched they may seem. This group's brainstorming list included the following:

Building a multistory parking lot in the center of campus

Constructing parking lots near the edge of campus

Reclaiming some faculty spaces for student use

Lighting and patrolling lots in the evening

Initiating bus service between apartment complexes and the campus

Encouraging students to carpool or to ride bicycles to campus

Evaluate Proposed Solutions. Now the group is ready to evaluate each proposed solution using the criteria listed in the third step. Next, the group considers the advantages of the proposed solution. Finally, they assess its disadvantages. The centrally located, high-rise parking garage may not be cost effective and may intrude on the beauty of the campus, but may use valuable land efficiently and limit the extent of late-night walking.

Select a Solution. After evaluating each proposed solution, you and your fellow group members should have a good idea of those solutions to exclude from consideration and those to retain. You will then weigh the merits and deficiencies of each. Your final solution may be a combination of several of the proposed remedies. For example, the group working on the campus parking problem could issue a final report advocating a three-phase solution: short-range, middle-range, and long-range goals. A short-range approach may involve converting a little-used athletic practice field to a parking facility, creating more bicycle parking areas, and encouraging carpooling. A middle-range solution could involve creating a bus system between student apartment houses and the campus or trying to get the city transit system to incorporate new routes. The proposal for the long range could involve building a well-lit multistory parking facility, not in the middle of campus, but near the athletic complex, to be used during the week for general student parking and on weekends for athletic and entertainment events.

Suggest Strategies for Implementing the Solution. Once the small group has worked out a solution, members would normally submit their recommendations to another body for approval, action, and implementation. Sometimes, however, decision makers should not only select feasible and effective solutions, but also show how they can be implemented. How would the small group incorporate suggestions for implementing its solution? Members would probably recommend coordinating their plan with the long-range master plan for the college. Other administrators would have to be included. The group would probably also suggest a timetable detailing short- and long-range projects and might also identify possible funding sources.

In summary, the reflective thinking model enables a group to define a problem, analyze it, determine the criteria for a good solution, propose solutions, evaluate solutions, select a solution, and suggest ways to implement it. Decisions made by following this process are generally better, and group members are more satisfied with their work. Not only can this model benefit groups in business, government, education, and other organizations, it can also improve your individual decision making.

The Responsibilities of Group Members

Whether your group is a self-directed team or a body of members with a traditional leader, the ideal leader–member relationship is not an active–passive partnership. To enhance the quality of the group's product, all members must participate actively. What do group members do? If you reflect on our example of the group tackling the campus parking problem, you can see how those group members handled their responsibilities. Productive group members undertake five key responsibilities.

Key Points

Responsibilities of Group Members

1. Inform the group.
2. Advocate personal beliefs.
3. Question other participants.
4. Evaluate ideas and proposals.
5. Support and monitor other group members.

Inform the Group. Group members should enlarge the information base on which decisions are made and action taken. A decision is only as good as the information on which it is based. If the group does not know all the causes of a problem, for example, its proposed solution may not solve it. The greater the number of possible solutions a group considers, the greater its chance of selecting the best one.

You enlarge the group's information base in two ways. First, you contribute what you already know about the issue being discussed. Hearsay information is worth mentioning at this stage, as long as you acknowledge that it is something you have heard but cannot prove. Another member may be able to confirm or refute it, or it can be put on the agenda for further research. Dispelling popular misconceptions so that they do not contaminate the decision-making process is important.

Second, group members contribute to a group's understanding of a topic by gathering additional relevant information. Ideas surfacing during a group meeting may help shape the agenda for the next meeting. You may hear ideas that you want to explore further. You may need to check out facts before the group can clarify the dimensions of a problem or adopt a particular plan of action. The research and thought you give to a topic before a meeting will make the meeting itself more efficient and productive.

Advocate Personal Beliefs. Group members should not only provide information to help make decisions, but they also should use that data to develop positions on the issues being discussed. Participants should be willing to state and defend their opinions. A good participant is open-minded, though—willing to offer ideas and then revise or retract them as additional facts and expert opinion surface. Your opinions may change as they are challenged throughout the discussion.

Question Other Participants. Effective participants not only give but also seek information and opinions. Knowing how and when to ask an appropriate question is an important skill. As one advertisement claims, "When you ask better questions, you tend to come up with better answers." Asking effective questions requires active listening, sensitivity to the feelings of others, and a desire to learn. Group members should seek clarification of ideas they do not understand and encourage others to explain, defend, and extend their ideas.

Evaluate Ideas and Proposals. Too often we either accept what we hear at face value or remain silent even though we disagree with what is said. Yet challenging facts, opinions, and proposals benefits the quality of discussion. It is the obligation of the group to evoke a range of positions on the issue being discussed and then separate the good ideas from the bad. Each idea should be discussed thoroughly and analyzed critically. A decision based on incorrect information or faulty reasoning may be ineffective or even counterproductive. Thus, all group members are obligated to evaluate the contributions of others and to submit their own positions to rigorous testing. This is sometimes difficult to do. Yet participants should not be defensive about their ideas, but instead be open to constructive criticism.

Support and Monitor Other Group Members. A group is a collection of individuals having different personalities. Some may be less assertive than others and may have fragile egos. Reluctant to express their ideas because they fear criticism, they may cause the group to lose important information and to rush into a decision. They may even foster the groupthink we discussed earlier. In addition to providing support for reticent individuals, members should also take note of possible dysfunctional, self-oriented behaviors that impede the group's progress. Ronald Adler and Jeanne Elmhorst describe some of these roles and behaviors:

"Freedom rings where opinions clash."

—ADLAI STEVENSON

- *The blocker:* Prevents progress by constantly raising objections.
- *The attacker:* Aggressively questions the competence or motives of others.
- *The recognition seeker:* Repeatedly and unnecessarily calls attention to self by relating irrelevant experiences, boasting, and seeking sympathy.
- *The joker:* Engages in joking behavior in excess of tension-relieving needs, distracting others.
- *The withdrawer:* Refuses to take a stand on social or task issues; covers up feelings; does not respond to others' comments.[8]

The climate of the group should encourage openness and acceptance. It is the job of both the leader and the group members to create and reinforce a climate of openness and acceptance.

The Responsibilities of Group Leaders

When individuals complain about the lack of cohesiveness and productivity of their group, much of their criticism is often directed toward the group's leader. Just as effective leadership depends on effective membership, so does effective membership depend on effective leadership. Leaders have certain responsibilities that, if fulfilled, will help the group meet its goal.

Key Points

Responsibilities of Group Leaders

1. Plan the agenda.
2. Orient the group.
3. Establish an information base.
4. Involve all members in the discussion.
5. Encourage openness and critical evaluation.
6. Secure clarification of ideas and positions.
7. Keep the group on target.
8. Introduce new ideas and topics.
9. Summarize the discussion.
10. Manage conflict.

Plan the Agenda. A group leader has the primary responsibility for planning an agenda. This does not mean dictating the agenda; rather, the leader offers suggestions and solicits group input into the process.

Orient the Group. How a meeting begins is extremely important in setting expectations that affect group climate and productivity. A leader may want to begin a meeting with some brief opening remarks to orient the group to its mission and the process it will follow. In analyzing business meetings, Roger Mosvick and Robert Nelson conclude, "The chairperson's orientation speech is the single most important act of the business meeting." They describe this speech as follows:

It is a systematically prepared, fully rehearsed, sit-down speech of not less than three minutes nor more than five minutes (most problems require at least three minutes of orientation; anything over five minutes sets up a pattern of dominance and control by the chairperson).[9]

For some groups that you lead, it will not always be appropriate or even desirable to begin a meeting with a structured speech. Still, leaders should try to accomplish several objectives early in the group's important first meeting. They should (1) stress the importance of the task, (2) secure agreement on the process the group will follow, (3) encourage interaction among members, and (4) set an expectation of high productivity.

Establish an Information Base.   Leaders may wish to introduce background information to the group in an opening statement or to forward some relevant articles with background information to members before the first meeting. This sometimes makes the initial meeting more productive by establishing a starting point for discussion. Leaders should encourage input from all members, however, as the primary means of ensuring sufficient information for making decisions.

Involve All Members in the Discussion.   A leader must make certain that participation among group members is balanced. A person who speaks too much is as much a problem as one who speaks too little. In either case, the potential base of information and opinion is narrowed. Leaders can encourage more thoughtful and balanced discussion by asking members to think about a particular issue, problem, or solution prior to the discussion and then asking each member to share ideas with the group before discussing each. This strategy often promotes a more thoughtful analysis of the topic and encourages each member to participate in the discussion. Remember our position that all members share the responsibility of group leadership. If someone is not contributing to the discussion, any member of the group can ask the silent person for an opinion.

Encourage Openness and Critical Evaluation.   After the group has shared information and ideas, the leader must guide the group in evaluating them. The leader may do this by directing probing questions to specific individuals or to the group as a whole. To achieve and maintain a climate of free and honest communication, the group leader must be sensitive to the nonverbal communication of participants, encouraging them to verbalize both their reluctance and their excitement about the ideas other members are expressing. At the same time, the sensitive leader will keep criticism focused on ideas, rather than on personalities.

Secure Clarification of Ideas and Positions.   Effective leaders are good at getting members of the discussion to make their positions and ideas clearer and more specific. They do this in two ways. First, the leader may encourage a member to continue talking by asking a series of probing follow-up questions ("So what would happen if . . . ?"). Even the use of prods ("Uh-huh." "Okay?") can force discussants to think through and verbalize their ideas and positions. Second, the leader may close a particular line of discussion by paraphrasing the ideas of a speaker ("So what you're saying is that . . ."). This strategy confirms the leader's understanding, repeats the idea for the benefit of other group members, and invites their reaction.

Keep the Group on Target.   Effective leaders keep their sights on the group's task while realizing the importance of group social roles. There is nothing wrong with group members becoming friendly and socializing. This added dimension can strengthen your group. However, when social functions begin to impede work on the task, the group leader must "round up the strays" and redirect the entire group to its next goal.

Introduce New Ideas and Topics.   We've already mentioned that it is important for leaders to prepare for the first group meeting, either by researching and preparing an orientation speech or by circulating background materials to group members. In addition, the leader should be the most willing researcher among the group. If discussion stalls because the group lacks focus or motivation, the leader must be willing and able to initiate new topics for research and talk. If a lapse in the group's progress signals that research and discussion have been exhausted, the leader must recognize this situation and be willing to move on to the next phase of group work.

Summarize the Discussion.   A leader should provide the group periodic reviews of what has been decided and what remains to be decided. These summaries keep members focused on the group's task. Leaders may begin a group meeting with an *initial summary,* a brief synopsis of what the group decided previously. They may offer *internal summaries* during the discussion to keep the group on target. At the conclusion of the group task, leaders should provide a *final summary* that reviews what the group accomplished.

Manage Conflict.   Conflict is not only inevitable in group discussion, it is also essential. When ideas collide, participants must rethink and defend their positions. This process engenders further exploration of facts and opinions and enhances the likelihood of a quality outcome. It is important, then, that a group not discourage conflict but manage it.

While conflict of ideas contributes to group effectiveness, interpersonal antagonism may undermine it. When conflict becomes personal, it ceases to be productive. Such conflict disrupts the group. Some members may stop expressing their opinions for fear of attack. If the climate becomes too uncomfortable, members may withdraw from the group. Thus, when conflict surfaces, it is essential that the group respond appropriately. At some point, it may become evident that conflict cannot be solved by the group or in

€thicalDecisions

Leader and Member Responses When Groups Fail

An anonymous benefactor has contributed funds to sponsor a Career Day on €mily's campus. The president of the Student Government Association appoints €mily, a first-year student, to chair a committee charged with drafting a detailed proposal for Career Day activities. Despite €mily's efforts to encourage open discussion and to distribute the workload, two of the five committee members have contributed little. Kate, a junior, opposes most of the ideas offered by others, seldom volunteers any concrete suggestions of her own, and often wants to discuss issues unrelated to the committee's task. Gary, a senior, seldom attends meetings, and when €mily asks for his input, he usually shrugs and says, "Whatever you decide is fine with me." After three unproductive meetings with all five members present, €mily is concerned that the committee may not meet its deadline for the report. She decides to call a private meeting with the two productive members and draft the report. They finish it in a few hours and then present it to the full committee at the next meeting, allowing all the members to discuss and vote on it.

Is €mily's strategy an ethical one for a committee chair? When a group is not functioning effectively, should the leader do everything possible to ensure that all members participate in the decision-making process, or is it more important to ensure that the group take action, even if it means giving more power to selected members? What responsibility do the members have to ensure equal participation?

the presence of group members. In this event, the leader may have to meet with the disruptive member and discuss the problem.

When a group, following the seven steps of problem solving, is composed of members and a leader fulfilling the various roles we have just outlined, it should produce results quickly. At times, the problem solving will benefit the group alone and no external report is needed. Often, however, the group will be requested or will want to present its findings to a larger group: co-workers, company stockholders, or just an interested public audience, for example. In such cases, the group must continue to work together to plan its presentation.

The Group Presentation

Next, we discuss two popular formats for group presentations and provide a systematic checklist to help you develop a first-rate presentation.

Formats for the Presentation

There are several different formats for a group presentation, two of which are the public discussion and the symposium.

The Public Discussion. In a **public discussion,** a group sits, usually in a semicircle, in front of the audience. Members are aware of an audience, but usually address others in the group. The audience, in effect, eavesdrops on the group's conversation. If your public speaking class includes group presentations, your small group may be asked to use this format to present its report to the class.

The problem-solving classroom discussion usually requires extensive preparation. The group has researched the topic, planned the discussion, and possibly practiced the presentation. Members have a general idea of the content and organization of their own and other participants' remarks, although the presentation is not memorized or scripted. The presentation is intended to inform and persuade the audience on the issue being discussed. Sometimes a question–answer period follows.

The Symposium. A **symposium** is a series of speeches on a single topic presented to an audience. It differs from a public discussion in at least two ways. First, there is no interaction among the speakers during the presentation, unless a discussion period follows. Each speaker has a designated amount of time to present his or her remarks. Second, speakers address members of the audience directly. Sometimes speakers are seated at a table; often they use a lectern. In most public symposiums, the speakers have not met beforehand to discuss what they will say. If you are assigned to a group for a presentation in this class, you will likely want to meet several times, following some of the guidelines we discuss in the following section.

Preparing a Group Presentation

A group presentation offers you a variety of learning experiences. You can enhance your research, organization, oral communication, and group interaction skills. This assignment, therefore, is a significant learning opportunity. In addition, your group presentation can be a positive learning experience for your classmates.

Although there is no one correct way to prepare for a group presentation, the following suggestions will help you work more efficiently and produce a more effective

public discussion: a small group exchanging ideas and opinions on a single topic in the presence of an audience.

symposium: a series of public speeches on a single topic, possibly followed by group discussion or a question–answer period.

In a symposium, speakers offer their perspectives on a topic and then discuss those issues with other panelists, often answering questions from the audience.

product. This symbol (•) denotes those steps requiring group interaction; the other steps can be done individually.

Key Points

Steps in Preparing a Group Presentation

- **1.** Brainstorm about the topic.
- **2.** Do some exploratory research.
- **3.** Discuss and divide the topic into areas of responsibility.
- **4.** Research your specific topic area.
- **5.** Draft an outline of your content area.
- **6.** Discuss how all the information interrelates.
- **7.** Finalize the group presentation format.
- **8.** Plan the introduction and conclusion of the presentation.
- **9.** Prepare and practice your speech.
- **10.** Rehearse and revise the presentation.

• **Brainstorm about the Topic.**   If you've read the previous chapters, our first suggestion for preparing a group presentation shouldn't surprise you. Through brainstorming, you will discover what group members already know, and you will uncover numerous ideas for further research. In addition to providing content, brainstorming also serves a relationship function. By giving all members an opportunity to participate, brainstorming affords you a glimpse of your peers' personalities and their approaches to group interaction. You get to know them, and they get to know you. Maintaining an atmosphere of openness and respect during this first meeting gets the group off to a good start. Once you have generated a list of areas concerning your group's topic, you are ready for the second step.

Do Some Exploratory Research.   Through brainstorming, you discover areas that need further investigation. The second phase of your group process is individual research. While there may be some merit in each person's selecting a different topic to research, research roles should not be too rigid. Rather than limit yourself by topic, you may wish to divide your research by resource. One member may search the Internet, another the library's databases, while a third may interview a professor who is knowledgeable on the topic, and so forth. It is important that you not restrict your discovery to the list of topics you have generated. Exploratory research is also a form of brainstorming. As you look in indexes and read articles, you will uncover more topics. Each member of the group should try to find a few good sources that are diverse in scope.

- **Discuss and Divide the Topic into Areas of Responsibility.** After exploratory research, your group should reconvene to discuss what each member found. Which expectations did your research confirm? Which were contradicted? What topics did you find that you had not anticipated? Your objective at this stage of the group process is to decide on the key areas you wish to investigate. Each person should probably be given primary responsibility for researching a particular area. That person becomes the content expert in that area. While this approach makes research more efficient, it has a drawback. If one person serves as a specialist, the group gambles that he or she will research thoroughly and be objective in reporting findings. If either assumption is not valid, the quantity of information can be insufficient and its quality contaminated. An alternative approach is to assign more than one person to a specific area.

Exploring *Online*

TEAM PRESENTATIONS
www.nsdc.org/library/publications/jsd/garmston 212.cfm
This website offers access to an excellent article by Robert Garmston. Drawing from his work with Suzanne Bailey, he provides helpful suggestions for effective group presentations. Especially interesting are the descriptions of five types of team presentations and tips for achieving a synchronistic style.

Research Your Specific Topic Area. Using the strategies we discussed in Chapter 7, research your topic area. Your focus should be on the quality of the sources you discover, not on quantity. While your primary goal should be to gather information on your topic, you should also note information related to your colleagues' topics. As you consult indexes, jot down on a card sources that may be helpful to another member in the group. If you are researching a relevant Internet source that gives you the option of forwarding the page to someone, send it to the email address of a group member who might find it useful. Group members who support each other in these and other ways make the process more efficient and, hence, more enjoyable. This usually results in a better product.

Draft an Outline of Your Content Area. After you have concluded your initial research but before you meet again with your group, construct an outline of the ideas and information you've found. This step is important because it forces you to make sense of all the information you have collected, and it will expedite the next step when you will share your information with the rest of your group members.

- **Discuss How All the Information Interrelates.** You are now ready to meet with your group. Members should briefly summarize what they have discovered through their research. After all have shared their ideas, the group should decide which ideas are most important and how these ideas relate to each other. There should be a natural development of the topic that can be divided among the members of the group.

- **Finalize the Group Presentation Format.** The speaking order should already be determined. There are, nevertheless, certain procedural details that the group must decide. Will the first speaker introduce all presenters or will each person introduce the next speaker? Where will the participants sit when they are not speaking, facing the audience or in the front row? The more details you decide beforehand, the fewer distractions you will have on the day you speak.

- **Plan the Introduction and Conclusion of the Presentation.** A presentation should appear to be that of a group and not that of four or five individuals. Consequently, you must work on introducing and concluding the group's comments, and you must incorporate smooth transitions from one speaker's topic to the next. An introduction should state the topic, define important terms, and establish the importance of the subject. A conclusion should summarize what has been presented and end with a strong final statement.

Prepare and Practice Your Speech.   By this time in the course, you know the requirements of an excellent speech and have had the opportunity to deliver a few. Most of our earlier suggestions also apply to your speech in your group's presentation. Some differences are worth noting, however. For example, as part of a group presentation, you will need to refer to members' speeches and perhaps even use some of their supporting materials. The group presentation may also impose physical requirements you have not encountered as a classroom speaker, such as using a microphone, speaking to those seated around you in addition to making direct contact with the audience, or speaking from a seated position.

• **Rehearse and Revise the Presentation.**   Independent practice of your individual speech is important, but that is only one part of rehearsal. The group should practice its entire presentation. Group rehearsal will not only make participants more confident about their individual presentations, but will also give the group a feeling of cohesion.

Following the procedures we have described should result in a group presentation that seems carefully planned, conscientiously researched, adequately supported, and well delivered. More than that, however, your presentation should also demonstrate the spontaneity, goodwill, and camaraderie that will likely have developed if members of your group have functioned effectively and productively together.

Speaking with Confidence

In my public speaking class I learned how to structure and present my ideas effectively. But team presentations offer an additional challenge. You need to care about other group members' opinions and input. Synergy just doesn't happen; it requires a lot of work. I've given team presentations in my English, communication, geology, and business classes. In my marketing class, for example, our group researched and presented a product analysis of the General Motors product line. Our presentation was more than just a collection of individual speeches. We met and planned our roles. Who would speak on what topics and in what order? Who was responsible for projecting visual aids? How would we dress to convey that we all took the presentation seriously? This required more preparation and practice than just rehearsing our individual parts. When each of us concluded our portion of the presentation, we previewed how it related to what the next person would talk about. A team presentation requires a smooth flow from person to person. Team presentations are a lot of work, but when they're done well, they can be exciting and rewarding.

—**Cynthia Opakunle,** *Radford University*

Theory into Practice
TIPS
Developing a Presentational Style

A team presentation is more than just a collection of individual speeches on the same topic. Coordinating your group's content and delivery will enhance your collective credibility and message impact. Consider the following guidelines to create a polished and proficient team presentation:

1. **Dress appropriately.**

   All presenters should be well groomed and dress up, rather than "dressing down."

2. **Introduce the presentation and team members.**

   Provide an agenda for your presentation. What will listeners learn and who will present each section? Will one person introduce all team members at the beginning, or will each person introduce the next presenter?

3. **Organize and deliver the team's ideas.**

   Use all those strategies you've learned in this class throughout the presentation.

4. **Incorporate smooth transitions from one person to the next.**

   A seamless presentation requires planning and practice.

5. **Have one person design and produce all presentational aids.**

   This will ensure that their design and appearance are consistent.

6. **Have one person display all presentational aids, except when he or she is speaking.**

   Assigning one person to handle and project all the aids will help the presentation flow smoothly and consistently.

7. **Assign someone to keep time and provide other signals to the group.**

   Use subtle but clear time signals so that team members do not exceed their time limits. This person may also signal when presenters are speaking too softly or too rapidly.

8. **Conclude the main part of your presentation.**

   Often the person who introduced the presentation also concludes it.

9. **Conduct a question-and-answer session.**

   If you are allowed a Q–A period, decide who will manage it. Will one person or several answer questions from the audience? Who will recognize those who want to ask questions?

10. **And, of course, practice, practice, practice, both individually and as a group.**

Summary

Whether they are part of our business, social, or personal lives, numerous formal and informal groups are important to us because they solve problems, get things done, and provide us with emotional support. A *small group* is a collection of three or more people influencing and interacting with one another in pursuit of a common goal.

Groups usually fulfill both *socially oriented* and *task-oriented* needs for their participants, though one of these types of needs will predominate depending on the situation. Three types of task-oriented groups include the *study group,* which learns about a topic; the *problem-solving group,* which decides on courses of action; and the *action group,* which implements proposals. The business and professional worlds are relying increasingly on *work teams,* groups of people who perform all activities needed to produce some product, service, or other goal specified by an outside leader, supervisor, or manager.

Self-directed work teams perform all the activities of work teams, but they also set their own goals and monitor their own progress. This chapter focused on the ways such groups and teams function and the tasks they accomplish: gathering, analyzing, and spreading information; and formulating, advocating, and implementing courses of action.

Group decisions are usually superior to decisions individuals make by themselves. To ensure valid decisions, groups must abide by five principles. First, group decision making is a shared responsibility and requires active participation of all members. Second, group members must share a goal that is specific and realistic. Third, groups make decisions best under a clear but flexible schedule or agenda. Fourth, groups can avoid *groupthink* and make the best decisions when members are free to express opinions openly. Fifth, group decision making requires and benefits from the research and information shared by all participants.

Problem-solving groups can speed their progress and simplify their task by following a seven-step modification of John Dewey's steps to reflective thinking. First, define the problem. Second, analyze the symptoms and the causes of the problem. Third, determine the criteria that an optimal solution to the problem must satisfy. Fourth, propose various solutions to the problem. Fifth, evaluate each possible solution against the established criteria. Sixth, decide on the best solution, and seventh, suggest ways of putting the solution into action. Following these steps in this order will streamline group problem-solving work.

Group participation involves five functions: sharing information, advocating personal beliefs, questioning other participants, evaluating data and opinions, and supporting other participants in the group. Responsibilities of group leaders include planning the group's agenda; orienting the group to the task at hand; providing background information on the prob-

lem to be discussed; involving all members in the group's discussion; encouraging a climate of open, honest critical evaluation; seeking clarification of members' ideas and positions; keeping the group focused on its task; introducing new ideas and topics for discussion; summarizing the discussion at various points; and managing interpersonal conflict. If group members and leaders perform these functions during the seven-step problem-solving process, they should reach a satisfactory conclusion and may then be asked to present their findings in a public presentation.

The presentation may take the form of a *public discussion* before an audience. In this situation, after researching, organizing, and practicing the presentation, participants speak to one another about aspects of the problem. Another popular form of group presentation is the *symposium,* a series of formal individual speeches on different aspects of a problem.

When given the opportunity to meet and plan a group presentation before delivering it, members should always do so. Both those experienced and inexperienced in preparing group presentations can benefit from a logical ten-step approach to developing them. First, brainstorm the topic with colleagues in the group. Second, do some individual exploratory research to gauge the scope of the topic. Third, discuss the topic with group members and divide areas of research responsibility by topic or source. Fourth, individually research your assigned area, noting sources in other group members' areas. Fifth, organize the data your research has yielded. Sixth, discuss with other group members how all the generated information interrelates. Seventh, determine the presentation format. Eighth, plan the introduction of group members and the material to be discussed. Ninth, prepare and practice speeches individually. Tenth, rehearse and revise the entire group presentation.

Practice Critique

Analyzing a Group's Interactions

Arrange to attend a meeting of a student, faculty, city, or some other decision-making group. Select a group with a limited number of members so that you can observe interactions among them. Take notes during the meeting and then, using the lists of responsibilities for group members and group leaders on pages 398 and 399 as a guide, write a brief analysis of the group's interactions. Which responsibilities did the group perform well? Which responsibilities seemed to receive little attention? What could the group do to foster more effective interactions? If the group had a leader, what strengths and weaknesses did you observe in his or her communication behaviors?

Exercises

1. Interview someone in a leadership position. The person may be a business executive, an officer in an organization, a school principal, a college president, or any other leader. Construct and ask a series of questions designed to discover his or her views on characteristics of effective and ineffective leaders. Record the answers and be prepared to discuss them in class.

2. Using the topic areas listed below, brainstorm and select a specific problem area. Word it in the form of a problem-solving discussion question.
   a. addiction and substance abuse
   b. education
   c. international relations
   d. political campaigning
   e. privacy issues

3. Choose four campus problems you think need to be addressed—for example, class registration. Word the topics as problem-solving questions. Analyze each topic, asking the following questions:

   a. How important is the problem?
   b. What information do you need to analyze and solve the problem?
   c. Where would you find this information?
   d. What barriers keep the problem from being solved now?
   e. Which steps in the problem-solving process do you think will generate the most conflict? Why?

   Based on your answers to these questions, select the best topic for a problem-solving discussion. Justify your choice.

4. Write a summary and evaluation of your participation in an assigned group discussion, using the five criteria for effective group participation. Write a critique of other members in your group using these same criteria.

5. Write a critique of your group leader using the ten criteria for effective leadership. If you served as leader, write a self-critique.

Appendix

Sample Speeches

Renaissance Fairs: The New Vaudeville[1]
Melissa Janoske, Radford University

Melissa took a public speaking class at Radford University during the spring of 2002. For her informative assignment she delivered a well-organized speech on Renaissance fairs. We asked Donika Patel, a classmate of Melissa's, to write a critique of the speech, using the guidelines we discuss in Chapter 4. Donika's critique is featured in the Theory into Practice feature on pages 78–79.

1 Imagine you're walking down the street, minding your own business, about to go into a store, when suddenly, someone calls your name. You turn around, and the person advances toward you. Immediately, you find yourself in the middle of a sword fight—right in the middle of the street! As you fight for your life, a crowd gathers, watching and cheering. The fight is treacherous, and your opponent is worthy, but finally, the fight ends when the gleaming edge of your sword pins your opponent onto the cobblestone path below him. Those who have gathered come up and congratulate you.

2 This seemingly outrageous scene is actually fairly commonplace in certain times and places. The year? Well, either 1521 or 2002. The place? Any busy street in Renaissance England, or your local Renaissance festival.

3 Elizabethan social historian Mike Bonk captures the excitement and fascination of this era on his current website, www.faires.com. He describes the Renaissance as "a period of intensity in all things: work, play, . . . the arts, world exploration, . . . religion and superstition. Renaissance faires resurrect [these extremes], both as reenactment and as a way of life."

4 Some people live and die by their ability to re-create pre-17th century Europe. They create elaborate costumes and have entire other personalities that they become on the weekends. Renaissance fairs are both exciting and educational, and anyone with curiosity and imagination can attend, observe, and even participate.

5 It's easy for you to experience present-day Renaissance culture through three easy acts: imagine yourself as a Renaissance figure, affiliate with your local kingdom, and participate in a local Renaissance festival or event.

6 To start on your journey into the Renaissance, imagine yourself becoming a part of the world of a Renaissance fair. This would mean becoming a person from the original world, letting that entire culture become part of who you are, and suspending normal belief about who you are in daily life. Renaissance fair enthusiast Mike Boar proclaims: "Monday through Friday, I'm Mike the Truck Driver. On the weekends, I'm the Barbarian King. Men fear me. Women can't get enough of me. Guess who I'd rather be?" And Mike isn't alone in his love of a personality switch for the weekend. According to Jules Smith, Sr., co-founder of International Renaissance Fairs Ltd., Renaissance fairs are the "new vaudeville," drawing a crowd of 193,000 people to the last fair he held in Maryland. That's a lot of people getting decked out in chain mail and corsets and going out for the weekend. Participants use traditional names and titles, wear period clothing, and even learn about a possible profession from that time period. Events are usually open to the public, and so even if you're not into wearing tights and riding horses, it's still fun to go and watch and learn about the diversity of the culture.

7 Learning how to do all of those character-altering activities is important, but the knowledge of all things Renaissance doesn't just come in a potion from the apothecary. It is instead often achieved through the second aspect of Renaissance life: affiliating with your local kingdom. The Society for Creative Anachronism, Inc., an international organization dedicated to Renaissance culture, has divided the world into sixteen kingdoms, spanning the entire globe and allowing everyone in the world in on the fun. A map of these divisions can be found on their website, www.sca.org. Many of these sixteen kingdoms have their divisions within the United States. Virginia is located in the Kingdom of Atlantia, and each kingdom has at least one university in a central location. These universities are run by kingdom officials and offer classes in how to become more immersed in the culture; how to be a goldsmith, or lessons in jousting; or even a lecture on the political methods of King Arthur. You can learn how to fence or ride a horse, cook medieval delicacies, or shop for velvet gowns and leather boots. Each kingdom also allows any of its subjects to gain membership, come to the annual events and fairs, and immerse themselves fully in any events or activities that might help them understand Renaissance Europe.

8 While each kingdom provides the learning opportunities for and access to these festivals, the actual participation in them is the third, and most important, aspect of Renaissance fair culture. Without this participation, all the character changes and kingdom knowledge don't mean nearly as much. It is the practice of Renaissance life that makes it worthwhile, and the actual Renaissance fairs are the easiest and most fun way to do that. There are lots of different types of fair activities to participate in, from jousting festivals to chain mail competitions to cooking parties. You can take classes on spinning and weaving and chain mail or participate in the annual Saint Patty's Day Bloodbath ($5 for a day of swordsmanship and excitement). All aspects of Renaissance culture are available and represented, and all you have to do is go out and look for it. Particular festivals are held around present-day holidays, such as Halloween and feasting days, or events that were important in Renaissance culture. There is a very popular fair held in Pennsylvania every year at Halloween called Renaissance Fright Night that includes renditions of "Frankenstein" and poetry from Poe, goblins and gargoyles that come alive, and street peasants, roasted chestnuts, and fighting for the plenty. This is just one example. There are many websites, such as www.faires.com, that offer detailed information about specific fairs in your area. These festivals are the culmination of the work that people do in learning about the way things were in Renaissance Europe. It's a chance to show off your costumes, present your new persona, showcase your work, or just go and be a part of the festivities. The festivals are a time to enjoy the culture and community that is created and to relax and bask in all the entertainment that is offered through a Renaissance fair.

9 Transforming yourself into a Renaissance figure, affiliating with your local kingdom, and participating in a Renaissance fair are three main ways to experience Renaissance culture today. To get started on your journey, visit www.faires.com. Just make sure you spell it the Renaissance way: f-a-i-r-E-s. Here you will find all sorts of suggestions on integrating Renaissance culture into your life in fun and exciting ways. So take the hint from Mike Boar, the truck driver: lose the college student in you for the weekend, and see how much you like being a Barbarian King with a penchant for chain mail.

Steganography: Hidden Messages[2]
Tiffanie K. Petrin, San Antonio College

Tiffanie found her informative speech topic during the flurry of Internet communication about national security following the tragedy of 9/11. She heightened listener interest in this novel topic by showing its ancient origins. Tiffanie won first place in informative speaking at the Texas Community College Speech and Theater Association state tournament in the spring of 2002.

1 In the movie *Along Came a Spider*, students of influential Washington politicians attend an elite, private school. The classrooms in this school don't look like what you might see in an ordinary public school. Here, students are assigned their own computers, all of which are networked together. As the instructor proceeds through his lesson, the students

are prompted to follow along on their own screens. The use of this kind of technology may suggest a wisdom beyond their years, but these students are still very much like other 4th graders. When the character Megan Rose wants to pass a note in class, she doesn't resort to the conventional folded up piece of paper. Instead, she uses her computer to send an innocent looking picture of a tiger to her friend, Dimitri. Dimitri then takes the picture and applies a simple program, thereby revealing a hidden message.

2 These students are using the very complex technology of steganography to accomplish a very simple goal. Steganography has existed throughout history, but just recently it has been given new attention. In fact, this old technique has been given new applications due to today's technology. This new use allows messages to pass, undetected, through many different media, including video, email, and digital photographs. This means that every image you view on your computer has the potential to contain a hidden message. This message can come in many different formats, including as a virus that can interfere with the files on your hard drive.

3 So today, we'll first discuss what steganography is and how it came into existence. Second, we will see exactly how steganography works. Finally, we'll look at its current uses and possible future applications.

4 First, then, what is steganography? As defined by Richard Lewis, of the System Administration, Networking, and Security Institute, steganography literally means "covered writing" and is the art of concealing the very existence of a message. The purpose of steganography is to hide a message within another form of communication in such a way that prevents an observer from learning that anything unusual is taking place.

5 Steganography has a long and rich history in warfare. One of the first recorded instances of its use is written in the *Histories* of Herodotus. In ancient Greece, messages were conveyed using wax tablets. In one story, Demeratus wanted to notify his hometown of Sparta that Xerxes was intending to invade the Peloponnesus. To ensure that the message would not be intercepted, he scraped the wax off of the tablets and wrote his message on the underlying wood. He recovered the tablets with wax so that they appeared to be blank. In this form, they could pass undetected back to Sparta. Once in Sparta, the wax was melted off, revealing the hidden message.

6 Another method of steganography is to use invisible inks. According to Declan McCullagh, in the February 2, 2001, edition of *Wired News,* these inks were used as recently as World War II. A covert message could be written between the lines of a seemingly innocuous letter. The most common inks used were milk, vinegar, fruit juices, and even urine. These liquids would darken when heated, thereby revealing the hidden messages. Later, with the use of other chemicals, the invisible ink became even harder to detect.

7 Just as Demeratus hid his message, we can now hide a message in an electronic format so that it's almost undetectable. The wax tablet has given way to the electronic file, but the goal remains the same: to obscure the message to all but the intended viewer. So, second, let's take a closer look at how steganography works.

8 In his article on steganography at the Johnson and Johnson Technology Consultants website, www.jjtc.com, last accessed on September 16, 2001, Neil F. Johnson, a professor at George Mason University, explains how these messages are embedded. In every computer file, there is a large amount of "empty" space, or space that is not integral to the file. These "low-order" bits can be changed slightly without alerting the human senses. Steganography takes advantage of this by embedding the digital message in these bits. You see, in a computer, an image is simply an array of numbers that represents light intensities at various points called pixels. Each pixel can contain up to three bytes of information, but most images do not require that amount of memory. So the steganographic program can simply utilize the "extra" bytes in those pixels. This creates a slight degradation in the quality of the photograph. Look at this picture of a chapel [showing Photograph 1]. Now, take a look at this picture [showing Photograph 2]. While they initially appear to be identical, you might notice the slight degradation in the second photograph. The reason for this is that Photograph 2 actually contains an aerial view of the Pentagon, encoded using steganography [showing Photograph 3]. The degradation, noted previously, is somewhat helpful in detecting a hidden message, but it's not a very effective tool. The degradation is so slight that most people won't even notice it, even when compared side by side with the original.

9 After hiding, then sending the message, the next step is to extract it. This is the easiest step because it's done by the computer. According to Dr. Johnson, using a steganalysis program, your computer can pull out the message and display it. Each day, many of us receive emails from various friends, family and co-workers. Many of these contain jokes or images. These images are perfect vessels for steganographic messages. Much like the U.S. postal workers were unwitting couriers of the anthrax virus, you too might just be propagating covert information without your knowledge.

10 Now that we understand how steganography works, let's look, finally, at some of its applications. One of the most unsettling aspects about this technology is its very nature: the sending and receiving of covert messages. Consider this example, given by Robert Vamosi, in the June 27, 2001, edition of the *ZDNet News:* You work for the National Security Agency monitoring terrorist activities. In the past week, you have recorded a large increase in the number of encrypted emails being sent. This may tip you off to a forthcoming event, or terrorist activity. At the very least, your suspicions will be aroused and cause you to take a closer look at those emails. Then consider that, instead of being able to monitor obviously encrypted emails, you had to monitor the subtle patterns of every single image on the Internet. This is the exact reason terrorists, including the infamous Osama bin Laden, use steganography to communicate. Because these embedded images can be posted to free websites, terrorists can convey their messages around the world without ever tipping off major security officials. Jack Kelley, in his June 6, 2001, article in *USA Today,* states that steganography has become so fundamental to the operations of these groups that bin Laden and other Muslim extremists are teaching it at their camps in Afghanistan and the Sudan.

11 On a more local level, steganography can be a very important tool for businesses. For example, let's say you work in New York City for a large software firm. You've just written a breakthrough program that has immense possibilities. The source code for this program needs to be sent to the parent company, located in California, but you're afraid that it may be intercepted. Prior to copyrighting the program, the only thing that keeps your program from being used by another developer is that they don't have access to your source code. Keeping this source code protected is very important and shouldn't be trusted to a simple encrypted email. So, you can embed the source code using steganography and send the email without worrying about its interception.

12 For the future, we can expect to see an increase in this type of communication. The technologies allowing messages to be hidden will increase in sophistication to reduce the amount of degradation, thereby making it even more difficult to detect these messages.

13 Today we have explored a new technology that can change the way we communicate. We have examined what steganography is and how it works. We have also explored current and future applications for this technology.

14 Current steganography is a new and exciting twist on an old form of communication. The uses I have shown you today are but a small portion of the possibilities for this technology. From terrorists to CEOs, this technology has a wide range of applications. So next time you open an email and see a picture of a family member or a familiar scene, you might think about what may be in the image that you're just not seeing.

A Sign of the Times[3]
Jared J. Johnston, West Chester University

Speeches sometimes gather impact by helping listeners consider a topic from a different perspective. Notice how Jared used sign language, vivid examples, statistics, and emotive language to help his hearing audience understand and appreciate Deaf culture. He delivered his problem–solution speech at the Interstate Oratorical Association contest in 2004.

1 [Jared signs the following sentence.] If you cannot understand what I am signing, you are part of the problem, not the solution. [Then, he signs and speaks the same sentence.] In spite of the fact that deafness is a common condition in our society, very few of us are equipped to communicate with Deaf people. According to a study by Gallaudet University as found on their website last updated March 14, 2004, every day 24 million

people across the United States are unable to communicate effectively because the hearing are unable to understand them. Twenty-four million—that is one out of every twelve of us. Every day we encounter Deaf people, but we just do not realize it. Unless we "catch" them signing, they remain invisible to us—invisible and silent. In our forensics community that places paramount value on the sharing of ideas in a symphony of individualized expression, we must be concerned when avenues of expression are systematically cut off.

2 The problems the Deaf face are real. Our inability to communicate with Deaf people we encounter has profound consequences for their ability to function in society. This situation is wrong and must change. We must make American Sign Language, or ASL, a part of our daily communication repertoires. In order to take appropriate action, we will first identify the real problems associated with being deaf in our ASL illiterate society. Second, we will confront the forces that perpetuate this problem for us. Before finally, addressing some solutions that must be pursued if we are to end the chronic isolation Deaf people experience on a daily basis.

3 First, we must identify the problem. Simply put, our ASL illiteracy has built a wall between the Deaf and the hearing. This lack of understanding causes daily inconveniences, chronic marginalization, and potential dangers for those who rely on ASL to connect with the world around them. The hearing impaired are practically cut off from day-to-day services most of us take for granted. A Deaf person cannot conveniently go to the bank or to a restaurant, because the tellers or restaurant staffs are generally ill-equipped to communicate with them. In the myriad of everyday interactions in which businesses meet and greet the public, accommodations for Deaf patrons simply are not present. As such, the Deaf are pushed to the periphery of society. What we have to realize is that being Deaf is not the problem; ignoring people because they are Deaf is. These inconveniences in everyday life are compounded by a marginalization of Deaf people in the workplace. According to the U.S. Department of Labor's website, updated daily, "only 43 percent of employers have accommodations for hearing-impaired individuals." This means that even in the confines of corporate America the Deaf are being isolated.

4 This isolation, however, pales in the face of the struggles Deaf people confront in medical situations—struggles that are a potential danger to their lives. Many hearing-impaired Americans receive inadequate healthcare, because communicating about medical conditions is very difficult. It is often assumed that all Deaf people are able to lip-read. This is not the case. Moreover, lip-reading is at best imprecise. As the September 1, 2002, *American Family Physician* notes, only 30 percent of English sounds are distinguishable on the lips. Add inarticulation and visual obstructions—well, you get the picture. The Deaf deserve better. Adequate medical attention means more than brief written notes like "You've only got a cold." or "You have to take these pills with food three times a day." Proper care requires forming a partnership with medical caregivers, which requires the ability to communicate in depth about one's condition. Moreover, in an emergency situation, the Deaf are often not able to tell the doctor what happened because there is usually no interpreter, because as [the] October 1999 *British Medical Student's Journal* notes, the Deaf are expected to provide their own. The bottom line is: being Deaf is unlike any other sensory handicap. Being blind, for instance, cuts you off from things; being Deaf cuts you off from people.

5 Now that we have some understanding of the problem, let's look at the forces that perpetuate this communication gap. The two main causes are a lack of support for ASL and our ignorance of Deaf culture. In the U.S. support for ASL is sparse. According to the National Association of the Deaf's 2003 report, only 14 states in the Union teach sign language in schools and universities. It's appalling that there aren't more schools that teach ASL when we consider that, according to Gallaudet University in Maryland, ASL is the fourth most used language in the United States. Moreover, there is no support structure to help bring ASL to fruition in language studies. ASL is not considered a legitimate language of study in most "speaking" universities; yet Latin, Russian, Portuguese, Chinese, and Japanese are. How many people do we encounter on a daily basis who speak Portuguese? One in 12? One in 1200? Ever? That's what I thought. This is because these languages are not prevalent in our country, and few of us are ever likely to need them.

6 In these presumably enlightened times you would think that this problem would be close to being solved, but it's not. This is because of society's entrenched attitudes to-

ward deafness. The Deaf are seen as people to be pitied, but mostly as people to be ignored. Michael Sattler, prominent author on Deaf culture, laments, "It is very common in our majority hearing culture to view the Deaf as a minority disabled group who are in need of our help, or of rescue by coddling or surgery." As a nation, we would rather ignore the problem altogether and hope it goes away. The Gallaudet University website informs us that even the government is trying to avoid the problem. The Census Bureau hasn't had a question about deafness since 1985. They can ask us about our hair color, our salary, and our families, but they can't ask us if we're Deaf. This is one of the building blocks of the wall that has been erected in our society between the hearing and the hearing impaired. In the way that our government bureaucracy works, official action can only take place on the basis of its own official numbers. In such an environment affirming attitudes and actions are difficult, if not impossible.

7 Now that we understand the problem and its causes, we can finally attempt to break down that wall and move toward the future. By examining what we should do on a governmental level, on an educational level, and finally on a personal level. First, the government through its census must take the first step by keeping records on the numbers of Deaf people in America. This can lead to an awareness that wasn't there before. Only by removing deafness from official invisibility can the government begin to create programs and incentives to integrate the Deaf into society. Change must start with our children. George Bush's "No Child Left Behind" program creates incentives for schools to hire qualified staff to optimize educational output. This program must live up to its name and not leave any student behind by creating incentives to schools who help the Deaf students live up to their potential. As well, the government, under the auspices of the Americans with Disabilities Act, should foster better customer service for Deaf people. Specifically, we should require businesses that provide a direct public service to have at least one person on duty that is proficient in ASL fingerspelling at the very least. Currently, the ADA is silent on this issue. With this simple change, the daily tasks that you and I often take for granted can be just as commonplace for the hearing impaired as for the hearing.

8 In addition to government action corrective steps must occur in our schools, colleges, and universities. According to the Center for Child Development found at Georgetown University, a child learns language best before the age of nine. Our schools should take advantage of this by offering a course in sign language. This could be learned right along with their alphabet in early schooling. Moving to the upper levels of K–12 learning, students should be allowed to learn ASL to fulfill a foreign language requirement. This also should be implemented on the college and university level. For instance, according to the Harvard University student catalog, there are ten languages that are acceptable fields of study. They include: Latin, French, Spanish, Italian, Russian, Portuguese, Japanese, Mandarin Chinese, Arabic, and Hindi. By adding ASL to the options, we give students the opportunity to participate in a language that is practical in everyday life. Until our government and school officials open their eyes, their ears, or their hands, we must take this initiative ourselves. Visit the ASL website at www.handspeak.com. Here you can learn fingerspelling, and the website will even test you to see how much you've learned.

9 We need to build a stronger support structure for the Deaf community. In our forensics community, a widespread knowledge of ASL would open our own doors to provide the benefits of our activity to more individuals. It has been suggested that I should sign my entire speech to be consistent with my argument. However, signing to an audience that lacks knowledge reduces such a gesture to mere distraction. Knowledge, on the other hand, opens doors and breaks down walls, and if we learn ASL, we can break down this wall into a new culture that many of us have never seen before: a world where sound is not an issue, but sights, smells, and feelings are magnified.

10 Today, we have confronted the problem of ASL illiteracy in our society, isolated the forces that perpetuate this divide between the hearing and the hearing impaired, and, finally, addressed some solutions that can bring down the wall of silence between us and them. Deafness need not and should not consign 24 million Americans to the periphery of our society. [Jared signs and speaks his final sentences.] Today, you can take matters into your own hands and start to make a difference. Be part of the solution, not the problem.

How Old Is He Anyway? Aging the Whitetail Buck[4]

Darla Goodrich, San Antonio College

Whitetail deer are common in the Texas hill country. When they wander into suburban areas, however, deer can annoy as many residents as they charm. A hunter, Darla knew that her audience would include both hunters and animal welfare advocates. She delivered the following speech in an Internet class during the spring of 2005.

1 Imagine for a minute that you're sitting comfortably underneath a huge oak tree, smack dab in the middle of a hundred acres of prime whitetail country. It's nearly dawn and suddenly from out of the shadows trots an 8-point buck! You look him over and realize that he's immature, only about 2½ years old. So you lower your scope, watch him a little longer, and then he's gone.

2 Can you really tell how old a buck is just by looking at him? Yes, you can, but until recently I couldn't and still feel badly that my first buck was so young. Had I only waited a couple more years, he could have grown into quite a trophy. And not only that, but even though the older bucks produce a healthier herd, you still need some younger ones around to reduce the breeding pressure on the older ones.

3 As you watch deer on the run around the city, or you watch them from your own back yard, have you ever wondered why one buck can look so different from another with the same point count? This evening I'm going to share some of the physical and behavioral characteristics of four different age groups of whitetail buck. I'm going to talk about yearlings, immature bucks, mature bucks, and post-mature bucks. So that whether you're a watcher or a hunter you too can age the whitetail buck on the hoof, and hopefully avoid the mistake that I made.

4 The first category that I want to discuss is yearling bucks. Now these bucks are actually a year and a half old, born late in the spring of the previous year. Their antlers are thin with short tines and they can range anywhere from one to ten points. This buck has a cute, little baby face. And as you can see from this illustration, his neck is rather skinny, and it's quite obvious where it meets the shoulders and the chest. His legs are long and lanky compared to the rest of his body and if, from a distance, you cover his antlers with your thumb, he looks more like a doe than a buck. All of my illustrations come from a poster entitled "Field Guide for Buck Deer," published by Wildlife Enterprises in 2000.

5 In addition to looking like a youngster, this buck behaves like a youngster. Often heedless of his surroundings, he'll be the first buck out to the food plot in the early evening. You can tell fairly quickly that a yearling buck is just that. He's young and impertinent and very entertaining to watch.

6 The second category that I want to discuss is immature bucks. These bucks range in age from 2½ to 3½ years and generally have antlers with thicker main beams and longer tines. The face is still rather long and if you picture it as a triangle, you'll see that the distance from the top of the head to the bottom of the jaw is actually shorter than the distance down the nose or from the jaw to the nose. The neck is beginning to fill out, but it's still obvious where it meets the chest and shoulders, and the legs still look a little long in proportion to the body. And if you look at the distance from the ground to the bottom of the chest and the ground to the waist, it's clear that the waist is smaller than the chest.

7 Immature bucks are more cautious than yearlings and will typically follow *them* out to the food plot in the early evening. This age group is the most tempting to harvest because they can have impressive racks and are fairly easy to shoot because of their aggressive pursuit of the doe in heat.

8 Immature bucks still appear much like does without antlers at this stage and because of their relentless promiscuity, more of this age group are taken than any other.

9 By the way you can find much of what I'm discussing, and a whole lot more, at www.whitetaildeer.com which I accessed on March 14th, and it's periodically updated.

10 The third category that I want to talk about is mature bucks. These are the 4½ to 6½ year olds. As you can see from this picture, the head creates an equilateral triangle and looks balanced. The neck is as thick as the shoulders and chest so there's no real distinction, and the legs are appearing a little shorter now in proportion to his body if you

note the straight line from the bottom of the chest to the waist with just a slight amount of sag. Mature bucks are the trophy bucks. Until now most of their growing energy has been concentrated on skeletal development, but at maturity most of their energy is now concentrated on antler development.

11 Unfortunately, these bucks also undergo a major behavioral change as well. This age group is much more reclusive than their younger brothers and you'll be lucky to see them out at legal hunting time. Mature bucks are in their prime with full-size bodies, impressive antlers, and an evasive attitude.

12 The fourth and final category that I want to talk about is post-mature bucks. These are the 7½ year olds and older. As a buck continues to age he exhibits many of the characteristics of a "senior citizen." His face becomes rather stubby and his skin starts to sag and droop. His legs appear much shorter than his body because of the sagging mid-section and swayed back. The antlers can still be quite impressive, but now they can begin to deteriorate because his teeth are getting old and worn, and so he's getting fewer nutrients.

13 Now this age group is the most challenging to hunt, having survived many hunting seasons already. And I was fortunate enough to see a buck at this stage. It was a few minutes past legal hunting time, and he was with a group of does that the younger bucks were herding out in front of them. He was an ugly old buck, and it looked like it really hurt his joints and his feet to walk.

14 Post-mature bucks look old, with pot bellies and sagging skin, and as white-taildeer.com puts it, they are like "old grandfathers, but still the kind who truly enjoy interacting with their young grandchildren."

15 So now we've talked about some of the physical and behavioral characteristics of four different age groups of the whitetail buck. We've talked about the size and the shape of the head and the nose as it relates to a triangle. We've talked about how the neck and leg looks in proportion to the body, and how the chest and the back and the torso are shaped. We've also discussed some behavioral characteristics, ranging anywhere from heedless and impertinent, to wild-eyed and raring to go, to very cautious and solitary. So whether you want to be able to judge the ages of your bucks for effective herd management, or to grow trophy bucks, or for whatever reason you may have, the basic physical and behavioral characteristics of each age group can aid you in determining just how old that buck is and, in so doing, hopefully avoid the embarrassing mistake that I made with my first buck.

Persuasive Speech[5]
Gene Fox, San Antonio College

A student in an Internet public speaking class, Gene delivered this persuasive speech at his final meeting to deliver speeches to his classmates. See whether you think Gene successfully appealed to these listeners, whom he had come to know only from emails and three previous meetings.

1 [Showing what is obviously a toy pistol] If someone pointed this at you, would you be able to recognize it as a toy gun, rather than a real gun? Probably so, huh? How about this one? [Showing a smaller toy pistol] I think it's pretty safe to say that, because of the classroom environment that we're in, it'd be pretty difficult to fool anyone. But how about this scenario?

2 Picture yourself: You're a police officer. It's 3:00 o'clock in the morning, and you're on a routine check of your business district. You know that there have been a rash of late-night restaurant robberies in your immediate area, and you're about to check a business that's situated right beside a 24-hour McDonald's. As you pull behind this closed business, you see a car that hasn't been parked there the rest of the night. So you radio in your location, and go to check out the vehicle. As a matter of policy, they dispatch a cover officer. But he's a ways away, and this is not an emergency—at least not yet.

3 As you make your way up to the car, you see there's an individual inside. He's watching every move that you make. As you get closer, you make contact with him and ask him

for some identification. He says, "Sure, officer. It's in my wallet. It's on the back seat." He opens his door and you're standing there; and as he's reaching inside, between the seats, toward the floorboard, you're scanning the area with your flashlight when suddenly the high-intensity beam of your flashlight comes across a heart-stopping, gut-wrenching object. It's a gun. You don't have time to think. You act. Your judgment, training, and experience take over. Your adrenaline starts pumping. Several things happen all at once: You hit the emergency toner on your radio. You're in too close proximity to draw your service revolver, so you pull this guy out of the car and slam him on the ground, face first. About this time your cover officer is showing up. He pulls up with his service weapon pointed at the subject. You can hear the sirens in the background as other officers are responding to a possible officer-in-trouble call. As more officers arrive, more guns are drawn and pulled on the subject. Eventually he's handcuffed, searched, and placed in the back of a patrol car. Now that things have calmed down, you go up to secure that weapon. When you pick it up, you realize that it's this. [Showing a realistic looking pistol] This is a Power Line Air Strike revolver, model 240, 24-caliber toy pellet gun. Would you have been able to tell the difference between that and a real gun? What if it was pointed at you or if it was laying on the floorboard of a car?

4 I know a little bit about this subject because this is an actual incident that happened to me one night. And, unfortunately, it's happened to almost every other police officer out there at one time or another. All the officers who were out there that night, with a variety of different levels of experience, handled that gun. None of them, until they handled it, could tell that it was a toy gun. So my purpose here this evening should be obvious: It's to persuade you that realistic toy guns, or nonpowder guns, as these are called, should be better regulated or even banned. I'm going to talk about a few of the startling facts surrounding toy guns like this and the lack of legislation regulating these toys. I hope you all leave here tonight angry that toy guns like this are out there.

5 First, we need to talk about the key facts involved in toy guns like this. Did you know that the minimum muzzle velocity for an object to penetrate the human eye is only 135 feet per second? The minimum muzzle velocity for an object to penetrate human skin or muscle tissue is only 350 feet per second? Well, this may seem like a lot to you. [Showing the realistic looking pistol] But this is bottom of the line in pellet guns and it has a muzzle velocity of 350 feet per second. After this are CO_2 cartridge pistols—pellet guns—that fire up to 450 feet per second. Top-of-the-line pump-action rifles and handguns like this can fire up to 900 feet per second. According to statistics from the Handgun Epidemic Lowering Plan, also known as HELP, in the 2001 statistical report published on their website at www.helpnetwork.org, combined with a January 30, 2002, news article by reporter Tom Atwood for the CWK Network on their website, www.channelcincinnati.com, "Each day, an average of 44 children and teens are treated for injuries from BB and pellet guns. In the year 2000 [alone], 21,000 people were treated in hospital emergency rooms for injuries related to BB and pellet guns. At least 63 deaths were reported to the Consumer Product Safety Commission in a twenty-year period from 1980 to 2000, and an estimated 3.2 million of these 'nonpowder guns' are sold each year in the United States." Now that's just injuries and deaths related to nonpowder guns like this. Unfortunately, most local police departments don't carry statistics on toy guns being used in criminal activities. But in an article written by Nancy Gibbs for *Time* magazine in 1993, she quotes the then surgeon general Joycelyn Elders as saying, "[W]e know that toy guns were used to commit [at least] 30,000 robberies in the last five years [alone]."

6 Now that we've covered just a few of the many startling facts surrounding toy guns like this, it's time to move on to our second point, which is the lack of legislation surrounding the regulation of these guns. Currently "[t]here are no national legal standards for the sale, ownership, or use of non-powder guns, as federal law leaves this regulation [up] to each individual state. Most states do not define non-powder guns as actual firearms and only fifteen states currently regulate their sale or possession." These statements I've just quoted come from the HELP Network statistical report 2001 that I talked about a few minutes ago. And, guess what, out of these fifteen states, Texas is not one that regulates these things. All Texas enforces is a variety of city ordinances that restrict the firing of these weapons within city limits. Companies are not even required to paint the muzzle a different color than the actual gun itself. And they are not required, as they are on that

one [Pointing to one of the first toy guns he showed], to put a plastic cover on it with a neon color so that you can distinguish it from a real gun. Companies basically just put a warning label on the package saying that this item is not a toy and you shouldn't handle it unless you're sixteen years of age or have a parent or guardian around. Local stores will go one step further than that, though. When you scan one of these on the cash register, it will prompt the sales clerk to verify your identification as being at least 18 years of age. But that's it. Nothing else covers the realism involved with these toy guns, the power behind them, or the possession of them in other than a recreational fashion.

7 Now an example of one of the fifteen states that does regulate these guns is the state of California. They finally got sick and tired of seeing these things out on the streets with people handling them. In the June 24, 2002, article featured on the California Assembly—Democratic Caucus web page, found at democrats.assembly.ca.gov, assembly member Herb Wesson, Jr., introduced a bill that "requires all toy guns sold, manufactured, and distributed in California to be completely made of clear plastic or of an approved neon color."

8 Now, don't get me wrong. I'm not against guns, as long as they are legally used. I'm not against toy guns, as long as they are responsibly used. What I am against are toy guns made so realistic that you cannot distinguish between them and a real gun, and so powerful that they will inflict serious bodily injury and even cause death in most children. Staff writer Elisa Schement of the *San Antonio Express–News* wrote in the metro edition on March 28, 2001, an article entitled "Project Seeks to Promote Peaceful Toys for Youth." In that article she quotes Kate Martin of the San Antonio Metropolitan Health District as saying, "I always hear, 'I grew up with toy guns and I'm not violent,' but," Martin goes on to say, "the world is different now. Drugs, alcohol and firearms are readily available to both kids and parents."

9 Realistic toy guns like this serve no legitimate purpose other than to create a large money market for toy companies. You'll hear some people argue, "But what about our second amendment right to bear arms?" Nowhere in the second amendment did I find "toy guns" or "nonpowder guns" listed. What we're talking about is saving the lives of our children and, in my opinion, regulating toy guns and nonpowder guns is not a violation of any rational second amendment objective.

10 Tonight we've talked about a few of the startling facts associated with nonpowder guns and toy guns. And we've talked about the lack of legislation involved with these types of guns. At classaction.findlaw.com you can view news release #95-009, dated October 17, 1994. It's a bulletin from the Consumer Product Safety Commission. In it Ann Brown, the chair of the CPSC, says it best: "Real-looking toy guns may be a small part of the problem of violence in our society, but it is the part of the problem we can solve." Unfortunately, our society these days is reactive rather than proactive. We don't react to a problem until we've experienced the results of that problem first. So instead of reacting to another child who is seriously injured or killed because of these realistic toy guns, instead of reacting to the shooting death of an individual by a police officer because he stupidly brandished one of these toy guns, instead of allowing easier access to realistic guns for criminals to use to commit a violent act against another, let's take that realism away from these types of guns. Let's hold our lawmakers and our toy companies responsible for our society's, and especially our children's, well-being.

Speech of Tribute to Charles M. Schulz[6]
Edwin C. Anderson, Jr.

Charles Schulz died on Valentine's Day 2000, just before the final Peanuts *cartoon appeared in Sunday morning papers around the world. At ceremonies in the Capitol Rotunda on June 7, 2001, members of his family received a posthumous Congressional Gold Medal in his behalf. Schulz's friend Edwin Anderson delivered the following brief, poignant words of tribute.*

1 Thank you. Mr. Speaker, distinguished members of Congress, and to all of the friends and admirers of Charles M. Schulz, known to many of you today as "Sparky."

2 President John F. Kennedy said that a nation reveals itself by those it honors, those it pays tribute to, and those it remembers. Today America, the most powerful nation in

the world, confers its highest civilian award upon a man who never sought power, never coveted wealth, and never courted fame. To the contrary, Sparky was humble; unpretentious; generous to friends and, as you've heard, to his community; devoted to his family; and always, always truthful to himself.

3 Interviewers often asked him, "What are you? Are you a philosopher? Are you a humorist? A writer?" His answer was always the same: "I'm a cartoonist. If you want to know me, read my strip. For everything I am is there."

4 Charlie Brown, Snoopy, and the *Peanuts* gang were in Sparky's heart and mind long before they became famous. They were with him when he was ice skating on the frozen ponds of Minnesota. And they were with him when he was playing sandlot baseball. They suffered with him on Valentine's Day, and they marched off with him when he went into the army in 1943. Virtually every experience that Sparky had—from raising his family to playing hockey, tennis, golf—would be reflected in his strip.

5 In 1750 Benjamin Franklin recommended that drawing be taught in the schools, the academies, and the colleges. He said, "It is a kind of universal language, understood by the peoples of all nations. Ideas," he said, "are better expressed when accompanied by a drawing." Two hundred years later, a young man from St. Paul would prove Benjamin Franklin right.

6 For the last half of the twentieth century, Charles Schulz was one of America's foremost goodwill ambassadors. The *Peanuts* strip, reflecting American humor and American philosophy, was read and enjoyed each day by hundreds of millions of people in seventy-five nations, making us realize that our fears, our frustrations, our hopes, our dreams are common to all.

7 Honored as he would have been personally by this prestigious award, what would have pleased him most is the recognition as a cartoonist. Cartoonists numbered among his closest friends. Many of them are here today, and they know he took much pride in their shared profession.

8 In one of Sparky's strips a dejected Charlie Brown was walking off of the baseball field when Lucy said to him, "Don't feel bad, Charlie Brown. Win some—lose some." His face broke out in a big grin and he said, "Gee, wouldn't that be great?" [Laughter.] I knew that would be understood in this town. [Laughter.]

9 Today Charles Schulz, as a cartoonist and an American, wins a big one.

10 And, finally, Charlie Brown gets it right: It is great.

11 The poet Sophocles wrote, "One must wait until the evening to see how splendid the day has been." Privileged to call him friend, honored that he walked among us, the life of Charles M. Schulz has indeed been splendid.

12 Thank you.

I Have a Dream[7]
Martin Luther King, Jr.

Speaking from the steps of the Lincoln Memorial on August 28, 1963, Martin Luther King, Jr., delivered the keynote address of the March on Washington, D.C., for Civil Rights. As you read his "I Have a Dream" speech, study the power of its language and see if you agree with many scholars that this is the greatest American speech of the twentieth century.

1 I am happy to join with you today in what will go down in history as the greatest demonstration for freedom in the history of our nation.

2 Five score years ago, a great American, in whose symbolic shadow we stand today, signed the Emancipation Proclamation. This momentous decree came as a great beacon light of hope to millions of Negro slaves, who had been seared in the flames of withering injustice. It came as a joyous daybreak to end the long night of their captivity.

3 But one hundred years later, the Negro still is not free. One hundred years later, the life of the Negro is still sadly crippled by the manacles of segregation and the chains of discrimination. One hundred years later, the Negro lives on a lonely island of poverty in the midst of a vast ocean of material prosperity. One hundred years later, the Negro is still languished in the corners of American society and finds himself an exile in his own land.

4 And so we've come here today to dramatize a shameful condition. In a sense we've come to our nation's Capitol to cash a check. When the architects of our republic wrote the magnificent words of the Constitution and the Declaration of Independence, they were signing a promissory note to which every American was to fall heir. This note was a promise that all men—yes, black men as well as white men—would be guaranteed the unalienable rights of life, liberty, and the pursuit of happiness.

5 It is obvious today that America has defaulted on this promissory note insofar as her citizens of color are concerned. Instead of honoring this sacred obligation, America has given the Negro people a bad check—a check which has come back marked "insufficient funds."

6 But we refuse to believe that the bank of justice is bankrupt. We refuse to believe that there are insufficient funds in the great vaults of opportunity of this nation. And so we've come to cash this check—a check that will give us upon demand the riches of freedom and the security of justice.

7 We have also come to this hallowed spot to remind America of the fierce urgency of now. This is no time to engage in the luxury of cooling off or to take the tranquillizing drug of gradualism. Now is the time to make real the promises of democracy. Now is the time to rise from the dark and desolate valley of segregation to the sunlit path of racial justice. Now is the time to lift our nation from the quicksands of racial injustice to the solid rock of brotherhood. Now is the time to make justice a reality for all of God's children.

8 It would be fatal for the nation to overlook the urgency of the moment. This sweltering summer of the Negro's legitimate discontent will not pass until there is an invigorating autumn of freedom and equality. Nineteen sixty-three is not an end, but a beginning. Those who hope that the Negro needed to blow off steam and will now be content will have a rude awakening if the nation returns to business as usual. There will be neither rest nor tranquility in America until the Negro is granted his citizenship rights. The whirlwinds of revolt will continue to shake the foundations of our nation until the bright day of justice emerges.

9 But there is something that I must say to my people, who stand on the warm threshold which leads into the palace of justice. In the process of gaining our rightful place, we must not be guilty of wrongful deeds. Let us not seek to justify our thirst for freedom by drinking from the cup of bitterness and hatred.

10 We must forever conduct our struggle on the high plane of dignity and discipline. We must not allow our creative protest to degenerate into physical violence. Again and again we must rise to the majestic heights of meeting physical force with soul force.

11 The marvelous new militancy which has engulfed the Negro community must not lead us to a distrust of all white people. For many of our white brothers, as evidenced by their presence here today, have come to realize that their destiny is tied up with our destiny. They have come to realize that their freedom is inextricably bound to our freedom. We cannot walk alone.

12 As we walk, we must make the pledge that we shall always march ahead. We cannot turn back. There are those who are asking the devotees of civil rights, "When will you be satisfied?" We can never be satisfied as long as the Negro is the victim of the unspeakable horrors of police brutality. We can never be satisfied as long as our bodies, heavy with the fatigue of travel, cannot gain lodging in the motels of the highways and the hotels of the cities. We cannot be satisfied as long as the Negro's basic mobility is from a smaller ghetto to a larger one. We can never be satisfied as long as our children are stripped of their selfhood and robbed of their dignity by signs stating "For Whites Only." We cannot be satisfied as long as a Negro in Mississippi cannot vote and a Negro in New York believes he has nothing for which to vote. No, no, we are not satisfied, and we will not be satisfied until justice rolls down like waters, and righteousness like a mighty stream.

13 I am not unmindful that some of you have come here out of great trials and tribulations. Some of you have come fresh from narrow jail cells. Some of you have come from areas where your quest for freedom left you battered by the storms of persecution and staggered by the winds of police brutality. You have been the veterans of creative suffering. Continue to work with the faith that unearned suffering is redemptive.

14 Go back to Mississippi, go back to Alabama, go back to South Carolina, go back to Georgia, go back to Louisiana, go back to the slums and ghettos of our Northern cities,

knowing that somehow this situation can and will be changed. Let us not wallow in the valley of despair.

15 I say to you today, my friends, so even though we face the difficulties of today and tomorrow, I still have a dream. It is a dream deeply rooted in the American dream.

16 I have a dream that one day this nation will rise up and live out the true meaning of its creed, "We hold these truths to be self-evident, that all men are created equal."

17 I have a dream that one day on the red hills of Georgia the sons of former slaves and the sons of former slaveowners will be able to sit down together at the table of brotherhood.

18 I have a dream that one day even the state of Mississippi, a state sweltering with the heat of injustice, sweltering with the heat of oppression, will be transformed into an oasis of freedom and justice.

19 I have a dream that my four little children will one day live in a nation where they will not be judged by the color of their skin but by the content of their character. I have a dream today.

20 I have a dream that one day, down in Alabama, with its vicious racists, with its governor having his lips dripping with the words of interposition and nullification, one day right there in Alabama little black boys and black girls will be able to join hands with the little white boys and white girls as sisters and brothers. I have a dream today.

21 I have a dream that one day every valley shall be exalted, every hill and mountain shall be made low, the rough places will be made plain and the crooked places will be made straight, and the glory of the Lord shall be revealed, and all flesh shall see it together.

22 This is our hope. This is the faith that I go back to the South with. With this faith we will be able to hew out of the mountain of despair a stone of hope. With this faith we will be able to transform the jangling discords of our nation into a beautiful symphony of brotherhood. With this faith we will be able to work together, to pray together, to struggle together, to go to jail together, to stand up for freedom together, knowing that we will be free one day.

23 This will be the day—this will be the day when all of God's children will be able to sing with new meaning, "My country 'tis of thee, sweet land of liberty, of thee I sing. Land where my fathers died, land of the pilgrim's pride, from every mountainside, let freedom ring." And if America is to be a great nation, this must become true.

24 So let freedom ring from the prodigious hilltops of New Hampshire. Let freedom ring from the mighty mountains of New York. Let freedom ring from the heightening Alleghenies of Pennsylvania!

25 Let freedom ring from the snowcapped Rockies of Colorado! Let freedom ring from the curvaceous slopes of California!

26 But not only that. Let freedom ring from Stone Mountain of Georgia!

27 Let freedom ring from Lookout Mountain of Tennessee!

28 Let freedom ring from every hill and molehill of Mississippi. From every mountainside, let freedom ring.

29 And when this happens, when we allow freedom to ring—when we let it ring from every village and every hamlet, from every state and every city—we will be able to speed up that day when all of God's children, black men and white men, Jews and Gentiles, Protestants and Catholics, will be able to join hands and sing in the words of the old Negro spiritual, "Free at last! Free at last! Thank God Almighty, we are free at last!"

Endnotes

PREFACE

1. Letty Cottin Pogrebin, *The Diane Rehm Show,* 6 Dec. 2002, WAMU, NPR, 12 Dec. 2002 <www.wamu.org/dr/shows/drarc_021202.html>. Pogrebin was quoting author Grace Paley.

2. Steve C. Beering, "The Liberally Educated Professional," *Vital Speeches of the Day* 15 April 1990: 400.

CHAPTER 1

1. Stacey A. Teicher, "Twenty-six Renaissance Men," *Csmonitor.com* 19 Feb. 2002, 12 March 2002 <www.csmonitor.com/2002/0219/p13s02-hehl.html>.

2. Stacey A. Teicher, "Reflecting on the College's Mission: 'A Life of Service.'" *Csmonitor.com* 19 Feb. 2002, 12 March 2002 <www.csmonitor.com/2002/0219/p14s01-lehl.html>.

3. L. Jackson Newell, "Deep Springs College: Loyal to a Fault?," *Deep Springs College* 12 June 1999 <www.telluride.cornell.edu/deepsprings/whatis/newell.html>.

4. Ernest L. Boyer, *College: The Undergraduate Experience in America* (New York: Harper, 1987) 73.

5. Cited in William E. Arnold and Lynne McClure, *Communication Training and Development,* 2nd ed. (Prospect Heights, IL: Waveland, 1996) 38.

6. *Planning Job Choices: 2000,* 43rd ed. (Bethlehem, PA: National Association of Colleges and Employers, 1999) 20.

7. Jerry L. Winsor, Dan B. Curtis, and Ronald D. Stephens, "National Preferences in Business and Communication Education: II." Speech Communication Association Convention, Marriott Hotel & Marina, San Diego. 26 Nov. 1996: 17.

8. Winsor 11.

9. This survey was conducted by Communispond, Inc., and is reported in "Executives Say Training Helps Them Speak Better," *Training: The Magazine of Human Resources Development* October 1981: 20–21, 75.

10. James Wyllie, "Oral Communications: Survey and Suggestions," *ABCA [American Business Communication Association] Bulletin* June 1980: 15.

11. Roger K. Mosvick and Robert B. Nelson, *We've Got to Start Meeting Like This!* (Glenview, IL: Scott, 1987) 224.

12. *The Oxford English Dictionary,* 2nd ed. (Oxford: Clarendon, 1989) 577.

13. Thomas M. Scheidel, *Persuasive Speaking* (Glenview, IL: Scott, 1967) 2.

14. C. K. Ogden and I. A. Richards, *The Meaning of Meaning,* 9th ed. (New York: Harcourt, Brace, 1953) 10–12. Chapter 1, "Thoughts, Words and Things" (pp. 1–23), explains in detail the relationships between symbols, referents, and interpreters.

15. HNN Staff, "So What Does Jihad Really Mean?," *History News Network* 6 June 2002, 18 June 2002 <www.historynewsnetwork.org/articles/article.html?id=774>.

16. " 'Jihad' Dropped from Harvard Student's Speech," *CNN.com* 6 June 2002, 18 June 2002 <wysiwyg://153/http://fyi.cnn.com/2002/f…dnews/05/31/harvard.jihad.ap/index.html>.

17. Karlyn Kohrs Campbell, *The Rhetorical Act,* 2nd ed. (Belmont, CA: Wadsworth, 1996) 119.

18. National Center for Educational Statistics. *National Assessment of College Student Learning: Identifying College Graduates' Essential Skills in Writing, Speech and Listening, and Critical Thinking.* NCES 95-001 (Washington, DC: GPO, May 1995) 122.

19. Robert Ennis, "A Taxonomy of Critical Thinking Dispositions and Abilities," in *Teaching Thinking Skills: Theory and Practice,* ed. Joan Boykoff Baron and Robert Sternberg (New York: Freeman, 1987) 10.

20. June Stark, "Critical Thinking: Taking the Road Less Traveled," *Nursing 95* November 95: 55.

21. National Assessment of Educational Progress. *Reading, Writing and Thinking: Results from the 1979–80 National Assessment of Reading and Literature.* Report No. 11–L–01 (Washington, DC: GPO, October 1981) 5.

22. Adapted from Robert J. Marzano, Ronald S. Brandt, Carolyn Sue Hughes, Beau Fly Jones, Barbara Z. Presseisen, Stuart C. Rankin, and Charles Suhor, *Dimensions of Thinking: A Framework for Curriculum and Instruction,* Alexandria, VA: Association for Supervision and Curriculum Development (1988) 66, 70–112. Reprinted by permission. The Association for Supervision and Curriculum Development is a worldwide community of educators advocating sound policies and sharing best practices to achieve the success of each learner. To learn more, visit ASCD at www.ascd.org.

23. Barbara J. Thayer-Bacon, "Caring and Its Relationship to Critical Thinking," *Educational Theory* Summer 1993: 323. Our emphasis.

24. Thayer-Bacon 325.

CHAPTER 2

1. Mark Monmonier, *Mapping It Out: Expository Cartography for the Humanities and Social Sciences* (Chicago: U of Chicago P, 1993) 140. We are grateful to Professor Jeremy Crampton of George Mason University for directing us to this source.

2. Fabien A. P. Petitcolas, "Digital Watermarking and Steganography," *The Information Hiding Homepage* 28 Jan. 2002, 15 March 2002. <www.cl.cam.ac.uk/~fapp2/steganography.> We are grateful to Jolinda Ramsey and her student Tiffanie Petrin for first introducing us to the field of steganography.

3. *Frasier,* NBC, 18 Feb. 1999.

4. Donald K. Smith, *Man Speaking: A Rhetoric of Public Speech* (New York: Dodd, 1969) 228.

5. Kenneth Blanchard and Norman Vincent Peale, *The Power of Ethical Management* (New York: Fawcett-Ballantine, 1988) 9.

6. Allan R. Cohen and David L. Bradford, *Influence without Authority* (New York: Wiley, 1990) ix.

7. Mary Cunningham, "What Price 'Good Copy'?" *Newsweek* 29 Nov. 1982: 15.

8. James C. McCroskey, *An Introduction to Rhetorical Communication* (Upper Saddle River, NJ: Prentice, 1968) 237.

9. Georgia Harper, "Using the Four Factor Fair Use Test," *Fair Use of Copyrighted Materials,* U of Texas, Austin, 10 Aug. 2001, 3 Aug. 2002 <www.utsystem.edu/ogc/intellectualproperty/copypol2.htm>.

10. USCS, Sect. 107, Limitations on Exclusive Rights: Fair Use.

11. Harper.

12. Harper.

13. Alexander Lindey, *Plagiarism and Originality* (New York: Harper, 1952) 2.

14. *Prentice Hall Author's Guide* (Upper Saddle River, NJ: Prentice, 1978) 9.

15. John L. Waltman, "Plagiarism: Preventing It in Formal Research Reports," *ABCA [American Business Communication Association] Bulletin* June 1980: 37.

16. Michael T. O'Neill, "Plagiarism: Writing Responsibly," *ABCA Bulletin* June 1980: 34, 36.

17. Carolyn Kleiner Butler, "The Old Ballgames." *Smithsonian Magazine* April 2005: 21.

18. *Paraphrase: Write It in Your Own Words,* Purdue OWL (Online Writing Lab), Purdue U Writing Lab, 16 June 2005 <http://owl.english.purdue.edu/handouts/print/research/r_paraphr.html>.

CHAPTER 3

1. Jerry Seinfeld, *SeinLanguage* (New York: Bantam, 1993) 120.

2. Virginia P. Richmond and James C. McCroskey, *Communication: Apprehension, Avoidance, and Effectiveness,* 5th ed. (Boston: Allyn, 1998) 41.

3. Garrison Keillor, "Monologue," *A Prairie Home Companion,* 13 Feb. 1999, NPR, 16 Mar. 1999 <www.phc.mpr.org/>.

4. David Wallechinsky, Irving Wallace, and Amy Wallace, *The Book of Lists* (New York: Morrow, 1977) 469–70.

5. John H. Greist, James W. Jefferson, and Isaac M. Marks, *Anxiety and Its Treatment* (New York: Warner, 1986) 33.

6. Richmond and McCroskey 45. The "Personal Report of Public Speaking Anxiety (PRPSA)" and directions for interpreting the scored results, reprinted in this chapter, appear on pages 135–136 and page 45, respectively, of Richmond and McCroskey.

7. James A. Belasco and Ralph C. Stayer, *Flight of the Buffalo* (New York: Warner, 1993) 327–28.

8. Belasco 328.

9. Ralph B. Behnke, Chris R. Sawyer, and Paul E. King, "The Communication of Public Speaking Anxiety," *Communication Education* 36 (1987): 140.

10. Howard Nemerov, *Figures of Thought: Speculations on the Meaning of Poetry and Other Essays* (Boston: Godine, 1978) 19.

11. Joe Ayres and Theodore S. Hopf, "Visualization: A Means of Reducing Speech Anxiety," *Communication Education* 34 (1985): 321.

12. Daryl J. Bem, *Belief, Attitudes, and Human Affairs* (Belmont, CA: Brooks/Cole, 1970) 57.

13. Jack Valenti, *Speak Up with Confidence* (New York: Morrow, 1982) 19.

CHAPTER 4

1. Bernard E. Farber, comp. *A Teacher's Treasury of Quotations* (Jefferson, NC: McFarland, 1985) 186.

2. Larry Barker, Renee Edwards, Connie Gaines, Karen Gladney, and Frances Holley, "An Investigation of Proportional Time Spent in Various Communication Activities by College Students," *Journal of Applied Communication Research* 8 (1980): 101–09.

3. Robert L. Montgomery, *Listening Made Easy* (New York: AMACOM, 1981) n.p.

4. William James, *The Principles of Psychology,* vol. 2 (Cambridge: Harvard UP, 1981) 380. This is a reprint of the original 1890 Henry Holt edition.

5. Michael Cronin, Rick Olsen, and Jan Stahl, *Mission Possible: Listening Skills for Better Communication,* computer software, Oral Communication Program, Radford University, Radford, VA, 1992.

6. Lyle V. Mayer, *Fundamentals of Voice and Diction,* 8th ed. (Dubuque, IA: Brown, 1988) 178.

7. Lyle V. Mayer, *Fundamentals of Voice and Diction,* 10th ed. (Dubuque, IA: Brown, 1994) 229.

8. This definition is adapted from Hendrie Weisinger and Norman M. Lobsenz, *Nobody's Perfect: How to Give Criticism and Get Results* (New York: Warner, 1981) 9–10.

9. This model of criticism is adapted from Beverly Whitaker Long, "Evaluating Performed Literature," *Studies in Interpretation,* vol. 2, eds. Esther M. Doyle and Virginia Hastings Floyd (Amsterdam: Rodopi, 1977) 267–81. See also her earlier article: Beverly Whitaker, "Critical Reasons and Literature in Performance," *The Speech Teacher* 18 (November 1969): 191–93. Long attributes this three-part model of criticism to Arnold Isenberg, "Critical Communication," *The Philosophical Review* (July 1949): 330–44.

CHAPTER 5

1. Mary Raymond Shipman Andrews, *The Perfect Tribute* (New York: Scribner's, 1906) 1–9.

2. Carl Sandburg, *Abraham Lincoln: The Prairie Years and the War Years* (New York: Harcourt, 1954) 443–44.

3. Newspaper reporters the next day began to reflect widely different public views of the president's surprisingly brief speech. The *Chicago Times* referred to "the silly, flat, and dish-watery utterances" of Lincoln; the *Harrisburg [Pennsylvania] Patriot and Union* simply reported, "We pass over the silly remarks of the President . . ." (Sandburg 445). Other newspapers, however, made entirely positive evaluations of Lincoln's speech. The *Chicago Tribune* predicted, "The dedicatory remarks of President Lincoln will live among the annals of man" (Sandburg 445). The *Philadelphia Evening Bulletin* noted that thousands who would not wade through Everett's elaborate oration would read Lincoln's brief remarks, "and not many will do it without a moistening of the eye and a swelling of the heart" (Sandburg 446). The *Providence Journal* reminded its readers of the adage that the hardest thing in the world is to make a good five-minute speech, and said, "We know not where to look for a more admirable speech than the brief one which the President made at the close of Mr. Everett's oration" (Sandburg 446).

4. Thomas M. Scheidel, *Persuasive Speaking* (Glenview, IL: Scott, 1967) 97. For a fuller account, see Mark E. Neely, *The Last Best Hope of Earth: Abraham Lincoln and the Promise of America* (Cambridge: Harvard UP, 1993) 154–55. Neely notes that Lincoln made these remarks to acknowledge a serenade celebrating recent Union victories at Gettysburg and Vicksburg.

5. Jeffrey F. Milem, "Why Race Matters," *Academe* September–October 2000: 28.

6. Robert Hughes, *Culture of Complaint: The Fraying of America* (New York: Oxford UP, 1993) 14.

7. Terry Sanford, quoted in "Commencement Remarks: Learning to Care and Share," *Representative American Speeches 1988–1989,* ed. Owen Peterson (New York: Wilson, 1989) 154.

8. John Jacob, "Racism and Race Relations: To Grow beyond our Racial Animosities," *Vital Speeches of the Day* 15 January 1990: 214.

9. "Transcript for April 24th," *Meet the Press,* MSNBC, 2 June 2005, transcript <www.msnbc.com/id/7619740/>. O'Neill attributes the quotation to Karen Armstrong, *The Spiral Staircase: My Climb Out of Darkness* (New York: Anchor-Random House, 2004) 298. Armstrong's actual words: "I tremble for our world, where, in the smallest ways, we find it impossible, as Marshall Hodgson en-

joined, to find room for the other in our minds." Armstrong is quoting from Marshall G. S. Hodgson, *The Venture of Islam: Conscience and History in a World Civilization,* 2 vols. (Chicago and London, 1974) I: 379.

10.   Madeleine F. Green, "Going Global: Internationalizing U.S. Higher Education," *Current* July/August 2002: 8.

11.   Abraham H. Maslow, *Motivation and Personality,* 2nd ed. (New York: Random, 1970) 35–47.

12.   Maslow 38.

13.   Maslow 41.

14.   Michael Pfau and Roxanne Parrott, *Persuasive Communication Campaigns* (Boston: Allyn, 1993) 70.

15.   Descriptions of categories are adapted from The VALS Types, 2001–2002, Stanford Research Institute, 18 Aug. 2002 <www.sric-bi.com/VALS/types.shtml>.

16.   <www.sric-bi.com/VALS/experiencers.shtml>.

17.   Ari Posner, "The Culture of Plagiarism," *New Republic* 18 April 1988: 19.

18.   Lawrence R. Frey, Carl H. Botan, and Gary L. Kreps, *Investigating Communication: An Introduction to Research Methods,* 2nd ed. (Boston: Allyn, 2000). We have drawn from advice in this excellent text in constructing our suggestions regarding audience questionnaires.

CHAPTER 6

1.   Ralph Fletcher, *What a Writer Needs* (Portsmouth, NH: Heinemann, 1993) 101.

2.   Borgna Brunner, "The Bloomsday Centenary: Joyce's *Ulysses* Unfolds over a Single Day in Dublin 100 Years Ago," *Infoplease Daily Almanac* 16 June 2004, 29 May 2005 <www.infoplease.com/spot/bloomsday.html>.

3.   Leonard J. Rosen and Laurence Behrens, *The Allyn & Bacon Handbook,* 4th ed. (Boston: Allyn, 2000) 68.

CHAPTER 7

1.   Patricia Senn Breivik, *Student Learning in the Information Age* (Phoenix, AZ: Oryx P, 1998) 2.

2.   Ann Marie Dull, "Clinton Selects Adelphi on Campaign Trail," *The Delphian,* 16 Feb. 2000, 6 Aug. 2002 <http://students.adelphi.edu/delphian/archive/51_1/clinton1.shtml>.

3.   "New Estimate Puts Web Size at 11.5 Billion Pages & Compares Search Engine Coverage," SearchEngineWatch, 17 May 2005, 30 Sept. 2005 <http://blog.searchenginewatch.com/blog/050517-07657>.

4.   Gary Ink, "Book Title Output and Average Prices: 1999 Final and 2000 Preliminary Figures," *The Bowker Annual Library and Book Trade Almanac,* ed. Dave Bogart, 46th ed. (New Providence, NJ: Reed Elsevier, 2000) 485.

5.   Jenny Sinclair, "The Information Challenge," *The Age* 6 Feb. 2002 <http://theage.com.au>.

6.   Breivik 1.

7.   Wayne C. Booth, Gregory G. Colomb, and Joseph M. Williams, *The Craft of Research* (Chicago: U of Chicago P, 1995) 35.

8.   Robert C. Jeffrey and Owen Peterson, *Speech: A Text with Adapted Readings,* 2nd ed. (New York: Harper, 1983) 169.

9.   "How Academic Librarians Can Influence Students' Web-based Information Choices," *OCLC [Online College Learning Center] White Paper on the Information Habits of College Students,* June 2002, 7 Aug. 2002 <www2.oclc.org/oclc/pdf/printondemand/informationhabits.pdf>.

10.   *OCLC White Paper* 4.

11.   Jaymee Soni, Sally Thomas, and Barbara Stone, "Dealing with an Information Glut," *School of Information Management &* *Systems,* 18 April 2002, 30 May 2002 <www.sims.berkeley.edu/courses/is206/f97/GroupE/infoglut.html>.

12.   Michael K. Bergman, "The Deep Web: Surfacing Hidden Value," White Paper, 24 Sept. 2001, 13 Sept. 2005: 5 <http://beta.brightplanet.com/deepcontent/tutorials/DeepWeb/index.asp>.

13.   Stephen Dingman, email to the authors. 2 Sept. 2005.

14.   Bergman 1.

15.   Chris Dodge, "Knowledge for Sale," *Utne* July/Aug. 2005: 73.

16.   "Preface," Ulrich's Periodicals Directory 2006, manag. ed. Dawn Lombardy Stoecker (New Providence, NJ: Reed Elsevier, 2006), in press.

17.   Lois Horowitz, *Knowing Where to Look: The Ultimate Guide to Research* (Cincinnati: Writer's Digest, 1988) 115.

18.   Alden Todd, *Finding Facts Fast,* 2nd ed. (Berkeley: Ten Speed, 1979) 14.

CHAPTER 8

1.   Ross Petras and Kathryn Petras, *The 365 Stupidest Things Ever Said* (New York: Workman, 1999) n.p.

2.   Amanda Ripley, "Grief Lessons," *Time* 29 Oct. 2001: 69.

3.   Ali Heidarpour, "Binge Drinking on College Campuses," *Winning Oration, 2003* (Mankato, MN: Interstate Oratorical Association, 2003) 59. Coached by Thomas Bartl, Stacy Schrank, Tiffany Mindt, and Weslynn Reed.

4.   John Ciardi, *A Browser's Dictionary* (New York: Harper, 1980) 206–07.

5.   *Encarta® World English Dictionary* (New York: St. Martin's, 1999) 1600.

6.   "Krumping," *Wikipedia* 28 July 2005 <http://en.wikipedia.org/wiki/Krumping>.

7.   George Lawton, "Invasive Software: Who's Inside Your Computer?" *Computer* July 2002: 15.

8.   Kimberly Paine, "Red Light Running," *Winning Orations, 2001* (Mankato, MN: Interstate Oratorical Association, 2001) 41. Coached by Susan Miskelly.

9.   Bill Gates, "High Schools Are Obsolete: Teaching Kids What They Need to Know," *Vital Speeches of the Day* 15 April 2005: 396–97.

10.   Ben Bradley, "The New College Disease," *Winning Orations, 2000* (Mankato, MN: Interstate Oratorical Association, 2000) 132. Coached by Terry West.

11.   Heidarpour 59.

12.   C. Everett Koop, address, National Press Club, Washington, DC, 8 Sept. 1998.

13.   Tony Martinet, "Ribbons: Function or Fashion," *Winning Orations, 2004* (Mankato, MN: Interstate Oratorical Association, 2004) 79. Coached by Christina Ellis.

14.   Travis Kirchhefer, "The Deprived," *Winning Orations, 2000* (Mankato, MN: Interstate Oratorical Association, 2000) 149. Coached by Ron Krikac.

15.   We adapted this checklist from Serena Fenton and Grace Reposa, "Evaluating the Goods," *Technology & Learning* Sept. 1998: 28–32; "Module IX: Evaluating Information Sources," 26 Aug. 2002, McConnell Library, Radford Univ., 2 Sept. 2002 <http://lib.runet.edu/highlanderguide/evaluation/intro.html>; Esther Grassian, "Thinking Critically about World Wide Web Resources," 10 Oct. 1997, UCLA College Library, 10 March 1999 <www.accd.edu/sac/lrc/gis/critical.htm>; and Keith Stanger, "Criteria for Evaluating Internet Resources," 31 July 1999, University Library, Eastern Michigan Univ., 30 August 2002 <http://online.emich.edu/~lib_stanger/ineteval.htm>.

CHAPTER 9

1. Robert Half, "Memomania," *American Way* 1 Nov. 1987: 21.

2. Robert L. Montgomery, *Listening Made Easy* (New York: AMACOM, 1981) 65–78.

3. Matthew Whitley, "Involuntary Commitment Laws," *Video User's Guide for the Allyn & Bacon/AFA Student Speeches Video I* (Boston: Allyn, 1997) 43–45.

4. B. Scott Titsworth, "Students' Notetaking: The Effects of Teacher Immediacy and Clarity," *Communication Education* October 2004: 317.

5. Glenn Leggett, C. David Mead, Melinda Kramer, and Richard S. Beal, *Prentice Hall Handbook for Writers,* 11th ed. (Upper Saddle River, NJ: Prentice Hall, 1991) 417–18. We have drawn on examples these authors use in their excellent section on connecting language.

6. Robert DiYanni and Pat C. Hoy, *The Scribner Handbook for Writers,* 3rd ed. (New York: Longman, 2001) 196.

7. DiYanni 197.

CHAPTER 10

1. Jake Gruber, "Heart Disease in Women," *Winning Orations, 2001* (Mankato, MN: Interstate Oratorical Association, 2001) 16. Coached by Judy Santacaterina.

2. David Slater, "Sharing Life," *Winning Orations, 1998* (Mankato, MN: Interstate Oratorical Association, 1998) 63.

3. Carl Wayne Hensley, "What You Share Is What You Get: Tips for Effective Communication," *Vital Speeches of the Day* 1 Dec. 1992: 115.

4. Bill Gates, "High Schools Are Obsolete: Teaching Kids What They Need to Know," *Vital Speeches of the Day* 15 April 2005: 396.

5. Brian Bauman, Untitled Speech, *Winning Orations, 2001* (Mankato, MN: Interstate Oratorical Association, 2001) 74. Coached by Al Golden.

6. Gruber 16.

7. Jayme Meyer, Untitled Speech, University of Texas at Austin, 2001–2002.

8. John Guare, *Six Degrees of Separation* (New York: Random, 1990) 46.

9. Elinor Donahue, "Writing Your Own Speeches," *Fund Raising Management* (Feb. 1996), 7 July 1999 <http://web4.infotrac.galegroup.com/itw/i_5!xrn_49_0_A18711219?sw_aep=viva_radford>.

10. Kimberly Paine, "Red Light Running," *Winning Orations, 2001* (Mankato, MN: Interstate Oratorical Association, 2001) 41. Coached by Susan Miskelly.

11. Paine 42.

12. Gruber 18.

CHAPTER 11

1. E. D. Hirsch, Jr., *Cultural Literacy: What Every American Needs to Know* (New York: Vintage-Random, 1988) 34.

2. Many people who teach creative writing prefer visual brainstorming, or "branching," to the traditional, linear outlines such as the ones we illustrate. For interesting discussions of how outlining by visual brainstorming draws on both sides of the brain, see Henriette Anne Klauser, *Writing on Both Sides of the Brain: Breakthrough Techniques for People Who Write* (San Francisco: HarperSanFrancisco, 1987) 47–55, and Gabriele Lusser Rico, *Writing the Natural Way: Using Right-Brain Techniques to Release Your Expressive Powers* (New York: Tarcher/Putnam, 2000).

3. Jeff Kirvin. "I Don't Really Have to Use Roman Numerals, Do I?" *Writing on Your Palm* 10 March 2003, 2 Aug. 2005 <www.writingonyourpalm.net/column030310.htm>.

4. "Getting Started: Outlining." *Guide to Writing Research Papers,* Capital Community College Foundation 2 Aug. 2005 <http://webster.comnet.edu/grammar/composition/brainstorm_outline.htm>.

5. This example is based on John M. Kennedy, "How the Blind Draw." *Scientific American* January 1997: 76+.

CHAPTER 12

1. Richard Lederer, *Anguished English: An Anthology of Accidental Assaults upon Our Language* (Charleston, SC: Wyrick, 1987) 8.

2. Gloria Cooper, ed., *Red Tape Holds up New Bridge, and More Flubs from the Nation's Press* (New York: Perigee, 1987) n. p.

3. Jeffrey McQuain, *Power Language: Getting the Most out of Your Words* (New York: Houghton, 1996) 6.

4. Gerald Parshall, "A 'Glorious Mongrel,'" *U.S. News & World Report* 25 Sept. 1995: 48.

5. Bill Bryson, *The Mother Tongue: English & How It Got That Way* (New York: Avon, 1990) 13.

6. This discussion of language is based on Roman Jakobson, "Closing Statement: Linguistics and Poetics," in *Style in Language,* ed. Thomas A. Sebeok (Cambridge: MIT P, 1964) 350–74.

7. Michael Balter, "First 'Speech Gene' Identified," *Academic Press Daily InSight,* 3 Oct. 2001, American Association for the Advancement of Science, 7 Sept. 2002 <www.academicpress.com/inscight/10032001/grapha.htm>.

8. Charles L. Barber, *The Story of Speech and Language* (New York: Crowell, 1965) 9–10.

9. Jefferson Graham, *Frasier* (New York: Simon-Pocket, 1996) 116–17.

10. "Top Ten Favorite Words (Not in the Dictionary)." *Merriam-Webster Online* 17 July 2005 <m-w.com/info/favorite.htm>.

11. This discussion of two different ways of responding to language is based on Louise M. Rosenblatt, *The Reader, the Text, the Poem: The Transactional Theory of the Literary Work* (Carbondale: Southern Illinois UP, 1978), particularly Chapter 3, "Efferent and Aesthetic Reading."

12. McQuain 3–4.

13. Miriam Ringo, *Nobody Said It Better!* (Chicago: Rand, 1980) 201.

14. Cherie Spurling, "Batter Up—Batter Down," *Winning Orations, 1992* (Mankato, MN: Interstate Oratorical Association, 1992) 12.

15. Peter Schjeldahl, "Cyclone! Rising to the Fall," *Harper's* June 1988: 68–70. Examples of visual, auditory, tactile, thermal, and olfactory sensory impressions are from Schjeldahl's article. Other examples are from Richard Conniff, "Coasters Used to Be Scary, Now They're Downright Weird," *Smithsonian* Aug. 1989: 84–85.

16. Kristin Lewis, "The Terrorists' Greatest Victory," *Winning Oration, 2003* (Mankato, MN: Interstate Oratorical Association, 2003) 78. Coached by Terry West.

17. Robert Claiborne, *Loose Cannons & Red Herrings: A Book of Lost Metaphors* (New York: Norton, 1988) 13.

18. "Speech, Figure of," *Encyclopaedia Britannica Online,* 30 July 1999 <htttp://eb.com:180/bol/topic?thes_id=503404&pm=1>.

19. Raymond Gozzi, "Metaphors around the TV Remote Control," *ETC: A Review of General Semantics* Winter 1998: 441.

20. "Metaphor," *Encyclopaedia Britannica Online,* 30 July 1999 <http://eb.com:180/bol/topic?cu=53596&sctn=1>.

21. Gozzi 438.

22. Elyse Sommer and Dorrie Weiss, eds., *Metaphors Dictionary* (Detroit: Gale, 1995) xi.

23. Schjeldahl 68.

24. Phillip J. Wininger, "The Unwanted Neighbor," *Winning Orations, 2001* (Mankato, MN: Interstate Oratorical Association, 2001) 36, 38. Coached by Judy Woodring.

25. Elie Wiesel, "The Shame of Hunger," *Representative American Speeches: 1990–1991,* ed. Owen Peterson (New York: Wilson, 1991) 70–74.

26. Travis Kirchhefer, "The Deprived," *Winning Orations, 2000* (Mankato, MN: Interstate Oratorical Association, 2000) 151. Coached by Ron Krikac.

27. Copyright © 1963 by Martin Luther King, Jr., renewed 1991 by Coretta Scott King. Reprinted by arrangement with the Estate of Martin Luther King, Jr., c/o Writers House as agent for the proprietor, New York, NY.

28. Mario Cuomo, Keynote Address, Democratic National Convention, *Vital Speeches of the Day* 15 Aug. 1984: 647.

29. Sarah Meinen, "The Forgotten Four-Letter Word," *Winning Orations, 1999* (Mankato, MN: Interstate Oratorical Association, 1999) 26–29. Coached by Dan Smith.

30. William Safire, "On Language: Marking Bush's Inaugural," *New York Times Magazine* 5. Feb. 1989: 12.

31. Our guidelines have been shaped and reinforced by suggestions in these two excellent publications: *Publication Manual of the American Psychological Association,* 5th ed. (Washington, DC: American Psychological Association, 2001) 61–76, and Rosalie Maggio, *Talking about People: A Guide to Fair and Accurate* Language (Phoenix, AZ: Oryx, 1997).

32. Rosalie Maggio, *The Bias-Free Word Finder: A Dictionary of Nondiscriminatory Language* (Boston: Beacon, 1991) 7.

33. Maggio, *Talking about People* 1.

34. Maggio, *Talking about People* 18.

35. Richard Price, interview with Terry Gross, *Fresh Air,* Natl. Public Radio, WHYY, Philadelphia. 9 May 1995.

36. *Ethnologue Language Name Index,* July 2002, SIL International, 10 Sept. 2002 <http://www.ethnologue.com/language_index.asp>.

37. Qtd. in George Plimpton, ed., *The Writer's Chapbook: A Compendium of Fact, Opinion, Wit, and Advice from the 20th Century's Preeminent Writers* (New York: Viking, 1989) 176.

CHAPTER 13

1. Elinor Donahue, "Writing Your Own Speeches," *Fund Raising Management* (Feb. 1996), 7 July 1999 <http://web4.infotrac.galegroup.com/itw/i. . . 5!xrn_49_0_A18711219?sw_aep=viva_radford>.

2. John Kao, *Delivering Successful Presentations,* FYI Video, American Management Association, 1992.

3. Myron H. Wahls, "The Moral Decay of America," *Vital Speeches of the Day* 15 July 1996: 604.

4. Mario Cuomo, "Introduction," *More Than Words: The Speeches of Mario Cuomo* (New York: St. Martin's, 1993) xiv–xv.

5. Steve Jobs, Commencement Address, Stanford University, 12 June 2005, *Stanford Report* 14 June 2005, 23 July 2005 <http://news-service.stanford.edu/news/2005/june15/jobs-061505.html>.

6. Achim Nowak, *Power Speaking: The Art of the Exceptional Public Speaker* (New York: Allworth, 2004) 11.

7. Mihaly Csikszentmihalyi, *Flow: The Psychology of Optimal Experience* (New York: Harper-Perennial, 1990).

8. Mihaly Csikszentmihalyi, "How to Shape Our Selves," *Psychology Today* January/February 1994: 38.

9. Deborah Blum, "Face It! Facial Expressions Are Crucial to Emotional Health," *Psychology Today* 19 Sept. 1998: 32. Blum uses Paul Ekman's estimate of 5,000 facial expressions. Ray Birdwhistell posited the number 250,000 in his *Kinesics and Context: Essays on Body Motion Communication* (Philadelphia: U of Pennsylvania P, 1970) 8.

10. Michael C. Corballis, "The Gestural Origins of Langauge," *American Scientist* March–April 1999: 140.

11. Donna Frick-Horbury and Robert E. Guttentag, "The Effects of Restricting Hand Gesture Production on Lexical Retrieval and Free Recall," *American Journal of Psychology* Spring 1998: 45–46.

12. "Gestures May Trigger Ability to Recall Words," *Roanoke Times* 10 June 2005: A12. See also Sharon Begley, "Living Hand to Mouth," *Newsweek* 2 Nov. 1999: 69.

CHAPTER 14

1. We adapted this chapter opening from four images described in an effective Nikon advertisement we saw for the first time in *American Photo* March/April 1991: 19.

2. Kit Long, *Visual Aids and Learning,* 12 Aug. 1997, U of Portsmouth, 21 Sept. 2002 <www.mech.port.ac.uk/av/ALALearn.htm>.

3. Michael Antonoff, "Meetings Take off with Graphics," *Personal Computing* July 1990: 62.

4. Achim Nowak, *Power Speaking: The Art of the Exceptional Public Speaker* (New York: Allworth, 2004) 192.

5. Ellen Braun, "Visual Presentation Tools Sharpen Communication Style," *The Office* June 1993 <http://web4.infotrac.galegroup.com/itw>.

6. Braun.

7. Jude Westerfield, *Giving a Presentation* (New York: Silver Lining-Barnes & Noble, 2003) 128.

8. Freddy Silva, *Secrets in the Fields: The Science and Mysticism of Crop Circles* (Charlottesville, VA: Hampton Roads, 2002).

9. Elizabeth Downs and Judi Repman, "Picture Perfect!," *Library Journal* Sept./Oct. 2001: 39.

10. USC Annenberg School Center for the Digital Future, *The Digital Future Report: Surveying the Digital Future, Year Four.* 21 July 2005: 29 <www.digitalcenter.org/downloads/DigitalFutureReport-Year4–2004.pdf>.

11. Martin Dodge, "Surf Maps: Visualizing Web Browsing," *An Atlas of Cyberspaces,* 9 May 1999, Centre for Advanced Spatial Analysis, University College London 14 Nov. 1999 <http://www.cybergeography.org/atlas/surf.html>.

12. Nick Morgan, *Give Your Speech, Change the World* (Boston: Harvard Business School, 2005) 139.

13. Edward R. Tufte, *The Visual Display of Quantitative Information* (Cheshire, CT: Graphics P, 1983) 121. See also Tufte's richly illustrated later works: *Envisioning Information* (Cheshire, CT: Graphics P, 1990) and *Visual Explanations: Images and Quantities, Evidence and Narrative* (Cheshire, CT: Graphics P, 1997).

14. We adapted this list of guidelines from two sources: Ann Luck, *Visual Aid Checklist for Interactive Video Presentation* (1997). Used by permission of the author. Also from Joyce Kupsch and Pat R. Graves, *Create High Impact Business Presentations* (Lincolnwood, IL: NTC Learning Works–NTC/Contemporary, 1998) 89–90, 95–96, 107–09.

15. Michael Talman, *Understanding Presentation Graphics* (San Francisco: SYBEX, 1992) 270.

16. Tufte, *Visual Explanations* 74.

CHAPTER 15

1. Pew Internet & American Life Report, "Internet Evolution," 25 Jan. 2005, 2 July 2005 <www.pewinternet.org/PPF/r/148/report_display.asp>.

2. USC Annenberg School Center for the Digital Future, *The Digital Future Report: Surveying the Digital Future, Year Four.* 14 Aug. 2005: 23 <www.digitalcenter.org/downloads/DigitalFuture Report-Year4–2004.pdf>.

3. Markus Geisler, "iPod therefore I Am," 15 Aug. 2005 <www.mymacexperience.com/ipod/html/introduction.htm>.

4. Andrew Sullivan, "iPod World: The End of Society?," 20 Feb. 2005, 15 Aug. 2005 <www.andrewsullivan.com/print.php?artnum=20050220>.

5. Susan Chontos, "The Amish: Seeking to Lose the Self," San Antonio College, Texas, Summer 1992. Reprinted with permission.

CHAPTER 16

1. "The 30-Second President," narr. Bill Moyers, *A Walk through the 20th Century,* exec. ed. Bill Moyers, PBS, 1984.

2. Charles U. Larson, *Persuasion: Reception and Responsibility,* 9th ed. (Belmont, CA: Wadsworth, 2001) 10.

3. Nick Morgan, *Give Your Speech, Change the World* (Boston: Harvard Business School, 2005) 1.

4. Neel Bhatt, Untitled Speech, *Winning Orations, 2004* (Mankato, MN: Interstate Oratorical Association, 2004) 21. Coached by David Moscovitz.

5. *The Rhetoric of Aristotle,* trans. Lane Cooper (New York: Appleton, 1960) 8.

6. James Benjamin, *Principles, Elements, and Types of Persuasion* (Fort Worth, TX: Harcourt, 1997) 122, 124.

7. James C. McCroskey, *An Introduction to Rhetorical Communication,* 7th ed. (Boston: Allyn, 1997) 87–88.

8. Gerry Spence, *How to Argue and Win Every Time* (New York: St Martin's Griffin, 1995) 47.

9. McCroskey 89. McCroskey credits D. K. Berlo and J. B. Lemmert with labeling these three dimensions of credibility in "A Factor Analytical Study of the Dimensions of Source Credibility," a paper they presented at the 1961 convention of the Speech Association of America, New York.

10. Benjamin 129. See also Robert H. Gass and John S. Seiter, *Persuasion, Social Influence, and Compliance Gaining* (Boston: Allyn, 1999) 89.

11. Jessica J. Jones, "Are You Guilty?" *Winning Orations, 2004* (Mankato, MN: Interstate Oratorical Association, 2004) 93. Coached by Barbara F. Sims.

12. William J. Clinton, Inaugural Address, 1997. *New York Times.* 20 Jan. 1997. Online. America Online/Newsstand. 21 Jan. 1997.

CHAPTER 17

1. Thomas Gilovich, *How We Know What Isn't So* (New York: Free, 1991) 6.

2. Aristotle, *The Rhetoric of Aristotle,* trans. Lane Cooper (New York: Appleton, 1932) 220.

3. For a more elaborate discussion of the structure of an argument, see Stephen Toulmin, *The Uses of Argument* (New York: Cambridge UP, 1974).

4. Ali Heidarpour, "Organ Donation Reform," *Winning Orations, 2004* (Mankato, MN: Interstate Oratorical Association, 2004) 69. Coached by Stacy Schrank and Thomas Bartl.

5. Kateri Mintie, "Failing Our Students: America's Misuse of Substitute Teachers," *Winning Orations, 2001* (Mankato, MN: Interstate Oratorical Association, 2001) 31. Coached by Alexis Hopkins.

6. Nicholas Barton, "The Death of Reading," *Winning Orations, 2004* (Mankato, MN: Interstate Oratorical Association, 2004) 32. Coached by Craig Brown and Robert F. Imbody, III.

7. Ellen Wartella, "The Context of Television Violence," Arnold Lecture presented at the Speech Communication Association Annual Convention, Marriott Hotel & Marina, San Diego, 23 Nov. 1996.

8. Mario Cuomo, Keynote Address, Democratic National Convention, *Vital Speeches of the Day* 15 Aug. 1984: 647.

9. John M. Ericson and James J. Murphy with Raymond Bud Zeuschner, *The Debater's Guide,* rev. ed. (Carbondale, IL: Southern Illinois UP, 1987) 139.

10. Mark Twain, *Life on the Mississippi* (New York: Harper, 1917) 156.

11. *The New York Public Library Desk Reference,* 2nd ed. (New York: Stonesong-Simon, 1993) 273.

12. "Super Bowls and Stock Markets," *Science News Online* 1 July 2000, 23 Aug. 2002 <www.sciencenews.org/20000701/mathtrek.asp>.

13. Bruce N. Waller, *Critical Thinking: Consider the Verdict* (Upper Saddle River, NJ: Prentice, 1988) 30.

14. Barack Obama, "Reclaiming the Promise to the People," *Vital Speeches of the Day* 1 August 2004: 625.

15. W. Ward Fearnside and William B. Holther, *Fallacy— The Counterfeit of Argument* (Upper Saddle River, NJ: Prentice, 1959) 92.

16. Raymie E. McKerrow, Bruce E. Gronbeck, Douglas Ehninger, and Alan H. Monroe, *Principles and Types of Speech Communication,* 14th ed. (New York: Addison-Longman, 2000) 153–61. See also: Alan H. Monroe, *Principles and Types of Speech* (Chicago: Scott, 1935).

17. See our discussion of Dewey's Steps to Reflective Thinking in Chapter 19, pp. 395–97.

18. James Chang, "Sustainable Giving," *Winning Orations, 2003* (Mankato, MN: Interstate Oratorical Association, 2003) 3–4. Coached by Liana Koeppel.

CHAPTER 18

1. Peter Bowes, "Sadness and Joy at Star's Funeral," *BBC News* 18 June 2004, 22 Aug. 2005 < http://news.bbc.co.uk/2/hi/entertainment/3820795.stm>.

2. Tom Singer, "Eckersley Relieved After Ceremony," *MLB.com* 25 July 2004, 22 Aug. 2005 <http://mlb.mlb.com/NAS App/mlb/mlb/news/mlb_news.jsp?ymd=20040725&content_id=810100&vkey=news_mlb&fext=.jsp>.

3. Diana Dean Schemo, "Holocaust Museum Hailed as Sacred Debt to Dead," *New York Times* 23 April 1993, natl. ed.: A1, 24.

4. Don Ochs, "Introduction of Samuel L. Becker, Central States Communication Association Convention, April 12, 1991," *The CSCA News* Spring 1991: 2.

5. Josh McNair, Speech of Presentation, Radford University, Virginia, Summer 2002. Reprinted with permission of the author.

6. Zachary Henning, Acceptance Speech, Radford University, Virginia, Summer 2002. Reprinted with permission of the author.

7. Cyrus Copeland, "New Life for the Eulogy," *The Boston Globe* 30 May 2005, 23 June 2005 <www.boston.com/news/globe/editorial_opinion/oped/articles/2005/05/30/new_life_for_the_eulogy/>.

8. Peggy Noonan, *What I Saw at the Revolution* (New York: Random, 1990) 253.

9. Cyrus M. Copeland, ed., *Farewell, Godspeed: The Greatest Eulogies of Our Time* (New York: Random-Harmony, 2003) xv.

10. Michael McDonough, "Untitled Speech," *1990 Championship Debates and Speeches* (Annandale, VA: Speech Communication Association, 1990) 86.

CHAPTER 19

1. Bobby R. Patton and Timothy M. Downs. *Decision-Making Group Interaction,* 4th ed. (Boston: Allyn, 2003) 1.

2. "The State of Meetings Today," *Effective Meetings.com,* 2002, 26 Sept. 2002 <www.effectivemeetings.com/meetingbasics/meetstate.sap>.

3. Paul E. Nelson, "Small-Group Communication," in Lilian O. Feinberg, *Applied Business Communication* (Sherman Oaks, CA: Alfred, 1982) 27.

4. Thomas E. Harris and John C. Sherblom, *Small Group and Team Communication,* 3rd ed. (Boston: Allyn, 2005) 156.

5. Richard S. Wellins, William C. Byham, and Jeanne M. Wilson, *Empowered Teams: Creating Self-Directed Work Groups That Improve Quality, Productivity, and Participation* (San Francisco: Josey-Bass, 1991) 4–5.

6. Irving L. Janis, *Groupthink: Psychological Studies of Policy Decisions and Fiascoes,* 2nd ed. (Boston: Houghton, 1982) 9.

7. John Dewey, *How We Think* (Boston: Heath, 1910).

8. Ronald B. Adler and Jeanne Marquardt Elmhorst, *Communicating at Work: Principles and Practices for Business and the Professions,* 6th ed. (Boston: McGraw, 1999) 241. These authors and other scholars base their discussion of these group roles on Kenneth D. Benne and Paul Sheats, "Functional Roles of Group Members," *Journal of Social Issues* 4 (1948): 41–49.

9. Roger K. Mosvick and Robert B. Nelson, *We've Got to Start Meeting Like This!* Rev. ed. (Indianapolis, IN: Park Avenue-JIST Works, 1996) 147.

APPENDIX

1. Melissa Janoske, "Renaissance Fairs: The New Vaudeville," Speech Delivered at Radford University, Radford, Virginia, Spring 2002. Used with permission.

2. Tiffanie K. Petrin, "Steganography: Hidden Messages," Delivered at the Texas Community College Speech and Theater Association State Tournament, Spring 2002. Coached by Jolinda Ramsey. Used with permission.

3. Jared J. Johnston, "A Sign of the Times," *Winning Orations, 2004* (Mankato, MN: Interstate Oratorical Association, 2004) 75–77. Coached by Mark Hickman.

4. Darla Goodrich, "How Old Is He Anyway? Aging the Whitetail Buck," Delivered at San Antonio College, San Antonio, Texas, Spring 2005. Used by permission.

5. Gene Fox, Untitled Speech, Delivered at San Antonio College, San Antonio, Texas, Summer 2002. Used by permission.

6. Edwin C. Anderson, Jr., Speech of Tribute to Charles M. Schulz, Congressional Gold Medal Ceremonies," Capitol Rotunda, Washington, DC, CNN, 7 June 2001.

7. Martin Luther King, Jr., "I Have a Dream," 28 Aug. 1963, Washington, DC. Copyright © 1963 by Martin Luther King, Jr., renewed 1991 by Coretta Scott King. Reprinted by arrangement with the Estate of Martin Luther King, Jr., c/o Writers House as agent for the proprietor, New York, NY.

Name Index

Subject Index

*Boldface page numbers indicate marginal glossary entries.

Photo Credits

Criteria
for Critiquing
a Speech

Content

- What audience needs and motivations did the topic address? Was the speaker's analysis of the audience on target?
- Was the topic appropriate for the occasion? Why or why not?
- Was the topic clearly focused enough to develop and support the speaker's specific purpose?
- Did the speaker use a sufficient array of sources to gather information for each idea?
- What supporting materials gave the speaker's ideas clarity, vividness, and credibility?
- Did the speaker cite the sources for those supporting materials?
- How did the speaker establish the reliability of the sources?
- Did the speaker develop the speech in an ethical way, presenting and supporting ideas that will benefit the audience?
- Did the speaker use presentational aids to make the ideas more clear, vivid, and credible? Did the speaker miss any opportunity to use presentational aids to his or her advantage?
- Were the presentational aids designed and prepared effectively?

Organization and Approach

Introduction

- What strategy did the speaker use to get the audience's attention? Was the opening statement effective?
- Did the speaker clearly state the topic and establish its importance? If not, did you have difficulty understanding the purpose?
- How did the speaker establish his or her credibility to speak on the topic?
- Did the speaker preview the speech's key ideas?

Body

- Did the speaker select a manageable number of key ideas to develop? What were they?
- Were the key ideas relevant to the specific purpose?
- What pattern did the speaker select to organize the key ideas?
- Did the speaker use the 4 S strategy to develop each key idea? If not, then what components were missing?
- What kind of transitions did the speaker use to connect the key ideas?

Conclusion

- Did the speaker summarize the key ideas?
- Did the speaker's closing statement take the speech a step beyond the summary? If so, what strategy did the speaker use to activate the audience and to provide closure?